CW01272866

# Without Favour or Affection

## A Novel

## James Leeds

Copyright 2015 © James Leeds All rights reserved. This book or any portion thereof may not be reproduced or used in any manner whatsoever without the express permission of the Author except for the use of brief quotations in a book review. The moral right of the Author James Leeds has been asserted.

# WITHOUT FAVOUR OR AFFECTION

*"It will be found an unjust and unwise jealousy to deprive a man of his natural liberty upon a supposition that he may abuse it"*
**Oliver Cromwell**
**Lord Protector of England (1653 - 1658)**

*"Everybody owes his Country some time in jail"*
**J.F. Kennedy (1917 - 1963)**

*"Point a gun at a Police Officer, in seconds he will be surrounded by his Colleagues, point a finger, he stands alone."*
**Anon**

This is simply a novel; all the characters and Police Officers described or named within are fictitious and are simply the product of the author's imagination. Any similarity to any person living or dead is purely coincidental. The Police Forces, stations and Divisions mentioned similarly do not exist, other than perhaps in the fading memories of any Police Officer who may have served in a large City Force during the seventies and eighties.

The realism of the incidents and occurrences described within, I leave to your own conclusions.

No apologies are offered for the language, violent acts, or the apparent mercenary attitudes of any of the Police Officers in the tale. Police Officers are drawn from the very public which they serve. Therefore, they are prone to the same conditions which affect us all, despair, anger, racism, lust, hatred and pride. These traits are manifest in us all. Look to your own frailties before rushing to criticize. We enjoy the liberty that comes with democracy, hard fought for and desperately defended. Anarchy erodes liberty; our Police Officers defend us from anarchy, despite the growing dissent from the not so silent minority.

*"The Public get the Police they deserve"* it was true when first quoted; it is still true to this day.

James Leeds

*****

**'Constable'** (Roman derivative) Count of the Stables. This was first heard of in the reign of Henry III around 1252 A.D. His main duties were to bring offenders before the Justices or 'Shire Reeves' (Sheriffs). He wore no uniform, collected no salary and for the most part, was despised and mistrusted by his neighbours and Townsfolk. He was required to serve a period of twelve months and at the conclusion, was then free to go about his lawful occasion. It was an odious task, so much so, that men of wealth and standing would pay some fellow to perform his duty period; the result of this was that these duties were often performed by ignorant and unsuitable men. *'Police before the Reform'*

*****

Regarded as being the finest Police Force in the world, the British Policing system has been emulated or adopted by nearly all Countries in the civilized world. It's judicial system, although painfully slow in process, bureaucratic and subject to the dogma and the whims of the politicians of the day, has nonetheless, formed the basis on which Courtrooms throughout the globe conduct and deliver justice. The administration of justice is the very pillar of society. Police Officers are sworn to protect life and property, to prevent and detect crime and to keep the Queens peace without favour or affection to any race, colour or creed.

*"Legum servi sumus ut liberi esse possimus"*

*****

## "What's past is prologue"

Station Sergeant John Stockley tamps the fine slivers of tobacco along the length of the paper which he holds carefully between the upper edge of his nicotine stained forefinger and thumb. Deftly, he folds one edge across and tucks it under its opposite edge before rolling it into a tube. Lifting the 'prison thin' cigarette to his lips, he runs the tip of his tongue along the gummed edge before running his finger along its length to form a seal. Satisfied with its preparation, he flicks it expertly up into the corner of his mouth.

He rolls up the sleeves of his blue nylon shirt and winces annoyingly at the collar stud which digs uncomfortably into his throat. He faces the aging Remington typewriter which sits atop the front counter. Striking a match, he squints as the end of the paper flares brightly and billows smoke up into his eyes. With the 'roll up' hanging limply from the corner of his mouth, Sergeant Stockley twists the knurled knob at the side of the typewriter and feeds an incident sheet down between the rubber covered roller and the brass face plate. Squaring the sheet, he releases the pressure handle and with the tips of his index fingers, he carefully types the date, '8th of July 1965'.

His labours are interrupted as the door to the Police station is rudely opened. Mr Maurice Manders, a resident of Wainwright Terrace enters; in his left hand, he is carrying one of the new 'Phillips' portable cassette recorders, in his right, a microphone.

At the annoying interruption to his daily duties, Constable Terrence Betteridge, the front office clerk, folds his newspaper and quickly places the half consumed bottle of Double Diamond into the drawer by the side of his desk. Showing a modicum of interest, he hauls his nineteen stone bulk from his chair and in preparation, casually walks to the rear of the front office and opens one of the heavy oak cell doors.

Sergeant Stockley doesn't divert his gaze from the typewriter keys or even bother to greet Mr Manders, who, on almost a daily basis, visits the station to make a complaint of some description.

Mr Manders purposefully places the cassette recorder on the scarred oak surface of the front counter. With shaking fingers he depresses the record/play paddles and flicks the small switch on the side of the microphone and starts to speak. "I am in the station; Sergeant 33 is at the front desk. Sergeant, I wish to know why Constable 202 Harrington, who came to my house this morning, was rude, uncivil and refused to take my complaint of damage."

Mr Manders thrusts the microphone aggressively into Sergeant Stockley's face.

Without looking up from his two-fingered typing, the veteran Sergeant sighs and speaks slowly.

"This is the third time this week Maurice. The reason my Officer didn't record a crime is because we both know that as usual, you caused the damage yourself to make a false claim on your house insurance. Now bugger off and let me get on, there's a good chap."

Mr Manders bangs his clenched fist against the countertop and with a hand shaking with rage, holds the microphone to his lips. "This is neglect of duty; I wish to lodge a formal compla..."

Before he can continue, Sergeant Stockley reaches across the counter and grabs the lapel of Mr Manders' duffle coat. "Terry" he calls back casually to his clerk as he drags the unfortunate Mr Manders completely off his feet and onto the top of the counter.

Constable Betteridge waddles across to his Sergeant and grabbing a handful of clothing, unceremoniously hauls the protesting Mr Manders bodily over the counter's time polished surface. As he is dragged away, Sergeant Stockley relieves Mr Manders of his cassette recorder.

"You're under arrest Maurice. Disorderly conduct in a police station…again."

Mr Manders is hauled unceremoniously through the front office and propelled bodily toward the white tiled wall at the rear of the cell. The heavy door is slammed shut behind him. "You can be sure that I shall be writing to Sir Frank Soskice." he shouts from within.

Mr Manders' protests regarding Police brutality are muted and what faint threats of a sure and certain complaint to the Home Secretary had been heard, are in any case, ignored.

Sergeant Stockley presses the rewind button on the recorder and when the tape has fully rewound, he disconnects the microphone and simultaneously, presses down on the record and play paddles.

Constable Betteridge, now sweating profusely, returns to his desk. He retrieves his bottle of beer from the drawer and resumes his morning read. "It says here that Ronnie Biggs as 'ad it away from Wandsworth Sarge."

Sergeant Stockley nods disinterestedly and unperturbed by the brief interruption, resumes his laborious typing.

*****

The old Police station now lies dormant, empty. Its sandstone mullion windows, pitted with the passage of time, are now hastily boarded over with Council plywood and adorned with notices of 'sale by auction'. The main entrance door of heavy oak, burnished smooth from over a hundred years of use is now locked and bolted closed. It sits between Tudor arches, resplendent with fanlights and heavy Tuscan columns which support a pediment hood, over which sits the intricately moulded City Coat of Arms.

Within, under the high ceiling with its baroque mouldings, the filthy threadbare carpets are now festooned with thin shards of emulsion which have fallen away from the sagging ceiling and intricately moulded covings. The main reception desk of thick oak extending from wall to wall, its polished surface scarred and scratched over the decades, now rests beneath a thick coating of dust, other than where shielded by an ancient discarded

Remington typewriter, yellowing statement forms and discarded incident reports.

Behind the desk, the Station Sergeant's domain is eerily quiet. The bold cast iron radiators now sag dejectedly from their mountings and the floor is spongy, rotting from the ingress of brackish water which has leaked from the joints. There is a pungent smell of mould, age and decay.

The two cell doors at the rear of the Station Sergeant's office, both of solid oak, their heavy hinges riven through with thick iron bolts, now sit ajar. The half tiled walls, the stone flagged floors and raised oak box platform beds within the cells, just visible. The brass oval viewing apertures once polished daily by the station cleaners, now neglected, are green and pitted by the onslaught of verdigris.

From the Station Sergeant's area run the stone flagged corridors down to the Collator's office and the main parade room. Here countless uniformed Officers once stood rigidly to attention, staff in right hand, handcuffs in the other whilst being rigorously inspected by the patrol Sergeants prior to commencing their allocated foot patrols.

The upper floors, accessed by a wooden staircase from the side of the Station Sergeants area, housed the offices of the patrol Inspector, the Clerk Typists, the Criminal Investigation Department and the Superintendent.

The building is silent now, decrepit, simply waiting for either development or demolition.

Set in the midst of the bustling, vibrant community, the old station has served local needs for over a hundred years. Redundant now like so many satellite Police stations since the reforms brought about in the late seventies and early eighties during the Thatcher regime.

Only in the farthest reaches of the Force area do the old Victorian Police stations still remain operational, most now with restricted opening times and vastly reduced resources. The City stations no longer served the needs of the Government of the day. They are no longer cost effective and simply unable to accommodate the now swelling ranks of Constables.

The old City stations and Sub Divisional buildings finally closed their doors and new 'state of the art' Divisional Headquarters were hastily built.

*****

## Historical note

In 1975, the basic starting wage of £1824 per annum for a uniformed Police Constable was simply not attracting sufficient recruits and Mrs Margaret Thatcher realised this issue when she achieved the 1979 general election. During that period, her Government introduced a number of political initiatives which were to prove profoundly unpopular with the Unions.

With unrest on the horizon, the Prime Minister needed a strong Police force on her side. In this respect, one of Mrs Thatcher's first initiatives on becoming elected Prime Minister, was to instigate the Edmund Davies regime on Police pay.

There were severe problems with both the recruitment and retention of Police Officers in England and Wales, mostly due to chronically low pay which had by then fallen far behind the pay for comparable occupations. This coupled with the fact that by 1975, a good percentage of those serving Officers who had joined the Police after being 'demobbed' from the armed forces at the conclusion of hostilities in 1945, were now completing their thirty years of service.

With a desperate haemorrhaging of uniformed rank and file Officers, in August 1977, Lord Edmund-Davies was appointed by Labour Home Secretary Merlyn Rees, to chair a commission of inquiry into the negotiating machinery for Police pay and conditions in the hope of staunching the flow. His terms of reference were enlarged in December 1977 to include the levels of pay.

His report was published in July 1978 and recommended a substantial increase in pay for Police Officers to the order of 45 per cent. Further drastic reforms were to follow.

By the early 1980's, the magma of dissent was bubbling up from the pit shafts of the Yorkshire and Nottinghamshire coalfields; there was the growing threat of public disorder.

Social unrest and a meteoric rise in the crime rate within the new 'super' Divisions, caused questions to be asked in the House.

In response, along with other sweeping measures, Senior Command rank Officers determined the requirement for the dissolution of the specialist Road Traffic Departments.

Once the 'flag ship' of the City Forces, largely autonomous and housed in large Central garages, they were staffed by highly trained Officers with a specific remit to patrol the Motorways and main arterial roads in and out of the Cities, to attend to and deal with all fatal and serious injury road traffic collisions and to prosecute road traffic offenders.

The Road Traffic Departments enjoyed their own rank structure and relative freedom from the repetitive tedium of 'call handling' suffered by their uniformed colleagues on the beat.

But now the Chief Superintendents at the new 'Super' Divisions looked with jealous eyes toward this elite Department. Envious of their experienced and highly qualified Officers, they coveted their ranks.

Harried by the Home Office and the City Fathers of the Police Authority to reduce response times and to combat the ever rising crime figures, to provide more cost effective policing, they appeased their masters' bleatings. They instigated the complete dissolution of the City Traffic Departments and the utilisation of the Traffic Officers, along with their expertise and high powered vehicles, within their own Divisions, to work as a further 'resource' in support of their struggling uniformed beat patrol Officers.

The Traffic Departments were emasculated; the Traffic Officers were posted to various Divisions through the whole Force area and attached to the uniformed patrol Groups. They were still tasked with attendance at road collisions where their skills at collision investigation could still be utilised, but now were also required to attend to more mundane issues, domestic disturbances, alarm calls, sudden deaths and shoplifters.

A massive increase in car crime and 'ram raids' which were becoming increasingly popular, provided a brief respite from call handling. The ever increasing numbers of pursuits begged the use of their advanced driving skills, but for the most part, the Traffic men were simply sintered with the beat patrols.

They were used as a 'first response' to any ongoing incident which the controllers in the Force Control Centers and Divisional radio rooms, considered required an immediate response.

Needless to say, the moves to Division were not well met.

## **The Ten Code**

| | |
|---|---|
| 10/1 | On duty |
| 10/2 | Contact your station |
| 10/3 | Return to station |
| 10/4 | Message acknowledged |
| 10/5 | Temporarily off air (meal, enquiries) |
| 10/6 | Arrival at (scene or incident) |
| 10/7 | Any messages |
| 10/8 | Repeat your message |
| 10/9 | Road Collision |

| | |
|---|---|
| 10/11 | Request for previous convictions |
| 10/12 | Arrest |
| 10/13 | Police Officer in trouble |
| 10/14 | Alarm |
| 10/15 | Suspects on premises |
| 10/16 | Resuming patrol – available |
| 10/17 | P.N.C. (Police National Computer) check |
| 10/18 | Request for services (Fire-Ambulance) |
| 10/19 | Fire alarm |
| 10/20 | Off duty |
| 10/21 | Request firearms authority |
| 10/99 | Degree of urgency - caution to be used. |
| 10/99ZZ | High priority-risk exercise utmost caution |

# It is the 1980's

### <u>One</u>

The parade room was warm, stifling and oppressive; the heating system had been left on at its maximum setting to assist with the drying out process. Minute cracks had started to appear where the hastily painted ceiling joined the plastered surface of the walls. The radiators gave off a heady odour as the newly applied gloss paint was baked hard as the metal heated. The station was newly built and had taken up operational duties prior to final completion. Multi coloured wires, still awaiting connection hung tendril like from the steel conduits which ran along the walls of the room and hastily handwritten cardboard notices still hung haphazardly from window latches and door handles, warning the occupants that the paint was still wet. There were, evident in the paintwork, the fingerprints of numerous Officers whose curiosity had got the better of them, these marks now indelibly imprinted in the hardening skin of the paint, visual proof of the cynical curiosity of both junior and senior Officers alike.

The odd item of uniform apparel had already begun to appear, draped over the radiators to dry. A tunic and a raincoat or two, steaming merrily away, giving off a smell not unlike that of a wet dog that sits in front of a fire, not offensive but well, peculiar.

The parade room was silent and Police Constable 868 Alan Pendle was alone. He had arrived early for the 2.00 pm late turn parade. It was fifteen minutes to the hour and most of the members of his shift would still be on their way to the station.

He could think of one or two who would just be finishing off the last mouthfuls of beer, vodka or whiskey, hastily glancing at their watches and popping the statutory extra strong mints to disguise the smell of the intoxicants. Alan could remember a time when Officers needed a drink *after* work to help them wind down and relax, more and more these days needing the mild euphoric effect of the alcohol to help them cope with eight hours on the streets.

Alan sat back in his chair and lit a cigarette, pondering over his pocket notebook which lay open on the chair next to him. He inhaled the acrid smoke deeply, sensing the pleasurable 'hit' at the back of his throat as he racked his brain trying to remember the events of the previous shift. The previous entry showed only the date which was underlined, his meal time and an initial entry which showed that he had attended a parade at 6.00 am that morning. The blank lines stared back at him, almost demanding attention. He picked up the notebook and rested it on his leg, his pen poised over the page as if this action alone would jolt something from his memory. Alan stared out of the window, his eyes unfocused and unblinking. He frowned and sucked on the filter tip of his cigarette.

"Christ, I'm cracking up." he thought. "I can't remember a thing about yesterday."

He shook his head slowly, deep in thought. A speeder perhaps, accident, alarm call. "I must have gone to something, God, I'm only in my thirties and senile dementia is already setting in, my memory cells are dying off."

Alan critically examined his reflection in the window. At thirty two, he was thankful that he still had a full head of dark hair, although lately, he had noticed a few grey wisps appearing at his temples. He sported a large flowing moustache, epitomical of his previous military service and almost a standard requirement amongst his Police colleagues. Six feet tall in his stocking feet, he still retained a muscular build, training with weights three times a week at the Police station gymnasium. His brown eyes peered back into themselves from the double glazed briefing room window; the window to his soul he mused.

He scrunched up the muscles in his face and noticed the deep laughter lines appearing at the corners of his eyes. Sighing dejectedly at the prospects of the inevitable onset of middle age, he returned his thoughts to the task at hand. His memory still failed him. Finally, he consoled himself with the fact that if anything important had happened, he would remember it and with resignation, he snapped the notebook shut, promising himself for the hundredth time that from today onwards, he would keep his notebook up to date *during* his shift.

It was still quiet in the parade room and as he stared vacantly out of the window, he was vaguely aware of the noises coming from the other offices which ran along the same lower corridor. The staccato click of the typewriter from the Admin Office as the office clerk prepared the week's duties for the four separate groups, the telephone ringing in the large C.I.D. Office at the far end of the corridor and the muted laughter and ribaldry emanating from the male changing rooms opposite.

The electric clock on the wall across from him clunked loudly as another sixty second cycle was completed, the minute hand shuddering slightly as it took up its new position.

A watery sun hung low over the main road which ran alongside the front of the Police station, its weak rays filtered through the trees, which were now quickly shedding their foliage. The grassed embankment which dropped steeply from the retaining wall bordering the footpath surrounding the visitor's car park was now thinly carpeted with brown wrinkled leaves, which danced a frantic jig as the November gusts whipped them up. Weak as it was, the sun's rays were still warm through the glass and as the blue smoke from his cigarette spiralled lazily upwards, he closed his eyes and listened with contentment to the droning of an aircraft high above the station.

The silence was abruptly shattered and Alan jumped, shocked from his reveries as the parade room door was opened and two members of the retiring early turn shift entered the room.

Alan opened his eyes fully and returned the nod from one of the Officers whom he had known for a while. His attendant colleague; a Probationer, was not yet worthy of acknowledgement.

"Lates Alan?"

Alan sighed and nodded wearily. "Yeah...another fulfilling day serving the great unwashed over is it?"

The other smiled as he pushed a half completed crime complaint into his personal tray. "Yes, thank Christ." he sighed. As he leafed through the various accident reports and offence files he muttered "Only another seven thousand two hundred and ninety to go, not that I'm counting...you?" he asked, looking back toward where Alan was slumped in his seat.

"Less than you mate." Alan replied. He winked and then looked across at the Probationer.

"How many is it for you lad, ten thousand and what?"

The Probationer, who looked about thirteen, smiled nervously, not quite knowing how to respond.

His Tutor nudged him playfully. "Come on Steve, he's only taking the piss, jealous of yer youthful looks…We're done for the day, see you later Al."

Alan smiled weakly and nodded. The two Officers left the room, leaving him alone.

The paint fumes were starting to give him a headache and he wished that he hadn't turned up so early. The room fell silent again; muted voices could just be heard from the outer corridor but the words were muffled by the plasterboard walls.

Alan sat and stared at the back of the chair in front of him, his eyes unblinking, lost in thought. Memories flooded back, washed over him and were lost.

The door opened again and shook him from his daydreams; the other members of his Group began to filter in.

There were thirty or more chairs in the parade room, all facing forwards to where two tables placed end to end were situated. Behind these, on the walls facing the chairs were the information bulletin boards. Pinned to these, were photographs and descriptions of those wanted for robbery, rape and burglary, a brief description of their particular M.O., their usual haunts and known associates. There were photographs of the usual suspects for offences of driving whilst disqualified, registration numbers and descriptions of their vehicles and where they were likely to be found. Bogus officials and 'prop' men, unscrupulous types who would prey on the elderly, the vulnerable and infirm, posing as Gas or Water Board officials just to gain entry into the house where pension books, jewellery or small amounts of hard saved cash would later be missed by the confused complainant.

The bulletin boards were filled with such descriptions and photographs, and it seemed to Alan, that more and more space was needed each month for the 'wanted persons' section; such was the way things were going.

Alan listened and smiled as one of his uniformed colleagues seated behind him complained to his crew mate for the day about how political correctness was ruining the job.

"I don't know what the job's comin' to. The job's fucked, that's for sure. Policewomen 'ave always had their arses date stamped on their first day, it's 'istoric, that's why the job issues them with stockings…for easy access to their bare arses."

"I'm not sure I'd like it if it was our lass." opined his crew mate.

"Bollocks Jack!" his mate retorted. "It's a rite of passage…You watch, they'll be promoting split arses next, then you'll really see the job go downhill. Bill Bexley's one of the best station Sergeants in the job, suspended after twenty years in; some split arse probationer makes a complaint about being stretched over the front counter and 'avin her backside stamped, puts pen to paper, official like…It's been crimed at Division, I tell you the job's fucked."

"So is Bill Bexley by the sound of it." uttered his mate.

"Joan Outhwaite didn't make a song and dance about that stunt at the Arndale." someone voiced from the back of the room, referring to a similar 'rite of passage' incident a few months earlier.

It had been her first shift, a night shift. Officer Outhwaite was extremely well endowed in the 'top bollocks' department, the source of much ribaldry amongst her male colleagues.

As with all new Probationary Officers, she had been crewed up for the first few months of her service with a veteran Tutor Constable.

During the early hours of the morning, the radio operator had passed Officer Outhwaite and her 'mentor' a bogus radio message regarding a burglary in progress at the Arndale shopping centre at the top end of the Division. The shift Sergeant and the night Detective had secreted themselves behind waste bins at the rear of the premises and were armed with shotguns which they had 'borrowed' from the station armoury.

Constable Outhwaite and her Tutor had attended at the premises and she had been told to go to the rear of the premises to check for any signs of entry. Armed only with her torch, she had tentatively walked down the alleyway at the side of the shopping centre and towards the rear loading yard, which was in darkness.

Her heart, no doubt pounding with fear and trepidation and a rush of adrenalin, her torch beam suddenly illuminated two figures squatting down by the side of the large industrial waste bins. The men were wearing balaclavas, again temporarily 'on loan' from the station connected property stores.

The two men held up their shotguns; she stopped dead in her tracks as the barrels were raised. She had somehow managed to stutter "Don't...don't." although her voice had wavered and cracked mid-sentence.

"Ditch the fuckin' radio." the first male had shouted, pointing the shotgun in her direction.

In panic, she had torn the pocket radio from its webbing harness around her neck and dropped it to the floor, unable to take her eyes from the barrel of the weapon pointed toward her face. The torch she had been carrying had fallen to the floor as her fingers had involuntarily lost their grip and she suddenly realised that she had lost control of her bodily functions and was vaguely aware of a warm, damp sensation emanating from between her legs which now trembled uncontrollably.

"And the fucken' rest." shouted the other, in his best effort at an Irish accent.

She did not know what he meant and stood transfixed and petrified.

"Get yer fuckin' kit off." shouted the first, taking a step towards her.

In utter panic, she looked about her for some sign of her Tutor, to no avail, she was alone. The alleyway remained in darkness, no approaching sirens sounded in the distance, no sound of her colleagues' boots rushing up the alleyway to save her. She tore at the buttons of her tunic and it fell from around her shoulders and dropped to the floor. Her hands were shaking and a sob gushed from her throat.

"The fuckin' rest then." one of the men had shouted.

She suddenly realised her predicament, it dawned on her...as clear as a summer's day.

"Please, pleeeeease." she had sobbed, as her trembling fingers had fumbled with the buttons of her blouse. She could not negotiate the small buttons through the button holes and sobbing, pulled the blouse free from the waistband of her uniformed skirt and unable to take her eyes from the barrel of the shotgun, tore the blouse open to reveal her ample breasts covered only by a thin filigree lace bra.

She was suddenly aware of applause, the sound of clapping from behind her. She turned sharply to see her Tutor and other members of her Group who were now cheering and clapping vigorously. The two 'burglars' had now removed their masks and she instantly recognised the Shift Sergeant and the night Detective, both of whom were now clapping and laughing uncontrollably.

"Welcome to 'C' Division love." the Sergeant chortled, barely audible over the cheers and applause from her colleagues now gathered behind her.

She closed her eyes slowly, knowing that she'd been 'had'.

Gathering the front of her blouse over her exposed breasts, she bent to pick up her tunic. She heard the distinctive popping sound of ring pulls and cans of beer were produced, one being hastily thrust towards her.

"Three cheers for Constable Outhwaite, a fully paid up member of 'C' Division" the shift Sergeant shouted.

"Hip hip."…and amidst the cheers from her colleagues, relief washed over her and she drank from the can, her hands still shaking.

Constable Outhwaite never had to buy a round of drinks in the Police bar from that day on and needless to say, successfully completed her probationary period.

"Joan's a different kettle of fish." said the first Officer. "Made C.I.D. within three years, kept to the code and didn't go howling to Discipline and Complaints."

"Just as well, else they'd all be in serious shit, I mean drinkin' on duty…fuck me."

The laughter from the Group subsided as two Patrol Sergeants entered the room.

Alan's usual shift Sergeant looked across and winked as he nodded towards the door. Seconds later, the door was reopened and the Inspector of the day entered carrying the briefing and disposition board. The Group stood as one as the Inspector entered. He walked toward the tables at the front of the parade room, not looking across to any of his Officers, or acknowledging the begrudged sign of respect.

"Christ knows why we do this." thought Alan. "This man's such a prick, another one with five years' service and only two of them actually out on the streets."

The Group was seated with a casual, somewhat limp, dismissive wave from the Inspector who seated himself without taking his eyes from the briefing board.

The Inspector of the day was not well liked and over the years had suffered at the hands of his despising junior ranks. The delivery of two tons of river sand (If there's no one in, just dump it on the drive, please). Countless volumes of Encyclopaedia Britannica and the odd request (under plain brown wrapper) for a subscription to 'Spank Monthly'. Or, the perennial condom trick, slipped casually into the pocket of his civilian jacket whilst it hung behind the door in the Inspector's office, in the hope that his Wife found same.

The Inspector was known to be a 'butterfly', flitting from post to post to enhance his promotional prospects, Headquarters, Training, Fingerprints or the Force Racial Harmony Unit. Any of these would assist in a meteoric rise through the ranks for a graduate entrant.

Street work was for Constables. Out there, you were just another face amongst many; get yourself into Headquarters as a Staff Officer or into 'Stats' and Planning, or, if you had the stomach for sucking up to the blacks, the F.R.H.U.

Twelve to eighteen months paying lip service to the black Community Leaders or spreading your arse cheeks for any of the local Clerics and Imam's was promotion guaranteed.

Alan had a natural distrust of non-operational personnel, the 'nine to fivers' or ESSO's (Every Saturday and Sunday Off). The Inspectors, who seemed to have little or no idea of what was really going on and in truth, couldn't have cared less about the escalation of street violence or assaults on Officers which was of late, showing an alarming increase.

The particular Inspector was in a class of his own, a flyer right enough, a Bramshill man, the Police equivalent of Sandhurst.

The recipe for disaster, take a twenty one year old University graduate, add an Honours degree in Tribology or some other subject totally irrelevant to Police work, place subject on streets for the statutory two year Probationary period, remove quickly thereafter so as not to expose subject to base rank and file humour and cynicism, place in Administration, Fingerprints or Planning and Logistics where delicate subject may be further groomed for rapid promotion and protected from the more colourful aspects of policing. Promote to rank of Sergeant and place subject within the hallowed halls of Bramshill College. Simmer for twelve months whilst subject is marinated in a fine stock of Racial Tension Indicators, Statistics gathering and the all-important subject of Command and Leadership. Finally, remove genitalia, perform frontal lobotomy and serve up to Division as a 'shake n' bake' shift Inspector.

Alan had sampled Bramshill logic earlier in his career; it had been during the Fireman's strike in the late seventies. The Army had been utilised and 'Green Goddesses', the Army fire tenders, had been stationed at most Divisions along with Army personnel to crew them. Alan had been part crew of a Traffic vehicle used to escort the tenders to the scene of a house fire where people were reported to be trapped.

The Team had arrived to find the semi-detached dwelling well ablaze, the roof was a billowing sheet of thick black smoke and the ground floor windows had been blown out, allowing the flames to roar out from the apertures and blacken the surrounding brickwork. It had been pandemonium at the scene; two 'Green Goddesses' had arrived along with their Army compliments.

The local beat Officers and the Community Constable were helping neighbours, some of them aged or infirm, away from the scene and vehicles had to be moved away from the blistering heat which radiated from the burning property.

One of the Community Constables had risked serious burns in entering the house to rescue a six year old child who had been trapped on the upper floor and had been too frightened to scramble down the smouldering staircase to safety. The house was now empty. The smoke from the house was receding as the heat from the flames vaporised the interior fittings and sparks leapt from the blazing roof timbers to engulf the Army lads or 'brown jobs' as they were affectionately known, as they lashed the building with water fed from the olive green tenders.

Two of the 'brown jobs' had been overcome by toxic fumes in the smoke. They had been led away, coughing and vomiting, their faces blackened with sweat and smoke filled spray. A patrol Sergeant had shouted to Alan to assist with the hose and Alan had run towards the house, seeing the 'brown job' silhouetted against the flames, fighting to control the hose on his own.

Standing side by side with the young Lance Corporal, Alan had taken hold of the hose and felt the pressure behind the nozzle and midst the screams of the children, the heat, smoke and confusion, together they leaned forwards against the pressure and played the water onto the roof of the house which was rapidly being gutted.

Alan's eyes had smarted from the intense smoke, his uniform quickly became soaked with the back spray and he could smell his hair singeing.

The Inspector of the day was a Bramshill man. On his arrival at the scene, he had been watching the blaze from the safety of the street. He had obviously noticed Alan and the 'brown job' struggling with the hose and when he had satisfied himself that there was no immediate risk to his personal safety, had casually sauntered up to where they were standing. The Inspector stood to the side, avoiding the heat and billowing smoke. Alan looked across and nodded. The Inspector had given no sign of recognition but after a moment, had returned to the safety of the main road. Alan was relieved by the second tender crew and he walked, wet, filthy and exhausted to the small garden wall which surrounded the gutted remains of the house. Sitting on the wall top, with his back against the wooden gate frame, he lit a cigarette and inhaled the clean smoke and watched as the flames subsided.

The Inspector approached Alan and expecting some small crumb of praise from his leader, he smiled, his teeth showing starkly white against his smoke blackened skin. The Inspector tapped Alan on the shoulder with one of his brown kid gloves and said "When you return to the station, read up on Force Order 13 paragraph 4." and without uttering a further word, walked away.

Alan had been dumbfounded and somewhat mystified and had laughed inwardly at first, but this had quickly turned to anger as he watched the Inspector walking away, the flat cap a little too large, the Gannex raincoat reaching almost to his ankles and the brown gloves held loosely between perfectly manicured fingers.

Alan had fought the urge to shout some obscenity at the man, strong as it was, he had resisted and stood up watching the pathetic figure walk away.

He was shaken from his anger by the Lance Corporal who slapped him on the back and said "Thanks mate."

Alan turned and looked at the smiling 'brown job', his teeth ridiculously white against his blackened face. Realising they both looked like caricatures from the Black and White Minstrel Show, they spontaneously burst out laughing.

The excitement of the day over, Alan had gone back to the station and stripped off his sodden tunic, laying it over one of the ever present radiators; he enjoyed a cigarette and a mug of steaming coffee made begrudgingly by the office clerk. He sank back into one of the easy padded chairs in the front office and closed his eyes.

Suddenly remembering what the Inspector had said, he leapt from the chair and reached over to the shelving by the radio shack where Force Standing and General Orders sat gathering dust. Snatching for the copy of Force Orders, he flicked through the yellowing pages until he reached the paragraph the Inspector had mentioned. He gazed at the print almost in disbelief; the paragraph was headed 'Saluting of Senior Officers in the field'.

Alan slammed the folder shut and laughed out loud. The office clerk looked around, wondering what anyone could possibly find amusing in Force Standing Orders.

*****

"Sit down please." the Inspector said without looking up. The two patrol Sergeants sat and only then, were the rest of the group allowed to take their seats. There were a few coughs and a little settling down before the Inspector began the parade. "Right, crimes for yesterday." the Inspector said, looking displeased and slightly more morose than usual. "We got a right caning on nine beat, God only knows what the night shift were doing, but we have suffered twelve thefts from motor vehicles on that beat area, all Vauxhalls and the same M.O., rear quarter light smashed and the stereo system ripped out of the dashboard. Someone's about doing this; it would be looked upon most favourably if a member of our group were to go 10/12 with the person or persons responsible." The Inspector looked up and cast a withering glance at the group as a whole. "With the rising crime figures in mind, if I hear of any member of this group spending half the night at the Esso garage on Tempest Road, take it from me there will be serious repercussions." The young girl who worked the night shift at the garage was reputed to be 'Cop friendly'.

The Inspector flipped the top page of the briefing sheet over. "The Animal Liberation Front is at it again as well, two butcher's shops defaced with spray paint, 'meat is murder' or some such. Get some checks done for likely suspects, anyone found with aerosol cans about their person wants their collar feeling, I want to see arrests."

"Does that include the ethnics in the 'Badlands' Sir?" asked one of the Group.

The young blacks were notorious for spraying their gang logos on the walls of local buildings to mark their 'turf'.

The Inspector looked up and for a moment there was a nervous silence in the parade room. He slowly removed his glasses and Alan noticed for the first time that there were two small indentations on either side of his nose, where the plastic bridge pieces had made impressions in his flesh.

"So, the bastard is human after all." he thought.

Totally ignoring the comments regarding the ethnic minority group now indigenous to the square mile colloquially known amongst 'C' Division Officers as the 'Badlands', the Inspector continued.

"I fail to see how any of these so called 'Animal Libbers' can stand on a busy thoroughfare and spray a butcher's shop window without being seen by someone. I want more foot patrols, Sergeant Robertson, see to it." The Inspector said and glanced up at the area beat Sergeant who pretended to make a note.

High visibility foot patrols were good for public relations, but the beat Sergeant knew that his lads and lasses had but fifteen minutes to respond to 999 calls which were very much on the increase. Response times were logged and recorded, the weekly figures being scrutinised by the Divisional Chief Inspector and it was his arse if his particular group were seen to be behind.

"I want the panda drivers out of their vehicles and walking their beat areas between calls. No more sitting with the engine running, wasting petrol with the heater on full blast. High visibility foot patrols promote public confidence and a feeling of well-being." The Inspector said, quoting directly from the Home Office Guidance.

"Foot patrols in the 'Badlands' as well Sir?" asked the Community Sergeant.

There was a hushed silence amongst members of the Group.

The Inspector slammed the briefing board down onto the table top. "I do not wish to hear eleven beat being referred to as the 'Badlands." he snapped. "It does nothing for community relations between the Police and the local ethnic minorities. The term bad, is indicative of a negative perception. From now on I will instigate misconduct proceedings against any Officer who I hear using this derogatory and insensitive term." The Inspector paused and looked across to the errant Sergeant. "And you should know better Sergeant Hicks; in fact, I'll see you after parade, my office if you please."

The Sergeant coloured slightly having been embarrassed by 'the boy wonder' in front of junior Officers. The Inspector continued.

"Right…just one or two more things from the briefing board. Item one, recent release from Her Majesty's Prison Holdthorpe, now resident on our patch, eleven beat, James Frederick Lyburn a.k.a. 'Midnight', 43 years, IC3 male, sentenced to five years for Section 18 wounding, slashed one of his working girls with an open razor. All Officers to make a note of his declared release address."

The Group Sergeant looked up and interjected. "Be careful with this chap Lyburn, he sounds like a nasty piece of work. Familiarise yourself with his photograph, he's got previous for weapons, in particular, the cutthroat razor which appears to be his weapon of choice…If seen, get those intelligence forms submitted. He's not the type to be rehabilitated and he won't be penitent. He'll be pissed off. Five years in Holdthorpe is no joke, he might just be looking for a little pay back."

The Inspector sat stone faced and pointed an accusatory finger towards the Group.

"Just remember, if any of you are called to the report of an assault in the prostitute area, or if this man is seen in the immediate area after an allegation of assault, by all means, let's have him brought to the station."

Alan noted that the Inspector had meticulously avoided using the term 'arrest'. Too long in the Racial Harmony Unit he thought.

The Inspector raised a cautionary finger. "I do not want to receive any complaints of excessive force or gratuitous violence from any of the residents of eleven beat. I shall send any such complaints straight to Discipline and Complaints so be warned…let's be professional."

One of Group raised a hand, the Inspector nodded condescendingly.

"Are we actually allowed to make arrests in the 'Bad…on eleven beat now Sir?"

The Inspector did not respond, but turned to the beat Sergeant, glowering as he gathered up his papers. "Deal with that issue Sergeant."

The Group rose as the Inspector left his seat, leaving the remainder of the briefing to his Sergeants; he walked from the parade room.

The Group now relaxed perceptively. Sergeant Dawson cast a disparaging glance at the Officer who had dared to mention arresting any of the ethnic minority in the now unspeakable area.

The Sergeant gave a swift sideways glance toward the briefing room door to ensure that the Inspector had indeed departed and satisfied that he now had sole charge over his minions, pointed at the errant Officer. "You ought to know better DeLacy. The Inspector is so politically correct, he makes Mary Whitehouse look like a two quid hand job hooker. Your card is well marked lad."

The Group collapsed with laughter at Pc DeLacy's obvious discomfort.

"Be careful with this one." the Sergeant continued in a more sombre tone, "He is destined for greater things and I strongly suspect that he will be the Chief Constable of some suffering Force before long and he doesn't care who he climbs over to get there. You have been warned."

There were various mutterings regarding the Inspectors parentage from the Group as they settled back in their seats for the rest of the briefing. Cigarettes were passed around and the Sergeant continued. "Right, those of you for special duty football tomorrow, you are to parade at the ground no later than two thirty and..."

The Sergeant rambled on regarding the general dress code and personal discipline whilst policing the match. Alan silently prayed that his name wasn't on the list.

Football, or 'special duty' was paid overtime and four or five hours at time and a half was very nice at the end of the month, but policing football matches was a pain, especially if the local Team happened to be playing Millwall.

If 'The Treatment' travelled north, there was bound to be grief. The fans wore surgical masks to prevent identification and were without doubt the most violent of the football hooligan element, axes, knives and even the odd handgun had been seized during previous arrests.

Some of Alan's colleagues actually volunteered for special duty weeks in advance. Paid overtime was at a premium and in any case, volunteers got the best duties, at the back of the South stand or in the Prisoner Reception Unit.

Alan never volunteered for football duty, not just because he didn't particularly enjoy football, nor because of the spitting or the odd bottle which took flight. 'Special duty' robbed you of a rest day and although the time and a half for payment was good, Alan had none of the domestic responsibilities which drew the married Officers with kids to give up their rest days.

The last time Alan had performed football duty; he had been standing at the edge of the pitch and had felt a sharp stinging sensation in his shoulder as a sharpened two pence piece fired from a catapult had struck him, cutting through the material of his raincoat and that of his tunic before nicking his flesh. Alan thought it must have been an airgun pellet at first and reached up to rub his shoulder and had felt the coin still wedged in the material of his uniform. He pulled the coin away and noted that it had been worked on with a degree of professionalism. The flat edges of the coin had been filed away to reveal a sharp cutting edge and had even been polished to remove all the file marks. Alan kept the coin to show to his colleagues. One had retorted whilst holding the coin up to the light. "Cheap bastards, you'd think they'd use a fifty pence piece so at least when it's ripped your ear off you could buy some fuckin' cigs."

The rest of the lads had laughed and Alan had tossed the coin into the box which contained the 'connected' property seized from prisoners brought into the reception area. It fell amongst the catapults, darts, marbles and 'Stanley' knives which were much preferred by the discerning football hooligan due to the fact that they were so sharp, the recipient didn't realise he'd been slashed until he felt the moist warmth and stickiness from the blood running down his back, by which time, the perpetrator was long gone.

There were darts to throw at the Police horses, marbles to make them stumble, knives, air guns, pellets and other essential paraphernalia required to really enjoy a good sporting fixture.

It wasn't even because of all that. He'd grown to accept the mindless violence aspect; it was more the fans themselves. They annoyed him; they annoyed him a great deal. It was the way they acted, like sheep, pushing and shoving each other to get into the ground, that along with the stupid songs, the banners, hats and scarves, the 'herd' behaviour. None of them seemed to be capable of independent thought. What one did was mimicked by the others, mindlessly and somehow magnetically drawn to disorderly and violent behaviour, just to 'belong'.

Alan considered that your basic football hooligan was required to have an I.Q. not exceeding double figures, have the minimum statutory tattoos on various parts of the anatomy, worth extra points if they were actually spelled correctly, a basic, fragmentary command of the English language where every third word was profane and the remainder made up of not more than two syllables.

It wasn't just the aggravation before and during the 'beautiful game' either. It was after the match, win or lose. Here the real senseless behaviour occurred.

In the City centre, the fans would fight, riot and destroy property. Shop windows would be assaulted and the City pavements and shop doorways would stink as a thousand rivulets of urine would meander towards the pavement cracks between shards of broken glass. The destruction was horrendous; cafes would be ransacked, with tables and chairs, having exited the premises through the plate glass windows, lying twisted and broken on the pavements. The interior walls would be reminiscent of the aftermath of the St Valentine's Day massacre, as sauce containers were used with the speed and dexterity of a Shaolin priest and streams of red, or the yellow equivalent, were sent with the much favoured double handed squeeze across the remaining fixtures and fittings of the chosen venue.

Such had been the cost of the destruction within the City centre over the years, that the fans were now escorted from the ground direct to the railway station or bus terminus, flanked by the Police Mounted Branch and Officers wearing protective headgear and every hundred yards or so, a Dog Handler, straining to control ninety pounds of extremely excited German Shepherd as the chanting fans 'trooped their colours'. The Police dogs it would appear were the only Police 'personnel' to actually enjoy football duty; one could almost see the evil intent in their eyes as they pranced at the end of their leashes.

Even the most raucous fan would fall silent as they passed the Police dogs, not wanting to be conspicuous or singled out by the Handler who may just, if the fan was sufficiently insulting or brave enough to goad his dog, be tempted to play out a foot or two of slack on the leash.

It never ceased to amaze Alan why members of the Public accepted these weekly invasions of the Queen's peace without demanding that the ground be closed, or moved to the wilds of the North Yorkshire moors or some disused airfield. Thousands of pounds were spent each week on Police wages, overtime and insurance claims. The senseless damage went unnoticed week after week during the football season.

Alan sat with baited breath as the last of the names were read out. "Pc 1402 Johns and last but not least, Pc 728 Morgan." The Sergeant closed the folder and Alan exhaled slowly. The group rose from their seats as if the parade was over.

"Just before you go." The Sergeant said, halting them.

"The pandas are like dustbins once again. When you've finished your shift, for Christ's sake clean the cars out, there's a waste bin by the petrol pump, so use it. I don't want to see Coke cans and fish and chip papers and the like strewn about, remember, the Officer who takes over from you does not want to start his or her shift by having to first get rid of your detritus, so clean it out before you leave it and furthermore, if it doesn't improve, the Inspector has warned that the Officers responsible will have their driving permits withdrawn for a month, so think on."

At this, the Sergeant stood and snatched up the briefing board. "That's it, there's plenty of calls waiting, let's have you all out."

The threat of a month's 'grounding' had fallen on deaf ears; most of the group would have given a month's wages to have their driving permits withdrawn. Beat patrol Officers generally drove 'pandas', so called because at their inception in the late sixties, the cars were painted light blue with white doors. They were small engined vehicles used as workhorses to get Officers from call to call and the drivers always ended up with a high work load, as it was generally quicker to send a panda than an Officer on foot. The panda drivers ended up with all the shoplifters and the burglars, the assaults and the arrests from domestic disturbances and the worst duty of all, ferrying the beat Inspector around, an unwelcome passenger who would sit in stony silence whilst you patrolled the Division. No smoking, no coffee stops and definitely no sneaking off to see Mrs Alsop, who's Husband was away working in Bahrain.

There was little or no advantage in being a panda driver. It was typically ridiculous to consider that taking someone's driving permit would be considered to be a punishment, however, the Police Force has never been strong on logic, far too many Bramshill types in existence for that. The practice of 'grounding' simply put extra work load on the other panda drivers who would now have to also attend to an increased number of calls due to the loss of a driver, whereas the 'offender', now on foot, heaved a sigh of relief and walked off casually onto his re-assigned foot beat and a pot of coffee with the lonely, yet reputedly sporting Mrs Alsop.

There had been more than one occasion, where a panda driver having come to the end of his clerical tether, had purposely backed the suffering vehicle into the petrol pump within the station back yard to put it out of its misery, or if the Officer was feeling particularly militant, into another panda, thereby disabling both, two birds with one stone as it were. This generous, selfless act by the Officer, would earn him the everlasting praise of his colleagues, having effectively given someone else a brief, yet welcome respite.

The erring driver could not be prosecuted for any offence under the Road Traffic Act as the 'accident' was not on a road; all that could be expected was a verbal lashing, a month on foot beat and his name forever stricken from the Inspector's Christmas card list.

The myth that all clouds have a silver lining is not altogether to be relied upon. There was always the threat that the ancient scrolls would be brought from the depths of the Police station and some medieval rite invoked and the Officer pursued by way of some obscure Force Standing or General Order. Even though the Officer was safe from any prosecution under the criminal statutes, a senior Officer worth his Bramshill qualification, could always find a little something lurking in one of the paragraphs which covered such a situation. Destruction of Police owned property (wanton) or failing to ensure that Police issue property was not so damaged or destroyed (wanton or otherwise) or, of course, the catch-all Conduct Unbecoming an Officer or CUBO as it was colloquially known. A CUBO could be anything from yawning on parade to actually getting caught in *flagrante delicto* with the frustrated, yet apparently adventurous Mrs Alsop.

"What the fuck's detritus anyway?" asked one of the Group, when the Sergeant had left and was safely out of earshot.

"Fuckin' skin disease innit?" replied another, raising chuckles from the group as they filtered out of the parade room.

Alan left the room immediately to make himself a cup of coffee in the Traffic office. He walked down the corridor, passing the spacious heated front office, where the clerks sat drinking tea and flicking through the 'dailies'. It was, so the clerks would have their operational colleagues believe, extremely injurious to one's health and safety being an office clerk. There were telephones to be argued with, and heaven knows that can be stressful. Crimes to type up and members of the Public who came to the station to bother the clerks with inane, trivial complaints of Burglary, Assault or Theft.

Office clerks were paid the same as their 'operational' colleagues. Some did it to escape the rigours of beat work, others were 'guests', having been removed from confrontational duties due to illness or a temporary disability, or in some cases, placed on 'restricted duties' whilst waiting for the outcome of misconduct proceedings.

Alan nodded to the clerk at the front desk, "Give us a nuisance box, then Derek."

The clerk smiled as he handed Alan one of the 'Burndept' personal radios along with a fresh battery which Alan clipped to its base, instinctively depressing the small button on the top of the radio to check that the red transmit light actually illuminated.

Satisfied that he had 'comms', he entered the office of the station Sergeant, who contrary to the belief of the Divisional Command Team, actually ran the station. Seated in his domain having just returned from the bar area with his winnings from the one armed bandit, was Police Sergeant 112 Ronald Dennison, ex Royal Navy and a man in his thirtieth year of service, who pleasant as he was, never stopped reminding his juniors of that fact. Sergeant Dennison was simply waiting for the last few weeks to tick away so that he could finally, in that most English of gesticulations, raise two fingers to the Police Force and retire to his narrowboat on the Norfolk Broads.

Alan felt something of a kindred spirit with Ron Dennison, this being due to the former's inbred distrust of anyone over and above the rank of Sergeant and the fact that he had once, some millennia previously, served in Her Majesty's forces *and* been a Traffic man.

"Hey Sarge, how's it hangin?" Alan said cheerfully, as he entered the station office and smiled at the large pile of pound coins stacked neatly in front of the aged Sergeant. Clearly the good Sergeant Dennison had recently enjoyed a modicum of success with the one armed bandit in the bar area.

"By the left as usual." the old man winked slyly. "What can I do for you Pendle lad, as long as it doesn't involve money."

Alan smiled, "Well, it does indirectly Sarge, but not yours, so if you'll be so kind as to shackle your bulwarks and raise the mizzen mast or whatever you old Navy types get up to on yer days off, you could issue me with some fresh batteries for my torch."

Dennison scowled in a friendly sort of manner. "What you doin' with 'em Pendle lad, sellin' them on the black market, you were only on the scrounge last week."

Alan raised a cautionary eyebrow, "You're not allowed to call it the black market anymore Sarge, you're clearly not keeping up with the times, it's a brave new world Ron." Alan said, sitting on the edge of his old mentor's desk. "The word black is now synonymous with something evil or bad, such as blackmail, or black magic. In schools, bah bah black sheep is now bah bah green sheep, get it?"

"What the bleedin' 'ell you bin smokin' Pendle?" The old man had one of his rare genuinely puzzled looks about him.

Alan leaned casually against the office door jamb. "It's like I say Sarge, the use of the word black is to be avoided if at all possible, says so in Force Orders, especially if you happen to be dealing with a member of the ethnic minority. 'Frinstance, if I'm dealing with a road accident and one of the driver's is coloured, see, not *black*...coloured, I would have to be careful not to describe the particular junction as an accident blackspot, insinuatin' by use of the term black, that that particular junction was bad, or worse than others, but that the junction in question was simply dangerous or more prone to accident activity. See what I mean Sarge?"

"I can see that the eunuchs at Force Headquarters 'ave got you successfully brainwashed, Pendle lad. Thank Christ I've only sixty days to do."

"You could do worse than to spend those few remaining weeks in the Racial Harmony Unit Sarge, it would give you a whole new outlook on life." Alan said smiling.

"Give me a pain in the arse more like. What was it you were on the scrounge for?"

"Batteries, torch for the use of, in triplicate Sarge."

"Come on then you bleedin' nuisance." The old man grunted as he heaved himself from his seat, grabbing the keys to the stationary store from the board above his desk.

"You leavin' that lot unguarded Sarge?" Alan said, pointing to the coins stacked in columns of ten on his desk.

The old Sergeant looked back and nodded his appreciation, "Good thinking Pendle lad." he said, tapping his temple lightly with his index finger as he turned the key in the Station Sergeants door and pocketed the key. "We'll make a Detective of you yet."

Alan snorted his disgust, "Christ Sarge, I thought we were mates..."

Alan fully expected to hear a quiet hiss as the stationary store door was opened, suspecting it to be hermetically sealed to protect the valuable (non-auditable) kit contained within. The door, however, opened in a disappointingly silent manner.

Inside was a veritable 'Aladdin's cave' of clerical requisites, pens, pencils, rubber bands, typewriter ribbons and of course the batteries, stacked like munitions in neat rows. Batteries however, were accountable and therefore subject to audit and with Christmas not too far away, highly desirable. Alan would not have been at all surprised to see a video camera installed somewhere in the store to protect the Forces' valuable assets against unofficial requisition and subsequent use in some kiddies radio controlled dune buggy or Albert the amazing talking bear (batteries not included).

"Thanks Sarge." said Alan, taking the offered jewel encrusted, solid gold, Faberge limited edition batteries and slotting them into the base of his issue torch.

Tossing the torch into his briefcase, Alan climbed the stairs to the upper corridor to where the Road Traffic office was situated. Entering the office, he grabbed the keys to his allocated patrol vehicle and looked up at the notice board for anything of interest.

The Traffic Sergeant had pinned a large, hastily scrawled demand for tea fund money alongside the advanced duties board. Alan smiled as he read "Mine will be a while coming Sarge, application to the International Monetary Fund pending." which someone had added across the sheet. Alan reached to the top of his uniform locker, took down his flat cap with its pristine white cotton cover and placed it purposefully on his head.

*****

The cold air bit into Alan's ears as he opened the outer door of the station and stepped out briskly towards the car park at the rear. His breath formed smoke like vapour as he exhaled and as he rounded the corner of the building, he smiled knowingly as he noted a fresh dent in the side of the suffering petrol pump. The ground was crisp and there was a glint of frost where the late afternoon sun cast long shadows from the corner of the building.

He shivered as he opened the rear door of the patrol car and tossed his briefcase onto the rear seat.

The Rover SD1 sat resplendent in its gleaming white livery and bright red fluorescent striping. The new 'American' style bank of rotating lights encased within a clear blue plastic bar, extending across the full width of the roof, disrupted the sleek lines of David Bache's British Leyland masterpiece, yet outwardly and necessarily displayed the demanding role performed by the vehicle.

Alan leaned into the car and after first ensuring that the gear lever was in the neutral position, he slotted the key into the ignition barrel and turned it clockwise. The three and a half litre V8 immediately purred into life. Whilst the engine warmed through, Alan rubbed his gloved hand across the windscreen; he was disappointed to find that a thin membrane of ice had formed across the glass. "First of the year." he thought. "It'll catch a few out tonight."

As the Rover warmed, Alan opened the rear tailgate; he checked that the emergency warning signs were all present and correct and that he had the required number of road closure cones. He shook the fire extinguisher and glanced at the small gauge on the brass top piece, the needle was hard across into the green and the safety pin was in place. Blankets, first aid kit, brush and shovel, the full complement, all as it should be.

Deciding that it was too cold to physically check the tyre pressures, Alan gave them a visual inspection; all looked well inflated with plenty of tread.

Shivering, he clambered into the driver's seat; he adjusted the seat rake and height, re-adjusted the rear view mirror and gently eased his foot down on the accelerator pedal. No faults were declared by any of the dashboard lights and as the engine revs increased, the oil pressure gauge rose reassuringly, to show fifty pounds per square inch. Alan nodded to himself appreciatively and maintained slight pressure on the accelerator pedal, allowing the tachometer needle to remain at the two thousand RPM mark. The hydraulic tappets ceased their initial chatter and the deep guttural growl from the exhausts echoed back from the walls of the station. He shivered again and turned on the heater blower, directing the blast of air towards the inside of the windscreen, to dissipate the thin film of condensation.

He punched the VHF button on the multi-channel radio set in the centre console and immediately, the interior of the vehicle was filled with static laden chatter. He waited for a quiet spot and keyed the handset to book on duty.

"Papa Yankee One Zero to control receiving."

"One Zero, go ahead." the operator replied through the static.

Alan adjusted the squelch button and the crackling static died to an acceptable level.

"Papa Yankee One Zero, 10/1 patrol, crew is 868 10/7 over."

"10/4" nothing at this time." replied the operator, acknowledging his call.

The radio fell silent and Alan settled himself down into the seat. Letting the engine revs die off, he flicked the switches on the bank within the dashboard facia and the emergency lighting and public address systems came to life. The blue lights were satisfyingly reflected back from the walls of the building and a quick flick of the siren button rewarded him with a brief screech from the wailers.

Happy that for once, Pc Oldfield had actually refuelled the vehicle, he zeroed the odometer reading and after checking that the vehicle's log book had been completed, drove slowly out of the car park and onto the perimeter track which led to the main road. The tyres crunched pleasingly on the gravel surface and the vehicle left a plume of condensation as the exhaust gasses were emitted from the twin pipes at the rear.

After nodding to a driver who had slowed to allow him out into the steady flow of traffic, Alan eased the patrol car out onto the main road and commenced patrol.

## **Two**

James Frederick Lyburn, was just the wrong side of 40, lean, muscular and two inches over six feet tall. He possessed the kind of intense, intimidating features, that coupled with his size, made most men cautious about remaining under his gaze for too long. His nostrils were flared, somewhat beyond the normal for his race; this involuntarily stretched the cheek muscles upwards, creating a snarling countenance which most would consider menacing.

Lyburn's street name was 'Midnight', adopted for two reasons. His skin colouring was of the deepest black, the heritage of his Masai ancestors and the fact that midnight was his time, rarely seen on the streets until this untimely hour.

Most coloureds who were anybody to be reckoned with, had street names and used them publicly, to avoid their real names being bantered around in the pubs and clubs which they frequented, the same premises, that were also frequented by the Detectives from the Drugs Squad or 'Vice'.

A street name, would mean very little to the Officers as no one would ever provide a name to the title. A given name could be one of choice, or one bestowed upon the recipient by the local 'brothers' due to an unusual practice or particular mannerism. Such names could also be the reminder of past incidents, such as the street name adopted by Leroy Lester Cannonier. 'Nightstick'. Cannonier received the dubious street name, due to a disfigurement on the right side of his face, where the cheekbone had been shattered and the lower part of his ear torn away.

After a profitable night's work, dealing in soft drugs at one of the illegal all night parties or 'Blues' as they were known, Cannonier had been stopped by a uniformed Officer whilst driving his vehicle home. An argument between the two had ensued, when the Officer proposed seizing the excise licence from the windscreen of Cannonier's motor due to the fact that the registration mark shown on the disk, bore little resemblance to the actual number of his vehicle. The Officer suspected that the tax disc had been stolen and demanded that Cannonier remove it from its holder and hand it to him for closer inspection.

Fearing immediate arrest and the subsequent discovery of over two pounds of good quality cannabis resin stashed in the boot of his car, Cannonier had protested. "Alright, alright, I'll get it, no big deal." He had reached back into the vehicle as if to retrieve the disc, but had entered the glove box and withdrawn a knife with which to threaten the Officer thinking that this one, like most, would back away. The uniform was single crewed and Cannonier reckoned that he wouldn't risk a stabbing over a 'bent' tax disc.

Unfortunately for Cannonier, this Officer was no Probationer, but a seasoned veteran of the coloured area of the City and was well schooled in the methods used by the blacks to evade arrest. He had been ready as the knife was produced and the Officer's heavy dark wood truncheon had arced across from the Officer's staff pocket and smashed across Cannonier's face, taking him down with a single blow.

The Officer panicked slightly, seeing the flow of blood and the devastation he had brought about the face of his 'prisoner'. He had quickly thrown the knife into the foot well of his panda and bundled the unconscious Cannonier into one of the rear seats to drive him to the local Infirmary.

Feigning unconsciousness, 'Nightstick' had effected his escape from the Officer's vehicle as it had stopped at the first set of red traffic lights and by the time the uniform had unbuckled his safety belt and wrenched on the hand-brake, Cannonier was long gone into the night.

Unable to attend the local Infirmary where the local Police would have been waiting, his cheek bones had knitted imperfectly and the tear across his ear went unsutured, so that the ends of the wound failed to join. He had been left with a hideous scar and a facial deformity which would remain with him until the end of his days. He had earned his street name the hard way. His street credibility, however, increased tenfold and to a young black on his way up, this was of far greater importance than a few unsightly scars.

*****

'Midnight' lay back on his bed, his hands behind his head as he looked around him. The room was dark and claustrophobic, any daylight that there might have been, failed to gain access through the accumulation of filth on the windows. A single naked light bulb hung from the center of the ceiling, struggling to emit light through the dust and nicotine staining on its outer shell.

Spartan though it was, 'Midnight' had missed his bedsit room whilst he had been away. Although the cell he had occupied with two others for almost five years had been infinitely cleaner and brighter than this, now he could leave any time he wished and come and go as he pleased. He'd been kept like a caged animal, counting off the days of his captivity with silent rage, one thousand eight hundred and twenty days, each one served with forced military precision.

The awakening bell, then the rapping on the cell door by the 'screws', slopping out, breakfast, then exercise, workshop, lunch, then slammed up for the remaining sixteen hours of the day. 'Midnight' could have secured an earlier release, but at first, he too easily showed his contempt for the screws, all of them white and who had called him "Uncle Tom", "Kunta Kinte" or simply "Nigger".

He had retaliated at first, with a head butt to the face or a knee to the groin, but the 'screws' had been ready with their sticks and they had beaten him. He had spent numerous weeks in solitary confinement, in total darkness. His meals, served up on plastic plates passed through a small aperture in the cell door, had reeked of urine or faeces or had glistened with spittle. His non-compliance with their rigid discipline, had earned him nothing but the right to serve the full term imposed.

He would refuse orders to leave his cell, having to be pulled out whilst he spat or punched out at the Prison Officers who entered to search for contraband, anything to show his contempt for their system. 'Midnight' didn't want to be rehabilitated; he wanted out, to pick up where he had left off. He was missing big money, every day inside was costing him.

He seethed when he thought of his girls out on the streets, working and keeping the punter's money for themselves. His revenge would be swift and terrible if they hadn't kept his percentage. None of them would argue that whilst he had been away, they had been left unprotected and so deserved all the hard earned money. They all knew what had happened to the 'Chinese'.

The days and months had dragged by with monotonous regularity. 'Midnight' made himself ready, he did press ups by the thousand, stomach pulls with his back against the coldness of the cell floor and his legs resting on the mattress of his bunk, raising his head until it touched his knees, pumping until the lactic acid burned him and his abdominals finally cramped and bulged.

The Prison gymnasium, he left to the other 'cons'. He worked out alone and in silence, his anger festering like an open wound. He fixed his eyes on a point across from him where the paint on the wall had either been dislodged as the screws had thrown the bunk across the cell during one of their many searches for contraband or weapons, or had fallen away through decay in the old Victorian Prison. The missing paint had a shape which vaguely resembled a man's head, a white man's head, a white pig.

He stretched out across the cell with his ankles resting on the ledge of the opposite lower bunk. He gripped his bunk rail, his palms pressing into the cold tubing as he lowered himself, pushing up slowly and breathing steadily, rhythmically as he felt the triceps muscle group in the back of his arms pumping. The pain started as the blood surged through the sinews, his eyes closed, hate, pump, work, pump, stare at the white pig's head and make ready.

He worked until the muscle was destroyed and could hold his weight no longer. He collapsed to the floor of his cell, sweat running from his forehead and into his eyes, the salt taste, the stinging in his eyes, the throbbing muscles. He would win, he would piss on their five years.

*****

'Midnight' looked about his single room bedsit. A fading Bob Marley poster was pinned up against wallpaper now so nicotine stained, that the pattern was hardly discernible. An old mahogany wardrobe stood by the wall opposite his single bed, the varnish peeling, looking as faded and tired as the carpet on which it sat. A chest of drawers, painted many years previously, leaned against the wall underneath the single pane window, the once white paintwork now yellowing, even with the lack of sunlight penetrating the room. The curtains rested their ragged edges along the top of the chest, too long by four or five inches, they sagged from the runners which barely held their weight. A single bar electric fire sat in the boarded up fire hearth and glowed with a faint humming sound and every now and then, the porcelain connector gave off a faint creak as it expanded with the meagre heat. Apart from this, the room was silent.

'Midnight' was out. He had survived the beatings and the solitary, he was back in circulation, harder and leaner than before. He was disappointed to find that news of his arrest and the reputation he had earned whilst in Prison was all but forgotten. Five years is a long time, things happen and situations change. Street credibility is not enhanced by anonymity.

He pulled himself up from the bed and crossed the room to the top drawer of the chest from which he withdrew a pipe and a crumpled polythene bag. Returning to the sweat stained mattress, he laid out and from the pocket of his jeans he took a battered tin containing tobacco, other than a well-thumbed, dog-eared pack of playing cards, this was the only souvenir remaining from his Prison days.

Opening the tin, he pulled away a wad of the damp strands and rolled them between the palms of his hands. With deft fingers, he separated the strands and added some of the contents from the polythene bag. He mixed the small seeds and crushed leaf in with his tobacco and filled the pipe bowl, tamping down the mixture with his finger until it was firm. Lighting the pipe, he leaned his head back against the wall and inhaled deeply.

The room was soon filled with the pungent heady aroma of the mix and 'Midnight' relaxed. He laid out full length on the bed and closed his eyes. The drug coursed through the microscopic capillaries in his lungs and flooded into his bloodstream. As the mild opiate found its way into the ventral area of his brain, he smiled at the onset of euphoria and his thoughts drifted back to the night causal to his demise.

*****

The night was warm and humid, 'Midnight' drove his car down the streets where his girls worked. Eddie Grant pumped out his heavy reggae from the cassette player, he felt good. The windows were wound down to catch what little breeze there might be. He cruised, now and then waving casually to a particular group of brothers who congregated at the street corners, their corners, their 'turf'. But tonight wasn't for socialising; he had business to attend to.

'Midnight' ran twelve girls, three of them black, eight white and a Chinese, very rare and much in demand. Her Father had owned a rundown take away in the black area of the City, 'Midnight' had learned that he was a user and that his supplier had fallen foul of a Detective Sergeant in the Drug Squad, earning eight years for possession with intent to supply. 'Midnight' entered his world and took over from the hapless dealer, making sure that the cadaverous old man was supplied with enough heroin to keep him happy.

The old man's business had started to falter as the soul food shops flourished as the blacks took up residence in the squalid three storey houses, now converted into flats. The old man's habit was desperate and now, extremely expensive. Such is the grip of the drug, the old man had 'sold' his Daughter to 'Midnight' in return for a constant flow of the light brown powder.

'Midnight' had weighed up the proposition, a fourteen year old Chinese girl on the streets would be worth good money, far more than it would cost him to keep the old man in the drug he craved. In any case, the old man's brain was addled, his speech incoherent and he would fall into bouts of semi consciousness on regular occasions. His time was short and the Chinese girl was young and slender, with blue black hair and classic almond shaped eyes. Just fourteen when he had first sampled her in his room, teaching her the finer points of what was soon to become her trade.

'Midnight' had helped the old man inject himself, slowly releasing the belt pulled tight around his withered bicep to allow the drug to surge upwards and into his bloodstream. The old man now lay slumped in a large easy chair in the room above the restaurant. Spittle drooled from the corner of his mouth and his eyes took on a distant, vacant expression.

'Midnight' had taken the young girl by the arm and led her to his car. They had driven in silence through the dimly lit streets towards his bedsit; 'Midnight' making no effort to calm the petrified expression on her face.

On entering the flats, he pushed her in the small of her back, ushering her towards the bare wooden stairs leading to the upper floor. As she climbed in front of him, he gazed at her coltish legs and lifted the hem of her skirt, smiling as he felt her stiffen to his touch. Reaching the top, he made some effort to calm the 'Chinese' who was trembling and had yet, uttered not one word, not even in protest. 'Midnight' put a muscular arm around her waist, not so much for consolation, more to let her know the difference in strength between them. He opened the door to his room and pulled her in. She had stood in the centre of the room, near to the bottom of the bed, her hands clasped tightly across her lap, her fingers nervously tying themselves together. 'Midnight' put on a record and the worn stylus had hissed out the strains of a reggae beat.

He crossed over to her and her eyes widened in horror; his hands went to her shoulders gripping her tightly before sliding them down the full length of her back and onto her buttocks. He was already hard for her, and he pushed his hips against her, causing her to whimper.

Taking hold of the bottom of the worn sweat shirt she was wearing, he slowly pulled it upwards. Forcing her arms upwards with his strength, he threw the shirt into the corner of the room and held her away from him to look at her. Her breast were small, not yet fully developed. He reached for them, feeling the softness of her skin, he could feel her shaking as he ran his thumbs across her nipples. 'Midnight' pushed himself against her as he toyed with her tiny breasts. "Take it out." he said and guided her small hand to the front of his jeans. She resisted at first, but he gripped her wrist tightly and pushed her hand down harder. She fumbled with the top button, unable to manipulate it with her trembling fingers. He slapped her hard across the face, she shrieked at the sudden pain and a sob forced its way from her throat. 'Midnight' gripped her tightly with his left hand and with his right, undid the buttons of his jeans which then fell to the floor. "Hold it girl." he demanded. "Take it out."

She pulled away from him, turning away from his breath which was now coming in short pants directly into her face. "Do it." he snarled.

She moaned with fright as he pushed her hand down the front of his briefs, curling his huge hand around hers, forcing her to take hold of him.

'Midnight' turned his head to the ceiling, eyes closed with delight. "Alright, alright." he whispered to himself in ecstasy.

She sobbed uncontrollably now, simply holding on to his hardness, too frightened to let go. Running his hand down over her buttocks he slipped it under her skirt and felt up her thighs. She stiffened and shrieked at his touch, but he gripped her tightly and with a single motion between finger and thumb, he snapped the thin side of her underpants and pulled them away. His hand went savagely between her legs, making her cry out.

'Midnight' was either unaware, or indifferent to her distress, he was too far gone. His eyes were still closed, he was panting hard and sweating, the small globules forming on his brow and neck. His fingers roughly probed her and ignoring her frightened sobs, he pushed her over onto the bed, pushing his muscular legs between hers; forcing them apart. He paused for a second to look down at her nakedness, apart from the skirt which was now bunched up around her waist. He looked up at her face and saw that it was contorted with fear.

"Lighten up girl." he said, "Just relax." and moved down between her legs.

Taking both her wrists in his left hand, he raised them above her head, gripping them hard. With his right, he guided himself into her.

She cried out with a long stifled scream as he pushed himself into her, and as he moved his hips with short jerking thrusts, her cries fell off to short sobbing gasps. She turned her head to one side and her body went limp as 'Midnight' emptied himself into her. He fell on top of her, now drained of all his strength.

Ignoring her doleful sobs, he lay for a while; his head against her breasts, listening to her heart pounding as his breathing slowed. She wept, yet he was unmoved. He withdrew himself from her and left the bed. He crossed to the chest of drawers and took out a stained syringe and a small bag of brown powder. A blackened spoon lay next to a candle in the drawer bottom, these he withdrew and looking across at her, lying motionless in the foetal position with her hands across her face, he lit the candle.

The first fix would be free, but thereafter, once the craving had taken hold, she would very soon be his to do with as he pleased.

'Midnight' had smiled to himself as he cruised the streets, remembering the first time with the 'Chinese'.

Over the months that had followed, he had fed her the heroin and taken full control of her and taught her the trade. Since then, she'd worked for him to pay for her habit and her Father's slow, lingering demise. She had learned something that 'Midnight' hadn't taught her, she'd learned how much her youth was worth on the streets, working extra tricks on different 'turf', holding out on him and making him look bad in front of the other 'brothers'.

'Midnight' cruised to the Chinese girl's patch, she was not there, although he wasn't surprised to find her absent, she never had been short of clients. He parked his car in a driveway which afforded him a view of the whole street. Most of the overhead street lights were broken, he knew that if she was working, she'd be back in fifteen minutes or so and make for a spot under one of the remaining lights. Like a moth he thought.

He turned off the ignition and sat in silence, the ticking of the cooling engine the only sound. 'Midnight' reached across to the glove box and his fingers went instinctively to the straight razor which he kept out of immediate view, but readily accessible. He took it out and palmed it, feeling the ivory handle cold in his grip. Holding it between index finger and thumb, he flicked his wrist and the stainless blade slipped silently out. He tapped the blade against his thigh as he watched up and down the street.

A pair of approaching headlights made him sit up straight. The oncoming car slowed and pulled over to the kerb between the street lights. 'Midnight' furrowed his brow and strained to see which one of his girls would leave the vehicle. The passenger door opened and the driver reached up to the courtesy light, quickly turning it off so that the interior of the vehicle remained in darkness. The driver looked nervously up and down the street, worried, fearing interest from Vice Squad Officers who worked in plain clothes and unmarked cars around the red light area. He'd finished with her now, the excitement now abated, his lust satisfied, he just wanted to go as quickly as possible.

'Midnight' made out the voice. It was the 'Chinese'. She closed the car door and the vehicle sped away. He watched as the 'Chinese' walked back to the lamp post, pulling down the hem of her short skirt and straightening the front of her blouse. She was illuminated by the dim yellow light and leaned back against the concrete post and shivered.

'Midnight' heard the car's exhaust note fade away and then there was silence. He watched her as she lit a cigarette and shifted her slight body weight from one foot to the other as she looked around her.

She stopped dead. The cigarette fell from her fingers. The 'Chinese' froze as she recognised the outline of 'Midnight's' vehicle. He opened the car door, allowing the interior light to illuminate his face and he heard her utter a short moan as she recognised him. She turned as if to run, then immediately turned back knowing that it would do her no good. If she ran, he would surely catch her and his rage would be without mercy and she would be beaten. Her good looks were her livelihood; she could not afford to be beaten, so she feigned a twitching smile as 'Midnight' walked across the road towards her. She glanced nervously up and down the street, in the vain hope that someone would be there, not that anyone would have intervened, not on 'Midnight's' turf. Here not a soul would utter a single word of protest even if he beat her to death in front of them.

'Midnight' approached her smiling broadly. She eased a little, but not completely convinced of his mood, she remained cautious.

"Bin holdin' out on me Mai Long, bin fuckin' with the man." he said, his face immediately losing its smiling countenance.

Her eyes opened wide as if to show her absolute surprise at the allegation.

"No, no I wouldn't, I give you it all." she stuttered, stepping backwards until further retreat was prevented by a low garden wall.

'Midnight' grabbed her by her long blue black hair, his face was drawn and tight, his lips curled back. "I got eyes and ears on the street, even when I 'ain't here bitch. You think I don't know every fuckin' move you make, every trick you pull and where." His voice raised as he spoke, each word louder than the one before.

He shook her head violently, still grasping her hair in a tight bunch at the nape of her neck. She wailed her innocence, which seemed to incense him further. He flicked the ivory handle and the stainless steel blade appeared in an instant.

He'd meant to just cut her, on her back or buttocks where it would cause pain, but not disfigurement. She was still an investment after all.

The 'Chinese' saw the blade as it flashed in the dull sodium glare of the street light and she instinctively twisted her body away from his grip to try to avoid the flashing blade. As she twisted, her legs buckled and instead of the blade slicing across her back, her body weight shifted and the blade bit deep into her back, sinking in through the sparse flesh and cutting at her entrails. She immediately went limp and 'Midnight' seeing the damage and the blood flowing freely from her side, released his grip and she fell like a discarded marionette to the pavement.

He stared at her for a brief moment, the blade still in his hand; he watched the pool of blood seep through the material of her skimpy blouse and gather in a dark cloying mass on the cold flagstones of the pavement. 'Midnight' snatched a look up and down the street and quickly fingered the blade back between the ivory handle, slipping the weapon back into the pocket of his jeans.

Running back across the road to where he had left his vehicle, he leapt in and fumbled with the ignition key, his fingers wet and slippery with her blood. The engine had cooled and was not quite warm enough to start straight away. The starter motor whined as he pumped the accelerator pedal. Convinced that the 'Chinese' was dead or at least dying, he shouted at the dashboard "Come on…COME ON!" His fingers feverishly twisted the ignition key once again. The engine finally caught and spluttered into life.

'Midnight' rammed the gear lever forward and dropped the clutch causing the vehicle to lurch forwards onto the road surface. He accelerated hard as he spun the steering wheel, the tyres screaming in protest as they lost traction with the cold road surface. The car carried him down the poorly lit street to the junction with the main road. He barely slowed at the give way lines and fought with the wheel as the vehicle skidded as it slewed around the harsh left hand turn.

'Midnight' was in panic and failed to see the oncoming motorcyclist approaching from his right. The rear tyre of the motorcycle howled as the wheel locked up solid and the rear of the machine snaked from side to side as the rider fought to control his bike.

Oblivious to this, 'Midnight' floored the accelerator pedal and the car responded, the engine screaming in protest. A number of oncoming vehicles flashed their headlights. He was mystified at first, until his eyes fell to the dashboard of his car. "Lights!

Lights nigger." he shouted to himself, throwing the switch. "Jesus, Jesus." he muttered. "Slow down man, cool it, fuckin' cool it." He became angry with himself, realising that he was attracting unnecessary attention.

He slowed his vehicle as he regained control of himself. He was shaking, not with fear or the enormity of what he had done, he was beyond that, it was the adrenalin flowing through him.

The 'Chinese' was dead, he was sure of that…So much blood.

His mind raced with the possibilities of what lay ahead. He stopped instinctively at a red traffic light and pulled across to the offside lane alongside a young couple in a VW beetle. After a moment or two, he looked across into their vehicle and noticed that the occupants were both looking at him; he looked away, fearing recognition. His heart tripped a beat as he caught sight of his fingers which gripped the top of his steering wheel; they were covered in blood, her blood, which now formed into sticky glutinous webs between his fingers as it congealed. He snatched his hands down out of view and jumped at the horn blast behind him. The lights had changed and the vehicle to his nearside, had now gone.

The headlights on the car behind him flashed impatiently and 'Midnight', his legs shaking as the adrenalin slowly dissipated from his muscles, let the clutch out too quickly and his vehicle lurched forwards. He quickly pulled over to the nearside lane and the impatient driver to the rear, sounded his horn as he overtook. Under normal circumstances, this would have not gone without any form of response, but tonight, he let it slide. "Jesus, get your shit together man." he told himself.

He closed his eyes momentarily and breathed in deeply, willing his heart to slow down and the pounding in his temples to subside.

He had no recollection of parking his motor, nor of fumbling with the key in the door of his bed sit, but when he palmed down the light switch and the room was bathed in the dull light, he could see that he was covered in her blood. It was on his shirt and down the front of his jeans, it was on his trainers where she had fallen and his hands and arms were covered with the sticky mess. He clenched his fists and the blood where it had dried on his skin; fell away onto the threadbare carpet in wafer thin translucent flakes.

He stripped himself naked and hurriedly gathered up his clothing and shoes and carried them down the unlit corridor to the shared bathroom. The bathroom was vacant. Locking the door behind him, he ran the taps and held his trainers under the running water, seeing it turn first pink and then darker red as the water dissolved the congealed blood. He rubbed at the material with his fingers, freeing the sticky mess from the welts and from where it had seeped into the lace eyelets. 'Midnight' reached across the sink and snatched up a toothbrush and squatting naked in the bath tub, he scrubbed the shoes until the water ran clear down the open plug hole.

He pushed the rubber plug into the drain hole and allowed the bath to half fill with tepid water. He cleaned himself with his bare hands splashing the water up over his forearms. He reached for the bundle of clothes and immersed them in the bath water, rubbing the material with his hands to dissolve the blood which was matted between the threads. His hands rubbed feverishly at the dark patches which dissipated and slowly disappeared as the water diluted the clots.

When he was satisfied that all the evidence of the 'Chinese' had disappeared, he stood in the bath and towelled himself dry, shivering in the cold.

He squeezed out his sodden clothing and dropped them into the sink. Pulling the plug, he watched as the pink water slowly swirled away. Cupping his hand, he threw the remaining water up the sides of the bath to dislodge the pink scurf which clung to the greasy ring which ran around the inner circumference of the chipped enamel.

'Midnight' returned to his room and turned on the electric fire. He hung his wet clothes over a chair which he placed in front of it. He sat on his bed, still naked and shivered as his clothes slowly started to steam. He held his head in his hands and sighed deeply, exhausted with the panic and expended energy. Try as he might, he could not rid himself of the vision of the lake of blood, which had spilled out over the pavement from the 'Chinese'. She was dead, he'd killed her hadn't he? Killed her with his blade, he'd seen her as she fell to the floor, dead for sure, so much blood from someone so small.

He was immune to the cold of the room, his body warmed with the exhilaration, yet he shivered uncontrollably, his thigh muscles twitched and he felt his testicles ache as his scrotal sac tightened and puckered. He needed his pipe and reached for it. Taking the polythene bag, he plunged the bowl of the pipe deep into its contents and pushed home the vegetable mixture, tamping it down tight. He added a little tobacco and noticed with a little satisfaction, that his hands were steady; he lit the concoction and inhaled deeply.

### **Three**

The evening flow of rush hour traffic droned past Alan as he sat in the patrol car which he had placed strategically on a small gravelled layby which overlooked a roundabout on the City Ring road. The parking spot was one which Alan favoured, especially at this time of day. It served a dual purpose, firstly, he was easily visible, the fluorescent striping down the sides of his Police car reflecting the headlight beams of the oncoming vehicles, having a salutary effect on drivers who may be speeding into the hazard, the fronts of those vehicles dipping sharply as brakes were hastily applied. Secondly, the position was such, that it afforded him a view of all four carriageways as the vehicles entered and egressed the roundabout. He watched for certain registration numbers, those which matched the ones he had scribbled onto the sheet of paper which hung from a small suction cup clipboard which he had attached to the windscreen, disqualified drivers, stolen vehicles and known document offenders.

The driver's window of the patrol car was fully down. Alan surreptitiously smoked a cigarette as he watched the traffic weaving from lane to lane. There was the odd horn blast as some irate driver felt cheated out of his position when someone cut across in front of him and every now and then, the tell-tale rubbery squeal of someone 'over cooking' it into the roundabout. He cupped the cigarette in the palm of his hand and turned his face into the patrol car to inhale. He looked out onto the Ring Road again, letting the smoke out slowly, disguising it amongst the vapour from his breath as it hit the chilled air.

Alan watched and smiled to himself as he watched the great public on their way home from work. The bored reps and the office types, the insurance salesmen and the clerical assistants, like sheep, day after day and he suddenly realised that he was humming a song he'd heard years ago *"Nine o-clock mornin's, five o-clock evenin's, I'd laugh in their face if I could"*. He concentrated, trying to remember the singer or the name of the song, but both escaped him. "Lemmings." he muttered to himself. He flicked the spent cigarette end into the long grass by the side of the layby and settled down further into the driver's seat.

Making their way over the cliff edge of life, he thought. Every morning down into Town, another boring day at the office and at night, same thing, the nose to tail crawl along the same route home. "No wonder they go daft at the weekends" he thought. "Christ, I'd go crazy if I had this to put up with every day."

Working shifts might be unsociable, but at least it freed most Police Officers from the drudgery of the rush hour. Starting at 6.00 am or 2.00 pm or 10.00 pm for night duty, meant that the roads were usually quiet, both to and from work.

Alan could hear one of the other Traffic patrols from the opposite side of the City, being called to a 10/9, an accident. Mildly curious, he turned up the volume a little and caught the operator advising the attending patrol of the location.

"Papa Bravo Three Nine, it's a 10/9, three vehicles, reported injuries, ambulance have been advised and are en route, junction of Waltham Road and Beckett Street."

"10/4 en route." the Traffic man responded and Alan just caught the sound of the wailers being activated prior to the handset being replaced.

Alan fixed the location in his mind and thought that he recognised the Traffic man's voice through the static of the radio; they'd done a short spell together on the Motorway Unit when Alan had first joined Traffic.

The radio fell silent and Alan shrank down further into the warmth of his yellow jacket. He pulled up the collar against the cold and allowed his eyes to stare unblinking, out into the rush hour traffic once more. As his eyes defocused, the red tail lights fused into one continuous snake like line. A slight drizzle started to fall and the windscreen became opaque, He could feel the small pinpricks of moisture on his face as the breeze blew the minute droplets into the vehicle and it roused him from his distant thoughts for a moment.

The road surface soon became wet and the shining surface now mirrored the red and white lights of the vehicles on the main road and now and then, the orange flash of an indicator. The lights and the constant humming from the vehicles had a hypnotic effect on him and he allowed himself to be lulled as he closed his eyes for a second, or perhaps two. His mind drifted half conscious, half dreaming back to the first fatal accident, he had attended; he had without doubt, been thrown in at the deep end, his initiation into vehicular carnage, severe.

He'd been to minor bumps before, names and addresses exchanged jobs, but this had been his first fatal, a life snuffed out in an instant, a horrific act of violence on the road.

He remembered thinking how good life was, parked on a raised platform at the side of the motorway. Him and his partner had opened their flasks of coffee and were eating their sandwiches in the vehicle instead of driving all the way to the Police post at the service area twenty miles away. Anyway, the motorway had been quiet, hardly anyone around to complain about a couple of Traffic Cops eating their sandwiches on duty.

His partner for his month's experience on the Motorway, was an ex RAF lad who had seen service at Kai Tak in Hong Kong and exotic faraway places such as Penang in Malaysia. He was telling Alan a tale, between mouthfuls of beef paste sandwich, probably colourfully embellished Alan thought, about how he and his mates had taken the City of Kowloon apart whilst on leave in Hong Kong. He graphically described the chariot races with the rickshaws, "Beatin' the slope 'eads with us webbing belts." after having consumed copious amounts of the local 'Tiger' beer. Alan had laughed until the tears had run down his cheeks at the tale of the luridly described sexual exploits in Singapore's notorious red light area.

"Bugis Street mate, Jesus, there was a bird there used to push a knotted silk handkerchief up your arse hole and then just as you was on the vinegar stroke, down it would come, one knot at a time…fuck me!"

Alan's laughter had become so uncontrolled; he missed the radio message calling them.

His partner stopped in mid speech and reached for the handset, his ears obviously more attuned to their call sign. He keyed the handset. "Charlie Mike One Four, 10/8 please." he asked, requesting the operator to repeat the message.

"Charlie Mike One Four, 10/9, reported as potential, request from Division, Walford Road near to the Three Nuns Public house, P.S.V. and one vehicle, ambulance advised and are en route."

His partner responded. "One Four 10/4." before quickly replacing the handset into its holder and nodding. "Let's go Al, hit all the go faster buttons."

Alan pulled the patrol car off the platform and glancing over his right shoulder, accelerated hard across the first two lanes, before checking again and entering the third lane. Flooring the accelerator, he felt the power of the V8 engine pushing him satisfyingly back into his seat.

The radio operator contacted them again and Alan's partner turned up the volume to hear the message over the loud growl of the engine and the doleful wailing of their sirens.

"Charlie Mike One Four, further to my last, Motorway Supervision are aware and permission to leave the Motorway is granted. What's your e.t.a.?"

"Minutes five to the scene, One Four over." his partner said and resting the handset on his lap, reached across to activate the bank of blue flashing lights on the roof of the vehicle. "Headlights Alan."

"Sorry." Alan said, slightly wary about releasing his two hand grip on the steering wheel as the vehicle powered past the 100 mph mark. Without allowing his eyes to leave the carriageways ahead, he flicked the switch to turn on the headlights.

"Charlie Mike One Four, any Divisional units in attendance yet?" his partner asked.

"Negative at this time One Four." the operator replied.

"Why am I not fuckin' surprised." his partner muttered, after making sure that the transmit light had gone out.

The tachometer needle bounced nervously towards the red line on the gauge as Alan changed gear, maintaining the revs to stabilise the vehicle as he cut across all three lanes towards the exit slip road, which lead to the roundabout thirty feet above the Motorway carriageways.

The Rover SD1 hurtled up the slip road and Alan let the revs die off slightly as he approached the give way lines. He doubled dipped the clutch and engaged a lower gear, remembering subconsciously the system he'd been taught at Central Driving School. He snatched a view to the right and seeing a gap, dived for it, accelerating onto the roundabout, his eyes searching for the Walford Road exit sign.

"It's the next one off Al." his partner said.

Alan's heart was pounding, not due to the exhilaration of the drive, although that would have been sufficient, but in anticipation of what he was about to encounter. He'd imagined all manner of grotesque images as he had listened to the Traffic lads during meal breaks, or in the office as they described the latest fatal or serious accident they had been to. Decapitations, missing arms and legs and badly broken bones, but nothing in his wildest imaginings had he mentally prepared himself for what was to come.

Hazard warning lights flashing up ahead told Alan that they had arrived; he allowed the speed of the patrol vehicle to fall away as his partner reached for the radio handset.

"Charlie Mike One Four, we are 10/6 at the scene over."

Without waiting for a response, he released his seatbelt and reached over into the rear seats and grabbed his fluorescent jacket and a hand lamp from the rear footwell. Alan envied his partner, he seemed to be unruffled by the prospect of the carnage to be dealt with. In the years to come, Alan would come to realise that his partner had been every bit as apprehensive as he was on that day, but had merely learned to conceal it.

Alan brought the Police vehicle to a complete stop some fifty yards or so prior to the actual scene and illuminated the rear matrix sign. Now the red 'Police Slow' lights sintered with the blue lights on the roof, which lanced out into the darkness and an eerie purple glow emanated from the rear of the vehicle.

His partner leapt from the passenger seat and went straight to the rear. He opened the boot and withdrew a 'Police Accident' fold away sign and a couple of extra battery powered blue lights. He ran back down the road to place them on the carriageway as a further warning to any oncoming vehicles.

In the sweeping blue lights, Alan could see people wandering aimlessly around in the carriageway ahead. A man vomiting, women crying and being comforted by their fellow passengers who had now left one of the vehicles involved. "Damn, no street lights." he thought and snatching for the radio handset, he requested Traffic back-up and emergency lighting and gave a preliminary report of the scene. "It looks like a thirty nine seater bus and some sort of light van, no details yet, the road is blocked and there looks to be numerous injuries. Request you expedite ambulance, Studio and Accident Investigation to the scene please."

"10/4." came the immediate response.

Alan hurriedly donned his fluorescent yellow jacket and automatically switched the radio over to the outside speaker. He left the vehicle and walked with trepidation towards the scene, his heart pounding fit to burst. He felt embarrassed, he had no idea what to do first and worst of all, he was afraid of showing that he was afraid. He remembered his Tutor Constable telling him, "You won't have time to be crapping yourself or throwing up, you'll have too much to do." Yet he felt slightly light headed and apprehensive as he attempted to walk, with feigned confidence towards the wreckage.

Other Police vehicles arrived at the scene. A Range Rover weaved its way into the centre of the incident and the driver leapt out and immediately twisted the hand throttle wheel at the base of his seat. The engine revs rose and the stem light emerged from its pod on the roof of the vehicle, the stainless steel tubing rising magically from within. The powerful circular arc lamp shuddered its way to maximum height and with a flick of a switch, the whole scene became as bright as a summers day. It was then that Alan could see the full extent of the collision.

A thirty nine seater coach was tilted at a severe angle with its nearside wheels hidden from view in a ditch at the side of the road; Alan could see that the offside bodywork of the vehicle had been ripped away from the front wheel arch to within a few feet of the rear of the coach. The alloy skin was ripped and torn and hung in huge shards from the coach's side, it looked as if an explosion had blown away the side of the vehicle to expose the shattered wooden frame along the lower half of the coach. The spruce spars from which the frame of the coach had been constructed, were smashed and splintered pieces, and were now strewn across the carriageway along with a sea of broken glass. Suitcases, from the storage area down the side of the coach had been scattered, some had burst open and items of clothing and possessions were venting from the vehicle.

The coach resembled a stricken animal, laid dying and on its side, the body ripped open by some massive claw to reveal the skeleton and entrails which now poured out onto the road surface. More Officers arrived at the scene and Alan saw elderly passengers being helped from the coach, they held handkerchiefs and field dressing wads to their bleeding hands and faces from where the windows of the coach had imploded, showering them with a million shards of glass. There were cries for help from those not yet seen by emergency services, they held hands over their faces, glass in their eyes and blood on their clothing. Some wandered aimlessly, unsighted, falling over the scattered debris in the carriageway. Others Alan noted, simply sat in silence on the grass verge, ignoring the damp seeping through their clothing, in shock and with eyes which simply stared out across the scene.

Alan stood dumbfounded for a second as he surveyed the horror; the pungent smell of spilled coolant mixed with battery acid assailed his nostrils. His partner's shouting shook him from his daze.

"Al, get more back up and Fire Brigade with cutting gear, we've got people trapped here."

Alan ran back to the patrol car and relayed the message, panicking slightly, afraid that he would not be able to cope.

Returning back to the scene, he saw that more ambulances had arrived. Harsh blue lights rippled across the open aperture along the side of the coach and momentarily, illuminated the passengers still trapped in the vehicle, some slumped over their seats. The ambulance crews leapt from their vehicles and set about seeing to the wounded.

Alan looked around for his partner and saw him standing on the opposite side of the road where the front of a van was embedded into a thick gorse hedge. Alan approached the wrecked vehicle, its offside completely torn away. The front wing and the driver's door were now lying in a twisted pile along with the debris from the coach. Someone had thrown a blanket over what was left of the roof and it draped down to the road surface. "Jesus." Alan whispered to himself, as he stared at the destruction.

His partner called him to come towards the front of the van. "Give us a hand Al." he said, pulling away the blanket from the exposed offside of the vehicle. Alan screwed his face into a silent grimace at the sight before him. He felt a slight rush of nausea as he looked down at the driver of the van, who was still seated in the vehicle, his hands still grasping the steering wheel. "What a bastard eh?"

Alan did not hear his partner's expletives; he was staring in disbelief at the horror visited upon the driver.

The van had struck the offside of the coach and the soft alloy panels which covered the wooden framework, had peeled back as the van had exploded into its side. The heavy spruce spars that ran horizontally and vertically along the length of the coach had shattered and one of the main cross spars had sprung outwards from the broken framework and punctured the bonnet of the van. As it had entered the engine compartment, the four by four length of hardwood had ripped off the carburettor and the air filter as it punched its way through the firewall bulkhead and into the interior of the vehicle. Tearing a hole in the dashboard facia, the spar had passed neatly between the spokes of the steering wheel and torn into the driver's chest. Passing completely through him, it had burst out through the back of his seat and its jagged, splintered end was now exposed, covered in an amalgam of torn muscle fibre, human flesh and particles of foam rubber which it had pulverised on its way through the seat. A thin trail of glutinous fluid dripped from the exit hole in the seat and ran along the length of the exposed spar, slowly dripping a dark viscous fluid onto the rear carpets.

As the van had ploughed into the side of the coach, its roof had been savagely pushed upwards and back towards the rear of the vehicle. It had folded in a concertina fashion. The windscreen pillar had snapped and on its way towards the rear, the roof had struck the driver on the forehead, ripping his scalp away. The hair covered scalp, now retained by a thin thread of flesh, hung down by the nape of the drivers shattered neck and the stark white of his exposed skull showed through the glistening red pulpy mass. The driver's eyes were glazed and lifeless; the eyelids drooped unevenly and were spattered with blood.

The smell from the interior of the vehicle made Alan retch and he quickly cupped his hand over his mouth and nose against the coppery smell of blood, mixed with faeces and urine excreted as the driver's muscles had instantly closed down and relaxed at the moment of his death.

The vehicle's drive shaft had bent upwards with the initial impact and had snapped at its joint with the end of the gearbox and forced its way up through the thin floor pan. The engine block and gearbox bell housing had been pushed through the firewall bulkhead and had pulped the driver's legs below his knees. The driver's left leg was completely torn away at the shin and the twisted metal of the bulkhead trapped his empty trouser leg against the front of his seat.

Alan couldn't breathe; he swallowed hard. Saliva flooding into his mouth and he fought the massive churning in the pit of his stomach. A veil of darkness started to fall over his eyes and his legs felt weak.

His partner slapped him on the back, bringing him back to his senses. "Come on mate, shake a fuckin' leg, things to do, get a plan started, I'll get one or two of the beat lads to help with measurements, ok?"

Alan, shaken from the grotesque tableau which had frozen him to the spot, turned. "Right, yes, right, I'll make a start." tearing his eyes away from the driver, who was totally unaware of his presence.

He didn't remember returning to the patrol car to retrieve his tape measure and clipboard, or in fact, preparing the plan drawing. His mind was in turmoil, all he could see as he drew the sweeping curve of the road and placed the positions of the two vehicles were the eyes of the driver, his drooping eyelids half covering the lifeless eyes, frozen in a last horror filled stare. He'd seen dead bodies before, quite a few in Ireland and the Middle East, but not like this, not ripped apart, torn into and invaded in such a grotesque fashion. Alan tried to imagine the last piece of information the dead driver's brain had received. He wondered if he realised that he was going to be killed, that this was actually his very last moment.

They say that things happen in slow motion at the very moment of your death. Alan wondered if the van driver had seen the splintered wooden stake as it had burst out through the dashboard. Had he felt the mind shattering pain as it lanced into his chest cavity, knowing that it was too late to do anything about it. Alan tried to capture that awful final moment and shivered at the thought.

"Who's dealing?" boomed a voice.

Alan looked up from his clipboard and saw the Motorway Sergeant standing amidst the debris. The three silver chevrons on his tunic illuminated brightly by the harsh arc lights in the raised pod.

"Me and Alan Sarge." his partner shouted, barely audible over the sound of the air powered cutters, now being used to cut the side door of the coach away so that the ambulance crews could safely remove the remaining passengers.

"Photographs organised?" the Sergeant enquired.

"Yes Sarge."

"Accident Investigation?"

"They're on their way." Alan replied, thankful that they seem to have remembered the basics at least.

"Who's doing recovery?"

"Local garage is turning out for the coach, I don't know about the van yet." Alan replied.

The Sergeant seemed to be satisfied that everything had been organised. "Get Division cracking on a rota garage for the van and tell them to make sure it's kept under cover; The Coroner will want full photographs of the deceased in situ, so get them on standby for when Studio have finished."

"Do we know who he is yet?" the Sergeant asked, nodding toward the wreckage of the van.

"No idea yet Sarge." Alan replied.

"Let's find out who he is then eh? Run a check on the registered number." he said to Alan's partner, "And don't let Division go to the address to do a death warning until we've confirmed it. We don't want Mrs Miggins telling that her Husband's been killed in his van if he sold the bleedin' thing to this chap last Friday…Oh, and tell 'em to check with neighbours first before they go blundering in." the Sergeant shouted to Alan's partner who was now making his way to the patrol car to begin the checks.

"You." the Sergeant said, looking back to Alan and crooking his finger. "With me."

Alan walked with the tall Sergeant as they made their way back towards the van. The nausea returning as he stepped carefully over the shards of wood and broken alloy panels, which were still strewn across the carriageway.

"Had a look at him have you?"

"Yes Sarge." Alan replied as they walked, hoping that the apprehension of seeing the dead driver again did not show in his voice.

"You're first fatal is it?" The Sergeant asked.

Alan chose not to reply, but held his breath as the Sergeant threw back the blanket to expose the decimated body.

"Poor bastard, least it was quick." said the veteran.

Alan nodded, feeling the impulse to retch again as the fetid abattoir smell, vented from the vehicle.

"Have a look through his pockets lad, see if he's got any I.D., driver's licence, club card or something."

The Sergeant went to the nearside door which was twisted badly out of shape. It had been forced slightly ajar, as the body shell had twisted with the initial impact. The door refused to open. The veteran Sergeant put his weight behind it and forced the door, it opened begrudgingly with the sound of tortured metal and glass particles crunching in the hinges.

Alan was in awe of the Sergeant who seemed to be completely unperturbed by the presence of the dead driver. The air became colder and steam now rose from the driver's open mouth, fixed in a last silent scream. A rivulet of congealing blood oozed from the torn chest wound and dripped in thickening globules down the front of his jacket.

The Sergeant rummaged through the glove box and looked up to see Alan staring at the driver.

"Come on lad, they'll be wanting to cut 'im out soon."

Alan hesitated, took a deep breath and tentatively took hold of the driver's jacket lapel between finger and thumb, hardly daring to touch the driver's body. He pulled back the jacket front and exposed an inside pocket. He reached with a shaking hand and felt inside the pocket and could feel the body heat from the driver. It felt somehow intrusive and irreverent. Fighting his fear and revulsion, he carefully reached over the wooden stake which still impaled the driver to the seat. Alan was fearful that touching it or disturbing it at all would somehow, be the cause of more pain.

He felt something inside the pocket. He tentatively gripped it between his fingers and withdrew it cautiously. As a small brown leather wallet appeared from within the depths of the pocket, the sleeve of Alan's fluorescent jacket caught on the rough edge of the wooden spar and Alan shot a glance at the driver, as if to apologise for any discomfort he might have caused.

The lifeless face gave no recognition of pain or indeed of Alan's presence. The eyes still stared blankly, half covered by the lids which drooped sadly, giving the face an expression of acceptance that in the last split second, its wearer had lost everything.

Alan felt the driver's warmth, not the normal bodily warmth, not like when you shake someone's hand or hold a woman and feel her warmth through her clothing, but clammy, wax like and fading. He felt as if he had somehow invaded the driver's privacy and wondered if he would have allowed Alan to go through his pockets if he'd been alive.

Still gripping the wallet between his fingers, Alan withdrew from the wreck to examine its contents.

It did indeed contain a driving licence; there was also a small amount of money and a membership card to his local fishing club. There was also a donor card which stated that the carrier's wishes were, that various parts of his anatomy could be used to save someone's life in the event of an accident. Alan pushed the donor card back into the wallet and thought that there wasn't much left of the driver that would be worth donating to anyone.

Flipping the wallet open, Alan found a well-worn photograph in one of the inner compartments. It was crinkled and dog eared at its edges, as if it was frequently withdrawn and produced proudly by the carrier. It had presumably been taken in the back garden of what appeared to be a small terraced house. A good looking woman was seated on a garden bench, she held up a young child with fat cheeks and curly blonde hair and faced the child proudly towards the lens as she smiled. It had obviously been taken during the summer months, the garden was well tended, the small lawn was well-manicured and the flower beds were glorious with colourful bursts of reds and yellows. A small tree in the background was in full bloom with what Alan took to be cherry or apple blossom.

Alan looked closely at the face of the young child. It had about it an expression as if he/she had recently been crying, or was just about to, the bottom lip pouting and curved outwards. He replaced the faded photograph and thought wistfully that there would be some crying done by both of them this day.

*****

The sound of shattering glass and the dull crump of buckling body panels wrenched Alan back to the present day. Sitting up sharply, he looked across the roundabout and saw that a Ford Cortina estate had embedded itself into the side of a double decked bus.

He groaned as he moved to a proper driving position and realised that he had been sweating and that his back felt clammy and cold. He shivered for an instant and had a feeling of déjà vu, as he looked across toward the bus and the car; his previous thoughts disturbed him just for a second. The two drivers had left their respective vehicles and Alan could see that there was a good deal of shouting and gesticulating going on.

"Shit." snarled Alan as he drove the patrol car from the layby and onto the roundabout. Activating the blue roof lights and the rear reds to protect the scene, he left the warmth of his car and approached the two drivers.

"Officer, for Christ's sake, look at this…Look at my bloody car, you must have seen what happened." the driver of the estate car ranted, whilst the bus driver stood, his hands deep in his pockets, surveying the damage to the side of his bus.

"He pulled straight out in front of me, I was already on the roundabout. I had priority."

The bus driver shook his head slowly. "You wanna try driving one of these things all day mate, I've got schedules to keep, if you'd shown a bit of bleedin' courtesy…"

"Gentlemen, gentlemen." Alan said, raising his voice and the palms of his hands to quieten the two drivers. "Firstly, are there any injuries?"

"I'll go and check my passengers." said the bus driver, returning his hands to his pockets and walking off towards the side entrance to the bus.

The other driver caught hold of Alan's jacket sleeve. "You must have witnessed this Officer, you were only parked over there." he said, nodding toward the layby.

Alan nodded slowly, looking back along the ring road at the traffic which was now backing up.

"Pulling out like that, you want bloody hanging." the estate car driver shouted, pointing an accusing finger at the returning bus driver.

"Yeah, alright Sir, that's enough." Alan said, allowing a little authority to creep into his tone. "I'm afraid that we've abolished capital punishment, especially for motoring offences. I'm sure that we can find some amicable way to deal with this, everyone ok?" Alan said, nodding toward the bus.

The bus driver nodded.

"Right, let's get your vehicles off the road so we can get the roundabout clear." Alan said decisively. Horn blasts had started from drivers within the increasing tail back and the rain started in earnest.

The two drivers returned to their vehicles and Alan pulled the collar of his yellow jacket up around his ears and squinted upwards toward the darkening sky. The Ford Cortina estate was struggling to start and Alan could hear the fan blades catching against the radiator cowling, as the starter motor cranked the engine over.

He walked to the first vehicle waiting at the roundabout, the first in a long line of vehicles now backed up as far as the eye could see.

"Won't be a minute." Alan said apologetically to the driver who had smiled at him and looked up to the sky and grimaced at the rain. "Anybody hurt?"

"Only their pride." Alan replied.

The driver smiled knowingly. "Sooner you than me stood out in this lot." he said and wound his window up against the downpour.

Alan got the traffic moving, favouring the vehicles travelling out of the City to try and clear the major backlog, which would no doubt by now, be effecting the City Centre.

A beige coloured Rover Coupe nudged up to Alan from his left hand side as he waved the outbound vehicles through. Two short horn blasts sounded and Alan looked slowly across to the driver who was edging his vehicle even closer. Alan continued to wave the outbound vehicles through, the rain now running in rivulets from the peak of his cap and seeping behind the collar of his jacket and shirt to run down his back. Another short blast from the Rover's horn. Alan walked slowly to the driver's door, as the window was wound down an inch or two.

The driver looked like a retired Colonel. His short cropped moustache and light brown, camel coat enhancing the overall military bearing. The driver grimaced at the rain which now blew in on him and he shouted angrily at Alan.

"Do get a move on Officer, get our lane cracking, we've got homes to go to don't you know." Alan considered whether a politely offered "Don't panic Captain Mainwaring" would sum up what he thought of the Colonel's impatience. He thought better of it and leaning down towards the partially open window. The rain now cascading from the top of his cap, entered the vehicle through the two inch gap and dripped onto the Colonel's expensive coat.

Alan smiled and said "I'm sorry it seems to be taking so long, why don't you come and stand in the lovely sunshine with me while you're waiting."

The Colonel's face flushed first red, then turned a rather worrying purple. "Well REALLY." he growled, clearly not being used to insubordination from the lower ranks. He snatched at the handle on the door panel, cranking it furiously so that the window snapped shut.

Alan shrugged his shoulders and continued to wave the outbound traffic through the roundabout. "I hope you're not in a rush Captain Mainwaring." he thought, smiling inwardly. "These traffic hold ups can last forever."

Both the damaged vehicles had managed to get themselves moving and Alan stopped traffic again until they had cleared the roundabout. He turned to the Colonel type and with a smile, waved his line of vehicles on. The old campaigner gave Alan an "If you'd have been under my command" look as he lurched his vehicle forwards and with a short protesting squeal from the rear tyres, sped off along the ring road, presumably towards the ancestral home for 'tea and tiffin' with the Memsahib.

"Prick." thought Alan as he walked back to his patrol car.

## **Four**

The two Detectives sat in their vehicle, waiting and watching. The car, an aging Vauxhall, bore no marks with which to announce the profession of its users. An attentive villain might notice the V.H.F. aerial which had been tucked away underneath the offside edge of the boot lid and if he knew where to look in the interior of the vehicle, he might just notice the multi-channel radio pack, shoe horned into the radio cassette aperture in the centre console.

The vehicle had started to rust, purposefully. The bodywork had been neglected to assist in its covert duties. The paintwork along the bottom edges of the doors and the curvature of the headlamp units, bore signs of advanced corrosion and the brown cancer bubbled up beneath the paintwork.

The Regional Crime Squad vehicle was innocuous. Designed to blend in, not one which you would single out or notice in a stream of traffic or whilst parked up at the side of the street, not one you would remember.

The Detective in the front passenger seat shuffled uncomfortably and scratched at the four days of growth on his face. He was dressed casually; blue jeans, a sweatshirt emblazoned with Status Quo's 'Whatever You Want' concert logo and a pair of grubby trainers. His long hair fell from a centre parting onto his shoulders and concealed the ear piece and the thin wire which ran from it to the personal radio pack which he wore in a harness under his armpit. He was bored with waiting.

His partner in the driver's seat was older, a Detective Sergeant. He also had a beard, but his was fully grown and neatly trimmed. A slight greying showed around the side of his chin and clashed with the darkness of the rest. He considered it to be distinguishing and would glare disapprovingly at his younger colleagues on the Crime Squad when they referred to him as the 'Old Man'.

He too was dressed casually, although more in keeping with his age. Light slacks and shoes and a cotton 'bomber' jacket. Serviceable and proving comfortable, whilst sitting in vehicles for lengthy periods. He watched the street intently as his younger colleague slouched in the passenger seat.

An empty Coke can lay on its side on the top of the dashboard, resting lazily against the windscreen, next to it, a packet of Benson and Hedges also thrown casually against the glass.

The radio pack, concealed by the 'Old Man's' jacket, hissed with a static filled message.

"Anything yet boss?"

Without taking his eyes from the street, the D.S. reached in under his armpit and depressed a small button activating the transmitter.

"No, not yet. The motor's still there, no sign of our man, I think he's out on foot somewhere."

The break in radio silence brought a brief respite in the boredom. The radio hissed again.

"Me and Derek fancy some chips, anyone else?"

A short pause, then "Yeah, obs three, we'll have some."

"Anyone else?"

"You can fetch me a large scotch." someone broke in.

The D.S. allowed himself a brief smile.

"Obs three to Derek."

"Yeah go on."

"Angela says she could fancy a Mars Bar."

"Like Marianne Faithfull?" someone replied.

"Oi!...watch it." a female voice protested.

"Enough banter." the 'Old Man' demanded.

"Received. Going off plot for the groceries then boss, ok?"

"Received." the 'Old Man' said quietly and releasing the transmit button, shook his head slowly and muttered to himself. "Chips and Mars Bars, for fuck's sake."

There were three vehicles in the team. Each of which had been positioned at various pre-arranged points where a building or street could be kept under observation. Each vehicle contained two Detectives.

At the briefing held earlier, the team members had huddled around a blackboard onto which was pinned a street plan of the area and as they adjusted the harnesses and tested their radios with squelch, the 'Old Man' as he was affectionately known, had passed round photographs of the target and given each team their observation points. There were to be the three cars and a footman call-signed 'Walker', who was designated a walking area around the target area between the three static points.

'Walker' was wearing and old R.A.F. greatcoat and dirty jeans. His plimsolls were frayed and dirty and his bare feet showed through where the rubber soles had parted company with the canvas uppers. 'Walker' was now slumped in a shop doorway, a half empty cider bottle clutched protectively in his grubby hands. He wore a greasy, matted wig under a woollen hat and the false locks fell about his shoulders to conceal the radio earpiece. His face was dirty, he having rubbed it with dust and grime from the briefing room floor as they had prepared for the stakeout. One of his colleagues had helped him with the wig, purloined some years previously from the premises where the local amateur dramatic society met and it where it was strongly rumoured that the 'Old Man' spent his days off perfecting his thespianism.

"There you go mate, you look like a right druggy." his colleague said, as the woollen hat was pulled down to his eyebrows.

"You look like my Son in Law." said the 'Old Man' smiling.

'Walker' stood in the centre of the briefing room whilst his colleagues circled him, laughing and joking, but behind the banter, searching for any tell-tale signs that he was not what he appeared to be. There must be nothing that could possibly identify him as a Police Officer. 'Walker' would be out on his own, in a potentially hostile environment, more so on this particular job which was in the 'Badlands'.

'Walker' was exceptionally good under cover, so good in fact that on a stake out a few months previous, he had been arrested by a uniformed Probationer and taken to the Bridewell for apparently being drunk and incapable, much to the amusement of the Bridewell Staff and the embarrassment of the Probationer.

'Walker' originated from the Midlands and would exaggerate the thick nasal accent, to convince a dealer that he was an 'out of towner' setting up new contacts. He was confident and tenacious, quite prepared to stand about for hours in the freezing cold or rain, as a desperate user would, to meet a dealer.

'Walker' was now laid, apparently much the worse for drink in the doorway of an Estate Agents. A silky strand of saliva hung from his open mouth and lazily swung down across his stubbled chin and onto the lapel of his grubby greatcoat. His eyes remained half closed as if he was in a drug or alcohol induced stupor and he muttered to himself, lines he remembered from the Bible and every now and then, he would shout them out to a passer-by.

He would go unnoticed in this area, the local inhabitants well used to seeing drunks slumped in doorways or laid out on the pavements, usually older end first generation blacks, poorly dressed and despondent.

After leaving Kingston or Port Morant, in pursuit of the promise of good jobs and a better standard of living, the blacks had found only discrimination and resentment from prospective employers other than in the most menial or demeaning jobs. They would slouch around the street corners amongst the overflowing dustbins which spewed their stinking garbage onto the pavements, where the hookers stepped casually around both it and the unending piles of dog shit, their garish colourful make up and dress somehow alien to the drab greyness of the area.

The area was poor and dilapidated, predominantly Afro-Caribbean, with a few Asians, Chinese and Poles thrown into the mix. The shops were run down, their frontages painted in the purples, bright greens and reds which the blacks preferred. The local Council would spend no money on developing the 'Badlands', considering it 'good money after bad'. The money went to the City centre and the Jewish quarter, where the Doctors, Accountants and Solicitors lived in good quality, privately owned houses. Here the streets were regularly resurfaced, the pavements kept clean and even and the street lights well maintained. Here they deserved and received a regular uniformed Police presence, high visibility patrols day and night, visits to the local schools and Parish Council meetings, all considered to be money well spent.

Any black face found to be 'abroad' in the affluent Jewish quarter, would be subjected to an immediate stop search and inevitably, subjected to a trip to the City Bridewell, arrested on the inevitable warrant or if all else failed, suspicious person loitering with intent or disorderly conduct.

In the 'Badlands', the record shops and Soul food take-aways had loudspeakers attached to their garish front hoardings and monotonous reggae music blasted out into the streets. Young blacks hanging around the corners in large, intimidating groups, practiced the latest dance moves to a plastic transistorized tape deck, more colloquially known in Police circles, as a 'third world briefcase' and due to their size, usually carried on the shoulder.

Whilst the rest of the City slept, the 'Badlands' awoke and the indigenous population crawled out of their filthy hovels to infest the streets they now owned. It was a night area, bright lights and loud music. The pavements were frequented by the hookers, pushers and dealers, the grey drabness hidden in the aurora of garish coloured lights, the sorry silence of extreme poverty masked by the mind numbing Jamaican music.

The dealing in drugs went on, for the most part, uninterrupted by the Police. The local Divisional Commanders advocating that a 'blind eye' be turned to the offence, after all, who gave a damn if they melted their own brains. The blacks were considered to be a lost cause anyway, as long as no drugs were being sold to school children outside the local Grammar school or Maccabee Junior. A simple arrest for possession of cannabis or amphetamine, wasn't worth the political backlash or damage to Police vehicles in the riot which would inevitably follow.

The 'Badlands' was a tinder box of simmering violence and the electricity of unrest lay heavily in the atmosphere. Police/Public relations were tenuous and closely monitored. A greater degree of leniency and discretion was shown to the local inhabitants for transgressions, which in any other part of the City, would bring about the full weight of prosecution.

The local eleven beat Officers were watched and monitored far more closely than the inhabitants. If he or she showed any bias against the blacks, engaged in any inappropriate racist banter or made jokes in the canteen at meal time, if overheard or reported to a Senior Officer, it would mean a swift move for the 'bad apple', sometimes overnight and a 'penal' posting to the City Bridewell for a period of 'restorative close supervision' or to a Division where the law abiding white folks lived. The tension could actually be felt as the beat Officers walked the streets; it was a tangible thing, indescribable, but present all the same.

Silence amongst the young blacks who sat on the pavements or slouched against the shop fronts as the uniform approached, and only after it had passed, would the caustic comments and laughter follow. A uniform learned not to look back, not to seek out his tormentor, nor offer any comment which could rupture the thin membrane holding back insurrection. A uniform could stop a young black to ask him innocent questions regarding a missing from home enquiry, or why he wasn't in school that day and within moments, the uniform would be surrounded by hostile coloured faces coming to the aid of a brother being hassled by 'Bumbeclart'. Safer to continue on his beat or get straight back into the panda and drive away. Better to ignore the catcalls and laughter, knowing that they'd won again. Better to suck up the humiliation, than the paperwork which would take until retirement as a result of a broken windscreen or a dent in one of the panda's body panels or worse still, complaints from the Local Community Leaders and the wrath of the Divisional Commander.

*****

The younger of the two Detectives sighed heavily with a grunt, reached for the packet of cigarettes on the dashboard.

"I wish I'd asked Derek for some chips now." he said dolefully.

The D.S. smiled. "I could just go for a nice succulent beef Wellington and a glass of Merlot myself."

His partner lit a cigarette and looked across to the 'Old Man', blowing smoke out through the partially open window. "I could nip across the road to Della's and get us a couple of bowls of mannish water Boss."

The D.S. chuckled. "You'd never come back alive and in any case, I couldn't bring myself to swallow any of that foreign shit."

"We're wasting our time here you know." the younger Detective said flatly. "We ought to be more like this lot." nodding his head towards the street. "Mister fuckin' Bojangles, lifestyle courtesy of the D.H.S.S. get up when you want, smoke what you want, shag yourself stupid, party all night, the odd taste of white meat every now and then and if the cash runs short, do the odd armed robbery to supplement the social. I mean…they plead poverty so the Social pays their rent and electric and even their fines. Christ! We're in the wrong job."

The 'Old Man' waggled his index finger in his ear and withdrew it to inspect a yellow waxy substance which had adhered itself to the underside of his nail. He frowned and rubbed the finger end into the palm of his hand. He sat back in his seat and rested his neck against the headrest, allowing his eyes to close for just a moment.

The radio hissed out a message, jolting him out of his weariness.

"Obs one from Walker, I think your man's on his way."

The two Detectives straightened themselves in their seats and looked out onto the street. The 'Old Man' thumbed his transmit button.

"Derek, you back on patch again?"

"Yes Boss."

"Can you see anything?"

"Not yet, where is he?"

"To all from Walker. I think it's him. He's in front of the Co-op, towards you Boss."

The radio crackled. "Break, break, from Obs three, target sighted, he's wearing a light green, looks like...a corduroy bomber jacket and black trousers, he's on your nearside Boss."

The radio messages bounced from car to car as the sighting was confirmed.

"From Walker, I've lost 'eyeball'. Obs two, have you picked up on him yet?"

"Yes, yes, he's made a left into Melbourne Terrace; he's on his own, looks like he's going home." The two Detectives watched carefully as the target crossed the street in front of their vehicle, ignorant as to its presence.

"He doesn't look worried." the 'Old Man' whispered, as if the target could hear him.

"I wouldn't be worried if I was his size." his partner said, raising an eyebrow. "He looks like a larger version of Marvin Hagler."

They continued to watch as the target walked from the main street into an unlit alley which formed the backstreet to the dingy tenement buildings. He was lost to them for a moment and the 'Old Man' stiffened and craned his neck up to the side window. The target re-appeared as a silhouette, climbing the rickety metal fire escape stairs to the second floor. The man hesitated, casting a glance up and down the alleyway out of habit as he fumbled his key into the door lock. The door swung open and the target disappeared inside the building. The 'Old Man' breathed out and nodded to his partner. "He's home then."

The younger Detective thumbed the transmit button. "From obs one, our man is home."

The footman replied. "From Walker, I'll get lost then, eh?"

"Don't go too far away. Obs three receive?"

"Yes, yes Boss."

"Dave, get onto Division, get a uniform down here to do the door knocking."

"From three, just the one Boss?"

"Yes, he's been briefed, any more than one 'woodentop' and you're guaranteed a fuck up. Our man won't expect grief from a single plod."

"10/4." the radio hissed.

"Obs three further, tell the uniform to get the target well away from his flat, onto the street, to his motor if possible."

"From three, received."

The younger Detective looked across to the D.S. a quizzical look on his face, "Just the one uniform Boss, on foot?"

The 'Old Man' straightened his radio harness where it chaffed under his armpit, "He's only there to get him out of his crib, there's a van coming to do the transport."

Twenty minutes passed whilst the Team waited for the arrival of the uniformed Officer from Division. "Fuck's sake, where is he?" moaned the 'Old Man'. "He's only got to get from the fucking station. Even on yer hands and knees it'd only be five minutes…Fucking plods."

Eventually, a uniformed P.C. strolled casually down Melbourne Terrace and as briefed, stopped in front of the target's vehicle. He looked it over and jotted down a few notes in his notebook. He cautiously glanced about him and recognised the firm's vehicle, careful not to give away any outward sign of recognition but making sure that the Detectives knew that he was aware of their position.

"'Bout fucking time." hissed the 'Old Man'

The uniform pocketed his notebook and playing out his part, walked slowly up the fire escape stairs.

"From obs one, the uniform's here and on his way up towards the flat."

"Derek."

"Yes, yes."

"If he gets him away from the flat, you and Matty nip round from Watson Street…crack a window if you 'ave to but get into his crib, we'll follow with the uniform."

"Received."

"Is the van about yet?"

"From obs two, it's with us Boss."

"Tell the driver to listen in. As soon as we've collared the target, I want the van in the alley to get him away quick, confirm."

"Yes, yes."

The 'Old Man' watched intently as the uniform knocked on the door to the target's flat. After what seemed an eternity, the door was opened and the uniform was bathed in a dim yellow light from the hallway. The uniform appeared to be engaged in conversation with the target. The Detectives watched as he pointed down to the rusting saloon which was parked on the main road a little distance from the flat. The uniform beckoned for the target to follow him down the fire escape stairs to the street. The target appeared to be hesitating, throwing his hands into the air gesticulating and waving the Officer away.

"Looks like he's getting' a hard time Boss."

"Uniforms round here wouldn't expect anything else. He'll manage it, give him a minute."

The 'Old Man' and his younger partner watched with baited breath as the 'target' continued to argue with the uniform. Finally, with more gesticulations, the man begrudgingly followed the uniform down to the street.

"Looks like he's managed it Boss." the younger Detective said, nodding excitedly.

The 'Old Man' depressed the transmitter. "Listen up, our man is out of the target premises and is with the uniform. He's clearly not happy but it looks to me like they're heading towards the motor. Derek, you ready?"

"Yes yes."

"From obs one to all. Wait, wait."

"Received."

The uniform and the 'target' entered the lit area of the main street and approached the battered vehicle. The uniform pointed to the excise licence and then pointed down to the registration number displayed on the vehicle.

The 'target' stood disinterestedly with his hands in his pockets. The uniform walked to the rear of the vehicle and shone his torch onto the rear tyres and beckoned the target to join him. The 'target' shook his head and gesticulated again, but walked to the rear of the vehicle where the uniform was now squatting down on his haunches, apparently inspecting the tyres.

"Nice one lad." the 'Old Man' nodded.

The side alley was now blind to the 'target'.

"From obs one. Derek, go, go."

"Yes, yes."

The two Detectives watched as the uniform took out his pocket book; the target looked nonchalantly up and down the main street and leaned disinterestedly against the brickwork of the wall which flanked the alleyway.

The 'Old Man' nudged his partner and nodded towards the alley, as the Team from obs two crept silently from the far end of the cobbled alleyway and approached the bottom of the metal steps.

"From obs one to Walker."

"Go Boss."

"Get onto Division and tell them to radio the uniform 'No Trace' on computer ok?"

"Received."

This was the prearranged message to let the uniform know that the Crime Squad were safely inside the target's flat. A few more stomach wrenching moments passed. The Detectives noticed the front end of an unmarked Ford Transit nosing its way into the far end of the alley, its lights extinguished.

The uniform pressed the button on the top of the Burndept radio in his top pocket and confirmed receipt of the message.

The 'Old Man' and his partner watched as the uniform pointed back towards the target's flat and the two walked back towards the alley and the metal stairs.

"He'll have asked to see his documents I reckon."

"Or if he can buy some resin." the 'Old Man' said jokingly, not taking his eyes from the uniform.

"From obs one, they're going to the steps, Derek, you ready?"

"Yes, yes."

The uniform followed the target up the fire escape and as they reached the half-way point, the 'Old Man' punched the transmit button.

"All Teams, move, move!"

The Transit at the opposite end of the alley entered the cobbled area and slowly made its way towards the metal steps, its lights still extinguished. The two Detectives hurriedly made their way from the vehicle to the alley entrance as a second member of the Team entered from a side street which crossed the backstreet halfway along its length. The 'target' stopped halfway up the stairs and looked back, sensing that something was not quite right. Something of his inner self, born of years of deception and street survival warned him. He saw the two Detectives approaching the bottom of the stairs and the Transit cruising over the cobbles and in an instant, he realised that he'd been set up. The target's eyes showed the instantaneous recognition of his predicament; he twisted away to avoid the outstretched hand of the uniform who reached out to grab his clothing and lunged for the door in desperation. The door to his own 'crib' was opened by the two Detectives who had gained entry and positioned themselves so as to block the entrance.

The 'Old Man' shouted "Get hold of 'im then." and the uniform leapt up the stairs, wary of the target's stature and the feral look in his eyes. The target turned on the uniform and let out a guttural scream. Penned in like a beast awaiting the captive bolt, he kicked out, the uniform took the blow on his chest throwing him back onto the 'Old Man' and his partner. The D.S. steadied the uniform and slowly, the three advanced on the target. In the dim half-light, there was a bright flash and the three Officers on the stairway halted as they were confronted by the stainless steel blade of the open razor. The target crouched like a cornered animal and his eyes darted from the Officers below him to the door at his back.

The two Detectives backed away slowly. The uniform instinctively held out his hands, palms forward, to protect his face from the wavering blade.

It was going wrong.

The target's breath was rasping from his throat and he swallowed frantically as he assessed his situation. He thrust the blade toward the uniform who flinched, throwing his head backwards.

"Move, mo'fucker...I'll fuckin' cut you." the target screamed as he waved the open blade viciously from side to side. He was wild and incensed. He knew what lay ahead and his mind centred on the only option open to him, escape.

The stand-off continued for what seemed to be and age. In slow motion, the Detectives and the uniform cowered back on the metal stairway but not retreating, the target staring at them, hatred and fear in his eyes.

A sound not unlike a football being kicked hard resounded through the alley. The target's eyes rolled slowly upwards and his facial muscles relaxed. The snarling countenance disappeared, his legs buckled and the weapon fell from his fingers as consciousness left him. He fell heavily against the uniform, who scrambled to keep his balance, as the dead weight of the target pinioned him against the metal stairs.

The 'Old Man' looked up and saw the Detectives from Team Two above them in the doorway, one still holding a large hardwood staff above his head, the type normally issued to the Mounted Branch Officers.

"Oh...take yer fuckin' time Derek...He could have 'ad me fuckin' face off." hissed the 'Old Man' visibly shaking.

The Detective shrugged his shoulders nonchalantly. "Forgot I 'ad it with me to be honest Boss."

The uniform, now joined by the van driver, dragged the unconscious prisoner down the stairs by his feet, his head rhythmically banging out the time against the metal rungs.

"'Cuff him." called out the 'Old Man' to the two uniforms, as they dragged the target towards the rear of the Transit.

"He's out cold Sergeant." replied the van driver.

"He is at the moment ...thanks to Derek's fuckin' cobra like reactions to the immediacy of the situation." he said, looking back sarcastically towards the members of the obs Two Team.

"But 'es going to be less than fuckin' 'appy when 'e comes round and one of you two heroes is going to be in the back with King Kong 'ere, and 'e might just want a little pay back."

The two uniforms paused, glanced at each other for a second and then hurriedly rolled the prisoner over onto his stomach. Now face down on the cobbles they wrenched his arms up towards the small of his back. Handcuffs were placed on the wrists, the ratchets clicking, lessening the circumference of the restraints until the case hardened steel bit into the target's unfeeling flesh.

"What about 'is feet?" the van driver said to the uniform, who seemed to consider the proposal for a second, before he recalled the blow he had earlier taken to his chest. He nodded quickly and a second pair of cuffs were hurriedly placed around the prisoner's ankles. The two uniforms lifted the limp body like a carpet remnant and tossed it unceremoniously onto the floor of the Transit van between the slatted wooden bench seats.

"Which nick?" the van driver called out, looking back to where the 'Old Man' and his partner were standing.

The 'Old Man' hesitated as if in thought, then called out "Moorwood." before disappearing inside the target's residence.

The uniformed van driver scowled at the now vacant doorway and whispered an obscenity to himself as he opened the van door and took his seat. He twisted the ignition key angrily and as the engine roared into life, he revved the engine hard, taking out his frustration on the suffering Transit. "Meal break down the fuckin' Swanee again, second time this week." He hissed as he slammed the clutch pedal to the floor and rammed the gear lever forwards. The Transit protested with a loud metallic crunch as the warn synchromesh failed to ease the gears together.

"Fuckin' Crime Squad." he muttered as he released the clutch pedal, the Transit lurching forwards and bouncing on the cobbles. The uniform in the rear was thrown back against the rear doors, the unconscious prisoner felt nothing as his head made contact with the steel legs which secured the wooden bench seats to the floor.

"Oi! fuckin' 'ell Mick, I'm in 'ere as well you know." shouted the uniform angrily from the rear compartment. He banged a fist against the bulkhead observation panel as the Transit van bounced crazily out of the alley and onto the main road, it's tail lights disappearing around the wall as it hastily left the 'Badlands' with its cargo.

The four Detectives rummaged through the contents of the flat, the 'Old Man' dismissed the rest of the Team and arranged a rendezvous for a de-briefing at Moorwood Police station.

"Derek, you and Matt get off. See to getting 'im booked in. Me and David'll go through this lot." The two Detectives turned to leave. The 'Old Man' added as an afterthought, "Better see what injuries he's got. Get 'im to the Infirmary if needs be, we can do without Civil Liberties pissing an' whining to the Chief about Police brutality."

"Oh, it's alright for him to carve 'is autograph all over us with 'is fuckin' cutthroat then." the obs two Detective sneered.

The 'Old Man' sighed. "Just do it Derek, eh."

"What about the razor Boss?"

"Bag it and get it off to forensic, and make sure you do an exhibit label."

The Detective nodded. Although the 'Old Man' was looking elsewhere, he stopped at the doorway and turned. "He would have used it you know Boss, his sort don't give a shit."

The D.S. sighed as if lost in thought. "I know Derek, I know." he whispered.

The two Detectives from Team two left.

The 'Old Man' looked across the room to where his partner was sifting through the contents of the chest of drawers beneath the window.

"Get Studio up here, I want photographs and fingerprints and get all the clothing you can find, bag it up for forensic."

The Detective nodded and left the flat to get the request sorted. The 'Old Man' stood alone in the flat and looked around. He wrinkled his nose at the smell of urine and stale sweat. The heady pungent scent of cannabis was strongly present in the room, permeating from the walls and the soiled clothing which was scattered haphazardly across the limited floor space of the bedsit. He looked around him at the squalor, the filth in which his prey had lived and felt a strange sense of inner triumph at having won the first round; he wondered how any human could live like this, without any form of self-discipline or motivation. His Detective was right, their target wouldn't give a shit.

Looking around the room again, the 'Old Man' conceded with a little dismay, that the threat of prison for the blacks in the 'Badlands' would never be a deterrent. A clean cot and three square meals a day, how bad could it be if you normally lived like this.

Checking the mattress for damp stains, he pulled the grimy, grey blanket over the corner of the bed and sat. He lit a cigarette, promising himself for the hundredth time that he would stop...but not today...Tomorrow... maybe.

*****

The Ford Transit pulled up outside the electronic receiving gates in the rear yard at Moorwood. At the sound of the horn, the radio operator inside, glanced out of the window and nodded to the driver as he thumbed the button on his desk to activate the van gates. The two Detectives from the obs Two Team stopped their vehicle behind the Transit as the gates slowly cranked open, reaching their full extent with a loud metallic clunk.

The Transit slowly entered the concreted prisoner reception area and the gates started to close. The two Detectives darted in through the closing gap as the overhead fluorescent yard lights flickered on. The steel backed cell area door was opened by the gaoler, the rivet heads on the steel sheet glistened in the harsh overhead lights where the grey paint had worn away by uncountable bodies which had been pushed against it.

The automatic gates slammed shut and only then, did the Transit driver leave his seat to join the two Detectives who were now hovering about by the rear doors. The driver took off the outer clip which secured the van doors and pulled the offside door open. The uniform inside scrambled out, scowling at the van driver, he rubbed his shoulder vigorously.

"Thanks for an emotional journey Mick, I hope you're not expectin' a fuckin' tip."

The driver ignored the sarcasm and opened the nearside door. Light flooded into the rear area of the Transit. The prisoner was seated on the rubber covered floor with his back against the rear bulkhead door and stared out at his reception committee with a face contorted with hatred and contempt. "Come on then Sooty." the van driver said, motioning to the prisoner with a sideways movement of his head. "Let's 'ave you out."

"Fuck you." the prisoner spat and continued to stare at his captors.

"Get 'im out then." the senior of the two Detectives said, nudging the van driver.

The Transit driver looked around. "Bollocks, 'es your fuckin' prisoner, I'm late as it is. You caught 'im, you skin the bastard."

The Custody Sergeant approached from the cell area, looking impatiently at the two Detectives. "Is he coming in or what?" he said angrily.

The Detectives pointed to the interior of the van.

"You two." The Custody Sergeant said, looking directly at the two uniformed Officers, "Get in there and fetch him out."

The smiles dropped from their faces. The van driver protested. "We're 'B' Division Sarge, just doin' transport, delivering 'im like. 'E's their prisoner." nodding towards the two Detectives.

"Then deliver him…to me, in here. Get on with it." the Sergeant snapped.

The two uniforms glanced resignedly at one another, then together, climbed onto the metal step at the rear of the van and bent almost double, they shuffled towards the prisoner.

"Come on then ya black twat, don't be fuckin' stupid." the van driver said as he reached out to take hold of the prisoner's handcuffed arms.

"Pull 'im to me." said the other as he moved over towards the offside of the van.

The prisoner lunged forwards, catching the two uniforms unawares. His forehead smashed down against the face of the van driver throwing him backwards against the side of the van. Blood exploding from his nose and spattered down the front of his tunic. The second uniform withdrew his truncheon from the deep pocket in his trousers and brought it down hard against the side of the prisoner's neck, deadening the muscles and preventing any further head butts.

The prisoner reeled at the blow and squeezed his eyes tight shut against the pain. The van driver staggered from the van, doubled over with cupped hands over his face, the blood seeping through his fingers and dripping to the painted concrete floor of the reception area.

The second uniform backed away from the prisoner and replaced his truncheon into its pocket. Grabbing for the link between the handcuffs around the prisoner's ankles, he backed out of the vehicle dragging the prisoner unceremoniously towards the rear doors.

"What the bloody hell is going on?" the Custody Sergeant growled as he strode to the rear of the van. "You two…get in there and help him out." he shouted to the two Detectives.

"And you." he shouted to the van driver. "Get to the matron and get that sorted...Bleedin' all over my fucking floor!" the Custody Sergeant said angrily.

The two Detectives scrambled up to the rear doors of the Transit and took hold of the prisoner's ankles. They slid him along the corrugated floor of the van whilst holding his legs tightly together, fearful of being kicked. The prisoner was dragged bodily from the vehicle, his hands still tightly 'cuffed to the rear. He was unable to support himself and his head struck the metal step as he was dumped on the concrete floor of the cell reception area.

"Straight through...cell three." the Custody Sergeant said, nodding towards the corridor.

The prisoner was grabbed under the armpits and dragged through the booking in area and taken down the long corridor containing the twelve cells, six to either side.

The prisoner was half lifted, then thrown, falling back against the wooden bench at the far end of the cell. As he fell, the ratchets on the handcuffs tightened further and bit into the flesh around his wrists.

The Officers retreated from the cell. The van driver, standing at the cell door, his hand still cupped over his nose, looked back down the corridor and seeing that it was clear, entered the cell and towered over the prisoner. He smiled at the manacled wrists and ankles, then sneered at the sweating face which looked up at him.

"You black piece of shit, fuck you too." he said. He glanced furtively toward the cell door and seeing that he was alone, raised his boot and stamped down hard on the prisoner's groin. The prisoner convulsed, his eyes screwed up against the searing pain in his testicles. Unable to put his hands out to protect himself, he curled up into the foetal position, bringing his knees up to his chest as the vomit welled up and was coughed out onto the cell floor.

The van driver smiled at the pain he had inflicted, the years of scorn and insolence suffered in the 'Badlands' were dissipated in one vengeful act. He leaned over the prisoner, enjoying the contorted features etched across the vomiting face. He whispered, nudging the prisoner's stomach with the toe of his boot. "You're in deep shit Uncle Tom, you're in my fuckin' world now and I promise you, you're not going to enjoy it."

The prisoner viewed his assailant through eyelids screwed into slits, a red veil of pain colouring his vision of the sneering uniform. His head fell back against the cold painted concrete of the cell floor. He was barely aware of the uniform leaving, but heard the empty acoustic clunk as the cell door impacted with its steel surround.

"Who is he and what's it for?" the Custody Sergeant said, now standing behind the reception desk. A blank detention sheet was laid on the wooden counter top. The Sergeant's pen hovered, expectantly waiting for the prisoner's details.

"James Frederick Lyburn, a.k.a. 'Midnight' 42 years, 36 Back Melbourne Terrace, Eastmoor. It's for section 18 wounding on Mai Long a.k.a. Annie Long' on the 27th of this month at Eastmoor" said the Detective.

"And you can chuck in possess offensive weapon, resist arrest and possession of a controlled substance." said his partner.

"And don't forget assault Police and generally being a twat." the van driver called out from the Matron's room.

## **Five**

Alan nodded to the female canteen manageress as he took his plate from the stainless steel counter top and joined some other members of his Group on early meal. Two of the Formica topped tables had been pushed together so that the lads could sit together, "Alright Al?" said one looking up.

"Yeah, not bad." he replied, reaching over for the salt and shuffling himself closer to the table edge.

There was an air of hilarity about the Group. One or two had reddened faces from the effects of laughter at a tale being graphically told, another was wiping tears from his cheeks with the back of his hand.

"No, it's right, 'onest." continued the storyteller.

"These two Detectives go down to London to collect a prisoner. Apparently, 'es bin nicked for something down there and 'e's wanted on our patch, so 'e gets banged up in the 'smoke' until our lads can get down there."

"Anyway, the two stalwart Detectives get off the train at Kings Cross an' there's two Met uniforms to meet them. They tell our lads that it'll be an overnight stop 'cos they haven't finished with 'im yet. Our lads get lodged in one of the section 'ouses and that night, they get taken out by the Met lads, usual courtesy, you know, loads of ale an' a filthy Paki curry on the way back."

Laughter rose from the Group, one, still totally overcome by the effects of the last tale, was weeping openly and uttering loud moans of laughter, which enhanced the effect of the current rendition. The teller continued. "Anyway, they're out all night aren't they, more ale, more curry, all free a'course, courtesy of the Met who as we all know are bent as nine bob notes an' pay for bugger all. Anyway, at about 4.00 am our lads roll back to the section 'ouse pissed as rats, 'onkin' an' fartin' all over the place."

"The Met lads tell our boys that they'll send a van for them in the mornin' so they can transport the prisoner back to Kings Cross an' then 'ome." Our lads, full of southern 'ospitality, get their 'eads down and sure enough, first thing in the mornin' a van arrives with the prisoner in the back and the two Met lads in the front. Our two lads get in the back of the van with the prisoner; identify 'emselves and re-arrest 'im on behalf of our Force. Due to the effects of southern ale, which we all know is like rat's piss, one of our lads 'as got a bad stomach. Anyway, 'e feels the need to vent wind an' farts, but unbeknown to 'im, the wind is of the liquid variety and when same is forced out between 'is well rounded cheeks, he 'as a rather childish accident."

Alan chuckled to himself between mouthfuls. He'd heard the story before, yet the tale itself and the manner in which it was told still made him laugh. The new members of the Group listened intently.

"Oh bloody 'ell, 'e says, I've shit meself, and the van fills with this 'orrible fetid odour. One of the Met lads pokes 'is 'ead through the hatch and says "Fackin' 'ell John, whose shit?"

The laughter fills the canteen. The teller's much exaggerated London accent enhancing the humour and even old Edie the canteen manageress who has also heard the tale before, cannot hide her chuckles.

"The other Detective points out 'is mate's predicament. "No fackin' problem John" says the Met lad, I've got a tailor on Saville Row what owes me a favour. What's your waist size?"

"Thirty eight says our lad, who is trying to lift his arse off the bench, 'cos by now, 'is trousers are stickin' to 'is arse."

"They gets to Saville Row an' the Met lad leaps out of the van and goes into this tailors an' a coupla minutes later, comes back with a brown paper parcel which 'e promptly chucks through the 'atch and they're off to Kings Cross. Our lads get the prisoner lodged on the train an' once it gets goin' the Detective says to 'is mate, "I'm off to get meself cleaned up". Off he goes to the toilet clutching the parcel right?"

Alan looks across the canteen to where the shift Inspector is seated; he has a blank expression on his face and is clearly not impressed by the uncontrolled inappropriate hilarity of his junior Officers.

The teller continued. "The train's givin' it clickety clack, clickety clack, 'e's in the bog and off comes 'is trousers. Oh Christ! 'e says, seein' the 'orrible damp stain. Anyway, 'e's got the parcel, so he rolls up 'is soiled strides and bungs 'em out the window. 'E drops his skiddies, thinkin' 'ow 'e can wash 'em out in the sink, but when he sees 'ow bad they are, 'e can't bring himself to wash 'em, so out the window they go as well." The Group howl with laughter as the teller stood up and continued with the tale, enhancing its impact with facial expressions and graphic descriptive movements.

"E manages to get 'is backside over the edge of the sink, which is no mean feat on a movin' train, right. 'E washes 'imself off with 'is 'ands, an' naked from the waist down, rips open the parcel and finds…a jacket!"

The Group explodes into screams of laughter, picturing the forlorn Detective standing in the swaying toilet, bare assed, forlornly holding up the jacket.

Alan joined in, the laughter was so infectious. He looked again to where the shift Inspector sat eating his salad alone. Not a thread of a smile cracked his sullen face, his head buried deeply into his copy of Police Review.

Alan finished his meal as the rest of the Group gradually controlled themselves enough to eat. The laughter erupting every now and then through the more sober conversation.

Alan stood up. He collected his plate and mug and walked to the server. "See you later lads." he said, walking towards the swing doors. "Yeah later Al." said one or two as the 'teller' started another tale.

Alan made his way to the canteen door, nodding briefly to another member of the Group who was late coming in for his meal.

"Pendle." called out the Inspector without looking up from his magazine.

"Sir." Alan replied, stopping in mid stride, wondering what gem was about to be offered.

"My office, six o'clock if you please." the Inspector said flatly, not taking his gaze from the page he was reading.

Alan waited for a second or two to see if he was worthy of a glance from the man. It wasn't forthcoming.

"Yes Sir, six o'clock." he replied and walked through the canteen doors.

Alan entered the Road Traffic office and passed the remainder of his meal break with the half night crew who were getting their kit ready for parade.

These were his own sort and he felt at home with them. Conversation came easy and it was of a common theme. There was a very strong 'espirit de corps' amongst the Traffic men. They were unashamedly elitist and extremely cynical regarding beat Officers, senior Officers and especially 'nine to fivers'.

"What's Mr fuckin' personality want of you then?" PC Oldfield asked, stealing one of his partner's cigarettes.

"I haven't a clue." Alan said, leafing through the papers in the Sergeant's tray and pausing for a moment as he glanced at a typed Minute Sheet from Headquarters.

"Fuck me sideways, I've got my basic firearms course." He beamed, as he waved the signed joining instructions across the front of Oldfield's face.

"You're welcome to it mate." replied Oldfield. "Job's dangerous enough without putting yourself in the firing line."

Alan continued to smile and read the Minute Sheet again, just to make sure. "Five day course lads, I'm off to Stretham, .38 and shotgun. Excellent!"

"Inspector'll want his Wife picking up from her Bridge Club." sneered Pc Barnett. "Don't worry dear, I'll get one of my Traffic men to collect you." he said, mimicking the sullen voice of the Inspector.

Oldfield leaned back in his chair and blew smoke back towards his young partner. "Shut the fuck up Barney, you're not a Traffic man yet. 'Aide's' aren't allowed to speak to us veterans, am I right Al?"

Alan winked at PC Barnett, who was now feverishly throwing 'V' signs towards the back of his Tutor's head.

"I've no doubt I'll find out." Alan said sighing, his mood lifted considerably at the prospect of the forthcoming firearms course. He glanced at his watch. "Christ! I'd better be off, he'll have my balls off."

Alan left the office and smiled as he heard Pc Barnett call after him, "Can I have your white top if he finishes you Al?"

Oldfield's laughter faded as Alan ran down the steps to the lower corridor.

*****

"Enter." said the voice from within the Inspector's office.

Alan opened the door and saw the Inspector instinctively look up at the clock on his wall opposite. "Shit, two minutes past." thought Alan.

"Sit down Alan." the Inspector said as he fussed his way through a pile of papers strewn across his desk.

"Oh Alan is it?" he thought, "Looks like it's a bollocking then." Senior Officers had a habit of calling Officers by their first names when they were about to tear them off a strip, it promoted a feeling in the recipient that the deliverer was offering it begrudgingly. "Sign of a weak man." thought Alan.

Alan noticed that the adjustable seat which he had been offered was set at its lowest height and it caught him off balance a little as he sat. He also noticed that the Inspector who was now seated opposite, had his seat at the highest setting. This was due to the fact that the Inspector had only just scraped through the height requirement for the Force and he suffered from a complex bordering on paranoia regarding his personal stature. It was also so that the Inspector was effectively looking down at his junior Officers during their yearly appraisals and general bollockings.

Alan sat and waited whilst the Inspector shuffled through the papers, segregating them into small piles in order of priority.

"Another ploy." thought Alan, "Gets me here at six o'clock, then fucks around with his papers for five minutes on purpose, increases his 'dominance position', hoping that I'm sweating over what he wants."

Alan fought the almost overwhelming desire to lean over the table and tell the Inspector that in fact he was very busy and that perhaps it would be better if the Inspector came to see *him* when *he* had more time, but immediately thought better of it and shuffled uncomfortably in the chair. From his lowered position, Alan effectively had to look up to the Inspector, physically if nothing else. This of course being the Inspector's desired result. He felt a little ridiculous looking over the desktop which was almost level with his chest and wondered if it would be prudent to adjust the chair to its proper height.

The methodical ticking of the electric clock pronounced the silence in the room which was only interrupted by the rustle of the papers and the clicking of a stapler as the Inspector continued with his clerical. If the Inspector was running true to form, he would let Alan sit until exactly five past the hour, thereby ensuring that Alan, without a word having to be spoken, was aware that he was in the presence of his superior. It would enhance the Inspector's personal gratification the more, due to the fact that he was painfully aware that Alan was over six feet tall.

Finally, the Inspector looked down at Alan, who glanced instinctively up at the clock. Five past exactly.

"Sorry to keep you waiting." the Inspector said, a false half smile stealing across his face, the same smile you get from a bank manager just before he tells you he's not authorising your loan application.

"You're not sorry at all, you fucking dwarf." thought Alan, smiling inwardly to himself in the knowledge that the Inspector also sat on a cushion.

The Inspector coughed, clearing his throat.

"I have earlier today, had the embarrassing task of explaining to one of the leading citizens in the community, why an Officer under my command, would be rude, ill-mannered and downright abusive. This is not a task which endears me to the Officer concerned and furthermore, I have taken time from my personal meal break, on the telephone, trying to avert an official complaint being lodged. I have also had to provide assurances to the Gentleman concerned, who I might add, is a personal friend of Councillor Middlemass who for your further information Pendle, is the Chairman of the Police Authority, that such reprehensible conduct as was displayed by the Officer concerned, will not go unadmonished. Do I make myself clear?"

Alan paused for a second, his brow furrowed in confusion. "Which Officer are we talking about Sir?"

The Inspector's face tightened. "You Pc Pendle...*You* are the Officer we are talking about. I understand that you dealt with an accident on the Ring Road yesterday evening, at the roundabout with George Road..... Ringing any bells yet?"

"No." Alan shook his head slowly. "I mean, yes, I dealt with a bump but......"

"You spoke to a gentleman at the scene Pendle...think...I know that might not come naturally to you, but give it your best effort." The Inspector said sarcastically.

Alan thought hard. Scratching the top of his ear, he leaned back in the chair. Suddenly, a light came on. "Captain Mainwaring!" he remembered, smiling. Alan nodded and looked up at the Inspector. "Yes Sir, I do remember speaking with someone, but I certainly wasn't abusive or ill-mannered, more of a joke, to lighten the gravity of the situation really Sir."

"I'm not interested in your weak bleating excuses Pendle." growled the Inspector.

"I don't suppose you are." thought Alan, as he sat pan faced in front of the man.

"What concerns me the most, is the apparent cavalier approach you seem to have with regards to our public image, how we come over professionally. Understand?"

Alan nodded, wishing that he did.

"What exactly did this Gentleman say I'd done then Sir?"

The Inspector waved the question aside. "Never mind that. I've placated the party concerned. You…can consider yourself reprimanded."

"For what though Sir. I don't know the full extent of the alleged complaint." stuttered Alan in his defence.

The Inspector pointed a warning finger and adopted a stern expression. "Look, you've a bit of a reputation as a 'Bolshevik' Pendle."

"Pendle now." thought Alan.

"And, it hasn't gone unnoticed, I can tell you. You'd better get yourself straightened out and start acting like a professional Police Officer, instead of some loose cannon not sufficiently proficient to work unsupervised within a specialist department, got it?"

Alan sat in silence for a moment or two and glanced out of the window to the car park beyond.

"I've had no complaints from my supervisors in Traffic Sir." Alan said, looking purposefully back towards the Inspector who, much to Alan's inward pleasure appeared to be slightly unsettled by the unexpected parry. With slightly raised confidence, Alan continued. "In fact Sir, I don't believe that I have ever been abusive or ill-mannered and if trying to make light of an unpleasant situation for all concerned is regarded as being unprofessional by the Gentleman concerned, then I can only assume that he is the type of person who revels in making trivial, vexatious complaints about Police Officers while they are trying to do their job in difficult circumstances."

There was a stony silence.

"I think you've said enough." said the Inspector, although somewhat quieter now.

"A little courtesy goes a long way Pendle. Sarcasm has no place amongst our ranks, it breeds insolence and denigrates our professionalism. I expect more from you in the future, understand?" The Inspector paused for a moment. "I note that you are due to attend a firearms course in the near future Pendle." He paused again, allowing Alan to reconsider his truculent stance.

"It is not too late for representations to be made to Headquarters regarding your behavioural profiling and perhaps…dubious suitability to become an authorised firearms Officer. Is my point made clear?" The Inspector said, with the merest hint of a raised eyebrow.

Alan inwardly slumped and nodded, knowing that he was beaten. Although he was Traffic, the beat Inspector had the final say regarding releasing uniformed resources from the Division to attend courses. In fact, Alan would have gladly bent over the Inspector's desk and spread his own arse cheeks to get the Inspector's final signature on his joining instructions. Stretham was a 'peach' of a course and very much in demand. Five days of tactics and instruction in the use of the Smith and Wesson .38 'special' and the Remington 870 pump action shotgun. At the end of the intensive course, if target grades were achieved and sufficient instructor's arses were kissed, a firearms authority ticket, special protection duty, Royal visits, as well as involvement in Divisional firearms operations, which were definitely on the increase and of course a chance at the pinnacle of all courses, Force Rifleman.

The 'serious rumour squad' had it that the Force was going to set up a specialised Firearms Department. Alan could see that the writing was on the wall for Traffic and if applications for the new posts were to be published in orders, Alan wanted to be ready. Those Officers already authorised to carry firearms would no doubt get priority consideration. Alan had waited years for a place on the basic firearms course to be offered and he had no intention of letting the 'boy wonder' or his personal pride get the better of him. Discretion being the better part of valour, Alan sighed inwardly knowing he'd been bested.

"I apologise for letting the side down Sir." he offered.

The Inspector allowed himself a moment to bask in Alan's total capitulation for a second, no doubt enjoying every moment. He nodded towards the door. "You're dismissed."

"Thank you Sir." Alan said, pulling himself up from the chair.

The Inspector returned his eyes to the pile of papers on his desk and Alan left him to the company of his paranoia and the ticking of his clock.

He walked from the Inspector's office feeling a little more than jaded by the man's attitude and slightly angry with himself for not having the courage of his own convictions to say more. Yet he knew that he would probably have said too much and the place at Stretham would have gone to someone else. The Inspector had got to him and it rankled, enough for Alan to have answered back. Polite as he had been, he'd lost his composure and that wasn't always wise when speaking with a senior Officer. The Fatherly concerned look, the ingenuous sympathetic nodding's of the head were not to be trusted.

"Anything said here will go no further than these four walls." was not to be believed.

Many a penitent confessing uniform had been whisked magically away to the farthest reaches of the County, or spent a year doing penance at the City Bridewell after 'confiding' in a senior Officer. Unfortunately, Inspectors and above are not tied to the ethics governing the sanctity of the confessional, especially when they consider their personal promotional aspirations weighed against the downfall, of what they consider to be a lesser form of life.

It seemed that the day was turning a little sour until Alan entered the front office.

There, standing with the Station Sergeant was a senior Officer's delight. A sight to purify and re-affirm belief in the rewards of command. An object to be taken in its raw, unadulterated, untainted state and moulded from the outset. To be taken under a Fatherly protective wing and nurtured, shaped and directed toward the paths of righteousness, before the single celled amoeba in the form of a beat patrol Tutor Constable could warp its delicate mind which in its virgin state, lay defenceless and receptive.

A new probationer.

The lad was being shown how to operate the 'Burndept' personal radio and Alan smiled as he noticed that the 'Proby' was standing gloriously to attention for the Sergeant. His eyes followed every move the Sergeant made, as he pointed out the various channel and volume controls.

"You going out?" the Sergeant called to Alan. Alan stopped in his tracks and winced, knowing what was coming. "In a minute or two Sarge, why, what's up?"

The Sergeant nodded to the mute probationer. "Take him out and show him round the Division if you've nothing else on."

The 'Proby' glanced across at Alan with an apologetic look, as if to seek forgiveness for becoming an encumbrance on what was clearly a veteran Officer and a Traffic man as a bonus.

Alan looked directly at the smiling face of the Station Sergeant and sighed. "Ok, five minutes."

The 'Proby's' dour expression immediately changed to one of rapturous joy and anticipation. Alan looked the lad up and down. "I'll get my kit and see you in the back yard, ok?"

The 'Proby' nodded quickly, his helmet almost falling from his shaven head.

"Thanks Alan." the old Sergeant said, walking away smiling wryly.

Alan walked across towards the radio room to check for any outstanding calls. Passing the Sergeant, he said with mock sarcasm, "Cheers Dave, thanks a lot."

The Sergeant smirked knowingly and his smile widened. "Don't mention it Alan, I reckon you of all people deserve a small favour, I understand you've just had your arse reamed by our illustrious leader…Think of it as part of your penance."

The probationer hung round Alan's ankles as he walked into the radio room, hovering like a moth around a bright light.

The Station Sergeant called after Alan. "Oi! I don't want you leading him astray. Keep him away from loose women and intoxicants."

Alan turned and smiled and they both paused for a second, looking at the 'Proby' and remembering their first days, days of innocence.

## Six

Alan arrived at the disused R.A.F. base in North Yorkshire to commence his basic training; it had been late in the April of 1975 and warmer than usual for the time of year. The trees that formed a long avenue leading up to the main gates of the base were well in bud and the sun was gloriously warm through the windscreen of his car as he drove. The excitement and anticipation of a new career, hopefully, a hot summer just around the corner and the prospect of thirteen weeks at the academy overrode any feelings of apprehension as he turned in through the large main gates and drove towards the Guardroom.

An immaculate uniformed Constable walked slowly and purposefully toward him. A spotless white glove on his upraised hand motioned Alan to stop.

He wore a tall hat, its raised chromium plated comb glistened in the sun and the peak, pulled harshly down onto the bridge of his nose, cast a shadow over the upper part of his face.

Alan was immediately impressed by the deportment of the Constable, who he considered must also be a student. His jacket and trousers were immaculately creased and the whitewashed frontage of the Guardroom was reflected in the mirror like toe caps of his 'bulled' shoes.

The Constable marched up to Alan's car and saluted crisply. "Good afternoon Sir, are you a recruit?" Alan was somewhat taken aback, he had risen to the dizzy heights of Lance Corporal in his last job and wasn't used to being saluted. "Thanks very much." replied Alan nodding. He would later find out that all persons in civilian clothing were saluted and called Sir, a safeguard against disciplinary proceedings being taken for failing to acknowledge a genuine Senior Officer who may be a visiting lecturer. Better safe than sorry.

"Yes, where do I report?" Alan replied.

The Constable leaned towards Alan's open window and pointed toward the brilliantly whitewashed building at the side of the entrance gates.

"You may park your vehicle in one of those marked bays for the time being Sir, the Duty Sergeant is in the reception area. Do you have your letter of authority?"

Alan rummaged inside his jacket pocket and produced the typed joining instructions.

"Give those to the Sergeant Sir. Thank you." The Constable said, taking one smart step backwards and saluting crisply.

Alan drove through and abandoned his vehicle in a space which was clearly defined as belonging to the A/Chf/Ins which was evenly painted in large white letters across the middle of the bay. "Any bay but that one please Sir." the Constable on the gate called out to him.

Alan peered out from the window of his vehicle and wondered why out of all the half dozen or so empty parking bays, this one was so important.

"Academy Chief Inspector's Sir." the Constable whispered surreptitiously out of the corner of his mouth, mimicking some 'spiv' trying to sell him silk stockings or some other illicit black market product.

Alan backed his car out of the bay. Assured that the A/Chf/Ins was obviously a man of some prestige. Whoever or whatever an A/Chf/Ins was, he'd certainly got the Constable on the gate worried.

The reception building had obviously been the Guardroom in its former R.A.F. days and Alan entered cautiously, just in case the dreaded A/Chf/Ins was present. As he entered, his nostrils were immediately assailed by the comforting smell of 'Cardinal' floor polish and 'Brasso'.

Alan enjoyed a fleeting moment of déjà vu and his recent release from his Regiment at Aldershot. The deep red linoleum floor shone as if covered in a thin film of water, due, no doubt, to the forced labour of thousands of airmen on 'jankers' over the years. The brass window and door fittings were burnished and worn smooth with polishing and the room was warm, orderly and strangely inviting. The old cell doors at the back of the guardroom had been removed, revealing the huge polished brass hinges which still protruded from the red painted brickwork of the interior walls. The wooden shelf beds, however, remained, their surfaces still varnished, but hardly visible due to 'No Waiting' cones and direction signs which had been stacked with military precision in rows. All in all, the room radiated an aurora of authority and discipline.

A Sergeant as immaculate as the duty Constable on the gate was standing behind the polished counter and looked up from a long typed list in front of him. He smiled, which Alan considered to be a good start. He asked Alan for his name and Force. Alan replied and the Sergeant ran his index finger swiftly down the line of typed names. "Pendle, Pendle, he muttered to himself. "Ah, here we are, Pendle A…Yes?"

"Yes." Alan replied.

The Sergeant paused and pointedly produced the left sleeve of his tunic for Alan to see. "Oh, sorry…Sergeant." Alan added quickly.

At this, the Sergeant nodded and smiled. "Might as well get used to it."

"Yeah." Alan laughed and again quickly added "Sergeant."

"You're in Block Three, room twelve. Can I see your joining instructions?"

Alan handed over the now slightly crumpled authority. The Sergeant perused the document for a moment, then looked up. "Do you know the camp at all?"

Alan was tempted to respond "Yes, I was a Spitfire pilot here during the last big one." but thought better of it. "No, Sergeant, not at all." was what actually came out.

The Sergeant handed Alan a printed map of the Academy and marked the position of Block Three. "You'll be expected to be in your allotted room by sixteen hundred hours to…that's four o'clock in civilian speak, to be present for roll call and Group assignment, ok?"

Alan resisted the urge to advise the Sergeant that he had only recently left one of the finest Regiments in the British Army, but decided to keep his own counsel and act as dumb as he obviously looked.

The Sergeant formally welcomed him to the academy in a genuine manner and told him by way of friendly advice, that all he had to do to succeed, was to work hard and to listen to his Instructors. He wished him luck and with a wave of thanks, Alan left the reception building and walked back to where he had abandoned his vehicle.

Alan nodded to the Constable on the gate and walked purposefully around the whole circumference of the bay marked for the A/Chf/Ins. He tossed the map in through the open window of his car, feeling like he belonged already.

He drove around the perimeter road to where the old billet buildings stood in imposing gargantuan rows of 'H' shaped blocks.

Alan found Block Three and parked his vehicle in one of the segregated bays, this time ensuring that there were no white letters proclaiming 'Visiting Pope', 'Queen' or 'God Almighty' at the head of any of the parking spaces.

The billet building was constructed of red brick, but the faint outlines of the grey and green camouflage could still vaguely be made out, a graphic reminder of the building's former use. Alan took his suitcase from the boot of his car, his stomach fluttering a little at the prospect of meeting a room full of complete strangers. He walked towards the twin polished wooden doors and glanced at the equally polished brass plaque which was riveted to the brickwork, the plaque simply said 'Bader' after the Second World War fighter ace.

A voice boomed out behind him.

"SIR!"

Alan jumped involuntarily and almost dropped his suitcase. He turned to be confronted by a huge barrel chested Sergeant wearing a bright red sash which ran diagonally across his upper uniformed torso. The Sergeant towered over six feet and looked to be all of seventeen stones. He carried a black, mahogany pace stick which was topped with a polished silver head. This instrument of torture was tucked purposefully under his left armpit, the white gloved fingers of his left hand resting lightly on its shaft.

The 'apparition' wore a flat cap, its peak so severely slashed that it ran parallel to his face. The peak of his headgear was highly polished and finished where it touched the Sergeant's bulbous nose just below the bridge, completely covering his eyes.

No hair at all showed beneath the cap, which Alan mused, was either due to severe premature baldness, an acute case of alopecia, or as he suspected with something of a grimace, the expected grooming standard of the Academy. The Sergeant was superbly turned out. The creases in his tunic and trousers were razor edged and twin rows of multi-coloured medal ribbons were emblazoned across the left hand side of his chest, just above the tunic pocket.

He spoke to Alan in what could only be described as a subdued scream. His voice was deep and gravelly, either due to a hundred 'Marlborough' a day or, through years of shouting at worthless students. How many threats of a fate worse than death had passed between those chiselled lips, how many Police recruits had burned themselves alive or wired themselves up to the mains simply to escape this man's attentions? Alan shuddered.

He accentuated his speech in the classic mode of the drill instructor as he pointed his pace stick towards Alan's car. "Is this your veeehicuarl Sir?"

Alan involuntarily glanced at the two front tyres and the excise licence. "Er, yes."

The monster stiffened perceptibly as if he'd been slapped. He tapped the gleaming white chevrons on his arm with the end of the pace stick.

"Sergeant." Alan added quickly.

"Thank you Sir?" the Sergeant responded. "And are you to be a student at this establishment?"

"Yes." Alan replied, inwardly cringing at the lack of confidence in his voice. The tip of the pace stick tapped the Sergeant's arm again.

"Yes Sergeant." Alan snapped quickly, wondering what obscure offence against the Private Vehicles on Police Academy Property Act 1975 he could possibly have committed so soon in his career.

"Then be appraised at this early juncture that student's vehicles are not allowed within the precincts of the Academy grounds. No expense has been spared in the provision of expansive parking facilities for said vehicles, behind the guardroom. You will have no need of a mechanically propelled motor vehicle, or indeed any form of transport whilst you are with us, a period, which in your case, I suspect will not be for long." The Titan paused. "We march everywhere here."

"Yes Sir." Alan blurted out. The chevrons were tapped again.

Alan slumped. Three chances of a remission were all he could possibly have hoped for. It was the electric cattle goad now for sure, or the dreaded anal insertion of the pace stick which would then no doubt, be opened to its greatest extent.

"Run along then Sir." his tormentor said quietly. "We don't want to be late in rooms for our first day do we?"

"No Sergeant." Alan replied, hesitating and glancing across his shoulder to his offending vehicle.

The Sergeant twisted his body and pointed with the pace stick towards the wooden doors of the billet. "Move it later Sir, get along with you now." At which, he turned sharply on his heel and marched stiffly away.

Alan turned and grasping the handle of his suitcase, he walked towards the entrance doors, almost suffering a premature cardiac arrest as the behemoth screamed at some poor unfortunate, who was walking towards the billets across the manicured grass.

"GET OFF MY GRASS SIR!"

Alan swore later that the glass in the wooden door frame actually vibrated as the Sergeant's vocal chords had clearly reached critical mass, probably causing the erring student Officer to immediately soil himself.

Alan leapt in through the double doors to avoid being the first to be chosen for the squad to execute the unfortunate who by now, had dropped his suitcase in abject fear and was running away from the scene as if his life depended on it. Alan mused that it probably did.

Slightly unnerved by his first experience of the Academy's discipline and slightly disconcerted, thinking that he had left all that behind at Aldershot, Alan made his way to his allocated room and entered.

Rows of grey, metal tubed bed frames were evenly spaced to either side of the room. Each bed head was an exact distance from the walls. At the head of each bed there was a bed pack made up of inner white sheets and grey blankets, each folded to an exact width so that the encompassing outer blanket which was wrapped around the bundle, made a perfect oblong. Two naked striped pillows rested on the top of each pack, the pillow cases, no doubt hidden somewhere within the bundle.

The wooden floor gleamed like a mirror and there wasn't a speck of dust to be seen. A few students were already gathered around the beds, each of which had a precisely folded cardboard name tag placed neatly on the pillows with a student's name and Force printed on it. Alan found his allotted bed space and heaved his suitcase onto the mattress.

The next half an hour or so was taken up with nervously offered handshakes and introductions as more students arrived. The students were from Forces throughout the Country. Alan found a student from his own Force and a friendship was struck. The room was filled with a myriad of differing accents and dialects and Alan overheard a deep Welsh voice utter "'Ave you seen that Sergeant then, the one with the stick? There's an evil man for you, screamed at me somethin' awful. Christ! I thought I'd run over somebody."

Alan laughed to himself, "Another Academy parking violation detected." he thought.

The buzz of conversation continued until the door was flung open and "Stand by your beds Gentlemen." was barked from a shape which completely filled the area where the door had previously been.

The students scurried to their respective bed ends and all heads turned pensively towards the door.

The body, which was blocking out all the incoming light from the open doorway, was owned by a Sergeant who made the first specimen look like a stick insect recovering from a serious case of anorexia. Silence fell across the room. The student's eyes widened and Alan noticed a few Adam's apples bobbing nervously.

The man entered. The studs on his immaculately 'bulled' boots resounded on the polished wood of the centre floor. He too carried a pace stick and Alan allowed his imagination to run riot for a second or two as to the possible purpose of such an item at a Police training Academy.

The scene of a defenceless student being bludgeoned to death with the heavy brass end of the stick flashed through his mind, the student's incriminating boot indentations still evident on the beloved grass.

The incoming Sergeant, who by his deportment and immaculate turn out, Alan guessed must be an ex Coldstream or Grenadier Guard, moved slowly and with purpose to the window at the far end of the room, wallowing in the awed silence.

He turned to face the students, allowing their gaze to soak up the atmosphere of the situation. His medal ribbons told of previous action in foreign fields and Alan recognised the blue and white of a Military Cross and a number of campaign ribbons one of which, was emblazoned with a silver rosette.

He told the students to sit and one could hear a distinct swish as twenty backsides broke the sound barrier to comply with the Sergeant's order.

The Sergeant commenced to read the students' names from a typed list and after the first had been vilified with a barked "On your feet!" each stood on hearing his name and replied with "Yes Sergeant" before resuming his seated position. "Any ex-servicemen among you?" he asked. Alan stood with at least half the room and the Sergeant noted down the various Regiments or Squadrons next to the student's name. "Right." he said, relaxing his tone a little. "You are still worthless civilians. You will not be sworn in as Police Officers until tomorrow. I am Sergeant Sharpe, your Drill Instructor, you will no doubt come to love me." A murmur of quiet laughter resounded about the room. The Sergeant smiled, to show that he was actually human and Alan almost believed it. The Sergeant paced the length of the room slowly, looking at each of the students in turn.

"You are free to leave this establishment at any time you wish. This is not Her Majesty's armed forces. We will not try to stop you, in fact, the opposite is true. We will openly encourage you to leave. We only want Officers who *want* to be Officers. You are about to enter a profession which is exacting, dangerous, poorly paid and for the most part thankless. Those of you who seek popularity, leave now and join the Fire service."

"Still all here? Good... You will throughout your thirty years of service, see the most grotesque, horrific, heart rending degrading levels of human depravity. You will be despised by most, respected by few, you will be spat at, sworn at and on occasions assaulted, anyone want to leave?" No one moved. Although the students looked around at each other to see if anyone was weakening.

The Drill Instructor slowly paced down the center of the room, the steel studs on his boots clacking against the polished floorboards. He looked at each of the students. "No?...Then I can also tell you that it can be the most satisfying, exciting and interesting job in the world. You are joining the most internationally respected Police Force in existence. We do not routinely carry or use firearms, forget what you have seen on television. The only time a precious few of you will come into contact with them is in the most dire of circumstances and then, only when all other avenues have been exhausted and firearms are the only method available to effect an arrest or to prevent an atrocious crime."

He continued in sombre mood. "I have been a Police Officer for over twenty years and other than the odd lazy student, I have not had to kill anyone." Laughter filled the room and Alan began to realise that he was actually starting to enjoy this.

The Sergeant relaxed his tone further and continued. "Tomorrow, you will be photographed and fingerprinted and we will reduce the length of your hair somewhat."

The room filled with murmurs.

"You will be sworn in as Officers after lunch tomorrow, after which you will be required to resign officially on paper if you wish to leave. Also, the academy Commandant can dispense with your services if at *any* time he feels, or if he is advised by any of your instructors, that you are not going to make an efficient Officer. It's up to you. In fairness to you all, I will tell you now that it is my job to find the weakest amongst you and to see that you never take to the streets of your respective towns and Cities. There are certain standards which we must protect for the benefit of the Public. For those of you who do not display the required common sense or skills, there will be no tolerance or compromise." The Sergeant let his words sink in for a moment.

"A word of warning. Although you will be sworn Officers and given the rank of Constable, you will not be allowed outside the confines of the Academy whilst in uniform. The reasoning here should be obvious. You will have all the powers granted to you under a multitude of Statutes and Acts bestowed upon you by the Government of the day, but none of the knowledge as to their uses and extents, so its civilian clothing at all times when outside the Academy grounds." The Sergeant paused and stared out of the window. He turned and paced the room again. "You will be with us for a period of thirteen weeks, during which time, we will endeavour to teach you the basic skills and knowledge you will require to graduate from here and become probationary Constables. Those of you who do manage to graduate." the Sergeant paused and then added "There is no shame in failing here Gentlemen; the standards are kept artificially high…will serve two years at your respective Divisions during which time, the Chief Constable of your respective Forces can also dispense with your services at any time if he feels that you will not become an efficient Officer. Any questions?"

A student at the far end of the room stood and asked "Are we free at the week-ends Sergeant?"

The Sergeant tutted theatrically and mocked him. "You've only been here five minutes and you're asking for time off already.

"The rest of the group laughed and the speaker's face reddened as he sat down.

The Sergeant silenced them by raising his hand. "You will finish here at sixteen hundred hours on Fridays and you must be back in rooms by twenty one hundred the following Sunday. For those of you without the benefit of a military background…learn the twenty four hour clock and the phonetic alphabet, a copy of which has been provided for your education and retention." He pointed his pace stick toward a notice board by the door.

The students nodded in unison.

"I'll mention sickness whilst on week-end leave later. Right, get your kit squared away into your lockers, I don't want to see any civilian rubbish laid about. If it doesn't fit in your lockers, it goes home with you and stays there. Understood?"

The students nodded in unison.

"The mess hall is on the right hand side of the parade ground. You can't miss it, just look for a line of students vomiting on their way back to the billets and you've cracked it. Walk across the parade ground or the perimeter grass at your peril."

There were a few chuckles, denoting those who had come across Vlad the Impaler previously.

"Evening meal starts at sixteen thirty. Meals are parades and as such, you are required to attend, whether you actually eat or not is up to you. Oh! Whilst we are on the subject of eating, a word to any aspiring Lothario's amongst you. The Policewomen's quarters are strictly out of bounds. Any male student found there, whether by invitation or otherwise will be immediately sent back to his Force and dismissed. This rule is vigorously enforced by the Commandant. There are no excuses, you have been warned. Nod your heads to confirm your understanding of this…immediate dismissal, ok." The room nodded in unison.

As he turned to go, he paused and as an afterthought added, "There are students here who due to the distance involved and time constraints, do not travel home for the week-ends, they may well be studying when you return on Sunday evenings, so no record players or musical instruments are allowed and in any case, you will be far too busy to bother with such trivial pastimes."

"Today, you are civilians, tomorrow you will be sworn Police Officers and as such, you will be expected to accept the discipline that will be meted out. The ex-Forces lads will help you with the discipline matters such as drill movements, your boots and uniforms. There is a very valid reason for instilling discipline, a reason which I will not dwell on at the moment. Accept the fact that it is necessary to prepare you for your future duties, embrace it and it will be tolerable, fight against it and it will be causal to your return to civilian life. Get yourselves squared away."

The Sergeant pointed his pace stick toward the rows of identical bedpacks. "Note how your personal bedpack has been constructed. Make a drawing if necessary, you will be required to replicate this each and every morning…for the first few weeks in any case….Your packs will be inspected daily. If they are not up to scratch, you will find yourselves parading at the Guardroom on 'nine o'clocks' under the watchful gaze of the duty Sergeant who will tutor you accordingly until you master the art." His tone softened slightly. "The ex-forces lads will be able to show you how it's done. It's about inter-cooperation lads. The ex-forces lads will be able to help with your personal discipline, kit and drill movements, but might not be able to readily grasp the academic side of things…especially if he happens to be an ex Para."

There were one or two chuckles. Alan felt his face flush slightly and the Sergeant smiled at him. "Conversely." he continued, "Those of you who were latterly consultant neurosurgeons or professors of economics, may readily grasp the majestic intricacies of English law, but make a complete bollocks of your drill and kit."

The students laughed. "Each is viewed with equal importance…so cooperate with one another and *maybe* you'll get by. Isolate yourself…and I guarantee you'll struggle. Lights out is at twenty two hundred ladies. I will see you all tomorrow."

*****

The next afternoon, Alan and the other students were sworn in as Police Officers. They all stood rigidly to attention as the Commandant of the Academy, along with his entourage of Senior Officers entered the long hall. Alan wondered if his old adversary the A/Chf/Ins was among them and subconsciously looked amongst the sea of silver coloured epaulettes and braided cap peaks, for a man ceremoniously carrying a set of car keys, a sign of his status and rank. The Lord Lieutenant of the City and his good Lady Wife were escorted into the Great Hall by immaculately turned out 'Phase Two' students, their helmets carried stiffly under their left arms.

The ceremony itself was rather short and sweet, there were speeches by the Commandant and a few anecdotal tales by one or two of the visiting dignitaries, who, Alan was much later to realise, knew as much about policing as he did then.

They were sworn in. Alan raised his hand and repeated the words in unison with his fellow students. "I Alan Pendle, do solemnly and sincerely swear that I…" The students repeated the solemn words of Office slowly and precisely, with a feeling of true conviction. "...and that I will diligently discharge my duties to the best of my ability, without favour or affection to any race, colour or creed." The oath was taken and the New Centurions glowed with pride and strong resolve. Congratulations were offered all round as the guests and dignitaries filed out for sherry and whatever else dignitaries consume after such occasions.

The rest of the day, their first as Policemen, faded into a vague memory. Uniform issue, horrendous haircuts, photographs and fingerprinting and the signing of various official documents, none of which Alan understood, nor had time to consider, as they were rushed around from one department to another. By the end of that first day, Alan was totally confused and exhausted. He had signed so many forms, for all he knew, he could well have signed up for a five year tour with the French Foreign Legion and agreed to donate his wages for the next ten years to the Lithuanian Baptist Church, he was too tired to care, or discuss it with his new Police colleagues. Alan, like the rest of them, had collapsed onto his bed at 'lights out' and had slept the sleep of the just until six thirty the following morning.

Reveille came as something like a cold wet flannel flicked against the gonads. The Sergeants rushed into the rooms with the usual clichés of "Hands off cocks and on with socks" and other colourful sayings which they had obviously memorised from cheap 'B' movies or earlier Army service. The obscene hour for those who had not previously served in Her Majesty's Forces, was met bleary eyed and drowsily. There were showers and shaves to be had before the morning parade at "Oh seven thirty ladies."

Alan shook the sleep from his eyes and glanced across the room. The Drill Instructor was beating some unfortunate who was experiencing difficulty in leaving the arms of Morpheus, with the brass end of his pace stick. The Drill Instructor was immaculate, too immaculate for this early hour and Alan nodded to his neighbour, an ex-submariner. They watched as the violent tableau was acted out on the opposite side of the room. "He must get up at four o'clock to practise this."

"No way Alan my man." his bed space neighbour said, shaking his head as he carefully pulled on his trousers, "I have it on good authority that he is the latest design from Hotpoint see? State of the art Drill Instructors. He's half man, half recycled washing machine. They plug him in at night, he just stands there whirring quietly away until five in the morning then he automatically switches on. Anyway, you and I have both met worse, eh?"

Alan chuckled and withdrew his boots from beneath his bed and carefully removed the soft cloth which had kept away the overnight dust from the mirror like toecaps.

The first parade was, of course, the utter shambles that the Instructors had expected it to be and Alan couldn't understand why they all seem to be so disappointed. They were verbally abused and their parentage put into question, except for the ex-Forces lads who slipped unconsciously back into effortless compliance with the Drill Instructor's commands. The rest obviously didn't know left from right and failed to stop when commanded. Their first morning parade was nothing short of a farce.

An Inspector and a man in civilian clothes approached the Drill Instructor and a few hushed words were spoken. The D.I. stood the parade at ease whilst the conversation between the three continued.

Alan nudged the man in front of him, an ex Scots Guard who's boots blinded everyone as did his rigid drill movements. "Oi Connor, lighten up for Christ's sake, you're making the rest of us look bad." The huge ex Guardsman smiled and without turning, told Alan in his broadest Glasgow accent that "You dinna' need me for that Alan lad, ye can manage that on yer ain", much to the amusement of the rest of the parade.

The D.I. called them all to attention and a number of names were called out and ordered to dismiss from the parade. The chosen students looked puzzled and apprehensive as they fell out and walked from the parade ground accompanied by the Inspector and the plain clothed Officer. They were never seen again.

Their curiosity was satiated during the first class that morning. One of the students asked the Instructor where the lads taken off the parade had gone. The Instructor explained that the missing student's fingerprints, along with the prints taken from them all had been fed into the system. Theirs had been found to match incriminating marks left at the scenes of previously committed crimes and that they had now been arrested. Alan had suffered a slight flutter of the nether regions at this news and had worried for the rest of the day. That Mars bar he'd nicked from Woolworths when he was nine…and what about his next door neighbour's cat, coaxed, then sealed into a biscuit tin and rolled down the stairs, maybe he'd left his prints on the lid or something, okay, he'd only been eleven at the time, but they'd never had his fingerprints before.

The days flew by. Alan enjoyed each one more than the last. Their drill got better and subsequently, the verbal abuse diminished as they came together as a single body. Friendships blossomed and there was talk of C.I.D. or Traffic and promotion in the future.

Their Instructors walked slowly between the rows of seats. The students gazed glassy eyed at the blackboards as they were force fed endless legal definitions.

"Crime, defined as an act of disobedience of the law, forbidden under pain of punishment. The administration of justice is the very pillar of society…Robbery, the force or threat of force, must be immediately before, or at the time of the stealing and must be for the purpose of stealing, if such force is used after the stealing, there is no robbery, it is Theft…Wounding…there must be a breaking of the whole skin, any person who unlawfully and maliciously by any means whatsoever, causes grievous bodily harm…Cannabis, the 1971 Act makes this substance a class three controlled drug and it's possession and use…Sexual Offences Act 1956, section 10 makes it an arrestable offence for a man to have sexual intercourse with a woman who he knows to be his Grand-Daughter, Daughter, Sister or Mother, it is also an offence…"

Alan's head buzzed with an overload of definitions, Acts and Sections. The students repeated them over and over, and practised amongst themselves during the evenings, until they could be faultlessly recited. There were also many Latin phrases to be learned, used frequently at Court and the pronunciation and knowledge of their meanings important.

The summer proved to be as hot as it had promised. Chairs were dragged from classrooms onto the beloved grass and lessons held outside in the fresh air. As the weeks passed, the Instructors treated them more as equals and even the Drill Instructors were heard to utter the odd first name from time to time.

Alan sat and watched the Policewomen playing volleyball as the Instructor attempted to deliver a lesson on rape. Phrases such as 'full insertion' and 'penetration' were met with lurid moans and deviant expressions as the sight of the unfettered breasts of the Policewomen's Academy Volleyball Team took precedence over their thoughts.

The students smiled and chuckled at the Instructor's efforts to keep his face straight as a particularly well-endowed specimen from Lancashire County ran over to retrieve the ball from where it had come to rest between their chairs. Heads turned in unison to gaze at her navy blue, scantily clad buttocks as she bent to pick up the ball. Tumultuous cheers and applause followed her as she ran back to her Team.

The days passed by all too quickly. Time goes hastily by when enjoyment is present and the thirteen weeks at the Academy drew to a close and Graduation Day loomed ominously nearer.

Alan sat in his room, spit polishing his parade boots. A student from Staffordshire burst into the room and hanging onto the door jamb, shouted "Dispersals are up." before disappearing to the next room along the corridor to deliver the same message.

Alan leapt to his feet and joined the rush to get to the Guardroom where the postings had been placed on view. They almost ran to the Guardroom, their exuberance restricted only by the knowledge that the Drill Instructor would no doubt be lurking somewhere, pace stick poised, ready to bludgeon senseless anyone running across the sacred grass.

Alan ran his finger down the list of names on the Dispersal list…Pc 868 Pendle A. Harrowford Division, Broughton Road Sub Division and next to it, the date on which he was to report.

The various dispersals were read with conflicting responses by his fellow students and Alan heard both groans and joyous expletives about postings.

"Oh Christ, not fucking Ricksworth! It's all niggers an' pakis…I'll be the only white face."

"Armsworth for me lad. Pit town, where men are men." said one.

"And the sheep are constantly worried." responded another.

The passing out parade, was executed with well-practised military precision and the Drill Instructor personally thanked them all for not making him look like a complete twat in front of the Commandant. Threats previously sworn out against his life, family and all his descendants for the next millennia, were shelved in the euphoria of the day and Alan shook his hand along with the rest of them.

Alan had slipped quietly away and returned to the empty room. He neatly folded his uniforms and packed his suitcase, leaving his locker and bed space as he had found them.

A Sergeant entered the room and Alan involuntarily stood up and fell to attention at the base of his bed. The Sergeant smiled and waved away the show of respect with a nonchalant shrug. "You can forget all that now. Graduation go ok?"

"Yes, thanks Sarge." Alan replied, relaxing and tightening the straps on his suitcase.

"Get the posting you wanted?" he asked, as he moved from one bed space to the next. Alan shrugged his shoulders. "I suppose so, I don't know the place, it'll be all brand new to me."

"Not your home town then?" the Sergeant asked.

Alan shook his head. "Not even my home County, I came back to the mainland on a seventy two hour pass during my last tour in Cyprus, walked into the nearest Police station and said I was interested."

"You'll be alright." the Sergeant said, as he placed small printed cards on the pillows of each bed ready for the next intake of students. "Look." he said, pausing for a moment and sitting on one of the metal bed ends. "A word of advice, you'll hear a lot of the older coppers ranting on about how the job's fucked. How the Public despise us, the Courts don't back us up and how we've more enemies inside the job than we have outside on the streets. You'll hear a lot of that. Make your own mind up lad, do the best you can and don't listen to the moaners."

"Foot soldiers privilege to moan isn't it Sarge?" Alan asked, smiling.

"Yeah." the Sergeant sighed. "Except it's all true."

He stood up and tossed the last card onto the bed beside the door and with a cursory nod, wished him "Good luck to you anyway." and left Alan alone with his suitcase.

Alan drove slowly through the Academy grounds for the last time on his way to the Guardroom gates, drinking in all the scenery and forcing the images into his memory banks. He felt a strange sense of foreboding, an uneasy doubt gnawed at his resolve as the Sergeant's words came back to him. He stopped at the gates and waved to the Constable on the gate before slipping his car into gear and driving along the tree lined avenue towards the main road. The dappled sunlight darted between the branches and spilled down across the windscreen. The warmth seemed to have gone somehow. He felt strangely vulnerable, like a child expelled from its protective womb. The Sergeant's prophetic words "It's all true." echoed again and again in the back of his mind and Alan knew somehow that the halcyon days were over and that things would never quite be the same again.

## Seven

Alan drove around to the front of the station, the probationer was waiting. The headlight beams picked him out as they swept around the corner of the building. Alan smiled as he watched the young Constable fumbling to get the bulky personal 'Burndept' radio into the black webbing harness that hung around his neck. The strap had caught on the rear of his helmet and as he stuffed the radio down the front of his tunic, the helmet flipped backwards and fell to the floor, bouncing on the flagstones. The 'Proby' snatched it up, fearing that his fumbling may have been witnessed and as he bent, the errant radio fell from its harness and clattered against the concrete kerb edge and fell onto the perimeter drive in front of Alan's patrol car.

The probationer looked horrified and prayed that the outer casing hadn't cracked. He grasped at it and held it up to the light from the headlights, rubbing it with his gloved hands. He looked across to Alan, guilt showing on his face, Alan smiled and shook his head slowly. The 'Proby' reddened with embarrassment.

"Need England tremble?" Alan muttered to himself softly as the lad gathered himself and his equipment together and ran to the front passenger door of the patrol car. Alan reached across and pulled at the door latch to release the lock. The 'Proby' still in a state of advanced embarrassment, smiled uneasily and as he attempted to get into the vehicle, his helmet caught against the roof gutter and again tumbled to the floor. It was again retrieved and the probationer straightened his cropped hair with his hands. Alan took the helmet from him and tossed it unceremoniously into the rear seats.

"We don't wear helmets in patrol cars mate, we can't see where we're going." he said, smiling.

The 'Proby' nodded and struggled with the seat belt.

"You'd probably be more comfortable without your raincoat." Alan said as he looked at the crumpled mass of material which had gathered up stiffly. "Haven't you got a car coat yet?"

The 'Proby' shook his head. "Not yet, I've got one coming. That is, I've signed for one, but it hasn't arrived from stores yet."

Alan frowned. "A tip from word go pal. *Never* sign for anything until you've got it in your sweaty hands. Yours is probably at this very moment, serving some 'nine to fiver' very well as a gardening jacket, never to be seen again."

The probationer looked confident. "It was the Inspector that got me to sign for it." Alan raised his eyebrows, amazed at the lad's naivety. "It's definitely a gardening jacket then." he said, as he adjusted the rear view mirror.

The 'Proby' looked puzzled. "You'll learn." Alan said and held out his hand. "Alan Pendle."

"John, John Pullman." the probationer replied beaming as he shook Alan's hand vigorously.

"Ok John. Let's take a run around, eh?" Alan said, unconsciously glancing over his shoulder as he eased the Rover away from the kerb.

"Thanks, sure you don't mind?" Pc Pullman asked with a genuine look of concern on his face. Alan laughed out loud, throwing his head back. The probationer smiled nervously, wondering what the joke was.

"I'm sorry." Alan said and smiled, "I'm laughing with you not at you. It's not my car, not my petrol and I'm getting paid lots of money just to run you around the Division, so don't feel bad about it ok?"

"Ok." the 'Proby' said, settling himself into his seat.

They talked as they drove. Various landmarks were pointed out as Alan took them out to the County boundary. The 'Proby' talked of the Academy and of lessons and passing out parades, Alan listened and smiled as memories flooded back.

The radio in Alan's pocket hissed. "Papa Yankee One Three receiving."

The 'Proby' looked across at Alan and fell silent. "One Three, go ahead." Alan responded, not taking his eyes from the road.

"One Three, report of a disturbance at 47 Harold Street. Sounds like a violent domestic, we're a bit short or units 'cos of meal times, could you have a look for us?"

Alan looked across at the probationer who was nodding his head vigorously.

"10/4. We're a fair way off, but we'll make our way." Alan replied, dipping the accelerator pedal and allowing the V8 to breath.

"Papa Yankee One Three, further." the radio hissed. Alan nodded across to his passenger. "Get that John." The probationer looked down towards the top of his radio and pressed the red transmit button. "Pass your message, over." he said tentatively.

"Alan, looks like we might have more than a routine domestic. Second reports of a woman screaming and sounds of violence from within the premises, there's numerous previous at this location. It's the Dennison's. He has previous for assault and damage and previous in '77 and '80 for assault Police and resisting. I'll try and get you some back up."

The probationer acknowledged the call and looked across to Alan, who was concentrating on his driving. "What do you reckon?"

"Just Mrs Dennison…she's obviously getting her nightly kicking…Nothing new in the Harolds."

Alan reached across and activated the rocker switch on the dashboard facia. The carriageway in front of them was suddenly illuminated by the beams of bright blue light, which swept down from the roof and lit the hedgerows and trees by the roadside as their vehicle roared back towards the City.

The City lights appeared as they topped the brow of a hill and approached the built up residential area. Alan's eyes darted from one potential hazard to another as their vehicle was accelerated toward the location of the call.

"Hit the sirens will you John." Alan shouted over the roar of the engine.

The 'Proby' searched frantically for the switch.

"It's the small red button on the public address handset." Alan reached across and snatched the hand held unit from its metal clasp and tossed it into the probationer's lap.

"There's a little red button on the front. Press it once for wail and again for yelp, ok?"

The handset was snatched up and the probationer pushed the button. Immediately, the car was filled with a loud sorrowful, undulating wail as they continued towards the City.

"Traffic lights at red." Alan shouted. "Check left John." He engaged third gear and allowed the vehicle to slow a little on deceleration. His passenger thumbed the button again, the wailing was replaced with a strident yelping tone and Alan took a position on the wrong side of the illuminated bollards which separated the carriageways at the traffic lights.

Quickly selecting second gear, he glanced left and right.

"He's stopping." shouted the probationer as he noticed a Vauxhall Viva, its front end dipping as it came to a halt to their left. Alan glanced just to confirm the probationer's advice, then floored the accelerator again, causing the rear of the SD1 to snake a little as the tyres fought to gain traction with the damp road surface.

Alan raised his hand in thanks to no one in particular and shot a glance across to the probationer who sat stiffly, staring out of the windscreen as the vehicle hurtled through the various hazards. His left hand grasped the door handle tightly, his knuckles were turning white.

"Almost there." Alan said, as he searched across the brickwork of the end terraced houses for the street names. "Cut the sirens John."

The probationer was sweating slightly and Alan smiled. "Relax mate, I do this for a living."

"I'm not a good passenger." the 'Proby' said, smiling apologetically. He slowly released the breath he had been holding and relaxed his vice like grip on the door handle as the vehicle slowed perceptibly.

Alan read off the street names as they passed the bleak rows of corporation owned terraced houses. "Harold Mount...Grove...Terrace...here we are, Harold Street. Tell 'em we're 10/6 John." Alan said, as he swung the front of the patrol car onto the cobbled street.

"Sorry?" the 'Proby' said, confused.

"Tell Control we're 10/6, we've arrived at the scene."

The heavy Rover shuddered as it drove along the cobblestones. The radio aerials on the roof snagged on the washing lines which hung limply between the opposing drain pipes. Feral mongrels snapped energetically at their tyres, excited by their presence, as Alan searched for a house number. The probationer soaked in the dankness and obvious poverty of the area. He frowned as he gazed at the cracked and peeling paintwork on the doors and window frames, the corroded fall pipes some of which hung threateningly at an angle away from the dark red painted brickwork. Many of them had long since parted company with the sagging gutters, from which grew small trees, sprouting from the leaf and moss mulch which filled them to capacity.

Old decrepit non-runners adorned the sides of the street. The MOT failures sat on partially deflated tyres, bonnets and roof panels dented inwards where the delinquents had jumped on them. Each vehicle showing the cancerous signs of oxidization which bubbled beneath faded paintwork.

The area was described as deprived, or so the left wingers on the County Council would have them believe. Most of the inhabitants were unemployed and for the most part, unemployable. Almost all were known to the local Police.

The Taggarts, Walsh's and Firths. Son's following Fathers into the criminal names index for offences of burglary, theft and drunkenness which was the natural pastime for the no-hopers who had neither the ability, nor incentive, to drag themselves out of the Council owned ghetto.

A Police presence was unwelcome in these mean streets. It usually pre-empted someone's arrest in the early hours of the morning.

No support for the Police here. They were neither trusted nor their presence tolerated or entertained. The estate wives, prematurely aged by poor diet and the drudgery of poverty, endured countless knocks at their front doors by the Law, who would inform them yet again, that their Husband or Son was in custody at Moorwood or down at the City Bridewell for driving whilst disqualified, burglary or assault. These warnings were generally accepted with the usual weary nonchalance and sagging acceptance that arrest was simply an occupational hazard. On the odd occasion, there would be a torrent of verbal abuse. "Can't you fuckin' leave 'im alone." they would scream, or "Why is it always our fuckin' 'door yer at?" The front door would be slammed shut long before the visiting Officer could explain, that if her Husband/Son stopped breaking into other people's houses, he could stop knocking at hers.

A small group of residents stood on the pavement at either side of the door to number 37. A woman waiting for the Police arrival, heaved her way up to the side of the patrol car as it pulled up to a halt in the street. She wore dirty fur lined slippers which looked as if they may have been pink a decade ago. A threadbare cardigan was stretched tightly across her pendulous stomach and the hem of a floral patterned dress flapped against bare legs which were darkly blotched between the varicose veins which erupted from behind her knees. Her huge arms were folded across the massive expanse of her breasts, which threatened to burst free from the restraints of her cardigan as she waddled towards the side of their vehicle. She was probably six or seven stones overweight and in her early thirties. She looked fifty.

"You took yer fuckin' time, 'e's fuckin' killin' 'er in there." she wheezed, nodding towards the front door of the premises. "I don't know why she fuckin' puts up with 'im. Drunken bastard that 'e is."

Alan and the probationer left their car. Alan made sure that the central locking mechanism had actually worked before withdrawing the key from the door lock and pocketing the keys. It was the Harold's after all and here, nothing was sacred.

Raised voices from within the premises filtered out into the street and the group of inhabitants now gathered by the front door showed consternation on their faces. More residents came out to watch the side show, as the shouting from inside the house grew louder and more profane. They leant against their door jambs, the ever present cigarette hanging limply from between their lips. They gossiped excitedly and pointed at the Police vehicle and slapped at the young children who peered out into the street, from between their parent's legs.

"Gerrinside you. Get to fuckin' bed, I've told you once. Its only't fuckin' P'lice."

"Excuse me." Alan said, pushing his way through the crowd. The 'Proby' stuck to his side like a limpet as they jostled their way to the front door.

"I'd fuckin' kill 'im if 'e were my 'usband." a grotesque female form uttered to her neighbour. A cigarette hung limply from her lips, it was hand rolled, prison thin and stained dark brown. Her hair was greasy and lank, it fell across her acne ravaged face and she swept the strands away with hands that were reddened with hard work and worry.

Alan grimaced at the smell of stale sweat emanating from her as he brushed past. "Death would be a welcome relief." he thought and he shuddered at the very thought of waking to see this 'Gorgon' like apparition lying next to him.

A man's voice, harsh and slurred with the effects of drink bellowed out from within the house. A woman screamed and the sound of a hard slap followed. Alan rapped on the door with the end of his truncheon. The knock was ignored, but then again, Alan would have been extremely surprised if it hadn't.

More screaming from within. Alan tried the door, it was locked. "Come on, open up, it's the Police." Alan shouted and banged on the door again with the end of his truncheon.

The noise from within increased and the sound of slapping could be heard and crockery or ornaments shattering. Alan beat against the door again. "Open up, or its coming in." he demanded. No reply, just the sobbing now and the man's grunts as he threw his Wife around the room.

Alan pocketed his truncheon and stepped back from the door. He turned to the probationer, "We're going in. Ready?"

The 'Proby' looked apprehensive, but nodded nervously. He tugged at Alan's sleeve and whispered; "Don't we need a warrant or something?"

Alan ignored the remark, considering that the 'Proby' had obviously been taught fuck all about 'practical' policing at the Academy, but decided that now was not the time to refresh his memory regarding lawful entry into any premises to prevent a crime.

The crowd, sensing impending action, backed away from the front door and nudged each other in anticipation.

The probationer watched as Alan took a step back from the door and ran at it, shouldering the woodwork near to the lock area. The area around the lock showed recent signs of replacement, indicative of previous forced entries. There was a splintering sound, but the door held.

A man's voice screamed drunkenly from within. "I'll fuckin' kill the first one in through the fuckin' door." Alan backed away from the door and motioned the probationer to join him. A cheer rose from the gathering crowd as they ran at the door together. The wood around the lock shattered and there was a tortured splintering of wood as the door was flung inwards.

The probationer lost his footing and sprawled out full length onto the filthy hallway carpet. He quickly scrambled to his feet and sniffed suspiciously at the brown, glutinous substance now smeared across the palms of his hands.

Alan was staring directly at the man who had backed himself away from the door and was swaying, fists clenched at the bottom of the stairs.

"When I say open the door, I mean open the bleedin' door, understand!" Alan shouted, his voice rising as he pointed directly toward the unshaven face of the man who, faced with two uniforms, backed away and tripped against the uncarpeted stairway. The man had a threatening sneer on his face and saliva glistened around his thick lips and trickled down through his greying stubble. He wore thick braces over a grubby white vest and a wide leather belt around the top of his baggy stained trousers. His protruding belly, the product of years of over indulgence in beer, hung over the top of the belt buckle. He was filthy, drunk and seething mad.

Alan gripped the handle end of his truncheon which he allowed to remain within its pocket, but ready to be produced at the slightest hint of violence. He glanced through into the front room of the house and could see a woman who was lying on a threadbare rug which was at the foot of a coal fireplace. She was thin, cadaverously so, the kind of thin you become when all the housekeeping is spent on beer and down at the bookies instead of in the Co-op. She was sobbing and held a skeletal hand up to the side of her face. Her nose was running and a single strand of bloody mucous ran through her fingers and onto the rug, where it was lost in the filth. Her undernourished body racked with sobs.

The probationer went to her and the man immediately made a move towards the front room door. "Don't you fuckin' touch 'er." he screamed. Alan moved between the drunken sloth and the probationer and pointed a warning finger between the man's glazed eyes.

"Enough, just calm down, right now." Alan's eyes burned into the man as they weighed each other up. The man's chest heaved with effort, his face glistening with sweat.

The probationer was trying to prise the woman's hand away from her face to assess the damage, yet keeping a wary eye towards the Husband. She moaned as her hand was gently, yet forcibly pulled away.

"Oh Jesus Christ." Alan heard the probationer gasp.

Alan took his eyes off the man for a split second and glanced across to the woman. Her lower eyelid had been almost torn away. Her eyeball seemed to hang precariously in its socket and Alan could see that she had a deep wound on her cheek. She was bleeding badly.

"Get her outside John and get an ambulance."

The probationer helped the woman to her feet, amazed at how little she weighed.

Alan pushed the man back against the stairs and leaned over him as the 'Proby' ushered the woman out of the premises. The crowd outside gasped with loud murmurs as they got what they had been waiting for. "Yer a bastard 'arry Dennison." a neighbour shouted from the street.

Alan faced the man. "You and me are going out to my car." he said softly, but with certain firmness.

"The fuck we are." the man spat venomously.

"You're coming out." Alan said quietly. "Conscious or unconscious, the choice is yours, I'm not bothered either way."

Alan watched the man's eyes darting around, frantically searching for a weapon of some kind. Behind him, and in his peripheral vision, Alan was aware of the probationer standing in the open doorway. He watched as the inevitable confrontation swelled before him. The man's body tensed, a kind of drunken resolve appeared in his eyes. Alan had wound him up with his quiet confidence and resolve and people were watching. His reputation as the hard man of the terrace was at stake. His huge hands were hung by his sides, but his fists were clenched. Alan read the signs and he slowly reached down and slipped his fingers through the leather thong attached to his truncheon.

The man let out a guttural scream and launched himself at Alan. In the same split second, Alan swept his truncheon upwards and into the man's solar plexus region, the blunt end sinking deep into the flabby area of the man's upper stomach. The man's eyes opened wide and his mouth dropped open, exposing the blackened stumps of his teeth. He sagged to his knees, trying to support his weight by gripping onto the front of Alan's jacket. His hands slowly slipped across the nylon material as he fought against the tightening vice in his lower chest which prevented him from drawing breath.

Alan watched him slip to the floor without emotion. He casually replaced the truncheon back into its pocket, the urgency had gone. Alan remembered the advice given by his self-defence instructor. *"If a man can't breathe, he cannot fight you, if he can't stand, he cannot fight you, strike for the solar plexus and you will achieve your man."*

Alan withdrew his handcuffs from within the leather pouch on his trouser belt and walked around the man who was now laid out on the hallway floor, desperately trying to suck air into his lungs. Alan pulled the hands away from where they clutched at his belly and one at a time, wrenched them around to the small of his back and tightened the ratchets around the fat wrists.

He looked across to the probationer who was gazing in admiration at the warrior who had dropped Goliath so calmly. Alan winked at him and lifted the man's head up, holding his stubble covered chin in his cupped hand so that he faced him.

"Listen to me, you're nicked for assault. You don't have to say anything unless you want to, understand?" The prisoner grunted and slowly vomited a lake of bile and beer onto the hallway carpet, coughing up the dregs over Alan's shoes.

"Let's have him outside and into the patroller John." Alan beckoned to the probationer.

Together, they lifted the man to his knees and pulled him out through the shattered door and into the street. A woman pushed her way through the gathered crowd and with a clenched fist, punched out and caught the prisoner at the side of his face. "You fuckin' animal." she screamed, lashing out again in a frenzy. Alan pushed her away with his one free hand. "And you'll be going with him if you don't behave yourself."

The woman returned in an effort to slap the heaving prisoner again, but she was prevented by a young man who caught her by her hair and pulled her violently backwards. She screamed as she fell back onto the pavement. "She's my fuckin' sister what 'e's nearly killed. You fuckin' bastard Dennison." Her obscenities faded as she was dragged back into one of the terraced houses and the door was slammed shut.

The prisoner's legs were not yet fully supportive of his weight and Alan and the probationer half dragged him to the side of the patrol car, where he was pushed against the rear door whilst Alan fumbled in his pocket for the car key. "Where's the ambulance for Christ's sake?" Alan asked, searching down the street towards the main road. "And I guess back up isn't coming."

The trick was to get the prisoner away as soon as possible before the gathered crowd's sympathies miraculously changed and the arresting Officers became the object of their pent up aggression. Now would be when the windscreen would go through, bottles would be lobbed from upstairs windows and doorways and Alan was painfully aware that they were vastly outnumbered. Alan managed to get the key into the door aperture. As he twisted it, he heard the satisfying click as all the doors unlocked and still holding onto the sagging prisoner, the probationer opened the rear door.

"If you spew up in my patroller, death will come as a welcome relief, got it?" Alan said firmly to the prisoner who was now able to breathe. He waited for the fat mess to nod, before he was bundled into the rear seats of their vehicle.

His feet had all but disappeared when there was a shrill scream from within one of the houses. Alan looked around in time to see the prisoner's Wife, still holding a grubby dishcloth against her cheek, as she ran shrieking across the street making a direct line for the patrol car. She sobbed and grabbed for the exposed feet of her Husband. Her wound forgotten, the dishcloth dropped to reveal the deep wound on her face. It flapped open grotesquely, dark red blood was clotting within the swelling flesh.

"No, no, no!" she screamed. Her sobs turning now to spitting hatred for the common enemy. Alan and the probationer now her nemesis, as she saw her Husband being taken.

"Get her away John." Alan shouted to the probationer as he pushed her away from the car door. He pushed at the door to force the prisoner's feet inside, eventually managing to force the door shut.

The Wife kicked out and spat at the 'Proby' as he led her back to the pavement as gently as he thought prudent under the circumstances. She swiped out at him and for the third time during his tour of duty, his suffering helmet fell to the ground and bounced on the cobbles.

The long awaited ambulance turned into the street and the crew dived out to assist the probationer with the struggling female. The 'Proby' was behind the frantic woman, holding her around her waist and had lifted her off the ground. She threw her head backwards in an attempt to head butt him in the face. The probationer anticipated well and arched his back, keeping his face well away from her thrashing head. Blood from her open facial wound sprayed back and lashed across the 'Proby's' face as the ambulance crew grabbed her legs and she was lifted bodily into the back of the ambulance.

Alan drove slowly back to the Police station. "John, contact the control room, tell them we're 10/12, we're coming in with one for assault. He'll need the 'drunk tank' for an hour or two."

The probationer nodded and quickly did as he was asked. He then looked across at Alan and glanced towards the rear seats where their 'prize' was now slumped, wheezing and coughing quietly.

"Alan?" the probationer asked, with an inquiring tone, nodding towards the rear seats. "Any chance…I mean…Could I..?"

Alan smiled, knowing what was coming. "Yeah, you want him, he's yours. I'll go second Officer."

The 'Proby' beamed. "Really? I mean, he's yours really of course. It's just…first day and all that. It'd look pretty good."

"No problem." nodded Alan. "I remember how it was."

Alan and the new Policeman booked the prisoner in and showed him to his usual cell to sober up.

The old Sergeant smiled at Alan and nodded to the probationer who was wiping the dried blood from his face with a damp paper towel.

"Pendle. I thought I told you to look after 'im. You've brought 'im back in a right state, his Mam won't let him come tomorrow."

The probationer's face reddened and Alan and the Sergeant laughed at his embarrassment.

"How did 'e do then Al?"

"Did well Sarge." Alan nodded. "The collar's his, not mine."

The Sergeant's eyebrows rose. "Impressive, first day here and a lock up. In at the deep end, eh. Lad show any promise then Alan?"

Alan nodded. "Shows promise Sarge…he shows promise." He nudged the blushing probationer. "Come on, we'll do our books and you can make the coffee."

They retired to the Traffic office and while they sipped the brew, Alan noticed that the lad looked puzzled.

"What's up?" he asked.

"Well." said the probationer, a puzzled expression on his face. "That woman, his Wife. If she didn't want us to take her old man, why'd she call for us in the first place? She must have known he'd get arrested."

Alan sat back in his seat. "Well, firstly, she didn't call us. It'll have been a neighbour. Moorwood uniforms have been to that house before, loads of times. Shit for brains, downstairs in the cells, goes out, he gets a skin full of ale and comes home and beats the crap out of his Wife."

"Why?" the probationer asked, even more puzzled.

Alan smiled. "Christ, you 'ave 'ad a sheltered life. Where the fuck were you brought up? This is the City pal, that's the way the great unwashed exist, hand to mouth, on the dole, drink, violence and crime. It's acceptable behaviour."

"So why doesn't she just leave him?" the probationer asked.

"Where would she go?" replied Alan matter of factly. "That's her house for what it's worth and he's her Husband. Her Mum lives three doors up the same street and her Granny before her.

It's all she's got and it's all she's ever likely to have. Next week, we'll probably be called to the house next door, same thing."

"Castle Hedingham." said the probationer, casually flicking through the pages of his Pocket Note Book.

"What?" Alan asked, puzzled.

"You asked where I was brought up. Castle Hedingham, a small village in northeast Essex, near Great Yeldham…"

"Yeah, look, sorry John, it was a metaphor. I'm not really interested where you…Well, I am, but that wasn't what I was getting at. Look, I suppose if you come from the garden of England, working at Moorwood will take some getting used to. This City has one of the largest Council house estates in Europe and unfortunately, it's in our Division. Fifty or sixty years ago, there was a waiting list to get a house on the Harold's, now it's a complete shit hole, why? 'Cos the Council filled them with shit and haven't spent a penny since on maintenance. When the steel foundry closed in the late sixties, there was massive unemployment. Most of the residents had gone straight from school at thirteen or fourteen and into the steel works, no qualifications, fuck all. The foundry was all they had. When it closed, they had no savings, there was no redundancy, it just closed. Result, social collapse. I saw exactly the same thing in Belfast. Falls Road, 'Andytown' and Whiterock in the West. After the Harland and Wolfe shipyards closed, there was nothing, and no-one gave a fuck about the Irish, 'specially during the 'troubles'. It was just row after row of dingy, cobbled back to back terraces. The Ebor's and the Kitchener's off the Donegal Road, the Rockville's an' La Salle's off the Falls. No difference to the street we've just been to John, fuck all to do and no money to do it with. It breeds social dissent, only difference in the Harold's, are the accents."

"There must be some way out for a few." the puzzled probationer asked.

"One or two I suppose." Alan replied dryly. "I know of a few that joined the Army, infantry of course, 'scum of the earth' as Wellington called them…Fuck all else on offer. There's a couple in the job mind…Dennis Greaves, a lad on the Mounted Branch grew up in the Brudenell's. He somehow managed to get to twenty one without getting locked up and he's one of the best coppers I've ever known."

The probationer sat quietly drinking the remains of his coffee. Alan sensing that he'd depressed him sufficiently for one shift, broke the ice.

"Right. What you 'avin' 'im for?."

"Section 47 assault. In fact, it's a Wounding, there's a breaking of the whole skin." said the new Policeman, proving his classroom knowledge.

"You've no chance." said Alan. "Breach of the Peace, charged and bailed before we go off duty."

"Why?" asked the 'Proby', somewhat astounded. "It's a straight up wounding."

"You're right." said Alan, turning now to look straight at the probationer. "Look John, she won't complain, not officially anyway, no statement, no complaint. Truth is, she'll get her face stitched up, discharge herself from hospital and by tomorrow morning, they'll be all love and kisses…'till he goes out on the ale again that is."

The probationer stuttered. "But we don't need a complainant for a wounding, it's an indictable offence against the Crown. We can charge him without a complaint from her."

Alan raised his eyebrows, impressed by his colleagues' knowledge. He paused, then added, "You're right John, we can, but we don't, it'd never see the inside of Court. Look, I'll try to explain. It's a domestic beating, man and Wife. The Courts are always loath to interfere with the marital situation which is to all intents and purposes, stable."

"Stable!" the 'Proby' exclaimed.

Alan smiled. "For that area, yes. Look, some poor bitch gets a fat lip nearly every night of the week, if we took them all, the Courts would grind to a standstill within a year, but that's not the real reason we don't push it." Alan paused, the probationer listened intently.

"I know what it says in the book John and in a perfect world we'd go by it, but what it says in the book doesn't always work out best when you're working the streets. Sometimes, there are more practical ways of dealing with things. Take this job." Alan continued. "We charge him and take him to Court right? After the third or fourth offence, the learned Judge sends him down the steps for a spell. They're a very tight community on the estates John, no one is going to call us to break up a family fight if they know that someone's going to go to the slammer for it…nobody. But they'll call us every time, as long as they know that it's just a night in the cells till he sobers up, then a quick ten quid fine for breach of the peace. If they thought it was prison, no chance. They wouldn't make the call, 'cos next time, it might be their Husband and if we don't get the calls, someone, sooner or later is actually going to get beaten to death. You saw the size of him compared to her, he's quite capable of killing her right?"

The 'Proby' nodded, as if he was slowly starting to get the picture.

"We keep the balance John, that's all we do. They call us, we turn up, break up the fight before anyone gets seriously hurt, but we only charge breach of peace. No one goes to jail and everybody's happy."

The probationer let it sink in for a while. "It's not right though is it?"

"No one said it was right mate, it's what works that's important. You'll see soon enough."

"I take your point Alan." replied the probationer, still looking slightly disturbed.

Alan recognised the expression. "I know how you feel, but you'll learn that what you soaked up for thirteen weeks at the academy is ok for examinations, but practically, it rarely works. Good coppering is only five per cent knowledge of the law and ninety per cent common sense and no one can teach you that. You've either got it or you haven't."

"What about the other five?" the probationer asked.

"Five what?"

"Per cent" the 'Proby' said.

Alan smiled. "Luck." he replied, opening his pocket book.

*****

Two hours later, the Rover SD1 purred effortlessly along the Ring Road towards the outer reaches of the City. The roads were quiet and as Alan drove, the probationer stared through the windscreen and reflected on his first day on the job.

"Not much left to do John, early turn will charge and bail him and leave the papers in your tray, come and see me and we'll do a file and bang it off to Prosecutions. We've only an hour or so to go. Let's see what's going on in the Badlands eh."

"The Badlands?" the probationer asked, looking across at Alan somewhat bemused.

"Approximately one square mile situated to the East of the City, the indigenous population being mostly of Caribbean origin and therefore, to be regarded as hostile. It's in our Division and it's where you will find the vast majority of your stolen vehicles dumped and drugs openly being sold. There's prostitution and violent gang related incidents, if you thought the Harold's were rough, wait till you see Melbourne Terrace." Alan chuckled as he purposefully slowed the patrol car as they entered the dismal square mile of eleven beat. 'C' Division.

The 'Badlands'.

The probationer's mouth hung open slackly, as he gazed through the passenger window at the lines of grey, run down tenements.

The once resplendent three and four storey town houses, once owned by wealthy Jewish bankers and wool barons at the turn of the century, had been bought up at knock down prices by property developers. They had converted them into flats for the Polish and West Indian immigrants who flooded into this part of the City in the sixties and early seventies. Neglect had followed, the unscrupulous landlords were unwilling to maintain the properties using any of the meagre rents paid by the local City Council.

The influx of immigrants and their lawlessness, coupled with the resulting decline in property values had effectively forced the white middle class population to leave. The properties, their Georgian frontages set well back from the road, were once resplendent. Long winding driveways lead to large polished wooden doors flanked either side by impressive stone pillars supporting delicately sculptured rotundas. Carefully tended rose gardens and neatly trimmed hedges, were all now overgrown and unkempt, their previously manicured lines now indiscernible. Dog faeces and empty beer cans now abundant midst the harsh field grass and rampant weeds which overflowed onto the driveways.

Left to their own devices, the blacks, for the most part unemployed, but quite happy to live in conditions far better than those they had left behind in Kingston, St Kitts and Martinique, simply allowed the area to deteriorate around them. The second generation blacks quickly discovered that there was a vast, untapped market for drugs. With frightening speed and efficiency, they made contact with their Jamaican 'Posse' counterparts, and the cannabis flowed through the Liverpool and Bristol docks and was transported via the motorway networks to the City.

Cannabis was soon superseded by cocaine and heroin as recreational use increased. It quickly became habitual and therefore much sought after. The risk of possession and supply of these hard drugs was far greater, but the risk of a serious custodial sentence was far outweighed by the incredible financial rewards.

Alan pulled the patrol car into a side street and up to where a tall black woman was leaning against one of the few working street lights. She was wearing a very short, flimsy fake leopard skin dress. It fully displayed her long ebony black legs, which she considered to be her best asset, to the greatest advantage. She wore silver high heeled shoes which, although completely out of character for the area, both accentuated her muscular calves and drew the eyes of potential customers up to the white lace panties which were just visible under the hem of her dress as she slouched against the lamp post. Her hair was dyed platinum silver and straightened. The long silver locks accentuated her blackness and draped over her bare shoulders, cascading onto the thin straps of her dress which struggled to contain her large unfettered breasts. A wide fox fur belt completed the gaudy outfit, but offered little protection against the cold. She peered hard and cautiously into the windscreen of the slowly approaching patrol car and on recognising Alan, her face immediately changed and she burst into a wide smile displaying brilliantly white teeth. She pointed a ring festooned finger towards him, as she shrugged herself away from the concrete lamp post and strutted across the pavement towards the kerb edge.

The probationer swallowed hard and looked inquisitively towards Alan, who pressed the rocker switch on the center console to open the passenger side window. As the glass slid noiselessly down into the door, Alan leant across and called out to her. "Evie, you bad girl, what's happening?"

The tall Negress leaned in through the passenger window, glanced at Alan, winked and then immediately turned her attentions to the fresh face of the probationer. The front of her dress gaped and her large breasts hung barely inches from his face, her ebony nipples partially exposed as the top half of her body entered the vehicle.

"I'll be dipped in shit, Mr Pendle. Long time no see…and who is *this* sweet motherfucker?" she beamed, and slowly reached into the vehicle to grasp the probationer's crotch. The probationer would have actually screamed had he not been struck completely dumb by the magnitude of his predicament. "You must be cold honey." she said teasingly, holding up her thumb and forefinger an inch apart.

She kissed the hapless 'Proby' on the cheek before slowly releasing her grip on the front of his trousers and winking at Alan.

The probationer sat stock still, shocked and breathing in short, shallow gasps, unable to take his eyes away from the fully exposed dark brown areola and protruding ebony nipples now perilously close to his face.

Alan threw his head back and laughed raucously at the probationer's obvious discomfort.

"Evie, behave yourself girl. This is Mr Pullman, he's new. My job's to show him round the Division. What's new with you?"

"Same-o, same-o Mr P. Things be quiet…must be losin' my looks."

"Never happen Evie." said Alan, leaning across the probationer, who seemed to have entered some form of catatonic state, to offer her a cigarette.

With painted fingernails, long and curved, she hooked the cigarette from the offered pack and as she withdrew her arm, she allowed her index finger to slowly trace across the probationers cheek. "He is so fuckin' sweet. Where'd you find this chil' Mr P?"

Alan chuckled. "He's fresh out of the box Evie. First day today, thought I'd show him a few of the sights."

The probationer was swallowing hard and Alan noticed that there was a thin sheen of sweat forming across his forehead.

She stood back from their vehicle and placed her hands on her hips, raising the hem of the dress slightly to expose the front of her filigree lace panties.

The probationer gulped, but could not help but look at the dark triangular mound bulging beneath the skimpy lace material.

"An' ain't I a sight to see honey?" she asked the probationer, a forced innocence in her tone.

The probationer stuttered. "Look, I'm a marrie…"

"They all fuckin' married hon', that's why Evie be here." she interrupted, lowering the hem of her dress.

Alan was smiling and slowly shaking his head. "Best leave him be Evie, he's had enough excitement for one day. You ok?"

"It is what it is Mr P." she said, sucking hard on the cigarette and tossing her head back to exhale the cloud of smoke up and away from the open window. "Vice be active. Who's the new bitch wid the red hair? Seen her smokin' aroun' wid some other dude in a shitbox Viva, tryin' they best not to look like cops."

"There's a lot of bad men around Evie. This drugs thing is getting out of hand, Vice cops are too busy with druggies to be bothering too much with honest working girls at the moment."

"Yeah well, I aint sellin' or usin' Mr P, jus' tryin' to make a livin' only way I know how." she said, her eyes darting up and down the street.

Alan noticed a number of slow moving vehicles quickly exiting the road into the various side streets in his rear view mirror. He saw her glancing back, noting the emptiness of the street, the presence of the marked Rover clearly a deterrent to trade.

"Yeah, I know." said Alan, noting her anxiety and feeling that he was now outstaying his welcome.

He dipped the clutch and eased the vehicle into gear. "You take care Evie, you know where we are if you hear anything interesting."

She nodded, stepping back onto the cracked paving flags and flicked the cigarette end out onto the road surface. "Keep the red head bitch off my ass Mr P, 'n I be grateful."

"I'll see what I can do Evie, stay safe." said Alan, closing the window as he eased the patrol car away from the kerb.

The probationer sat in silence for a moment, then looked across at Alan, an incredulous look across his face. "That woman is a prostitute!" he blurted.

Alan nodded, glancing to his right as he eased the patrol car out onto the main road. "Fuck all wrong with your observations John, very astute." replied Alan sarcastically. "Don't you have hookers in Castle Yerdingham?"

"It's Castle Hedingham, and no, it wouldn't be tolerated. Look, surely we should have been arresting her." he protested. "I'm in my probation. She grabbed my cock for Christ's sake, what if someone reports it?"

Alan roared with laughter and looked across at his passenger who looked extremely anxious and far from amused, his distressed state further fuelling Alan's mirth.

"Lighten up John for fuck's sake, Evie's old school, she's…"

"She's a common prostitute is what she is." the probationer protested. "We could get done for discreditable conduct, or neglect of duty. Section 1 of the Street Offences Act 1959 clearly states, that it shall be an offence for a common prostitute to loiter, or solicit in a street or public place for the purpose of prostitution."

Alan continued to laugh, but nodded his head vigorously agreeing with his passenger. "How do you know she's a common prostitute?" Alan asked, wiping moisture from his eyes.

"Oh come on Alan." the probationer protested. "The way she was dressed, she exposed her breasts and her vagina in public, on the street, it's clear that…"

Alan cut him short. "She didn't ask you to pay for the pleasure did she? An' anyway, as my old Dad used to say…You don't pay a hooker for sex, you pay her to fuck off afterwards."

The probation threw up his hands in exasperation.

Alan's tone took on a more sombre note. "Look John, Evie's profession may offend your delicate moral sensibilities, but she is, and has in the past, been an excellent source of information. It's that balance I was telling you about earlier. Evie has no problem with us 'cos we're Traffic and she knows that generally, we don't bust hookers, that's Vice's job. She won't ever be seen talking with Vice, but she'll drop us the registration numbers of weirdo punters asking for young children or those who offer her coke for a blow job. I've had some good lock ups from Evie's 'intel' and so have the Drugs and 'Kiddie' Squads. In return, she gets a little slack from Vice. Balance John, it's all about balance."

"I'll be sure to mention that to Discipline and Complaints when I get my Reg 7 for neglect." the probationer moaned.

"Well, my lips are sealed…as opposed to Evie's." Alan said with a smirk. "Anyway, "Evie has been known to service the odd cop during periods of personal domestic strife, Detectives from D n'C included. I think you're safe. Come on mate, cheer up, it's home time."

## **Eight**

'Midnight' Lyburn needed money, lots of money and quickly. After five long years out of circulation, the small empire which he had built now lay in ruins. The girls he had managed had gone free-lance at first, happy to see him out of sight and mind after what he had done to the 'Chinese'. They had all lived for too long under the threat of his violent outbursts.

Word had quickly spread that 'Midnight' had gone down the steps for five years and they, all knowing his temperament fuelled by his bitter hatred for whites, knew that his term would be fully served. The rival pimps and dealers also learned of his removal from the scene and quickly moved in on his 'property'.

The working girls were taken under their protective wing and 'Midnight's' turf had been divided between them, disappearing altogether as new boundary lines were agreed. Had he only gone down for twelve or eighteen months, his girls would have been looked after for a small percentage and there for him on his release, along with a good deal of back pay.

The circuit Judge at the Crown Court had bowed to Government pressure in respects of a crackdown on knife crime and handed down the maximum term which the sentencing guidelines allowed.

"Five years Lyburn…There you have it, take him down Officer."

'Midnight' Lyburn had been taken over, lock, stock and women. His turf fought over, like carrion over a carcass.

His name once feared, had faded into obscurity, now only mentioned by a few of the older brothers when they met at 'blues', or when they hung around the street corners to reminisce. New factions had risen up from the streets, the old methods were gone.

The gangs ruled the streets now with a single leader at the head; he remained untouchable and for the most part unseen. His minions and 'mules' laboured for him. They took all the risks. He organised the buys and the transportation of the drugs from neighbouring Cities, such as Manchester, Bristol and London, never actually involved. He was simply the overseer providing the organisation, muscle and finance. The offer of a large sum of money to simply transport a package along the motorway network and back to the City, provided for a never ending stream of 'mules'.

A second car would shadow the vehicle actually transporting the drugs and should the Police be seen anywhere in the vicinity, the 'interference' car would attract attention by passing the patrol car at high speed, initiating a pursuit. This would allow the 'carrier' to leave the motorway network at the very next exit. If, however the Police had good intelligence and the 'mule' got taken with the package, he would be 'down the steps' for a long stretch, but the 'man' remained anonymous and untouchable.

Had 'Midnight' not gone away, he could have consolidated with the 'brothers'. A coalition could have been formed to protect each other's turf and the street gangs would never have been allowed to gain a foothold. The original 'brothers' had grown older and as such, weaker. They had either moved away, fearful of the violent turf wars, the slashing's, stabbings and 'drive by' shootings, or had been sucked into one of the gangs to enjoy the obscurity and safety in numbers in exchange for the high risk, high profit one man operations they had enjoyed previously.

The main man was all powerful and was obeyed without question. He allowed his lieutenants a certain amount of tolerance in the day to day running of the organisation of the gang, movement of money and the product to the various dealers and ordering the necessary beatings where a lack of respect might have been shown.

The junior soldiers, lower gang members and street dealers took the inevitable arrests quietly. They admitted full responsibility and accepted the consequences of Borstal or Prison readily. They protected the 'man', knowing that whilst they were away, they would be looked after and money put away each month to be paid in a lump sum on their release, payment for their loyalty and silence. The rule of 'Omerta' was not a concept singularly owned by the Mafia. The consequences of revealing the identity or any involvement of the main man were in any case, too devastating to consider. Better to take the time, hard as it was, than to be gang raped or shanked in Borstal, or maimed, the loss of fingers or an arm, as one was held against one of the many moving machines in the Prison workshops, the price to be paid for 'indiscretion'.

'Babylon' would offer incentives, of course, deals would be offered, immunity in some cases, *if* the information was good and a high quality arrest followed. But the new wave wouldn't crack. Loyalty was bought through the fear of emasculation, a severe beating at best, at worst, a shot to the head if 'bumbeclart' grassed to 'Babylon'.

'Midnight' had heard of the slow but positive rise of the gangs whilst he had whiled the days and months away. The news from the streets filtered in from the new inmates as they sat playing poker for matchsticks and cigarettes during 'association'. He had shrugged the gangs off as unimportant, merely 'tenants' on his turf during the enforced absence from his rightful seat of power. He'd make his move against them as soon as the white man set him free. But unbeknown to him, the gangs had become strong, stronger than he had realised. They had seized power by violence and fear. The Police had acted as the gang leaders had expected, true to form, ineffective and tied by political restraints. Racism was a dangerous word and the gang members used it to their best advantage. A brother arrested for a minor breach of the Misuse of Drugs Act, suddenly becoming a direct assault on the local ethnic minority by the racist Police.

Divisional Officers quaked in their golfing shoes at references to apartheid in scathing letters, received by the media alluding to racist comments or discrimination by the Police from the ever increasing number of black Councillors and Community Leaders.

The gang leaders saw the cracks in the Police armour and capitalised on it, prostituting their racial principles to evade justice.

The capitulation of the Police was not total. Arrests were made and successful prosecutions gained, but the main man remained untouched and unknown. His power grew like a social cancer, untreated and ignored. The flower of coloured youth were devoured by promises of easy wealth and street respect.

The local schools and youth clubs became a never ending source of volunteers. Young blacks, eager to become recognised by their peers as loyal gang members, wore their colours with pride. The 'Street Lords' and the 'Sons of Judah', the 'Panthers' and Jo'burg Bloods' now had the streets in the palms of their hands. The heroin, in white or brown form, a derivative of morphine, flooded the streets. Worth far more than its weight in gold, along with the crystalline 'Crack', the mind killer, seven seconds to heaven and a life of hell thereafter.

'Midnight' pondered all these things as he remained in his room, out of sight and mind of the gangs as he tried desperately to formulate some kind of plan. For once in his life, he had become the victim, he had been robbed and it gnawed at him. His intended redress was not through the judicial system, however, the answer was in his own hands and he planned to use all his resources and street smarts to reinstate himself to his rightful position. He was broke, a previously unknown experience. He needed money, a massive influx of cash with which to make his move. The new gang leaders were by and large, young men, not seasoned or fully proven as far as he was concerned and 'Midnight' concluded that they held onto their status by a very thin thread which in turn, was kept under constant tension by the soldiers and lieutenants. Envious of the wealth and power just out of reach, a sudden bid for power was known but uncommon. A full takeover was as yet unheard of, as the consequences of failure were swift and final.

Young blacks had been found on a number of occasions in rubbish skips or derelict buildings, of which there was no shortage. A single shot to the forehead, throats cut and genitals removed, the victims of a disastrous 'coup', and as a result, the recipient of a 'Yardy' funeral.

'Midnight' listened to the street talk, watched the envy and the jealousy, storing the names of the bearers for future consideration.

He had changed considerably since the time of his arrest for the attack on the 'Chinese'. The dreadlocks were gone, his hair was now close cropped, with a side parting shaved in. He was two stones lighter, leaner and harder in spirit as well as body. He had learned how to survive in prison. The beatings and the constant torment from the screws had hardened him, he was unafraid and unimpressed by the self-proclaimed rulers of his turf. He was happy to bide his time and prepare himself fully for his return to power. He had no car, no weapons and no contacts, at least none that could be relied upon. A small job would do to start with, just to get hold of some working cash.

'Midnight' shrugged himself up from the bed and pulled on his shoes. Grabbing his jacket from the peg on the back of the door, he quickly thrust his arm into the sleeve and with it hanging from his shoulder, he patted his jeans pocket to make sure he had his key before opening the door and stepping out onto the metal platform of the fire escape. He instinctively glanced up and down the street for anything that looked out of place and his body shivered with a single violent movement as the cold air bit into his body. He pulled the jacket on and zipped it up, pushing his hands deep into the side pockets as he descended the metal rungs. The sound of his shoes on the steps brought back the memory of the Detectives running up to him to effect his arrest, the blinding white light in his forehead and the sudden sickening pain which had seared up from the back of his neck as the long wooden staff had felled him.

His thoughts went back to cell door being opened. He had curled up in the foetal position, his hands still wrapped protectively around his aching swollen testicles where the uniform had stamped on him. The vomit had dried on his face as he had lain on the cold cell floor, trying to ease the dull pulsing throb in his groin. "Come on then sooty, let's be 'avin' you." a hollow voice had called out to him, the speaker's impatient tone echoing in the acoustic bareness of the cell. 'Midnight' had ignored the demand, raising his head slightly to observe the owner of the voice. It was the Detective, one of those who had arrested him. He let his head slip back to the concrete floor and curled himself up tighter. The voice shouted back to the reception area. "Give us a hand in 'ere."

'Midnight' waited and heard footsteps entering the cell. He recognised the Detective's voice again. "Get 'im cleaned up and bung 'im in an interview room for us."

"Oh yeah, no problem." replied a new voice with a hint of sarcasm. 'Midnight' sensed that the owner of the voice was close.

"Has sir enjoyed his stay, room service ok? I hope the massage and handjob by the Policewoman was to your satisfaction."

'Midnight' had ignored the uniform now towering over him. He felt a nudge in the small of his back, a boot toe cap tapping him.

"On your feet, the 'cloth' wants a word."

Again 'Midnight' had ignored the demand. The voice grew angry and impatient, its tone now raised and menacing.

"I said on your fuckin' feet rastaman." The nudge from the toe cap was again applied but this time with more force. 'Midnight' turned his head to look up at the voice. He saw the two uniforms, one leaning over him, the other leaning against the metal door frame of the cell, casually swinging his truncheon by the leather strap, a knowing smile across his face.

"Am in pain man." 'Midnight' groaned softly.

Again, came the nudge with the size twelve.

"You don't know what fuckin' pain is yet sooty, now on yer feet unless you want to feel my mates staff round yer knackers."

The look on the uniform's face told him that these two would like nothing better than to have a chance at 'remonstrating' with him. His testicles would hardly stand touching let alone stand a tap from a truncheon. He slowly rolled over onto his back, the dull pain from his groin causing him to snatch at his breath. 'Midnight' looked down at the handcuffs which still shackled his ankles. The uniform glanced at them and then back to his colleague who was still standing by the door jamb. He nodded and the second uniform knelt down and inserted a small metal key into the body of the handcuffs.

"Don't get any ideas about kicking off again either, or I'll fuckin' bounce you round this cell like a bleedin' football." the uniform sneered. 'Midnight' looked up at the uniform with a discerning eye, weighing him up and concluded that out on the streets, truncheon or not, he could take him in ten seconds flat. However, now was not the time.

The two uniforms had heaved him to his feet and pulled him from the dimly lit cell into the brightness of the reception area. He brought his hands up quickly to shield his eyes and the uniform in front, caught the movement in his peripheral vision and whirled round, staff in hand.

'Midnight' flinched seeing the raised wooden staff. "It's the lights you dumb fuck." he snarled, glancing up at the bright fluorescent strips, forcing his eyes to become accustomed to the glare after the dinginess of his cell.

The uniform said nothing, but slipped the truncheon back home into its pocket and 'Midnight' was pushed towards a small open room within the reception area.

The medical room was clinical and clean, but smelled of disinfectant and urine and the pungent smells assailed 'Midnight's' nostrils. The room contained a stainless steel sink and toilet and a polished square of the bright metal had been screwed to the wall above the sink. 'Midnight' held out his arms to the uniform standing next to him, the handcuffs still in place around his wrists, the chromium now dulled and blackened in places where his blood had smeared over them. The ratchets had been tightened to such a degree, that the hardened steel had bitten savagely into the soft flesh of his wrists.

The uniform hesitated, then withdrew his 'cuff' key from a small pocket just below the waistband of his trousers. 'Midnight' winced as the uniform twisted the handcuffs around to expose the keyhole aperture. "You enjoyin' yourself man?" he hissed, glaring at the uniform.

The uniform smiled and twisted the cuffs again. "About as much as you enjoyed headbuttin' my mate, you black twat." he said, not taking his eyes from 'Midnight's' as the 'cuffs were released. "Get yourself cleaned up." the uniform sneered, nodding towards the steel sink. "You stink like a pig."

'Midnight' looked directly into the eyes of the uniform. "We got more in common than I thought mo'fucker."

The sneer disappeared from the uniform's face and 'Midnight', having won the verbal confrontation, was pushed towards the sink. He ran the taps, the water ran cold and his wrists stung as he immersed them. He washed the dried vomit from his face, cupping his hands and lifting the cold water to his mouth, sluicing it around between his teeth to rid himself of the bitter metallic taste. He looked up at the polished square of steel above the sink. There were bags under his eyes and abrasion marks on his cheek where it had lain against the cold concrete of the cell floor. He looked like shit and felt worse.

"Come on, that's enough, it won't fuckin' wash off you know." the uniform said impatiently. His colleague chuckled and pulled off a length of paper from a dispenser above the fingerprinting table. He screwed it loosely into a ball and tossed it towards 'Midnight'.

"Thank God for the sickle cell eh Charlie." he laughed.
The other uniform took hold of 'Midnight's' arm and lead him away from the sink. "Come on sooty. The 'cloth' awaits."

He sat in silence throughout the interview, the two Detectives running the 'good guy' 'bad guy' routine which mused

'Midnight', was as pathetic as ever. These two had obviously been watching far too much American television.

'Midnight' remained silent.

The evidence was damning right enough. They had his razor and even though he had washed it, they would find traces of her blood in the swivel joint. His car had been seized and he knew there was blood all over the interior. Even his clothes that he had washed out so carefully would show traces of her blood and clothing fibers.

There was a statement from the motorcyclist that he'd almost totalled on his way out onto the main road and worst of all, the slant eyed bitch had lived to tell the tale. He was fucked all right.

"Look man, enough of this we can help you shit, just do what you got to do, ok?" 'Midnight' said and sighed, showing his boredom at the Detective's efforts.

"Why make it harder on yourself Jimmy, tell us how it happened. Let's get it sorted out, eh? There's trace heroin and a good amount of cannabis in your flat. Where did that come from? Save yourself some down time. You cooperate and it'll go better for you. Come on, we've all got homes to go to."

The Detective offered a cigarette; 'Midnight' shook his head. "*You* might be going home man, but don't shit me about gettin' bail."

The two Detectives looked resignedly at each other; one shrugged his shoulders. "Get 'im back to 'is cell." the D.S. shouted out to the reception area.

A uniform appeared, a large bunch of keys swinging from his crooked index finger. He nodded, motioning 'Midnight' out of the interview room.

"You're well in the shit my son." the D.S. called out after him.

"We all in the shit man." 'Midnight' said quietly as he was led back to his cell.

The two Detectives retired to the CID office for a well-earned glass or two of scotch whilst they wrote up 'Midnight's interview and his subsequent confession.

*****

'Midnight' shuddered and wondered if it was the cold or the fleeting recollection of his arrest and detention at Moorwood. He pulled his jacket collar up around his neck as he walked out onto the street, his hands stuffed deep into the pockets against the biting cold. The freezing air found its way through the thin weave of the material and nipped at the tips of his fingers. He nodded to an old acquaintance as he walked, a 'brother' he had known back in the day, who was leaning against a shop doorway with a group of other unknowns. The man sauntered up to him, a smile stretched across his face as he recognised someone from the old streets.

"Midnight my man. Motherfucka its bin some time…was' happ'nin' man?"

'Midnight' allowed himself a half smile and offered his upturned palm to be slapped in the almost traditional greeting. He cast a fleeting critical eye toward the shop doorway and the faces he did not recognise.

"Same ol' shit man, y'know how it is." 'Midnight' replied.

"Yeah, I know how it is." his old friend said. "Hard is how it is…Hard for a nigger to make a livin' is how it is."

'Midnight' shrugged and nodded, looking again at the faces of the young blacks huddled in the shop doorway against the cold.

"How long's it bin man? four years, five?"

'Midnight' nodded slowly, "Five fuckin years man, did the man's time."

"How was it?" his friend asked.

'Midnight' waited for a second, pausing to look at the bright lights that spilled out across the pavements from the shop frontages. The bright colours somehow managed to hide the filth and drabness of the street, a disguise almost. Perhaps that's why we come out at night he thought, the days too bright, natural light shows all the shit and badness.

He looked back to his old friend who hopped nervously now from one foot to the other, perhaps through the cold, perhaps because he was 'coming down'.

'Midnight' looked again, looked closer and saw the glazed eyes shrunken back into their sockets, the whites yellowed by the effects of the 'crack' cocaine, the skin of his face stretched tight across his cheekbones.

"Hard for a nigger inside." 'Midnight' said, looking away and up the street, anxious to be on his way.

The other noted 'Midnight's' reluctance to stand and talk. He nervously nodded his head. "Yeah, right. Good to see a nigger back anyways, keep in touch man."

'Midnight' walked on, breathing in hard, letting the freezing air sting his lungs.

He stood by the bus stop, hands still deep in the pockets of his jacket as he leaned against the concrete post. He looked up the side streets which ran off in straight lines from the main road, the street lights at the junction mouths throwing their hazy yellow beams into the darkness of the narrow cobbled alleys. "All the shit and badness." he thought, shivering against the cold.

He shrugged himself free of the concrete stanchion as the double decked bus heaved its way into the nearside kerb and with a hiss of escaping air, the folding doors opened and he stepped up onto the low platform and paid the Asian driver.

He ran up to the upper deck and took a seat by the nearside window, wiping the condensation from the glass with the sleeve of his jacket. The bus juddered as it set off and 'Midnight' settled back in his seat. He stared out through the grease smeared glass at the surrounding area, with its boarded up buildings and broken down cars and wondered why he had missed it so much.

The bus made its way onto the Ring Road. 'Midnight' lifted himself from the seat and struggled with a piece of paper which he had folded up and placed in the back pocket of his jeans. He unclipped a ballpoint pen from the inside pocket of his jacket and as he stared out across the cold and depressing landscape. He clicked the retractor button unconsciously as the bus meandered its way around the City. The bus continued in an endless loop around the City Ring Road and by the completion of the fourth circuit, he had all the likely prospects down to a short list of three. As he passed each location for the last time, he scored plus and minus points against them.

"Too new, they'll have floor safes." he muttered to himself as he scored the name from his list.

The night shift had obviously just started at his second choice and as the bus passed the forecourt, he drew a line through the name as he noticed that this particular garage employed two assistants for night duty.

The Ring Road all night bus trundled on and he waited impatiently for a last look at his first choice; he lit a cigarette and craned his neck forward, to gain a view of the premises.

"Good size, nine pumps, open twenty four hours." He glanced at his watch as he muttered to himself. "One on duty, no cameras, and access to the shop...Perfect." he nodded to himself. His mind made up, he folded the paper and pushed it back into his jeans pocket.

The room was cold when he returned, bitterly cold. Damp had appeared in sodden patches on the walls and the dingy wallpaper hung like loose skin from the coving at the ceiling joints. A thin film of ice coated the inside of the glass of the small window, the crystalline fingers spreading upwards from the pool of condensed water on the window sill to slowly cover the filthy panes. 'Midnight' turned on the electric fire. It hummed and ticked slowly into life.

He sat cross legged in front of it and looked around his room. The air was still and cold and his breath formed vapour as he breathed. He sighed heavily. A deep and sudden depression gripped him as he surveyed the squalor and poverty in which he lived and he made a silent pact with himself then and there, a personal maxim by which he would abide.

He pulled a faded denim covered cushion from a chair which stood by the side of the struggling fire. He lay out in front of the single glowing bar, pushing the cushion under his head, he brought his knees up towards his chest and thrust his hands between his thighs to gather what little body warmth was available. He stared at the small sparks which flashed minutely within the coils of glowing wire as pieces of dust and moisture droplets settled on its red hot surface. His eyes closed and in the cold silence, sleep overcame him.

The dream was vivid and almost surreal. The 'Chinese' lay on his bed, fondling herself between her legs in readiness for him. She beckoned him with a lustful smile and tossed her head back laughing, her blue black hair whipping out across the stained pillows and falling back across her pale shoulders.

His vision crossed from the bed, blurred at the edges, yet crystal clear in the centre and in colours clear cut and defined. He saw the old Chinese man laid out on the floor at the side of the bed, his arched back against the wall, his frail body racked with the coughing and violent tremors of his withdrawal. A crab like hand scurried from side to side across the floor, searching frantically for the restricting band which lay coiled snake like, just out of his reach.

The 'Chinese' laughed again and dragged his attention away from the disgusting vision of the spittle, which ran silk like from the old man's half open lips. She opened her legs wide and held out her arms, beckoning him to come to her.

He wanted desperately to go to her, needing her warmth. He struggled with his own weight, his arms refusing to lift him from the floor. Dragging his legs, which for some reason, would not seem to work, he edged himself across the floor towards her, but the closer he got, the fainter her outline became.

A shadow came over him. He looked up, terrified as he saw the uniform standing over him, a sneering smile distorted the face. He heard maniacal laughter as a booted foot was raised in slow motion and then plunged downwards onto his testicles.

'Midnight' screamed and sat bolt upright, breathing rapidly in short gasps. The dream left him. In an instant and as conscious thought returned, he realised that he was sweating, even in the numbing coldness of the room. He sat for a moment, disorientated and troubled by the memory of the 'Chinese'. He snapped his neck around to look at the bed, it was empty, the blanket ruffled as he had left it. The urge to go to the bed to feel for any warmth that she may have left, was strong, yet as reality returned to him, he let himself fall back to the floor. He breathed in deeply, letting the air slowly out through his nostrils.

'Midnight' felt the stiffness in the muscles of his back and thighs and he stretched out and rolled himself over as he scrambled to his feet. He reached for the jacket which he had thrown over the corner of his bed and hurriedly pulled it on. Zipping it fully up to his throat, he walked towards the door, reaching for the key which was hanging from a small hook on the door jamb.

He opened the door allowing the freezing air to flood in. Stepping outside and onto the metal platform, he quickly closed the door behind him, leaving the electric fire to fight against the plunging temperature, at least offering some meagre form of welcome on his return.

The hour was early and the streets all but deserted. The pavements glinted with frost as he walked towards the City center, the air biting at him through the thin cotton jacket. He pushed his hands deep into his pockets and clenched his fists against the cold.

A few of the coffee shops were still open and he was tempted to enter, to be warm for a while even at the expense of unwanted conversation. He shrugged off the idea annoyingly as he realised that he didn't even have the price of a drink, although he had no doubt that the proprietor would give him a coffee and a warm for free if he asked, only too pleased to offer services for gratis. One never quite knew who the request was coming from and how he made his living. By the grace of the ruling factions and for his generosity, he was never robbed, his windows remained intact and his Wife and daughter were ignored, in an area where rape and robbery were more of a hobby than an isolated incident.

A free meal or a cup of coffee was a small price to pay and he paid it gladly…often.

'Midnight' walked on, the collar of his jacket pulled well up in an effort to prevent the freezing air from nipping too hard at his ears. There were still one or two faces around on the street, even on a night as crisp as this, it would never be totally deserted. Addiction cut no slack whatever the weather or time of day.

'Midnight' recognised no one. They were young, newcomers to the early hours, young enough to brave the cold conditions and the rare presence of a prowling Police vehicle to show off their newly earned colours. Swaggering with the false machismo of reckless youth who had no other place to be, no responsibilities, or with little or nothing to lose, and no fear of consequences.

He caught sight of one of the young blacks as he walked passed the doorway to Della's Soul Food café. The lettering and motif sewn onto the back of the thick cotton jerkin he wore, stood out brightly and colourful in the lights from the shop interior. A clenched black fist outlined in white and held up defiantly, stood out starkly against the red background. The words 'Jo'burg Bloods' in gold and black were stitched above and below the motif. An arrogant, visual gesture worn by a young black with no money, no job or prospects of ever having one. Having turned to the only source of recognition he was ever likely to achieve, he wore his colours for all to see.

'Midnight' walked on with a steady pace. After a time, he left the predominantly Afro-Caribbean area and entered the outskirts of the City. The area was as bad, if not worse than the black area. The houses, all back to back and constructed of red painted brick, faced out onto narrow cobbled streets which bristled with weeds and discarded rubbish. Washing lines were strung out between the guttering fall pipes, faded articles of clothing, now frozen stiff as boards and white from the frost, hung motionless, waiting patiently for the little warmth that the coming day might bring.

Old rusting vehicles in various states of disrepair were prevalent up the side streets. Most sported sun-strips across the upper parts of their windscreens or cheaply made magnetic door signs denoting one private hire company or another. Run on a shoestring and operated out of hastily erected ramshackle offices in the Asian area. The companies were family run, Uncles, Cousins and brothers worked around the clock, all using the same vehicle, bed and driving licence.

The area was drab and dirty, no effort being made by the inhabitants to improve their standards, or to maintain the properties. Living in one of the run down back to back terraced houses in the cold and damp of the City being infinitely better than eking out an existence in one of the slum dwellings in Orangi Town or Islamabad.

An all pervading smell of curry hung heavily in the air and 'Midnight' wrinkled his nose at the fetid odour and looked up the streets with distaste.

"Mo'fuckin' pakis deserve all they get." he muttered to himself as he quickened his pace toward the City.

He wanted something in particular, something familiar with which he would feel a little less vulnerable.

His strong legs kept up the steady pace towards the bright lights of the City center. He was conscious that he was well out of his own area now and his eyes scanned the streets for 'Babylon'. The Police in the City center would be out on foot, usually in two's, walking the pavements of their particular beat areas, looking at the goods in the brightly illuminated shops on the main streets, just passing the time until six o'clock when they could go off duty.

There would be a Ford Transit floating around somewhere, intermittently picking up the beat Officers for a smoke and a warm. After the Sergeant had checked their pocket books and given them a 'chalk', they would be dropped off again to continue their beats. The beat Officers would be bored and would certainly make a point of stopping a solitary black at large in the City at this untimely hour. There was always a chance of winding him up until there was a breach of the peace or at least a hint of 'disorderly conduct'. The inevitable arrest would follow, then it would be off to the Bridewell with their 'prize', taking their time over the required paperwork, remaining warm for the rest of the shift and an arrest to show the Inspector.

But tonight it was really cold, bitter. Most of the uniforms would be warming their arses in the kitchens of one of the many hotels in the City center, drinking coffee or perhaps something stronger with the night porter, dutifully listening with forced interest to the incessantly repeated war stories, just to humour the old fart, to be out of the cold until the Sergeant called up asking for their location.

'Midnight' entered the heart of the City; his eyes darted across the many shop frontages until he found what he was looking for. The shop was a gift, not too new, obviously coming to the end of its lease and starting to look a little run down and neglected. An unlit alley ran between the side of the shop and its neighbouring building.

'Midnight' could just make out the wooden framed door at the side of the building and his eyes ran quickly over the frontage, searching for an alarm box. He could see none fitted at the front, neither could he detect any tell-tale aluminium strips on the glass panel in the front door. He glanced quickly through the glass on the twin panelled door and searched the interior for any passive infra-red detectors in the upper corners of the shop interior. Seeing nothing, he slipped quickly down the alley between the two buildings and entered the small courtyard which was littered with dustbins and empty boxes.

The yard was bordered by a small wall, less than six feet in height and offered him a little visual security and an avenue of escape should anything unforeseen occur.

'Midnight' walked stealthily up to the side door of the shop, noting the peeling paint and the poor condition of the wood. There was a small window to the right of the door; he noted that this was semi opaque due to the wire mesh which reinforced the glass. Not knowing what lay behind the window, he decided on a direct entry approach.

He felt around the door frame and pushed the wood panel gently with his shoulder to ascertain the position of the securing points. There was no keyhole in the door, nor any handle. He pushed again and found that the door bulged inwards slightly in the middle where it met the door frame. Kneeling down, he pushed against the bottom of the door and found it to be solid, concluding that the door was bolted top and bottom without any securing device in the center. 'Midnight' stood quietly for a while; he studied the door, his ears tingling in the icy crispness. He listened for any sound, but heard nothing over the sound of his breathing. He searched around the small yard and caught sight of the old metal dustbins; he shot a glance back at the door then returned his gaze to the bins.

He walked silently up to them and tentatively felt their individual weight, rocking them gently on their metal rims. One of the bins felt satisfyingly heavy. Not bothering to see what it contained, he tipped it on its side and rolled it towards the door, letting it come to rest where his measured eye had determined that it would yield the most use.

A vehicle passing the front of the shop froze his movements. He stood stock still, holding his breath until the engine note had faded completely out of earshot. A glance around the yard reassured him and he sat down on the icy flagstones, the cold immediately attacking his buttocks through the thin material of his jeans. With his legs bent at the knees, he placed his feet against the door where it felt more solid. He placed his back against the dustbin and arched upwards, raising his shoulders so that he could press downwards on the rim handles of the dustbin with both hands. Now half his body weight was resting on the heavy container which felt now solid against the flagstones. He had doubled his leverage power.

'Midnight' drew back his knees towards his chest and slammed them forwards. The bottom panel of the door shrieked and then shattered. With what sounded like a gun shot in the stillness of the air, the impact from his feet burst the bottom bolt from the door frame. The bottom edge of the door was now twisted inwards and 'Midnight' was able to identify the upper securing point where the door was still flush with the frame.

He held his breath and listened intently for the sound of running feet and any static filled requests for assistance over an approaching Police radio.

The seconds passed without incident. He got to his feet and carefully and quietly replaced the dustbin near to the base of the wall at the end of the yard, a good jumping off point, if he had to make an escape over the wall.

'Midnight' returned to the door. Placing his shoulder against the now spongy woodwork, he pushed the door inwards, opening the gap at the bottom until it was large enough to wedge his foot between the twisted panel and the door frame. Letting it ease back, he felt the pressure from the door, squeezing against his foot through the thin material of his shoe. He took a half step back and shouldered the door with all his weight. The top bolt was ripped from the old wooden framework and as the door burst inwards. He heard the metal securing bolt and clasp bounce with a metallic tinkling sound as it skittered across the floor inside the shop.

'Midnight' entered and immediately, his eyes darted from wall to wall for any tell-tale pinpricks of red light which would denote a beam, activated by his movements or the noise or vibration of the door being sprung. Cautiously, he turned and satisfied that his presence had not been electronically noticed, he swung the door back towards the shattered frame. He pushed it gently back into place so that to all intents and purposes, the shop appeared secure.

'Midnight' considered that it would at least pass a visual test from any torch beam played down the alley by 'Babylon' as he walked past on his beat. The chances of the Officer actually coming into the yard to physically check the property on his beat, were slim to none. Too much effort on such a cold night. If it looks right, it probably is and probably, would be good enough.

The aromas within the shop assailed his nostrils. The heady smell of the perfumed astringents, the shampoos and cigar smoke which had seeped into the fixtures and fittings over the years.

He paused and stood perfectly still, allowing his eyes to become accustomed to the blackness inside the premises. Slowly, the various forms took shape, the row of vinyl covered chairs facing the washbasins, shower heads on long chromium hoses which hung from the walls above the sinks like so many cobras, frozen at the very point of striking.

'Midnight' moved silently and cautiously towards the Formica topped work surfaces between the sinks. He immediately froze as he caught sight of his own dark shape reflected in one of the mirrors. His heart burst into triple time as a sudden surge of adrenalin rushed through his body. Feeling light headed and hearing his own heartbeat pounding loudly in his ears, he quickly kicked off his shoes and resting an arm across the back of one of the chairs to steady himself, he took off his socks and pulled them over his hands. He searched the worktops in the dark, feeling each of the inanimate objects through mittened fingers, identifying them by shape. Scissors and electric razors, a hand mirror, combs. His fingers closed around a familiar shape, the ivory handle retaining a certain warmth even in the coldness of the shop. He gripped the razor between his thumb and index finger and flicked his wrist. The stainless steel blade swung out silently, a little stiffly he thought, but nothing that a few minutes work wouldn't resolve. Palming the blade back into place, he felt its weight and noted that it felt right in his palm, as if somehow, it belonged.

The lights of a vehicle swept across the interior of the shop as it rounded a corner from the main road. The interior of the shop was illuminated brightly as the headlights chased the darkness from one corner to another, then as quickly and as unexpectedly as it had arrived, the light disappeared, plunging the shop once again into total darkness. 'Midnight' stood motionless and listened to the blood pounding in his temples. He slipped the razor into the back pocket of his jeans. His stomach felt suddenly tight and he had an irresistible urge to relieve himself.

Quickly, he undid the top button of his jeans and pulled down the zip, allowing the material to fall to his ankles. He pushed down his briefs and squatted down onto his haunches, holding on to the back of one of the swivel chairs to steady himself. He pushed his feet outwards and at the same time, his bowels suddenly opened, their contents rushing out onto the carpeted floor.

The room was immediately filled with a foul stench as the watery contents of his bowels seeped into the carpet. 'Midnight' let his head fall backwards and he exhaled slowly, tensing his stomach muscles then allowing them to relax slowly. The tightness was gone.

He reached out to one of the sinks and grabbed a towel from where it hung limply through a chrome ring attached to the wall.

He cleaned himself with the towel and rose to his feet, carefully avoiding the slurry of his excreta; he threw the towel into one of the sinks and stepped backwards. He dressed himself quickly and with his socks still covering his hands, he rummaged further along the work surface until his hands touched upon a small wooden box. He lifted the box carefully, noting that it was satisfyingly heavy.

'Midnight' pulled on the small brass handle fitted across the face of the box and a drawer slid outwards. His eyes, which were now reasonably accustomed to the darkness, peered into the drawer. There were a few notes, not enough for him to retire on, but better than nothing. Grabbing the notes up, he stuffed them into the front pocket of his jeans. Tipping the drawer upwards and to one side, a number of coins fell out into his palm. Quite pleased with the small financial bonus the job had produced, he allowed the coins to join the notes in his jeans pocket. 'Midnight' pushed the front of the drawer and it slid home, he replaced it on the work surface. He stood motionless in the shop, allowing his eyes to sweep across the interior of the shop once again.

His inner mind told him that he had got what he had come for and to get out. He still had to get safely back out through the City center. He had work to do, but now he was carrying a weapon. Stripping the socks from his hands, he quickly pulled them back over his feet and replaced his shoes. Reaching into the back pocket of his jeans, he retrieved the razor, feeling with some satisfaction, that the ivory handle had become warm from his body heat as if they were one already. 'Midnight' pushed his hand down the front of his jeans and let the razor lie across the top of his genitals. Even if he was stopped, no cop was going to search him there. Cops never did for some strange reason, embarrassed to touch another man's penis, too afraid of a complaint of indecency, especially on another male, too much of a stigma attached and no uniform would want to carry that sort of complaint throughout the rest of his service.

He peered cautiously out through the doorway and seeing it was clear, he stepped out into the yard, breathing in the cold freshness; welcome now after the fetid stench from within the shop. 'Midnight' Lyburn, burglar, and now in possession of an offensive weapon, quietly disappeared into the darkness.

## **<u>Nine</u>**

The young girl slouched back in the worn seat behind the counter and cursed as she felt the rough metal edge of the chair nip at the skin on the back of her legs. She sighed as she bemoaned her fate. She was slim, good looking, or so her boyfriend said. She was nineteen and bored.

She looked down at her hands as they rested on her lap; she clicked her thumb and second fingernails together as she examined them. The 'Oyster Glo' varnish was starting to look chipped and she considered repainting them. She opened her fingers wide, holding her hand out in front of her and twisted it directly under the overhead strip light to examine what remained of the mother of pearl effect. She breathed in deeply and despondently, let her hand fall back into her lap.

Reaching for her cigarettes, she took one from the pack and looked guiltily across at the ashtray which was overflowing with the many discarded remains of her habit. Three hours into her shift, she was bored. Bored with her home life where her Step Father and her Mother constantly nagged her about the length of her skirts, her makeup and her boyfriends, not that there was much time for the latter these days.

She was bored with the job, although it was a job she supposed and most of her friends were unemployed, she at least, did have a little money. The financial gains of employment only just outweighed the monotony which she suffered; eleven at night until seven in the morning, six nights a week. Her social life was almost non-existent.

She was missing a party tonight. One of her old college friends was eighteen at last and her Parents had promised to stay out until at least two o'clock. She'd been invited of course, although invitations were becoming scarce due to her commitment to night work. Her friends just seemed to stop asking, knowing what the response would be.

She couldn't even have a drink before work, the petrol delivery man would report her to her employer if he smelled alcohol on her breath as she 'supervised' the delivery of petrol into the huge tanks deep beneath the concrete of the garage forecourt.

She had pleaded her case with the other members of staff, hoping that someone would swap shifts. No one had offered, who wanted eleven sevens?

"Sorry love, the old man's on nights and there are the kids to look after."

"What? Nights on Saturday? No chance love…Sorry."

She had turned up for her shift in a bad mood, after telephoning her friend to once again, make her apologies. She hardly spoke to the girl from whom she took over, going through her duties like an automaton, checking the till totals, the receipts and the digital counters on the petrol pumps. Smiling weakly, and not without a little jealousy, at the girl on three elevens as she had waved back, before clambering into her boyfriend's car which had screeched to a halt on the forecourt. They set off at equal pace towards the City and the night life.

"Creep." she muttered to herself, as she watched the tail lights of his car disappear from the forecourt and out onto the Ring Road.

The garage premises fell silent and she was immediately bored again.

There had been the odd highlight to her night. A man in his early forties had struck up a conversation with her and asked her out for a drink. He was well dressed, perfectly groomed and the smell of his expensive aftershave had wafted across the counter top as he had filled out the charge card invoice. She'd glanced fleetingly across the forecourt, to where his gleaming Mercedes sat, and for a second, she allowed herself to consider his proposal, imagining the expensive meal and the wine with liquors afterwards, all on expenses no doubt. Perhaps a night club, cabaret, then afterwards, the smell of the leather from the seats in the back of the huge saloon, his warm, manicured hands inside her blouse.

"Maybe." she'd said. "But not this week, I'm on nights."

He had smiled, exposing perfect teeth. "More's the pity, later perhaps?"

He had waved at her from within his vehicle as it purred away from the pumps. She had been flattered and more than a little tempted by his offer. She knew exactly what he was after of course, but she'd never been out with a real man, a man of means who would know just how to treat a girl. She allowed her imagination to wander. He was probably a Managing Director or an Executive, or something equally as important. He'd be married of course, probably with children and a cultured Wife living in a huge, sprawling country house filled with expensive carpets and soft furniture all the way from Madrid or Paris.

She decided that if he came in again and asked her out, she would accept, just for the experience.

The passing traffic had died off and it was quiet. The takings of the day were in neat rolls of one hundred pounds and crammed into grey plastic tubes. She would recount them and check the amount against the till receipts and the charge card invoices and then drop the lot into a canvas bag, ready for the day shift to bank in the morning.

The night was starting to drag. The local radio station had closed down at three a.m. and she had forgotten to bring her cassette player. The silence annoyed her. She settled back into the seat again and looked around the shop at the bulbs and fuses, the batteries and the cans of top up oil and anti-freeze, all the motoring paraphernalia and accessories she'd looked at a million times before.

The late night Ring Road bus broke the silence briefly as it meandered its way past the forecourt. She leaned forwards and rested her elbows on the counter top, taking the weight of her head in her hands. She sighed and wondered how the party was going. She could almost hear the music and the shrieks of laughter, feel the frantic groping's, the hurried lovemaking in the bedrooms, inhibitions forgotten, cast aside just for a single night of alcohol fuelled euphoria.

She breathed in and sighed heavily. "Shit." she muttered to no one. She lifted her head slightly as she heard footsteps. "Christ, another human being." or maybe, she thought, in a fleeting moment, the man with the Mercedes. If he'd been out to a night club, he could still be out and about. Perhaps he'd seen a little weakness in her earlier refusal and was coming back to try his luck again.

She quickly decided that if it was him, she would make him a coffee in the back office and if he asked her out, she would accept. She could call in sick, even her Parents wouldn't know. She grew excited at the prospect and involuntarily ran her hands through her hair as the footsteps grew louder.

"He'd have come back in his car though." she thought quickly, and at the same moment, she felt her heart sink as she saw the huge Negro walking in through the door.

'Midnight' smiled and shivered violently as he walked up to the counter.

"Hi…Listen. I'm out of petrol on the Ring Road. You got a can I could borrow?" he said, as he slapped his arms across his body to show how cold it was outside.

"We don't usually lend cans out." she said, letting disappointment show in her voice. "They have a habit of disappearing."

"Hey, I'll be back, promise." 'Midnight' said and nodded out towards the petrol pumps. "I'll have to fill the car up anyway."

He leaned casually up against the edge of the counter. She looked directly at him for a split second; there was something about his eyes.

She tore her gaze away from him, feeling slightly uncomfortable. She hesitated, then said "Hang on, I'll see."

She disappeared beneath the counter.

'Midnight' heard the empty acoustic clang of a can clattering against something as the girl rummaged around beneath the counter. He readied himself, gave a quick glance back across the garage forecourt and quickly donned the smile again as the girl reappeared holding the can.

"Cheers." he said, as he reached over to take it from her.

"As long as you bring it ba…"

She stopped in mid speech as 'Midnight' grabbed her wrist tightly and pulled her violently forwards, winding her as her stomach struck the counter edge. She started to form a scream as a stark realisation formed in her brain. The reasoning was cut short as 'Midnight's' clenched fist swung out in a blur across the counter and struck her hard on the side of her head. She recoiled slightly, but his grip was still tight on her wrist.

A veil of darkness started its descent across her eyes and she was vaguely aware of intense pain as he struck her again and for a brief moment, she was aware of a strange coppery taste in her mouth, salty and warm as she felt her legs fold under her.

'Midnight' let the girl slump back onto the floor behind the counter. He acted quickly, running to the glass doors, he dropped the latch and slid a small aluminium knob in a plastic frame attached to the middle of the door. The sign now read CLOSED. He ran back towards the counter, throwing a glance at the deserted forecourt before pulling himself up and swinging his legs over to drop down to where the girl now lay unconscious. His eyes darted up to the petrol pump isolator switch and he snatched down the handle, his heart pounding in his chest.

The lights on the forecourt pumps flickered then died. He heard the diminishing whine, emanating from the rear store room as the generator wound down and starved the pumps of their power.

'Midnight' fumbled with a bank of switches on the wall by the side of the cigarette display until the overhead strip lights in the awning above the forecourt died. To all concerned, the garage was closed.

Squatting down behind the counter and leaning over the prone form of the unconscious girl, his eyes fell to the pile of plastic tubes stacked on a small ledge beneath the counter top; the sight of the tightly rolled notes within, made his heart race with excitement. Grabbing for one of the canvas bags lying in a small heap on the floor, he scooped the tubes from the ledge and in rows, they toppled into the bag. He felt no need to count the tubes, they were full of money and money was enough. He satisfied himself that he had gathered all the tubes which contained money and cautiously, showed his head above the level of the counter top to scan the forecourt. Seeing that it was still deserted, he stood up and felt his legs shivering with the infusion of adrenalin.

The girl moaned softly as 'Midnight' randomly punched the buttons grouped on the side of the till. Feverishly, he tapped at them all, until he was rewarded with a hollow metallic clunk as the till sprang open. He flipped up all the spring clips which held the bank notes flat against the base of the separate drawers. Grabbing up the twenties, tens and fives, 'Midnight' pushed them down into the canvas bag. He scooped up the pound coins from the plastic receptacle and allowed them to drop from his cupped hand into the front pocket of his jeans.

Wiping the till buttons with the sleeve of his jacket, 'Midnight' closed the drawer with his forearm. He pulled at the draw string which was woven around the upper seam of the canvas bag until it closed up tight. He glanced down at the girl. She was still.

'Midnight' roughly ran the canvas bag over the ledge underneath the counter top, and anywhere he felt that he may have touched. He pushed the bag down the front of his jacket which he quickly zipped up. Again, he nervously scanned the forecourt. Still it was deserted.

He knelt down over the girl, his eyes involuntarily falling to the hem of her skirt which had ridden up as she had fallen. 'Midnight' looked at her exposed thighs; she wore no tights, only ankle socks within her soft shoes, her legs were smooth and white. He smiled to himself and his eyes searched over the motorist's accessories section at the far end of the counter. His heartbeat was loud. He felt the blood pounding in his temples and he felt the sweat trickle from his armpits under his shirt. The sight of her bare legs caused the beginnings of an erection and he felt tight and uncomfortable in his jeans.

"This is madness man." he told himself. "Get out now, we've got what we came for."

His fingers flicked up the hem of her skirt and exposed her almost transparent briefs. "Oh shit." he murmured to himself. He knelt beside her and sunk his hand into the soft dark mound between her legs, feeling the softness and warmth there. He felt himself growing harder and his eyes darted again to the car accessories, noting the rows of brightly coloured plastic insulating tape, which hung from long chromium plated pins evenly spaced along a pegboard.

Grabbing at a roll of the tape, he tore wildly at the outer cellophane wrapper with his teeth and spat the slivers onto the floor. All sense and reason now having fled, driven by animal lust, he was unable to take his eyes from the helpless girl lying prone at his feet. 'Midnight' stuffed the roll of tape into his jacket pocket and stood over her. Lifting her under her armpits, he half pulled the girl from the floor and dragged her still semi-conscious body from behind the counter area and along a narrow corridor which led to a small office.

He elbowed the office door handle downwards and applying a little pressure with his shoulder, the door swung inwards.

The office was sparse. A single wooden desk, which was strewn with invoices and charge card receipts, sat in a corner next to a battered metal cabinet. A padded chair in faded green leather, had been pushed tightly up against the table, its four legs splayed crablike on the linoleum floor covering.

'Midnight' lowered the girl onto the office floor and returning to the corridor, snatched up a linen drying cloth from where it hung over the rim of a small stainless steel wash basin. The girl moaned and her body twitched as she returned to consciousness. All his senses told him to leave, but he was drawn by an animal force beyond his control. Unable to stop himself, he tore the cloth in two. He rolled one of the halves into a tight ball and standing over the prone figure of the girl, he roughly rolled her over onto her back. Her eyes flickered for a second as 'Midnight' knelt down astride her and forced the ball of cloth into her mouth. He fumbled in his jacket pocket for the roll of tape and finding the end with his teeth, he pulled two feet or so from the roll and wound it around the back of her head. With a finger through the cardboard inner core, he rotated the tape around her head, again and again, stretching the strips of thin plastic over her mouth to hold the ball of cloth in place, stifling any sound she might make.

'Midnight' folded the remaining piece of cloth and placed it over her eyes, again repeating the process with the insulating tape, wrapping it around her head so that the mask would stay in place. The girl returned to consciousness quiet suddenly and 'Midnight' sensed her immediate panic. Her screams were muffled as she thrashed her head from side to side; she flayed at the air with her hands and clawed at his clothing. 'Midnight' forcefully turned the girl over onto her stomach and he felt her stiffen at his touch. She screamed constantly into the tightly packed roll of cloth which held her jaws slightly apart. Her nostrils flared as she pulled the vital air into her lungs between screams.

She fought uselessly against him as he pulled her left arm into the small of her back and held it there tightly with his knee. He pulled her right arm across, and holding her twitching fingers with one of his huge hands, he wound the tape around her wrists. Her panic increased as he pinned her to the floor with his body weight and her panting screams withered to moans and stifled sobs as she gradually weakened.

'Midnight' took his weight from her and knelt at her side. As he rolled her over onto her back again, she screamed in agony as her own body weight fell against her pinioned arms and she involuntarily arched her back to ease the pressure. Her body shuddered with terrified sobs as she struggled uselessly against the tape which was tightly binding her wrists.

Grasping the hem of her skirt, 'Midnight' slowly pulled it up over her trembling thighs exposing her briefs. He paused for a second, savouring the moment before pulling her skirt all the way up and onto her stomach. He pushed a hand roughly between her legs, feeling the sheer material of her briefs and the warmth beneath his fingers. 'Midnight' forced the girl's legs apart and positioned his legs between her thighs, her body arched and thrashed.

Ignoring her terror, he gazed down at the darkness of her pubic hair where it showed through the thin material of her briefs. Like a mauling animal, he ripped at the front of her blouse, tearing the material like damp tissue.

Immune to her sobs, 'Midnight' reached into the back pocket of his jeans and took out the new blade. Flicking it open, he slipped the warm steel between her skin and the front of her bra.

Without effort, the blade whispered through the material and the bra fell away to either side of her breasts.

He leaned forwards and took one of her nipples in his mouth, biting gently at first, then with more ferocity as his excitement increased. The girl let out a long mournful sob as her body was violated by his mouth and she thrashed beneath him as she felt his hand grasping at the material of her briefs. She felt a moment's tightness across the small of her back as the waistband dug into her flesh as he ripped them away.

'Midnight' tossed the briefs across the office, neither knowing nor caring where they fell. Straightening his back, 'Midnight' freed himself from his jeans and taking his upper body weight on his elbows, he entered her slowly.

His eyes flickered and his mouth fell open as he felt the warmth of her. The girl thrashed, violently shaking her head from side to side. She involuntarily arched her back, which allowed 'Midnight' to insert himself fully. His movements quickened as he felt his climax approaching. He squeezed his eyes tightly shut and he felt his muscles flex beneath his sweatshirt. His mouth opened in a silent expression of ecstasy. He froze rigid and his seed flowed into her.

The girl lay still. Her forehead glistened with sweat. Her breathing was shallow between her gasping sobs.

'Midnight' eased himself away from her and searching across the greasy linoleum floor, found his razor. Snatching it up, he forced the stainless steel blade back between the ivory handle and replaced it in the back pocket of his jeans.

A moment of panic seized him and he wondered how long he had been with the girl and as sense and reason returned, he darted from the office.

Straightening his clothing as he entered the corridor; he stopped to peer around the wall and out onto the garage forecourt. Apart from the muted moans from the girl in the back office, there was silence.

'Midnight' patted the bulge beneath the front of his jacket, making sure that the bag was still there. He slipped over the counter, rubbing his hands in a circular motion across its surface to destroy any tell-tale marks peculiar to him. Quickly, he glanced around the shop and seeing nothing incriminating, he slipped the Yale latch on the door and pulled it open.

The cold damp air rushed in and chilled the sweat on his face. He stepped out cautiously, looking across the forecourt and out onto the Ring Road. A slight fog was swirling in on a light breeze and he was pleased to see that he could hardly see across to the other side of the main road. 'Midnight' closed the door behind him, hearing the latch click home.

He briefly ran the sleeve of his jacket over the smooth surface of both sides of the handle before once again, patting the bag beneath his jacket as he walked quickly across the garage forecourt and onto the Ring Road where he disappeared like a wraith, into the freezing fog.

*****

As 'Midnight' sat cross legged on the bed in his room counting the notes and coins, a bright yellow Ford Transit pulled up to one of the pumps on the garage forecourt. The driver was a regular visitor to the premises, to both fill up his vehicle and hopefully, to have a chat and a coffee with the girl who worked nights. He immediately thought it strange not to see the bright fluorescent strip lights bathing the forecourt; only a solitary emergency backup light flickered dimly from within a recess in the large overhead canopy.

The man glanced through the window of the shop where the girl usually sat. He normally got a wave, or at least a smile of recognition, yet there was no one there behind the window to welcome him. The driver pulled his vehicle alongside one of the diesel pumps and noticed that none of the delivery nozzles were padlocked to their retaining stanchions as they would certainly be, if the garage was closed. He had also noticed with growing consternation, that the lights behind the delivery counters on the pumps were not lit.

With a puzzled look on his face, he set the handbrake and got out of his vehicle. He looked across the forecourt and once again to the till area within the shop where he had expected to see the girl. He noted that the sliding sign on the door advised customers that the garage was closed.

He leaned back against the side of his van, the twin black letter A's standing out starkly, even in the dim yellow glow of the emergency light. He took off his beret and tossed it onto the dashboard of the van and reached across to the horn stalk. The shrill, strident tone shattered the silence, but attracted no attention. Seeing no one, he walked up to the door, pressing his nose against the cold glass. He cupped his hands around the sides of his face to cut out any reflection, as he peered into the interior of the shop.

He frowned and his brow furrowed. "Bloody closed?" he muttered, "They're never closed."

He was slightly annoyed. If truth be known, he'd driven a fair way off his assigned route, to come for a coffee and a chat with the girl during the quiet hours of his night shift. His curiosity nagged at him, this garage was open twenty four hours every day except for Christmas Day and if it was closed for some unknown reason, it worried him that none of the pumps had been locked.

The AA man knocked tentatively on the door and strained his head to one side listening intently for any sound. He walked to the window where the girl normally sat and knocked again, still he heard nothing.

Walking back to the door, he grasped the handle and rattled the door within its frame, finding it indeed locked; he shook his head as he looked back across the forecourt to see the fog swirling in around the desolate pumps. It was eerie and he felt slightly disturbed. The cold was now seeping through the material of his jacket and he shuddered. "Well, if they're closed, they should have locked the bloody pumps." he thought to himself.

Suddenly resolute, the AA patrolman returned to the cab of his Transit and picked up the radio transmitter from its clip on the dashboard, he looked again at the deserted garage premises. He paused, if he radioed it in to his controller, they would know that he was way off his area, but something was definitely wrong here.

He sucked on his teeth as he considered his options. He depressed the transmit button, but then released it. "Bollocks." he whispered in frustration, slumping back in his seat.

The memory of a blue rotating sign not a few miles back down the Ring Road flashed through his mind. "Moorwood nick." he muttered to himself as he twisted the ignition key to start the Transit's engine.

*****

The AA driver entered the warm reception area and pressed the small button on the counter top. His eyes gazed over the colourful crime prevention posters and informative literature on the wall as he waited. A young P.C. in shirtsleeves answered the buzzer and smiled as he came to the counter from the front office.

"Morning." said the AA man.

"What can we do for you?" the Constable asked, stifling a yawn and shaking his head. "Sorry." he said apologetically. "First night shift."

The AA man smiled knowingly and nodded. "I know just how you feel." He leaned against the counter top and adopted a puzzled expression. "That garage up the road." he said, pointing out towards the main road and in the general direction.

"Oh yeah, the all-nighter." the uniform replied, leaning on the counter trying his hardest to look interested.

"Well, it usually is." the AA man replied. "The place is in darkness, the door's locked, but there's no locks on the pumps. I've never known it to be closed."

"No, neither have I. Hang on a minute mate." the P.C. said, as he disappeared back into the front office. He returned a few moments later with the Station Sergeant.

"You say the pumps are unlocked then?" the Sergeant asked.

The AA man nodded. "I just thought it was a bit strange."

"It's not just strange, it's a fire hazard." said the Sergeant and turned to his Constable.

"Go find the key holder list lad. Make contact an' ask what's going on, see if the place is supposed to be closed."

"Sarge." the young P.C. said, acknowledging the order as he made his way back into the front office.

"And make sure you tell 'em that the pumps are insecure." the Sergeant shouted after him.

The Sergeant reached under the counter top and lifting a telephone handset, he rang the internal number for the radio room.

The AA man could hear the muted sound of a telephone ringing from somewhere within the station. He lifted one of the many leaflets on crime prevention, which were strewn across the counter top and read it with feigned interest as he waited.

The Sergeant looked slightly displeased as he attempted to raise someone in the radio room. There was a click and the AA man could just make out the metallic voice on the other end of the line.

"Radio."

"So sorry to wake you PC Jackson." the Sergeant said sarcastically, his displeasure at being kept waiting clearly evident in his tone. "Sergeant Mellors here, front office."

The AA man noted the embarrassed silence from the Officer on the other end of the phone and chuckled as the Sergeant shook his head in mock despair.

"Get a car to 'ave a look at the all night garage on the Ring Road. It's Hammond's, the place looks closed up, but all the pumps are unlocked. We're getting the key holder out."

The Sergeant replaced the telephone handset without waiting for a response from the radio operator. He nodded to the AA man. "Sorted. Fancy a brew while you're 'ere?"

"Oh cheers, very nice, thanks." The AA man beamed. The Sergeant shouted through to the front office for someone to get the kettle on.

"I don't suppose you've got time to 'ave a look at my alternator while you're 'ere 'ave you?" the Sergeant asked pensively.

\*\*\*\*\*

Alan shone his torch through the driver's window of the blue Ford Capri on the dealer's frontage. Wiping the condensation away with the sleeve of his jacket, he winced at the mileage as the beam illuminated the odometer and he looked again at the asking price which was splattered across the windscreen in bright orange self-adhesive figures.

"Robbing bastard." Alan muttered and frowned as he swept the beam of his torch over the bodywork, casting a critical eye over the vehicle's lines and noting with satisfaction, a tell-tale line of paint overspray on the rubber surround at the base of the windscreen.

He clicked his tongue against the roof of his mouth and glanced wryly at the plastic roof sign which proudly pronounced 'One careful owner'. Alan snorted. "Yeah, Hertz Rentacar, you cheatin' twat."

Dismissing the Capri, Alan sauntered over to a red Granada 28S marked up at £3995. It was a good looker and he ran his fingers behind the inner edges of the rear wheel arches to detect any sign of filler or repair.

He faintly heard his call sign over the radio he had left in his patrol car. "No peace for the fuckin' wicked." he muttered, as he left the Granada and reached in through the window of his patroller to pick up the personal radio.

"Papa Yankee One Five, you calling over?"

The radio crackled. "Alan, 'ave a run up to Hammond's garage for us. The night AA man says it's all locked up, but the pumps are insecure."

"From One Five. John, I'm across the other side of the City, anybody any closer?" Alan said hopefully, looking wistfully back at the Granada. He wanted to give it a good looking over without the dealer hovering over him, pushing all its good points. There was also a very nice black Ford Capri 2.8 which was certainly worth a second look.

"You're all we've got at the moment Alan." The radio operator replied.

Alan sighed and glanced at his watch. "That's right John, don't make any fucking effort to raise anyone else, good ol' Traffic'll deal." he muttered to himself.

He thumbed the transmitter. "10/4 John, I'll have a look. I'll be five or ten minutes."

Alan threw the radio onto the front passenger seat and got in behind the wheel, muttering as he fired up the engine. "Can't a man have five bleedin' minutes to himself?" he cursed under his breath and casting a last look across to the Granada and the black Capri, eased the vehicle into gear and set off.

He fumbled for the cigarettes in his jacket pocket, pulling one out with his teeth; he tossed the packet onto the passenger seat to join his personal radio and steering with his knees, held the cigarette steadily as he lit it. Alan inhaled deeply and took out his frustration as usual, on his patrol vehicle. Pressing down hard on the accelerator pedal, the big V8 growled in protest and the rear wheels slithered slightly on the damp road surface.

Within ten minutes, Alan pulled onto the forecourt of the garage and reached over for his radio.

"Papa Yankee One Five."

"Go on Alan" the operator replied.

"I'm 10/6 John. Doesn't seem to be any sign of life."

Alan leaned across to the passenger seat and looked at the pump nozzles opposite.

"From One Five. The AA man's right, the pumps are unlocked, I'll 'ave a look round."

"10/4 Alan, we've raised the key holder. He's not 'appy, says the garage should be open as usual, he's turned out from Bridgeford Road, so he shouldn't be too long."

Alan glanced at his watch. "Christ! Bridgeford Road's fuckin' miles away, I'll be 'ere till going home time." he cursed quietly to himself, wanting to get back to the Granada to complete his examination and do a PNC check on it before seeing the dealer when he got up off nights.

*****

Alan took his torch from where it was wedged between the edge of the passenger seat and the center console and left his patrol car. He shone the beam over the building as he walked across the forecourt. He was pleasantly surprised to see a taxi pulling up beside the pumps. The interior light came on and after a few moments, the passenger door opened. Alan depressed his transmit button. "One Five, looks like the key holder's arrived."

"Received Alan, let us know what's going on. Sarn't Mellors is still with the AA chap, I think he's out in the back yard getting a 'freeby' on his motor, but he'll want to know the result."

"10/4 John, did you say Mellors was getting a 'freeby' in his motor." chuckled Alan. "The AA's service is better than I'd heard."

The radio operator double clicked his transmitter to let Alan know he'd received his last.

Alan walked over to the taxi as the key holder struggled to remove his huge girth from his seat. With one hand on the top of the window surround, he hauled himself upwards.

The taxi, which had previously had a significant list to the nearside, suddenly righted itself as its passenger alighted. The man was sweating profusely even though he wore no jacket against the biting cold, Alan noticed a large damp patch on his shirt between his fleshy shoulder blades. The obese key holder sported heavy gold rings on the majority of his pudgy fingers and a heavy identity bracelet the width of the Forth Road Bridge, clearly worth more than Alan earned in a month of Sundays.

The man was clearly unhappy at having been turned out; his face was bloated and reddened, probably due to the inconvenience of the hour and the fact that he had an eighteen inch neck which had somehow been forced into a seventeen inch collar.

"Morning." Alan called out cheerily, trying to suppress a grin at the sight of the waddling mess approaching. The Capri was forgotten for the time being. Alan was heartened at being instrumental in getting some fat 'nine to five' civilian out of his stinking pit. The fat key holder scowled and muttered a begrudging "Morning Officer." under his breath as if it was costing him a fortune to speak.

"What's going on then?" asked Alan. "Is it supposed to be closed?"

"No, it isn't." the key holder snapped as they walked towards the door of the shop.

"But I can guess what's happened." he wheezed. "The girl that's supposed to be on nights asked for time off, to go to a bloody party or something." Alan tried to look genuinely sympathetic and watched with growing amusement as the morbidly obese key holder hauled the overhanging paunch of his stomach, up over his trouser waistband and shoved his right hand deep into the pocket of his trousers to search for the keys to the premises. "I said no, unless she could get a shift swap. She's obviously waited until it quietened down and locked up and pissed off. Anyway, she's finished now, I can tell you…finished."

The sweating key holder heaved and wheezed as he withdrew a small bunch of keys from his trouser pocket. Separating one from the cluster on the ring, he pushed it into the lock barrel in the door frame. The lock refused to accept the key, and angrily, the key holder yanked it out and ran his banana like fingers along the circle of keys dangling from the ring. Another key, another attempt. Again the lock defied him. The sweat was now running freely down the sides of his neck and a damp ring showed around the collar edge where it bit deeply into his flesh. Alan grimaced as he got a whiff of the sour sweat emanating from the key holder and took a half step to the side.

"Bloody staff these days." he muttered angrily. "If they're not stealing sweets, its cigarettes or letting their boyfriends do drive offs." Again the lock refused him entry.

Alan smiled to himself at the frustration and effort the key holder was expending. It was probably the nearest thing he'd ever had to a workout and as Alan watched his fumbling's, he could not help but notice the vast expanse of his backside and the voluminous rolls of fat belching out over the top of his trousers and wondered somewhat disturbingly, how the man could actually physically manage to wipe his own arse. Alan grimaced as a ghastly image formulating in his mind. 'Fat boy' sat on the toilet trying to get his hand around his copious rolls of fat, the huge apron of his stomach rolling out over this thighs as he reached around to pull the cheeks of his backside apart.

He shuddered as the key holder continued to do battle with the unyielding lock and complain about his staff.

"I provide coffee and tea for them you know, all out of my own pocket. You'd think I'd get a bit of loyalty, but oh no, that's too much to ask." he wheezed. Another key inserted into the lock without success.

"Three mugs broken this week." he ranted.

"Try that one Sir." Alan said, now bored with the man's puerile whining and pointing to a specific key on the ring. "The one that's actually got Yale stamped on it."

"What?" snapped the key holder. "Oh, yes, right."

The key slid home and the door opened. The fat key holder entered the garage premises, closely followed by Alan, who by now had considerable sympathy for all his employees.

"Look at this, see what I mean." wheezed the key holder, as he walked toward the counter; Alan smiled at the dangerously stretched material of the man's trousers as he waddled. He chuckled to himself. As Sullivan, his regular partner would have said. "It looked like two dogs fightin' in a sack."

"The bloody heating's been left on full blast, blatant waste. They wouldn't like it if I docked their wages to pay for the electric, oh no."

"She might have been taken ill or something." Alan said, trying to subdue the apoplectic key holder.

"There's a contingency plan for such an occurrence. No, she'll have pissed off to her party, brains in her knickers that one. Well, she'll have plenty of time for partying from now on, I can tell you."

Alan cocked his head slightly to one side and placed a hand on the man's shoulder, feeling the damp warmth seeping through the material. "Listen." he said.

There was a faint moaning from somewhere within the shop.

"Hear it?" Alan asked softly, pointing towards the rear of the shop.

"Did you hear something?" the key holder asked. His expression of anger changed to a puzzled frown as he crossed the shop floor to a door leading to the rear of the counter area.

Alan followed and as the door was opened. The fat man hesitated, allowing Alan to enter first. "Where's this lead?" Alan asked, pointing up the narrow corridor.

"Er, to my office, why?"

Alan ignored the question and shone his torch up the corridor as he walked cautiously towards the office door.

Alan entered the darkened office and searched with the flat of his hand along the surface of the inner wall for the light switch. As his hand felt across the cool plaster, the torch beam fell on the girl who was still lying on the office floor.

Alan froze. "Jesus fuckin' Christ." he uttered, seeing the tape which bound her and her skirt up around her waist. Alan shouted back to the key holder. "Get the power on…NOW!"

He whirled around to try to find the elusive slight switch with his torch beam. It was already turned on and as the key holder activated the main power switches, the strip light on the ceiling hummed momentarily, flickered, and then flooded the room with light.

Alan dropped his torch and rushed over to the girl who still unsighted, flinched as he approached. He saw her fright. "It's alright love, it's the Police." he said softly.

He knelt at the side of her and carefully taking the hem of her skirt between finger and thumb, pulled it down to cover her nakedness. He pulled gently at the tape which secured the cloth around her eyes, it stuck to her hair and he felt panic for a moment. Not knowing if he should actually be touching her at all, but at the same time, wanting to reassure her that she was now safe.

She squinted and blinked as the light struck her eyes. She was trembling and moaned faintly as her body rocked slowly backwards and forwards. She appeared to be in some form of catatonic trance. Her eyes had a vacant insane glaze, unseeing, even though they were now uncovered.

Alan drew closer to her. The girl arched away from him, her eyes opening wider and she let out a muffled scream as he pulled the tape away from her mouth. The wet ball of cloth spilled out onto the office floor. The key holder appeared at the doorway. Alan heard him gasp.

"Oh my God!"

"Get out." snapped Alan. "And don't touch anything; keep your hands in your pockets."

The key holder had suddenly gone very pale and was swallowing hard as he backed away from the doorway.

"I'll be back in ten seconds love, ok?" Alan said reassuringly.

The girl stared up at Alan, her eyes fixed and staring, as if she were no longer aware of his presence.

Alan darted from the room and ran along the short corridor, cursing himself for leaving his personal radio in his patrol car and having to leave her.

The key holder was leaning against the counter top, his head in his hands, his fingertips sinking into the thick flesh on his forehead.

"The takings...all the bloody lot." he snapped. He reached out to grab the sleeve of Alan's coat as he rushed passed. Alan tore his arm free of the man's grip, ignoring his protestations regarding his financial loss and ran from the shop to where he had left his patroller on the forecourt.

"One Five urgent."

Alan tapped the side of the radio impatiently. "Come on, come on." he whispered. Again, he transmitted "Papa Yankee One Five urgent."

"Go ahead Alan."

Alan took a deep breath. "John, it's genuine at the garage, robbery, possibly a rape, 10/18 ambulance and supervision to the scene. Oh, and try and get hold of the night Detective...and a female Officer."

"10/4." the operator snapped back.

Alan frantically pushed the radio into the front pocket of his jacket and ran back to the shop.

The key-holder was slumped in the threadbare swivel chair behind the counter, his eyes unmoving. Clearly, he was in shock.

"We're not insured for this you know." he said, without looking up. "Can't get insurance without cameras and a floor safe these days. Do you know how much that costs?" he shouted to Alan, who ignored him, running quickly down the corridor and back to the office.

The girl was where he had left her; she had curled herself up into the foetal position and was whimpering softly. Searching the desktop, he found a pair of scissors and dropping to his knees, Alan put his hand gently under her head.

"It's alright love." he said softly, his hands shaking slightly, as he slid one of the scissor blades between her skin and the tape which was still dangling like a hideous snake around her neck.

Cutting through the tape, he pulled it gently away, taking hold of strands of her hair before pulling the tape away.

She started to weep freely as Alan held her; he gently moved her into a sitting position and reached behind her to cut the tape which bound her wrists. Pulling it away, he noticed that her hands had turned a deep shade of purplish blue where the circulation had been stemmed. Alan talked to her, not knowing the right things to say, but just so that she could hear a voice, any voice, a comfort Alan hoped.

She held her blouse front together to cover her breasts once her hands were free. Alan carefully placed the stretched and crinkled tape on the table top, noting the shiny surface of the adhesive tape, muttering "Prints" to himself.

"The ambulance will be here in no time, nothing to worry about now." Alan said, feeling useless and almost ashamed to be a male in her presence.

She rocked slowly backwards and forwards, emitting long sorrowful moans, as if her mind had gone. Her fingers gripped

Alan's jacket sleeve tightly and she stared, unblinking across toward the office door. Her legs flailed wildly across the surface of the floor as if she was trying to get to her feet to escape some terrible thing which only she could see.

Alan silently cursed the time for passing so slowly, but at last, after what seemed to be an eternity, he heard voices in the shop area and footsteps running along the short corridor. Two ambulance men appeared in the doorway to the office. Alan acknowledged their presence, then nodded toward the crumpled tape which still lay on the desktop and pointed to the torn briefs in the corner of the office.

The first of the ambulance crew paused for a second, then said "Yeah, we know mate, your Control Room told us." He turned to his colleague. "David, get a blanket round her, I'll get a lifter."

The second ambulance man draped a deep blue blanket around the girl's shoulders. She was shivering violently and Alan doubted that it was entirely from the cold.

Leaving the girl with the ambulance man, Alan left the office and as he walked down the corridor to the shop area, he updated the radio operator. The second ambulance man re-entered the shop carrying an aluminium folding chair.

Alan leaned against the cold wall of the garage shop and spoke quietly into his radio. He could see the blue flashing lights of approaching Police vehicles, and he watched as the girl was carried out from the office, through the shop area and out across the forecourt toward the rear of the ambulance, the blanket still draped around her shoulders.

He realised that he was shivering and all of a sudden, he was desperate for a cigarette. He paused for a moment as he watched the girl being lifted into the back of the ambulance. He shivered again in the damp mist and tried to imagine the horror that she had endured.

A Police vehicle skidded to a halt on the forecourt and Alan was thankful to see the shift Sergeant accompanied by a female

Officer, as they alighted from the vehicle. The Policewoman went directly to the ambulance, where the crew was helping the girl into one of the side beds and covering her with a blanket.

"Sarah, keep a written note of anything she says." the Sergeant called out to the Policewoman as she scrambled into the back of the ambulance. The young Policewoman looked back and nodded as the doors were closed.

"Right Alan. What's the score?" the Sergeant asked, as Alan shrugged himself away from the coldness of the shop wall. He held his hand up as Alan was about to reply and keyed the transmitter on his radio. "John, inform the Inspector that the ambulance is 10/6 and get me some more units down here to secure the area. Where's the night D.C.?"

"Received Sarge. Paul Dobson's aware, he's en route."

Alan then quickly briefed the Sergeant on what he had found. He nodded towards the shop interior and to where the fat key holder was still seated behind the counter. The Sergeant looked directly at Alan. "You ok Al. You look a bit peeky?"

"Yeah, I'm fine, thanks Sarge." Alan replied, nodding. "Jabba the Hutt there's in a bit of a fuckin' state though." he said, indicating toward the counter area.

"Get the 'circus' organised Alan and make a note as to who comes in and out."

The Sergeant walked into the shop area and approached the key holder who looked in worse shape mentally, than the girl recently removed from his premises. Perhaps, because of all his previously unwarranted accusations, or just with the shock of it all. A violent, vicious occurrence had entered his secure, organised life and he simply didn't know how to cope with it.

An unmarked Vauxhall Cavalier pulled up to a halt on the forecourt and Alan recognised the driver as the night Detective. The Shift Inspector sat at his side. Alan thumbed his transmit button. "Papa Yankee One Five." There was a short pause before the operator replied.

"John. We'll want Studio up here ASAP, can you get it organised?"

"10/4 Alan, has the Boss turned up yet?"

"He's just arrived with the night D.C." Alan replied.

"Let him know that Sarah Mills is at the hospital with the victim. He'll need to authorise her overtime, she's due off at six."

"10/4" Alan replied and released the transmit button.

"Morning Sir." Alan said as the Inspector walked across the forecourt.

"Where is your head dress Pendle?" were the first and only words from the Inspector's mouth.

"Well, Sir...I..." Alan replied to no one as the shift Inspector brushed briskly past him to enter the shop area.

Alan realised that the Inspector was wearing his cap and had probably expected a salute. He had no doubt noted, that Alan's white topped cap was resting on the dashboard of his patrol car.

The night D.C. chuckled, as he joined Alan at the shop frontage. "Fucked up again, eh Al?" he said.

Alan nodded resignedly and surveyed the night Detective. His suit was crumpled and looked as if it had been slept in, which, mused Alan, was probably not far off the mark, noting his tousled hair and bloodshot eyes.

"What's the score then?" he asked, breathing beer laden fumes into Alan's face.

Alan grimaced and stepped back a pace. He explained what he had found on his arrival and what he had done in the first instance. "I touched the tape getting it off her, but only at the edges, I've got Studio en route, the victim's away to the Infirmary. Sarah Mills is sitting with her."

The Detective nodded sombrely. "Is it a rape then Al?"

"Looks like it to me." Alan replied, scratching at the side of his head. "Her blouse had been ripped open, skiddies torn off and chucked to the other side of the office, an' she's had a beating. I haven't actually crawled around looking for splotches of jizz on the lino, that's your job, but even as a shiny arsed petrol waster, I'd say it's a fair bet."

"Who's the victim?"

"I haven't a clue to be honest, not one of my regular tea spots. She looked to be eighteen, maybe twenty, white, good looker…"

The Detective looked across the forecourt and into the shop area. "No Video?"

"Fuck all. No wonder it got screwed."

The night D.C. raised an eyebrow.

"You know what I mean." replied Alan, suddenly realising that his choice of words had been clumsy. "You'd think that this prick." Alan said, nodding towards the key holder, "Would at least have a night pay window fitted so she didn't have to rely on customers coming into the shop. I mean, who wouldn't have video fitted these days. Petrol at £1.60 a gallon, he must 'ave ten 'drive offs' a week." Alan suddenly realised that he had been raising his voice and paused. "Her employer's with the Boss." Alan said, looking back to the counter area where the key holder was now throwing empty canvas money bags across the shop area, as he continued to rant.

"All he cares about is the money. He couldn't give a fuck about her, callous bastard."

The night D.C. put his hand on Alan's shoulder. "Go an' 'ave a smoke mate, calm yourself down a bit. Do me a quick statement about your time of arrival an' what you saw, what you did, touched etc, the usual." Alan nodded and walked back across the forecourt to where he had abandoned his patrol car.

"Pendle." the Inspector called out, Alan stopped in his tracks.

"Take Mr Papadopoulos back to the station. Organise a witness statement and make sure he gets some tea, he's in shock. Get full details of the victim, name, age, address, what time she started, names of any of her boyfriends, you know the drill."

The fat key holder nudged the Inspector and whispered something. "Oh yes...and the amount missing Pendle, takings and what have you."

"Sir." replied Alan.

"And see if that AA man is still about, we'll want to talk to him."

"Sir." replied Alan, wishing he had the balls to say "Stick a brush up my arse and I'll sweep the fuckin' forecourt as well if you like."

The key holder squeezed himself through the shop door aperture and waddled across the forecourt to where Alan, standing by his patroller, was holding the rear passenger door open. The key holder looked in dismay at the space available in the rear of the SD1.

"It'd be better if I got in the front Officer." he said, wiping at the sweat on his brow with his shirt sleeve.

"Insurance." Alan said dryly, opening the door further and nodding towards the rear seats. "Passengers have to be transported in the rear. We wouldn't want you suing us under health and safety. You know...for reckless negligence...if anything were to 'appen."

Alan stared directly into the key holder's eyes, accusingly and with just a hint of sarcasm. Not enough to substantiate a Public complaint, just enough to let the key holder know, that Alan held him partially responsible for what had happened here tonight.

As Alan drove away from the forecourt, the rear nearside of his Rover now noticeably lower than usual, the wheels of the detecting machine groaned, shuddered and started to turn, slowly, but with determination.

The girl's clothing was carefully and separately wrapped in brown paper. Each article in its own wrapping, to prevent any cross contamination prior to it being sent to Forensic. Her fingernails would be pared, again over brown paper and tested for skin fragments. Her ordeal was far from over. Vaginal swabs, pubic combing, photographs and examinations were about all she could look forward to for the next eight hours, then, if she was fit for interview, a protracted witness statement and questioning by Detectives.

The girl would only remember that her attacker was black, wearing a dark jacket and jeans and that his breath smelled.

'Midnight' slept peacefully and deeply. His outstretched hand lay across the piles of notes and coins which he had scattered across the blanket on his bed.

## **Ten**

Alan sat in the Traffic office and stared at the typewriter which sat on the desk in front of him, a sheet of blank paper wrapped around the roller. His pocket note book lay open, inviting the entry of the night's events. It was almost five o'clock, the early turn crew would be in before six and he had a statement to do regarding the garage job before he went home.

The radiator behind him ticked as it expanded with the growing heat, the station warming itself for the nine to fivers.

Alan felt drained and fatigued; he found it difficult to concentrate on either his book or the statement. He reached into his jacket pocket and pulled out his cigarettes.

He leaned back in the chair, tilting it onto its rear legs so that the backrest touched the radiator. The heat slowly seeped through the padding and into the small of his back.

Inhaling deeply, he slowly blew out the blue grey smoke. He looked around the office at the uniform jackets and the high visibility fluorescent jackets hung in rows along the opposite wall, each with a flat cap, adorned with its white cover, resting on the hook.

His eyes reluctantly returned to the typewriter and he allowed the chair to fall back onto all fours and his fingers stiffly jabbed against the plastic keys and he commenced his statement.

A notice in the Sergeant's 'IN' tray caught his eye. Alan reached across the desk for it and read through the typed script. It was a report regarding the suitability of the Traffic 'Aide'.

Pc Barnett. An Officer taken from normal beat duties and taught the preliminaries of the system of car control and traffic law for three months, to assess whether he was suitable for the Department.

If acceptable, he'd start the long haul through intensive advanced driving tuition and the Road Traffic Act, hazardous chemicals and movement orders, special types and heavy goods vehicles driver's hours and records. There were all the drink driving statutes to learn, along with the thousands of offences which the motoring public inadvertently commits against heights, widths and lengths, speed limits and driving licence types. All this, prior to any recommendation by his Tutor, that was ready to attend at the Police Driving School for an intensive four week course on Traffic Law.

If during the final exam the 'Aide' attained 86% or more, he would go straight to the Advanced Driving Course to hone his skills on the skid pan, pursuit training and commentary. If he failed in any one of the academic or practical subjects, or didn't show that he was made of the 'right stuff' during high speed pursuits, he would simply be returned to beat duties, his personal file stamped 'Not Suitable'.

Alan read through the Tutor notes within the 'Aide's' personnel file. Police Constable Barnett it would appear, was still weak on his forward observations and showed a tendency towards a lack of concentration during pursuit practice. On the plus side, his Tutor had written that he displayed an excellent grasp of road traffic law, was highly motivated and actively sought a high volume self-generated work. He was popular with the other members of the Department and had a good humoured disposition. Someone else had obviously got hold of the confidential report. Alan smiled as he read the anonymous comment written in pencil under miscellaneous remarks. "Barney fails miserably at roadside sarcasm and doesn't make coffee, he'll never make it."

A gentle rain spattered against the office window. Alan turned in his seat and looked out at the street lights on the main road. The yellow glow from the overhead shrouds was distorted through the glass as the water ran down in rivulets to the window ledge.

"Roll on bloody summer." Alan sighed and returned his concentration to the typewriter, noting disappointedly, that his cigarette had burned completely down to the filter where it had rested in the glass ashtray.

He picked up the report on Police Constable Barnett and slipped it back into the Sergeant's tray and wondered how the new boy would feel, coming into the closely knit Traffic Department as a newcomer. He would be made welcome enough, he supposed, but the lads would be sceptical until he had proved himself, not just with his driving, but whether he could be trusted. Would he back you up if the evidence was a bit 'thin'? The first few weeks were nearly always a bit of a drama. Alan was aware of a warm, comfortable euphoria sweeping over him, his eyes became heavy, too heavy to support…Perhaps just a moment or two.

*****

Late July 1975, Alan had arrived for his first day as a Police Officer at the small Police station on Broughton Road with a slight feeling of foreboding, which he considered was natural enough. The nervous fluttering in his stomach was coupled with a liberal dash of excitement and an unswerving and distinct picture of what was lawful and was not. He was eager to take up his duties in the Office of Constable.

The station itself was a Victorian stone built detached house. It was situated on the outskirts of the town and had been purchased by the Police Authority from the local Church Authority who had for many years, used the large residence as a Manse for the local Minister.

The parish had been dissolved and the house had lain empty until converted into the Town's local station, when the population had grown to a sufficient level to warrant a Sub Division within its own boundaries. It had been hacked about a little on the inside, but maintained much of its Victorian charm.

What must have originally been the drawing room, with its high ornate ceilings and delicately carved covings along with a vast open fireplace, were the first things that Alan had noticed when the office man had shown him into the room.

He was told to wait to see the Chief Inspector. The office clerk, who Alan noticed with some amusement, was wearing a pair of worn carpet slippers and an open necked shirt, told him to hang around and amuse himself until the Chief Inspector was ready to see him.

"I'll try and organise a pot of tea if Vera's about. The Boss won't be long."

"Cheers." said Alan, sitting down in one of the two high backed chairs which sat at an angle facing the open fire.

As he looked around the room, he found it hard to believe that this was the seat of law enforcement for the whole Town. A large oval wooden table, delicately inlaid with marquetry around its outer edge, faced the single casement window. Four chairs were evenly spaced around its somewhat scarred surface. The chairs were of the same high back design and ornately covered with tapestry, the design of which was distinctly ecclesiastical and Alan guessed that they had been inherited from the previous owners.

The statutory portrait of the Queen, hung serenely within a heavy and ornate gilt frame in the center of the fire breast. The walls were adorned with a few faded sepia photographs of the Town as it had been prior to the Great War.

Alan reached out to run his fingers over the wallpaper which appeared to be some sort of fabric. He guessed it was silk and touching the smooth texture, confirmed his suspicions.

All the contents of the room, the furniture, carpet and light fittings seemed somehow to be from some bygone age, not the trappings of the modern Police force that he had expected. It reminded him of a stage lay out for a Dickensian play, where scrupulous detail had been adhered to.

Other than the portrait of the present Monarch and the electric light fittings, they'd managed pretty well.

He was debating whether to light a cigarette when the door swung open and Alan involuntarily stood up. A man approached him, his right hand outstretched, proffering a shake. Alan took the man's hand, which was pumped vigorously.

"Constable Pendle no doubt." the man beamed.

"Er, yes, Sir." replied Alan, not quite sure who he was talking to.

"Chief Inspector Welton. How are you?"

Alan snapped to attention and pushed his chest out, staring straight ahead.

"Very well Sir, thank you."

The man appeared to be in his late fifties perhaps, with large soft cheek jowls which hung to his chin line. His skin was shiny and the evidence of fine capillary lines on his cheeks gave his face a cheery glow. He had the persona of a self-neglecting professor. Huge black eyebrows sprouted wildly over his soft brown eyes, the hairs unkempt and falling over his upper lids, twitching as he blinked.

"Oh sit you down lad, sit down, we don't go in for much of that sort of thing here."

He waved Alan towards one of the seats and looked quite excited with himself as he crossed over to the fireplace and leant his elbow against the mantle.

"Fresh from the factory, eh?" he nodded, as he banged his pipe bowl haphazardly against the Adams style fire surround. He pointed to the medal ribbon over the left pocket of Alan's tunic. "Military man, eh?...Good, good…Ireland?"

"Yes Sir." Alan replied.

As the Chief Inspector dropped into one of the chairs opposite and stretched his legs out in front of him, Alan was unable to help noticing that he too wore faded tartan carpet slippers.

The fire roared up the massive expanse of the soot covered fire back and they were both bathed in the warmth of its cherry glow. From a pocket in the stretched and threadbare dark blue cardigan he wore, the old man took a cracked leather pouch. Without taking his eyes from Alan, he began to fill the bowl of his pipe from the contents.

He beamed across at Alan. "Tell me about yourself then lad."

Alan stuttered as he began.

The Chief Inspector eased himself down further into the chair and crossed his hands over his ample stomach and puffed contentedly on the stem of his pipe, nodding every now and then, when Alan mentioned something of interest.

The door opened and Alan stopped in mid speech. A lady entered carrying a tray, on which was two mugs of steaming liquid. She smiled at Alan as she carefully placed the tray onto a small bow legged table which she drew up towards the fire. The Chief Inspector glanced down at the tray. "Any biscuits Vera?" he asked, looking up hopefully. The lady looked down at him. "I'm sorry Mr Welton, but no. Your Wife says you're not to have them." she wagged a finger at him as if scolding him for asking. The old man's face dropped and his eyebrows knitted themselves together as he frowned disappointedly.

"Ah well." he sighed, as if resigned to the fact that he must do as he was told.

He perked up after a second. "Vera, this is Pringle, new lad." he beamed again, the lack of biscuits and the scolding now apparently forgotten.

"Er, it's Pendle Sir." said Alan as he stood to shake the ladies hand. She smiled warmly. The old man winked up at her and sucked on his pipe.

"She's as good as gold is our Vera, wouldn't know what to do without her. Bit tight with the biscuits mind." the old man chuckled.

Vera left the room, giving the old man a stern but friendly smile. The old man winked and chuckled to himself. He nodded as if remembering some long ago tryst with the Lady Vera as he stared into the flames, oblivious for a brief moment to Alan's presence. Then, as if suddenly remembering the purpose of the meeting, he focused and said "Now, where were we?"

Alan continued with his antecedents and lowered his voice as he noticed that the Chief Inspector's head had started to nod. The smouldering bowl of his pipe fell gently onto his chest as his eyelids first drooped and then closed. Alan stopped talking and watched as the old man napped. The logs, crackling and hissing in the grate, now the only sound in the room.

The pipe fell suddenly from his mouth and dropped to the carpet. Alan dived for it as the old man snorted, his eyes opened quickly and his hand came up to brush away the glowing particles of ash which had fallen onto the front of his cardigan.

"And that's about it Sir." said Alan, as if nothing had happened. He handed over the pipe to the old man, who didn't seem the slightest bit embarrassed. He simply took it with a nod of thanks and placed the worn stem back in between his teeth. He looked down at the front of his cardigan, brushing it again with the back of his hand, the fresh scorch marks mingling with the old, which Alan took as evidence of previous daytime naps.

"Other than I'm pleased to be here Sir." Alan added quickly, reminding the Chief Inspector of the general drift of their conversation, prior to Morpheus interrupting his flow.

"And we are glad to have you lad." The old man said and smiled, lighting his pipe again. "We're a small sub Division, quiet, perhaps a little too quiet for you, being naturally keen and excited to get on with the job. We like to get on with people, you know, help each other. You'll do just as much good here, being friendly and helpful to the members of our small community as you would kicking backsides all day in the City." He paused and drew on his pipe as if deep in thought. Alan fully expected his head to start its slow but inexorable descent to his chest again. The old man had after all, been fully awake for well over five minutes now.

"We have our own way of doing things here you see Son." He stood up and turned his back to the fire, reminding Alan of everyone's favourite Grandfather.

"I've no doubt you'll be full of powers of arrest and arrestable offences and the like, keen to get on with it, as well you should be." he paused. "But take your time, listen to what your Tutor Sergeant and Constable tells you. Be guided by them, you'll have no trouble settling down with us, I'm sure."

The old man nodded and smiled.

"Thank you Sir." Alan said, not quite sure if the interview was now over.

A pregnant silence followed and Alan looked around the room as the old man rocked on his heels and stared down at the carpet.

"Cricketer are you Brindle?"

Alan let the Chief Inspector's short term memory loss slide. "Er, I did a bit at school Sir, but just lately…"

"Oh, we'll soon change that. Good team here, good team." he winked as if letting out some well-kept secret. "Always short of new blood though."

Alan watched the old man stare upwards towards the ornate plasterwork in the center of the ceiling. He clenched his pipe stem between his teeth as he continued to rock slowly, probably reminiscing about the Divisional cricket team that had toured the County just prior to its members being called up for the Crimean war.

Alan sipped at his coffee, fully expecting Vera to re-enter to remind the Chief Inspector that it was time for his afternoon nap. He was in truth, slightly disappointed, laid back was one thing, but this place was virtually comatose.

"Yes, we had an exceptionally good team last year." the old man continued. "Best ever some reckon. Lost Morrison though, good left arm bowler, Traffic man, got promoted, moved on, you know."

The old man clicked his tongue against his teeth and slowly shook his head, as if Morrison (whoever he was) had been lost over the Channel on his return from a night bombing raid.

"Never mind." the old man suddenly brightened. "We'll see eh?"

"Yes Sir." Alan nodded.

"Digs alright are they?"

"Oh yes Sir, fine thanks. I can walk to work, they're only across the park, its qui..."

"Good, good." The old man cut him off, holding out his hand again. The interview was clearly over. Alan stood up and took the soft hand.

"My door is always open, that sort of thing. Anyway, I must get on."

"Thank you Sir." said Alan, wondering what on earth the old man could possibly have to get on with. Pruning the roses in the station garden, or a bit of model making in his office perhaps.

Alan smiled to himself as the old man shuffled out of the room.

Finishing his coffee, Alan wandered round the old house, noting the small C.I.D. office and the equally small charge room.

He entered what he took to be the canteen. A small Baby Belling stood on top of a metal cabinet, the white enamel of its doors chipped and discoloured with age. There were two Officers in the canteen and Alan introduced himself and hands were shaken.

"Met the Boss yet 'ave you?" asked one.

"Yes, just a minute or so ago." Alan replied, wondering what the two were smiling about.

"Fall asleep did he?" asked the older of the two, the other bursting into laughter.

Alan smiled. "As a matter of fact, he did, yes."

"Has a habit of doing that has our mister Welton. Did it in Court once, halfway through prosecuting a double yellow liner, Magistrate adjourned until he woke up."

Alan laughed, imagining the scene.

"He's a bit eccentric is our Harry, but he's as sound as a pound, as long as you don't make waves."

The other nodded in agreement. "You'll find they're not too keen on arrests here, 'specially on nights…Alan isn't it?"

Alan nodded.

"It means getting a Sergeant to come in. They only work days here see. If it's after four o'clock, it's a callout job to open up the cell area and do the custody record. Stick to tax discs and the odd double yellow lines offence and you'll do alright."

Alan nodded at the advice and looked out of the canteen window to the yard at the back of the station house.

Two grey Mini Vans were parked up at the top corner and dwarfing them, a gleaming white Ford Consul with red striping along its sides. A single blue light sat in the center of the roof and twin radio aerials raked back at a sporty angle. There was also an old ex-Army Land Rover, still in its original drab olive livery. The word POLICE had been stencilled along the rear wing in large white letters and the soft canvas top had obviously been recently re-whitened. Alan recognised it as an old series two air-portable, the type he'd used during his first tour in Londonderry, before things had gone from bad to worse.

"That your Traffic car?" Alan asked, nodding out towards the rear yard.

"It is." said the older Officer. "You'll have a spell with us while you're in your probation. Fancy Traffic do you?"

"Give 'im a fuckin' chance Jack, it's 'is first day."

"Got to get 'em indoctrinated to proper policin' young." his colleague added quickly. 'Afore they get snapped up by the piss'eads in C.I.D."

The Traffic man winked at Alan as he turned to the table top and started to pack up his Tupperware box and flask.

"Looks like senior Officer material to me." his partner said. "We'll be salutin' 'im in five years." he said, smiling as he pulled on his bright orange jacket.

Alan smiled and decided that he liked these two. He was envious of their partnership and the easy manner they seemed to have with each other.

"Right, we're off...motorin' public to persecute, see you later. Alan wasn't it?"

"Yes, Alan...Pendle...See you later."

The two disappeared from the canteen and Alan watched as they entered the rear yard, jostling each other as they seated themselves in the gleaming Consul.

Apart from the fact that there didn't seem to be much going on, he decided that he would probably enjoy his time at Broughton Road.

What was left of the summer months, Alan spent in company with his Tutor Constable. They talked constantly as they walked each foot beat around the Town center, the older Officer constantly holding him back when he walked too quickly.

"Slow down Alan, you'll be knackered by the end of your shift. Nice steady pace, give folks a chance to see you."

Alan listened, constantly asking questions, soaking up his Tutors responses and storing them for future use. He was proud of his uniform which he kept immaculately pressed. His boots, he still spit shined until they glistened in the sunshine as they walked, his Tutor pointing out this shop, or that office where they were always welcome for a cup of coffee. "As long as you don't tear the arse out of it."

Alan nodded, noting the peculiar expression used by Policemen to describe outstaying your welcome.

It was a country Town, steeped in traditions of farming and local crafts, with a little light industry thrown in. The people seemed to be naturally friendly and not a bit suspicious of the Police, offering information freely, in the knowledge that they also had to play their part in the quiet running of the Town. The Queens peace had never been so easily kept.

Tourists abounded. They came to see the castle, built at the end of the first millennium and seated high up on a grassed mound at the head of the High Street. They were mostly Americans who couldn't wait to shake hands and have their photograph taken with a real English 'Bobbie' and Swedes and Germans who just wanted to wear a British Policeman's helmet.

There was a market held each Wednesday during the summer. The local tradesmen erected stands on the cobbled area to each side of the main road. Brightly coloured canvas awnings flapped gaily in the warm breeze. Alan and his Tutor would stand on the pavement and watch the world go by. "It's amazing to consider that we're actually getting paid for doing this isn't it?" Alan said as he smiled at a young Chinese girl, a camera slung around her neck. As she slinked past them, her head turned to look back seductively as she passed.

His Tutor nodded in agreement. "One thousand eight hundred a year, just to stand here smiling at the tourists. I should say so."

"Be different working nights in winter I imagine." Alan said.

His Tutor looked surprised. "If you actually find yourself standing on the High Street, cold and wet in the middle of the night in winter, then I clearly haven't tutored you properly." he replied, looking knowingly at Alan and inviting a response.

"Ah yes, sorry. I forgot about the Bewerley Hotel, the signal box at the railway crossing and who could forget your lurid tales regarding the very sporting Mrs Evans of Bridge End Road, whose Husband works permanent nights." Alan replied and laughed.

"You might laugh Pendle lad, but I guarantee that in ten or twelve years' time, you will be giving the same advice to some young 'Proby'."

"How old will Mrs. Evans be by then?" Alan asked, smirking.

The warm days dragged gloriously by. Alan, now out on his own, walked the High Street and mingled with the locals, the sun hot on his back through his tunic as he enjoyed the hustle and bustle of the various street incidents.

His 'Pye' radio hissed. "Where are you Alan?"

Alan pulled the light blue radio transmitter from the top pocket of his tunic and pushed the small transmit button on the side. The small aerial automatically extended. "High Street, by the cenotaph." Alan replied.

"Hang on there. Sergeant Deal wants you."

Alan was curious, it was rare that the Sergeant called on him, unless it was to pick him up to go in for his meal, accompanied by the statutory game of dominoes which Alan detested, but knew that his Sergeant loved. The loss of ten pence a day wasn't so bad, it was the ignominy of constant failure that made it hard to bear.

Alan walked out across the cobbles and to the kerb edge of the High Street and a few moments later, he saw the battered Land Rover bouncing up towards him.

"What's up Sarge?" he asked as the Sergeant opened the passenger door.

Sergeant Deal had a wry smile on his face. "Get in lad." he chuckled, causing small sparks to fly up from the bowl of his pipe which was the constant companion to the veteran Sergeant.

Alan glanced down to see whether he was wearing carpet slippers. Pipe and slippers seemed to be a requisite of working at Broughton Road. Alan had not yet acquired either.

"Job on at the Abbey." he chuckled. "Just up your street."

The Land Rover lurched forwards, throwing Alan back in his seat. Sergeant Deal continued to laugh, causing Alan to smile with the infectious mirth which filled the cab.

"Nude bathers." the Sergeant guffawed, his face now turning an unhealthy shade of red.

"Nude bathers Sarge?"

"Nude bathers lad, heinous offence and an affront to the decency of the blue rinse set of Broughton." The Sergeant laughed, as he gave a cursory glance to the right and entered the roundabout at the top of the High Street, totally heedless of an oncoming vehicle which braked harshly to avoid the bouncing Land Rover.

The driver of the vehicle screeched to a halt on the roundabout, narrowly avoiding a collision. He threw up his hands in disbelief at the cheery wave from the Sergeant as the Land Rover continued round the roundabout.

Sergeant Deal's driving, was historically the cause for much concern amongst the local inhabitants of Broughton, although no actual complaints had ever been officially lodged. He loved the old Land Rover and would not be seen driving anything else. He just didn't seem to have any concept of the system of car control or hazard perception as he hurtled through the streets of the Town. Whilst the locals dived for cover in shop doorways and side streets, fists would be raised, only to be greeted by a cheery wave from the oblivious Sergeant, as he smoked his omnipresent pipe and tapped his fingers on the steering wheel, to the strains of the radio which he had fitted surreptitiously. Sergeant Deal still bemoaned the fate of the 'Light Programme' but was getting quite used to Radio One; fortunately, he was also quite hard of hearing and normally had the radio on full volume, which at least gave the locals some warning as to his approach.

The ancient Land Rover lurched and bounced its way out of the Town toward the local beauty spot, a medieval Abbey situated by a slow running river where people flocked in their hundreds to sun bathe and picnic and take the kids for a paddle in the safe shallow waters.

"How many bathers are we talking about Sarge?"

"Oooooh 'undreds lad." the Sergeant laughed, clenching the stem of his pipe between his teeth.

"We 'ad a phone call from a very irate member of the Public. She says there's men and women engaged in naked debauchery and public copulation on the river bank and as 'ow it was frightening 'er dog."

The Sergeant became helpless with laughter and tears sprang to his eyes. The Land Rover veered alarmingly towards the nearside grass verge and Alan grabbed for the steering wheel.

"I'd quite like to live to see it Sarge…if you don't mind me saying." Alan said, as he glanced at the needle of the speedometer which twitched erratically from side to side, around the sixty miles per hour mark.

"Oh dear me." the Sergeant said, his voice wavering as he regained his composure and wiped away the tears on his cheeks, with the sleeve of his tunic.

"I immediately thought of you for this job Pendle lad. Good experience of 'ow to deal with a delicate situation."

"Thanks Sarge." Alan replied sarcastically, amazed at his Sergeant's apparent utter contempt for human life, as the Land Rover rolled unnervingly around the winding country roads, towards the Abbey.

As they hurtled towards the grounds of the ancient Cistercian Abbey, the Land Rover suddenly left the carriageway, such as it was, and launched itself into an open field between a pair of tall, substantial stone pillars. The Sergeant had either gauged the available width perfectly on this particular occasion, or had driven between the stones previously, thereby knowing at exactly what speed and angle at which they could be approached. The alternative, Alan thought with some concern, was that his Sergeant simply hadn't seen them.

"Jesus Christ Sarge, steady on." Alan gasped, involuntarily squeezing his arms into his sides, as if it would somehow help the vehicle fit between the two monolithic stones.

"That's the trouble with you young lads today, no sense of adventure." Sergeant Deal said, winking as he smiled.

"It's the sense of pain which is my immediate concern Sarge." Alan said, as he was thrown wildly around the cab interior as the vehicle bounced across the rough grassland.

He could see the crowds of people gathered alongside the river bank as they approached the Abbey. It was a hot day and tourists and locals alike were taking full advantage of the glorious weather.

There were a few cheers from the crowd as they spotted the Land Rover approaching, to all intents and purposes, completely out of control as it lurched along the rough embankment at the side of the river.

A few of the locals, recognising the Police Land Rover and suspecting that it was probably being driven by Sergeant Deal, moved away from the river bank, hurriedly gathering up their children, well away from the flight path of the oncoming hazard.

Alan had no difficulty in spotting the complainant. She came scurrying towards them as they approached, which Alan considered to be quite brave under the circumstances. She was elderly, yet approached in a sprightly fashion. She wore rimless glasses and her hair was indeed a pale shade of blue. Her brightly coloured summer dress clashed harshly with the whiteness of a manicured toy poodle which she was clutching to her ample bosom.

The Sergeant stopped the Land Rover and set the handbrake, his one and only concession to the Highway Code.

"Police, police." she panted, as she ran toward the driver's door of the Land Rover. "Thank goodness. It's disgraceful, they're over there." she said, pointing a bony finger toward where the river banking dipped gently down to the water. "Do your duty Sergeant." she said, with the pompous air of a frustrated spinster and again pointed down toward the river. She covered the shivering poodle's eyes with her hand.

"It's quite alright madam." the Sergeant said, placating the woman's ranting, calmly raising his hand. "My Constable will soon have this lot sorted out."

"I should hope so too Sergeant. Lord knows what the world is coming to."

The poodle shivered and whimpered, clearly traumatised by the whole incident.

Alan and his Sergeant ignored the further protestations regarding the state of the world and received more cheers as they walked purposefully down the banking toward the river's edge.

There, lying by the river's edge were three people, two females and a male, naked as the day they were born, basking unashamedly in the sunshine.

A battered acoustic guitar lay by the side of a jumbled heap of clothes. They were obviously 'hippy' types, all three had long unkempt hair, which hung down to their shoulders. The male of the species sported a long straggly beard and a wispy moustache. He was desperately thin and Alan thought he looked like Jesus. His facial hair and uncanny resemblance to the Son of God, however, was not the most distinguishing feature exposed to public view. For a consumptive man of peace, he appeared to be extraordinarily well endowed.

His flaccid penis, the tip of which lay nonchalantly on the short cut grass, was roughly the dimensions of a baby's arm.

Alan looked across to his Sergeant and raised his eyebrows. "Impressive."

Sergeant Deal smiled and whispered through the side of his mouth. "You watch it doesn't turn nasty."

The crowd of people on the opposite bank were now standing and watching intently, their attention focused on the actions of the two brave Officers, who had arrived to restore the tranquillity of the day.

Alan stood transfixed and let his eyes roam from the four perfectly formed breasts to the two mounds of pubic hair exposed to the sunshine for all to see. He tried desperately to resist staring at the ninth wonder of the world, in the form of the anaconda sized penis which emanated from between the male's legs. It reached completely across the width of his stomach, snaked down the side of his leg and the tip actually touched the grass on which 'Jesus' lay.

"Oi!" his Sergeant called out. Alan looked up, tearing his eyes reluctantly away from the resplendent female forms.

"Get on with it then."

"What Sarge?"

"Get 'em sorted out."

"Oh, right Sarge." Alan replied nervously.

Squaring his shoulders, Alan walked towards the three 'hippies' who were either totally unaware of the massive Police presence, or were choosing to ignore it.

"Right, you three, get dressed." Alan said in his most authoritative voice.

One of the females opened an eye and squinted against the glare of the sun.

"Sorry?" she said innocently.

"I said get dressed, all of you."

The 'Son of God' then spake, and he sayeth unto Alan. "What for man? This is natural."

"It might well be natural, but it also happens to be an offence." replied Alan, exposing his trump card and turning to look at his Sergeant who nodded and winked, clearly appreciating Alan's swift summing up of the situation.

The male stood up and exaggerated a stretch, his gargantuan penis now swaying gently in the breeze.

Alan heard the blue rinsed complainant gasp. The poodle yelped alarmingly and even Alan took a half step backwards, just in case.

"Against what man?" asked the Jesus 'lookalike'.

"What?" asked Alan, somewhat taken aback that his authority under the Crown was being challenged.

"What is it an offence against?" asked Jesus, yawning casually and scratching the underside of his testicles.

Alan squared his shoulders at this flagrant show of disrespect, even if it was from the Son of God.

"The Public Order Act of 1936 and indecent exposure under Section 4 of the Vagrancy Act 1824, if you must know. Now get dressed all of you, or I can promise you that you will be finding out all about the said Acts, from first-hand experience."

Alan looked around. His Sergeant was nodding slowly, clearly impressed.

Alan returned his attentions to the male, the smug, self-indulgent smile fading from his face, when he saw that the 'Son of God' had now laid down again and was spread eagled, soaking up the sun.

"I'll ask you one last time." said Alan, now desperately trying to sound as if he meant it, but unable to tear his gaze away from the four tantalizing breasts exposed to the bright sunlight.

"Get on with it then." someone on the far river bank shouted, this being quickly followed by a tirade of cheers as the agitator was applauded.

"Are you going to get dressed or not?" Alan demanded.

A smile crept across the face of the male as one of the girls rolled slowly over onto her side, to face Alan. One of her huge breasts flopped softly onto the grass. She purred with exaggerated seductiveness. "Are you going to manhandle us Officer?"

The other girl giggled and Alan felt himself reddening.

Unperturbed, Alan squared his shoulders. "Right, you leave me no choice. You're none of you obliged to say anything, but anything you do say may be given in evidence. You are all under arrest for conduct likely to cause a breach of the peace."

Sergeant Deal leapt forwards and grasped the man's arm and pulled him bodily from the ground and towards the rear of the Land Rover.

There was no crack of thunder, no deep heavenly voice from above. Sergeant Deal was neither struck by a bolt of lightning nor turned into a pillar of salt and Alan surmised, that as his Sergeant was not being assailed by a plague of frogs or boils, the male could not actually be the second coming and although his nether regions had clearly been touched by a divine hand, he was locked up and that was that.

Alan walked towards the two girls who were giggling. They obviously hadn't grasped the fact that the wheels of law enforcement had begun to grind inexorably forwards. It came home to them as Alan took hold of the first girl's arm and pulled her forcibly to her feet. "Come on, pick up your clothes, you're both nicked." Alan said forcibly, trying desperately to avoid his hand touching any intimate parts of his prisoner's anatomy.

"You pick them up pig." the other girl spat venomously.

"Oh, very original, pig…that's a new one." Alan replied sarcastically, as he led the naked female to the back of the Land Rover.

Sergeant Deal held up the canvas flap above the rear tailgate of the Land Rover and watched as the first girl clambered in over the metal gate to join the male.

Alan looked to his Sergeant and raised his eyebrows, smiling as the girl's buttocks reached head height and as she bent to avoid the roof bars, she fully exposed her most intimate parts not inches away from his face.

The second girl had by this time, collected all their clothes and belongings and approached the Land Rover unassisted; the fun had now gone out of the day.

She looked annoyed and shot the Sergeant a disgusted glance as she moved to the vehicle. "Fascist." she hissed, as she threw the bundle of clothes and the battered guitar over the tailgate.

"Thank you." Sergeant Deal said sarcastically, smiling as she too clambered in over the tailgate.

The cheers now rose from the not inconsiderable crowd which had gathered to see justice done and there was a good deal of clapping and cheering.

The last girl in, pushed her head through the canvas and shouted "Morons." loudly. Her outstretched fist protruded through the gap and a single middle finger was raised in defiance.

Alan tied the canvas flap securing ropes around the cleats on the tailgate and shouted, "Now get your clothes on" to the occupants in the rear.

"Fuck you pig." a female voice snapped from within.

"Nice…Nice." Alan muttered, as he opened the passenger door and got in.

Alan slid open one of the side windows of the cab and lit a cigarette as they left the Abbey and headed back towards the Town.

"Bad for your 'ealth them you know lad." Sergeant Deal said, tutting and shaking his head.

"With respect Sarge, if your driving is anything to go by, my life expectancy is not going to be particularly affected by smoking."

"Cheeky young prat." Sergeant Deal scowled, then smiled. "Bugger all wrong with my driving, forty years now, never 'ad an accident."

"Caused thousands." thought Alan and wondered fleetingly if anyone had ever kept statistics on fail to stop accidents in and around the Broughton area, especially those involving an old olive green Land Rover with a white canvas roof.

The High Street was crowded as usual and Alan had not noticed the laughter at first, nor the clapping. He did wonder though, why the men outside the public houses were holding up their pint glasses and cheering. The laughter increased in volume and Sergeant Deal looked across to Alan, a puzzled expression on his face. "What's going on?"

Alan shook his head and shrugged his shoulders, catching as he did, a glimpse through the rear Perspex window into the rear of the vehicle.

"Oh fuckin' hell Sarge."

The Sergeant looked around and noticed the daylight streaming in through the rear of the Land Rover. "Oh Christ!" he said dejectedly, raising his eyes slowly to the heavens.

The 'hippies' had managed to untie the canvas flap and had rolled it back over the metal roof frame and were now standing, still naked and were waving to the hundreds of people thronging around on the High Street. Tourists in profusion, meant cameras in profusion which in turn, meant photographs, most of which, found their way to the editor of the local Telegraph and Argus, who in turn, printed them up, with discreet blurring around the exposed intimate parts of the females and a very large exclamation mark covering the 'divine one's anaconda sized member.

A copy of the front page of the paper remained pinned up on the noticeboard in the front office of the station, until it yellowed into obscurity.

*****

Alan's first summer at Broughton Road, had been enjoyable and satisfying, long and hot. But all things must pass, and the evenings slowly drew in and it stayed darker for longer on each early turn.

Alan would set off well before six o'clock, walking across the dew soaked grass in the park, on his way to the station. He liked to get into work early to have a coffee and a chat with the night man in the office before his shift started. The old station house was warm and welcoming; the rain beat heavily against the glass panes of the radio room, its ferocity exaggerated by the strong wind which swept in unopposed across the park and hurled the droplets against the window.

"Sooner you than me out in this Alan lad." the radio operator said, as he stood wearily. He leant backwards to stretch his back and rubbed his face with his hands. The large open fire which the night man had kept well fed, roared loudly as the wind pulled the heat violently up the stone flu and dissipated it immediately as it was whipped away and cooled by the rain.

Winter was on its way, and it was historically hard out in the rural area of the Division. Alan hoped that he would soon be given a one day driving assessment, so that he could take one of the plain grey Minivans or Sergeant Deal's beloved Land Rover, to patrol one of the outlying beats. He stretched himself out in front of the fire and watched the steam rising from his damp shoes as he finished his coffee. "I'll be going out in a minute Tom, anything you want?" Alan called over his shoulder to the radio room. The operator shook his head. "No, I don't think there's owt." but then as an afterthought, called back. "Oh, you could fetch us an ounce of 'baccy when you come in for your meal."

Alan walked to the radio room. The radio man reached into his trouser pocket for the money, his teeth clenching the stem of his pipe. Alan saw where it had worn his two front teeth down with the years of constant abrasion and the enamel was stained dark brown.

"How you can smoke that thing at this time of the morning beats me." Alan said, grimacing as the plume of thick blue smoke assailed his nostrils.

"Takes years of practice lad and a good deal of will power. Now piss off out on yer beat and give me some peace."

The old radio man settled back into his chair and opened his paper, crossing his outstretched legs under the table.

There were only a few Officers on a shift at Broughton. Because of annual leave being hurriedly taken before the year end, Group Two at the moment, consisted of Alan and the radio operator. He, having completed over twenty five years of service, was quite happy to let Alan do the street duties, whilst he took care of the monotonous administrative tasks and the radio room.

This arrangement actually suited Alan quite well; he had no desire to remain indoors and was afraid of missing out on a job, as much as the radio operator was clearly afraid of actually having to deal with one.

"See you at meal time Tom." Alan called out, as he left the warmth of the office and opened the front door. Tom as usual, ignored him, in a friendly enough manner Alan supposed.

Tom regarded Alan as an occupational hazard, calling up over the radio for vehicle checks and the like, disturbing his tranquillity and he often made the point that until Alan had at least ten years' service in; he was obtaining his wages under false pretences.

The truth of the matter was, that Alan was becoming quite bored; the jobs just didn't seem to come in.

The Traffic lads seemed to have plenty to do, but as a foot beat Officer, trapped in the Town, there wasn't much on, other than the odd report of dogs worrying sheep and movement of pigs orders to see to and worryingly, Alan was beginning to feel the odd twinge of doubt about his decision to leave the Army.

The wind whipped at the tails of his raincoat and Alan pulled on his leather gloves against the chill of the morning as the rain lashed against his helmet and into his face.

Perhaps old Tom had a point after all he thought. The streets were as yet deserted and Alan steadily made his way to the far side of the Town.

The sky started to brighten a little as he left the High Street and the rain petered out to a fine drizzle by the time he had reached the bus terminus.

The air smelled fresh and clean and Alan breathed in deeply, easing his pace as the road took on a slight incline out of the valley in which the Town sat.

Grey, stone built houses bordered each side of the road. Well-kept gardens to the front were separated from the pavements by small stone walls and wrought iron gates provided access up the paths to the front doors. The roofs of the houses glistened darkly, where moss and lichen deposits had coated the Yorkshire slate slabs over the years. The rims of the red pots on top of the chimney stacks were blackened from coal fires and the grey smoke was whipped quickly away in the wind.

Alan shivered against the cold. Dampness from the earlier rain now passing through the seams of his heavy raincoat and into the material of his tunic.

He looked at each of the three storey houses as he made his way up the hill and just as he reached the brow, he saw a woman watching him from where she stood by a downstairs window. She was cupping a mug of something between her hands and her eyes followed him as he walked.

Alan raised an arm and waved politely and in response. He saw the woman smile and raise her mug so that Alan could see it.

She first pointed to the mug and then to Alan, who fleetingly wondered if she was making the analogy between Alan out walking in the cold and rain, and the receptacle from which she was drinking.

With a motion of her hand, she motioned Alan to make his way to the side of the house and she held up the mug again before disappearing from the window.

Alan hesitated for a second, not quite sure of the woman's visual instructions and wondered as he walked up the flagged pathway to the house, if he had totally misconstrued her meaning. She could well have been telling him to piss off from the front of her house, as he was spoiling her view as she drank her morning coffee. However, full of resolve and not a little curiosity, Alan walked under the stone archway which separated the woman's house from that of her neighbour, not quite knowing why he was going, but going anyway.

The tunnel under the archway opened out to a large back garden which served both the houses, but was separated into two sections by a tall wooden paling fence which offered privacy to each of the rear gardens.

Alan approached the rear door of the house and it was opened as soon as his shadow fell across the upper glass panel. Warmth flooded out from the house and the woman beckoned him inside. "You lookin' wet through." she said, motioning him to step inside. Alan carefully wiped his feet on the coconut fibre doormat, before entering the kitchen.

She closed the door behind him, scurried over to the work surface and plugged in an electric kettle.

"Yes, it's a bit rough out there this morning." Alan replied, casually glancing around the kitchen.

"Nice cuppa warm you up eh." she said and turned to face him as she leaned back against the Formica topped work surface.

She saw that he was still standing and rushed across to a small glass topped table and pulled a chair out from between its chromium plated legs.

"Sit, sit." She beckoned towards the chair. "I make you coffee, jussa moment eh, for water to boil up."

Alan took off his soaking helmet and placed it on the table top, taking a seat on the offered chair, feeling slightly uncomfortable, but for no reason that readily came to mind.

The woman had a strong Italian accent. She was small, Alan guessed about five one or two, but with large breasts, which seemed to be struggling to free themselves from the constraints of her blouse. She was perhaps in her late thirties or very early forties, slightly overweight, but in a voluptuous way he thought, as his eyes flitted discreetly from her breasts to her waistline.

She had well-formed legs with muscular calves which were accentuated by a tightly fitting short skirt and high heeled shoes. Her hair was a veritable waterfall of glossy black curls, which fell to her shoulders, characteristic of the Mediterranean female; it was tinged with electric blue as the light caught it.

Alan felt a little uncomfortable and the kettle seemed to be taking an age to boil. Perhaps if he stopped watching it he mused.

"You from Broughton eh?" she asked, seating herself next to him.

"Er, yes. I've only been here a few months, just joined you know."

She nodded and seemed to be searching his face for something.

"You bin busy?"

"No, it's too early yet; another hour or so, perhaps a job will come in." Alan replied, trying to keep the somewhat strained conversation alive.

The kettle intervened and clicked off noisily. She leapt to her feet and as she attended to making him a drink, Alan's eyes swept up her legs and the shape of her backside. He could just make out the outline of her briefs beneath the tight material of her skirt and he looked away quickly as she turned with his coffee, noticing that as he took it from her, he was having difficulty in keeping his hands steady. He gripped the mug between both hands as he sipped the hot liquid.

They swapped names and pleasantries. Alan told her about his time in the Army before the Police and she explained how she had come to England from Italy some twenty years previous to marry her English Husband, who worked at the local cotton and yarn mill, on the small industrial estate on the outskirts of the Town.

Alan glanced at his watch and realised that he had been with her for almost an hour; he took a last sip of his coffee, which had now gone cold and stood up as if to leave. She looked out of the window at the rain which was now lashing down again.

"You wanna somethin' to eat eh Alan?" she said quickly, as if trying to entice him to stay a little longer.

"No, thanks very much, I'll have to be off, thanks for the coffee though, very welcome." Alan said, squaring his damp helmet back on his head.

"Any mornin' you passin', you know, call in eh?" she said innocently, as she leaned back against the sink unit, her breasts straining against the material of her blouse.

Alan tried not to look, but couldn't help but notice her raised nipples. It had suddenly either got a lot colder in the kitchen or she was excited.

Alan on the other hand, had left ninety eight point six well behind and he could feel his ears glowing and the uncontrollable beginnings of an erection.

The situation had trouble written all over it, but Alan was suddenly suffering from a severe reduction of his cognitive skills. "Leave, leave now, immediately this instant, thank her for the coffee and fuck off. Do *not* allow this situation to progress." his conscience screamed at him.

But she was sex on a stick and it is a well-known adage that a raised cock has little or no conscience.

The 'Italian job' oozed sensuality. She was clearly sending him a message, which couldn't have been more obvious if she'd handed him a note saying 'I'm yours if you want me'.

Her burning, pent up, unfulfilled sexual desires were dangled before him and in a moment of weakness, Alan gulped down the bait.

He laughed nervously. "Oh, I'm sure your Husband would love that."

She immediately adopted a distasteful expression at the mention of her Husband, as if someone had just farted in her mouth. "He's out alla day, froma six in a mornin' you know, he work alla day at the mill, you come for coffee Alan eh?"

Alan's mouth was suddenly very dry and he was having difficulty in swallowing. He walked past her, turning slightly away to the side in the hope that she would not notice his raging erection and opened the kitchen door.

"I'll see you then, thanks again for the coffee."

Their eyes met, and in that fatal gaze, Alan instantly knew what was on offer.

"Ok," she smiled. "I watch for you, lika today eh?"

Alan smiled back and walked out into the driving rain. As he turned briefly to wave, she was standing by the door, wistfully watching him leave.

Walking back in towards the Town, Alan's mind raced. She was good looking right enough and she had gone to great lengths to let him know that she and her Husband didn't get on. But he knew that he was on thin ice.

His conscience nagged at him. "Women, money and property." The Sergeants had constantly told them during training. "They are source of all grief and the downfall of many a good Officer, stay clear of the former and dutifully record the latter."

He told himself that it had been innocent enough. "I only had a cup of coffee for Christ's sake." but his stomach churned and as much as he told himself that he would purposefully steer clear of her house, he knew that the next day, he would find himself there and looking up to her window.

The next morning, Alan was awake at four thirty and into the shower. He shaved closely and applied more aftershave than normal for a working day, telling himself that he was a being a pillock, but doing it anyway.

"She probably won't even be there." he told himself as he pulled on his uniform.

On the short walk across the park to the station, Alan thought of things to talk to her about. Conversation had been a bit strained and as usual, in the presence of women, he tended to dry up a bit.

Alan entered the station office and relieved the night Officer who nodded gratefully at his early arrival. A cheery fire was already blazing in the briefing room and Alan sat in front of it, deep in troubled thought.

"Look, if it worries you that much, don't go." his conscience warned.

"I probably won't." he lied to himself.

His reveries were interrupted as Vera popped her head around the door. "Morning Alan…Coffee?"

"Smashing Vera, thanks."

"Two minutes then."

She disappeared, humming to herself as she walked up the short corridor towards the canteen.

The two halves of his inner conscience struggled for primacy as they sat, one on each shoulder, nagging at him.

"You could get finished for it you know, its conduct unbecoming an Officer, shagging someone's Wife whilst on duty." Reckless Eric cautioned.

"You only pop in for coffee." Peter Perfect responded.

"At the moment yes, but don't tell me that if it was offered…"

"She's probably just lonely; people like to talk to a Policeman."
"At half past six in the morning! Fuck off Pendle."
"She probably won't be there."
"So you won't bother going then."

The two ethereal gremlins suddenly disappeared as Vera returned, still humming happily and carrying a mug of coffee and a slice of toast.

"Vera, you're an angel."

She smiled. "You young lads, you go out without anything in your stomachs, it's not good for you."

Alan could have remarked that on this particular morning, his stomach felt full to capacity with half the residents of the local bird sanctuary, all of which were flapping their wings at the same time.

As he sipped at his coffee, he fought with his conscience again. Reckless Eric in the blue corner was considerably ahead on points. There was a brief scuffle, but then Peter Perfect in the red corner took a straight left and fell to the canvas.

By the eight count, Alan had convinced himself that his intentions were quite in keeping with the Chief Constable's policies of keeping the Officer on the beat, in close touch with the local community and less than half an hour later, he found himself walking up the incline in the semi darkness towards her house.

She was of course at the window and as she spotted him approaching, immediately disappeared from view.

She was waiting at the back door as he walked through the tunnel into her back yard. She smiled and beckoned him into the kitchen.

Alan said "Hi." cheerfully and noticed that she was dressed in a very short white skirt and a virtually translucent blouse which left little to the imagination. She had obviously taken a long time over her makeup. In truth, she looked glorious.

"Ello Alan, bit better day today eh?" she said, as she quickly closed the door behind him.

"Yes, not too bad, at least it's dry."

Alan realised that this condition also aptly described the interior of his mouth and that his pre-rehearsed witty banter and repertoire had suddenly deserted him.

"Come into the front room." she said, taking his arm. "I'll make coffee, you wanna somethin' to eat?"

"No thank you, coffee's fine."

She walked him out of the kitchen area and showed him into the lounge.

He sat on the spacious settee, it sank lower than he expected, causing him to throw his legs out to steady himself, thank God by which time, she was back in the kitchen making coffee. He could hear her humming some local Italian tune, probably sung to her by her Father, who was probably the leader of the local Cosa Nostra who, when he found out what Alan was up to with his Daughter, would cause a 'contract' to fly out from some small dusty village outside Turin to the local Broughton hit man. There would be a knock on the door of his digs at three in the morning and a short barrelled Lupara poking through the letter box.

Alan stood up to take off his helmet and raincoat. Looking around the room, he could see that it was clean and furnished neatly. A huge picture of Pope Paul the sixth hung on the wall above the gas fire and on the tiled fireplace surround, there stood numerous cheap looking trophies for snooker and darts. "That's obviously how he spends his evenings." Alan thought.

She returned to the lounge carrying a tray containing two mugs of steaming coffee and a small plate of biscuits. Alan sat down again carefully and remembering the free fall he had experienced earlier, he steadied himself with the padded armrest.

She sat across from him and turned to face him as she handed him his coffee. Alan's hands still shook a little and although performing microsurgery would be out of the question, he felt slightly more in control of himself than he had on the previous day.

"How are you today then, alright?" Alan asked, trying desperately to maintain eye contact so as not to stare at her bra, which showed temptingly through her nylon blouse.

"Oh I don' know, just a bit fed up." She replied coyly.

"Why, what's up?" Alan asked, trying to sound genuinely concerned, mindful of his Chief Constable's policies.

He involuntarily snatched a momentary glimpse of the dark 'V' between her legs as she shifted her weight. He quickly looked away and regained eye contact, afraid that she'd noticed his indiscretion. He'd either got away with it or she wasn't bothered. He noticed that her eyes were glistening and she put a hand to tears that were welling up.

"Here, what's the matter?" Alan asked, putting his coffee mug down and shuffling up next to her to tentatively put a comforting arm around her shoulder.

A few tears fell onto the front of her skirt as she hung her head. Alan could feel the heat from her body even through his tunic and a strange rushing sound filled his ears.

"What is it?" he said, using his best, genuine caring Policeman tone.

"I don' know, jus' get 'unappy sometimes." She lifted her face and dabbed at her eyes with a tissue and for a split second, which seemed like an eternity, they were still.

For reasons totally unbeknown to him, throwing caution to the four winds, Alan kissed her gently on her lips.

It was as if he'd plugged her into the mains.

The dramatic result of his simple, comforting act was totally unexpected as she threw her arms around his neck and pulled him tightly to her.

A 'half nelson' applied by Kendo Nagasaki would have given him more opportunity to breath. She kissed him violently on the mouth, forcing her tongue between his lips as she moaned and squirmed. Alan surmised that if it became local knowledge that this was how she reacted when she was unhappy, the few Policemen that there were at Broughton Road would be racing round the Town in the Mini Vans like men possessed, trying to run her husband over so that they could deliver the death message personally.

By now, clearly possessed by some demonic force, she pulled feverishly at the buttons of his tunic; Alan helped her, neither of them saying anything. The room filled with the sound of heavy breathing as she pushed her hands inside his tunic and clung to his back, squeezing his flesh.

Alan, all vestiges of sense and sensibility now thrown out onto the main road, kissed her with equal fervour. She was his first 'older woman' experience and come hell or conduct unbecoming, he was going to enjoy it.

She moaned and twisted like a wild thing, pulling him tighter to her; Alan slid his hand round from her back and slowly cupped one of her large breasts. He felt her stiffen for a second and wondered if he had gone too far. Perhaps in Broughton, the heavy kissing stage had to go on for a week or two before any important flesh was fondled.

She moaned again and continued her assault on his person. Her tongue slithered into his ear and Alan felt her hot panting breath coming in short rasps.

"In for a penny, in for a pound, a faint heart never fucked a pig." goaded Reckless Eric, as Alan fumbled with the miniscule buttons on the front of her blouse.

She lay back against the padded settee to help him; Alan looked directly at her half closed eyes and her front teeth biting gently onto her bottom lip. He pulled the blouse fully open to reveal her bra; it was sheer and lightly laced. Her nipples were dark and pushed solidly against the soft material. She smiled and reached behind her back, unclasping the strap herself and Alan drew in his breath sharply as the bra fell away to expose her full breasts. They were as he had fantasized, large and firm, not a hint of sagging. He cupped one in the palm of his hand and his mouth fell instinctively to the erect nipple.

She groaned and twisted her hands in the hair at the back of his head, pushing his face harder into her. He allowed his hand to stray slowly from beneath her breast and gently onto her lap as he kissed her again on the mouth.

Again she tensed, but clung onto him as his hand fell to her leg. Alan pulled her closer and slowly slipped his hand beneath the material of her skirt, savouring the feel of the heat emanating from the inside of her thighs.

She was breathing harder now and suddenly, she let go of him and lay back against the settee's arm rest, her eyes fully closed. Alan eased her legs apart, there was no resistance. His eyes rested on the front of her briefs. Beneath the thin material Alan could see that she was gloriously natural and his heart skipped a beat as her hand immediately went to the front of his uniform trousers.

He eased himself onto his knees on the settee, facing her and lifted the hem of her skirt over her buttocks. His heart pounded in his chest and the rushing sound in his ears was now deafening as he slipped his thumbs under the elastic of her briefs and eased them down.

She lifted herself up from the settee to help him and Alan felt her hands fumbling with the buckle of his belt. He stopped and as she had done for him, he helped her, unclasping the buckle and undoing the buttons on his trousers, before resuming his silent undressing of her.

Alan groaned out loud as she took hold of him, the heat from her hand seared into him. Her chest was heaving and her breasts rose and fell excitedly.

Alan pulled her briefs completely away and stared down at the black mass of pubic hair, which glistened damply as she opened her legs wide and pulled him down onto her. Alan slipped into her.

His lovemaking was crude, hurried and clumsy. He could exercise no self-control, she had excited him too much and he spent himself, feeling the breath leaving her body as she tensed to receive him.

They lay panting and exhausted on the settee. She smiled and kissed him on the forehead where it lay against her breasts.

Alan got up slowly, not knowing what to say and turned away from her as he dressed himself. He sat back down to button his tunic, his legs unable to carry his weight. She pulled her blouse together and fumbled with the buttons. Her face was flushed and shining with tiny beads of perspiration as she pulled the hem of her skirt down.

Alan was embarrassed at his performance and stuttered. "Look, I'm sorry I didn't last ver…"

Her fingers immediately went to his lips to silence him; she smiled knowingly and removing her fingers, she kissed him again on the mouth.

"Better next time eh?" she whispered.

"What about going out for a drink one evening, if you can get away?" Alan blurted out, not knowing why he had said it.

She nodded enthusiastically.

"We could go back to my digs, if my landlady was out."

"That would be nice. More time eh?" she said.

Alan looked down at her. "Look, I'd better be off, we've been ages."

She got up from the settee and finished straightening her clothing, running her hands through her tousled hair.

Alan grabbed up his raincoat and helmet and followed her into the kitchen. The moment was over and he was desperate to get away, although he felt guilty for leaving her so soon afterwards. As he reached for the back door handle, she put a hand on his arm, holding him back for a second. She seemed unconcerned at his apparent haste to leave. She simply smiled. "See you later Alan, I watch for you eh."

Alan merely nodded and slipped quietly out into the back yard. Once under the cover of the tunnel, he made sure that his coat was fastened properly and that he'd remembered to do up his trouser buttons.

Still feeling slightly weak at the knees, he did his best to adopt the slow steady pace of the beat Officer as he walked onto the pavement at the side of the main road, forcing himself not to look across to the window as he walked his beat, back in towards the Town.

He felt guilty about his actions, yet somehow, strangely elated. He was only too aware that although he'd committed enough breaches of the Code of Conduct to keep the Discipline and Complaints Department busy for the next decade, he consoled himself with the knowledge that at least while he'd been up to his nuts in the 'Italian Job', he'd kept his radio turned on.

*****

The door to the Traffic Office suddenly opened and shook Alan from his reveries as the early turn crew tumbled in.

"You still 'ere mate?" Oldfield shouted.

Alan was startled and realised that he had dozed off.

"Just going." Alan said, as he stretched and yawned. He pulled the unfinished statement form out from between the typewriter rollers.

Pc Oldfield and Pc Barnett, his 'Aide', grabbed their caps and hurried down to the Parade room for the morning briefing.

Alan closed his notebook and pushed it into his docket, pausing for a second or two over the memories which were fading quickly.

A nostalgic smile crept across his face, as he grabbed his 'civvy' jacket and made his way downstairs to the main outer doors.

## **Eleven**

'Midnight' cast a critical eye over the lines of the Ford Cortina on the forecourt of the used car lot. He ran his hand across the smooth paintwork on the bonnet as the salesman hovered impatiently, nervously snatching glances at other potential would be customers, who walked slowly around the array of cheap vehicles he had for sale.

"It's not a bad example for the year." he said, adopting his well-practiced, honest smile.

"It's an expensive example for the year." 'Midnight' said brusquely, leaning his back against the nearside wing, his face impassive and looking directly into the eyes of the salesman.

The salesman felt strangely uncomfortable, threatened by this man's presence, although he did not know why. There was something in his eyes that seemed to bore into his very soul. The salesman shivered involuntarily.

"Well, I'm sure we can come to some amicable arrangement, was Sir thinking about a cash deal or a part exchange of some sort?"

"Its cash." said 'Midnight', turning his back on the salesman and looking again over the interior of the vehicle.

He had netted just over two thousand pounds from the garage job, but had brought only a thousand with him, the wad of notes sitting uncomfortably in his back pocket.

The car was a red Ford Cortina Mk4, the most common car on the road. It was a little on the high side, price and mileage, but it was perfect for him. Anonymous and discreet.

"What will you take?" 'Midnight' asked.

"Well, why don't you make me an offer and let's see what we can do." the salesman said, smiling.

"Five hundred cash." 'Midnight' said flatly, continuing his unnerving stare.

The salesman laughed nervously. "I asked for an offer not an insult." he replied, immediately regretting his choice of words as he noticed 'Midnight's' dour expression suddenly change to a more threatening glower.

The salesman stuttered. "No…look, I didn't mean that you were insulting. I meant…well, you know, it's just a salesman's joke…The car's worth more than five hundred, you can see that."

"There's no road tax and it needs tyres." 'Midnight' said, as he tapped the front nearside tyrewall with his foot to emphasise his point, again looking directly into the salesman's eyes.

"Look." the salesman said, nodding in acquiescence. He pondered for a moment. "It's up at six fifty, I'll meet you half way on the road tax, call it six hundred for cash."

The salesman looked slightly more confident. 'Midnight' looked again over the vehicle and nodded.

"Ok, six hundred."

'Midnight' did not take the offered hand to shake on the deal and after a moment's awkwardness; the salesman withdrew it and smiled nervously, gesturing towards the far end of the forecourt. "Right then er…come to the office and we'll do the necessary."

'Midnight' followed the man into a ramshackle office and counted out the cash onto the desk top, watched eagerly by the salesman.

The salesman rooted around in a battered filing cabinet and withdrew an equally tattered registration document which had an MOT certificate stapled to it. "There's still a couple of month's test on it, I'm sure she'll sail through the next one."

'Midnight' took the offered document and folded it before pushing it into the back pocket of his jeans. "Keys?" he asked.

"Oh yes." The salesman attempted a laugh. "Won't get far without those, eh."

'Midnight' didn't feel like wasting his breath advising the salesman that he could enter and start the engine in ten minutes flat, but simply took the single key and left the office without further words passing between them.

The salesman called out after him. "What about your recei..."

'Midnight' ignored him and walked across the forecourt, towards his newly acquired wheels.

The salesman watched 'Midnight as he started the Cortina. Something about the tall, muscular negro had disturbed him, as if some violent aurora had oozed out from the man and clung to the air in the office. He shuddered involuntarily as he picked up the loose notes, shuffling them into a pile before wrapping a rubber band around the wad, as he watched the vehicle being driven off the forecourt.

'Midnight' drove the vehicle carefully into the City, maintaining the speed limit and keeping a wary eye out for 'Babylon'. If he was seen and identified in the vehicle, local intelligence reports would be submitted, sighting him, a known and habitual criminal, drug offender and recent prison release in a recent vehicle. There would be 'markers' placed on his file for weapons and drugs, violence and assault Police indicators. The information would be logged by the Collators at the Division where he was registered as being resident and read out on daily parade briefings. Once known, the Traffic men would harass him relentlessly, using their powers under the Road Traffic Act as an excuse to stop him.

He would be followed by one of the brightly liveried patrol vehicles and stopped to be informed that they had checked the speed and distance of his vehicle and that he had been exceeding the speed limit. No amount of protestations of innocence would prevent 'producers' or the inevitable Fixed Penalty Tickets, all designed to add up to 'totting up' until he had attained twelve points, where he could be disqualified from driving. No point arguing, if the Traffic Cop said you were speeding, you were speeding, that was the game.

Once disqualified, you were on the system and it gave any Police Officer an immediate power of arrest if they found you driving. Once arrested and in custody, they had the keys to your place of residence as well.

A good Traffic man could always find *some* defect with a vehicle. They were entitled to carry out roadside examinations, which could also include carrying out a cursory glance within the boot area to examine the petrol filler connection, to ensure that 'fuel wasn't leaking into the confines of the vehicle', or at least that was the excuse provided to allow the Officers to carry out the search. Battery not properly secured, windscreen washers not maintained, defective exhaust or tyres, excessive play in the steering, horn not maintained, all good Construction and Use offences and all carrying penalty points.

They could 'mix him a powder' easily enough. He played by his rules, they played by theirs. That was the game. It all depended on who the Magistrate believed at the end of the day and a black ex 'con', in a dodgy Ford Cortina had little or no chance against the sworn evidence of two Road Traffic Officers.

'Midnight' pulled up in front of the barrier at the multi-storey car park in the busy City center. A ticket appeared with a metallic clunk from the robot dispenser as he drove over the pressure pads. He reached out and took the ticket and the barrier rose automatically. He drove up the ramp into the heart of the grey, concrete parking facility and cruised slowly around between the rows of parked vehicles, not searching for a space, but for a particular vehicle.

Further up the ramp onto the next floor, 'Midnight' slowed further as he passed the front of the Ford Cortina and drew almost to a stop, so that he could see the date on the excise licence displayed on its windscreen. Noting the Cortina's position, he continued and looked for a space to leave his vehicle for a while.

'Midnight' walked back to the old Ford. Looking around, he noted that the multi-storey was still quite busy and vehicles filed past him as drivers squinted in the darkness looking for vacant spaces. He ambled up to the front passenger door of the vehicle and withdrew the half inch wide strip of stiff vinyl packing strip from his pocket and doubled it to form a loop. He had a further glance around the parking lot, before forcing the looped tape between the trailing edge of the passenger door and the rubber surround of the central pillar. The stiff plastic loop passed easily into the gap and pushing a further two to three inches of the loop into the interior of the vehicle, he slid the strip downwards until the loop passed over the locking stud which stood just proud enough of the inner door panel.

'Midnight' pulled one side of the loop tight and then pulled the strip upwards, he was rewarded with a faint audible click as the door unlocked.

Quickly looking around to ensure that he was not being observed, 'Midnight' opened the door and reached into the interior of the vehicle. He peeled the polythene tax disc holder from the inside of the windscreen and slipped it into his jacket pocket. Wiping the door handle with the sleeve of his jacket and after having a last look around to satisfy himself that his crime had gone unnoticed, he walked to the nearest pedestrian exit and out to the City Centre.

He had some shopping to do.

*****

Alan sat in the driver's seat of the patrol car and watched his partner devouring a bag of chips. He sighed and depressed the electric window switch in the center console, opening the window to dissipate the stringent smell of the vinegar and ketchup saturated meal.

"You eat like a fucking camel Sully."

"Uh." his regular partner grunted, wiping ketchup from his chin.

"I said...I see your recent sojourn to more exotic climes has failed to educate your palate."

"What?" Sullivan said, stuffing the limp ketchup soaked oblongs of potato into his mouth.

Alan sighed again. "What I mean is, after three weeks in the sultry heat of Greece, no doubt imbibing copious amounts of refined aniseed spirit along with mousaka, kleftico and tara masawhatsit, I'm surprised to see you so quickly return to your usual casual approach to healthy eating."

His partner chewed briefly and swallowed. "You don't half talk some shit Al." he said, spraying Alan's yellow jacket with small particles of the semi masticated mess.

Alan grimaced and brushed the speckled pieces from his jacket. "Christ, Pete, you could spend six months with the Royal Household and still come back with the table manners of an Aborigine."

"Well, thanks mate." his partner spat, with mock contempt. "It's good to know you've been missed. What makes you so lahdy fuckin' dah these days?"

Alan adopted an affected serious expression. "I just think we ought to be aspiring to heighten our cultural awareness that's all. Attempting to dispel the widely held theory that just 'cos we're PC's, we read the Beano and have difficulty with joined up writing."

His partner wiped his mouth with the back of his hand. "You mean like, go to the theatre or the opera, Madame Butterfly and all that other Spanish shit."

"Italian, not Spanish. Puccini was Italian Peter, Christ you're a Philistine."

"Not me pal." retorted his partner, screwing up the paper which had recently contained his meal into a tight wad and tossing it into the glove box of the patrol car. "I'm C of E." he said, lifting himself away from the seat and breaking wind loudly.

"You've missed me, admit it." his partner said, nudging him playfully in the ribs.

Alan grimaced, shaking his head and depressed the door switch again to lower the window fully, as the sickening rancid odour expelled from his partner's arse assailed his nostrils. "Christ Pete, that is fucking outrageous. I can taste that bastard. You need to seek medical help." Alan said and screwed up his face in disgust. He quickly poked his head out through the open window to gulp in the fresh air.

"Anyway." his partner responded, settling himself down into the passenger seat. "It's no good getting' ideas above yer station, 'arbourin' elusions of grandeur will only leave you disappointed mate."

"That's delusions Pete, not elusions, an' I haven't got ideas above my station as you so eloquently put it. I'm just sick of being treated like a twat by the bosses."

"Sit yer Sergeants then mate." his partner said. "You might even pass, but don't blame me when you get 'made' and posted to the fuckin' Bridewell."

A thin drizzle of rain hazed the windscreen and Alan flicked the windscreen wiper arm on the steering column. The twin blades swept across the screen clearing it for a second.

"I bet you didn't miss this bleedin' weather." Alan said, peering up through the screen at the black clouds gathering over the City.

"You are so fucking right Al, you are so right…Not forty eight hours ago, I was sitting on the old veranda, sipping the Ouso with the warm Mediterranean breeze waftin' across me bollocks, while our Linda slaved away over the barbequed lamb chops."

"Still, you'd be looking forward to getting back on nights though eh?" Alan said sarcastically. "Oh yeah, nights…nights makes life worth livin'." his partner scoffed.

"He's still there." Alan said, sighing and glancing at his watch.

"Course he is, ten minutes drinking up time yet." his partner reminded him. "Anyway, what's the rush, the longer 'e's in there, the more 'e gets down 'is neck."

Alan sighed and screwed up his nose. "You're not going to leave those chip papers in the glovebox all night are you, it'll stink for weeks."

Pc Sullivan retrieved the soggy ball and tossed it across the front of Alan's face and out through the open window. "'Appy now, Mr fuckin' perfect?"

"That's an offence you know, litterin'. I feel it is my duty to report the incident to a senior Officer." Alan said teasingly.

"Report it to who you want mate, I'm doin' my bit for the community like the Chief says."

Alan looked puzzled. "Go on then, amaze me. How on earth do you come to the conclusion that you chuckin' your chip papers out on to the street helps the community?"

Sullivan leaned back in his seat and lit a cigar. "I look at it this way see, there's people employed by the local Council as litter collector's right? If no one chucked litter, they'd have fuck all to do, redundant so to speak. I therefore, am ensuring 'is continued employment and financial future, my bit for the community, see?"

"An astounding piece of logic." Alan admitted, as he flicked the wiper arm again to provide a clear view of the aged Ford Escort van which was still parked across the main road, in front of the Public House.

"You don't suppose 'es sold it, do you?" his partner asked.

"Would you buy that?" Alan said, sarcastically.

"No, I guess not." his partner admitted, smiling as he drew on his cigar. The bluish grey smoke slowly filling the patrol car with its pungent aroma.

They sat in silence for a while. Alan watched the miniscule pinpricks of drizzle haze down across the windscreen obscuring his view, until they gathered together and ran in rivulets down the glass.

The silence between them was not an embarrassment, not present because they had nothing to say to each other, but a silence that can be entered into without the need for an explanation, such as would be demanded by a girlfriend or Wife, if such a silence prevailed. Partners of long standing could be silent without the other questioning it. Partners, who know each other back to front, mannerisms, temperaments, strengths and weaknesses and the sharing of a course, base type of humour, usually at someone else's expense, within the private confines of their patrol car.

All these things, borne out of spending countless hours, weeks and years in the same company. Known company, safe, reliable company.

A partner could disclose his innermost confidences and fears to his crew mate, sometimes, before he would be prepared to disclose them to his Wife, due to the fact that for the most part, a Traffic man actually spent more time with his partner.

Alan had partnered with Sullivan for over five years. They matched each other well. Sullivan was well over six feet four, slow to lose his temper, but awesome when he did. He had a quiet manner about him and could rip a strip off a member of the Public and it would be accepted without complaint, whereas, exactly the same delivery by Alan, would have them screaming down the 'phone to Discipline and Complaints before he could close his pocket note book.

Sullivan was a calming influence, a thinker and although Alan would never admit it, the more intelligent. Alan preferred the more Neanderthal approach to Police work, with more of a "Let's do it anyway and worry about it later." attitude.

They had shared most things together, the bloodletting in the City on Friday and Saturday nights, the limbless, headless bodies at countless accidents, along with the boredom and monotony that comes with most jobs. They had shared the bollockings and laughed about them afterwards and like most crews, sat for hours, watching and waiting for a disqualified driver to finish his nights drinking and clamber into his vehicle.

Alan had parked their patrol vehicle in a cobbled side street which looked out over the main through road. The street, which was more of an alley than a thoroughfare for vehicles, was in total darkness and disguised the presence of the marked patroller well. The area was dirty and run down and gave an overall impression of poverty. The residents looked tired before their time, lack of education kept them in place. They ran up the cobbled streets as children with the friends they would grow up with, all in the same hand me down or second hand clothes and shoes. They would go to school for a while, before the Juvenile Courts sent them to Youth Custody Centers or Borstal and inevitably and for the majority, prison.

Eventually, they would marry, live in the same streets and drink in the same pubs as their Fathers and in time, their children would once again complete the same cycle of despair, as they in turn waited to grow old.

Drinking and drunkenness was the regular social pastime enjoyed by most of the residents. The public houses in the immediate area were low class and poorly maintained.

Fights were a regular occurrence. A broken beer glass pushed into someone's face, a bar stool over someone's head, or a good kicking out in the car park over something as ridiculous as an argument over football, or the fact that the recipient had allegedly looked sideways at someone's Wife or girlfriend. 'The great unwashed' as Sullivan described them.

"They drink 'cos they're depressed. They want to forget their worries 'bout not 'avin' any money or prospects an' they don't 'ave any money or prospects 'cos they drink." His partner opined casually.

Alan nodded slowly. "Your theory on the cause and effect of the downward spiral of the working classes, is quite profound Sully…I'm impressed…you should give lectures". Alan held up his hands depicting an imaginary headline. "Social deprivation…The cure?...close all the fucking pubs says Professor Sullivan. Government to consider ground-breaking recommendations."

His partner chuckled. "Fuck you Al."

The van they were watching belonged, so advised the Police National Computer, to a disqualified driver, sat on a three year ban for his second conviction for drinking and driving.

The local residents looked upon periods of disqualification as something of a recreational hazard. Alan and his partner saw things a little differently. They had donated a significant amount of effort in placing this particular driver, convinced that he was failing to comply with his ban. So far, he had eluded them. They would 'sight' the van and sit on it for an hour or so, only to be called away to deal with an accident or an alarm call somewhere. On their return, inevitably, the van would be gone.

Tonight he was theirs. Offering to pay a month's tea fund, the half night Traffic crew had reluctantly agreed to deal with all the calls, leaving Alan and his partner free to sit on the van. All night if need be.

"Come on." Alan said quietly, glancing once again at his watch.

"Patience mate." Sullivan replied. "Your trouble is, you've no fuckin' tenacity. You want to take up fishin' mate…you'd learn 'ow to control yer impatience."

Alan snorted derisively. "Fishing…Now there's a complete fucking mystery. Sit for hours an' hours in the cold and rain, dippin' a rod in the fucking lake or whatever. Then if by some miracle you *do* manage to catch something, you don't even get to eat the fucking thing! You chuck it straight back where it came from and start again!...Go fishin', I'd sooner stick pins in my eyes."

His partner parried the latest verbal debasement of his favourite off duty pastime. "Lot of skill in fishing, tactics, strategy, knowin' yer adversary, 'ow he thinks, where 'e's likely to be, where to drop yer feeder or ground bait, more to it than you think mate. It's a bit like chess."

"Like *chess*?" Alan guffawed. "It's like chess…fuck me!…Well viewers, it looks like Sullivan is going for the classic Sicilian defence with this particular trout." Alan mimicked the hushed tones of a snooker commentator…His partner ignored the sarcasm.

"That's why you've no patience." his partner scoffed. "Cos you've the concentration span of a fuckin' 'amster."

"Well, I'm certainly getting seriously bored with this." Alan said, glancing at his watch for the umpteenth time.

"The more 'e drinks, the better the score mate." his partner said.

Alan looked across to his partner with raised eyebrows. "A rather cavalier attitude if you don't mind me saying so Officer Sullivan."

"Bollocks to 'im." his partner spat. "I didn't force 'im to drink an' drive. Nobody's tied 'im down an' poured ale down 'is fuckin' neck… anyway, it was the Magistrates what banned 'im not me, an' now 'es out as usual, same old shit box van parked right outside the pub, blatant as you like, no fuckin' tax or insurance, bollocks to 'im. Do you honestly think 'e gives a shit?"

"Probably not." Alan said. "But I bet if we parked up in full view, he'd come out, see us and lock his vehicle up and walk home."

"More than likely." Sullivan said and shrugged nonchalantly. "So what?"

"Well, my point is, that in effect, we're allowing him to commit the offence, which we could just as easily prevent, just so we can have the satisfaction of locking him up. We're almost aiding and abetting the commission of the offence."

His partner thought for a second, opened his mouth as if to speak then paused again. Alan's argument seemed to have some logic.

Alan continued with his argument thread. "See Pete, if the job's about protecting life and property and the prevention and detection of crime an' all that shit, we'd go into that pub in uniform and tell everyone that we were going to be sat outside with a breath kit."

"And." Alan continued, "If we had a Traffic car sat on the car park of every public house in the country, breath testing at random, there'd be no drinking and driving. Consequently, there'd be a massive decrease in the amount of fatal road accidents and bearing in mind that each fatal cost the tax payer half a million quid, it would almost be cost effective."

"An' where's the fun in that?" his partner said, looking genuinely astounded at his partners apparent leftist attitude.

"You're right of course." Alan acceded. "And I suppose, we'd be out of job sooner or later. No need for Traffic Cops if there's no traffic offences being committed, yeah, can that last idea." His partner thought for a moment. "Yer last argument doesn't hold water Al, see...we also get paid to *detect* offences an' we need to be able to evidence the act. So to actually detect 'disco' driving, we 'ave to actually see 'im drive." Sullivan looked pleased with himself having countered Alan's argument. "Anyway, bollocks to it. When 'e comes out, 'es ours."

"Talking of which." Alan said, nodding towards the street.

His partner sat up straight. "About bleedin' time we were under starter's orders."

The doors to the public house opened and the unsuspecting public filtered out. There was much raucous laughter and shouting as they slowly dispersed back toward their hovels. A few car engines started up, ignored by Alan and his partner as they watched the roof of their 'target' vehicle intently. The rain had stopped and Alan swept the wipers once across the screen to clear it.

"Here we go mate." Alan said, as the van slowly pulled away from the kerb opposite the public house frontage and set off onto the main road.

"Which way do you reckon?" Alan asked, without taking his eyes from the van.

"If 'es off straight 'ome, he'll 'ead towards the Saxtons. If 'e's managed to pick up a slag, your guess is as good as mine." his partner said, glancing at his watch and noting the time for the offence report.

Alan slipped the gear lever forwards and let the clutch out slowly, the patrol car crept forwards out of the alleyway entrance. His partner lifted himself from his seat slightly to keep sight of the roof of the van over the top of a small wall, which had previously served to conceal their presence.

"City." he said, dropping back into his seat.

Alan let the clutch out fully and eased the patrol car out onto the main road, flicking on the sidelights and pulling his seatbelt across his chest. He snapped the clasp into place as he accelerated the patrol vehicle towards the rear of the unsuspecting van driver.

They allowed the target vehicle to clear the immediate area of the public house, not wanting to advertise the fact that they had been sitting on it.

The van turned right onto the main City bound road, its nearside wheel nudged the kerb edge as the driver misjudged the turning circle, it lurched forwards erratically, its engine still cold.

"What'd I tell you, pissed as a rat." Sullivan said, with a satisfied chuckle.

"Ok." said Alan. "Let's have him stopped."

His partner reached forwards to the dashboard facia and flicked the switch operating the bank of blue lights fitted across the roof of their patrol car. Alan accelerated up to the rear of the van and flashed the headlights through the glass panels in its rear doors, illuminating the interior of the van. The driver neither slowed nor accelerated, but chose to ignore them. Alan flashed the headlights again and saw the driver look up to the interior rear view mirror.

The van slowed slightly and Alan reached down to his seat belt release clip, holding his thumb on the button ready to be out quickly when the van stopped. Disqualified drivers had a nasty habit of running off. They were approaching a major crossroads; the traffic lights ahead of them were on red.

"We'll 'ave 'im at the lights. Cheeky bastard, 'e knows we're 'ere."

Alan nodded. "Let's invite him to join us in our office eh."

The noise of the van's engine suddenly revving hard, made Alan take his hand away from the seat belt clasp, instinctively knowing that the van driver had no intention of stopping.

He was about to speak when the van leapt forwards and accelerated toward the red traffic light.

"Hey up, 'es 'avin' a dabble." his partner shouted excitedly.

Alan was already on the accelerator, the patrol car's V8 growling at the harsh demand made of it, from a near standstill.

The van weaved in the road and raced towards the junction, heedless of the red light ahead. Alan's partner turned on the sirens and the night air was filled with the eerie tormented sound of the wailers.

The van swung hard left into the junction mouth and straight through the red traffic light, its rear wheels losing traction on the wet road surface.

Alan saw the rear of the van snaking from left to right as the driver fought to maintain control of his vehicle as it slewed left and away from the main road. The rear offside of the van swung out wide and encroached into the opposite carriageway, where it collided with the front of an oncoming vehicle halfway into the junction. There was a dull thud and the explosive sound of a headlamp bursting, as the front offside wing was ripped away.

Alan's partner casually glanced at the registration number of the crippled vehicle, quickly scribbling it down on the back of his hand and looking across to its driver. He saw his eyes wide open, his mouth frozen into a silent scream, knuckles white, as his hands gripped the steering wheel as the offending Ford van, followed closely by the wailing patrol car, swept past.

"Go, go." Alan's partner called out, his eyes sweeping across the junction to corroborate Alan's judgment that they were clear to continue.

"Fuck me, this fella's in deep shit." Sullivan chuckled, as he snatched up the radio handset and keyed the transmitter. "Papa Yankee One Five in pursuit."

"One Five, talk through is on." The operator at the Control Room answered quickly.

The radio tone took on a hollow sound as Sullivan's commentary was placed on the open channel. Every Traffic crew in the City would now be listening, engines started and caps thrown into rear seats in anticipation of joining in with a pursuit. Each crew member praying, that the chase would last long enough for their vehicle to become involved.

"Papa Yankee One Five. We are in pursuit... dark blue Ford escort van. Yankee Victor Alpha Fiver One Four Lima...City bound on Watson Road, driver is believed OPL and disqualified."

The van continued to weave and accelerate, wildly overtaking, heedless of oncoming traffic. Headlights flashed and vehicles pulled in sharply to the nearside, as the fleeing van sped down the center of the road.

"Left onto Wellington Road, still City bound, sixty plus, traffic is moderate and road conditions tolerable. For the log, target vehicle in previous 10/9 with red coloured Vauxhall, Papa Yankee Golf Eight One Three Tango junction Watson Road."

"Received One Five." the operator quickly responded.

"Now approaching Fell Street fly over, speed is seventy plus."

Alan accelerated toward the offside of the van in an effort to overtake and caught a glimpse of the driver who turned his head around for an instant before snatching at the steering wheel in panic. The van swung wildly out towards the side of the patrol car and Alan quickly took evasive action, quickly dabbing on the brakes and adopting third gear to maintain stability.

"He'll 'ave the fuckin' front off us mate, I wouldn't bother." Sullivan said, shaking his head, "He's got 10/9 written all over 'im. I'd hang back and wait for 'im to fuck up, won't be long the way 'es going."

Alan settled himself into his seat and concentrated on his forward observations. His partner was right of course, any damage to their patroller would keep them tied up with paperwork for hours and incur the wrath of the Inspector. There was a time when a ramming was the only option, but it wasn't yet. The call signs of the other patrol cars could be heard over the radio, announcing their positions. Sullivan continued with his commentary giving speeds and directions of travel.

Traffic cars throughout the City closed in for the chase.

The van entered a stretch of dual carriageway on the approach to the City center. Alan's partner glanced at the speedometer situated in a large pod on the top of the dashboard. He keyed the handset. "Fell Street, speed is six zero, still toward the City, traffic is light to moderate."

"One Five received."

Alan allowed their speed to drop off momentarily so as to allow for a slight increase in the distance between them. He hung out to the offside to maintain a view as far ahead of the speeding van as possible. At almost sixty miles per hour, Alan needed increased reaction time, the van was obviously struggling and the worn engine emitted plumes of oily smoke from the exhaust, as it protested against the demands of the panicking driver.

"He's a fucking looney." Alan shouted, as he watched the van racing towards the blind junction where the stretch of dual carriageway ended.

"Approaching Ring Road with Fell Street, lights at red, he's not stopping." Alan's partner spoke into the handset with unruffled tones.

"Papa Bravo One Five on Edward Street, we have you in view."

A second Traffic car had found them; Alan could see the sweeping arc of its blue lights being reflecting from the buildings along the side of the entry slip road which dipped down to the dual carriageway.

Alan decelerated harshly and felt the seat belt pull reassuringly across his chest as he applied the brakes in readiness for the junction. The front of the Rover dipped and Alan doubled the clutch to allow the engaging of second gear. The V8 growled in protest, as he craned his neck searching for an early view to the nearside.

"Yes, yes." shouted Sullivan, as his eyes swept from side to side taking in all the emergent junctions. Trusting his partner's judgment without question, Alan kicked down on the accelerator, feeling the Rover immediately surge forwards as they crossed the stop line at the traffic lights. There had been no brake lights displayed on the Ford van, the driver was fully committed to making good his escape whatever.

"Papa Bravo One Four, we see him." A second Traffic car had joined the fray and was making sure their call sign was entered on the running log at the Control Center.

"One Four received." the operator acknowledged.

The chatter on the radio was now taken over by the attending Traffic Officers, as they planned positions and tactics.

"One Five, we'll take Oxford Place."

"One Four. Roger that Dave. We're on Melbourne Street."

Acknowledgments were not needed between the Traffic crews, each driver stating his intention and acting upon it, to place his vehicle for maximum inconvenience to the vehicle being chased.

"Time to feed him." Alan said to his partner. Dave Mercer's on Oxford Place."

Sullivan nodded. "Ave a go mate, but watch 'e doesn't trip you up."

"Can't let him into the City center Pete, he'll end up killing someone." Alan said, and without taking his eyes away from the Ford van, he eased the gear lever forwards whilst maintaining the engine revs.

As the Ford neared the junction with Oxford Place, the Rover SD1 shot forwards and caught the driver of the Ford Van unawares, overtaking it on its offside. Alan aggressively moved across the front of the target whilst braking heavily. The van driver, as expected, also braked heavily and expecting to be rammed, swerved his vehicle into the junction to his nearside.

The Ford van was still going too fast to complete the manoeuvre and as the front brakes bit hard, the front end dipped, causing the rear end of the vehicle to become light, too light to maintain a good grip on the road surface and the vehicle rocked violently.

The driver's fine motor skills, dulled by the effects of the alcohol, fought with the steering and to keep control of his vehicle. Alan braked hard and swiftly engaged second gear. The rear tyres of the Rover howled in protest as he swung the steering wheel to the left and powered the patrol car into the junction directly to the rear of the Ford which continued directly towards the waiting Traffic car.

"Got the bastard." Alan muttered.

"From One Five, 'e's towards you on Oxford Place."

"One Five, got 'im."

The weaving van screamed up the street towards the waiting patrol car, which was now positioned diagonally across the road a hundred yard ahead.

The driver of the Ford was suddenly greeted by a blinding array of blue lights, reflecting both in his rear view mirror and directly ahead, as Papa Bravo One Five announced its presence.

Alan pulled back slightly to give himself an escape route and plenty of time for braking. The van seemed to slow momentarily as if the driver was undecided as to what to do.

Alan saw a huge plume of smoke from its exhaust and instinctively knew that he had made his decision. The van accelerated hard, and drove directly towards the waiting Traffic car.

"He's not having it Dave!" shouted the observer to his crew mate in the waiting patrol car.

The driver reversed quickly. The van hurtled towards the gap which had now opened on its nearside, between the front of the patrol car and the far kerb edge.

"This is gonna' to be fuckin' tight." muttered the driver of One Five.

He eased out the clutch and allowed the front of his patrol car to edge forwards, then immediately braked again.

The van driver reacted as expected and wrenched his steering wheel harshly to the right to try to avoid the impending collision. The van driver had feared he was about to be rammed, the ploy had worked. It usually did.

The front offside wheel of the Ford van struck the high concrete kerb slab and there was a gunshot like rapport as the tyre fragmented.

Due to its speed and the violent frontal impact, the rear end of the van released its tenuous grip on the road surface and lifted as the body of the van twisted violently, now half on the pavement, its rear end swung out wildly into the center of the road.

Alan held his breath and whilst still braking, watched the inevitable collision. His field of vision narrowed and the death throes of the Ford van seemed to unfold in slow motion. Alan was unaware of any voices over the radio, or of any sounds at all, other than the tortured screech of metal against concrete.

The van's front wheel, its tyre flapping uselessly on the buckled steel rim, bit into the flagstones of the pavement. Sparks spat out from beneath the vehicle as the metal was friction melted against the concrete of the pavement.

The steering rack, torn away from the front wheel hub, rendered the steering useless. It refused to answer to the driver's wild flailing's and the front nearside wing crumpled slowly backwards, as it was compressed at almost fifty miles per hour against a metal lamp standard.

The van seemed to climb up the unforgiving, immovable post as the vehicle's body panels buckled and were torn away to fly away from the vehicle in large shards, to ricochet back into the road from the adjacent walls.

The glass from the shattering windscreen, rose like a dust storm as it exploded outwards from the front of the vehicle, the miniscule glass particles reflecting the rotating blue lights from the patrol vehicles like so many glittering sapphires, before cascading to the road surface.

The Ford's body panels, already badly weakened by years of corrosion, inevitably folded backwards and the vehicle pivoted around the metal post. It keeled over onto its nearside like a stricken vessel before sliding along the road surface. Its metal panels shrieking like fingernails across a blackboard.

The van pirouetted to a halt. A plume of steam rose slowly from beneath the crumpled bonnet of the vehicle and, other than the ticking from the cooling engine, for a moment there was silence.

"Papa Yankee One Five, he's stuffed it, Oxford Place."

Alan's partner didn't wait for a reply from the Control Room operator, but threw the handset onto the dashboard. He leapt from their vehicle as Alan set the handbrake.

The wreckage of the van, was strewn across the whole width of the road and there was a pungent smell of hot oil and coolant in the air. The blue lights from the patrol cars still danced across the adjacent shop windows, office walls and the silver reflective stripes on the fluorescent jackets worn by the Traffic men. The street took on something of a carnival appearance, belying the actual horror at the scene.

Alan along with his colleagues rushed to the overturned Ford.

Sullivan crawled halfway into the stricken vehicle through what was left of the crushed windscreen aperture and reappeared quickly to give Alan a questioning look. "Better get an ambulance Al."

Alan looked perplexed and peering down in through the upturned driver's window, saw that the driver was only semi-conscious and moaning, his face a bleeding mass where the steering wheel had pulverized the bridge of his nose. His breathing was very laboured and weak, signs that his chest had taken the initial impact with the steering wheel.

His front seat passenger was still, completely still, her eyes wide open, yet blank and unseeing. Her mouth hung open, the lower part of her jaw hanging slackly down towards the shattered passenger door window.

Alan was still shaking slightly from the adrenalin rush, but reached into the vehicle to feel for a pulse. Her head seemed to be laid at an impossible angle and as he pulled the collar of her coat aside to touch her skin an inch or so beneath her ear lobe, he noticed a strange disfigurement on the side of her neck, as if something was pushing outwards from beneath the skin. Alan snatched back his fingers in horror, as if she had died from some contagious disease. The sight of her broken neck sent shivers down his spine.

The sound of the two tone horns of the ambulances setting off from the City Infirmary, filtered through the maze of adjoining streets and echoed eerily from the walls.

Alan stood up slowly, taking in the gravity of the incident. The passenger was dead, and the driver looked as if he was likely to go the same way.

Sullivan had disappeared back to the patrol car to request Police supervision, Accident Investigation and Studio, for the photographs and measurements which would now be required.

The Traffic man from the crew of Bravo One Five, sidled up to Alan and took out a packet of cigarettes as he stared at the macabre scene inside the van. He nudged Alan with his elbow; Alan looked at the offered packet, and with shaking fingers managed to take one of the cigarettes.

"Cheers Dave." he said, thrusting the filter tip between his lips. He bent down slightly to where the offered flame cupped by his colleague's hand, flickered and fluttered in the breeze.

"Looks like we might be up shit creek with this one." he said quietly, not looking at his colleague, unable to tear his gaze away from her eyes which stared back accusingly from within the vehicle.

"Why?...we did fuck all wrong. Anyway, could be worse mate." his colleague said matter of factly, shrugging his shoulders. "Could have dented your patroller."

Alan drew hard on his cigarette and inhaled deeply, the night wasn't going exactly as planned.

*****

"I'll have full statements from you two before you retire from duty." the night Inspector bellowed.

Alan and his partner stood loosely to attention in front of his desk. Hands down at their sides in the Home Office approved stance for receiving bollockings.

"What the hell do you think you were doing? You weren't even in our Division." the Inspector shouted, the decibels ascending with each word.

"We were in pursuit Sir, he's a disqualified driver and to be fair, the chase did start in our Division." Alan offered meekly.

The Inspector shot up from his chair, his knuckles white where he had pressed them against the table top, his voice now raised to the level of a minor scream.

Alan instinctively leaned backwards fearing that the Inspector had finally lost it and was actually going to physically assault them.

"You knew who he was." the Inspector hissed, now pointing an accusatory finger directly at Sullivan. "You could have visited him at his home address and reported him for the offences tomorrow."

Sullivan opened his mouth as if to speak. The Inspector pre-empted the expected flow of pathetic excuses and raised the palm of his hand as a visual warning not to bother. Sullivan closed his mouth again, now looking slightly less sanguine.

"Now." he shouted, as his accusing stare alternated between them, "We have a dead passenger and a driver who will, no doubt, if and when he gets out of intensive care, scream from the bloody rooftops that she died as a result of Police action. Haven't you got a brain between you?...Christ!"

The Inspector collapsed back into his chair, apparently in despair. "The Coroner's going to have a fucking field day with this one."

"All he had to do was stop Sir." Alan said, growing a little tired of the unwarranted tirade of criticism, from a man who hadn't been out from behind his desk for fifteen years.

"What!" the Inspector howled, his eyes staring at Alan in disbelief.

For a moment, Alan felt a little like Oliver Twist, just after he'd asked for more, but he was tired now and suffering from an extremely low shit tolerance level, especially from an office dweller, he pressed his point anyway.

"I said, all he had to do was stop Sir, he's disqualified from driving. He was driving a motor vehicle on a road, that gives us a power of arrest. We correctly challenged him to stop, but he took off. We didn't force him off the road and there was no contact made."

The Inspector became apoplectic and slowly, but determinedly rose to his feet, his face now an unhealthy shade of purple. "Don't you quote fucking definitions to me Pendle." he screamed, all vestige of self-control apparently having fled the scene.

The Inspector paused; he closed his eyes and breathed out slowly through his nose to regain his composure. "I shall be advising Discipline and Complaints regarding tonight's fall from grace, I won't be at all surprised if *you* get arrested for causing death by reckless driving." he said pointedly, his withering stare directed toward Alan. "Now, get out both of you and get on with your statements, before you go off duty…and I don't want to see any claims for overtime."

They both saluted loosely and turning in unison, left the still fuming Inspector to his paperwork. Alan made coffee and entered the Traffic office, nudging the door open with his elbow, the coffee slopped over the sides of the mugs and splashed onto his shoes.

"Shit." he hissed.

"Who's in the shit?" his partner asked, smiling, his feet up on the desk as he leaned back in the Sergeant's chair. Alan pushed one of the steaming half-filled mugs across the table top toward his partner and tutted despondently as he looked down at his sodden shoes.

"We are, if you hadn't noticed mate. You will no doubt recall that just a few moments ago, we received a little less than the expected support from our illustrious Inspector who is no doubt, as we speak, putting pen to paper in colourful diatribe to the black rats in D n' C."

Sullivan swung his legs away from the table top and sat up straight as he reached for the mug of coffee.

"You worry too much mate, 'e's crapping himself 'cos 'e thinks 'e'll 'ave to answer questions at Division. You an' me are quite legit and that wanker knows it, fuck me! It's come to a fine state of affairs if Traffic cops can't stop motors for fear of a chase coming off."

Alan sighed heavily and stared blankly out of the window at the first watery signs of a grey dawn. He felt weary and strangely depressed.

"All he had to do was stop Pete." Alan said quietly, looking across to his partner for some sort of reassurance.

"Yeah, 'an all we've got to do is get our statements right and make it all fit. I've already squared it with Dave Mercer and his mate, we're squeaky clean on this one Al. Now fucking strap on a pair and give us one of your cigs, we've got writing to do."

*****

Alan closed his eyes, yet sleep evaded him. He lay awake, unable to drive the images from the night's occurrence from his mind. The clock on his bedside table showed almost eight thirty. Normally, off nights, by that time he would have been asleep for over an hour. In his mind, the van rolled over and over in slow motion. He imagined the intense, searing pain as the vehicle's bulkhead was compressed rearwards, first crushing her legs, then powdering her pelvis. Her head, first catapulted forwards by the impact, then snapped backwards, as the metal lamp post crushed the front panels of the vehicle. As it rolled over onto its side, the window glass shattered and the roof collapsed onto the top of her head, separating, then crushing the vertebra in her neck. The spinal cord severed. Instant oblivion.

Alan shuddered and pulled the duvet further up over his ears.

The sound of the early morning rush hour traffic droned along the main road under his bedroom window and his senses dulled as fatigue finally won him over. He finally felt himself enter the preamble to sleep, a mild feeling of euphoria, a feeling of well-being as Morpheus finally swept him away.

## **Twelve**

Whilst dreaming it came back to him, crystal clear, in glorious technicolour, as if it had happened only yesterday. The room smelled old and slightly musty, like a church hall or an old suit not worn for years then taken out to air.

The fire in the huge expanse of the open grate hissed and spat small wooden fragments which ignited and soared away up the blackened flu, iridescent for a brief moment before being swept away. The room was familiar, welcoming, like an old friend.

"Morning young Pendle." Sergeant Deal said, as he entered the room carrying a fat, buff coloured folder. Alan thought that he looked unusually wide awake for the hour.

Pc Ian Fielding followed the Sergeant into the room, hurriedly buttoning his tunic. He nodded to his Sergeant.

Sergeant Deal made a point of glancing at his watch, knowing that by this action alone, Constable Fielding would know that his late arrival had not gone unnoticed.

Fielding made a point of arriving for work as near to the hour as possible, his personal maxim seemed to be to do as little as possible for maximum gain. He had thirteen years' service in, all of it spent in the quiet Broughton sub Division. Harbouring no aspirations toward promotion or transfer to a specialist department, Broughton suited him well enough. He remained courteous and friendly towards the inhabitants and helpful enough, when it suited him. It usually suited him to turn a blind eye to those small misdemeanours, such as the local Publicans parking on double yellow lines, or shopkeepers stealing half the pavement width to display their boxed goods, along with the poultry dealers who hung pheasant carcasses over the Public footpath.

Fielding was understanding and had a sympathetic ear for the local shopkeeper's problems. They in turn, understood that Policemen were usually hard pressed to make ends meet. A little too much month left at the end of the money and so, Fielding could always get the odd pint 'on the house' and his groceries on a slate, which was miraculously wiped clean. Not bent exactly, just a little suspect.

"Right." Sergeant Deal said, opening the folder as Vera brought in the coffee. Alan winked and Vera blushed as usual.

"There's all 'ell on upstairs. CID are all runnin' round like 'eadless chickens."

He looked across to Alan then to Fielding. "We 'ad an armed robbery last night."

Sergeant Deal paused to let the impact of the news sink in. Alan's face dropped, an armed robbery in Broughton was about as common as a case of the bubonic plague.

The Sergeant did not look best pleased; he pushed his glasses up the bridge of his nose and read from the yellow flimsy copy of the crime report.

"M.O. as follows, at approximately 1700 hours on Friday the 17$^{th}$ etc, two men entered the premises of Walmsley's Turf Accountants on Mill Hill at Broughton. The perpetrators had disguised their features by way of stocking type material which had been pulled over their faces. One of the males, who is described as being between five feet ten to six feet, was wearing blue denim type jeans and a black blouson style leather jacket. This male produced a short barrelled shotgun from within a blue coloured sports bag with the logo 'Adidas' thereon in white letters. He demanded cash from the Manager of the establishment, a Mr. Robert Shaw. The second male, described as being of similar height, thin build, had a noticeable moustache under the stocking material and was similarly dressed to the first male. He was armed with what appeared to be a large tyre iron or crowbar which he had concealed about his clothing."

The Sergeant paused again and took a sip from his coffee mug and shook his head slowly.

"The complainant had cashed up the day's takings, which are reported to have been in excess of fifteen hundred pounds. This was contained in a dark brown leather satchel with a clasp lock fastener bearing the embossed words Midland Bank thereon, and the company logo stamped on the brass clasp. This, under the threat that violence would then and there be used, was handed over to the male holding the firearm."

The Sergeant took a deep breath and continued. "The complainant was then ordered to turn around. This he did, whereupon he was struck a single blow to the back of his head. It is believed with the tyre iron, which was in the possession of the second male. This blow rendered Mr. Shaw unconscious. He was discovered by a Mrs Irene Cullen at approximately 17.15 hours when she attended the premises to carry out her cleaning duties. The two raiders apparently left the premises via the rear fire exit door, which they left insecure and made good their escape along the canal bank. The second male is reported to have had a local accent."

Sergeant Deal looked up and placed the crime report back in the folder. He was clearly furious, "I don't know what its bloody well coming to, this is Broughton not bloody Chicago." He shook his head in dismay. "C.I.D. requests that the usual checks are to be made with local dry cleaners, for blood stained clothing, apparently Shaw bled like a stuck pig when they belted 'im". Sergeant Deal looked up from the crime report and reached into his tunic pocket for his pipe.

"Alan, we've only got one, Formby's on the High Street, but there's that laundromat on Beck Hill, you never know, someone might have noticed something. See to that will you and let C.I.D. know."

Alan nodded, then added, "Well, I reckon they're either local men or they've been keeping an eye on the place for a week or two, how else would they know what time to go in?"

"Either way." Sergeant Deal continued, "Keep your ears open, someone will have seen something. Ask around…shopkeepers opposite, people living in the flats above the shops, make a point of seeing yer local informants. Ian, I want you to check every shop on Mill Hill and the flats, ok?"

Fielding nodded.

"Oh and Alan, while I remember, some Italian woman phoned up for you. Can't remember her name and Tom didn't make a note. She wants to complain about vehicles parking in front of 'er 'ouse. Asked for you by name, ring any bells?"

Bells rang alright, but not the sort that the Sergeant was referring to; Alan's heart skipped a beat, but he shrugged his shoulders and adopted a vacant expression.

The Sergeant glanced at the briefing sheet. "Before two p.m. if you can…42 Bentham Terrace, ok?"

Alan nodded and pretended to make a note of the address in his pocket book.

His 'older woman' fantasy had run its course and had been totally dissipated in the form of a nineteen year old counter clerk in one of the local banks. It had been almost a month since he had called to see the 'Tigress of Turin'. Better keep her sweet though he thought, woman scorned and all that. Alan didn't want her getting all vexatious and grassing him up to Discipline and Complaints.

The Detective Sergeant entered, looking greyer than usual and Alan guessed that his night had passed without much sleep. Armed robbery wasn't out of his league by any stretch, but he only had a staff of three, namely himself, and two junior

Detectives and one of them was an 'admin' type, working all hours on his precise for Bramshill.

The D.S. was obviously worried that Division would take over and usurp his right to detect this heinous crime.

"Have you had a word John?"

Sergeant Deal nodded. "I've got them doing all the usual checks, cleaners, house to house, shops and the like."

Alan briefly wondered if he could write off an hour or so doing 'house to house' at Bentham Terrace and was surprised to find that he had the beginnings of an erection just at the thought of seeing her again.

The D.S. nodded his thanks and sat on the edge of the table. "Not much we can say at this stage. All I ask is that you don't wait to be told. Ask, ask, and ask again…Everybody you meet on your beats. Somebody's seen something and nothing's too trivial and I'll tell you this, the Officer who gathers the information leading to an arrest will be in C.I.D. the same week, I can promise you that."

Alan made a mental note to pass on any good information he got, on to one of his colleagues just in case.

"Can I have a word with you John, if you've finished with your lads?" the D.S. asked.

Sergeant Deal gave them their beats and meal times and Alan and Fielding were dismissed.

Back in the front office, Alan nudged Fielding's arm. "Jesus Christ Ian! An armed robbery, here in Broughton."

Fielding shrugged his shoulders. "I don't suppose anyone's considered old Shaw doing it 'imself."

Alan frowned, "What do you mean?"

"Just as I say." Fielding said, shrugging again. "Think about it. Old man Shaw rigs it up 'imself, cashes up as normal, hides the takin's, waits till the old bag as does the cleanin' is due, cracks 'is 'ead against the counter top an' lays down till she comes in. 'E groans a bit an' carries on alarmin' as to 'ow 'es bin robbed.

Easy, fifteen 'undred quid's well worth a coupla' fuckin' stitches."

Alan thought for a moment, mulling over the proposed scenario, then shook his head. "Can't see it Ian…C.I.D.'d crack that in ten minutes."

Fielding snorted in disgust. "Christ, what a fuckin' innocent. C.I.D?…this lot 'ere? They couldn't crack a fuckin' walnut. Look, old Shaw's fifteen 'undred quid up and 'es got us lot runnin' round like fuckin' loonies, lookin' for non-existent robbery merchants."

"Look at it this way." Fielding continued, leaning back against the office table, "'Ow much do you reckon old Shaw's paid out in bets in say, the last six months, ten, twenty grand? Maybe 'e's 'ad a bad spell, what better way to recoup 'is losses. I bet C.I. fuckin' D don't ask to see 'is receipts."

Alan shook his head slowly. "I see your point Ian, but I still don't think he could make it wash."

Fielding cocked his head. "You mark my words. It's an insurance 'bake'."

The local Telegraph and Argus seized the opportunity to extract an interview from the complainant, which was printed up on the front page of the weekly edition. The journalists pestered the beat men for a week or two, following them around like flies, seeking a bit of 'inside info'. The subject was avoided as politely as possible and in any case, there *was* no inside info.

It would have stayed that way, if it hadn't been for Sergeant Deal's roses.

Crimes have a sickeningly nasty habit of becoming detected by the simplest of means and the armed robbery at Broughton had been no exception.

Just by pure chance, three weeks to the day of the robbery, Sergeant Deal telephoned the offices of the Broughton and District Telegraph. He'd won first prize for one of his roses, a bed of which, he lovingly nurtured whilst both on and off duty.

The Stainborough and District flower show, organised by the local Women's Institute had bestowed the golden rosette on his 'Elizabeth of Glamis' and Sergeant Deal, pipe stem clasped firmly twixt his teeth, had posed proudly, holding the golden accolade as the reporter had captured the moment for posterity.

The young delivery boy cycled up to the Police station and leant his pushbike against the stone wall by the boiler house door. He took a single copy of the local paper from the canvas bag which he had draped across his shoulder and walked up to the rear of the building and tapped on the window through which, he could see the Sergeant flicking through a glossy magazine full of pictures of women without their clothes on.

Sergeant Deal had jumped at the unexpected tapping on the window and his face and neck flushed as he closed the magazine hurriedly and tossed it onto his table top.

The paperboy held up the folded tabloid and the Sergeant threw open the window, grabbing for the paper and frantically thumbed through the pages, searching for the article on the flower show.

"I see you caught 'em then." the paperboy said blandly, straining his neck to an almost impossible angle to look at the front cover of the Sergeant's magazine. A naked woman with large bosoms smiled back at him from the glossy page.

"Caught who lad?" asked Sergeant Deal.

"Them robbers what did Shaw's."

The Sergeant looked up from the pages and across to the innocent face of the paperboy who was still waiting for his sixteen pence, but was too embarrassed to ask for it.

"What do you mean lad?" Sergeant Deal asked and noting that the youth's attention seemed to be directed elsewhere, he followed his gaze to where the magazine lay open and quickly swept it from the table top and tossed it into his top drawer.

"What was that man doing with that woman?" the lad asked, his face a picture of innocence.

"Never mind that lad…its…erm…evidence…" Sergeant Deal said and coughed with embarrassment. He turned to face the boy. "What about the robbers?"

The lad pointed to a blue Fiat, which was parked at the top of the Police station yard. "Nearly 'ad me off me bike it did."

"When was this then?" Sergeant Deal asked, slowly folding the newspaper, the flower show competition temporarily archived to the back of his mind.

The boy sighed heavily, exasperated at the apparent stupidity of the Sergeant.

"The day that Shaw's got done." he emphasised his words.

"What do you know about that car?" Sergeant Deal asked, nodding towards the top of the station car park.

"I was ridin' me bike to Morrises to collect the papers for me round. I always go along the canal bank, see if there's anyone fishin'. You know, sometimes there's four or fi…"

"Yes, yes, never mind the fishing, what about that car?" Sergeant Deal asked impatiently.

"Like I said, it come along the canal bank, nearly knocked me off, must've been doin' 'undred at least."

Sergeant Deal stared at the youth for a moment; the casual innocence of the remark caused an awful realisation to sweep through him. He leaned through the window and pointed to the small door at the nearest end of the building.

"Come round into the station lad…David isn't it?"

The boy nodded.

A few minutes later, the Detective Sergeant seated himself opposite the lad and leaned across the table in the C.I.D. office; Sergeant Deal stood by the door and sucked pensively on his pipe.

"How come you know it's the same car then David?"

The boy was confident. "The number's the same. I 'ave to remember numbers for me round, I practice, an' anyway, the corner of the boot's grey, same as the one what nearly 'ad me off."

Sergeant Deal walked slowly to the window and peered out to the top corner of the station car park. Sure enough, the corner of the boot lid had been sprayed with what looked to be a coat of grey primer. He turned to the boy.

"What makes you say it was used by the robbers then David?"

The boy shrugged as if it should have been obvious. "Getaway car innit, two blokes wi' stockin' masks and that…"

"They were still wearing stockings over their faces when they drove past you?" the D.S. asked.

"Yeah, they looked really scary like. All their skin was pulled tight." the boy blurted.

"Why didn't you come to tell us what you'd seen before today son?"

The boy became defensive and quickly said, "I told me mam, she says not to make stuff up or I'd be in trouble, she says P'lice 'ave got enough to do an' they wouldn't b'lieve me anyway."

The Detective Sergeant looked straight at the boy, deep into his eyes.

"Are you making it up David? It's important that you tell us the truth."

The boy twisted his fingers together nervously as he looked across at the Detective. "It's the same car, honest."

"Good enough son." the D.S. smiled and patted the paperboy on his shoulder.

Sergeant Deal looked across to his old time colleague, his eyebrows raised, a questioning, yet knowing expression about his face.

"Will your Mum be at home now David?" Sergeant Deal asked.

The lad nodded.

"You on the telephone at home?"

The lad shook his head.

The Detective Sergeant took the lad's address and simply nodded to Sergeant Deal, who without further words, left the office to organise transport for the lad's Mother.

"What about me round?" the lad asked.

"Don't you worry about that son; we'll get that sorted out later eh."

The lad sighed deeply and as he waited, he looked disinterestedly around at the photographs and artists impressions festooning the walls of the C.I.D. office. "Can I look at that magazine the other man had?" he asked innocently.

*****

They sat in the interview room together, the paperboy and his Mother now gone.

The D.S. shook his head and read again the last few lines of the boy's statement which had been countersigned by his Mother.

"Is there a car handy John?"

"Harrowford?" Sergeant Deal asked, questioningly.

The D.S. let his shoulders drop and shook his head slowly. "We can't sit on this John; it'll have to go to Division."

"Rushin' things a bit don't you think Pat…He could've lent that car to anyone."

The D.S. rubbed his eyes with the tips of his fingers and sighed deeply.

"Give up John, I know he's one of yours, but he's bent. He's always sailed close to the wind and we don't owe him a bloody thing. If it's right, there'll be enough of a stink when this caper comes out. It's got to be done straight John, or we'll all end up going down the steps."

Sergeant Deal sighed despondently. "What if young David's imagination's got the better of 'im? Let's be right Pat, 'e's not the sharpest knife in the drawer is 'e?"

"Then your lad's got nothing to worry about has he." The D.S. said flatly.

*****

"Look, I'm sorry mate." Alan said, exasperated. "But look at the tailback you've caused, it's up to the High Street."

"I've only been five minutes Guv." the driver pleaded.

Pc Fielding stood in the center of the road junction and directed traffic around the heavy articulated goods vehicle whilst the driver pleaded his case.

"You can't just abandon your forty foot artic anywhere you want just 'cos you fancy a couple of meat pies Use a bit of common." Alan said, pointing to the queue of vehicles. "Look at this lot."

The driver raised his hands in exasperation. "Loadsa' people park 'ere to nip into Robertson's, I've seen it meself. There's no double yellow lines or owt."

"That's right, there isn't, but you will have no doubt noticed." Alan said, practicing his roadside sarcasm, "That not many, are thirty eight ton five axle 'artics' which, I'm sure you'll agree, take up considerably more room than your common or garden Hillman Avenger. Get my drift?"

The wagon driver sighed heavily and looked resigned to his fate. In his hand, a white paper bag, presumably containing two of Robertson's finest hot pork pies.

"Can I see your heavy goods licence please driver?"

"Oh come on pal, 'ave a day off eh" the driver pleaded. "Five minutes. Five bloody minutes and you're bookin' me for it?"

Alan was unmoved, and as the driver wasted his efforts appealing to his better nature; he watched the paper bag intently. It had now become quiet translucent along the bottom edge where the juices from the hot pies, had soaked through the crusts and got to work on the absorbent paper.

The driver swore under his breath and fumbled in the top pocket of his grimy overalls and produced his licence.

Alan carefully jotted down the licence number and the driver's name and address, keeping a keen eye on the bottom seam of the paper bag as he handed the licence back to the driver. The driver snatched it back, all hope of a reprieve gone.

The sudden movement was sufficient. The bottom seams of the bag parted company and vented the two pies onto the road surface where they both impacted with a dull wet thud and split open to reveal their pink contents. Two plumes of steam rose slowly up from the loose gravel surface.

The driver lifted the bag, staring incredulously at the sodden ragged hole in the bottom. He slowly looked down at the pies, his shoulders dropped and his eyes closed as he mouthed a silent obscenity.

Fielding was trying desperately to control his laughter. Alan bit down hard on his bottom lip as he snapped his notebook shut.

The driver looked wistfully at him. "Go on then, bugger off." Alan said, nodding towards the cab.

The driver beamed. "Oh cheers mate, you're a gent." He looked casually back across to the shop, "I don't suppose I could…"

"Don't push it." Alan said with authority and began to open his pocket book again.

"Ok, ok." the driver said, holding up the palms of his hands and backing away quickly towards the door of his cab.

The huge seven litre diesel roared into life. Plumes of oily black smoke shot into the air from the twin upright exhaust stacks at either side of the cab. The air brakes hissed as the vacuum was released and the juggernaut lurched forwards, running over the pies.

Fielding joined Alan on the pavement and they laughed at the two flattened greasy piles on the road surface. "Nicely timed that Alan." he said, nodding slowly with an approving look on his face.

"Make a good photograph for Sporting Life." Alan said, clicking an imaginary shutter, one eye closed and leaning over the decimated pies. "I can picture the headline, Hedgehogs in suicide pact. They were always so happy together said surviving son Harry."

Fielding chuckled as Alan's radio hissed.

"Alan."

"Go ahead Tom." Alan replied, still smiling.

"Is Ian with you?"

"Affirmative. He's ten six days; we thought we'd double up for a while due to it being so busy."

"Sergeant Deal wants you both to 10/3."

Alan frowned. "Any reason? Over."

"No idea mate, just passing the message." the radio operator replied tersely; Alan mused that the day's crossword must not yet be completed.

"10/4. Five minutes." Alan said and pushed the radio back into the top pocket of his tunic.

"What's that all about?"

"Search me." Fielding said, shrugging his shoulders.

Ten minutes later, Alan followed PC Fielding up the solid stone steps and through the front door into the Police station's public enquiry area, a small foyer with a bench seat facing the fold down counter giving access through to the front office.

Neither had paid much attention to the smartly dressed man seated on the wooden bench seat, who had watched them enter.

Sergeant Deal suddenly appeared at the other side of the counter. Pc Fielding put his hand under the hinged wooden flap.

The Sergeant pressed his weight down onto the scarred woodwork, and at the same time, nodded to the waiting man who stood and walked up to Fielding. He placed a hand on his shoulder.

Alan frowned, as Policemen do, even when very young in service, when they instinctively realise that something is not quite right. He looked inquisitively across to his Sergeant and opened his mouth as if to speak. Before any words could be formed, Sergeant Deal shook his head and his stern look silenced Alan immediately.

The man in the fawn camel coat and the expensive looking brown brogues, spoke softly and slowly.

"Constable Ian James Fielding?"

Fielding whirled around as he felt the man's hand on his shoulder.

"Yes, and you are?" Fielding said defensively, frowning as he shrugged the man's hand from his shoulder.

"I am Detective Superintendent Adrian Preacher. I am with discipline and complaints, I must caution you that you are not obliged to say anything unless you wish to do so, but that anything you say will be taken down and given in evidence. I am arresting you on suspicion that you, with another, on Monday the 17th of March of this year, committed an offence of robbery on a certain Dennis Shaw at his premises on Mill Hill at Broughton."

Alan realised that his mouth had fallen open; he snapped it shut and swallowed hard.

Fielding said nothing and stared through the senior Officer who had now taken hold of his arm.

Sergeant Deal opened the counter top and stepped through into the foyer area.

Alan was struck with sudden panic as the quiet man looked across to him. His heart almost stopped and there was a curiously loud buzzing in his head. *"That you, with another."* echoed back at him and for one ghastly moment, Alan thought that he too was about to be arrested.

"Officer." the quiet man said, looking directly at Alan, still grasping the material of Fielding's tunic sleeve.

"Sir?" Alan said, his voice wavering, not quite believing what was happening.

"Relieve him of his accoutrements if you please."

"Sir?" Alan said questioningly, and looked across to his Sergeant for guidance.

Sergeant Deal nodded. "Staff and handcuffs."

Alan licked his dry lips and looked across to PC Fielding, who was now slumped against the information board attached to the foyer wall. Ironically, his forehead was resting against the information sheet offering a reward for information leading to the arrest of the robbery suspects.

Alan reached across for the leather thong which hung limply from the staff pocket in Fielding's trousers; he drew the staff out with shaking hands. The handcuffs hung loosely from the belt around his waist and Alan fumbled to release them, feeling Fielding's body trembling through his shirt.

Sergeant Deal took Fielding's other arm and together with the quiet man, they led Fielding through the front office and towards the cell area, leaving Alan shocked and stunned, still holding the staff and handcuffs.

The radio operator appeared and from the other side of the counter, he whistled at Alan through his teeth to attract his attention.

Alan looked across at him, still in shock. "What's going on Tom?"

The old radio operator walked up to Alan and took the staff and cuffs from him, patting him gently on the shoulder. "Go and see Vera. Ask 'er to put the kettle on, eh."

Alan looked up to the knowing eyes, confusion and shock still showing on his face. "We've walked the beat together for Christ's sake."

The radio operator nodded sombrely. "You'll see it again before your service is through Alan, I've seen it a time or two and it never gets any easier to believe."

Sobbing could be heard from the cell area and raised voices.

Alan recognised Sergeant Deal's voice, raised as he had never before heard it, then the unmistakeable sound of a loud slap, a chair toppling over and what sounded like a body falling to the floor. Alan looked around, wide eyed, searching for answers from the radio operator who by which time, had disappeared back into his shack.

For the first time ever, he closed the door behind him.

*****

The news that the robbery had been committed by one of their local Policemen, hit the small town like a tidal wave and the Magistrates Court was filled to capacity for the first hearing.

Alan sat with his Sergeant on the Police bench as they listened to the evidence given by the prosecuting Police Inspector.

Fielding stood in the dock along with his fellow accomplice, their heads hung low as the Inspector related the details of the complaint to a disbelieving Magistrate.

Both entered pleas of not guilty, before being remanded in custody awaiting trial at the Crown Court at Harrowford.

Some five months later, Sergeant Deal, whilst taking the early turn parade, informed Alan that Fielding had gone down the steps for eight years and his co-accused for six. "Good fucking riddance." he spat.

The town had changed since the arrest. Alan now felt strangely unwelcome on the streets he had walked for almost a year. There was curious mistrust in the eyes of the shopkeepers and gone were the cheery waves from the market stall holders across the High street.

After weeks of silence, other than the calls of "Goin' down the bookies?" from unseen mouths as he walked his beat, Alan made formal application to transfer to the City.

## Thirteen

As Alan slept fitfully, 'Midnight' Lyburn carefully filled a fountain pen from the cup of hydraulic fluid which sat on his chest of drawers. He immersed the nib of the pen into the clear liquid and squeezed the thin rubber tube, causing bubbles to rise from the oily, viscous fluid.

Releasing the pressure on the tube, the liquid reacted to the vacuum and eased its way through the fluting beneath the nib and filled the rubber sac. 'Midnight' placed the stolen excise licence on a piece of pink blotting paper, making sure that the disc was placed towards the top, so that there was sufficient space for the blotting paper to fully fold over to cover the whole disc. He screwed the body of the fountain pen back over the rubber sac and after shaking the pen gently, drew a single line down the blotting paper, noting with an appreciative nod, that the hydraulic fluid was drawn from beneath the split nib and was immediately absorbed into the paper.

Resting the side of his hand against the top of the chest of drawers, 'Midnight' carefully wrote over the original letters and numbers of the registration mark on the disc. He folded the blotting paper over after working on each symbol, pressing down to allow the fluid and the ink, which it had emulsified, to be transferred to the blotting paper.

He checked his handiwork carefully, making sure that all traces of the original ink had been dissolved and transferred. The disc was now blank, ready to be dried out and the registration mark of his newly acquired vehicle to be added in bold black ink. 'Midnight' smiled at the disc, confident that when completed, the forgery would stand even the closest scrutiny.

A current excise licence being displayed, was usually a good indication that there was also insurance in force, as one had to produce an insurance certificate in order to obtain one of the expensive tax discs from the Post Office.

Tax and insurance was expensive and 'Midnight' needed his money for other more important things. In half an hour, at no cost, he had produced a visual assurance to all, that that his vehicle was taxed. Only if the disc was seized and subjected to the expensive forensic Ninhydrin testing, would the forgery be detected. He held the disc in front of the electric fire until the hydraulic fluid had completely dried. Then carefully, and in black ink, he added the registration number of his Ford.

He lay back on his bed, holding the disc up to the naked light bulb which glowed dimly from the ceiling. Smiling with self-admiration, he reached over for the tax disc holder and deftly rolled the licence into a thin tube which he then inserted between the vinyl, before rolling the forged disc out flat with his index finger.

'Midnight' tossed the disc holder back onto the chest of drawers and stretched out full length on the bed. Placing his hands behind his head, he concentrated on the various shapes formed by the damp flaking plaster above him. His eyes grew heavy and fearful of falling asleep; he leapt from the bed as if electrified.

It was time he decided. He grabbed for his jacket and made for the door. Remembering the tax disc, he took a half step back and took it from the top of the chest of drawers and pushed it into his pocket.

Once out in the street, 'Midnight' breathed in deeply. He inhaled the fresh early evening air, appreciating the sweetness after the dank staleness of his room.

Although it was warmer, the evenings were still quite short. It was almost five thirty and dusk was beginning to cast its grey shadow over the tops of the slate roofs, which glistened with damp at the first hint of condensation.

The stillness of the air allowed thin fingers of smoke to drift unmolested from row upon row of chimney stacks. Grey wisplike tendrils reaching upwards into the darkening sky. The street lights flickered into life and as the sodium filled bulbs warmed after being activated, the half-light from their dim, orange glow still disguised the dirty streets and cracked pavements. No shadows yet from those who stood beneath, to ply their ancient trade.

'Midnight' walked the short distance to where he had parked his vehicle. Never leaving it too close to home, not wanting it to be associated with him. He unlocked the driver's door and slid in behind the wheel. Reaching into his pocket, he withdrew the tax disc and licked around the edges of the vinyl holder. He attached it to the windscreen, placing it directly in the center, behind the rear view mirror and slightly tilted toward the offside. A uniform walking his beat may just glance at the disc to make sure that it was current, but would probably not bother to walk out onto the street and lean over the wing of the vehicle to check its details.

The car started easily, a trait of the most popular Ford ever made. 'Midnight' had a cursory glance over his shoulder before pulling away from the kerb edge. The streets were quiet as they would be for some time. Most of the coloureds would still be sleeping, getting up around eight to roam the streets for a while. They would then make for one of the many 'blues' where cannabis, cocaine and 'Red Stripe' Jamaican lager, would be consumed in great quantities until five or six the next morning.

He pushed a cassette into the car's tape deck; the rhythmic pounding strains of the reggae filled the car as he cruised slowly around the streets he used to own. He glanced up and down the cobbled side streets which ran off in endless rows from the main road. All the same, all dirty, all neglected; the only certainty here was a lack of Police presence, on foot at least.

The only time the uniforms were to be seen, were the Task Force Officers as they poured out from the rear of a Transit van as a team to affect an arrest. Strength in numbers, insurance against the natural hostility and violence they would undoubtedly encounter from the indigenous population. One to affect the arrest, four or five to assist, two to stay with the van and a Dog Handler with an excitable Alsatian hovering not far away.

Task Force arrests, usually for drugs and firearms offences, were hard and uncompromising. The invariable complaint of assault or gratuitous excessive force, would of course have to be weighed by Discipline and Complaints against the sworn statements made by the Officer and his colleagues, all of whom would state that they were present throughout the whole of the incident and the only violence they witnessed was that offered by the subject during his arrest and that the injuries sustained by the prisoner, although regrettable, were as a result of lawful and justifiable force used in response.

That was the code, carved in stone, unbreakable, an *auto de fe*.

The prostitutes favoured the dimly lit streets. They were poor for identification purposes and effectively disguised the drabness of the tired, painted faces of those with no hope of bettering themselves.

Some would take their 'clients' into shabby rooms in one of the back to back tenement buildings to do business. Or, work in the time honoured practice of getting into the company cars driven by fat businessmen in their Burton's suits and Timex watches, keeping an ever vigilant eye out for the Vice Squad.

The girl's high heeled shoes tapped out a staccato rhythmic beat as the heels clicked against the concrete flags of the pavement as she walked. The shoes were black patent leather, the cracked uppers were now separating from their soles and the sides of her bare feet showed, grimy and calloused through the gaps. Her legs were bare and slightly rough where she had neglected to remove the stubble from her shins. She wore a short red pleated skirt which she had rolled up at the waist to leave the hem hanging just a few inches below her black briefs. The cheap plastic handbag she carried swung lazily from her shoulder as she sauntered casually to her 'plot'. Business was quiet tonight.

She leaned against the waist high stone wall and lit a cigarette. Her face half in shadow as the street light above her flickered on in response to its wakening pulse, but as yet, only gave out a dim orange glow. In a few minutes, its inner heat would cause the gas to glow bright yellow and cast eerie shadows over the broken walls and neglected outhouses.

She was twenty seven years old, yet could easily have passed for forty. The many years of street work now telling about her face. Crow's feet wrinkles spread out from the corners of her eyes and disappeared beneath her lank mousy hair. Her forehead was now lined with permanent creases. She wore long sleeves to hide the pin prick marks on the insides of her forearms, the ones which never quite seemed to heal completely.

She danced nervously from one foot to the other as the afternoon heroin induced euphoria dissipated. Her small breasts, unfettered for convenience, had started to sag, mauled a million times by sweating hands, which wandered over them, squeezing and kneading as she performed her art. An art she practised well; the deftness of her hands and mouth left her clients feeling relieved and rejuvenated, free from any obligations, no ties, no promises to keep.

She provided a service to the community in her own way; the frustrated fantasies of respectable men were waged out upon her body. The masturbation into the tissues she carried in her handbag, or into her mouth at extra cost. Straight sex was slightly more, and anal was negotiable. All these services, provided by her, kept the dark, sordid desires away from the bedrooms of the suburban housewife. She'd serviced them all over the years, men of the cloth, bank managers, accountants, and solicitors. All venting their innermost fantasies upon her, letting her know in embarrassed whispers, how and what they required of her.

Her career had been pre-ordained long before her birth. Her Mother's Mother having worked the same streets where she now plied the ancient trade. The streets where she, and the Officers from the Vice Squad, now performed a kind of ritual, a 'pavane', a song of sixpence.

The wailings of the City Fathers, those be-suited gentlemen in the cloistered ivory towers of the Civic Hall, who answered directly to the scathing letters from 'decent' womenfolk (God bless them) with their constant demands to rid the streets of these evil women, were subsequently transmitted down the chain of command to the Divisional Police Officers. It was after all, an election year.

In turn, to placate said City Fathers and the Police Authority, along with the decent righteous women who drafted the original letters of complaint (whose Husbands, unbeknown to them frequented the same evil women with monotonous regularity) loosed upon the streets, the Vice Squad. A peculiar animal, not uniformed yet not quite C.I.D. and held in minor contempt by both.

The Vice Squad. The universally accepted stepping stone to a place in the Criminal Investigation Department.

Two or three years in Vice, the latter part of which spent buying the Detective Chief Inspector's scotch, would usually mean support in any application for a course at the Detective Training School at Force Headquarters. Here, much like the basic training Academy, students would pore over their books, purely concentrating on criminal matters. Murder, Theft, Burglary, Conspiracy and a myriad of other heinous offences which could be committed against the person or property. Only on successful completion of the intensive ten week course and the statutory gift of a case of Scotch to the Senior Instructor, could a PC become a DC, a Detective Constable.

To the greater number of uniformed Officers, both male and female, notification of a temporary secondment to the Vice Squad was an unwritten licence to party whilst on nights, drink on duty, or, if there was a good film showing, a trip to the Odeon, on the pretext of observing gays masturbating each other in the back seats or in the toilets. Or, there was always 'obs' on the Public toilets, those red bricked wanking emporiums, provided by the City Council and regularly frequented by the gays.

In unmarked vehicles, the Vice would sit for an hour or so, observing the local 'fruits' coming and going at regular intervals into the filthy, urine smelling conveniences.

Vice smoked, joked and ate their Mars bars and crisps as they noted the frequency of visits of those afflicted with an alternative sexual orientation.

On the third visit within the same hour by the same person, they would swoop on the assumption that the gentleman was incontinent, suffering from a weak bladder or looking for business.

Vice would creep into the toilets and listen. A pair of well-worn heels facing forwards and protruding from the gap beneath the trap door was a good sign of wrongdoing, especially if on closer inspection; a second pair of shoes could be seen, outstretched and positioned on either side of the wearer of the first pair.

The door would be kicked open and there would be looks of abject horror on the faces of the 'fruits' as unlawful cotious was interrupted and a Police warrant card produced.

"Vice, you're under arrest for gross indecency." The hapless pair, one seated, his trousers about his ankles, his 'friend' knelt between his legs, still grasping the recipient's penis, now returning to a flaccid state at the speed of sound, are dragged to their feet, whilst they hurriedly pull up their trousers.

The Vice Officers are struggling to keep their faces straight. "Hello Melvin, givin' 'im the kiss of life were you?"

The recipient, perhaps unknown to Vice, would blurt out his denials. "I'm partially disabled Officer. This man, who I do not know by the way, kindly offered to lend me a hand with my clothing."

Vice smiles knowingly. "I see Sir, that's why that colourful little ring around your dick just 'appens to match the colour of Melvin's lipstick. You're nicked, the both of you."

More protestations of innocence. To no avail, Vice has seen enough. Warrant cards are hastily stuffed into the back pockets of their jeans and the two red faced prisoners are handcuffed and led to the waiting unmarked car.

One arrest a week would do, just to keep the figures looking right, but not too right, or the Gay Liberation Front would howl to the papers with complaints of harassment and discrimination by the Vice Squad, whereupon, Senior Officers, to avoid having to answer questions regarding justification of their deployment of resources targeting minority groups, would direct Vice to concentrate on the drug and prostitution problem for a while instead.

This delicately maintained balance between law enforcement and toleration was played out carefully by both parties.

The poor arrested unfortunates would be taken to the station and photographed and fingerprinted prior to being charged with Gross Indecency or Male Person Importuning. The regulars no longer given to tears of humiliation at the wry quips from the Custody staff. "Hey up Melvin, how's tricks?"

Tales of a particularly gruesome or perverse act, would be embellished upon and told and retold during meal times or during evening drinking sessions, preferably the latter, as alcohol has an exaggerating effect on the humour of a tale being told.

The most popular at the moment being Gateley's tale.

Gateley, a young uniformed Officer but a few weeks into his service and dutifully walking his foot beat in the City center late one evening, came across what appeared at first glance to be a common drunk who was sprawled across the pavement, which carried foot passengers across a large Victorian cast iron bridge spanning the canal. Gateley thought it was strange, as the man seemed to be quite expensively dressed and well-manicured. Not the usual deportment of your common or garden variety of wino.

The man's face was wax like and ashen and on closer inspection, Gateley noticed that the man seemed to be close to death. His lips were blue and his skin, cold to the touch.

Gateley's eyes fell on an axe, which was heavily blood-stained and laying on the pavement next to the prone body of the man. Panic quickly set in and Gateley blurted out a call for assistance over his personal radio, as there had obviously been murder most foul, plain for all to see.

The good Officer Gateley, whilst waiting for the cavalry to arrive, noticed that the man's left hand was stuffed deep into his trouser pocket from whence spread an ominous dark stain. Now more than slightly perturbed, he nudged the semi-conscious man with the toe of his size ten, causing the 'body' to emit a reassuring groan.

Gateley heaved a sigh of relief at not having to deal with a 'snaggy' sudden death and took it upon himself to help the poor unfortunate to his feet. He struggled with the weight until he managed to get his hands under the man's armpits and he heaved the moaning man to his knees. At this, the stricken man's arm came away from his trouser pocket and Gateley was presented with a gory stump, from which was pumping away the man's life's blood. The hand had been hacked away at the wrist.

One glance at the bloody carnage which had been visited upon the wrist, the white splinters of bone and the muscle, sinew and tendons hanging limply out from the stump, was quite sufficient to cause Gateley to immediately heave a lake of vomit down the man's reasonably expensive suit, and then to fall across him in a dead faint.

Seconds later, the air was filled with the wailing of sirens as his colleagues made good speed from all points of the City to his assistance. With a screech of tyres, they rushed from their vehicles to be presented with the ghastly scene which in fairness, even to the longer serving members of the cavalry, must have looked as if their colleague had been bludgeoned to death with an axe, whilst affecting an arrest.

Gateley laid there, quite still, mouth wide open, his eyes rolled back and a pool of congealing blood emanating from his crumpled form.

Officer Gateley was whisked away from the scene by an ambulance which had been summoned by the Inspector of the day. He demanding that his Officer receive immediate treatment at the Infirmary or heads would roll.

Fortunately, Gateley came to his senses whilst still en route to the house of healing and much to the amazement of the ambulance driver and his mate, asked to be dropped off at the Police station.

Owing to the failure in the request for a second ambulance and the fact that those Officers arriving at the scene had little or no first aid training, the handless man shrugged off his mortal coil whilst still laid out on the bridge pavement. He sadly relinquished his last grasp on life, to the sounds of Policemen vomiting their early meals of shepherd's pie and chips over the bridge parapets. This, much to the displeasure of the Underwater Search Officer who had to wade through the congealed entrée as it sat on the still waters of the canal whilst he, when the fullness of the story came to light, was forced to retrieve the severed hand from the canal basin.

At the Coroner's Inquest, it transpired that the hapless victim had been arrested by Vice whilst in the act of masturbating a young accounts clerk from the offices of the City Council.

He had been charged and bailed to an address where he resided with his 'live in lover', a balding quantity surveyor in his fifties, who wept openly during the Inquest as he told how Julian, the deceased, had come home after being released from custody and in a fit of remorse had decided to come clean (no pun intended).

A savage and bitter domestic dispute had ensued and the adulterous deceased had been ejected from the love nest in a fit of hissing, spitting and scratching.

In an effort to prove his undying love for the quantity surveyor and in a fit of remorse, the deceased had taken an axe from the shed at the back of the house and had walked to the canal bridge.

Placing the errant hand on the iron parapet stanchion, with a single blow, had hacked it off at the wrist. The hand had fallen twenty feet or more into the murky canal waters, and he, to the pavement, where Officer Gateley had happened upon him.

"If thine eye offends thee, pluck it out." the Coroner remarked sadly.

The quantity surveyor nodded slowly, his head hung low, tears running down his cheeks onto the front of his lime green trousers.

The Court fell into a respectable period of silence, as the Coroner returned a verdict of suicide whilst 'the balance of the deceased's mind had been temporarily disturbed'.

Officer Howard Gateley was thereafter referred to as 'Andy' by all ranks.

Unable to accept that if one was seen to have the slightest physical or psychological weakness, one's Police colleagues would identify the deficiency and exploit it to the full...relentlessly, Gateley resigned his Office of Constable three months after the Inquest.

*****

The girl flicked the cigarette end casually over the small wall onto which she leaned. The evening had become decidedly cooler and a breeze infused with the smell of curry, blew the strands of lank hair across her face. She wished that she had brought a cardigan and shivered. Business had been quiet of late. 'Vice' had been paying more frequent visits around the area where she and her colleagues plied their trade.

Most of the Vice Squad cops knew her and used their discretion, more often than not, pulling up in their plain cars simply to have a chat. Sometimes, she would tell them about a particularly weird client, one who had maybe asked her where he could get a very young girl or if she had a younger brother. She might describe him briefly and give them a vehicle type or part of a registration number if she could remember. A good bit of 'info' might just offset her arrest next time she was caught with a punter. The details of an indecency merchant or a potential child molester, being far more important to Vice than a simple arrest for soliciting.

The girls knew most of the Vice cops, some of them by their first names. The male Officers would always have a laugh and a joke with her, it was the Policewomen she despised the most. They looked down their noses at her, contempt showing in their eyes as if in some way, she was belittling their sex, cheapening them somehow.

She was safe from 'Vice' for a while; she'd played out her part of the ritual only a week or so ago. It would be someone else's turn this week.

The Vice cops would sit and watch, sometimes from a parked car or from the window of one of the many derelict buildings. The street dealers, winos and glue sniffers scurrying away like flies at the first sign of Vice. They would watch as the girls approached the cars as they slowed and pulled over to the kerb edge, taking down the make and registered numbers of the vehicles, checking them on the Police National Computer and obtaining names and addresses, logging the frequency of their visits to be used later in cases of Murders or serious assaults.

Any vehicle seen too regularly may prompt a visit to the keeper's address, but usually a telephone call from the Vice Squad office would ensure that the owner of the vehicle would very quickly offer, in hushed tones, to attend at the Police station to 'save them a trip' to his home address.

Vice had noticed the increasing numbers of vehicles which had the bulbs removed from over the rear registration plates as they cruised the red light area of the City. A minor infringement, likely to warrant nothing more than a polite bollocking from a Traffic Cop for failing to illuminate the rear number plate, yet a reasonable deterrent from the prying eyes of the Vice squad cops as they observed from within their vehicles. So prevalent had this practice become, that Vice had borrowed an image intensifier from the Regional Crime Squad, which in almost total darkness, could pick out the registration numbers in an eerie green light.

The girl breathed in and exhaled deeply. She allowed her body to relax against the wall, flicking the wisps of hair from her eyes as she glanced up and down the street. The street lights, now at full intensity, cast a yellow glaze over the sagging roof tops of the terraced houses and highlighted the craters in the road surface, where the asphalt had crumbled away to reveal the shiny surfaced cobbled stones beneath.

She glanced at her watch and sighed again, wondering whether to go for a drink. Della's coffee bar and Soul Food Shop would be open by now. It would be warm and there was a good chance that a few of her friends would have gathered there, it being so quiet.

The car's headlights approaching slowly along the street focused her attention and she watched it approach. It was the slow 'drive by' favoured by the punters, looking to see the goods on offer before committing to buy.

The car slowed further as it approached her. She instinctively hitched her skirt a little higher and leant back against the wall, stretching out her legs in front of her.

The tyres of the vehicle squealed a little as they rubbed against the kerb edge. The car stopped and she shrugged herself away from the wall and glanced quickly up and down the street before approaching the passenger door which had been pushed open from within the vehicle.

She leaned against the top of the door frame, allowing her breasts to press invitingly against the glass. The driver moved the top half of his body over the center console, his left elbow resting on the passenger seat and slowly with his right hand, 'Midnight' reached up and switched on the interior courtesy light.

The girl's confident, business like smile fell from her face like a veil and for a second, she felt a cold tingling sensation at the nape of her neck.

"Trina McKnight as I live an' breath." 'Midnight' said. He smiled as the girl backed away from the vehicle, glancing quickly up the street, for once, hoping that the Vice cops would take an interest in the old Ford Cortina.

The roads were empty and with her heart pounding in her chest, she looked back to the cold, hard eyes.

"Midnight, Jesus…Long time no see man." she blurted, her voice wavering, trying desperately not to show her fear.

'Midnight' raised a hand slowly. "Hey Trina, I'm cool, don't back off girl, I need to talk is all."

"Look, I er, I'd love to man, old times an' all, but I'm waiting, booked, you know how it is. He'll be here any second." she said, glancing at her watch and suddenly realising how false she sounded.

'Midnight' pushed the passenger door further open. "I said all I want to do is talk, no big deal." He looked at her knowingly. "You aint got no trick booked Trina, anyways, I'm here and I'm buyin' so get in."

She gave a last hurried glance up the street, then resigned to her fate, she clambered into his car.

"Close the door Trina."

"Look Midnight man, I never said a fuckin' word I swear I…"

'Midnight' cut her short, waving off her frightened excuses with a raised hand.

He noticed how she instinctively flinched and he smiled to himself.

She fell silent as the vehicle pulled away from the kerb and drove slowly down the street. 'Midnight' eased the car out from the side street and onto the brightly lit main road. She sighed with relief, yet kept her fingers resting gently against the door release handle.

'Midnight' reached across to the tape deck in center of the dashboard and he saw her flinch again as he pushed the cassette home. He turned down the volume as music filled the interior of the vehicle.

"So, what's happ'nin' Trina, bin a long time you know." 'Midnight' asked softly, tapping his fingers against the rim of the steering wheel as he manoeuvred the vehicle though the traffic and out towards the Ring Road.

Trina laughed and nervously chewed her bottom lip. "Oh, you know, same ol' shit. Get busted every now an' then, can't seem to get ahead. Same as always."

She glanced quickly across to him, noting the soft smile playing on his mouth, the prominence of his forehead and the squat nose spread halfway across his face which made him look threatening and intense. She twisted her fingers together nervously as he drove.

"Streets are quiet." he said, not looking at her.

"Yeah, back end of the holiday season. Their all away, fuckin' their wives in Benidorm. Always like this, remember?"

'Midnight' nodded slowly. "Yeah, I remember."

She remembered, she remembered only too well. How she had been petrified of him when the week's money had been short when punters were down because of the holiday season; she remembered the look in his eyes when she knew that he suspected her of keeping money back from him. She remembered the vicious rages, when his eyes would open wide, filled with anger. She remembered the slaps and punches. Never in the face, but on the body where the real pain came from. She remembered the open razor and the coldness of the stainless steel as it had softly but threateningly, caressed her cheek.

She remembered what had happened to the 'Chinese'.

"Look Midnight." she said, drawing on what little confidence she had. "If you wanna reminisce, great, but can't it wait till tomorrow man, during the day. Things are bad enough you know…" She leapt away from him and her fingers tightened on the door handle as he lifted himself up from his seat and pushed his hand into the back pocket of his jeans.

She swallowed hard, fully expecting to see the dull ivory sheen of the razor. Her body fell limp as he tossed a crumpled twenty pound note across into her lap. Again he smiled to himself, noting the reaction she had displayed. "It's still there my man, you can have it all back and more. Five years away and it's still fuckin' there." he thought. "I'm payin' for your time Trina." he said. "All I want is a little information, so you've no need to be crappin' yourself, ok?"

"Sure Midnight, it's just kinda strange seeing you around again after, well, after you know…" Her voice trailed off and she stuffed the note into her handbag and for a moment, considered the irony of him giving her money. "Whatever." she said quietly.

'Midnight' pulled the car off the main road and into the car park of the municipal sports centre, now closed for the night.

The tyres crunched on the loose gravel as he drove to the bottom end of the car park away from the main lights on the main road. He killed the engine and turned off the lights.

She sat in silence, listening to the engine ticking as it cooled.

'Midnight' reached under the front edge of his seat and pushed the small lever across. The seat slid back on its runners. He stretched his legs so that he could reach into the small ticket pocket in the front of his jeans and from it; he withdrew a crumpled hand rolled cigarette. He twisted the ends of the thin paper around the cardboard tube which served as a filter to protect his lips from the heat which the mix would generate;

'Midnight' took the tube between his lips and lit the twisted end of the roach. Immediately, the heady aroma of the bush filled the interior of the vehicle and he inhaled deeply.

She looked across at him, relaxing slightly, but ever mindful of their deserted location.

'Midnight' pulled on the smoke again and inhaled, holding his breath as he turned to face her, offering her the joint. She accepted it with shaking fingers and squinted as the hot oily smoke which sputtered upwards as the small seeds within the wrap ignited.

She drew on the damp end of the cardboard tube and inhaled the pungent brew. He shuffled himself further down in his seat and opened his window slightly to let the smoke drift out.

"So who's the man now Trina?" he asked nonchalantly. He took the joint from her fingers as she offered it back. "Or are you freelancing these days?"

She snorted and looked away, out of the window to the deserted rear of the sports center. "There's no freelancing in this City, you oughta know that."

"I've bin away Trina, things change." he said softly, his left hand now slowly caressing her leg.

She turned slightly sideways, her back against the door panel as she looked at him, his passive features at the moment, belying the violence of his nature.

"Lots of things 'ave changed, it's not like the old days anymore, fuckin' Vice are everywhere man. The AIDS thing, everybody's shittin' 'emselves."

"Who's the man Trina?" he snapped.

She winced as his fingers tightened around the flesh of her thigh. His stare bored into her, but he relaxed his grip on her leg.

"You won't know 'im." she said, looking down at her hands, which lay on her lap, gripping her fingers together to disguise the shaking. "'Soldier'…Garrison. He came in from Bristol, two, maybe three years ago."

"You payin' 'im rent?" Midnight asked.

She nodded. "We all are." Nervously, she pushed her hair behind her ears and stared out through the windscreen.

"How much?" He asked.

Trina diverted her eyes and looked wistfully out through the passenger window. "Eighty a week."

'Midnight' shook his head slowly and released the grip on her leg, patting her knee to put her at ease. "No wonder you look like shit girl, how much you makin' for yourself? I presume you're rippin' him off a piece."

She paused for a second, not sure of his drift. "I can clear twenty, thirty a week if I get lucky."

"Who be runnin' the girls an' the blues?" 'Midnight' asked, nudging her arm gently with his fingers to focus her attention.

"Fastener's his main man' she said softly.

"Fastener, what sort of half assed name is that?"

Trina shrugged. "His name's Zippleman, calls himself the Fastener, his old man must've been Jewish or somethin' I don't know."

"Where's he at?" he asked. He reached across and ran his hand up from her knee and onto her thigh.

"Look Midnight, I don't know, 'onest." she blurted, her voice quivering. "I just don't know."

'Midnight' considered the fact that she may be more afraid of this 'Fastener'' than she was of him. He gripped the inside of her thigh to prompt her.

"I don't see 'im, none of us do." She sighed deeply. "He sends a collector once a week or so, I pay 'im an' 'e leaves me alone. That's all, I like it that way an'…It's the same for all of us."

"How many he runnin'?" 'Midnight' asked.

"Twelve…fifteen maybe. They come and go, some of the girls you used to run, Helen Tebb, Jean Moores and a few others you'd remember, but most only stick around for a month or two, then do a runner, Manchester, London, they always seem to turn up again, usually with an arm or a leg in plaster..." Her voice trailed off again. She turned to stare out of the windscreen, steaming up with condensation now and blurring the view of the main road which might just as well have been a million miles away.

"The 'Chinese', where's she at?" he asked, gripping her leg again.

Trina winced and her ears roared with the rushing of blood as her heart rate quickened.

He had cut the 'Chinese', cut her with his razor. She had almost died, would've done if Vice hadn't come across her laid out on the pavement.

"Gone, gone ages ago." she shook her head. "'Er old man croaked an' she just disappeared, 'onest, I havn't seen her in…must be three years."

'Midnight' released his grip on her thigh.

"What's this 'Fastener'' mo'fucker look like?"

"Look, I don't see 'im, it's like I said." Trina stuttered. Tears welled up in her eyes and spilled over to run in dark rivulets down her cheeks as her mascara dissolved. She wiped her face with the flat of her hand, smudging the darkness across her cheekbones.

'Midnight' sighed impatiently. "S'right Trina, I'm cool. Don't go weepin' an' fuckin' moanin' on me now."

She sniffed and fumbled in her handbag for her cigarettes. Lighting one with trembling hands, she inhaled deeply and wound down the passenger window to blow the smoke out into the chilled air.

'Midnight' slouched down in his seat again. "Just want to know where the competition is at that's all, no big deal."

"Oh yeah!" Trina blurted out with a sob. "No big deal for you, I get my fuckin' legs broken." She sucked nervously on the cigarette. "You don't know 'im, but 'e knows about you, 'e jumped in as soon as you got lifted. The fuckin' rent went up as well as the rough stuff, I wouldn't be able to work for a month if 'e found out I'd bin talking to you."

'Midnight' moved towards her. "Look, Trina, I bin away. Now I'm back, an' I'm takin' it back, all of it. You tell me about this 'Fastener' an' you get to work freelance with my protection."

She shook her head fiercely and pulled away from him. "Look man, no way you can jus' move back in. 'Soldier' runs things now. You can't just move in on a man like 'im, e's into everything, it's all sewn up, the girls, the dope, the blues." She sobbed again, not wanting anything to do with the dangerous game that she could see was hatching.

'Midnight' snorted his disgust. "Shit Trina, he's just another nigger, same as the rest. I'm tellin' you girl, he's finished…history, with or without your help. But you come along an' you work for free."

She shook her head slowly. "You don't know what 'e's like…People've turned up dead, he doesn't give a shit. He's got too big, he's untouchable."

'Midnight' snorted again. "Aint no such thing as untouchable Trina, you just got to have a plan is all. You could come out of this good girl…Look, how long do you think you've got left on the streets, five years, maybe ten at the outside? Lookit you girl, you all fucked up even now." he said, grabbing for her wrist and forcing the sleeve of her blouse up over forearm to emphasise his point. She pulled her arm away, embarrassed at the small bruises and scabs which the needles had caused. She pulled the sleeve back down.

"What you gonna do then?" he asked. "Look, you could be runnin' your own show girl." His voice softened. "Runnin' the girls with me, instead of humpin' yo' ass dry."

She looked across at him, wary, yet interested in his proposition.

"I mean it." he said, nodding his head. "I run the blues and the dope, you handle the women. All it takes is someone to off this 'Fastener'' fuck, an' we're both in business."

She sat in silence, mulling over his words, dropping her cigarette end out of the window.

"You'll never get within a yard of him." she said. "He surrounds himself with the gangs; they do exactly as he tells them."

"An' if he's replaced." 'Midnight' asked questioningly.

"What do you mean?" Trina asked.

"Say this 'Fastener' fucker suddenly died of a heart attack tomorrow, who'd step up?"

She shrugged.

'Midnight' pointed a finger. "I'll tell you who girl, the man with the money an' connections for the dope. Fucker's only there 'cos he in the know. We both know how it works Trina."

There was a silence in the car as Trina considered what he'd said.

The quartz clock clicked away the seconds from where it sat in the middle of the center console.

"What the fuck you got to lose girl?" 'Midnight' urged.

"I don't know about his crib." she said softly. "No one does, but he runs a big blues on Marbury Avenue."

"You work there?"

"Some nights." she admitted.

"What's he like?" 'Midnight' asked.

She turned to look out of the passenger window and wiped away the condensation with the tips of her fingers. "Big dude, flashy, wears lots of rings an' shit like that, you know, 'spensive suits an' ties an' stuff."

"He drive?" he asked.

"Never." she said, shaking her head. "Uses private hire everywhere he wants to go. He leaves the blues about four, five in the mornin', walks down to 'Dellas' Soul Food place and gets a cab from there."

"Same firm every time?" 'Midnight' asked.

"No idea, I just know that he goes by taxi everywhere. They reckon he's shit scared of driving."

"Just how big is this blues?" he asked, his interest intensifying.

"Massive…always plenty there." she said.

"Locals?"

Trina shrugged. "Yeah, the usual's, although you might not know 'em now. They come over from Manchester a lot."

"Brothers?"

"Whites as well." she replied.

'Midnight' considered the information for a while. He watched the girl as she lit another cigarette, her hands were steady now. "She's not so frightened anymore." he thought.

He reached slowly across with his hand and placed it on her knee and ran his fingers up to the hem of her skirt. She instinctively opened her legs and he toyed with the soft flesh between her inner thighs.

"He do the deals from there?"

Trina nodded. "All the blues do big business now, guns, dope, women, whatever you want, they're safe."

"How so?" he said, frowning.

Trina laughed nervously. "Jesus, you have been away a long time. It's safe 'cos the fuckin' cops don't bother with them anymore. They'll pull someone off the street, but they're scared shitless of a riot startin'. The blues 'ave bin safe for two, three years now."

"I heard there'd bin trouble." 'Midnight' said, lifting the hem of her skirt to look between her legs.

"Trouble." she laughed. "Last time a blues was raided, the cops took a right kickin', cars turned over, shop windows through, loads of cop cars wrecked, it was fuckin' great."

"How much bush he movin?" 'Midnight' urged, wanting to get back to the matter in hand.

"As much as 'e wants." she replied. "But bush is out for the blues. You can sell a joint out on the streets, cops aren't going to risk a kickin' for the sake of a few joints. It's all coke now, they sniff it up through rolled up fivers. Give 'em a few minutes an' you can charge what you like, most of 'em so stoned, they couldn't get it up with a fuckin' fork lift truck."

"What about smack?" 'Midnight' asked.

"Yeah, loads." she shrugged. "China white, Mex brown, Meth, whatever."

'Midnight' smiled.

She glanced at her watch. More than an hour had passed since he had picked her up.

He saw the anxious look on her face and he reached into the pocket of his jeans and pulled out a handful of money. Her eyes lit up at the sight of the crumpled mass of notes. He tossed them into her lap. "You in with me or what?" he asked.

She looked across at him. "What sort of business?" she asked cautiously.

'Midnight' reached across and gently ran a finger across her cheek. "You're on the inside; you see what I need to know. I need times, regular things, his habits, like when he arrives, when he leaves an' with who. You come see me at my crib…No one's any the wiser."

She swallowed hard. "I've told you man, I'm dead if 'e finds out."

"Finds out what?" 'Midnight' said, becoming exasperated. "There's nothin' for 'im to find out, an' you aint gonna be involved until it comes off."

"Till what comes off?" she asked, a little frightened.

"Bes' you don't know right now. You want in on the deal or what?" 'Midnight' asked.

"You'll really give me eighty a week?" Trina asked flatly.

"And some." 'Midnight' replied, nodding. "An' after I off this 'Fastener' fuck, you run the girls an' the street work."

"What about 'Soldier' and the gangs?" she asked questioningly.

'Midnight' shook his head. "You let me worry 'bout that. One nigger at a time. The gangs be comin' across when the real money starts comin' their way."

She hesitated, then scooped up the notes and stuffed them into her handbag. "Ok."

"We in business girl." He smiled as he reached across, cupping one of her breasts in his hand.

She looked across at him, a questioning look about her face.

"To seal the deal babe." he said.

She snorted and laughed nervously, but reached across to the zip on the front of his jeans, drawing it down slowly.

She shivered slightly in the cold air of the vehicle and felt the hairs on her arms standing up as her skin expanded to gain what little heat there was.

'Midnight' groaned as she took hold of him, gently pulling back his foreskin and running her thumb over the head of his engorged gland.

She felt his hand grip the hair at the back of her head and the pressure as he pushed her face down towards his lap and so, with experienced efficiency, she went to work.

## **<u>Fourteen</u>**

The telephone warbled its shrill beckoning tone from the top of the glass coffee table in the corner of the lounge. Alan sighed annoyingly and pressed the pause button on the remote control device which lay on the padded arm of his settee. The picture on the TV screen froze, leaving the olive green clad troopers from the 101st Airborne Division, tableau like amongst the ruins of Khe Ta Laou in the A Shau valley. He groaned with annoyance and pulled himself up from the comfort of the chair, silently cursing at being interrupted whilst he was watching a film, especially as he was off nights.

He'd slept restlessly during the day, the visions of the previous night's incident gnawing at his subconscious, denying him much needed sleep whilst he mentally defended his actions. By lunch time, Alan had given up all hope of sleep and had lain in bed, listening to the sounds of the day.

When at one o'clock, the Water Board jack hammers began their assault on the road surface further down the street; he had thrown the duvet cover back and staggered from his bed towards the bathroom. He'd showered and whilst still drying himself, wandered zombie-like into the kitchen area and thrown the switch on the kettle.

Pulling on a pair of his favourite tracksuit bottoms and a faded sweatshirt, he'd lit his first cigarette of the day.

Walking through into his lounge, he pressed the rewind button on the video unit which sat on a glass and chrome unit by the window. The motor whined as it rewound the film, which it had magically captured from the night before.

Notwithstanding the lack of solid sleep, there was a certain satisfying feeling about lounging about all day when everybody else was at work. Nights were sacrosanct and Alan religiously avoided making any plans for the seven or eight hours that he had completely to himself between waking and resuming night duty.

His coffee cup was empty and sat on the small table by the side of the settee. He munched his way through a large bowl of cereals as he watched the best equipped, best supported army in the world, getting its arse kicked by small, slant eyed men wearing loose black pyjamas.

Alan picked up the handset, more interested in stopping the annoying warble than who was actually on the other end of the line.

"Hello." he said, the unwelcome intrusion obvious in his voice.

"Hello yourself, you crabby bastard."

Alan smiled as he recognised the dulcet tones of his partner through the amplified earpiece. His tone immediately changed. "Hey Sully, what's up?"

His partner laughed down the telephone. "You bad tempered prat, called you at an inopportune time 'ave I? The good Officer Prestwick kept you busy off nights? Or yer cleanin' lady doin' 'er bit for the troops?"

"No, I was watching a vid from last night and you know full well that I don't have a cleaner." Alan replied.

"Nympho Nurses again, eh? You'll go blind mate." His partner said, chuckling.

"Look Pete, much as I appreciate your lurid humour, can we get to the point. I suppose there's a valid reason for this unwarranted intrusion into my personal leisure time?"

Alan reached across and pressed the pause button again. The scene on the flickering screen advanced a frame or two and the forward sight of a Kalashnikov assault rifle appeared from behind a shattered tree stump, a bright flash of light rushing from its vented barrel end.

"There is indeed. Our illustrious leader has called. We've to go in at seven tonight. There's a job on."

"What sort of job?" Alan asked.

"Christ knows, does it matter, its three hours overtime." His partner replied.

"Apart from the financial ramifications, did you actually ask what it was about?"

"No knowledge mate." his partner replied. "Very secret squirrel. I picked up the telephone, a cloud of cigar smoke billowed out from the earpiece an' Roger just says you an' me are to parade at seven sharp, when all will be explained."

Alan reached across for his cigarettes, holding the handset between his ear and shoulder as he fumbled with the lighter.

"Yeah, ok Pete, I am so warned. I'll see you at seven."

"Couldn't pick us up could you Al? Linda will still 'ave the car."

Alan gave a much exaggerated sigh down the phone. "No problem you bleedin' nuisance. I'll see you 'bout twenty to then."

"Cheers mate." His partner replied cheerily.

"See you." Alan said, although the line had already gone dead.

He slouched back into the settee and touched the play button. The tall Negro trooper on point sagged to his knees as a .762 fully jacketed round burst through the rear of his helmet, spraying the R.T.O. behind him with small shards of metal and brain matter.

*****

The Traffic Sergeant rolled the end of his cigar amongst the ash and dead matches in the glass ash tray on his desk. The hot ash flaked off and revealed the dull red glow of the burning tobacco.
He listened condescendingly to the Chief Inspector on the other end of the telephone line and rolled his eyes toward the office ceiling.

"Yes Sir, I'll personally ensure their presence at seven thirty. I'll make sure that they are aware Sir…yes Sir." The veteran Traffic Sergeant replaced the handset onto the body of the telephone and cursed under his breath as he leaned back in his chair.

The door to the office opened. "Hi Sarge, what's up?" Alan asked as he entered, casting an inquisitive glance across to his partner, both noting their Sergeant's dour expression.

"Firstly." the Sergeant scowled. "That." he said, pointing down to the telephone, "was Mr 'shit for brains' Parkin who annoys me simply by his very presence on the same planet as me, tellin' me how to organise my lads for the job of the century, secondly" he said, peering disappointedly into the dead end of his cigar, "my fuckin' smoke's gone out. Give us your lighter Alan."

Alan tossed his lighter across the table top as his partner collected three empty mugs from the window ledge; grimacing at the sight of the wizened tea bag, which had seemingly time welded itself to the bottom of one of the mugs.

"Look at this shit." Sullivan said, tipping the mug towards his Sergeant, exposing the hairy green bacterial growth which was permeating through allegedly two thousand perforations.

The Sergeant screwed his face up and backed away. "Yes, very nice Peter, thank you for that." he said, waving the mug away from his face.

"It's fuckin' Oldfield an' 'is tea." Sullivan spat contemptuously. "Tea's for civilians an' old people, Traffic men drink coffee." he muttered, striding out for the door clutching the mugs.

"What's the job then Sarge?" Alan asked, rummaging through his docket to see what grief had arrived as a result of the previous night's incident.

Relieved not to find any form of a notification of complaint from Discipline and Complaints, he pushed the docket drawer closed and took a seat.

"Believe it or believe it not, I'm not able to advise you." the Sergeant replied, drawing heavily on his cigar. "I am not involved, therefore, I have not been made privy to the night's entertainment. You and the 'long one' will find out when you attend his little soiree at seven thirty. Conference room, second floor. Prompt attendance expected."

Alan looked around, "Why all the secrecy?"

"'Cos he doesn't fuckin' trust us is why." his Sergeant replied.

The Sergeant sucked on the cigar which rendered fresh air into his mouth. "Shit." he said scowling as he peering at the blackened end of the damp chewed cigar. "Give us a light Alan."

Alan pointed to the lighter which was still lying on the Sergeant's desk. "Ever considered buying one of those Sarge, they're quite cheap and available at most good retail outlets."

"What grips me." the Sergeant spat, ignoring Alan's sarcasm, "is that I was taking the oath of allegiance whilst that prick was still pissin' 'is bed."

Alan smiled, "At which unfortunate is this tirade of abuse directed?"

The Sergeant adopted a distasteful expression. Chief Inspector, I'm going to be Chief Constable one day Parkin."

"Oh him." Alan said, raising his eyes toward the ceiling, "I've heard he still pisses the bed."

"Bramshill man." the Sergeant muttered. "Fuckin' eunuch."

Sullivan re-entered, carrying the mugs which now held steaming water. He pushed aside the various boxes and containers in the coffee swindle locker, spilling most of the contents of the mugs onto the carpeted floor as he rummaged. "No bloody milk chaps, sorry."

"Steal some from the nine to fiver's fridge downstairs Sully. Use yer fuckin' initiative lad." the Sergeant smiled and settled himself down into his chair. He reached out once again for the 'Team' lighter. Squinting his eyes, he ignited the two inch stub which was firmly clenched between his teeth and exhaled a thick blue cloud of smoke into the confines of the office.

"He must have given you some inkling of what it was about Sarge." Alan said inquisitively.

The Sergeant shrugged. "Huh…what, me?..a mere Sergeant with only twenty seven years' service in. Why! I am unworthy to flush the rascals from 'is toilet. No, we shall 'ave to wait Alan lad."

"Suspense is killin' me." Alan said, smiling and returned his attention to his clerical docket.

The Sergeant chuckled. "I 'ope whatever it is 'e's got organised goes better that 'is famed raid on the fuckin' Polish Centre last year."

Alan was engrossed in reading the long awaited joining instructions from Stretham, advising him of the start date for his basic firearms course. "So, the shit for brains Inspector didn't mix me a powder after all." Alan whispered to himself, tucking the document into his shirt pocket.

He sat down opposite his Sergeant and gave him his undivided attention. The firearms course was in the bag and all was well with the world.

"Which was that?" Alan frowned, not being able to bring it to mind.

"It was a fuckin' classic." the Sergeant said and winked. "Parkin gets wind that they're serving after hours at the Polish Club so 'e takes it upon 'imself to organise a raid on said premises. 'E organised half a dozen beat lads, a Tranny van full of Task Force Neanderthals and a Dog Man for good measure. At the appointed time, Parkin blows that fuckin' whistle 'e always carries around and they all barge in. Must've bin like the first day on the fuckin' Somme."

Alan chuckled as the Sergeant continued to graphically describe the scene.

"The lads all pile in and start seizin' all the glasses, sealin' the tops with fuckin' cling film and start takin' names and addresses. Parkin, gawd bless 'is cotton socks, leaps up onto the stage and grabs the microphone off the "turn", some fuckin' Rumanian fire eater from 'alifax, an' promptly informs everybody that they are under arrest. All would 'ave bin well, 'cept Parkin 'adn't checked the licensing register. It was a Polish weddin' with an extension till two am."

Alan laughed as his Sergeant coughed and choked on the fetid smoke from his smouldering cigar. "'is faux pas may well 'ave bin forgiven 'cept the dog man's pup bit the groom on his knackers." The Sergeant's eyes filled with tears and his shoulders rocked with mirth. Alan laughed more at his Sergeant's warped sense of humour, than the tale itself.

Alan thumbed through his pocket note book and ruled off the previous night's entries. "You hear 'bout him in the toilets with Ron Dennison?"

The Sergeant shook his head, regaining his composure slightly.

"I was in trap three last week, when they were havin' that promotion do for Dave whatsisname, the lad from Task Force. Anyway, old Ron Dennison and Parkin come in to take a leak. I'm sat there mindin' me own business and I can hear Parkin extolling the many virtues of Bramshill to old Dennison whist they're stood at the piss stones. I don't know what service Ron's got in now, but 'e must be about ready for off."

"Joined up just after the relief of Mafeking." Sullivan added, as he stirred the coffee noisily.

"Anyway." Alan continued. "I hear zips being pulled up and Dennison goes to the sinks 'cos I can hear the taps runnin'. Parkin must've gone straight for the door 'cos I heard old Ron call out to 'im. 'Don't they teach you to wash your hands after you've been to the toilet at Bramshill then Sir?'

Parkin shouted back. 'At Bramshill Sergeant, they teach one how not to piss on ones fingers.'

The Sergeant chuckled and spilled coffee down the front of his shirt. "I'm more surprised to hear that Parkin stands up to piss to be 'onest."

*****

19.30 hours, Alan and his partner entered the spacious conference room office where thirty or more uniformed Officers and a handful of Detectives, were already sitting around in various groups awaiting the commencement of the briefing. The room was heavy with conversation and cigarette smoke. Detectives from the Division were laughing and talking with colleagues who had moved away from normal divisional duties to the Drugs Squad. Long hair and beards, patched and faded jeans and sweatshirts belied their profession and set them apart from the smartly dressed Divisional jacks in their suits and ties.

Groups of Task Force Officers with their reinforced helmets and heavy boots, stood around in a tight group, reminiscing about the differing amounts of action they had seen during the Miner's strike.

Sullivan moaned, "Oh fuck me, its Serpico and the Storm Troopers." He nudged Alan, directing his attention to where the Drugs and Task Force Officers were standing. "Looks like a B.J."

Alan glanced around the room and spotted a white top, another Traffic man from an adjoining Division. He nudged his partner. "Must be mate, they've roped Dave Mercer and his mate in from City."

They made their way through the crowd of Officers, nodding every now and then at a face they recognised.

"Alright Al?" One of the City men asked and smiled as Alan and his partner joined them on the row of seats at the front of the office. Sullivan nodded and accepted the half empty plastic cup of vending coffee from his colleague from across the City.

"Much said about last night's job Al?" he enquired.

Alan shook his head, lighting a cigarette whilst glancing across at the clock, to make sure that he had time to finish it before the briefing started.

"We took a right bollocking from the night Inspector, but that was to be expected." Alan said.

"Not grounded are you?" the City man enquired.

Alan shook his head and settled back in the chair listening to the snippets of conversation that filtered through the general hubbub of noise.

"Horgreave, that were a fuckin' picnic, you should've bin at Frickley mate, we took some right stick there…doled some out as well a'course, it were like a bad day on Falls Road, you ought to 'ave seen…"

"I hope it kicks off big style tonight." another said. "For once we've got the lads and the kit, all we want is some senior Officer with enough balls to…"

"What do you reckon then Al?" the City Traffic man asked.

Alan shook his head and pursed his lips in thought as he looked around the room at the gathering of Task Force, Drugs Squad Officers and Detectives. "Haven't a clue Dave. The 'Squad' are here so it looks like a drugs raid maybe. Our boss was pretty tight about it. Me an' Sully can usually torture him into submission, you know, hide his cigars or the coffee stuff, but he wasn't havin' any of it, only that Parkin was organising it."

"Not Bramshill Parkin!" the City traffic man exclaimed, a look of abject horror on his face.

"The same." Alan smiled; clearly the rumours of Parkin's incompetence and ineptitude had spread to all the outlying Divisions within the Force.

The swing doors of the C.I.D. Office burst open and a loud, authoritative voice cut through the barrage of conversation.

"Thank you gentlemen, please be seated. We've got a lot to get through."

Chief Inspector Reginald Parkin and George Denholme, the Beat Inspector of the day, walked hurriedly up to the desk at the front of the office and the conversation in the room quickly died away. Chairs were shuffled into position as the Officers settled themselves down.

"Gentlemen, you may smoke." the Chief Inspector said, not looking up from the briefing board that he and the Inspector were engrossed in. Had he bothered to cast an eye over the amassed group of Officers, he would have noticed that most were smoking anyway.

"Good evening." Parkin said, placing the briefing board squarely and precisely on the desk in front of him. "For those of you who do not know me, I am Chief Inspector Parkin and I am in overall command of this evenings exciting operation."

"We're all in the shit then." said a voice toward the back of the room, just loud enough for most to hear. Parkin obviously had not and as bottom lips were bitten and coughs feigned to conceal laughter, he raised a clipboard for all to see and said proudly, "Gentlemen, Operation Home Front."

The Beat Inspector took a half step backwards and coughed into his clenched fist to stifle a smile.

"Rather apt Gentlemen, as I am sure you will all appreciate as I make you privy to the nature of this operation."

"Berlin tonight is it then Sir?" one of the more senior Detectives called out from the back of the office.

There was a brief ripple of laughter across the room, but it quickly died away, as the beat Inspector glowered and peered amongst the sea of faces in an effort to identify the heckler.

Parkin, either too thick skinned to realise that the lads were taking the piss out of him, or so engrossed in his brainchild, continued, oblivious to the smiles and slowly shaking heads.

"The nature of this operation has been kept from you, except those Officers from the Drugs Squad who I might add at this juncture, have worked long and hard on the logistics of this particular operation. Thank you gentlemen." Parkin said, and nodded appreciatively toward the long haired weirdo's leaning casually against the wall at the rear of the office.

"Where was I?...Ah! yes. The nature of this operation is delicate and because information has a nasty habit of leaking out, innocently enough sometimes I grant you, but nonetheless, out, the intrinsic details of this operation have therefore, not previously been disclosed."

The Chief Inspector looked out across the sea of expectant faces and added, by way of admonishment. "I only wish as much information found its way into the Local Intelligence Office as that which gets leaked so freely to the editor of the local newspaper."

Parkin stared long and purposefully at one of the uniformed Officers whom he strongly suspected was responsible for a letter which had been sent anonymously to the local paper regarding the 'discretion' employed by certain Senior Police Officers. This being in respect of personal friends, golf club associates and members of the local Masonic Lodge who had received 'leniency' in respect of various parking and speed infringements.

The 'mole' had alleged that a number of these influential pillars of society had escaped prosecution for offences which under normal circumstances would certainly have led to prosecution.

An article which was printed on the second page of the local Telegraph caused not a little consternation in the Senior Officers Dining room for a week or two.

Parkin dropped his stare from the Officer who retained an innocent expression throughout the psychological interrogation and he returned his attention to the clipboard. "This operation has been formulated from its inception, on a need to know basis and you" he said, passing the clipboard slowly over the heads of the gathered multitude, "did not need to know until now." Mutterings of dissent broke out at the obvious distrust Parkin had in his Officers.

Unperturbed, he continued. "It is planned to raid a blues party where it is believed, large amounts of cannabis, heroin, cocaine and other mind altering substances are freely being sold and abused."

The room erupted into excited whoops and a clamour of conversation.

Parkin held up a hand to silence his troops. "It has I know, been a long time, too long in my opinion, since this Force has initiated an action such as this, however, such is the quality of the information received," again Parkin nodded with gratitude toward the Drugs Squad Officers before he continued, "that the amounts of controlled drugs involved are so great and the sale and abuse so widespread, it has led the Divisional Officer to sanction this operation. His vacillations finally set aside by the gravity of political fervour and pressure from the anti-drugs campaign group."

"What the fuck's vacillations?" Alan heard one of the Task Force Officers seated behind him ask.

"It's that jelly stuff queers smear on their dicks." a colleague whispered.

Alan chuckled and returned his concentration to the ranting's of the Chief Inspector.

"I cannot stress strongly enough however, the need for the utmost tact and professionalism to be employed by all the Officers engaged in the actual raid. I need not, I am sure, labour on the known sensitivity of the target area and the volatility of the indigenous population. Our cause is just gentlemen, but we must be ever mindful, that the success of the operation will be measured against any public complaints alleging the unnecessary use of force, the use of any racial epithets, or verbal impropriety in respect of race, colour or creed. Bear this in mind at all times."

Loud murmurings filled the room and Officers smiled knowingly at one another in anticipation of the night's forthcoming action.

Alan noticed that a number of the Task Force Officers were already removing the epaulette sleeves containing their collar numbers.

"Right gentlemen, thank you, settle down." Parkin banged the clipboard onto the table top to restore order. "Time is pressing."

The room fell to silence again.

"Please listen for your names."

The list of Officers was read out, each responding with a loud "Sir" or "Present" depending on how near they were to promotion, or how much respect they had for the Chief Inspector.

"Road Traffic."

There were loud theatrical hisses, mostly from the Detectives at the rear of the office. Laughter followed.

Parkin cast his gaze on the bright yellow fluorescent jackets and white tops. "The Moorwood Traffic contingent. Pendle and Sullivan?"

"Sir." Alan murmured and nodded. His partner half raised a hand.

"You two will be responsible for Transit van Hotel Foxtrot Three."

Alan looked slightly puzzled as he considered the strange callsign. Moorwood Traffic always had a 'papa yankee' prefix. A wry smile crossed his face as he made the connection. Hotel Foxtrot…Home Front.

"…with a Sergeant and ten, who will be…" Parkin's finger scrolled down the prepared list of names on his clipboard. "Sergeant Robertson with Constables West, DeLacy, Neadly…"

The names of the ten Officers were read out and Alan scribbled their assigned callsign on the back of his hand.

Parkin continued with his briefing. "The Traffic Officers will be utilised as drivers. Primarily responsible for the transportation of the serial units to the target area, to remain with their allocated vehicles so as to provide security for same, and subsequently, to transport detained persons to the Police station after arrest."

The Chief Inspector looked to the Beat Inspector standing at his side. "It will be the Central Bridewell I believe."

The Inspector nodded and Parkin continued. "I will say this. The Traffic contingent are to keep a low profile and are to avoid any verbal or physical confrontation with any ethnic groups who may gather around the target area once the operation has commenced. The vans must, I repeat must, remain attended to at all times. On no account are you to leave your allocated positions, no matter what the provocation or abuse from local gang members who will no doubt, gather in numbers and attempt to disrupt proceedings. The vans must be able to carry out the transportation of prisoners immediately after arrests are made, rotationally replaced by their following callsigns, who will then take up the same position in order that arresting Officers will know exactly where to bring their prisoners. If the intelligence bears fruit, I have no doubt that there will be some high profile arrests and I do not want to get into the position, where Officers are having to stand about on the streets with their prisoners, waiting for transport. It's into the vans and away, the next van takes its place, understood?"

Parkin looked directly across at Alan and his partner and then to the Traffic crews attending from the adjoining Divisions.

"Transits are extremely expensive, I want them looked after." he said, with a cautionary tone.

"And they burn well, as some of you may remember from last year's bonfire night riots."

The Beat Inspector adopted a sober expression and looked directly across at Alan and his partner. "Any damage caused to Police vehicles used in this operation will come out of this division's annual budget for which I am responsible, the very same budget gentlemen, which pays your overtime. Do I need to say more?"

Alan shook his head, wondering why he and his partner in particular had been singled out as being causal to Mr Denholme's budgetary concerns.

Parkin paused, having lost the flow of his oratory. "I must be kept appraised of the volatility of the situation and informed immediately of any increase in agitation indicators, is that clear?"

"Agi...what Sir?" asked one of the Task Force Officers.

Parkin waited for the brief sputter of laughter to diminish. He looked down over the top of his glasses and said quietly, "It's a Bramshill term Morrison, designed I concede, to be received and understood by Police Officers with an I.Q. marginally over and above that of a potted plant. But for the benefit of the Task Force contingent, I shall use more base terminology; it means trouble Morrison, trouble."

"Sir." the Task Force Officer said and shrank back in his seat, realising that he had just been verbally defecated upon.

The briefing continued, each Officer being assigned to a specific task, arrest, containment, exhibits, transportation or Supervision.

Parkin was an insufferable prick, but Alan had to concede that the planning of the operation had been meticulous.

Parkin placed his clipboard down on the table. "The Detective Inspector will now outline the preamble gentlemen...Frank?"

D.I. Frank Ellis stubbed out his cigarette and casually rose from his seat; he reached out and grasped a large buff coloured envelope being handed to him by one of the Drug Squad Detectives.

"Thank you Mr Parkin." Ellis said, taking his place at the front of the room and purposefully avoiding the term "Sir" when addressing the man who he personally regarded as being professionally his subordinate, yet was actually one rank higher then himself.

Parkin simply nodded and sat back in his chair, noting with a visible look of disdain that the D.I. already smelled of drink.

The two were like oil and water, neither making any pretext at their dislike for each other's methods, yet tactfully stopping short of any verbal or written criticisms. Parkin was a 'by the book' man, everything done precisely and meticulously as per Standing Orders with no deviation from written instructions and protocols, even when logic may sometimes point toward a more practical solution. Parkin accepted with absolute, unswerving stringency that the 'book' had been conceived and ordained by an all knowing, all seeing higher echelon to which he desperately aspired.

Parkin was not popular, this he knew and accepted the fact with a warped form of contented logic, that popularity may well be a hindrance to his planned meteoric rise through the ranks. It was part of his personal life plan, formulated during his thirteen week basic training period at the Police Academy, when he came to the conclusion that *his* intelligence far surpassed that of any of his peer group.

He planned his career structure, firmly set out in his mind, in clear, concise mathematical terms of rank, relating to specific periods of service. Each rank interspersed with an acceptable number of years, the fewer between each promotion the better.

Parkin did not feel the need for interaction with his colleagues, he felt himself to be just what the modern Police Force required. He was young, motivated, totally committed and educationally superior to the vast majority of his colleagues. He was also obstinate and pedantic to the point of frustration. Parkin was not actually 'in' the Police Force, he was merely 'using' it as a vehicle by which he would reach his personal goal. There was little doubt amongst his suffering troops, that he would eventually become the Chief Constable of some Force, well before he was forty.

D.I. Frank Ellis was on the other hand, plainly and simply, a taker of thieves.

He was a copper who had taken twenty seven years to reach the rank of Inspector. He spoke his mind with particularly colourful colloquialisms and used industrial language unashamedly in the presence of all ranks. He smoked and drank to excess, with an apparent zeal which caused consternation amongst his colleagues (and his G.P.) and he couldn't have quoted the definition of aggravated burglary if he was promised a gold pig.

To Ellis, the most important things in life were his long suffering Wife, his kids and a bottle green Jowett Javelin, which he had rescued from a dusty barn somewhere up in the wilds of North Yorkshire. He had lovingly restored the classic over a number of years, to a pristine, concourse winning example of Northern engineering's claim to vehicular fame.

Frank Ellis was slovenly and dressed to his moods, which normally meant jeans, a faded sweat shirt and a worn out hacking jacket with brown leather patches at the elbows. His utter contempt for long established methods of crime detection was legendary, yet he was begrudgingly tolerated by his seniors simply due to his superb track record. Ellis was a 'copper's copper'.

His popularity with the junior ranks was an embarrassment to those of his peers, as was his tenacity. Ellis used logic, common sense and guile and had detected more serious crime than any other Detective in the Force. He was, as his doting Detectives would have it, a legend in his own time.

He was a crafty bastard as well.

On one occasion, famous throughout the Force, Ellis had been dragged kicking and swearing down the tiled corridor from the prisoner reception area and thrown bodily into a cell which was at the time, occupied by a robbery suspect. Ellis had thrown a well-aimed punch at the face of the Custody Sergeant which he had luckily been able to avoid, but which had earned Ellis a pre-arranged slap across the mouth, splitting his lip. The heavy metal cell door was slammed as Ellis, stinking of beer, three days growth on his face, vented a stream of foul obscenities at his captors, which would have earned an appreciative nod even from one of the local Hell's Angels chapters.

The whole charade carefully planned and executed purely for the benefit of his cell mate. Ellis stayed in the cell for almost three days, being periodically removed for the purpose of interviews which would be held conveniently in an interview room near his cell and therefore just within earshot of his captive companion. Ellis would feign total non-cooperation and verbally abuse his interviewers. There would be the sounds of scuffles and tables would be overturned. In fact, during this charade, Ellis was enjoying a 'tailor made' smoke and a decent cup of coffee whilst his D.C's kicked the chairs around the small interview room and noisily promised him a further three day 'lay down' if he didn't come up with the goods. Whilst this was going on, he was busily writing out a report on the information which had so far been able to glean.

Thrown unceremoniously back into the cell, he refused clean clothes and food which he threw back at the custody Officer through the open hatch when offered. Slowly but surely, he built up a rapport with his cell mate, winning him over with stories of previous jobs born purely out of his imagination and associating himself with well-known names, which he knew his cell mate would be acquainted.

He cleverly wormed his way into the man's confidence, demanding nothing, raising no suspicions, simply relying on the inherent inability of your common or garden villain to keep his mouth shut or to resist bragging. Ellis listened with false adulation as his cell mate explained how they had beaten the alarm system and foiled the closed circuit televisions; he promoted the man's bravado with smiles and appreciative nods.

The robber had actually asked Ellis if he knew their driver and when given the name quite freely, screwed his face up as if deep in thought and admitted that he had used him once, but a long time ago in a notorious jewellery blagging in the City. His cell mate's eyes had opened wide with admiration. "The one at Reids with Hanksy and Danny McCardless, yeah, I 'eard about that?"

"That was the one." Ellis nodded and added with a whisper, "If you want a cheap Rolex, I know where there's a few still stashed away."

Having just cleared up a long standing good class robbery, Ellis stored the names inadvertently disclosed and after two more days, during which Ellis implicated himself in being instrumental in the planning of a series of good class burglaries in the Jewish area of the City, extolling his own brilliance unashamedly. His cell mate, not to be outdone, coughed up the names of his co-accused in the robbery for which he was being held suspect and described in detail how it had been planned.

Ellis was subsequently taken from his cell and charged within earshot of his cell mate and was told that he would now be remanded in custody awaiting Trial. In fact, he was driven home, for a hot bath, a good meal with his beloved Wife and of course an hour or two polishing the Jowett. Not exactly what the Judges Rules had in mind in relation to the obtaining of evidence, but Ellis's ruse had worked.

*****

"Right lads," he coughed and pushed another cigarette between his lips. Pausing to light it, he squinted as the plume of smoke drifted up and into his eyes. He turned his back on the Officers and pinned a well-drawn street map onto the hessian wall board.

"Thirty three Marbury Avenue." he said, pointing vaguely toward a location on the map. "A three storey shit hole, one of three properties known to be owned by one Dexter Lloyd Garrison a.k.a. 'Soldier'. An arsehole 'Yardy' late of Trenchtown, Jamaica, now unfortunately, incumbent on us."

Alan noted with pleasure that Parkin was squirming uncomfortably at D.I. Ellis's flagrant lack of political correctness.

Ellis continued. "Garrison and his substantial team of fellow ne'er-do-well's, are suspected of dealing in Heroin and Cocaine which is brought across in quantity from Manchester and sold at the 'blues', not only to those attending to party but also distributed in viable quantities to the various sub gangs operating at street level. 'Soldier' Garrison is the main target gents, certainly from the Drugs Squad's point of view, but personally, I wouldn't expect to find him in attendance at a low level 'blues'.

The D.I. drew long and hard on his cigarette. "Garrison's elusive, he's very street smart…and he's dangerous…the Don Corleone of the 'Badlands' His lieutenant's and mules take the fall, Garrison has never been convicted of a criminal offence lads. He's effectively 'clean'. The way to bring him down is to hit him where it hurts…at his 'blues'. So…anyone possessing sufficient quantities to qualify for a possession with intent to supply should have their collars felt."

D.I. Ellis slipped a grainy black and white surveillance photograph from the envelope and pinned it up alongside the map. "Take a good look at this before you go out. The one in the middle is Garrison. The one wearing the thousand quid suit on his left, is one Lester Addai Zippleman a.k.a. 'Fastener', an interesting nominal, his Father was Jewish, so he'll no doubt be the only circumcised sooty on the block."

Again Parkin squirmed and looked up at Ellis as if to remonstrate at what he felt was a step too far, but his disparaging moan was drowned out by the laughter emanating from the floor.

D.I. Ellis continued, totally oblivious to Parkin's distress or if he was aware, simply didn't care. "Zippleman is Garrison's main man. He runs the hookers and the street deals in the 'Badlands'. The third male is as yet unknown to us, but needs to be…It's the drugs we're there for lads; we're not too interested in the illegal sale of alcohol. There'll be enough Red Stripe and white rum to float a battleship, seize it if you want but it's the powder and rock we're after. Anyway, the arrest teams will be given their specific targets, but any of these three…" Ellis tapped the photograph with his finger… "Seen in or around the premises by any of you, needs to be nicked and the lucky one amongst you who lays his hands on 'Soldier' Garrison actually in possession, will not 'ave to buy his own beer for a month."

Loud cheers from the floor erupted and Parkin could tell that he was losing the military precision with which he had intended to conduct the briefing.

The D.I. resumed to the business end of the matter, thoughtfully scratched his head and directed his gaze to the Traffic men. "Alan, you and your mate in Hotel Foxtrot Three should approach Melville Road from the Ring Road end, nice and steady, no white tops either. The sooties might be ugly, but they're not daft. They'll twig that there's something amiss if they spot a Traffic man driving a Transit."

Alan smiled and nodded.

Ellis continued. "Slowly into Marbury Avenue, as if you're just patrolling. Don't go drawing attention to yerselves and I don't want any of the vans anywhere near their static points until two a.m. and by that, I mean it's got to be as well timed as that. I've got an informant already in the place and I want my man out of the premises and well out of the way before we show our hand, so you and the other van drivers, get your watches sorted…Jim Hubbard and Dave Mercer." he said, looking down at the City Traffic men, "You and your compliment, Hotel Foxtrot Two, with Sergeant Steel…" Ellis paused and turned to Parkin who examined his briefing sheet and nodded to confirm the crew… "and ten uniforms, approach from Buckingham Road. Two a.m. at the static point to the rear of the premises. The other Traffic crews are to float and attend the static points immediately they are informed that either of the other vans are leaving for the Bridewell."

The D.I. pointed to the map and the City men nodded.

Ellis emphasised his last few words. "Any worries with Traffic?"

"We all worry about Traffic Boss." shouted one of the Detectives at the rear of the room.

Again the room was filled with theatrical hissing.

D.I. Ellis chuckled. Alan looked across to his Traffic colleagues, heads were shaken. "No problems Boss."

The D.I. looked at his watch. "I've got eight twenty two and we're going by my watch."

Alan checked his Seiko. It read eight eighteen and it hadn't been wrong in over four years. He wound the minute hand begrudgingly forwards to twenty two minutes past the hour, making a mental note to claim back the four minutes immediately after the job was over.

Officer Wrigley, one of the other Traffic men brought in to assist from one of the satellite Divisions, fumbled with the small buttons on the side of his newly acquired digital watch. He cursed under his breath as the liquid crystals changed from day of the month, to stopwatch mode, completely bypassing the minute display.

The D.I. had moved on to the Task Force Officers duties when he was stopped in mid-sentence by a metallic rendition of 'I wish I was in Dixie' which plinked merrily out from the small speaker in the watch as Pc Wrigley assaulted the various buttons with the sharp end of his pen.

"For fuck's sake borrow one, ok?" Ellis said impatiently.

"Sorry Boss." Wrigley apologised. He tapped the watch against the radiator grill on the wall, to no avail, finally stuffing the watch deep into his trouser pocket in an effort to silence the Confederate mewings, which could still faintly be heard even with his fluorescent jacket pulled tightly across his thighs.

"Sergeant Forester with your valiant Task Force lads..." Ellis continued, unable to mask a slight smile, as Officer Wrigley's watch suddenly broke into a rendition of the 'The Yellow Rose of Texas' from within the deep recesses of his clothing.

A faint ripple of laughter rose to a crescendo as Ellis shook his head in despair.

"Officer Wrigley. As much as I in particular, fully appreciate the necessity of staying on the good side of Traffic, I swear, if you don't do something with that fucking watch..."

The room exploded into laughter as Wrigley, his face reddening with embarrassment, pulled out the errant plinking watch by its strap and held it aloft. "The bloke set it up for me in the shop Boss, I haven't got a clue how..."

Chief Inspector Parkin, worried that his briefing was fast becoming a farce, intervened. "Er...yes, I believe that the Traffic contingent have their duties. Collect the vans from Central garage and carry out normal pre-patrol checks please. I want any current damage and defects recorded in the log books prior to signing for them. Be outside the station at no later than 00.30 hours to load up. You can all be dismissed."

The Traffic men stood up. Alan grabbed his headgear and nodded to D.I. Frank Ellis, who smiled and shook his head as he looked at Officer Wrigley, who was still struggling with the errant watch.

Muted robotic tones of 'John Brown's body' faded as he left the conference room and hurried off down the corridor.

*****

"Well, what's the Fuhrer dreamed up for tonight then?" the Traffic Sergeant asked, leaning back in his chair, hands clasped behind his head, his upper torso barely visible behind the pall of blue grey smoke from his cigar. "A night raid on the Oxfam shop is it, or perhaps a long overdue Trading Standards check on Billy Wong's take away on Watson Street."

"Nothing so mundane Sarge." Alan said, lighting a cigarette and wondering why he had bothered, as the nicotine content of the air in the Traffic office was well above the minimal body craving level.

"Tonight Sarge, is the real McCoy. The Moorwood Police Amateur Dramatic Society's rendition of the re-enactment of the battle of Rorke's Drift."

"'Cept for convenience sake, were holdin' it in Marbury Avenue." his partner added dryly.

"No shortage of extras then." the Sergeant chuckled…"A blues raid eh! I'm impressed." Then with a sudden afterthought added "I 'ope you're not plannin' on using our patrol cars."

Alan shook his head. "Trannies from Central garage." he said, as he rummaged through his small locker searching for his cricket box and a pair of shin pads.

"Good luck with gettin' a Transit out passed the swamp monster." the Sergeant said, flicking his ash casually onto the office floor. "Young Parkin's got more balls than I gave 'im credit for." the old Sergeant mused. "Mind you, the Police Authority'll want 'em on a plate if it goes wrong."

"Will that be with, or without chips do you reckon?" Alan asked, as he inspected the cricket box for random pubic hairs before pushing it down the front of his trousers to carry out a comfort check.

The old Traffic Sergeant shook his head slowly. "You lads watch out for yerselves, that's all I've got to say…Thank fuck I'm off at ten…Rorke's Drift!" he snorted, "More likely to be Isandlwana."

Sullivan's face took on a confused expression. "Who?"

Alan looked across to his Sergeant and they shared a knowing smile.

The old Sergeant chewed at the end of his cigar and leaned back in his chair, his hands clasped behind his head. "The day before, the glorious twenty fourth regiment of foot went about winnin' no less than eleven Victoria crosses at the Drift Sully, the British army got a right 'arsolin' at a small place called Isandlwana….You need to spend less time drownin' defenceless worms an' more time readin' Sully lad."

"That's one of the things I love about being a member of this department." Sullivan said sarcastically, "One always knows that one's supervisory ranks are constantly reassuring their men in respect of the infallibility of the forces of law and order."

"You can fuckin' joke young Sullivan." the Sergeant said, scowling before tossing his cigar butt causally out of the window. "But when the black 'ordes of the Zulu Impi come sweepin' down the Marbury's, spears bangin' in unison against cow'ide shields... an' the 'orns of the buffalo close in around yer rapidly diminishin' ranks. Just remember, form a square, put yer 'ead between yer legs an' kiss yer arse goodbye."

Alan laughed as he took the keys to their allotted patrol vehicle from the hook on the vehicle disposition board. "You or me?" he asked, dangling the keys in front of his partner's face.

His partner thought for a moment. "What do you reckon Sarge, who's likely to get maimed if Parkin's job goes pear shaped tonight, driver or observer?"

The Sergeant pursed his lips and thought for a moment. "Driver, definitely, no question." he said nodding slowly.

His partner grabbed the keys from Alan's fingers. "Me to push first tour then. You can drive the Tranny for the job."

"Oh! by the way lads." the Sergeant said, as he concentrated on peeling the cellophane wrapper from a fresh cigar. "You *will* pay yer coffee subs before your imminent deaths. I'd hate for the rest of the lads to have to divvy up the shortfall as well as 'avin' to give a quid for flowers an' a condolence card."

Alan picked up his personal radio and his briefcase. His partner pushed past him, leaving the office as quickly as possible at the mention of coffee subs.

"See you later, Sarge." Alan said, smiling at his partner's panic.

As he placed his hand on the door handle to leave, the Sergeant called after him. Alan turned, his leg propping the door open.

"You be careful tonight, the both of you." his Sergeant said quietly.

Alan winked. "Yeah, see you tomorrow Sarge."

The old Sergeant nodded and returned his attention to the mound of traffic offence reports strewn across his desk.

*****

"Jesus Al, let's get the bleedin' heater revvin'." his partner said, shivering violently, exaggerating the movement to press home his point.

He twisted the ignition key and the engine of their patroller coughed into life.

Sullivan glanced down at the fuel gauge and groaned as it crawled its way up to the half way mark and stopped. "Lazy bastards." he whispered. "Who had our car last Al?"

Alan reached down and pulled the dog-eared vehicle logbook from where it sat wedged between the passenger seat and the center console. He flicked through the pages until he came to the last entry.

"Oldfield." he said, snapping the book shut.

"I might 'ave bleedin' well known." his partner snarled. "You'd think 'e 'ad to pay for the fuckin' stuff 'imself."

"You'll get an ulcer mate, getting all fractious like that." Alan said, as he reached for the radio handset. "We booked on?"

Sullivan shook his head and took a roadside breath kit from his jacket pocket and tossed it into unceremoniously into the glove box.

Alan punched the VHF button on the multi-channel set that had been shoehorned into the central dashboard facia. "Papa Yankee One Five, we are 10/1, crew 868 and 418 available until twenty three hundred over, 10/7."

The static hiss was broken by the controller's voice.

"Papa Yankee One Five, 10/4, nothing at this time."

"That's whoisit's Wife isn't it." Sullivan asked, motioning his head toward the radio.

"Who?" Alan asked, shaking his head. "No knowledge mate."

His partner continued. "You know, 'er that was found down by the lake, in the Transit with the young copper from City."

Alan looked puzzled and shook his head.

"Ah…must've been while you were away on yer jollies with the voluptuous Sandra Prestwick. Big scandal at City." His partner's voice took on a lurid tone, betraying the sexual nature of the incident. Sullivan eased the patrol car out of the parking bay, casually glancing over his shoulder to make sure the perimeter drive was clear.

"Well?" Alan prompted, his interest now well and truly kindled.

"She got moved, under a cloud as it were, servin' out 'er penance in the Control room." his partner offered temptingly, as he paused to light a cigar.

"Well get on with it then." Alan urged.

"I'm amazed you 'avn't 'eard about it mate, it was all over the Division." His partner prevaricated, feeding off Alan's curiosity.

"Sully, for fuck's sake…"

His partner relented. "Ok, ok, she's supposed to be out in a panda right."

Alan nodded.

"Anyway, they're callin 'er an' callin' 'er, no response. So the Sergeant does a street trawl an' finds 'er panda parked up in the Belmonts, unattended, insecure an' she is nowhere to be seen. The Sarge rummages through the glove box and finds 'er pocket book, torch an' personal radio."

You're joking?" Alan said, shaking his head in disbelief.

"As true as I'm sittin' 'ere." his partner said forcefully.

"So…?" Alan reached over and turned down the volume on the VHF radio.

"Well, after a while, 'e gets worried, as you would, an' contacts the Inspector. 'E comes out, surveys the scene and reckons that she might have bin abducted by the local 'groids'. Huge search gets underway, no gain right. All the lads get called out from meal and the Inspector requests assistance from City an' 'C' Division to carry out a street by street."

"Jesus Christ." Alan exclaimed, his attention now fully captured.

"The Inspector and the Sergeant 'ave a roam about and half an hour or so later, they come across the Divisional Tranny van, parked up, no lights, down by the lake, secluded spot an' all that...Anyway, they get out of their motor and they can 'ear screams comin' from inside the back of the van an' it's rockin' about like a good 'un, side to side, like some prisoner's gettin' a right arse'olin' in the back."

"Oh no." Alan groaned, imagining the grief.

"No listen...nothin' like that." his partner exclaimed. "Much worse than that! The Inspector pulls the back doors wide open and there, in the back, is her off the radio." Sullivan again nodded toward the VHF set.

Alan sat aghast; his eyes wide open with anticipation.

His partner continued. "She's wearing fuck all but 'er skiddies an' she's standin' over this cop from Fuller Road nick. 'E's laid out on the floor of the van, starkers."

"What!" Alan gasped.

"I shit you not, an' it gets better." his partner laughed. "This cop is cut to fuck. All over 'is back an' e's bleedin' like a stuck pig. She's 'oldin' the VHF aerial what she's got from the roof of the van and she's bin whippin' the poor bastard with it an' 'e apparently, as got the biggest 'ardon you've ever seen."

Alan listened to the tale, spellbound, his mouth open in disbelief.

"On bein' caught flagrante delicto as it were, the Policewoman leaps out of the van, straight into the arms of the Inspector, shoutin', 'e made me do it sir, 'e made me do it." At which, the good Inspector whips off 'is jacket and throws it around 'er shoulders, casually, but covertly takin' the opportunity to cast a glance at 'er large pendulous breasts, an' then whisks 'er off back to the station."

"What about the cop?" Alan asked, his tone incredulous.

"I'm comin' to that." Sullivan's voice dropped almost to a whisper and Alan moved closer. "The Sergeant drives the van back to 'eadquarters with the cop still in the back, whimperin' an' still bleedin' all over the place, straight to the Force Surgeon where 'e gets examined."

"Yeah...and?" Alan urged, now totally captivated by this tale of wanton debauchery.

"Well." his partner said, pausing and then looking directly across to Alan. "The Force Surgeon reckoned it was the worst case of *van aerial disease* 'e'd ever seen."

His partner howled with laughter, his cap falling from his head and into the rear footwell.

Alan remained straight faced and looked across to his partner. "You've got a very deranged mind Sully. I'm genuinely worried about you."

Sullivan composed himself slightly and wiped a tear from the corner of his eye. "You ought to 'ave seen your face." he laughed, "No!"..."Never!" his partner mimicked and then choked as his cigar smoke got the better of him.

Alan shook his head, but conceded a smile. One of his partner's better tales he thought.

The radio was quiet and neither Alan nor his partner had the incentive to get involved with any routine police work.

There was Parkin's 'Op' coming up and neither wanted to get unnecessarily tied up with anything. They parked up on one of the raised platforms on the Ring Road and for a while, simply watched the late evening traffic making its way to and fro.

"She's a foxy little bugger is that one." Sullivan said out of the blue, reaching over his shoulder for the seat belt clasp and waving to the young girl cashier in the garage as he pulled their patroller away from their parking spot opposite.

"Mmmm, you might come away with more than you bargained for as well." Alan said, with a cautionary note in his voice.

"Oh yeah, you know something I don't?" his partner asked, a wicked smile creeping across his face.

"No." Alan protested. "All I'm saying is, you go dipping your toilet parts into that one mate, and you might just have some embarrassing questions to answer…from a medical point of view I mean. You being a married man and all." Alan reached into the side pocket of the door panel for his cigarettes, flicking the top of the box open with his thumb; he drew one out with his teeth and lit it.

"Oh, come on." his partner said, not letting the subject drop. "All the times we've been in there for a brew an' you've never considered it?"

Alan sucked on the filter tip and looked casually across at his partner and smiled at the deviant leer spread across his face. "You ever considered seeking psychiatric help Sully?" Alan continued with a more sombre tone. "There is a very interesting theory, that the male of the species formulates a sexual thought every seven minutes. You Sully seem to be the exception to the rule; you are clearly something of a medical anomaly. Your whole existence seems to consist of one continuous deviant sexual fantasy, only briefly interspersed with the odd dip back into reality. I suspect that the medical profession would probably pay a considerable amount to observe you."

"Huh!" his partner snorted, tapping his forehead lightly, "Nuthin' wrong with me up here pal, which is more than I can say for the likes of Parkin. Did you see 'im when Frank Ellis was givin' 'is brief? 'E was literally cringing."

Alan mused on it for a moment. "You're talking about a totally different breed of animal Pete. See…Parkin's not a Policeman any more, he's a manager. In fact, as soon as you make Sergeant, other than the odd exception to the rule, Ron Dennison for instance, you cease to be a copper in the truest sense of the word. In fact, the further up the promotion scale you go, the less you have to do with actual police work. It's all about bullshit meetings with various Rotary Groups and discussions with ethnic action forums, civil liberties groups and the like."

"'E must know that the lads take the piss out of him." his partner said.

Alan shook his head slowly. "If he does, it doesn't bother him. It's like water off a ducks back. Parkin's a clone from the old type of senior Officers at Headquarters. He's where he is today because of how he is, he doesn't give a toss about the welfare of the rank and file." Alan snorted. "Nor does he care about how much work you turn in. Forty names a week in the back of your pocket book wouldn't impress him, but he would check to see what percentage of that forty were from minority ethnic groups. See…blokes like Parkin get promoted by blokes like Parkin. The senior ranks see him and recognise him as being one of their own, politically correct, highly educated and good with statistics. That's all that matters Sully, it's not about coppering, it's about keeping the organisation stable. Same as the Army and the commissioned ranks. Right school, right background, right name. I mean, if your first name's Digby, Julian, or Tarquin, some shit like that, especially if you've got a double barrelled surname, you've got it cracked."

His partner frowned. "But what about members of the Public, they're not exactly getting' value for money are they, I mean, 'e earns a fuckin' sight more than you an' me, an' we're the ones actually doin' the job."

"Oh give up Pete, don't be daft. You don't honestly still think that the Public still count for anything. Nobody gives a shit about members of the Public, certainly not the likes of Parkin. Members of the Public aren't going to promote Parkin. Oh, outwardly, he make all the right noises 'bout us being in the public service and how we should strive to 'maintain the principles of policing by consent' and all that shit, but it's all a game mate, nobody really cares about actual crime figures 'cos they don't exist. They make the reported crime fit an acceptable rate, murder down to manslaughter, street robberies down to theft, even rape down to sexual assault. You know that's what goes on Pete. If members of the Public actually knew how bad things were, there'd be a shitstorm of protest. In fact, if our Force published the correct statistics on drug related murder and robberies, half the Command Team would be for the chop."

Sullivan sat quietly, listening to his partner having a rant about the failings of the system.

"Another thing that grips me." Alan continued, flicking his cigarette end out of the window, "The Public are all too quick to complain about a policing method that they themselves have demanded, low key, softly softly, let's not upset anyone. I mean, what about the bloke that gets his new motor nicked? We might pick up on it, even give chase, but if it drives into the 'Badlands', especially Marbury Avenue, we have to stop and watch the bleedin' ethnics strip the alloys and the stereo from the damn things…why? 'cos the bosses are shit scared of a riot starting if we go in to make a perfectly lawful arrest. Wouldn't happen anywhere else in the City."

Alan sighed.

His partner sensed that there was some mileage in Alan's mood and decided to fuel the fire. "Yeah, you're right there Al, I mean, some fucking 'groid' breaks into yer 'ouse, 'as it away with yer video an' stereo deck, shits on the carpet for good measure an' what do we do? We go round and make all the right noises, the sympathetic touch whilst we fill in a crime report, but what happens in reality is, fuck all. Chances of nickin' the bastard are thin to start with an' even if we do, they'll be screamin' racial prejudice as soon as 'is arse 'its the cell floor. Then, some 'do gooder' social worker type, with green peace stickers plastered all over 'is 2CV, will turn up at Court for 'im with 'is social enquiry report, as 'ow poor Leroy didn't 'ave enough toys when 'e was a kid or 'ow 'e is findin' it 'ard to adjust to the social demands of a black youth in a white society…Bastards!"

"That's if he doesn't get a caution in the first place." Alan responded. I'm sick of the whole system. What ever happened to the punishment fitting the crime? I mean, all the Magistrates and Judges live on three beat. They don't get 'groids' sloping round at three and four o'clock in the morning. They haven't got hookers hanging round their street corners, no used needles tossed over into their cultivated front gardens right? I mean they seem to live in this protected cocoon, a nine to five existence, the golf club, the Masons and the bridge club. They should have to come out on patrol with us for a month or so, just to open their eyes."

His partner nodded. "Yeah, I mean, look at that little shit Colin Spencer, lives in the Harold's. John DeLacy locks 'im up for a string of burglaries and 'e ends up at Juvenile Court. It's 'is fourteenth conviction an' 'e's only sixteen. The Magistrate in 'is infinite wisdom, grants 'im bail with conditions, curfew, eight till eight. What 'appens?...Two days later, Davy Muscroft locks 'im up for burglary at half one in the mornin'. He gets remanded and put up before the same Magistrate the followin' day. What does 'e do?...Grants 'im bail, same conditions. You tell me, what's the bleedin' point?...If it were the Magistrate's 'ouse..."

"Papa Yankee One Five a message."

Alan's personal radio hissed into life and interrupted their reveries. "Not a minute's peace." He scowled as he depressed the transmit button. "One Five, go ahead."

"Alan, report from a passing motorist of smoke from a fire of some sort on the side of the road near to Wensley Bridge. Can you have a run out?"

"Jesus Christ." Alan cursed, it's ten miles away. Don't they know we're on standby for the job of the century.

Alan pressed the button on the top of his Burndept. "Yeah, 10/4, any further info, car, barn or what?"

"Negative Al, I've given you what I've got." the operator replied apologetically.

Alan muttered under his breath as his partner accelerated out into the nearside lane of the Ring Road. "Smoke at the side of the road, what's wrong with calling the bleedin' fire brigade."

"Hey Al, could be one of them Buddhist monks what's set fire to himself in protest over Moorwood's fraudulent crime figures. 'E'll be sat there at the side of the road, a blackened, charred, bubblin' mess."

Alan turned to look across at his partner, a worried look on his face. "Where did that thought come from? You definitely need help Sully...This Walter Mitty world you're living in gets weirder by the day."

His partner snorted loudly. "Huh, you're going out with Sandra Prestwick and I need help?" Alan's face dropped. "What's wrong with Sandra Prestwick?"

"Nothin' mate." Peter said quickly, pretending to stifle a smile. "All the lads say she's...." he paused, pretending to choose his words... "Accommodating."

"Whoooa! ...What do you mean accommodating...and what the fuck do you mean *ALL* the lads?" Alan demanded over his partner's laughter, as the patrol car sped out of the City towards the open countryside.

*****

A thin pall of grey smoke wafted across the road surface, hugging the rough tarmac as it was swept sideways by the breeze. Its source was not readily visible until Sullivan eased their patrol car onto the soft grass verge to the nearside of the carriageway and turned on the four way flashers. The smoke in fact, emanated from a small fire in a ditch some two feet deep and two or three feet wide, a natural soak away for the heavy volume of water which drained from the raised fields which bordered the busy main road.

Alan peered across the top of the ditch and saw a semi opaque sheet of polythene which had been placed over the top of the ditch and secured with small rocks and sods of grass, giving rude, but apparently effective shelter to a wizened old man who sat hunched over a small fire in the bottom of the ditch. He held a small battered aluminium pan over the flames which were enclosed within a small ring of stones to prevent them spreading. Alan looked down into the ditch and guessed the man's age as being perhaps 55 to 60. His hair was long, matted and dirty. It curled stiffly outwards over the greasy collar of an equally dirty calf length waxed coat, which the tramp had tied tightly around his waist with a length of baling twine.

The old man gave Alan and the patrol car a cursory glance and without further ado, returned his rheumy gaze to the pan.

Alan looked across to his partner who appeared to be as disinterested in the event as he had been when they had set off. "It's a tramp mate, that's all. Come on, let's go." he urged.

"I'll just go and have a word, see if he's ok." Alan said, opening the car door.

His partner caught hold of his arm. "Look Al, it's just a dirty festerin' old tramp with pissy trouser legs. 'E's probably crawlin' with hepatitus or somethin', so what, we can write the call off as no danger caused an' leave 'im to 'is cookin'. Come on, let's fuck off. Anyway, I don't want you to be embarrassed."
Alan frowned. "Embarrassed?"

Sullivan nodded sombrely as he craned his neck to look down into the ditch. "Mate...I think its Sandra Prestwick's dad."

Alan sighed and shook his head as he left the patrol car and walked across to the side of the ditch, ignoring his partner's protestations.

The tramp looked up at Alan as he squatted on his haunches at the top of the ditch. The old man remained silent and unconcerned as he fumbled with dirt engrained fingers, through a battered shoe box which he produced from beneath the polythene roof.

"You alright then?" Alan called out cheerfully.

The tramp ignored him as he shook two well used tea bags free of clinging debris and dropped them into the pan. With a well-practiced wrist movement, he swirled the boiling water over and around them, immersing them and causing the water to take on at first, a pale yellow tint.

He returned the blackened base of the pan to the flames, shuffling it down into the glowing embers causing sparks to fly upwards towards Alan's face.

"Al, for Christ's sake." his partner called out impatiently from the patrol car.

Alan looked around and scowled.

"I said, you alright then?" Alan again called down into the ditch, returning his attention to the tramp.

The old man looked up at Alan. His eyes glistened from the smoke which billowed up into his face. The part of which was visible behind the voluminous beard and flowing moustache, was weather tanned and like his hands, had the appearance of well-polished leather.

"He's probably Polish or somethin'. 'E won't understand a word, come on mate." his partner called out from the patrol car.

"Hang on." Alan called out over his shoulder, his impatience with his partner's incessant wittering now evident in his voice.

Alan smiled down at the tramp who had lifted the pan from the fire and was swirling the darkening liquid over the tea bags until it met with the approval of his critical eye.

"You'll have the County on fire." Alan said, nodding towards the sputtering flames as he climbed gingerly down into the ditch and stood in front of the filthy bundle of rags attending to his brew.

The tramp placed the pan on the grass in the bottom of the ditch and it hissed loudly as the hot base made contact with the dampness.

He slowly looked up at Alan again and smiled, exposing the stumps of brown teeth beneath the nicotine stained hairs of his moustache. "May I offer you a little liquid refreshment Officer? I've nothing stronger I fear. Beggars as they say, can't be choosers, but I do find that hot tea is a most effective remedy against the cold."

Alan smiled in confusion at the unexpected eloquence of his softly spoken voice. His offer was neatly cultured and perfect in its delivery. The tramp offered up a chipped enamel mug, heavily stained with tannin.

Alan smiled politely and shook his head. "No…thank you, I've just had coffee."

"Ah yes, coffee." the old man said softly, closing his eyes for a moment as if in ecstasy.

He breathed in deeply through his nose, as if trying to recall or conjure up the smell of freshly roasted grounds. He seemed to come back to reality with resolve and lifted the mug tentatively to his lips, sipping the tepid concoction slowly, as if savouring and evaluating its taste.

Alan watched as the old man sipped his tea in silence.

"How is it?" he asked, smiling and settling down on his haunches in the ditch, consciously remaining a yard or so away. He was acutely aware of the pungency of the fetid aroma wafting out from the old man's clothing and remembered his partner's throw away comment regarding hepatitis.

The stillness of the evening was broken as the fire crackled and spat, as the moisture in the broken twigs fled from the heat which lapped up from the glowing embers. The tramp sluiced the liquid around in his mouth, then swallowed. "Not quite Lapsang Suochong." he paused, "Camellia Sinensis to give it its correct name Officer." he said and smiled. "But quite adequate under the circumstances, you're sure?" he said, again offering the mug across the fire.

Alan smiled politely and shook his head, holding up the palm of his hand.

The tramp shrugged his heavy shoulders and again raised the mug to his lips and sipped in silence.

"You'll catch your death of cold, sat down here in the damp." Alan said, pushing his fingertips into the soft damp ground in the bottom of the trench.

The tramp leaned his back against the side of the ditch, half under the polythene sheet. He squinted up at the darkening sky as if sensing rain. "I have been rather fortunate on that score of late Officer, in fact, I haven't suffered from a cold in…" he paused, as if trying to drag a memory back from somewhere in the recesses of his mind. "…oh, must be fifteen years or so." He smiled again, exposing the rotting stumps of his teeth.

Alan frowned at the cultivated voice and something in his puzzled expression must have been identified by the old man, who laughed briefly at his visitor's confusion.

"One develops immunity to certain malevolent airborne viruses." the old man said, then coughed to clear his throat. "Nasopharyngitis, rhinopharyngitis or acute coryza.". He smiled knowingly to himself. "The common cold to you Officer. "It can be resisted by extended exposure to an outdoor existence you see." he said matter of factly, as he patted his coat pockets and ran his wrinkled hands over himself as if trying to remember where he had mislaid something.

Noting the old man's nicotine stained moustache, Alan smiled knowingly and reached into the pocket of his yellow jacket and withdrew his cigarettes, also noting how the old man's eyes lit up as he saw them.

"Smoke?" Alan asked, offering the packet.

The old man reached out for one of the cigarettes which Alan had half withdrawn from the pack. He paused as if afraid to submit to the temptation. "Very kind Officer." he said, quickly overcoming his hesitation and snatching the filter tip from the pack with a pair of stained fingers. "Not too often one realises the opportunity to partake of the real thing. Tailor made as they say." he said, drawing the cigarette full length under his nose as if savouring a fine cigar.

Alan lit his cigarette and held his lighter across the flames to the old man who ignored the device, but reached down into the fire and withdrew a small twig, holding the glowing end to the cigarette and inhaling deeply.

The old man closed his eyes as he slowly let the smoke drift out from his mouth and nose. He laughed a little nervously as he became aware that Alan was watching his reveries and quickly took the cigarette out of his mouth. He held the filter tip between finger and thumb, rolling it gently and squinted as he attempted to scrutinize the brand name. "I recall" he said, pausing and staring out over the top of the ditch, "A time when I could smoke five or ten of these a day."

"When would that be then?" Alan asked, now curious as to the old man's antecedents.

The old man smiled wistfully and drew on the cigarette again, allowing the smoke to roll out slowly between his teeth. "A time young man, if you will forgive the familiarity, when I used to take things such as the enjoyment of a fine cigar, a well-dressed female upon my arm and haute cuisine for granted." Again he smiled as if the memories pleased him. "When finances were in good order as Mr Micawber would say, that is, if you recall your Dickens, and I was not as you see me today."

"How long you been a…on the road?" Alan asked.

"Oh, fifteen years or so I suppose." he sighed and stared down, deep into the depths of the glowing embers of the fire, apparently lost in some secret within his past.

Alan broke the silence. "What made you become a tram…you know, a traveller?"

The old man laughed. "A tramp?…Yes, I am a tramp, plain to see." He paused and held out his arms as he surveyed himself. The grubby clothes, the unkempt appearance and his worn out, salt stained boots. "I do seem to fit the generally accepted definition I suppose."

He paused as if considering his next words carefully. "Quality of life Officer, quality of life." he said softly.

Alan looked puzzled; the old man recognised his confusion and laughed. "You wouldn't understand at your age Officer, nor could you be expected to. You have all that you desire?"

Alan looked at him questioningly.

"A car, somewhere nice to live, a healthy bank account, a Wife?" the old man asked.

"All but the latter, thankfully." Alan replied.

The old man chortled, throwing his head back. "A wise decision, I concur. Women are fine when taken in small and intermittent quantities. Now, a bottle of Henri Jayer Richebourg enjoyed with a fine hand rolled Habanos premium is a totally different matter."

Alan smiled at the old man's priorities, not recognising any of the fancy names which he presumed were exclusive.

"I was." he paused, "Still am, I suppose, a Consultant Opthalmic Surgeon. Mr Ralph Arnold Swinton at your service." he bowed his head theatrically. "Still on the register at a guess."

Alan looked at him warily.

"Ah! I detect a hint of cynicism, rightly so I suppose, given my obvious persona and your occupation. Yes, it's all perfectly true, I assure you. I was the senior partner of Swinton, Melbourne and Hargreaves, with exclusive consultancy rooms on Harley Street." he said with exaggerated grandeur and a hint of sadness.

"What happened?" Alan asked, shifting his position to ease a cramp gripping his calves.

"Happened?" the old man said softly. "Oh, I see what you mean. No, no, nothing like that, no malpractice suit, no scandal involved, I simply gave it all up for this." He smiled, sweeping his hand emphatically over his few possessions.

Alan frowned. "I see you're confused." the old man said laughingly. "I had all a man could desire, a Rolls Royce, suits by Willing and Basker." He frowned and his voice took on an imperious tone, "Saville Row of course. Shirts hand made by Benborough and Danks and a conservative, yet comfortable set of rooms in the more fashionable quarter of Chelsea. Oh! yes, not to mention an income of twenty thousand a year. That was a considerable amount of money in those days."

"It still is." Alan offered.

"Is it?" the old man asked, raising his eyebrows. "I had everything you see, yet." he paused. "I had no…quality of life, no time to enjoy what really matter, d'you see?"

Alan shrugged, not sure of the old man's sanity and starting to seriously doubt his own, sat in a damp ditch, talking to some dirty old looney. "Sounds pretty good to me." he said.

The tramp smiled wistfully. "At your age, yes, I concede the point. When I was your age, it was important to me as well, but I wanted…rather, I craved, a certain freedom from all that. His face brightened perceptibly. "Which I now enjoy, to the detriment of no one but myself."

The horn on the patrol car sounded, its strident note making both Alan and the old man jump. The tramp smiled and nodded toward the car above them. "Your colleague is a perfect example of what I am talking about, you won't be able to see it yet of course." he paused. "But you may …someday."

"It's meal time." Alan said, glancing at his watch. "My partner's hungry and he's got the patience of a hamster."

The old man laughed and nodded knowingly. "You're tied to a system, willingly I have no doubt, same as everyone these days, breakfast, lunch, dinner, work and play. A set time for everything and no time for anything."

"Bloody 'ell Al." his partner called impatiently from the patrol car.

The old man looked saddened. "Your Mother's calling." he whispered, looking down into the dulling embers of his fire.

Alan stood up and rubbed his thighs to get the circulation going, still slightly disturbed at the old man's apparent resignation from society. "Well, take care old man." he said, stepping up onto the brow of the ditch.

The tramp looked up and smiled as if he knew something of Alan's future. "I will." he said and set about poking the remains of his fire with a twig.

Alan took a couple of steps toward the patrol car, and then paused. He reached into his jacket pocket and turned to face the pathetic figure hunched up in the ditch. "Mr Swinton." he called out.

The old man looked up quickly, surprised at hearing the sound of his name after such a long time. Alan tossed the cigarette packet down into the ditch. The old man caught the pack deftly with one outstretched hand. He looked up to Alan, who was silhouetted against the orange flashes from the patrol car's indicators; he touched his forehead lightly with his index finger and nodded just once.

"Live a little." Alan called out and walked back to the patrol car where his partner sat tapping his fingers against the steering wheel.

He looked back down into the ditch briefly as his partner eased the patroller away from the grass verge and accelerated away.

"D'you check 'im out then?" his partner asked, looking across at Alan, who was staring out through the windscreen, a blank expression on his face.

Slightly disturbed by the tale the old man had told, it took a moment for Alan to gather his thoughts.

He took a deep breath. "What?" he asked, glancing across at his partner.

"Did you check 'im out?...Christ Al, you were down there with 'im ten minutes."

Alan shrugged. "Nah, you were right mate, just an old tramp. Nothing to write home about."

## Fifteen

The metal slatted roller door at the entrance to Central Garage creaked and groaned in protest and rattled against the steel runners which held it captive along both sides of its full height.

The pitted and much repainted grey door, rippled against the buffeting wind which howled around the sides of the red brick building. Angry at being denied entry, it rushed at the side windows, seeking out a loose pane in the painted transom window above the oil store, and rattled it until it cracked within its metal frame.

The wind screamed in frustration as it scorched down the long sides of the building, picking up dead leaves and broken twigs which carpeted the car park and hurled them wildly upwards at the air intakes beneath the eaves of the asbestos corrugated roof.

Still the door persisted as it had for years, allowing only a crisp draught to sweep underneath its bottom edge, where it rested against the uneven concrete floor of the garage.

Inside, the invading draughts were warmed and dissipated by the flow of hot air which was blown downwards from the ducted heating outlets in the ceiling and kept the interior of the garage at a constant fifty degrees.

The garage was cavernous, hanger like, dating back to the early nineteenth century, during which, it had been a wool mill. Until the early eighties, Central Garage had been the home of the City Road Traffic Department and had housed the Mini Cooper 'S', Ford Consuls and Rover P6's which were replaced over the years by the Rover SD1's and Ford Granada's. Each car allocated to a specific crew of two Traffic men per group.

All the cars were gone now, other than those for storage, service or repair. All sent out to the various Divisions, along with all the Traffic men.

The parade room, the canteen and the report writing room at the rear of the garage, now echoed emptily as the wind battered the roof panels.

The ornate cast iron roof ribs and beams were still present, now painted a dull grey, originally used to support vast metal shafts which ran the full length of the building and the massive pulley wheels. On these had ridden wide leather belts, driving the heavy carding machines and spinners.

The beams now simply supported the galvanized heating conduits and the numerous double tubed fluorescent strip lights which hung lazily from chains.

Released from the weight of their original burden, the roof ribs and long beams, now served only as a reminder of a bygone industrial age, when the building would have hummed and clanked with the sound of the heavy machinery and reeked from the smell of the emulsifiers and the soft soaps, used to release the oil and dirt from the wool brought in huge bales, carried along the canals in long boats from the Yorkshire Dales and the Lancashire sheep farms.

The original stone flagged floor had been coated in rippled concrete to provide a slip free surface and was now painted with a thick grey, oil resistant resin.

The long hall to the right of the roller door had been partitioned off with a low brick wall. There was a separate hand operated chain driven roller door providing access and exit to and from the workshop area. Here stood the massive hydraulic lifting ramps, the engine hoists and the bright red boxes containing the mechanic's tools, all lined up against the far wall.

Here the patrol cars were serviced and maintained. Damaged body panels were replaced and sent to the spray booth for painting and restriping.

The patrol cars sat neatly in rows awaiting attention by the mechanics, or collection after service or repair by the various Divisions to which they were allocated. The work sheets, placed under their windscreen wipers, fluttered every now and then as the warm air was deflected along their long white bonnets, upwards again toward the impellers which hummed quietly in unison as they collected, re-heated and re-circulated the warmed air around the cavernous interior of the garage.

Against the far wall, stark with its whitewashed brickwork, directly opposite the suffering roller door, the Transits were parked. Some still bore the scars of repairs carried out during and after the great strike, where half bricks and bottles, thrown angrily by frustrated Miners, had dented and ripped their thin metal skins. Their light blue paintwork had bubbled and blackened with the burning petrol that had cascaded over wings and bonnets as the 'Molotov cocktails' had shattered against them.

The B.M.W. motorcycles leaned methodically against their side stands, like dominoes frozen at the point of toppling. The overhead strip lighting was reflected brilliantly in their chrome plated exhausts and the fluorescent striping on the fairings and panniers.

The night security man, known colloquially throughout the Force as 'The Swamp Monster', waddled slowly down the length of the garage between the ranks of parked vehicles, his soft shoes noiseless against the painted surface of the floor.

He stopped every now and then to inspect a worksheet trapped between wiper blade and windscreen, his huge girth resting against the bodywork as he leaned across to read the fault report. Main crank case journal oil seal (replace front) check cam followers and re-time, 'K' Div.

He moved to another vehicle, wheezing slightly, the warm, dry air not helping his asthma. Ignoring the tightness in his chest, he paused to light a cigar, his twentieth of the day in defiance of the advice from his G.P. The extra seventy pounds he was carrying didn't help either and he grunted as he glanced at the worksheet, noting the reported fault. Compression loss, excessive oil consumption/heavy exhaust emissions, 'C' Div. Below the fault, the garage Foreman had scrawled "Check rings and valve stems" across the advice column and had left an oily thumb print across the fine blue lines.

The night security man understood neither the faults nor the remedies. The intricacies of the internal combustion system were a mystery to him, drive shafts, differentials and overhead whatsits were equally Greek and he was the first to admit it, but the vehicles themselves were his responsibility, for ten hours at least, eight in the evening until six the following morning, five nights a week.

He knew all the cars and the motorcycles, knew all their registration numbers and without looking at the fault reports, which Division they belonged to. He meticulously washed their bodywork and vacuumed their carpets during his tour of duty, replacing them in their allotted parking bays where he would leather off the glass work and chromium body parts under the warm buffeting air.

Often, in the early hours, he would sit in one of the big patrollers, fastening the seat belt across the wide expanse of his stomach. Careful not to drop any cigar ash on their carpets or seat covers, he would listen to the VHF radio, running the palms of his hands lovingly around the circumference of the smooth, leather covered steering wheels. He listened to the controllers dispatching various Traffic crews to the various incidents; he listened intently to the vehicle checks and occasional comments regarding a disqualified driver or crew acknowledgments which were passed over the air, the hollow sounding messages echoing from the whitewashed brickwork of the garage.

He especially liked to listen to the exciting commentary passed between the vehicles during one of the frequent chases in the City, hurriedly turning up the volume and holding the steering wheel tightly in the 'ten to two' position as the Traffic men were taught, he imagined himself being involved, racing through the streets at breakneck speed, sirens and tyres screaming and blue lights flashing.

Sometimes whilst listening to a particularly exciting pursuit, he would get an erection.

He took another few steps and ran his hand over the bonnet of a Motorway Unit Ford Granada, caressing the smooth white paintwork wistfully as he looked across to where he had parked his own vehicle.

The Lada was rusting badly now and the sills and lower edges of the doors appeared leprous with the brown, tell-tale bubbles which erupted like acne, through the dull green paint. The red oxide which he had applied in copious amounts in an effort to stem the onslaught, had long since surrendered unconditionally and the vehicle seemed to sag with fatigue.

He stood with his hands somewhere in the region of where his hips used to be and he surveyed the garage. He looked quickly across to the roller door as it shuddered violently within its runners. A violent gust of wind rattled the slats and blew a few dead leaves into the garage beneath its bottom edge. Glancing at his watch, he realised that it was almost midnight and his stomach gurgled. As if on cue, a large bubble of gas fought its way upwards through the mass of his body and he belched loudly.

His office was warmer than the rest of the garage, separated from the shop floor by plasterboard walling with a small window through which he could view his domain. An oil filled radiator by the vehicle disposition board, sent shimmering waves of heat upwards toward the brown stained ceiling.

He eased his girth into the aged swivel chair and sucked wetly on his cigar, noting with a little annoyance that it had gone out. Placing the damp stub carefully in the ashtray, he reached out across the table top for the Tupperware box which contained his sandwiches. A faint hiss emanated from the box as he lifted the corner of the lid and the airtight seal was broken. Immediately, the strong, recognisable aroma of egg filtered upwards and assailed his nostrils. With a look of distaste, he peeled back one of the slices of bread and groaned to himself. "Christ on a fuckin' bike Norma, egg and mayonnaise again?" he said dejectedly, peering into the sandwich box and replacing the lid. He pushed it to the back of the desk and angrily reached for the stub of his cigar.

"Soft egg and mayonnaise, cream cheese, milk products, Jesus Christ, what I'd give for a plate of fish and chips or a steak pie, just every now and then."

His mind wandered and he could almost smell the vinegar on the hot battered fish and his mouth watered. His stomach gurgled again and deep within his glistening entrails, a small ulcer wept acid and slowly ate into his stomach wall. He winced and pushed his fist into the folds of fat which hung voluminously over the top of his trousers.

The night security man heaved his weight around uncomfortably in the chair, trying to ease the pressure in the muscles around the small of his back and he sucked on the cigar stump, tasting the bitterness of the tar on his tongue as he gazed out of the window and onto the shop floor.

His eyes fell on the wrecked shell of a Rover SD1 in the far corner; its twisted bonnet sneered at him above the gaping mouth of the torn grill and collapsed suspension. The car was a 'write off'; being stripped for whatever parts could be salvaged.

The front of the vehicle was hideously distorted, as if the car had ripped itself open to scream at the moment of impact before whatsoever it had collided with, had torn into the thin metal panels like wet tissue.

His curiosity aroused, with a grunt, he heaved himself from the chair and closing his office door behind him to conserve the heat. He shuffled across the garage floor to where the stricken vehicle sat.

He stood directly in front of the patrol car, his hands deep within his trouser pockets, shaking his head slowly as he perused the damage. "Cowboys, fuckin' cowboys that's what they are." he said softly to himself, as he peeled off a particle of splintered paintwork from one of the buckled wings. "Traffic cops…fuckin cowboys…in their fast cars, swannin' round in their fancy white tops, lordin' it over everyone. Give 'em push bikes again like we 'ad in the war, see 'ow they like that." he muttered to himself.

His eyes skipped over the damaged parts of the vehicle. The radiator, ripped away from its bottom housing points had been violently impacted against the water pump which now showed its cracked shell through the ruptured honeycombs and dripped brackish brown coolant onto the garage floor. Through the gaping opening where the bonnet had been so violently distorted, he peered further into the engine compartment. He noted the firewall bulkhead which had buckled as the heavy eight cylinder engine block had been catapulted rearwards. The suspension struts had burst through the inner wings and the vehicle sagged unevenly, its shattered front panels resting against the floor.

The night security man sighed heavily, noticing quite suddenly, that the wind had ceased its howling and, other than the humming of the overhead heaters, the silence in the garage was almost total.

He shuffled his way back to his office, his wheezing along with a disturbingly rattle deep within his chest, now more audible in the quiet stillness.

The chair creaked ominously as he eased his weight back against the backrest, trying to gain some relief from the pressure of the metal framework which was now exposed through the frayed hessian material.

Reaching out over the desk, he held a magazine up lengthways and feasted his eyes on the naked form of the centrefold. Her long blonde hair cascaded down onto her shoulders. Her tongue voluptuously caressing her upper lip in a lewd expression of ecstasy as her hands cupped her large breasts, her thumb just touching the dark nipples which jutted out proudly. "Christ, they're like chapel hat pegs." he whispered. "She can't be more than eighteen." he muttered to himself as his eyes dropped to the mass of blond pubic hair.

He was conscious of his quickening heart rate and the first stirrings of an erection and was shocked to find himself forming a mental picture of his daughter's face over that of the model.

His wayward teenaged offspring was seeing some unemployed leather jacketed moron. His acne ravaged face, clashing colourfully with his fluorescent green Mohican hairdo as he arrived at the house to collect his daughter in his hand painted M.O.T. failure.

He despaired at them both and remembered the scene that there had been at the house last Saturday evening. Norma, his suffering Wife pleading with her to put something decent on instead of the short black leather skirt which showed off the crack in her backside as she walked.

His daughter had laughed mockingly as she'd pulled on her leather jacket with the name of some inane rock group emblazoned across the back and ignoring further protestations from her Mother, had rushed out of the house to greet the borstal reject, who sat in his car outside the front gate, the stereo blasting out an insane wailing noise, consistent with a cat being castrated. This cacophony, just managing to drown out the noise from his defective exhaust until he accelerated away, eager not to have to confront her geriatric parents.

He leered guiltily at the centrefold. He imagined his daughter's squeals of laughter as she was mauled by the moron in the back of his wrecker. His grimy hands running over her small breasts beneath the 'T' shirt and up between her legs, which she opened invitingly.

He squeezed his eyes tightly shut and tried to force the vision from his mind, his daughter, his little angel, being willingly ravaged by that useless pile of shit.

His self-recriminations exacerbated by the full erection he had not been able to prevent.

His guilty imaginings were shattered by a horn blast outside the roller door. He jumped involuntarily and glanced quickly at the closed circuit television monitor on the table top and picked out the brilliant white glare of a pair of headlamps on the grainy black and white screen. He snapped the magazine shut and pushed it hurriedly away into the top drawer of the desk. His erection disappeared as quickly as it had arrived as he pushed the small button on the office wall to open the outer door.

A solenoid clicked and activated the electric motor which groaned and creaked in protest as the heavy door was hoisted upwards and rolled around the spindle between the outer gear wheels.

Alan glanced up through the windscreen watching the door shudder its way upwards and as the bottom edge passed the safety mark which was painted on the red brickwork, the after product of many a dented roof. He eased the patroller into the warmth of the garage. His partner looked across to the office window as Alan pulled up opposite and turned off the engine.

"Oh shitty death, I forgot about the swamp monster." he groaned.

Alan laughed. "Let's get in there pal and make him have it. It's your turn to do battle with the colossus".

"I wouldn't mind." his partner moaned. "But you'd think 'e owned the bleedin' things the way 'e carries on."

Alan laughed as he reached for the radio handset to advise the control room operator that they were 10/3 at Central Garage.

"We'll be call sign Hotel Foxtrot Three from now on. Crew is as previous."

"10/4" the operator replied.

Alan opened the door to the night security office and stepped in breezily, closely followed by his partner.

The fat night security man scowled at the two clowns as the hot air fled from his office and dissipated into the outer garage area.

Smiling, Alan turned and winked at his partner and swept off his cap pressing it against his chest. He bowed low at the waist, facing the Buddha like security man who glared at them warily.

"Good morrow oh mighty one." Alan said, bowing theatrically. Sullivan smiled and leaned against the door, peeling the cellophane wrapper from a cigar.

"May I rise oh giver of foul wind, for we have travelled long and far over the sands of Arkos. We have braved the godless dark skinned ones of the Badlands, to bring you greetings from our liege lord Parkin, who begs thee to entrust us with one of thy metal chariots."

The security man sat, unimpressed and unsmiling at Alan's efforts at humour. He reached across the desk for his lighter and purposefully lit the stub of his cigar.

Alan turned to his partner and shrugged his shoulders. Returning to face the fat night watchman; he leaned across the counter top and smiled. "Give us a Transit John, any Transit, we're not proud."

"That's a fact." the watchman wheezed. "Where's your request form?"

He held out a pudgy hand and looked directly at Sullivan, ignoring Alan completely.

Sullivan shrugged himself away from the door frame and leaned across the counter top alongside his partner. "What request form?"

"Must have been something I said." remarked Alan, a puzzled expression on his face.

The Buddha like security man sucked on his cigar and leaned back in his seat, smiling victoriously.

"Can't let you have a vehicle without a form 118…Standing Orders." he said smugly, confident that he had won the day.

Alan sighed, "Look John." he said dryly. "You might recognise this uniform, it's a Police uniform…look…it even says so here." Alan pointed to the cloth badge and Force crest sewn above the pocket of his yellow jacket. "See all those vehicles out there?" he nodded his head toward the office window. "They're Police vehicles. They've even got Police stickers on the sides so you can tell straight away just by looking. I'm a Policeman, those are Police vehicles, which makes them ours, not yours. Now…be a good chap, stop fuckin' around and give us the keys to one of those Trannies and we'll be on our way."

The security man remained unmoved. "Without a 118 form, I am not authoris…"

Alan's partner, who ran on a much shorter fuse, opened the hatch in the counter top and walked across to the fat man's desk. He snatched up the telephone handset and punched at the buttons on the body of the phone, glaring down at the security man as the extension number rang out.

"You're not allowed in here." the fat man wheezed, yet noting Sullivan's excessive height, remained seated. "It's a secure area; I'll have your numbers."

Sullivan lowered his shoulder towards the sweating Buddha so that the chrome numbers on his epaulette could be seen.

The watchman grunted and stretched up from his chair to read the numbers then sat down heavily. With shaking hands, he jotted down the time and Sullivan's collar number.

"Sir. It's Pc Sullivan, crew of Hotel Foxtrot Three. We're at Central Garage Sir, trying to requisition a Transit for tonight…Yes Sir there are, but the swam…gentleman on night security refuses to release one…I don't know Sir, something about a 118 release form…Yes Sir."

Sullivan handed the telephone handset down to the security man and smiled across at Alan. Perspiration stood out in tiny droplets on the security man's forehead as Parkin's voice spilled out angrily from the earpiece. "Yes I see…Well…they come in here demanding a van…I'm not to know…Yes I appreciate that, but…well, yes."

Sullivan heard the handset click as Parkin hung up. The night security man was left holding the dead handset up to his ear and slowly replaced it on its holder.

He reached up to the row of hooks on the vehicle disposition board above his radiator and took down a set of keys which he dropped into Sullivan's open palm.

Sullivan smiled knowingly. "Cheers John, as always, it's been a pleasure to see you, if ever we can be of assistance to you, just…"

"GO ON, BUGGER OFF." the fat security man shouted, leaping from his chair with amazing dexterity. "You're cowboys, that's what you are, cowboys."

Alan and his partner ignored his ranting's, fearful now of witnessing a cardiac arrest as the fat man trembled, sweated profusely and wheezed.

They closed the office door behind them and walked laughing towards the row of Ford Transits.

The office door was thrown open and a voice called after them. "I'll be checking it for damage when it comes back as well, any marks and you two buggers are for it."

Alan smiled at his partner. They both turned quickly and standing rigidly to attention, together raised their right arms in the Nazi salute. Alan shouted "Jahwohl mein grossenfuhrer."

The security man ran from his office and waddled toward them, his face now a worrying deep shade of red.

The rolls of his flesh moved loosely beneath his shirt as his pace quickened. The sweat marks under his armpits spreading quickly to join the damp patch which now ran down the full length of his back. His breathing was now coming in short rasping gasps as he lurched towards them. He mouthed obscenities which neither Alan nor his partner could decipher over the roar of the engine as the Transit fired up and spewed a cloud of oily black smoke against the whitewashed brickwork.

"Come on Al quick, before the old fart throws a 'thromby'. I'm not giving that old bastard the kiss of life."

"Wait 'till he gives you his I was at Arnhem routine." Alan said, allowing the van to lurch forwards as he dropped the clutch a little harshly.

The fat security man leapt quickly to one side. Sullivan wound down his window and smiled at the heaving security man. "Give our patroller a wash over while you've nothing to do. Oh, and if you could vacuum the carp..."

"YOU BLOODY COWBOYS, FUCK OFF, GO ON, FUCK OFF." The night watchman screamed. He coughed alarmingly and held a clenched fist tightly against his chest.

"CALL YOURSELVES POLICEMEN." he howled, "I WAS AT BLOODY ARNHEM." His voice cracked as he screamed over the noise of the revving engine.

"Here we go." Alan said flatly, as the van crawled forwards.

"YOU BUGGERS WOULDN'T HAVE LASTED FIVE MINUTES." the watchman wheezed, his voice becoming fainter as Sullivan wound up his window and waved politely to the frenzied security man.

"Where the fuck's Arnhem?" his partner asked casually, as they cleared the doors and the front of the Transit dipped down onto the main road.

Alan glanced quickly to his left and accelerated. "Somewhere near Rochdale I think."

*****

Sergeant John Robertson waited impatiently outside the Police station and checked his watch for the umpteenth time. The ten young Officers with him were in good enough spirits he supposed, eager at the thought of some action at last, a little payback for the years of verbal and physical abuse they'd suffered in the 'Badlands'. He on the other hand, could well have done without this foray.

He was cold, hungry and pissed off and the chin strap on his helmet rubbed annoyingly against a shaving rash he'd developed, this only adding to the foulness of his mood.

Sergeant Robertson had made plans for the night shift which had now been seriously disrupted by Parkin's impromptu raid. He glanced at his watch again, zero zero forty.

He shoved his hands deep into his pockets and looked down the perimeter drive, watching and waiting impatiently for the arrival of the van. "Bollocks to you Parkin." he hissed to himself. Over the past few weeks, he'd been cultivating a relationship with a woman from the Brandlea's, a council estate at the bottom end of the Division. Her young Son had been locked up for shoplifting whilst he was supposed to be a school and Sergeant Robertson had arranged for him to be brought to the station to receive an official caution from the Divisional Inspector as it was his first offence, well, the first time he'd been caught.

Sergeant Robertson had noticed that the lad's Mother seemed very grateful and given that she was not by any means unattractive, in a housing estate sort of way, Sergeant Robertson had offered to call round to her house every now and then, just to see how the lad was shaping up you understand, anyway, that was the excuse he was using. She, in turn, a young divorcee with a young Son who she felt was mixing with the wrong company, gladly accepted his kind offer.

At first, it had been a cup of coffee and a chat whilst the lad had been at home. It had progressed of late, to a cup of coffee at weekends whilst the errant youngster was away enduring his Father's visitation rights.

He'd noticed that she had been taking more care over her appearance and had been nicely made up when he had called to see her a week or so ago when he was on a late turn shift. He'd been bold enough to kiss her as he left, having assured himself that he had read her 'body language' correctly, not wearing a bra under her thin sweater, he'd considered it worthy of the risk. She'd responded eagerly enough to his kiss and in fact, had slipped her tongue into his mouth and moaned favourably as he slipped his hand under her sweater to caress one of her breasts.

Tonight was the night, he'd been sure of it…That bastard Parkin.

Sergeant Robertson had phoned her during the day whilst his Wife had been out collecting the kids from school. He'd arranged to see her at about half eleven that night after the pubs had kicked out and it had quietened down a bit. He'd even covered his absence from the shift with the Inspector, making up a non-existent shotgun licence enquiry with a bloke that worked nights. That would have given him at least two hours.

"Bollocks" he hissed again, realising that he'd started to get an erection. He'd even tucked a covertly purchased packet of condoms into the top pocket of his tunic, on the strength of the inviting tone in her voice. The condoms were for his protection not hers; she was nice enough, but her antecedents were unknown and if she'd cave in so easily for him, who knows where she'd been.

"What's up Sarge, you don't look too 'appy." Constable West said, as he sauntered up to his Sergeant and offered him a cigarette. He accepted one with a nod. "Crawling little prat." he thought as he bent down to accept the offered light.

West was still in his probationary two year period and was on monthly reports. He wasn't doing too well in the paperwork department; his street work was suspect as well. He tried too hard to be popular with his colleagues and it grated.

John Robertson was West's shift Sergeant and as such, had to write out the monthly reports on the lad's progress, or lack of it and dispatch them to Headquarters. Some eunuch in a white shirt would subsequently assess West's suitability for Office and the likelihood of him becoming a good and efficient Officer which, the Sergeant thought to himself, was far from being a certainty.

"What do you think then Sarge eh? 'Bout time we got stuck in. I reckon the niggers 'ave 'ad it their own way for too long, what do you say?"

Sergeant Robertson scratched at the irritating rash on his throat with his fingertips. "I say that kind of talk could well cost you your job these days."

West flicked the ash nervously from the end of his cigarette. "Yeah, well, I'm only sayin' what everybody knows is the truth."

"Nobody's disputing that West." the Sergeant said, looking out over the fields toward the main road. "It's just that it's against Force policy to let anyone hear you saying it."

The probationer grunted and drew on his cigarette. "Anyway Sarge, what else is there to do at this time of night eh?"

Sergeant Robertson saw the Transit turn into the station perimeter road. He tossed the part smoked cigarette onto the flagstones and ground it out with his boot. "Don't be naive West." he said, as he walked out onto the road.

He left the young Constable looking puzzled and raised his voice as he turned to face his Officers. "On your feet lads, the van's here. Come on, waken yourselves up. DeLacy, you're in charge of the shields, I want them stowed properly."

*****

Alan set the handbrake and flicked the switch on the dashboard facia and the interior light in the passenger compartment illuminated.

The cold air rushed in as the rear doors were flung open and the van rocked on its springs as the uniforms clambered noisily in.

Sergeant Robertson approached the driver's window. Alan wound it down. "Alright Sarge?" he said, immediately realising by his glowering countenance, that the Sergeant was not alright, not by any stretch of the imagination.

"No, I'm not alright. Where the fuck have you two been?"

Sullivan leaned across from the passenger seat and peered out of the driver's window at the Sergeant.

"We Sarge, have had the odious task of trying to pry this fucking heap from the sweaty grasp of fat John down at Central garage for the past half hour."

The Sergeant realised that it was no good biting the heads off his lads just because he'd dipped out on his 'extra maritals' and forced a smile. "Fair enough lads, but we'd better get cracking." he said, glancing at his watch again.

Alan nodded and opened the bulkhead door behind the front seats and secured it to the side of the van with the small metal hook. Sullivan moved across into the center of the three front seats and the Sergeant clambered in. He turned to face the Officers in the rear.

"Right, listen." He waited for silence. "This is not a licence to do untold damage to Police community relations. I don't want anybody overstepping the mark, you all know what I mean. It's a drugs raid and that's all. Let's not go fucking stupid." he paused and looked at each Officer individually. "The target premises has three floors, the blues itself will be on the first floor. The main stash of drugs will probably be somewhere in the basement. We're looking for controlled drugs, they will be cleverly secreted. Look in the backs of the speakers, taped up under the tables, behind pictures on the walls, they hack out the brickwork behind and stash the gear. It'll be in large quantities. Seize the fuckin' bag and make a note of where it was found, make sure the exhibits Officers make a note of your collar number for continuity…Look after yourselves and your mates. If it kicks off, form a group, back to back, don't expose yourselves unnecessarily. We only have our staffs and cuffs and a couple of dogs for backup, *they* have a habit of carrying knives, and the odd handgun isn't unheard of either, so for fuck's sake think on."

He looked back at all the young faces in the rear of the van and failed to see one which he knew for sure he could rely on. "Anyone found in possession gets nicked, cuffed, and out of the premises quickly and into one of the vans. Don't waste your time identifying type and quantities in the premises, if it looks like drugs, it will be. Shove it back in 'is pocket or wherever you found it on 'im and deal with it at the Bridewell. This job will be tricky enough without us helping it to deteriorate, which these jobs have a nasty habit of doing, as those of you who remember last bonfire night will agree. For those who weren't there, I can tell you, we got a right stuffing. I do not want to see any Officer on his own…You go in pairs, everywhere, understood?"

The uniforms nodded in unison and a more sombre mood enveloped them all.

"If you lose a prisoner in the melee, let 'im go, get another. Christ knows, there should be plenty to go around. I don't want to see anyone running away from the scene after a prisoner, you get caught in the back streets, and the gangs will 'ave you. Let the dog handlers deal with any runners from the premises, got it?"

The uniforms nodded.

"These bastards come out of the woodwork from nowhere and they don't play fair, so be careful." He emphasised the last words to impress his point upon them, not that it should have been needed. "All of you." he said, and looked back to Alan and his partner. "Take your numbers off; I don't want any complaints coming in about any member of my unit. Not that it gives you carte blanche to do damage or engage in gratuitous violence, I mean that, understood?…West?"

"Sarge." the probationer nodded.

"Have we all actually got our staffs and cuffs, tell me now if you haven't." He searched their faces as they took off their epaulettes, stuffing them into the top pockets of their black jackets.

Each Officer nodded and the Sergeant seemed satisfied.

"Right Alan." he called out to the front of the Transit. "Let's get off."

Alan turned in his seat and started the engine, securing his seat belt into the securing clasp as his partner contacted the Control room.

"Hotel Foxtrot Three a message."

## **Sixteen**

The old man's eyelids fluttered then opened. His chest ached with a deep numbness beneath his sternum and a constricting band of pain tightened across his rib cage, making him pull in his breath sharply. He coughed quietly and winced against the stabbing pain that shot across his chest. He squeezed his eyes tightly shut against the torment which relentlessly reminded him that it was the angina which determined how long, or how well he should sleep.

He turned his head stiffly on the pillow, grimacing at the pain which the slightest movement exacerbated. He looked to see if his coughing had wakened his Wife, she lay beside him as always, the wisps of fine white hair, falling over her forehead and cheeks.

He remained motionless for a moment and looked lovingly across at his Wife as the thudding pulse beats in his temples subsided slightly. He remembered when her hair had been black, black as a raven and lustrous. He smiled briefly to himself as he thought how coy she had been as she had let it down on her wedding night, the tight folds falling open and cascading down onto her shoulders and across the whiteness of her nightdress. Blue black it had been, even in the dim light from the gas lamp, no electricity back then, just the faint hiss of the gas as it escaped into the tulip shaped filament and burned with a warm yellow glow.

She lay facing him, her mouth slightly open, the skin stretched tightly across her cheekbones, parchment like, dry and ancient looking. She breathed lightly with a slight wheezing sound and he was relieved to see that she slept on, knowing how many nights he had disturbed her of late. With a claw like hand discoloured with brown liver spots, he reached across to the bedside table and sought out a small metal box. Its shape, he could just make out in the dull yellow light filtering through the curtains from the lamp post, directly outside their bedroom window.

He grimaced again as he grasped at the familiar shape with his arthritic fingers. His knuckles were distorted and swollen, yet the box was designed for those with such deformities and the large luminous button on the front, responded immediately to his touch.

The top of the box snapped open to reveal the small white tablets, one of which he fumbled from the shallow tray and with a trembling hand, dropped onto his tongue. The tablet immediately sucked at the sparse dampness in his mouth and started to dissipate, its bitter contents attacking the taste buds on the back of his tongue. He swallowed hard and reached for the plastic tumbler of tepid water that he had prepared earlier, he gulped eagerly and the bitterness faded.

His Wife stirred and mumbled incoherently.

He lay, silent and unmoving, allowing the Glyceryl Trinitrate to filter through his system and ease the constrictions in the paper thin fibers that surrounded his heart. He breathed easier as the pain slowly subsided and he leaned gently against the wooden headboard and closed his eyes. The dull pulsating beat of the music resonated through the still cold air outside and filtered into the room.

He sighed quietly to himself and cursed the Council yet again for housing him and his Violet in this area. Things had been good at one time.

Just after the war, property had been at a premium of course and they had considered themselves fortunate to have been offered the house. He'd been given preferential treatment because of his war service, helped by the fact that he had been wounded during the re-occupation of Akyab in Burma back in '45.

On his return to England, he had taken his new bride into the Council owned three storey terraced accommodation, grateful in the knowledge that he had done his duty and now the Council in turn, were doing theirs.

The gardens had been neatly tended, the paintwork maintained well and not always by the Council. People had pride in those days; he smiled to himself as he remembered the women scrubbing their front door steps with pumice stones, as if it were some sign of ungodliness to have a dirty step leading to your house.

The summers had somehow seemed longer as well. The old man remembered the menfolk out on the street, after a day's work at the factory, talking and smoking, them that could afford it, their trousers pulled in tight around their stomachs with thick leather belts as they reminisced about the war. Most had been in work as well, trudging like so many automatons to the wrought iron factory gates at first light, their old Army back packs slung over their shoulders, the brass buckles dulled through neglect now. Their steel studded boots scuffed and worn out, but still casting off the odd spark against the cobbles on the back streets, as those that had survived the conflict, went back to work.

They had no money, or very little at least. Every family had a pawn ticket somewhere around the house, yet it seemed to him to have been a still time, peaceful after the dreadful conflicts in Europe and the Far East and he had been thankful to have made it home and for what little they had.

The first coloureds to move into the area, invited by the Government of the day with promises of employment and a better standard of living, were something of a curiosity. Most of the local inhabitants never actually having seen a coloured before and those that had, remembered them in the drab olive green of the U.S. Army. That first generation of blacks had been God-fearing and industrious and had accepted the menial jobs that the white man at that time, thought to be beneath him. The coloureds worked hard and were uncomplaining. To 'work like a black' became the coined phrase of the day.

For the most part, they attended the local Baptist and Wesleyan churches, with a reverence which could only be emulated by the white locals who seemed to display their piety more with lip service than with the genuine devotion displayed by the immigrants. The blacks turned up regularly for work, as opposed to their white co-workers, who were steeped deeply in Socialist fervours after the war. The 'English Disease', having gained a strong foothold in the tenement areas of the City.

That had been forty or so years ago. The area had gradually degenerated. The immigrant offspring, generation by generation, showing less and less regard for the community life or the integration which had been hoped for. The upkeep of the streets and houses had declined as the blacks slowly took over.

The drugs trade had started and the prostitution. Not that prostitutes hadn't been there before the immigrants had arrived, they had simply brought it to the fore, organised it, realised the demand, supplied it and then monopolised it.

The drugs scene was a new thing. The blacks had brought it with them from Jamaica. It had always been dark stout and cigarettes in his day, that's all a man had needed, a paying job, a good Wife and a bottle of 'Forest Brown' stout and a Woodbine of an evening. Now the once proud streets from whence had come the 'salt of the earth' were littered with syringes, used condoms and broken down vehicles.

The black children shouted out their foul obscenities as they jumped from the crumbling garden walls, onto the bonnets of the cars and kicked at the empty beer cans which littered the gutters up and down the street until the early hours. And it was the music now, incessant loud music, the heady throbbing of the black man's lyrics which echoed from the vehicles as they passed beneath his window and boomed out from the houses, each resident, seemingly in contest with their neighbour.

The old man thanked God that his Violet was housebound. It would have frightened her to have shuffled her way down to the shops through the groups of young blacks who hung around the street corners, shouting abuse as they did, to the old or infirm.

He glanced at the clock on the bedside table and dragged his legs out from beneath the quilt, taking great care not to disturb her. He sat for a moment, quietly on the edge of the bed and reached for the clock. He pulled it closer and tilted its face toward the window to catch the dim light across the glass. Almost two o'clock, the old man sighed heavily and carefully replaced the clock on the table top and sat in silence. He rested his hands against his knees. Sleep was over for tonight. Although he felt weary, he knew that he would lie awake until daybreak.

He stood up slowly and his knees cracked as they took his weight. He crossed the small room to the window which overlooked the street; he looked out in an effort to see which house the music was coming from. Tomorrow, he would go down to the Council offices again and ask for a move to the new sheltered housing complex on Pemberton Way. He knew that there were vacancies. Mrs Shaw from the Post Office had told him so and he decided that he would no longer be 'fobbed off' by some snot nosed young social worker who had never faced the end of a bayonet in his life. He'd fought for his Country and they owed him.

There were bungalows on Pemberton Way, no stairs to climb and that in itself would be a Godsend. They were centrally heated too, and that would ease his arthritis.

It saddened him to think of leaving the area. He'd lived there for most of his adult life, worked there and raised his children. But the blacks had ruined it, damn them, ruined it as they ruined everything they came into contact with.

He supposed that he was admitting defeat, but he had Violet to think about. The blacks were welcome to it now, damn them. Damn them all to hell.

The old man placed his twisted hands against the flaking paintwork on the window sill and eased the curtain to one side to look down onto the street. The music came as usual, from the house directly opposite, one of those parties again. Their shouting would surely wake Violet as the revellers left at four or five in the morning. No wonder they couldn't get up for work he thought.

He pushed the discoloured netting further across as a glint under one of the street lights caught his eye. He looked down toward the main road and noticed a solitary van being driven ever so slowly up the street.

*****

Alan glanced up to the rear view mirror and although the interior light was off in the rear passenger compartment, he could just make out the faces of the Officers who were seated nearest to the bulkhead door. He looked across to the Sergeant who was fastening the press stud on his chin strap, "You ready for this?"

"Fuckin' right we are." the Sergeant snorted, still annoyed at having to cancel his sojourn to the willing divorcee in the Brandlea's. "Parkin's spoiled my evening; it's time to cheer myself up by asserting some long overdue authority on the indigenous lower forms of life."

"Very diplomatic Sarge." Alan said smiling. The Sergeant simply shrugged and glanced at his watch.

Alan nodded to his partner and Sullivan depressed the transmit button on the personal radio clipped to his jacket pocket. The red light on the VHF set in the dashboard facia illuminated as the talk-through facility was activated. "You about Dave?"

The radio hissed quietly for a second, then Alan recognised Pc Mercer's voice as it came faintly through the speaker.

"Go ahead."

"Where are you?"

"End of Cowper Street."

"Can you see the rear of the premises?"

"'firmative. I've got one fifty six…You?"

Sullivan glanced at his watch and nodded to Alan.

The Transit gradually slowed to a halt as Alan depressed the clutch pedal and eased up the handbrake lever, gauging the distance to the target premises.

"You call it Dave, it's close enough." Sullivan said quietly into the top of his radio.

The radio hissed again. "10/4, stand by. You seen anything of Task Force yet?"

"Negative." Sullivan replied, scanning the street behind the van through the large nearside wing mirror.

"A couple of minutes should do it lads." Alan said, looking up to the rear view mirror.

He recognised the sound of press studs being fastened on reinforced helmets and the dull sound of a sledgehammer being dragged out from beneath the slatted wooden seats.

"Sully." the radio whispered.

"Go ahead." Alan's partner said, looking directly out through the windscreen.

Alan's calf muscles twitched as he held the clutch pedal down, one hand ready on the handbrake lever as he stared at the gate leading up to the target premises.

"Dog van's here and so is Task Force, if we're…"

"NOW, NOW, NOW." the radio screamed.

Alan dropped the clutch and revved the engine.

The nose of the Transit lifted as the van surged up the street towards the house onto which Alan had focused his vision.

All six wheels of the Transit locked up and there was a shrill screech as the van skidded to a halt. The rear doors were thrown open and the van disgorged its contents, in the shape of ten uniformed avenging angels, out onto the street.

Sergeant Robertson exited the van and ran toward the wooden gate. He kicked it rudely open and ushered his troops up the short path toward the front door of the premises. "Call it in Alan." he called back to the Transit, as he ran up the path to join his troops.

Sullivan grabbed up the VHF handset, stabbing at the button to release it from talk through and advised the control room operator, that Hotel Foxtrot Three was active. "This is going to end in fucking tears, I just know it." he said and scowled as he replaced the handset in its holder, noting the groups of young blacks quickly dispersing from the street corners and scurrying down the cobbled alleys between the houses.

Alan clambered out of the cab and went to the front offside to watch the action as the first of the Task Force contingent arrived, smiling at his partner's discontent. "All the fun of the fair, eh, Sully?"

His partner shook his head disconsolately.

Sergeant Robertson reached the front door just as the first sledge hammer blow fell against the woodwork.

The fourteen pound head shattered the old wooden panelling, sending slivers of wood flying out onto the path. "Try the fucking handle first you idiot." Sergeant Robertson shouted.

The hammer head froze in mid-flight.

The Sergeant twisted the door handle and put his shoulder sharply against the splintered door which swung inwards easily. The uniforms surged forwards into the premises. Already, loud, panicked shouts of 'Babylon' could be heard from the occupants within, as the blue clad warriors poured into the hallway.

"Well done Williams. Fucking well thought out." Sergeant Robertson said angrily. He sneered sarcastically at the Constable who stood at his side, still holding the hammer aloft. "Remind me of this incident when I come to do your appraisal next month will you."

Williams lowered the hammer ruefully. "I just thought…"

"Christ! Don't do that Williams, you're dangerous enough." the Sergeant mocked, grabbing for the hammer handle. "Just get in there and join your mates eh…and try not to cause any more damage to property. Think you can manage that?"

"Right Sarge." Constable Williams said sheepishly, slinking away into the hallway.

Sergeant Robertson stood for a moment at the doorway, listening to the mayhem from within. He shook his head slowly and looked back to where Alan and his partner stood watching, leaning over the bonnet of the Transit.

Alan chuckled, his hands thrust deep into the pockets of his jacket. He nodded to the Sergeant who shook his head in despair and dropped the lump hammer by the front door before disappearing into the house.

"First blood to us then Pete, chalk one up to the Police for a bit of unnecessary gratuitous damage. Police Complaints Authority'll have a field day with this."

Sullivan shrugged his shoulders. "What d'you expect, Parkin's wound them up tighter than a virgin's ring piece with all his military style 'gung ho' shit. In the space of half an hours briefing, he's managed to transform twenty odd reasonably mannered beat lads into a mass of seething shock troops. Bit of damage is the best we can hope for and the fuckin' Task Force 'avn't even got started yet."

Alan laughed and scratched the side of his head. The music from within the premises stopped abruptly, with a heavily amplified shriek of a stylus being snatched across the face of a record.

The second Task Force van screeched to a halt. Ten uniformed Officers, all wearing black overalls leapt from the rear of the vehicle and charged down the path toward the suffering front door. The Sergeant in charge of the Task Force contingent, wandered casually over to where Alan and his partner were leaning against their van.

"Anything yet?"

"Only just gone in Sarge. We've attracted a fair bit of attention though."

Alan nodded toward the end of the street where four or five groups of young blacks had gathered, their colours standing out starkly even in the dim street lights. One member of the group spoke sharply and the groups immediately dispersed in different directions.

"You know where they're headed." The Sergeant said pointedly.

"Reinforcements." Alan replied.

The Sergeant nodded as they watched the young soldiers disappearing down the side streets.

He turned back to face the house as the first prisoner was dragged out onto the pathway with a uniform at each arm. He was kicking out and mouthing the usual colourful obscenities as the uniforms dragged him unceremoniously toward the rear of the van.

Sullivan glanced at his watch, "I'd better let the Ayatollah know it's started."

The Sergeant adopted a puzzled expression. Alan put him out of his misery. "Parkin Sarge, he'll be in the control room coordinating his operation."

The Sergeant smiled, "Yeah…bit like Churchill in his war room, eh?"

Alan raised his eyebrows and scratched his chin. "Yeah, 'cept Winston actually knew what he was doing Sarge."

The Sergeant turned to the arresting Officers. "Right lads…Who's this sorry looking piece of shit and what's it for?"

The uniforms, clutching their 'prize', dragged the young black up to the rear doors of the van.

"Name and address refused, suspicion of being in possession of a controlled substance Sarge."

One of the uniforms held up a small plastic bag which looked to contain a considerable amount of white powder.

"Oh dear." the Sergeant said dryly, looking down with a disapproving expression at the young black who he now noticed, was bleeding from his mouth. "There's enough there for a possession with intent to supply…fall over did he Wilson?"

The prisoner spat at one of his captors. The blood streaked saliva clung to the uniform's jacket and slowly ran down the material leaving a shiny streak in its wake.

"Motherfucka drop it in ma poke is what." the prisoner screamed, struggling against the hands which gripped his arms tightly behind his back.

"Course 'e did." the Sergeant said with mock condescension. "You've obviously been well stitched up. But don't you worry; I shall personally take it up with the Chief Constable on your behalf as soon as we get back." He nodded to the uniforms. "In the back with 'im then lads."

The protesting prisoner was bundled into the back of the Transit whilst he continued to cast doubts as to the marital status of the uniform's parents at the time of their births. The sound of a hard, solid sounding slap echoed around the van's interior. Alan winced and the Sergeant tapped on the side panel of the van. "Wilson." he said sternly.

"Sarge?" came the muted reply, loaded with schoolboy innocence.

"Watch it."

"Right Sarge."

Alan smiled at the Task Force Sergeant's half-hearted efforts to suppress the young Officer's exuberance. There was little doubt, that the prisoner would receive a physical reminder to extend a little respect for the forces of law and order, but that should be delivered on the way to the Bridewell, not in the back of a Transit whilst at the scene. Cameras and witnesses had a nasty habit of appearing from nowhere in the 'Badlands'.

"That's telling him Sarge." Alan nodded sternly, emphasizing the sarcasm in his voice.

The Task Force Sergeant grunted. "Look…the only thing your basic street nigger understands is a knotted rope across the arse. Does 'em good to get a crack every now and then. Niggers are a cursed race, hewers of wood and drawers of water, if you know your bible."

"A rather colonial attitude if you don't mind me so opining Sergeant." Alan said, in his best Magistrates voice. "And if I may go further, without appearing too liberal. Your views on curbing the inner City unrest amongst our ethnic minorities are a maxim to which we should all aspire."

"It's alright you taking the piss." the Sergeant snapped, catching Alan a little unawares with his sudden change of temperament. "I've had this fuckin' lot for over ten years. You just wait, when the bleedin' heart, tree huggin' lefties have finished, it'll be a disciplinary offence to look sideways at these bastards." He cocked his thumb toward the house. "We should 'ave gripped this fuckin' drugs thing in the bud when it first started. But oh! no, as usual, the bosses are too shit scared of any hint of discrimination or racism. We've left it too late. We 'ad all the troops together during the Miner's strike. We should 'ave let the Met lads go in while we 'ad 'em up 'ere. They know 'ow to deal with yer ethnics."

Alan nodded, not wanting to enter into the same old argument, where although everybody agreed that it was the right thing to do, no one actually had the balls to go ahead and do it. Except Parkin, it appeared.

Alan sighed. "Yeah, you're right Sarge, although I think you'll agree that the Broadwater Farm fiasco didn't end too well for the Met."

The Sergeant pondered on that one for a moment and without responding, wandered back towards the house.

Alan climbed back into the cab of the rocking Transit; his partner flopped down wearily in the passenger seat. He lit a cigar, winding the window down to allow the smoke to escape.

"Jesus." Alan exclaimed, reaching across and releasing the bulkhead door from its hook and slamming it shut to isolate the cab area from the rear.

"What's up?" his partner asked.

"That Task Force Sergeant." Alan said, nodding back toward the house.

"Bill Elmsley, what's up with him?"

Alan snorted. "Ferkin 'ell Pete, you're joking. It's no wonder the Task Force lads get into so much shit, they've got Genghis Khan as a supervisor."

The van rocked on its springs as another prisoner was bundled into the rear. Alan could hear his muted protests through the plywood bulkhead door.

He half turned to look through the small aperture, when a loud metallic thud resonated through the van, like someone wearing heavy boots kicking a dustbin.

Alan snapped his head around to face the front. "What the fu…"

The windscreen of the van suddenly imploded, showering him with powdered glass and small splinters.

Alan shook his head involuntarily; his eyes had closed tightly at the first crack against the screen which had now folded slowly inwards, falling away from its rubber surround.

Alan was vaguely aware of the sound of something heavy thudding against the floor pan near to his feet. His heart rate doubled in a millisecond as the shock of the attack dawned on him and the adrenalin rushed through his system. He was covered in small shards of glistening glass particles which fell from his hair and the front of his jacket. He quickly gathered his senses and slowly and tentatively opened his eyes to peer out through the open aperture where the screen should have been.

He caught sight of a group of young blacks as they dodged into a garden, some twenty yards or so away from the Transit. The stone wall which had separated the garden frontage from the pavement now lay in fragments over the flagstones. It had been pulled down and the heavy sandstone coping stones used for ammunition.

His wits returned quickly and Alan reached out across for the radio handset. "FUCK ME!... come on mate, it's starti..." Alan stopped in mid speech, starting in disbelief at the darkness of the blood which was now cascading over his partner's eyebrows and onto his flickering lids.

Sullivan's chin now sagged sideways and hung slackly against the lapel of his jacket. An obscene swelling had already appeared over his partner's right eye and an ugly gash oozed blood at an alarming rate from within its ragged edges.

Alan froze for a millisecond, his peripheral vision closed down. His vision withdrew inwards, became tunnel like with a worrying dark veil around the edges. Time slowed and the shouting from those outside the van, seemed muffled and incoherent.

In slow motion, his eyes returned to the floor pan as he recalled the dull thudding sound at his feet.

The large coping stone still rocked on the rubber matting at his partner's feet. In immaculate detail, Alan could see miniscule particles of glass embedded in its surface. They glistened and turned to ruby red as his partner's blood spattered onto the rough surface of the stone.

His breathing quickened and he uttered a single sob of panic, raising his hands to his partner's face but not daring to touch.

The Transit rocked again and Alan was vaguely aware of the sound of boots pounding against the tarmac as uniformed Officers ran past the van, charging toward the black faces which now seemed to be everywhere.

Another deafening thud against the bonnet of the van brought Alan to his senses. Another rock disintegrated as it smashed against the pale blue paintwork and he felt the stinging of the particles which spattered against his face.

He shrank back behind the dashboard of the vehicle and although shielding his eyes against the glass particles, he was unable to take his eyes from the unconscious form of his partner now slumped in his seat. He shook his head and the shouting and the sounds of shattering glass snapped back to full volume.

Alan fumbled for the radio handset again, dropping it to the floor. He snatched it up and his voice wavered, his throat strangely dry as he started to shout even before he had depressed the transmit pad. "Hotel Foxtrot Three, urgent."

"Go ahead over." the control room operator replied quickly, identifying the urgency in Alan's voice.

"10/13...10/13" Alan shrieked, ducking involuntarily as a bottle shattered against the front wing of the Transit. "10/13...Officers require urgent assistance Marbury Avenue, my partner is down."

The radio was silent for a moment, then Parkin's unmistakable voice broke in. "Hotel Foxtrot Three. What is the current situation?...Over."

"Ambulance required and further assistance." Alan shouted. "We've got Officers injured and we are under attack with stones and bottles. My partner..."

Alan's transmission was interrupted by a Task Force Officer who pulled the driver's door open violently, the studs on his boots screeching against the road surface as he skidded to a stop.

The young Officer's face was damp with sweat, his eyes filled with panic.

"Gerra a fuckin' ambulance quick. Robbo's bin stabbed!"

The Task Force man didn't wait for a reaction, but glanced quickly across to Alan's partner and grimaced before running off towards the rear of the van.

Alan heard a loud whining in his ears and for a second, wondered what it was, before he realised somewhat shamefully, that it was his own panic.

The sounds of the escalating riot outside the van faded again and Alan could just hear his own breathing over a curious pounding in his ears. He flinched involuntarily as more missiles struck the van. He ducked down below the level of the vehicle's dashboard and keyed the radio handset.

"Hotel Foxtrot Three." He shouted into the mouthpiece. He could hear nothing but the loud ringing in his ears.

"Hotel Foxtrot Three. 10/13…10/13." he shouted.

Parkin's demanding tones over the radio shook him back to his senses. "Hotel Foxtrot Three, 10/4 your last. What is your operational status?"

Alan pressed the handset hard up against his ear to try and block out the ringing and the noise from the street.

"Hotel Foxtrot Three." Alan replied, ducking further down behind the dashboard as another missile bounced off the bodywork. "Officer has been stabbed, require immediate ambulance and Police Support Units to the scene."

Alan heard the rear doors of the Transit being flung open and there were shouts and swearing as the prisoners were thrown bodily, still handcuffed, out onto the road surface to be dragged away to one of the other waiting vans.

The inner bulkhead door was flung open and the form of the Task Force Sergeant half entered the cab from the rear compartment, his face streaked with perspiration and smeared with blood. "Move it…NOW!.. Infirmary and fuckin' quick."

Alan quickly glanced through the bulkhead aperture and saw the injured Sergeant being laid out on the rubber flooring between the slatted seats. An Officer knelt beside him, his hand pressing hard against the Sergeant's side whilst a rolled up uniform jacket was pushed hurriedly beneath his head. Blood welled up between the Officer's fingers and he pressed down harder against the wound, forcing a moan to escape from between the Sergeants tightly clenched teeth, his eyes screwed up tightly against the pain.

The Task Force Sergeant looked across at Alan's partner, then quickly back to the floor of the Transit to where his fellow Sergeant writhed in agony. He pushed Alan's shoulder roughly. "Fucking get on with it then." he screamed.

Alan fumbled with the ignition key, his hand shaking. The engine fired up and howled in protest as he wrenched the gear lever forwards. His left ankle was shaking uncontrollably as he released the clutch. His right foot slammed against the accelerator pedal and the van lurched violently forwards.

The windscreen sank further inwards, down onto the top of the dashboard and as Alan punished the van in first gear, with his left hand, he pushed the flaccid glass out onto the bonnet, ignoring the cuts from the shards which clung to the inner polythene membrane as he pulled the remaining edges out from the rubber surround. The whole screen fell away from the dented aperture and slithered away across the bonnet and out of sight as Alan raced the Transit away from the scene.

*****

The old man glanced quickly back into the semi darkness of the room and saw that his Wife, oblivious to the noise outside, slept on. He looked back to the street below and watched as a Transit van screamed away toward the junction with the main road. The unsecured rear doors of the van flapped wildly and slammed against its side panels as the vehicle slewed out onto the main road and out of sight.

Uniformed Officers spilled out of the house opposite, running out onto the street, some of them dragging handcuffed blacks, some of whom, having lost their footing, were kicked and heaved violently to their feet.

The old man watched, transfixed by the scene being played out on the street below his window. All semblance of order seemed to have gone; one of theirs was down.

The uniforms lashed out with their truncheons, striking at anyone as long as it had a black face and happened to be in the immediate area.

He looked across the road to where a second van which had stopped opposite the house. It now sat with a broken windscreen. One of its headlights was out and he could vaguely make out a large dent in the center of its bonnet and the shape of a large stone laying on the road surface illuminated by the one remaining headlight.

He looked further down the street to the left of his house. Under a street light, a Policeman was struggling with a young black man. They had both fallen to the pavement and the Officer's helmet lay on its side in the gutter, the chrome metal badge reflecting the yellow light until it was sent skittering down the road as it was kicked by one of the struggling pair.

The old man watched as the Officer fought to free his truncheon from his trouser pocket.

The black man gripped the Officer's wrist in an effort to prevent its withdrawal, knowing what was coming, his knee stabbed wildly around the Officer's groin area. Their arms flailed wildly around each other like two demented lovers.

The truncheon was eventually drawn free and it was brought down in a blurred arc across the face of the Officer's adversary. All the pent up anger of a decade of policing the coloured area was released. All the nights that he had cleaned the spittle from his uniform, all the verbal abuse that he had suffered, was cleansed from him in an instant as the heavy wooden staff was brought down again and again.

The young black curled up into the foetal position, his arms folded tightly across his face and head as the truncheon lashed down again and again. The surface of the pavement suddenly darkened with a widening pool of blood, or was it just shadows?

The old man rubbed at his eyes to clear his blurred vision, but clarity failed him.

The uniform had scrambled to his feet, bettering his victim and was now standing over him; his feet placed methodically either side of the prone figure as he vented his anger. The dull thudding sound of his truncheon striking the unprotected body was barely audible over the shouting and the shattering of glass.

The old man's eyes darted to the opposite side of the street where three coloureds were kicking the prostrate body of a man wearing a dark blue uniform. He saw the splashes of colour emblazoned across the backs of their jackets, but the letters were a blur to him.

The man in the uniform put up no resistance. His head lolled from side to side as the kicks landed about his body.

A new sound filtered into the street, growing in strength as it approached.

A small white van, its two tone horns drowning out the sounds of the melee as it swung into the street from the main road.

A second similar vehicle appeared and the horns fell silent, allowing the sound of loud, excited barking to fill the air.

Officers ran from the vans and threw open the ventilated rear doors. The barking became louder as the heavy Alsatians leapt from their mobile kennels, their front legs prancing with excitement as choker chains were slipped over their upraised ears.

More vans arrived into the street, large blue ones, like the first ones which had arrived. Their rear doors burst open and uniformed men spilled out, quickly forming into ranks, shuffling hurriedly into line as sharply barked orders were given.

The dogs barked, and one, freed from its retraining steel chain, raced forwards. Its ears were now laid flat against the fur on its neck, the stark whiteness of its teeth plainly visible as it launched itself into the air a few feet behind one of the coloureds kicking the unconscious Officer.

The gang members, seeing the approach of the Police dogs immediately ran off in different directions.

The first dog ignored the other two and brought the nearest black down heavily. The beast's claws skittered on the road surface as it slewed to a halt and bit deep into the flesh of the man's back. Its huge head swung wildly from side to side, shaking its prey like a puppet, until its handler slipped the heavy chain back around its neck and pulled it away from the fallen man.

With a single word of command, the dog reluctantly released its grip. The handler placed a booted foot against the back of the man's neck forcing his face down against the road surface. Another sharp word of command was shouted and the dog leapt forwards again, sinking its fangs into the soft flesh of the coloured man's thigh, before looking up excitedly to its handler, who patted its head lovingly.

*****

The old man frowned as he watched the ranks of men move forwards. They didn't look like normal bobbies, these men wore dark blue crash helmets like motorcyclists. Their faces were hidden behind shiny curved visors and they wore no uniform that he'd ever seen before, they were wearing what looked like overalls. They had long batons clasped in their gloved hands and carried small shields as well, like dustbin lids but clear, plastic maybe, he thought. They wore them strapped on their forearms.

Each one had a wide, white strip across the center. Large black letters stood out starkly, he furrowed his eyebrows against the half-light and saw the 'POLICE' lettering.

He turned again to look at his Wife, she slept on. He considered waking her, this was something she should see.

The barking of the dogs dragged his attention back to the streets. The ranks had started to move forwards, their shields held up in front of their chests as they paced evenly in two ranks down the street. The Police dogs were yelping and straining at their leashes, they pulled their handlers forwards as they walked behind the slowly moving lines. Bottles burst against the road surface as the ranks marched inexorably forwards. Some were deflected by the shields, most falling short of their target and shattering against the tarmac, sending showers of glass across the road surface. The shards of glass were crunched beneath the soles of their heavy boots as the lines trudged forwards.

He watched, holding his breath, transfixed as the ranks of men moved. Apparently unperturbed by the flying missiles. The front rank increased in width, as Officers from the rear rank stepped forwards one at a time and methodically took their places between those in the front rank until a single file of Officers stretched across the whole width of the street.

They moved perfectly in step and in single file, ignoring the prone bodies of their uniformed colleagues. They struck out with their heavy batons at any blacks daring to try to force a way through the shield wall.

Those laid out by the strikes from the batons, were set upon by uniformed Officers following up in the rear. Knees were dropped heavily down between shoulder blades and hands were wrenched up behind backs so that handcuffs could be applied.

The leashes restraining the prancing Police dogs were loosed. Those unfortunate enough to be arrested, were bitten about their legs and thighs as they were hauled to their feet by the snatch squads and dragged unceremoniously toward the waiting Transits.

The shouts and taunts from the coloureds that dashed forwards to throw their rocks and bottles grew fainter as they retreated down the street. They pulled down the walls as they went, gathering fresh ammunition.

The ranks of men marched out of his view. The whining and yelping of the dogs, grew faint.

The old man stared down onto the street which was now littered with broken glass and powdery pock marks where the sandstone rocks and coping stones had impacted and disintegrated against the tarmac.

He was suddenly aware that his hands were aching and realised that he had been gripping the woodwork along the edge of the window ledge. His knuckles had whitened and stiffened with the cold. He crossed his arms across his sunken chest and tucked the swollen hands under his armpits, hoping that the small amount of warmth there would alleviate the nagging in his joints.

"Tomorrow without fail." he whispered to himself, turning from the window. "Nine o'clock sharp. I'll damn well be outside that Council office and I'll not leave until I get something in writing. Pemberton Way…that was it. That's where they should be. Enough of this…enough."

Crossing back to the bed, he stepped out of his slippers and gently pulled back the corner of the quilt and eased himself softly down onto the mattress.

Perhaps all the trouble tonight had done them a favour he thought, more likely that folks our age will get moved if the darkies are going to start this sort of thing on a regular basis. Might just have done us a good turn old girl, he thought.

He turned and looked down at his Wife. Her eyes were closed and her mouth was slightly open as usual, yet something was different. The gentle wheezing had stopped.

The half-smile fell from his face. He leant over her and whispered her name sorrowfully, realising the truth immediately. He touched her face gently with the back of his hand and brushed away the few white wisps of hair from her cheek, feeling the coldness there.

## Seventeen

6.17 am. The first fingers of light appear. The thinning rain clouds that have washed the City clean now move slowly on. Their dark elephantine shapes silhouette the high rise office buildings against a leaden sky. A grey day.

Alan drew on his cigarette and threw the remains out across the flagged area onto the tarmac ambulance turning zone, it sputtered and died with a faint hiss as it rolled into one of the puddles which had formed on the uneven surface of the asphalt.

He exhaled and chewed on fresh air, grimacing at the coppery tasting fur that coated his tongue, the product of too many cigarettes during the night.

His back ached where the coldness had crept into his muscles from the brick wall against which he leaned.

He shrugged himself upright, stretched and walked wearily back towards Casualty Reception. The electronic eye above the doors noted his approach and with a click, barely audible, automatically opened the glass sliding partitions.

Alan walked up the rubber coated ramp, through the doors, and into the sterile smelling warmth.

Bright green plastic moulded seats, garish in the brightness of the reception area, sat in neat rows facing a hatchway in the wall opposite. To either side of the hatch, pinned to the wall, were posters graphically illustrating the ravages of various venereal diseases and the new harbinger of doom, the Acquired Immunity Deficiency Syndrome.

One of the posters depicted a syringe; half full of what Alan supposed was Heroin, the needle of which, was inserted partially into the recipient's arm. The muscle was wasted, with track marks running raggedly down the length of the inner forearm and oozing some disgusting yellow substance from suppurating, blackened veins.

Alan stared at the poster until his eyelids slowly started to close through sheer weight and lack of will power. He shook his head to waken himself and smiled as he remembered his partner's views on the unparalleled plague which was sweeping its way unopposed through the uncivilized world.

"It's God's way of riddin' the world of queers and junkies. That's all, no big deal, you an' me are safe Al."

Alan had laughed at his partner's theory, stated somewhat dispassionately after the lecture at the station, given by some leading Virologist or other from a University down South.

"I mean it's not like you can catch it from a toilet seat or anything right? Keep yer 'ampton tucked safely away in yer trousers and don't do drugs, you're home and dry, right?" Sullivan said.

Alan pondered for a while. "What about road accidents, we must be at risk."

His partner paused, the assault on his sandwich forgotten for a moment. "Al, you can't catch AIDS off a wrecked Skoda...They just look sick." he said, spraying Alan with the half chewed remnants of a canteen cheese sandwich.

Alan threw his partner a disgusted glance and wiped the yellow speckles from his jacket. "You really are a moron Sully; you didn't listen to a word of that lecture did you?"

His partner shrugged. "Well, truth is…"

Alan nodded knowingly. "Look, I'll remind you, Say we go to a nasty bump, there's people bleeding all over the place. You're reaching into the wreckage to apply direct pressure to an artery or something, yes?...and you get their blood all over you…and say that you've cut yourself working on that wrecker of yours the day before. If their blood gets into your cut, if they've got AIDS…bingo, your H.I.V. positive mate."

"Bollocks." his partner sneered.

Alan noted his partner's cynical tone. "As I'm sitting here pal. You heard that Virologist or whatever he was. Blood to blood contact. You don't have to be a shirt lifter or a druggie Sully. Somebody with AIDS bleeds on you and you've got a small cut, its goodnight Vienna."

His partner was silent for a while and chewed on the remains of his sandwich. "Fuck me, I'm gonna wear gloves from now on." he professed dramatically. "No more bare handed stuff from now on, an' you remind me…every time, ok?"

Alan laughed and closed his pocket note book. "Come on mate, time we were out and about." he grabbed the car keys from the disposition board.

His partner grabbed him by the arm.

"You can just imagine me explaining it to our Linda. "Look, I got it from a road accident, honest."

Alan smiled. "If you contract AIDS mate, I should think that the trauma of explaining it to your Linda would pale into insignificance. What about when your dick turns gangrenous green and drops off?"

His partner's face dropped. "What?" he said, turning to face Alan, a disbelieving look about his face.

Alan stared at his partner. "Seriously Pete. You heard what Dr whatsisname said. Oh, course you didn't did you, concentration level nil during that riveting lecture. Well, apparently"…Alan flipped opened his pocket note book and pretended to read from the 'notes' he had made during the lecture. "Due to an enemic hormonal imbalance caused by the induction of the immuno virus into the pancreas, within twenty four hours from initial contagion, the male genital member takes on a greenish hue, withers and in due course, will fall away from the scrotal sac."

Sullivan's hand involuntarily fell to his genital area and he cupped his testicles as he winced. "Jesus." he said disgustedly. He looked up to Alan, who was now standing with a sick smile on his face.

Sullivan's face dropped, then broke into a smile, knowing he'd been had. "Fuck you Pendle." he chortled.

Alan burst out laughing and walked out of the office into the corridor screaming "Sarge, Sarge, me dick's goin' green Sarge…Aaaargh! it's fell off."

They had laughed all the way down the stairs and out into the car park.

*****

Alan's eyes drifted across from the poster to the reception hatch. A young coloured nurse had appeared and was looking at him. He forced a smile, she looked bored and tired. Her eyes looked like his felt.

"Nights?" she asked. Alan nodded. "You?"

"Yeah, my last one thank God, you hurt?" she asked, with a concerned tone.

Alan shook his head. "No, my partner's down though. Another grim night in the Badl…sorry." he checked himself, feeling his face reddening.

She shrugged and smiled. "That's ok. I wouldn't like to work there either, let alone live there." She busied herself with a small bundle of papers on her desk. Alan stretched out his legs in front of him; his mind was numbed, almost twelve hours on duty. He imagined slipping beneath the cool duvet and snuggling his head down onto the soft pillows and allowing sleep to wash over him.

"How is he?"

"Uh." Alan jumped, realising that he had started to doze and he quickly wiped the back of his hand across his chin in case he had dribbled.

"Your mate. How is he?" she asked.

Alan scratched his head. "I don't know, haven't seen him."

The nurse stood up. Involuntarily, Alan glanced at her body, there was something definitely erotic about the white starched uniform, especially on a coloured female and a good looking one at that.

"I'll see if I can find out. What's his name?"

"Sullivan, Peter Sullivan. You can't miss him, he's six four and hideously ugly."

The nurse smiled and disappeared into the surgical room from which, all the curtained cubicles extended, like spokes from a square wheel.

Alan yawned and stared down at the polished linoleum flooring, not at any point in particular and not even in focus. The 'thousand yard stare' the American Victnam veterans called it. A glazed, vacant look brought about by apathy, fatigue and total weariness throughout the body.

"He's in seven if you want to go in." the nurse said smiling, exposing her perfect white teeth. Alan looked up. The nurse had returned to the hatch.

"Sorry?"

"Time you went home." she said in a sympathetic voice. "I said, your mates' in cubicle seven, five minutes, that's all. He'll be going up to the ward shortly; they'll be keeping him in for observations with him having been unconscious."

"Is it because he gives the impression that he is feeble minded?...Is he babbling incoherently? 'cos to be honest, that's quite normal for my partner." Alan said in an attempt to get her to smile again.

The nurse rewarded his efforts with a broad smile as Alan heaved himself wearily from the chair.

"Five minutes." she called after him as he walked toward the green plastic drapes surrounding the various cubicles.

Alan glanced up at the numbers on the drape support rails and pulled the material aside and poked his head in.

"Hey Bro' wa'ppnin'" he said in his best Jamaican accent. His face immediately dropped when he saw his partner. "Jesus! You look like shit."

Sullivan was laid out on a stainless steel tubular trolley, the type you see the stiffs laid out on at the mortuary. Alan hoped that it wasn't indicative of the junior Doctors prognosis of his partner's recuperative prospects.

His uniform had been discarded hastily and was crumpled into a ball and thrust onto a rack beneath the bed of the trolley; the blood staining on his jacket had now turned to a dark crispy brown and was falling away from the material in small flakes.

Alan bit his bottom lip to stem a smile, mindful of his partner's obvious discomfort.

The sight of the fetching light green 'Airtex' gown, obviously designed by a man with reverse jointed elbows, who thought that everyone could reach from their arses to the nape of their neck to tie the cords, looked ridiculous. The sight was accentuated by his hapless partner's long hairy legs, which poked out from beneath the short hem of the flimsy material and stood out starkly white against the dark blue of the vinyl covering of the mattress.

"Christ, I wish I'd brought the Polaroid mate, your street 'cred' would go straight down the 'S' bend…On the plus side, I'm glad to see that you've stopped shaving your legs."

"If you've come to take the piss, you can bugger off." his partner snapped, wincing against what was obviously a mammoth headache.

The right hand side of his face was turning a nasty shade of blue and had swollen around the eye and cheekbone.

Alan counted the sutures in the wound which was still weeping slightly.

"Nine stitches." Alan whistled in admiration. "That should be worth a few quid compensation…Is Linda coming down or what?" Alan asked, sitting on the side of his partner's trolley and scrutinizing the angry gash in his forehead. "That's not going to assist your quest in notching one up with the lass from the garage mate. Nasty that, it's gonna leave a hell of a scar."

"Oh, cheers Al. Yer genuine concern for my looks 'as touched my 'eart and in answer to yer original question, no. There's no point worrying Linda. We going home or what?" his partner asked.

"I am…you're not." Alan said matter of factly. "I have it on good authority from the rather stunning receptionist that they're keeping you in for twenty four hours, being as how you were unconscious."

"Great." his partner sighed. "Al, you let Linda know I'm ok eh? I don't want silly bollocks Parkin calling round. If she sees a ranker at the door, she'll think I've croaked on duty."

"As you very well might have done mate." Alan said thoughtfully. "You won't have heard about John Robertson."

His partner shook his head and looked apprehensive.

"Stabbed mate…stomach. He's in a bad way by all accounts. You were out for the count by the time they brought him out of the house, bundled him into the back of our Tranny and I whizzed you both down here. Parkin's job turned out to be a complete clusterfuck after all. It kicked off big style after you got whacked, loads of vans are wrecked, had to call for a PSU. Dogs went in, it was like last year's bonfire night all over again."

"What's the news on Robbo then? How bad is he?" Sullivan asked.

"No knowledge yet mate." Alan said, looking again at his partner's wound. "Anyway, I'd make the most of it Sully old lad. Look on the positive side, least you won't have to work nights tonight. Fuckin' typical of you that…self, self, self."

The curtain partitioning the cubicle from the surgical area swished open and a young coloured doctor entered.

Frowning at Alan's presence, he snatched up the medical notes attached to a progress board clipped over the end of the trolley.

"You will have to leave now; you can visit him on the ward later."

The doctor waved Alan aside and bent over his partner. He shone a small torch into his right eye whilst holding open the upper eyelid. Alan saw the pupil retract quickly and feeling that he was in the way, he opened the curtain and waved his hand over the stooped form of the doctor to catch his partner's attention, called out. "I'll call Linda before I go home; let her know you're malingering, but that they're keeping you here."

The doctor reached for his partner's left eye and turned toward Alan. "Go now; do as you are told please."

Alan sneered behind the doctor's back and fought the urge to point out to 'Mr Bojangles', who would probably start casting bones and shaking a gourd filled with dried seeds over his partner as soon as he left, that if it hadn't have been for his sort, his partner wouldn't be here in the first place. He thought better of it and stepped out into the corridor and closed the curtain behind him to afford his partner some privacy.

*****

The day had brightened, the clouds had thinned with the full dawn and a vague hint of blue was visible between the dispersing grey wisps. Alan rummaged through the pockets of his jacket for the keys to his patrol car and shuddered involuntarily as the morning chill seeped through his clothing. The door panel button snapped up as he turned the key in the driver's door of the patroller. He turned as the flash from an approaching pair of headlamps caught his eye. Alan leaned back against the side of his car and watched as the Range Rover pulled alongside.

The craggy faced Traffic Sergeant looked as if he'd worked a week of nights without sleep. He obviously wasn't used to early turns.

Six a.m. starts were the penalty for remaining as a Traffic Constable; Traffic Supervisors earned the right, by divine right of God, to start at seven.

The first cigar of the day was well under way and the Sergeant's eyes looked like the small yellow holes which appear when one urinates in fresh snow.

"Alright Al?" the Sergeant asked through the open window of his patroller, blowing on the end of his cigar to revive its embers.

Alan scratched his neck, the night's growth uncomfortable against the collar of his shirt.

"Not bad Sarge, knackered."

"How's Sully?" the Sergeant asked, nodding toward the Casualty entrance.

"Nine stitches and a massive fuckin' headache. They're keeping him in overnight; he was out cold for a while. How's Parkin's job progressing?"

The Sergeant frowned. "What job?"

"Last night's job Sarge." Alan said incredulously. "All the prisoners from last night's blues raid. Christ Sarge, the nick must've been packed."

The Sergeant dropped his eyes to the floor and tossed the cigar butt out onto the flagstones. His eyes met Alan's. "All refused charges." he said quietly, as if he were ashamed to admit the truth. Alan stared at his boss, his eyebrows furrowing in the center of his forehead. "What all of 'em?"

The Sergeant nodded. "All the ones nicked by uniform for simple possession. Drugs Squad claimed a few collars, but just those names of note by all accounts."

"What about breach of the peace, assault, criminal damage, stuff like that?"

The Sergeant breathed in and exhaled slowly, looking across the car park at the vehicles arriving for the early shift at the Hospital. "Eighteen locked up all told, that was by half past three. At four fifteen it would appear, the Civil Liberties people,

Community Leaders and the Police Complaints Authority were ringing the Chief at home. Seems our lads might have gone a bit over the top."

Alan stared at his Sergeant in disbelief. "Over the fuckin' top? I was there Sarge. Pete was there with me." His voice was raised and wavering with frustration as he pointed back toward the casualty reception area. "'Cept Pete isn't going home. We took a right kicking, my partner's going to be off on sick for a month and that's if he's lucky. John Robertson got stabbed for fuck's sake."

The Sergeant swallowed. "Look, I know how you must feel…"

Alan fell back against the door of his patroller and laughed insanely. "Oh great. So Parkin gets us all wound up about unlawful possession of drugs and as 'ow the Chief has sanctioned the raid. We go into the 'Badlands' like John fucking Wayne, next thing, its windscreen's through and Christ knows how much damage done to firms vehicles. A coping stone nearly takes my partner's fucking head off and you're telling me they've let all the bastards go?" Alan stopped himself, realising that he had been shouting and looked away embarrassed.

There was silence between them for a moment. He looked back to his Sergeant. "Sorry Roger, you didn't deserve that. I'm pissed off about Sully and I'm knackered that's all."

The Sergeant waved off the apology and looked convincingly disgusted at the outcome of the night's events. "Mayhew rang the control room personally. Told Parkin to ensure that all those nicked for possession were to be refused charged and informed him that he wanted to see him in his office at ten a.m. sharp."

Alan rubbed his eyes with his fingertips and sighed heavily with fatigue. "Wonderful. Remind me to ring in sick next time Parkin organises another little foray into the now unmentionable territory. What about the bastard that stabbed Robbo?"

"No trace." The Sergeant shrugged and shook his head. "Plain cloth's workin' on it though; our very own Detective Inspector

Miller has assured the Chief that he will close the case within a week."

"Miller!" Alan groaned. "Miller couldn't close a fucking umbrella."

The Sergeant glanced at his watch. "Get off home Al. Get some sleep, you look like shit. Come on at ten tonight. I'll sign your overtime for last night. I'll see you later, ok?"

Alan nodded and opened his car door. A bone numbing tiredness came over him in waves. "You going in to see Pete?"

The Sergeant nodded. "Where is he?"

"Cubicle seven, but watch out for Doctor M'buto, he doesn't take to visitors, especially Traffic cops. You'll recognise Sully straight off though, he'll be the one covered in dried bones and chicken entrails."

The Sergeant allowed himself a wry smile; he turned and with a wave, walked toward the Casualty reception doors.

Alan slumped down into the driver's seat of the patroller and fired up the engine. As he clipped his seat belt retainer into the anchorage block, his Sergeant returned to the car. Alan activated the electric window as the Sergeant lit another cigar and squatted down on his haunches, resting his elbows against the top of the driver's door.

"You made your note book up yet?"

Alan shook his head. "No. I was going to do it tonight, why?"

"Just be careful that's all. There'll be a fucking witch hunt over this job, you mark my words. Don't drop yerself in the shit."

Alan looked puzzled. "All me and Sully did was drive the van. We didn't arrest anyone, didn't even go into the house."

The Sergeant nodded knowingly. "That'll have fuck all to do with it. There's been a monumental cock up and heads will roll, believe me, I've seen it time and time again. Some senior Officer makes a balls up of a job, but it's a Pc that ends up suckin' the 'ammer for it.

D n'C are gonna be on this like flies round a witches twat and you can bet yer arse that all pocket books will be seized. All I'm sayin' is, be brief and say only what you've got to say an' no more. Don't go overboard. The less you've got in yer book, the less D n'C 'ave got to stitch you up with....get my drift?"

"Do you know something about this job that I don't Sarge?" Alan asked.

The Sergeant wagged a warning finger. "No, but I've seen this before. Parkin will cover his arse nicely and D n'C will miraculously discover that it was some Pc that fucked up. Once the scapegoat 'as bin found, everybody will avoid 'im like the fuckin' plague an' it won't matter a fuck what 'e says, he'll go for it. Don't be that person, ok. Get just enough in yer book to cover Sully's injury an' 'ow 'e was non-contributory. Other than that it's like you weren't even there, kapeesh?"

Alan nodded.

"Are you lettin' Sully's missus know?" his Sergeant asked.

Alan nodded again. "I'll give her a bell, go round on my way home if she wants."

The Sergeant stood up and flexed his knees. "I'll see you later."

"Yeah, later Sarge…and thanks." Alan called after him.

The Sergeant nodded and walked towards the glass doors. Alan watched him disappear into the Casualty reception area.

He sat for a moment, the engine ticking over quietly as he thought about what his Sergeant had said before easing his patroller into reverse and backing it out of the parking bay.

The Rover seemed to make its own way back to the station. Alan drove like an automaton and as he pulled into the station yard, he realised with a little consternation that he couldn't remember anything about the journey at all. He turned the ignition key and the engine died. The silence in the car park was beautiful and he allowed his head to drop back against the head restraint as he closed his eyes and savoured the peace.

A few seconds elapsed and then with a grunt, he forced himself back into action. The log book was wedged firmly between the front passenger seat and the center console. Wearily, he opened the page and scribbled in the end mileage column, squinting as he read from the odometer. Snapping the book shut, he tossed it unceremoniously onto the top of the dashboard. He slouched in his seat and debated whether to have a last cigarette. His eyes felt heavy and there was a strange buzzing in his ears again. His Sergeant's words of warning came back to him.

He was right of course; anything to do with the blacks would be closely looked at. Allegations of racism, the unnecessary or gratuitous use of force. The local Community Leaders would be pulling the Chief's strings and he would dance as usual. D n'C would be all over it and any hint of impropriety would attract a rigorous investigation.

D n'C...Discipline and Complaints, a.k.a. Internal Affairs, a.k.a. the Rubber Heel Squad.

A fine and necessary institute admired by one and all. Epitomising all the qualities of a particularly virulent incurable disease. A visit from the 'Black Rats', was about as welcome as seeing blood in your stools.

The personal motto of their Department, describing quite admirably, the caring professional and thoroughly unbiased principles of the investigators. *'Here to Police the Police'*.

The Geheime Statspolizei of the modern Police force. The ankle length leather trench coats may have gone, the black fedoras, now unfashionable, may have been discarded, but the ideology and techniques remained as ever, the same.

An interview conducted with the feather light touch of an electric cattle goad to the genitals, was guaranteed to spoil your day.

A specialist Police department formulated from within its own ranks to investigate those niggling little complaints made by

Members of the beloved Public, such as unlawful arrest, assault, oppressive or inappropriate behaviour, harassment or racism.

D n'C. A necessary evil. An ache in the molars of tranquillity. A cuckoo in the nest of complacency...A complete pain in the arse.

A radio message passed to a patrolling Officer to the effect that investigators from D n'C were at the station to see him would, without fail, even in the squeakiest of clean Officers, raise the heart rate a beat or two, dilate his anus by the odd centimeter and raise his stress factor by fifty per cent.

The trembling of an accused Officer, as he sits in front of his 'inquisitors', it is said, can actually be detected on the Richter scale.

Ignorant of his presence and discomfort, they peruse and sift through various statements obtained from witnesses miraculously produced by the complainant; with demands that the Officer's life be forfeit, or at the very least, that he should be relieved of his testicles which should then be displayed on the Town Hall steps.

The investigating team normally appeared in pairs. One, usually a Superintendent or above, the 'Fatherly' type, the sort who goes to Bude in Cornwall for his holidays and owns a Lada estate. He directs his faithful sidekick, usually an Inspector, who hangs on every word spoken by his Liege Lord, in the desperate hope, that his grovelling will be mistaken for capability and that during some evening of drunken debauchery in the local Masonic Lodge, after the chests have been bared, trouser legs rolled back down and the funny handshakes dispensed with, that his Lord will mention his name to the Chief as a likely candidate for promotion.

The Superintendent's job was to actually put the question to the quivering mass of subservience seated before him. The Inspector's, to hurriedly write down any response the Officer may offer through his chattering teeth whilst pools of water form on the carpet at his feet through the constant wringing of sweaty penitent hands.

Meekly, the heretic is brought before the Inquisition.

The Superintendent looks up and smiles condescendingly and the *auto de fe* begins.

*****

The Town Hall towers proudly, grandiose. Its classical baroque style, dominating the skyline of the main thoroughfare into the City, a stunning visual statement of the power of the City Fathers and the Town Council of the 1850's.

Its rows of Corinthian columns flanked by four lions in repose, carved from Portland stone, sit atop imposing marble plinths which stand on gargantuan sandstone blocks. The columns are evenly spaced, providing access to the intricately carved oak doors set back in the centre of the building frontage.

A clock tower, set atop a smaller row of carved columns surrounded by a marble topped balustrade, soars to over a hundred feet above street level. Domed and capped with thick lead sheets, now gloriously faded to white. The four Romanesque clock faces are visible from each point of the compass.

From the expanse of the stone flagged frontage, wide sandstone steps rise steadily upwards toward the imposing oak doors through which, those who enter to visit the Council Offices or those of the Alderman of the City, are directed by a uniformed Commissionaire toward the left and thence up a gently spiralled stone stairway. Those who are directed to the right are destined for the Magistrates or the Crown Courts.

Those who enter and walk the well-worn stone flagged corridors toward the closed oaken doors of the Courts, are presented with intricately carved over boards, advising those in attendance to '*Be just and fear not*' They are perhaps destined to leave through another portal, with the bewigged Judges' adjudication ringing in their ears, after he has peered down from his raised throne like chair. His voice loaded with suitable condemnation, he scowls at the convicted felon over the top of his glasses…"Well, there you have it Johnson…four years."

With a suitably solemn nod, he indicates to the waiting Officer, who waits dutifully by the trapdoor entrance and thence, to the ancient steps leading down to the Bridewell below street level. "Take him down Officer."

The street entrance to the City Bridewell however, is innocuous, understated. It is accessed via a small painted door to the far left of the building, almost hidden from view by two of the huge plinthed lions. The proud head of the one to the right of the door entrance faces away to the side as if to show indignation or indifference to the plight of those who have flouted the law.

*****

Alan sits lost in his thoughts, staring blankly out through the windscreen of the patrol car.

"Ow bad was it?"

Alan blinked, refocused himself and rubbed his eyes with his fingertips. He was exhausted.

He had slept off nights, but fitfully, replaying the previous night's incident over and over.

"Bad Charlie, it was bad…We took a right kicking if truth be known. Sully's gonna be off for ages. Linda says there might be a problem with his eye, might not be able to focus properly. I don't know mate…Robbo's still in intensive care, I mean he's probably gonna be ok, but if you could have seen the blood on the Tranny floor…Jesus."

His temporary crew mate sat quietly, not quite knowing what to say. He was a Traffic man, he worked out of the same office as Alan, but partners were partners and he knew that he didn't share the close brotherly like bond which Alan shared with Sullivan.

"Pete will be fine Al, you can bet yer arse he'll be back in a week or two…Anyway, you're off to Stretham next week aren't you?"

Alan brightened a little. "Yeah mate, start next Monday, finish nights. Two days off, clear a bit of clerical. I should be able to spin that out for a day or two, then its weekend off."

"Pete'll be back by the time you get qualified, you'll see." his crew mate said confidently.

Alan nodded, but didn't look convinced. "We should have had a Tranny with a screen shield Charlie. That rock came in through the screen like a fucking Exocet."

He sighed and sat up straight in his seat. "Anyway, look mate, I'm really grateful for you stepping up to do full nights…"

His crew mate shook his head. "Hey, no sweat Al, to be fair, it's four hours 'OT' which I could do with at the moment. Fucking child care's killin' me…"

They sat in silence for a while, watching the traffic as it filed past, in and out of the City. Alan's crew mate decides that what is needed is a spot of light entertainment to bring Alan out of his dark place.

He scans the vehicles as they stop at the traffic lights across from where they have parked, on the flagged area in front of the Town Hall.

"There you go Al. Tonight's sinner has arrived."

Alan's temporary crew mate nods through the windscreen toward the main road at the battered Vauxhall Viva estate which is stationary at the traffic lights.

It is 10.30 pm, that time of night for Traffic men.

Two lanes of traffic wend their way out of the City center toward their homes, or on to the numerous Night Clubs and Casinos which have just thrown open their doors for another night of violence and drunken debauchery which, briefly interspersed with bouts of dancing, vomiting and casual sex with a complete stranger in some garbage strewn back alley, constitutes a good night out.

The old Vauxhall sits at the traffic lights in a queue of vehicles waiting for the green. It displays no lights and the driver, for reasons best known to him alone, chooses to ignore the headlight flashes from the driver of the vehicle behind him.

The green light illuminates and the vehicles in front of the Viva pull away smoothly.

Alan and his crew mate watch with growing interest as the sagging Vauxhall lurches forward like a cat pouncing, then stalls halfway across the stop line. The vehicle behind it, not expecting the sudden failure to proceed, brakes harshly to a halt and as the traffic is brought to a standstill. The horns begin their impatient wails of protest.

"Doin' well this lad." Alan's crew mate smiles knowingly and reaches into the glovebox for the roadside breathalyser kit.

A plume of oily blue smoke belches from the rear end of the Vauxhall as the engine catches and rattles back into life. The driver releases the clutch and the vehicle wheezes its way through the traffic lights which by this time, have unfortunately changed back to red.

"Oh dear." Alan said mockingly, looking across to his crew mate. "We seem to be experiencing a degree of difficulty in mastering the controls of our vehicle."

"Well, you do all sorts when you're pissed." his crew mate sneers. "Let's 'ave 'im in eh?"

Alan slid the gearlever forward and set off, looking to the left and right as his crew mate activated the bank of lights on the roof of their patroller. The raking blue lights demanded access across the two lanes of traffic. Their entry into the line of traffic is granted willingly and a gap is provided. It's the 'at least it's not me' syndrome and those drivers who may have imbibed the odd after work drink, are more than happy to have the Traffic men now concentrating on some other poor unfortunate.

Alan pulled up behind the Vauxhall and flashed his headlights. The blue lights across the rear screen of the Viva have an immediate effect. The driver turned on his lights and gave a cheery wave of thanks as he looked up into his rear view mirror.

"Too late my lovely…too late." Alan muttered with determination, as his crew mate touched the small red button on the handset controlling the sirens.

The air was immediately filled with a strident single yelp and a further flash of the headlights caused the driver to again look up into his rear view mirror.

Alan made eye contact and pointed over to the nearside.

The errant driver realised that his wave of thanks for the reminder to turn on his lights was not going to wash and as the Vauxhall braked and veered in toward the kerb edge, Alan and his crew mate both smiled as they noted that only the offside brake light illuminated.

"Oh dear, a triple sinner. No lights, red light, no light." his crew mate said chuckling.

The Vauxhall eventually shuddered to a halt, its front nearside tyre howling in protest as it ran along the polished kerb edge.

Alan checked his door mirror and thumbed the release clasp on his seat belt stalk. "Let's see what he has to say for himself shall we?"

Alan glanced back down the road over his shoulder as he walked up to the driver's window and tapped on it lightly with his knuckle.

The driver hastily cranked the window winder and the glass juddered its way downward, its erratic and hesitant descent, helped by the driver who pressed down onto the upper edge of the glass with the palm of his hand. A strong smell of intoxicants mixed with stale cigarette smoke immediately assailed Alan's nostrils, notwithstanding the valiant efforts of the 'Feu Orange' air freshener, which was hanging limply from the interior mirror.

Alan looked back to his crew mate and nodded with a knowing smile. The driver, bucolically thin and sporting a small teardrop tattoo at the corner of his right eye, smiled up at Alan, displaying brown rotting stumps where his teeth had long since given up the ghost.

His passenger conversely, was morbidly obese; clearly the prize for 'slimmer of the month' was out of the question for a while.

Her seat belt was stretched taut over massive pendulous breasts and the rolls of her stomach bulged out between the belt crossovers and hung slackly across the top of her gargantuan thighs. She sat unconcerned and ignored Alan's presence as she stared straight out through the windscreen.

Alan smiled inwardly at the self-administered tattoo on the side of her neck, just beneath her right ear lobe, which declared to the world that she was an '*Angle*'

Perhaps it was an ancient cultural declaration Alan mused, giving the dyslexic tattooist the benefit of the doubt.

He returned his attention to the driver who waited pensively. "I wonder how far you would have actually driven without lights driver."

The driver nodded his acceptance and tutted, berating his stupidity. "Yeah, sorry mate, just din't notice, sorry."

The fat passenger sighed heavily, clearly bored with the proceedings.

"You also managed to travel through the last set of lights at red. Is there a problem?"

"No, no…the motor's a bit dodgy at the moment; I think it needs a tune up."

Alan nodded. "Lucky there wasn't anyone coming out of Richmond Street."

The driver nodded again. "Yeah, yeah, really sorry 'bout that mate."

His passenger sighed for the second time and muttered "For fucks' sake." under her breath.

The whispered expletive was not lost on Alan who leaned further into the vehicle.

"Sorry love. What was that?"

The passenger could contain herself no longer. Obviously she harboured scant regard for the forces of law and order and she turned to look directly at Alan, her face glowing bright pink. "It's a shame you've fuck all better to do." she spat vehemently.

The driver looked horrified and pushed her shoulder roughly with his hand. "Fuckin' shurrup Tina." He turned to Alan despairingly. "She's not 'erself Officer, she buried 'er Mam yesterday, you know 'ow it is."

Unfortunately, Fat Tina was on a roll (no pun intended)…"Ooooooh, a red light." she howled theatrically… "You lot were nowhere to be seen when our fuckin' 'ouse got broken into. Oh no…Too busy sat on yer' fuckin' arses waitin' for some poor cunt to go through a red light. You fuckin' wasters."

The driver sat forlorn, his head now in his hands. He then found courage from somewhere and slapped his fat Wife/girlfriend/other across her face with the back of his hand.

"Ah said, fuckin' shut it Tina." he howled and looked up at Alan, who was now nodding appreciatively at the driver's bravado and total disregard for his own life.

Unbeknown to Fat Tina, she had strayed unwittingly or otherwise, into an area of expertise honed to razor like perfection by veteran Traffic men.

Roadside sarcasm.

"Ah…" said Alan, directing his gaze across to the delectable Tina. "You see madam, what you needed when your premises was attacked was a Detective. What you've got tonight…"

She cut Alan short and despite numerous slaps from the despondent driver, she continued. "It's no fuckin' wonder everyone hates you lot." She was heaving now and thin rivulets of sweat ran from beneath her hairline across her tasteful, misspelt tattoo and onto the grimy neck line of her blouse, which swiftly turned from light, to dark blue.

Alan was not to be bested. "Well madam…Tina isn't it? …If I craved popularity I'd be the payout man for Littlewoods Pools, or perhaps Father Christmas at the local orphanage, but God called upon me to be a Traffic Cop, I answered his call as did my partner here." Alan nodded toward his crew mate who had by now joined him by the driver's door.

"Oh fuckin' 'ilarious you two, Little an' fuckin' Large." Fat Tina spat contemptuously and wheezed audibly. She reached for the packet of cigarettes which had been tossed casually onto the dashboard top. With shaking hands, she withdrew one of the few remaining cigarettes and stuffed it between her trembling lips. Alan, certainly claiming round one, returned his attention to the driver.

"I notice that you have a brake light out as well driver, have you been drinking tonight?"

The driver's pupils immediately dilate with a rush of realisation. "I've 'ad one pint Officer, that's it."

Alan nodded. "Really, just the one eh?…Well you'll have no problem with a breath test then." The hapless driver's shoulders slumped. "Come on mate, I've 'ad one pint." he offered hopefully.

Alan ignored his protestations and reached in through the open window and turned off the ignition. The ancient Viva's engine rattled with a serious timing overrun, before finally dying after a sudden rush of revs.

"You have committed a number of moving road traffic offences driver. I can smell intoxicants on your breath and I suspect that you may have above the prescribed level of alcohol in your body and I require you to provide me with a specimen of breath for a breath test. Just step out of your vehicle and join me at the patrol car, ok?"

The driver capitulated and took off his seat belt. Alan stood back as the driver's door was opened. It groaned in protest with a dry metallic screech. Clearly there'd been no expense spared on regular servicing.

Alan placed his hand on the open window surround and pointed back toward the waiting Rover. The hapless driver left the Vauxhall. He sloped off toward where Alan's crew mate was now holding the rear door of the patroller open invitingly. As the driver approached, he stepped back onto the kerb, just in case there was a sudden change of heart and the driver decided to do a runner.

Alan, not quite finished baiting the delectable Tina, leaned into the interior of the Vauxhall.

"I'm afraid you may be a little late getting home this evening madam. I also suspect that you will be walking the rest of the way. It may be some poor consolation, but I'm sure the local tandoori take away will deliver…Oh,…but I'd only order for one if I were you." Alan said and smiled sweetly, winding her up even further.

Round two to Traffic, Alan thought to himself.

"Go fuck yerself." she muttered defiantly.

Alan smiled as he walked back towards his patroller.

The driver had flopped down into the rear seats and the door was firmly closed. Charlie remained by the door and waited for Alan to join him.

Once back in the driver's seat, Alan flipped over the cover on his pad of HORT/1's and pen poised, he turned to face the driver who was staring dejectedly out to the street through the passenger window.

"Before we start the roadside breath test proceedings driver, this…" Alan said, holding up the small pad in his hand. "Is what we call a HORT/1, it stands for home office road traffic form number one, although in your case, I'm sure that I'm preaching to the converted. Once I serve you with your copy, you are required to produce your driving documents at a Police station within seven days. In your case, that means your licence, insurance and MOT certificate. The form is self-carbonated; you get the white top copy, the blue…" Alan lifted up the virgin front sheet. "Is for the prosecution file when you subsequently fail to produce the said documents. The yellow bottom copy just stays in my pad for future reference. Need me to go through that again?"

The driver simply stared out through the window, ignoring the sarcastic slight on his intelligence.

"Let's make a start then eh?...Name ?...Oh." Alan paused and held up a cautionary finger. "Just a word to the wise driver, you only get one chance at this…The name you give me will be the name I write on the form. If it turns out to be 'stiff' or if I suspect you are telling me porkies, you will be arrested."

The driver turned to face his tormentor. "Rawlinson…Edward, Eddie, to my friends."

"Where are you living Eddie?"

"I said to my friends." the driver retorted, trying his hand at a little 'back seat of the patrol car sarcasm'.

"I'm cut to the bone Edward. Just when I thought we were getting on so well." Alan replied dryly. "I'll still need that address"

"Harold Square…eighteen." Eddie to his friends replied.

"Date of birth?"

The driver reluctantly reeled off his details as Alan recorded them on his pad. His crew mate reached for the radio handset.

"Papa Yankee One Four a message."

There was a brief silence before the operator replied. "One Four go ahead."

"It's a 10/17 person and vehicle please. Victor Uniform Alpha…"

Alan continued writing as they waited for the result of the check. "Where would you like to fail to produce your documents Eddie?"

"Moorwood." Eddie to his friends replied and sighed with resignation, either missing or choosing to ignore the quip.

Alan noticed in his peripheral vision that Eddie's hand was casually straying up toward the door handle.

"We only look stupid Eddie, the child locks are on." he said, without looking up from his pad. The driver's hand fell back onto his leg.

The radio cackled and broke the silence. "Papa Yankee One Four."

"One Four go." Alan's crew mate said and immediately thumbed the mute button on the main set. He wedged the handset between his ear and shoulder as he scribbled hurriedly in his green supplementary note book.

Alan glanced across at his mate's scribbling's and tore off the top white copy of the HORT/1 and handed it to the driver who took it impassively.

"Right Eddie. Listen to what I have to say to you. Take that form with you, you have seven days to produce your driving licence, certificate of insurance and the MOT certificate at Moorwood Police station. If you fail to produce any of the documents you will be reported for failing to produce, or as an alternative, for driving without a licence, insurance etc, ok?"

Eddie nods. They both know there will be no production, but giving him the form is required foreplay.

"Right." Alan produced the Lion Alcolmeter from where it waited in readiness on the top of the dashboard facia. "This is a roadside breath testing device; it will give me a visual indication as to whether you may have above the prescribed level of alcohol in your breath."

Eddie stared disinterestedly out through the passenger window again; he knows the game is up. "Eddie, listen to me, it's important."

Eddie looked back and Alan pointed to the small set of traffic lights on the device.

"There are three lights, green, amber and red. Green is a pass, amber is a pass, amber and red is still a pass. Red on its own would be a positive test."

Alan withdrew a mouthpiece from the pocket of the device's leather cover and broke away its thin cellophane cover. He pulled the business end of the white plastic tube partially free of the wrapper. "When I attach this tube to the device, I will invite you to pull off the wrapper so only you will have touched the end which you will be placing in your mouth."

Eddie threw up his hands in supplication. "Come on lads, I've 'ad one fuckin' pint" he pleaded. "Don't tell me you lads don't drive 'ome after just the one."

"You're right Eddie, we don't." Alan replied, as he shuffled himself around in his seat so that he was fully facing the driver.

"An' I don't suppose you've ever forgot to put yer lights on either." Eddie spat derisively.

Alan smiled sarcastically. "You're right again Eddie, that's twice. You should go on Family Fortunes. Now, back to the breath test, if you've only had the one, you'll have no problem passing the test. How long is it since your last drink?"

Eddie slowly shakes his head in resignation. He knows it's not the last pint he just managed to get in at the Old Bank before closing time, it was the previous gallon he'd consumed at the local working men's club which would without doubt seal his fate.

Alan's crew mate looked up from his green book. "It's more than twenty minutes since we stopped him Al." he offered, as he waited for the Area Control Room operator to respond with the information he had requested.

After a moment he nodded and depressed the transmit bar on the handset. "One Four, all received. We are Park Place just doing a roadside, I will advise you further over."

"Papa Yankee One Four, received."

As the radio fell silent, Alan's crew mate opened his green book and tapped the top of the gear lever with its spine; Alan glanced down and read his crew mates hastily scribbled notes.

"Eddie, I'm shocked and...to be honest, a little disappointed in you. There's a warrant; it appears that you failed to attend at Bamborough Magistrates last August. Ring any bells?"

The driver shrugged nonchalantly and again looked out from the passenger window, trying to appear casual, but the pulsating vein in the side of his neck told Alan all he needed to know.

"Drive whilst disqualified and no insurance." Alan continued, staring directly at the driver. "Eddie, another moment of your valuable time if you don't mind. When were you first disqualified?" The driver looked back, but lowered his eyes and stared vacantly to the area between the two front seats.

"E's still only half way through a three year ban Al." Charlie offered. "An' the warrant's not backed for bail."

"Eddie." Alan nudged the driver's knee to focus his attention. "Forget the warrant for the time being, I still want a breath test."

"Bit fuckin' pointless innit?" Eddie shrugged.

"Procedure driver. I've made the request for a specimen, whether you provide one is up to you. But I have to warn you, that if you fail or refuse to provide a roadside specimen you will be arrested." Alan said.

"Am fuckin' arrested any'ow." Eddie protested.

Alan nodded slowly, mulling over his response.

"That is essentially true Eddie...I won't lie to you. I can see that you are giving your present dilemma a considerable amount of thought. However, being as how you will no doubt be detained overnight and fronted up before a Magistrate tomorrow morning on the warrant, any spanking you might get, will only be exacerbated by a failure to cooperate during the breath test procedure."

"Exacer...what?" Eddie asked, looking puzzled.

"Made worse...It means makes things worse Eddie." Charlie assisted.

Alan pressed the white plastic tube onto the top of the device and offered the sealed end of the tube up toward Eddie inviting him to remove the remains of the plastic cover.

Eddie snatched at the wrapper. Pulling it free, he dropped it to the carpeted floor of the patroller and shuffled himself forwards and took a deep breath. Alan pulled back the device. "Whoa, hang on a second Eddie, I haven't finished my spiel yet. It's got to be done right."

Eddie exhaled and looked exasperated. "What I want is one continuous breath and for you to carry on blowing until I tell you to stop. You can't cheat the device. If it doesn't get a sufficient puff, it will show me by way of these two little lights here." Alan pointed casually toward the two small button lights on the front of the machine. "When both those little lights have illuminated, it tells me that you have blown long enough and hard enough. I will then press the read button and we'll see how you get on, ok?"

"In your own time then." Alan said.

He offered the end of the tube to Eddie, who again took a deep breath and slowly delivered it into the device through the open ended tube.

Alan depressed the button on the right hand side of the device and watched as the traffic light sequence on the left, completely disregarded the green and amber and went directly to red.

Alan turned the device around so that Eddie could view the result; Eddie shrugged disinterestedly. A foregone conclusion.

"It's a positive test driver." Alan said with the briefest of smiles creeping across his face.

Even knowing what the outcome would be, Eddie's mouth had gone strangely dry.

He heard Alan running though the set procedure, he'd heard it all before of course, knew it almost off by heart.

"You're under arrest for providing a positive breath specimen, for driving whilst disqualified and on the strength of a warrant not backed for bail issued by the Bamborough Magistrates in August. You're not obliged to say anything unless you wish to do so…"

Charlie again reached for the handset. "Papa Yankee One Four."

"One Four go ahead."

"We are 10/12 with a positive roadside test in Park Place, on to the Bridewell. Where is the warrant over?"

*****

The relatively simple traffic lock up deteriorates rapidly and the scene is acted out.

Charlie experiences a sense of foreboding as he spots fat Tina heaving her bulk from the Vauxhall and commences a frontal assault on the patrol car. She waddles purposefully toward the rear nearside door; Charlie gets out to confront her.

"Ow long am I supposed to fuckin' wait?" she demands. Charlie points out to her as sympathetically as possible, that the driver is under arrest.

"What for?" she screams, leaning down to the rear window, shadowing the side of the patroller in a total eclipse of the nearby street light.

She ignores Charlie as he explains that the driver has provided a positive breath test and that in fact, he is wanted on a warrant.

"You alright Eddie?" she shouts at the glass which seems to concave in its rubber mounting, either from her fetid breath or the force with which it is delivered.

She turns on Alan's crew mate. "If you've fuckin' touched 'im." she howls and reaches for the door handle.

Eddie flinches away from the door, either because he is petrified of the demented Tina or because he senses a chance at freedom. His head snaps to the left and right, searching for a possible escape route once liberated. His hand snatches at the door handle, the door locks are indeed on, the doors can only be opened from the outside.

Alan kneels on the driver's seat and faces Eddie, who has started to wind down the window.

"Don't even think about it." Alan's voice is forceful and threatening, Eddie's hand retracts from the handle.

"Wind it up." Alan demands as he reaches into the leather pouch attached to his trouser belt. They stare at each other as Alan slowly withdraws his handcuffs.

Charlie is leaning his weight against the rear passenger door and is struggling with the behemoth. She is kicking out and screaming, her hand seemingly welded to the rear door handle.

Despite Charlie's grip on her other wrist, her handbag swings out wildly; Charlie fends off the blow with his forearm and the bag bounces harmlessly against the roof of the patroller.

Eddie screams through the closed window, "Get yer fuckin' 'ands off yer fat bastard."

Alan feels that Eddie's loyalties seem to be a little misguided, unless of course he is shouting at Tina.

Eddie's hand grabs for the door handle again and he twists his body around in the seat. His legs are drawn up to his chin and he kicks out at the door panel and the glass which thuds ominously.

Charlie is slowly losing his battle with fat Tina. You can only go so far with a female, even if she does outweigh you by four stones. Knee dropping a female to the pavement, even if she is the bare knuckle champion of the local housing estate, is against the code of ethics of most male Police Officers, and in any case, by now, a considerable crowd had gathered to take advantage of the free entertainment. A plethora of potential witnesses for Discipline and Complaints.

Things are going badly.

Alan leaps from the patroller and enters again through the rear offside door; Eddie has wound himself up and is now fighting mad.

Alan kneels over the seats and grabs Eddie gently by the throat restricting his breathing; after all, if a man can't breathe, he can't fight you. With a twisting motion at the throat, the body follows and Eddie is rolled over onto his stomach.

Eddie's teeth are bared and his eyes are bulging. Alan squeezes a little harder, a little further pressure against the windpipe.

Noting that her beloved Eddie is now being throttled into submission, Fat Tina lets out a demonic, banshee like wail. She kicks out uncontrollably against the outer door skin of the patroller whilst simultaneously raining blows on Charlie's head and shoulders.

Alan pulls Eddie's right arm out from where he has tucked it beneath his stomach and places a restraining knee in the small of his back. He pulls back on Eddie's arm until it is extended and snaps the handcuff around his wrist.

"Give me the other." Alan demands. He squeezes the ratchet on the applied cuff. A little 'pain compliance' has the desired effect and Eddie quickly produces his left arm. The opposing cuff is snapped around the wrist. Eddie is secure. With a final squeeze on both retaining ratchets, a little 'reward' for disrespecting Alan's patroller, the handcuffs significantly reduce in diameter and nip tight against the flesh of Eddie's wrists. Now the more he struggles, the tighter the cuffs will become.

Alan backs himself out of the patroller and slams the door shut. He runs around to the nearside to assist his crew mate. The alcohol fuelled crowd now cheer and applaud Tina's stalwart efforts; there is a full semi-circle of onlookers around the patrol car, but none willing to assist.

Fat Tina is weak now. In her present state it would probably only take seven rounds for Mike Tyson to defeat her. She is in tears from fatigue and frustration, yet still she will not relinquish her grip on the door handle. Her knuckles are white from exertion.

Charlie still has hold of her wrist. The contents of her handbag are now strewn across the pavement, a small plastic mirror has shattered against the kerb and a lipstick rolls across the flagstones. As it drops from the kerb edge onto the road surface, it passes between the cast iron slats of a gulley grate and plops incongruously as it hits the water below.

Alan grips Tina's swinging arm and pushes her up against the door panel allowing Charlie to withdraw his handcuffs. With little remaining resistance, Tina is secured behind her back. She sobs now as she is bundled through the well dented rear nearside door, to join her precious Eddie in the back of the patrol car.

The gathered crowd roar their appreciation, but as Charlie withdraws his baton and turns to face them, interest in any further goading the forces of law and order are quickly diluted and the dispersal is instantaneous.

Charlie checks that the rear door is fully closed and leans his back against it to catch his breath; the torrent of verbal abuse from within the vehicle is muffled, but now in stereo.

Charlie rubs his ear where he has been caught a blow from Tina's Gucci 'rip off' handbag.

Alan inspects the door panel; it is rippled and dented where her frenzied kicks have made contact.

"Shit." Alan curses under his breath as Charlie retrieves his cap from the pavement.

"Never mind the door, what about my fucking ear?" Charlie protests, rubbing the bruised appendage.

Alan leans toward his crew mate and inspects the ear. "It's still attached mate, not to worry. In fact bright red suits you." He runs his hand over the rippled metal of the door skin and shakes his head in dismay.

"Besides, we don't have to explain your ear on a minute sheet to our illustrious leader. Twiggy here, will have to be charged with criminal damage."

"And assault." Charlie adds quickly, still rubbing his ear.

Alan looks quizzically at his crew mate. "Charlie, you're seventeen stones if you're an ounce. You're a prop forward for the Force rugby team; do you really want the whole office to know that you got cracked by a sweet little thing like that?" Alan nods toward the rear seats of the patroller. Four letter expletives still flow freely between hysterical sobs.

Charlie considers Alan's point for a moment. He knows that his crew mate is right, the lads would be merciless.

"Damage it is then." Charlie says in agreement.

Alan smiles knowingly and opens the door for his crew mate. "Call it in mate, let's get off."

"I'd best lock 'is motor up first." Charlie says, loping off toward the aged Vauxhall, still rubbing the glowing ear. Alan takes his seat and turns to gaze at the two prisoners.

Eddie appears to be somewhat resigned to his fate. The Sumo wrestler still sobs and saliva runs from her nose. It drips, leaving a glistening silken thread between her many chins and the collar of her blouse.

She is cautioned and informed that she also is under arrest for criminal damage to the Police vehicle and Alan throws in a breach of the peace for good measure. She continues to sob, the patroller rocks on its springs as her body convulses.

"Big fuckin' brave men." Eddie spits, his machismo returning in the presence of his woman.

Alan turns and clips his seat belt into place; he looks up into the rear view mirror and adjusts it so the he has a clear view of the two in the rear.

"Eddie, language please. There are ladies present." Alan admonishes.

"Yeah, you two cunts." Eddie sneers.

Charlie returns to the patroller and reaches for the handset as Alan pulls away from the kerb edge. The blue lights are switched off.

"Oi! warrabout my fuckin' car?" Eddie shouts politely.

"What about it?" Charlie responds, half turning in his seat to look at Eddie.

"You're not just fuckin' leavin' it there." Eddie tells them, leaving Alan and his crew mate in no doubt as to who is in command of this situation. "If it gets nicked, you two twats are in big fuckin' trouble."

Alan looks up into the rear view and returns Eddie's stare. "Eddie...be honest...Would you steal *that* car?"

Charlie chuckles as Eddie responds with incomprehensible obscenities. He depresses the radio handset bar.

"Papa Yankee One Four message."

"Papa Yankee One Four, go ahead." the operator responds, expecting the call.

"From One Four, we're 10/12 from Park Place. As previous, one for O.P.L. drive whilst disqualified and the warrant. Oh, and one for criminal damage, a female, over."

The controller replies. "Papa Yankee One Four, to the Bridewell over?"

"Affirmative, is there a Matron on duty over?"

"One Four, Matron is present. I'll inform the Bridewell, over."

"I'm obliged." Charlie nods at Alan and replaces the handset.

The patroller weaves smoothly through the City traffic on its way to the Bridewell.

Eddie sits in stony silence in the rear, no doubt plotting nefarious methods with which to rid the world at large of his captors.

The Sumo still blubbers. She wails again as she notes the state of her clothing.

"Eddieeeee, they ripped my b..b..bes' fuckin' blouse."

Eddie remains impassive. He half turns to the grotesque visage of his wife/girlfriend/other, she was no Da Vinci before the incident, but the hysterical sobbing has reddened her eyes and her neck has swollen with exertion. Her mascara has run, dampened by her tears and sweat, it has diluted and formed into large black patches beneath the bags under her eyes. She looks to all intents and purposes like a grossly overweight panda that's been on the piss for a week.

Alan considers that he may have misjudged Eddie; he is obviously a very brave man.

"Lo…ok at m…m…my b…b…blouse Eddie." She chokes between sobs, now obviously near to complete exhaustion as she holds up the torn edge of the blouse.

Eddie shakes his head slowly. "Shut the fuck up Tina." he says lovingly.

She breaks into secondary sobbing at this touching outward sign of affection from her man.

"'Er fuckin mam died yesterday you know." Eddie screams from the rear and kicks out at the back of the front seat to give his message impetus.

Charlie half turns toward him, "Is that a fact?"

"Yeah, it's a fuckin' fact." Eddie spits.

"Well Eddie", Charlie says with feeling. "I'll be frank with you…" Alan holds up a hand and interrupts his crew mate's oratory "Mate, you were Frank yesterday, you're Ronald today."

Charlie smiles. Eddie sneers contemptuously as Alan's crew mate continues.

"Well, to be honest Eddie, I'm amazed that whilst racked with grief over the sad loss of her Mother, she still finds it acceptable to go out for a skin full and kick off with the law. If you don't mind me saying, having experienced your girlfriend's pleasant disposition at first hand, I can only surmise that her Mother's passing has come as something of a welcome release."

Fat Tina continues to whimper and wipes her nose on the sleeve of her blouse; Eddie looks across to her, a look of disgust on his face. He mouths some indiscernible obscenity and then stares up at the rear view mirror.

"You've fuckin' ruined my life. All for a fuckin' light out. I 'ope you're fuckin' appy that's all."

Alan looks up to the rear view mirror. "Oi! Eddie." Their eyes meet in the reflection.

"I don't recall tying you to a chair and pouring ale down your neck against your will, nor do I remember forcing you to drive yer MOT failure at gun point afterwards. So how is it that *we're* to blame? Enlighten me."

Eddie ignores the logic and returns his stare to the passing buildings as the patroller negotiates the series of traffic lights and junctions which take them back toward the Town Hall steps.

The patroller pulls up outside the Bridewell gates and the ultimate trip in degradation begins.

*****

The City Bridewell, its aged corridors and dungeons snake labyrinth like beneath the bowels of the Town Hall. The small entrance gates, innocuous and insignificant to the casual passer-by, is the portal to a terrible place. The corridor which leads to the main electronic gates from the street is stone flagged, worn away at the centre by untold size thirteens since time immemorial.

At the far end of the entrance corridor stands the steel covered door, which when opened only from within, allows the prisoner and his escort entry. Once entered, this inner portal slams shut ominously with a loud clang of finality and all contact with the outside world is lost.

The City Bridewell is older than time, older than the grandiose building which stands above it, splendid with its Gothic arches and marble pillars, overarched by grotesque gargoyles which vomit the rain water from beneath the balustrade eaves onto the heads of the Keyworth lions guarding the entrance door.

From early Neolithic times (or so it seems) the Bridewell has incarcerated drunkards, rapists, thieves and burglars, along with a myriad of murderers and arsonists along with the general ne'er do wells of the City, since well before the original Jack the Ripper hacked his way to notoriety.

It is strongly rumoured, that the Bridewell has been repainted just the once since the end of the Punic wars.

A move to the Bridewell is regarded by some as a punishment posting, a penal retreat for those unfortunates ranking Inspector and below, who, having sinned against one of the numerous disciplinary offences committable both on and off duty, find themselves dispatched to the Bridewell for an indeterminate period or, until sufficient 'penance' has been performed and the transgressor is allowed to return to Division.

Those Officers who perform gaoler duties as a career choice, are generally known as the 'pissed off, lame or lazy'. Their interest in active policing totally eroded for one reason or another. Others remain, simply eking out their last few years of service doing as little as possible before collecting their pensions.

Whether there by choice or otherwise, the Bridewell staff are not be relied upon to provide a helpful or sympathetic ear to either the plight of those dragged unceremoniously down the stoned flagged outer corridor and 'fronted up' before the Inspector, or indeed, the arresting Officers. Perhaps if they are 'veterans', known to the Bridewell staff for a minimum of ten years, then...maybe.

Such institutes of incarceration have always existed; the British Empire in its heyday had the Antipodes when transportation for life was in fashion. It was either that or a slow death from malnutrition or disease in the dreaded Newgate Jail.

The French favoured penal servitude for life, although served out in warmer climes. Guiana and 'Le Iles du Diable'.

The Soviets, famous throughout the civilised world for their touching concern for the health, safety and welfare of political dissidents and common criminals, not only incarcerated for life, but froze your ass off for good measure in the Siberian Gulags.

The Police Force has the Bridewells.

\*\*\*\*\*

The Bridewell Inspector greets Eddie and the blubbering Tina cheerfully as they are brought down the 'short walk' from the street. Alan grips Eddie's arm and releases it only when he hears the click of the solenoid against the metal rods securing the inner door behind him.

Charlie removes his hand from Tina's upper arm and subconsciously wipes the palms of his hand down the seams of his trousers. She leans against the yellowing tiles by the entrance door and whimpers.

The Inspector glances up at the quivering mass and touches the button on the intercom unit which sits gathering dust on the counter top. "Matron, wouldst thou come hither please."

A hollow, indiscernible response hisses from a small speaker which hangs precariously from the coving behind the Inspectors' chair.

Eddie leans nonchalantly against the polished counter top and considers the advice provided by home-made sign pinned to the wall facing him: '*Do not ask for bail as a refusal often offends*'.

Alan and Charlie stand one either side of Eddie. Charlie reaches behind and releases the handcuffs and hands them back to Alan, who stuffs them back into the leather pouch at his waistband.

Eddie rubs at his wrists and scrutinizes the deep red wheals where the ratchets have bitten him. He scowls at Alan.

The Inspector smiles.

"Officer Pendle." he says by way of acknowledgment and glancing toward his crew mate with a puzzled expression. "Paired on this occasion with the good Officer Morrisey if I'm not mistaken. What ill fate hath brought about this marriage of convenience?"

Inspector Cawthorne is a keen amateur dramatist and something of a thespian. He is worryingly going through what is thought to be a profound Shakespearean period, best ignored and not to be encouraged unless you were willing to while away the wee hours discussing the 'Scottish play' or any other of the great Bard's works.

Inspector Cawthorne is at the Bridewell through choice, which is a further worry, but probably best for all concerned, at least until his mind returns to the twentieth century.

Mr Cawthorne is well known and much loved by all who experience the pleasure of his distinctly unique and often bizarre supervisory qualities.

He is the owner of a battered (yet seemingly reliable) Yamaha FS1E moped which he rides daily to work.

On day shifts, which start at 9.00 am, Mr Cawthorne would as ever, ride his moped into the City, make his way across the Town Hall forecourt and arrive at the outer door to the Bridewell to be viewed by the early turn staff via the security camera. Wearing his normal full length khaki trenchcoat which rain or shine was always buttoned to the neck, a red and white 'Stirling Moss' type peaked crash helmet and Long Range Desert Group goggles, Mr Cawthorne was readily identified.

The outer door would be activated by the Bridewell staff seated behind the charge desk and Mr Cawthorne would ride his 'fizzy' down the corridor, toward the inner security door. By which time, the outer door had closed, allowing the inner door to be nudged open by the front wheel of his machine.

It would be at about this time that all the remand prisoners produced from prison to have their cases reviewed in either the Magistrates or Crown Court, along those unfortunates incarcerated for the night on no bail warrants, would be gathered in the long corridor under the watchful eyes of those Officers parading for Court and tasked with escort duty, until their particular case was to be heard.

The early turn Bridewell Sergeant would at this time, be standing in the long corridor clasping his clipboard to call out the names of those Officers previously warned for Court duty and designate them a prisoner to be escorted up to the Courts.

Mr Cawthorne would enter the long corridor from the charge area, still astride his moped, the exhaust throwing out clouds of oil laden smoke; he would stop and casually raise his goggles.

"Ah! Sergeant. I seem to have missed my way. City Square?"

The Sergeant having replayed this scenario on a number of occasions, would think for a moment, scratch the side of his head with the end of his pen, then point down the long corridor which ran between the cells.

"Oh, you're well out of your way Sir...Down the corridor to the end, make a left and go through the traffic lights at George Street. Carry on and you'll come to the Square."

Mr Cawthorne, polite as ever would thank the Sergeant and pedalling furiously until the FS1E gained sufficient inertia for the engine to take over, would disappear down the corridor leaving the waiting prisoners wondering what the fuck was going on. Much to the amusement of those escort Officers who knew Mr Cawthorne.

"Sullivan will be out of the game for a while Sir. Last night's soiree in the Badlands."

"Ah yes." Mr Cawthorne sighs, nodding sympathetically. "I noted that in the Chief's log, any news on the good Sergeant Robertson?"

"Nothing yet Sir, but no news is good news I 'spect."

"Indeed." The Inspector nods again as if deep in thought and then suddenly brightens as his focus returns to the matter at hand.

"Well met Officer Morrisey! What of these two miscreants?"

"A moving road traffic offence Sir. Positive breath test at the scene. PNC shows him to be a disqualified driver and there is a warrant not backed for bail, issued in the first instance from Bamborough Magistrates Court in August."

Mr Cawthorne looks across to Eddie who still slouches against the counter edge. "Oh dear." he says sombrely, shaking his head and tutting. "And this mountain of mad flesh?" he asks, nodding inquisitively toward Tina, who is still slumped against the far wall sniffing and still inspecting her torn blouse.

"She Sir, has kicked the shit out of our patroller whilst attempting to assist an offender...Eddie here...to escape lawful custody. So it's criminal damage."

"Good heavens!" Mr Cawthorne exclaims dramatically, directing his gaze toward Tina. "What will your Mother have to say about that young lady?"

This brings about a fresh outburst of wailing and sobbing from the now totally exhausted Tina.

"Actually Sir." Alan intercedes, "That's something of a sore subject at the moment."

The Inspector looks to Alan and his crew mate and just short of asking for an explanation, pauses as his attention is diverted. He frowns. "What has happened to your ear Constable Morrisey, it appears to be a tryst discoloured."

Charlie scowls and looks back toward the quivering mess in the doorway. "We had a slight difference of opinion regarding her boyfriend's loss of liberty Sir."

The Inspector's facial expression changes significantly. "Thou jarring motley minded strumpet." he utters, as he stares at Tina and shakes his head slowly.

Tina is shocked and bewildered by the Inspector's incantations. She hasn't a clue what he has just said, but considers that it can't be good. She holds her breath as Matron shuffles into the charge area from her office down the corridor.

Mr Cawthorne points theatrically toward Tina. "Out of my sight, thou dost infect my eyes."

Matron rolls her eyes despairingly at the Inspector and tuts as she takes hold of Tina's arm to lead her from the charge area.

"I wish he'd watch telly like normal people." Matron mutters to herself, as she half drags the disconsolate Tina out into the main corridor and down to the female search room.

Constable Wainwright and Sergeant Makepeace enter the charge area from the small office at the side of the charge area carrying the remnants of their meal break.

Eddie watches the twenty five stone Constable Wainwright approaching and cautiously steps back from the edge of the counter. Constable Wainwright is six feet five and wears 'tailored' shirts. Constable Wainwright's shirts are tailored because extra material is required; the Force simply does not have any issue shirts in XXXXXXL. Therefore, two five inch wide side panels have been added between the side seams under his armpits, to envelope his enormous stomach, the bulk of which sags over the top of his trouser belt and onto his thighs. The material across his stomach is stretched to bursting point and gapes alarmingly between the button holes, to reveal the white ripples of his stomach flesh, liberally covered in thick, black matted hair. He is unshaven and unkempt, which only adds to his frightening visage.

Constable Wainwright is a perfect choice for the Bridewell.

Sergeant Makepeace nods casually to Alan and his crew mate as he takes his seat alongside the Inspector. He reaches underneath the counter top and withdraws a blank detention sheet. He looks up at Eddie enquiringly. "Name?"

Eddie glances suspiciously at Constable Wainwright who has moved to the left hand side of the counter which runs at a right angle back toward the entrance door. It houses a drop down partition, allowing access to a *very* chosen few into the inner sanctum.

Alan nudges Eddie. "The Sergeant is talking to you."

Eddie seems to garner a little confidence and again leans casually against the polished front edge of the counter.

Sergeant Makepeace, carefully places his pen to one side and makes eye contact with Eddie.

"Firstly. Stand back from my counter whilst I explain a few rules of the house."

Eddie shuffles back to stand between Alan and his crew mate.

"This is a charge office, not a Police station. You are wholly my responsibility and what happens to you while you are in my charge, is entirely up to me. Now you can fuck around all night for all I care, but if you fail to comply with any of my instructions or requests for information, my gaoler here…" Sergeant Makepeace nods toward Constable Wainwright who is flexing his fingers backward, resulting in an ominous cracking of joints. "will assist me in focusing your attention and compliance. Understood?"

Eddie shrugs but remains silent.

"All your property. Out of your pockets and placed onto my counter top."

The Inspector reaches under the counter and produces a clear plastic property bag which is placed on the counter in readiness.

Eddie notices that the leading edge of the counter against which Constable Wainwright has now eased his bulk, is devoid of varnish and the wood beneath is polished smooth. Eddie has heard about the 'stretching's' at the Bridewell and decides that compliance will be a lot less painful. He places the few contents of his pockets onto the counter top as he provides the Sergeant with his details.

"Right Mr Rawlinson. These two fine Officers have satisfied me that the reason for your detention is lawful. Shortly, you will be taken to another room where you will be asked to provide two samples of your breath. You can have a Solicitor, if you can find one that is willing to turn out for you, or you can telephone one for advice. But it won't delay the breath test procedure, understand?...Sign here for your property."

Eddie nods in acquiescence; he's heard it all before. He leans forward and makes his mark on the offered sheet, on the line just below the Sergeant's indicating finger.

Sergeant Makepeace nods to Alan. "Sit him on the 'fed up' bench 'till I get someone to do the breathalyser."

Alan takes hold of Eddie's arm. He walks him out of the charge area toward an open area at the top of the long corridor which houses the cells to either side. There is a long wooden bench placed against the tiled wall, it is time polished, scarred and defaced with hastily carved graffiti, Eddie flops down on it. He is indeed fed up and the bench is aptly named.

Charlie stays in the charge area; he is leaning up against the counter top discussing rugby with Sergeant Makepeace, who also plays for the Force team.

The Town Hall clock, a hundred feet above them booms out the hour.

"I shall take my repast Sergeant, as we have heard the chimes at midnight." Inspector Cawthorne says to Sergeant Makepeace as he stands and stretches.

"It's actually only eleven o'clock Sir" the Sergeant replies dryly, not bothering to look up from his paperwork.

Mr Cawthorne ignores the sarcasm and disappears into the side office; he closes the door behind him, presumably so that he can return temporarily to the seventeenth century.

Sergeant Makepeace has noted that Mr Cawthorne was carrying a copy of 'A Comedy of Errors' and considers his choice of reading material to be quite appropriate given his Inspector's present state of mind.

Whilst Eddie languishes on the 'fed up' bench, Alan stands opposite, waiting for the breathalyser operator. He leans his back against the door frame of the breathalyser room as he makes notes of pertinent times in his green book.

From the Matron's room there is the sound of raised female voices, just audible over the drunken howls of protest and veiled death threats from those unfortunates already in residence along the length of the corridor. Eddie can just make out Tina's protests at being forcibly searched and there is the sound of a slap. Tina has obviously upset Matron and reprisals have followed, swiftly and no doubt painfully. Matron, rumour has it, was dishonourably discharged from the Totenkopfverband Division of the Waffen SS for cruelty and in fact, bears an uncanny resemblance to Ilse Koch, that quintessential mother figure of Buchenwald.

The breathalyser room is small, insignificant yet wholly functional. Purpose built, it contains two chairs, one for the operator and the other, a tired sagging effort, threadbare through the friction of a thousand trousered (and skirted) backsides, which have palpitated throughout the clinical procedure and suffered the ignominy of an equal amount of rectal contractions and expansions, as the 'victims' wait for the outcome of their test.

The chair creaks in protest as Eddie slouches against the backrest. He watches as the machine begins to test itself.

The ethanol solution bubbles and gurgles through the innards of the thing and the illuminated display panel flashes up the first result whilst the infernal thing tests itself yet again. If ever a man was at the mercy of a machine, it is here.

The operator glances casually, disinterestedly at the first of the self-test results and continues to scribble across the pre-printed proforma.

Charlie joins Alan to stand behind Eddie; they watch the machine rotating through the self-testing stage, more through habit, than any genuine interest. Alan nudges Charlie and raises six fingers then five; Charlie muses for a while and looking down at the despondent Eddie, shakes his head and silently shows nine fingers. Alan smiles and digs into his pocket and places a small silver coin carefully between them on the scarred metal shelf, against which they both lean. Charlie covers his crew mates bet with a coin of similar value. They settle back to watch Eddie's performance.

"Right. The machine has self-tested and is found to be correctly calibrated ok." the operator says dispassionately, as he pulls out a length of clear plastic tube from within the bowels of the machine. He has attached an equally clear plastic square block to the offered end of the tube and he waves this in front of Eddie's face.

"Blow into that end of the tube till I tell you to stop. Yer can't mess wi' it. If yer try suckin' instead of blowin', the machine'll abort yer test. It'll gi' yer another try, but if yer fuck about again, it's a failure to provide an' you get charged anyway."

Eddie grasps the end of the tube and after inhaling deeply, does his best.

The machine buzzes and after a few moments, emits a loud click. The lights flash and Alan and Charlie peer over Eddie's shoulder to note the reading. The operator also glances at the machine and notes the first result on the form.

Eddie searches the operator's face for a sign. Something, *anything* to give him a vestige of hope. The operator's bored expression gives nothing away.

"Am I over or what?" Eddie asks, looking first to the operator, then twisting at the waist, looks up to where Alan and Charlie stand mute.

Alan points casually to a small dog-eared sign on the wall opposite which states:

'DURING THE PROCEDURE, ALL OFFICERS TO REMAIN **SILENT**' the word silent is in grossly oversized letters.

The sign has been placed as a result of a successful not guilty plea to a drink driving offence when the defendant's Solicitor, grasping at any form of defence no matter how futile, had submitted to the Magistrate that whilst attending to his Client in the breathalyser room, the two arresting Officers had laughed and joked throughout the whole of the procedure and in fact, his instructions were that the Officers had almost been in tears of mirth as his Client's final reading was displayed. All this he submitted, had caused his Client to miss the part of the procedure where the operator was supposed to have given his Client the opportunity to provide a specimen of blood, which he, the defendant, would have preferred to have done.

The Magistrate in his unquestionable wisdom had deemed this to be a reasonable departure from Home Office procedure and promptly dismissed the case, much to the surprise of the defence Solicitor and total disbelief of the arresting Traffic Officers. So the sign had appeared and was dutifully signed by some aged Superintendent or other, probably long since retired.

It had of course been defaced, someone had added in what space remained along the bottom edge:

'PRISONERS, WHILST BLOWING INTO THE MACHINE, REFRAIN FROM FARTING, AS THIS <u>COULD</u> EFFECT YOUR RESULT'

Its placing had also prompted the usual satirical backlash and handwritten signs now appeared at various locations within the Bridewell. One of which, placed conveniently above the urinals, at eye height in the Gents toilets advised:

'OFFICERS MUST BE MINDFUL OF THE IMPORTANCE OF REMOVING THE PENIS FROM WITHIN THE CONFINES OF UNIFORM TROUSERS PRIOR TO COMMENCING URINATION'

"Same again" the operator says, nodding to Eddie, making a note of the first result on the form.

Eddie's second blow is higher than the first; Charlie smirks and pockets the two coins gleefully, but in compliance with the sign, silently.

The operator turns and informs Eddie of the result. With genuine concern, with feeling. As heart rending as a surgeon advising the expectant Father that his Wife and child have just died on the delivery table. "On yer first puff, yer blew ninety, on yer second, yer scored ninety four. Looks like yer fucked kid."

Eddie turns slowly around and looks up at Alan and his crew mate, who both return his stare impassively. To the victor the spoils.

"Just the one pint was it then Eddie?" Alan asks with just a hint of sarcasm.

Eddie sucks at his teeth.

The operator hands Alan the completed proforma with a copy of the print out from the machine. He winks and offers a sly smile as he stands to leave the room.

"You know the old sayin' don't you Charlie?"

Charlie smiles inquisitively. "Go on."

The operator looks down at Eddie and methodically lights his fortieth cigarette of the day. "The day shit is worth money, 'is sort'll be born without arse'oles."

Alan and Charlie chuckle. Their mirth somewhat enhanced by the confused look on Eddie's face. He doesn't quite know whether he's been insulted or not.

## **Eighteen**

The all night Ring Road traveller, bumped and jostled its few remaining passengers over the potholes and poorly finished roadworks as it continued its endless repetitive journey.

Each full circuit, twenty three miles around the outskirts of the City, an hour and a half later and you were back at the terminus on Bellows Lane.

Twenty pence for a ticket and you could ride all night, eleven until seven, if your spine could stand the endless buffeting and your nostrils the stink from the winos who paid the princely sum to stay warm all night, as they drank and argued their way around the City limits.

Drunkenly and nonsensically with wide and rapid arm flailings, they extolled their personal politics and made the world a better place in great detail, to equally soporific companions or perhaps, to no one at all.

The stale urine and tobacco stench seemed to cling to the graffiti covered seats. The stained interior panels of the bus, are ignored or go unnoticed by the drunks, whose nasal sensory capabilities had long since been destroyed by vapours of methylated spirits, solvents and cheap cider.

The winos generally congregated under the dark railway arches and the bridges which spanned the canal, however, as the weather turned colder, they were to be seen in ever increasing numbers riding the Ring Road traveller.

The aged Atlantean creaked on its springs and the tyres screeched and sang to its half dozen or so passengers as it ran along the scarred surface of the outer Ring Road, the top surface of which, had been chewed and ripped away by the heavy steel teeth of the scarifier prior to new asphalt being laid.

A studious looking man, perhaps in his twenties, lifted his head from where it had lain against the window leaving a greasy filigree print in the condensation. He yawned, the screaming from the tortured tyres had awakened him. He sighed and glanced about the interior of the bus, disorientated by the period of sleep and now, momentarily unsure of his whereabouts.

He reached into the pocket of his Army greatcoat and withdrew a battered cigarette packet. A copy of Karl Marx's 'Das Kapital' lay open, spine upwards, next to him. He lit a cigarette and inhaled deeply, putting his hand on the book as if undecided whether to continue with his reading.

He wore John Lennon style glasses, small circular lenses trapped within thin wire frames. A popular design adopted by the National Health Service in the fifties and sixties. No one wanted them then of course, it smacked of poverty, that is, until the style was immortalised by the modern day Liverpudlian Bard.

He yawned again and decided on the book. He pushed the glasses further up the bridge of his nose with an index finger and slouched down in his seat to continue his studies.

'Midnight' grimaced at the hot taste of his cigarette and noticed that it had burned down to the filter tip. He dropped it unceremoniously to the floor and ground it into the rubber flooring with his foot.

He glanced at his watch and wiped the window with the sleeve of his jacket, peering out into the darkness through the rivulets of condensation which streamed down the glass. He noted that he was nearing his destination. His window now had a small porthole shaped area which reflected the interior of the bus against the darkness outside and he watched with some interest, the reflection of the young couple who were seated in the aisle opposite him, but a few seats to the rear. The girl, who was seated nearest to him, was half turned in her seat and faced toward her male companion. She was masturbating him as covertly as possible and looking timidly every now and then, toward the front of the bus.

She returned her gaze to her boyfriend's erect penis as she sensed his nearness. Her movements quickened.

'Midnight' smiled as the young man reached out and gripped the back of the seat which hid them from general view. He arched his back and uttered an ecstatic grunt, almost masked by the howling of the tyres, as he ejaculated against the plastic backrest of the seat in front.

'Midnight' stretched. He reached up toward the curved roof of the bus and pressed the thin ribbed slat which ran the full length of the vehicle on either side of the centre aisle. A strangled buzz was barely audible, emanating from somewhere near to the driver's cab and 'Midnight' felt the bus start to decelerate.

He stood and briefly glanced back toward the young couple whose earlier sexual activities he had witnessed. As he entered the aisle, he just noticed the young man's hand being withdrawn from beneath the front of the girl's creased sweatshirt before he walked down the rubber floored gangway toward the opening door of the bus.

*****

'Midnight' turned his face away from the billowing cloud of diesel laden fumes which belched out from beneath the rear of the bus, as it pulled away from the kerb edge, to continue its never ending circumference of the City.

The singing from the tired transmission finally faded, leaving him standing alone in silence on the pavement. He remained still for a moment or two, allowing his eyes to become accustomed to the darkness. The nearest working street light was a good way in the distance, its yellow fluorescence fighting against the grime which seemed to hang in droplets, suspended in the damp air of the night.

He walked now, his hands deep in the pocket of his jeans, back towards the City.

After a ten minute walk, 'Midnight' stopped and leaned back against a high stone wall which bordered the pavement on which he stood. He felt the harsh coldness of the stone seep through his clothing whilst he surveyed with a critical eye, the forecourt of the used car lot across the road from him.

The lot contained twenty or more vehicles which stood expectantly in two rows, each vehicle set diagonally for maximum visual effect. 'Midnight' scanned the tops of the poles, which stood at each corner of the lot and the small box like office to the left.

He squinted against the poor light, searching for the presence of any passive infra-red detectors, which if activated by movement, would suddenly flood the forecourt with light. A deterrent to thieves, or those who would cause damage, and to provide sufficient light for the video cameras to record the crime.

Bunting, comprised of cheap plastic flags in grimy red, white and blue, hung from thin wires stretched between four corner poles at the outer reaches of the lot. The flags slapped lazily against each other in the slight breeze, as if applauding the potential customer's good taste.

Under the flags and in a similar state of repair, were gaudy plastic signs within corroded wire frames. They sat on the roofs of the offered vehicles, proclaiming each particular model to be the 'bargain of the week' or 'close inspection invited'.

'Midnight' noted with satisfaction, that the forecourt seemed to be free from any security devices and he shrugged himself free of the stonework, flexing his muscles against the cold numbness which by now had crept into his back.

He glanced up and down the Ring Road before sauntering across the road. He walked tentatively across the forecourt, to peer into the sales office through the single window which overlooked the lot, cupping his hands around the side of his face to block out what little ambient light there was.

Through the grime covered glass, his eyes quickly scanned the single desk and cheap plastic folding chair; the only other fittings were a metal filing cabinet which listed at a precarious angle, where the wooden floor of the office, seemed to have partially collapsed. The office was similarly unprotected, a cheap padlock and latch was all that secured the flimsy wooden front door and given the Spartan state of the office and fixtures, burglary was clearly not a concern.

The cars for sale were definitely at the lower end of the market, catering mostly to the needs and pockets of the residents of the nearby council owned back to back terraces. The cost of automatic lighting or video security was neither financially justified nor worthwhile.

Pulling on thin woollen gloves, his eyes skittered from one vehicle to another on the front row and finally rested on a dull brown Austin Allegro, which was, if the sign on its roof was to be believed, a 'credit to its former owner'.

'Midnight' squatted down beside the driver's door of the vehicle and unrolled a small canvas tool holder. He withdrew a small flat bladed screwdriver from within one of its many pockets and with a cursory glance down the Ring Road, slipped the blade of the tool between the edge of the driver's door and the central door pillar. He took out a small length of stiff plastic banding from the roll and folded it in two to form a loop. With a minimum of pressure on the screwdriver handle, he prized the edge of the door outwards, sufficient to allow the loop of plastic to pass between the perished rubber door seal and the pillar.

'Midnight' 'see sawed' the loop of plastic downwards, until it was level with the top of the mushroom shaped door locking stud which protruded from the top of the inner door panel. Dropping the screwdriver, he pushed one edge of the plastic strip forwards and the band naturally formed a loop within the interior of the car. This he carefully worked downwards until it dropped over the top of the door stud. Pulling the two ends of the band tight, he locked it around the plastic stud beneath its mushroom head and with a slight upward pulling action, the door stud snapped upward with a dry click.

'Midnight' methodically replaced the screwdriver and the plastic band back into the tool holder and from it, he took a small steel tyre lever which he placed on the tarmac just beneath the sill of the vehicle.

Tentatively, he opened the driver's door and immediately reached up to flick back the switch to extinguish the courtesy light by the interior mirror. He noted with some satisfaction, that at least the battery of his chosen vehicle appeared to be well topped up.

Kneeling on the cold tarmac, he opened the door fully and leaned in over the sill kickplate. He ran a gloved hand over the plastic lower steering column shroud. He felt for the two cross headed screws and without looking, felt his way across his toolholder and pulled out a Phillips screwdriver. Within seconds, the two screws dropped to the floor of the vehicle and 'Midnight' eased the lower part of the shroud free, to expose the ignition barrel.

'Midnight' wedged the end of the tyre lever between the alloy casting and the steel tubing of the steering column and ensuring that a sufficient amount of the hardened iron was between the two, he heaved downward with his body weight. The casing of the ignition barrel split with a loud crack, exposing small brass plugs, which when correlated to the correct equation by the insertion of the correct ignition key, released the steering lock pins.

Not being in possession of the ignition key posed little inconvenience and 'Midnight' pushed the tyre iron further in between the opened gap and pushed down again. The cheap alloy outer casing of the barrel shattered and fell away onto the rubber floor mat, followed by a shower of the small brass plugs. He pulled out the locking pin and tossed it out onto the forecourt, hearing it rolling away underneath the vehicle which still invited 'close inspection'.

Pausing, he listened, but hearing only the flapping of the flags, he returned his attention to the ignition system.

The four coloured wires parted company with the rear of the plastic switch cover more easily than he had expected and as he ripped the wires free of their soldered joints; his right elbow rocketed backwards, smashing into the central door pillar, sending a lance of pain up into his shoulder. Cursing under his breath, 'Midnight' rubbed frantically at his elbow to ease the numbness which had extended from his ulnar nerve to his fingertips.

Taking the unwelcome opportunity to look again up and down the Ring Road, he watched until the numbness slowly receded from his fingertips.

Briefly, using his lighter to identify the colour coding of the four wires, 'Midnight' dug his thumbnail into the soft plastic sheath of the battery feed wire and bared half an inch of the shiny inner core. Stripping the black and yellow ignition wire in the same fashion, he feverishly twisted the two wires together to form a crude connection. He was rewarded with a bright red glow from the ignition and oil lights on the dashboard facia.

'Midnight' quickly stripped the remaining wires and left them hanging as he hurriedly replaced the tyre iron and refolded the tool roll and tossed it into the rear seats. He threw the lower part of the steering cowl into the passenger footwell before seating himself in the driver's seat and closed the door.

It had all but clicked shut when he suddenly remembered that the plastic roof sign was still attached to the roof of the vehicle. Cursing himself for his stupidity, he leapt from the vehicle and frantically unclipped the rubber retaining straps from the roof gutters and threw the sign across the forecourt.

Twisting the wires that he had joined into a single thick strand, 'Midnight' pumped his foot down onto the accelerator pedal, to infuse a little fuel into the bowl of the carburettor.

Holding the wires he had joined in his left hand, he glanced again up and down the Ring Road and satisfied that it was clear, he touched the bared solenoid wire against the pair he had previously joined.

The Bendix spring in the starter motor whipped its small gear wheel forwards and up against the teeth of the flywheel and as 'Midnight' held the wires together, the Allegro's cold engine churned over slowly.

'Midnight' pumped the accelerator pedal frantically and willed the engine to come alive. The engine turned reluctantly, yet remained lifeless. A thought rushed coldly through his brain and his eyes darted to the fuel gauge. He saw that it sat quite healthily above the red empty mark.

He released the solenoid wire and sat in silence, fully expecting a dozen Police vehicles to come screeching to a halt in front of the car lot, spilling out uniforms, all eager to 'chastise' him.

Holding his breath, 'Midnight' wondered why in hell's name he had chosen to steal one of the most unreliable cars in the world.

He touched the wires together again and pumped the accelerator pedal, whispering encouragement and subconsciously nodded his head in time to the cranking of the flywheel. The engine churned, coughed and fired.

Quickly, he released the solenoid wire, cutting off the power to the starter motor. He revved the engine hard.

'Midnight' rammed the gear lever forwards into first. There was a crunching thud as the synchromesh complained bitterly at the abuse. With a cursory glance to left and right, he let off the handbrake and drove the screaming Allegro from the forecourt, across the pavement and down onto the road surface.

The vehicle lurched across to the nearside carriageway and 'Midnight' accelerated hard towards the City. Only when he considered that he was a safe distance from any unseen witnesses, did he flick the plastic rocker switch, activating the lights.

*****

The heavy gold rings sparkled expensively, even in the dull light of the smoke filled basement room. The fat fingers on which they sat, moved with practised dexterity as the edges of the notes were flicked upwards. The fingers paused and an index finger was raised to a thick pair of lips which parted momentarily to allow the digit to be moistened on a tongue, which darted out with the speed of a striking snake. The digit then returned along with its four like appendages to the beer dampened table top where the counting continued.

The broad gold links of the man's identity bracelet rattled against the wooden surface as the notes were patted satisfyingly by the huge hands into an even oblong wad, which with equal dexterity, was secured with a rubber band.

As the notes were secured, the man's wrists were exposed and the nameplate on the bracelet twisted upwards. The smoke filtered shafts of light picked out the word 'Fastener' in deeply etched gothic style lettering.

The lips parted again, this time in a smile. He exposed perfectly formed teeth, brilliantly white even in the dim light.

The man nodded his appreciation and pushed the wad of notes into the inner breast pocket of his jacket which he purposefully patted back into shape, the bulge still evident beneath the expensive cut of the material.

'Fastener' looked up, his eyes shaded by the snap brim of the light grey fedora which was his trademark and rarely seen without. His fingers fluffed up the white silk handkerchief which spilled out from the top pocket of the Italian silk jacket and the heavy gold Rolex on his wrist, earned a cursory glance, before the jacket cuff was carefully adjusted to cover it.

The smile continued as if it were painted on his face. He stood, holding his manicured hands up to shoulder height as a young soldier wearing 'Sons of Judah' colours on his sleeveless denim jacket, draped a heavy Cashmere coat over the shoulders of the man. He shrugged, allowing the coat to fall comfortably against his shoulders and briefly, the black custom grip of the snub nosed Smith and Wesson 617 he carried in the waistband of his trousers, was exposed momentarily for effect.

The young black stepped back and resumed his rightful position to the rear of the man, silently waiting for the next visual order.

'Fastener' expected his soldiers to know what was expected of them. His personal guard was hand-picked. He never asked for respect, never had to. Like the Dons of Sicily from a bygone era, lack of respect, a disparaging look, or a critical remark, was indelibly memorised, stored for future reference. Recrimination like vengeance, is, as they say, a dish best served cold.

Across from the man, still seated, an act of disrespect which had not gone unnoticed, the Manager of the 'blues' nervously bit at the soft skin on the inside of his cheeks. He distorted his facial muscles so that the molars could nip at the flesh and pull away small slivers of the soft tissue which he ground between his front teeth. It was a nervous habit, it displayed a weakness in his character, like smoking or excessive drinking and 'Fastener' despised weakness in anyone.

The Manager's eyes fled quickly from the butt of the small pistol and flitted across the cut of the man's suit and to the gold draped across his fingers as 'Fastener' adjusted his coat. He quickly looked back to the table top in case the envy in his eyes became evident.

'Fastener' spoke, his voice deep, guttural. "Done good Lester." he said, nodding approvingly. He offered a half smile to his Manager as he patted the bulge beneath his coat.

"What'd we lose when the man come aroun' las' night?"

The Manager shrugged. "It was a minor gate, nutt'n' to speak about. Some minor bush weight lost, a few brothers got busted, but they was all out 'fore daylight. 'Babylon' got fucked over man. Soldiers done good, few heads cracked, but dat's to be 'spected, no loss of revenue, as you kin see, eh?" he said, nodding toward the prominent bulge beneath his boss' coat.

'Fastener' stopped. The rictus like smile dropped like a stone from his face. He placed the palms of his hands face down on the table top and peered down, deep into the eyes of his Manager. He spoke softly, but there was a force behind his words, a threatening undertone, he almost whispered. "But how'd they know where to come Lester?"

He let his words sink in and stared questioningly into his Managers eyes…"How'd the motherfuckers know where it was at?…dat's the fuckin' point. See, someone talkin' and' dat's why the 'Soldier' pays me, an' I pays you, to know shit like this. If you aint up to it…I finds someone who is…Think on it."

The Manager averted his gaze, fearful that his boss should mistake any alarm in his eyes as a sign of guilty knowledge. A Judas sign.

Moving his lips close to his manager's ear, 'Fastener' whispered threateningly. "You bes' be tellin' me the motherfuckin' stash is safe Lester."

The manager felt his boss's hot breath on the side of his face. Almost overcome by the overpowering smell of his expensive cologne; he nodded quickly and cast a furtive glance toward the massive Wharfedale speaker tucked away in the corner of the room.

The Wharfedale, was a trademark double cabinet model, large, heavy and robust. The space between the inner and outer shells being filled with sand to reduce resonance. Also assisting in resonance reduction, although the four foot speaker was now redundant, was a large canvas bag which was wedged between the inner shell and the two enormous speaker cones.

'Fastener' allowed his gaze to linger on his Manager for a while, that was his prerogative. He was slightly perturbed at his sullen manner and wondered fleetingly if he was being ripped off. The thought dispersed as quickly as it had arrived. No…the raid had been random, a one off, just 'Babylon' flexing a little muscle. He had too many soldiers frequenting the 'blues', too many eyes to see and too many mouths too quick to tell if there was something amiss.

He stood up straight and took a last look around the room. A few of his girls sat smoking and talking with the sisters of their profession. He made a mental note. They were looking cheap and spending too much time in each other's company instead of working. Clothes dirty and ill fitting, hair not washed and brushed, standards were slipping. His eyes floated over them, each one in turn lowered her eyes to avoid his gaze. He looked at them critically as a collector would peruse a fine work of art. He determined to have a word with his people tomorrow, time to get some discipline back. "Makin' a motherfucker look bad." he thought to himself.

His decision made, he turned to leave with a swirl which caused his coat tails to sweep across the table top. He strode toward the steep stone steps which led up to the ground floor from the converted cellar.

'Fastener' smiled inwardly as he felt the wad pressing tightly against his chest as he climbed the steps, good takings. The Manchester imported white was selling well, not that he had ever sampled the fine white powder, it was much too valuable to waste on personal gratification. He needed his mind clear, money was what counted. Money bought respect and respect bought the power that he had craved since he had moved to this depressing cold, damp country.

Another glance at his watch. The bold heaviness of it pleased him, as did its outward opulence. Such a fine watch said something about the wearer. In 'Fastener's' case, it said that he was a receiver of stolen goods.

A house boy wearing the statutory sleeveless denims, as yet without colours as he had not yet proved himself sufficiently, slid back the heavy duty bolts on the outer door. The sliders were almost an inch thick, the brass now showing through the fine abrasion lines in the chromium plating. Necessary at one time, when the local uniforms had taken it into their heads to raid his 'blues' on a more regular basis.

The heavy bolts would submit to the sledgehammer blows eventually, but they would buy valuable time in which cannabis resin could be flushed down sinks and toilets and marijuana tossed into an open fire before 'Babylon' flooded in.

Coke was easier to dispose of; one simply sniffed it away or blew it into a fine dust to fall on the grimy carpet, no exhibits, no prosecution.

'Fastener' nodded briefly to the houseboy, recognising the show of respect as the door was held open for him. He stepped out onto the stone flags which led down toward the street. The door closed behind him and he paused, waited and listened. He heard the bolts being slammed home again and he nodded, pleased with security.

He walked the short distance to the waist high wooden gate at the end of the pathway; the gate screeched satisfyingly from its rusted hinges when opened. He stepped through the opening and onto the pavement, the gate swung back automatically on its spring. 'Fastener' glanced back to the house and noticed that a curtain in one of the upstairs rooms had been pulled to one side and an unrecognised face appeared. A 'watcher', warned of someone's presence, by a small bulb attached to the window sill which went out when the gate was opened. The bulb now glowed dimly, as an electrical contact was made when the gate catch snapped back into its latch.

Cops always opened gates, never climbed over them...ever.

A hand was raised briefly as the 'watcher' recognised the man.

'Fastener' touched the brim of his fedora, again, suitably impressed by the maintained vigilance.

The chances of a raid on this 'blues' was slim, but last night proved that they could still happen. Cannabis wasn't too bad, marijuana was worth a caution as long as you only had half an ounce or so, but the fine white powder or the brown crystals brought with it heavy down time, especially in any quantity. 'Babylon' would make it so and charge possession with intent to supply. That could be three to five 'down the steps' and the law was playing a different game these days.

He almost preferred the old days of the raids, at least you knew when the law was coming down on you. Each 'blues' could reckon on being raided every third week or so. Nowadays, it was electronic gadgets and sophisticated, covert deceit by the law.

'Plants' would come to the 'blues' posing as buyers. Crime Squad usually or a Drugs Squad man, on loan from the Met, or brought in from Newcastle or Birmingham so the accent would provide credibility.

'Fastener' shook his head at the deviousness of it all. "Mo'fuckers even got brothers in the squad these days, dreadlocks an' all."

He shivered at the thought and briefly considered the suspicious attitude of his Manager tonight. He reminded himself that he allowed all his employees to snort a little Coke from time to time. This he tolerated and in fact when new prospects showed up, he insisted on it, on the assumption that no undercover Cop would actually do a 'one on one'.

'Babylon' might smoke a little bush in the line of duty…but not Coke.

'Midnight' waited and watched intently. He saw his man leave the house and step out onto the deserted street. From midway down an unlit cobbled ginnel between the three storey houses, he'd noticed the 'watcher' and the bulb trick. He'd smiled with a little admiration and in the silence, had heard the heavy bolts on the front door of the house being slammed home.

His man had his act together alright. His 'blues' was secure, but the 'blues' wasn't the target, it was the man. He was vulnerable, he'd shown a weak link, his weakness betrayed by one of his own women.

'Midnight' felt his heart thudding in his chest and quickly wiped away the small pinpricks of sweat which had gathered on his upper lip.

He twisted in the seat and searched the street, up and down through the semi opaque side windows where condensation had gathered. It was hot inside the vehicle, or it seemed so, the heater was fully over its cold setting and the fan was softly blowing cold air onto the inside of the windscreen to keep it clear. The engine ticked over sweetly.

He watched as 'Fastener' walked passed the ginnel entrance, where 'Midnight' had secreted the stolen vehicle. He cast an appreciative eye over the man's threads as he walked along the pavement in front of the vehicle. "Trina was right, he is a flash fucker." he thought to himself.

'Fastener'' gave the vehicle not a solitary thought. Just one of many cars parked up on the darkened side streets, engines running for the heater, lights off, of course, while some punter got a blowjob or relief from the old 'five fingered widow'. Nothing worthy of a glance, nothing suspicious. If he gave it any thought at all, it would have been the hope that it was one of *his* girls doing business.

The sound of the steel tips on the heels of his Enzo Bonafe handcrafted leather shoes, clacked against the flagstones on the opposite pavement. The staccato tapping faded slowly as the distance between the two rivals increased. For the 'Fastener's' part, a rival he had no idea existed.

Yet the usurper watched and waited.

'Midnight' momentarily lost sight of his target. He released the handbrake and let the car roll forwards until the 'Fastener' appeared again as the front of the vehicle cleared the edge of the high brick walls to either side of the ginnel.

He was aware that his breathing had quickened and that his temples were pounding. Annoyed at himself for the onset of mild panic, he forced himself to take control of his breathing, gripping the edges of the steering wheel and taking deep breaths, exhaling slowly through his nostrils, his eyes never leaving his man.

He could smell himself; he smelled fear in his sweat, tangy and fetid.

'Fastener' walked on and 'Midnight' eased off the handbrake again, careful not to touch the footbrake pedal, which would illuminate the rear brake lights and perhaps give away his presence.

The vehicle rolled forwards a short distance, then stopped as its front tyres gently nudged up against the lip formed by the raised tarmac surface of the street.

Quietly, 'Midnight' slipped the vehicle into first gear, releasing the clutch slowly, noting with a little dissatisfaction that his calf muscle was twitching. He comforted himself with the thought that it was purely the constant pressure of the clutch pedal and nothing to do with his frayed nerves.

The Allegro strained a little as the front tyres made contact with the lip of the road surface. The engine rattled in protest at the lack of fuel. 'Midnight' brushed the accelerator pedal with his toe and the vehicle gently surged forward, allowing him a view of his man again. He was now some two hundred yards up the street, the tails of his coat swaying cloak like from where it draped across his shoulders.

'Midnight' watched and tried to judge the distance. A single rivulet of sweat emerged from beneath his close cropped hair and trickled down the side of his face, he wiped it away quickly with the palm of his hand and was surprised to find that it felt damp against his cheek. He looked at his palms, they glistened even in the darkness of the vehicle. As if they were coated with something vile and disgusting, he grimaced and wiped them quickly along his thighs, the denim material quickly soaking up the moisture.

'Fastener's' lower body had all but disappeared, as the slight curvature of the road surface had reduced his view of the nearside pavement as it fell away below the cambered crown of the road.

'Midnight's' left leg juddered. The calf muscle now in spasm. No pretence at the reason now, he needed to piss badly and his breath came in short, uneven gasps.

He was sweating freely, the fat beads emerging from within his pores at the side of his head and laying glistening tracks as they trickled down onto the collar of his shirt.

'Fastener' hummed softly to himself as he walked, a nameless tune which had slipped into his head from somewhere. Its origins evaded him and he hummed the refrain over and over, trying to remember where he had heard it.

He had considered taking a taxi from outside 'Della's' to Benny's Casino in Town, instead of going straight back home. The wad in his pocket was tempting him, and he felt lucky. He mulled over the idea as he continued to walk. An hour or so at Benny's then back to his crib. He could contact one of his people, get them to run one of his girls up to his place. The McKnight woman would be good. The last time, he recalled, she had been clever with her mouth and tongue and she had convincingly moaned with pleasure, even as he had eased himself into her anus.

'Fastener' nodded to himself, having decided on the evening's entertainment and only fleetingly noticed the lights from a vehicle approaching from his rear.

He noticed his own shadow growing rapidly in length and heard the engine of the oncoming vehicle revving hard and wondered why the driver didn't change gear. The sound of the protesting engine caused him little concern; some youngblood in a stolen vehicle was all.

Now he was on his home turf and enjoying the exhilaration of a high speed jaunt through the streets at someone else's expense. No eerie sirens split the night, 'rasclart' would be hesitant in entering the area after the previous night's abortive raid. Tension indicators would be high and the 'Badlands' would be a 'no go' area for a while.

That had happened before, after the riots in the late seventies. It had been weeks before even the Community Cops had ventured back onto the streets to try to heal the rift.

'Fastener' smiled when he recalled how business had been good. It had flourished in the streets, for the time being, free from the attentions of the Police.

The engine tone grew louder.

'Midnight' reached across and pulled down hard on the seat belt where it crossed his heaving chest. The inertia mechanism locked and he leaned forward into the webbing, keeping it taut against his chest as he wrenched the steering wheel across to the right. His mind was set, set on murder and his rival's death was but a sharp intake of breath way.

He'd mulled the idea over and over in his mind. The information he'd got from Trina had been reliable enough. 'Fastener' had one weakness, he was predictable, too safe in his own skin. A man of set routine was vulnerable and 'Midnight' had capitalized on it.

It would be death by collision.

At best, it would get dealt with by local Traffic Cops. They would deal with it as a fail to stop fatal. Stolen vehicle involved, one fatality. Single black male, known nominal. A 'home goal' in the 'Badlands'.

There'd be an accident report of course, Studio would attend to take photographs and the vehicle examiners would be all over the wreckage looking for defects.

But, that would be for the Coroner and his Inquest. No team of Murder Squad Detectives, no incident room, probably wouldn't even make the papers. Just another nigger drug dealer killed in the 'Badlands'.

The Traffic men would make a show of appealing for witnesses, knowing that their perfunctory efforts would be a waste of time. Knowing equally, that the only time any of the indigenous residents of eleven beat would assist 'Babylon', was when the Detectives from Discipline and Complaints called to take their statements of complaint.

It was murder, with malice aforethought. Even if he was later taken, the law would have to prove it beyond any reasonable doubt. It would be fifteen years if they did and it would be Parkhurst on the Isle, the Scrubs, or Wakefield. No easy time in Holdthorpe this time, not for murder.

If they came for him and *if* they could prove he'd been the driver, he might 'cough' to causing death by reckless, ran from the scene 'cos he'd panicked, didn't know the nigger but knew he was dead. Four years, three if his 'brief' could 'reach out' to the prosecutor. A deal, maybe a guilty plea to driving without due care and attention.

Chance of a lengthy period of disqualification, but no 'down time'.

*****

The front offside tyre of the Allegro exploded with a loud gunshot like rapport as it struck the raised kerb edge at speed. The outer tyre wall fragmented with the immediate increase in pressure and the steel rim screamed momentarily as it first distorted, then collapsed against the hard kerbstone.

The steering was almost wrenched from his hands and 'Midnight' gripped the edges of the strangely square shaped wheel to keep the vehicle on track.

As the wheel rim collapsed against the kerb, the massive forces exerted, tore the lower suspension arm free of its lower wishbone joint. The nearside wheel cranked crazily upwards into the wheelarch, and in the same nanosecond, the thin, pressed metal of the engine's sump pan exploded against the unforgiving kerb, spewing hot black oil onto the flagstones, as the vehicle launched itself up onto the pavement.

It was the gunshot rapport from the bursting tyre which sent a wave of dread coursing through him. Instinctively, 'Fastener' reached for the waistband of his trousers, his fingers fumbling for the grip of the small revolver. Now it dawned on him, it was a 'drive by'...He was being taken down.

'Fastener' started to turn, twisting his head around and following it with his upper body. The shock of seeing the vehicle up on the pavement on which he stood, froze him for a micro second. Forgetting the revolver, he whirled, facing the vehicle.

The sudden realization dawned on him and he held out his arms full length toward the oncoming dazzling headlights, palms facing forwards as if he were capable of halting the screaming vehicle. He filled his lungs to scream.

'Midnight' screwed his eyes tightly shut and braced himself for the inevitable impact. He kept his arms slightly bent at the elbows, knowing that shattered bones in his arms wouldn't serve any useful purpose.

The Allegro's chromium bumper bar struck 'Fastener's' legs below his knees at over sixty feet per second.

The thin flesh of his shins instantly compressed against the thick tibia bones which flexed fractionally before fragmenting. Sharp shards of bone exploded backwards and into the soft calf muscle tissue. The thinner fibulas snapped in the same fraction of a second and the razor sharp stumps tore through his flesh, ripping their way out through the expensive material of his trouser legs as they exited.

His body was bent forwards with the natural momentum of the initial impact, he was as yet, capable of conscious thought. His brain, however, was still unaware of the devastation which had been visited upon his legs, only registering a dull, numbing thud.

The Allegro's speed had been reduced as a result of mounting the pavement and with the initial impact with 'Fastener's' legs, but so fractionally, that it would not be possible to discern with the naked eye, nor was it sufficient to lessen the effect.

As his legs fractured and folded backwards, 'Fastener's' chest smashed down onto the leading edge of the vehicle's bonnet. His sternum shattered, allowing the upper ribs to compress to beyond their tolerance. They were ripped away from their cartilage fibres and stabbed unopposed, down into his plural cavity, through the spongy flesh of his lungs and tearing through the gossamer thin wall of his aorta.

The sharply inhaled air with which 'Fastener' would have screamed, was exhaled at seventy times the normal pressure and carried with it a rich mist of oxygenated blood, which sprayed onto the windscreen.

His fractured breastbone tore into the lower ventricle of his heart. Swollen and racing with the instantaneous flood of adrenalin, it spasmed, fluttered and stopped. 'Fastener's' shoulder struck the base of the windscreen. He died at the same time as the glass bulged dangerously inwards before fracturing.

A myriad of small octagonal particles freed from the inner membrane sprayed needle like back into 'Midnight's' face.

The carnage was as yet unrelenting, even with his death, the collision was not over. 'Fastener's' broken body travelled further up the bonnet of the vehicle. His twisted legs, flailed marionette like as if on hidden strings, as the windscreen pillar slammed into the side of his face, tearing away the cheek muscle, shattering his jaw and pulsing broken tooth particles into the back of his throat.

The Allegro had not escaped; it was damaged just as fatally. It had slammed into the sturdy wall at the far side of the pavement. Instantly, the headlight units exploded, showering the brickwork with powdered glass and miniscule shards of bright reflective coating.

The windscreen which had at first become concave as it had shattered, now with the sudden loss of inertia and with equal opposite force, suddenly became convex and tore itself from its rubber surround and skittered down across the crumpled bonnet.

The concertina'd front grill, compressed the radiator back into the spinning blades, which prior to the collision had provided the engine's source of cooling; now the steel blades ripped mercilessly into the fine honeycombs and the inner core. The coolant, no longer under pressure, burst out through the ruptured vanes of the radiator and boiled immediately, evaporating in a cloud of sweet smelling anti-freeze.

The inertia of the collision with the wall, was returned with deference to Newton's third law and the Allegro rebounded violently backwards, throwing 'Fastener's' body forward and off the crumpled bonnet onto the unforgiving flagstones of the pavement.

'Midnight' opened his eyes, which he had screwed up tightly at the moment of impact. Less than a quarter of a second had elapsed since the front of the Allegro had made contact with 'Fastener's' legs.

As the vehicle lost its momentum, it rolled slowly backwards from the pavement toward the road surface.

'Midnight' fought to release the seat belt which still gripped him vice like across his chest. The engine howled and he realised that he still had his foot hard down on the accelerator pedal. What little lubricating oil remained within the engine, started to boil and without the necessary coolant circulating through water galleries, the inner temperature of the engine rapidly increased.

The pistons within the cylinder walls of the now super-heated block, rapidly expanded. They tightened within the bores and the piston rings shattered. The power plant was failing, compression was lost and smoke, heavily laden with the last of the burned oil, billowed out from the exhaust tail pipe as the engine finally gave out its death rattle.

'Midnight' panted uncontrollably. He fumbled frantically with the seat belt clasp.

After what seemed an eternity and only when he forced himself to relax and sit back in his seat, did the tension release sufficiently so as to allow the belt to shimmy across his body and disappear back into the door frame.

It was done. 'Midnight' heard the blood rush in his ears and the pounding in his temples. His legs were shaking, almost uncontrollably, as the adrenalin which had rushed into his bloodstream now dissipated. His breath came in short rasping gasps as he tore back the handle and shouldered the door open. It howled with a metallic screech of protest against the distorted panels which had been pushed up tight against its forward hinged edge.

He stumbled from the vehicle, instantly smelling the sickly sweetness of the radiator coolant and hot oil. His legs, still unable to hold his body weight, failed him and he fell scrambling to the pavement, feeling the slickness of the hot oil against the palms of his hands and the pinprick stings where the shards of broken glass bit into his skin.

Like a drunkard, he rose unsteadily to his feet. Seconds had passed, yet it seemed like an eternity.

His eyes scanned the area, across the garden, the retaining wall of which he had collided with, to the upstairs windows where he saw that a light had come on, but as yet, no curtains twitched. Across the road to the flats above the fast food take away and the betting shop, another upstairs light and the sound of a casement window shuddering noisily upward.

No cars approached and no footsteps could be heard.

'Midnight' looked quickly across to the motionless body of his victim. He grimaced at the unnatural position of his legs, snapped cleanly at the knees. The glistening white of the exposed bones slicked with blood, showing starkly where they had burst out through the material of his trousers, themselves now darkened where the expensive Italian cloth had become soaked with blood.

His thoughts were of flight, to flee the scene, the job was done, yet his eyes lingered for a second to 'Fastener's' coat, which had been thrown from his shoulders and lay open, exposing the wad of banknotes within the inside pocket.

'Midnight's' eyes widened, as he noted the huge thickness of the wad and his heart raced again as he saw the grip of the small revolver, still trapped tight between the 'Fastener's' trouser belt and his lifeless body.

Voices now, one shouting obscenities at being woken at the early hour, but still a good way off. 'Midnight' glanced left and right. He knelt on the oil spattered pavement, sharp glass particles digging into the denim material covering his knees, as he plundered his victim.

He wrenched at the wad of notes from the inner pocket of the man's coat, feeling the sponginess of the flesh where it was no longer supported by his rib cage. His distaste was eroded by the obvious thickness of the wad which he immediately pushed down the front of his jeans. 'Midnight' hurriedly snatched at the grip of the revolver, pulling it free of 'Fastener's' waistband and without examining it, pushing it forcibly down the back of his own jeans, momentarily feeling the warmth of the chromium plated steel against the skin of his back.

"Now, go, go, get the fuck out, it's done." his senses screamed at him.

More voices now, louder and nearer, yet his eyes fell on the heavy gold watch which still adorned the wrist of his victim.

Just two seconds more.

He flicked open the wrist band clasp with a fingernail and pulled the watch from the wrist, across the twisted broken fingers and grasping it, took to his heels and ran.

*****

Inspector Cawthorne shuffled the thin pile of papers into a rough semblance of order and holding the edges lightly between his fingers, tapped them against the top of the charge desk, before placing the neatened bundle in front of him. Alan and his crew mate stood with their backs against the wall by the inner door. There was just the clerical to organise now, the fun part was over, they were bored. It was time for coffee and a smoke.

Charlie nudged Alan's elbow and smiling, nodded toward the vast expanse of Tina's backside as she stood facing the charge desk in front of them. The material of her leggings was stretched taut to contain the mass of her arse cheeks which seemed to commence from somewhere in the middle of her back. They had clearly stretched to their maximum tolerance and the outline of her knickers showed white between the weave. Alan mimed a vomiting motion and the Sergeant looked across to them reprovingly, but allowed the hint of a smile to play around the edges of his mouth.

Mr Cawthorne coughed to clear his throat and directed his gaze toward his charge.

"Tina Lofthouse, you are charged that you did without lawful excuse, destroy or damage property belonging to another, intending to destroy or damage any such property or were reckless as to whether any such property would be destroyed. That's contrary to section one of the criminal damage act of nineteen seventy one."

Pen poised, he waited expectantly for a response, an enquiring look about his face.

"Worrabout Eddie?" she asked.

"Mister...? The Inspector paused and looked enquiringly across to his Sergeant.

"Rawlinson boss."

"Ah yes...Unfortunately, Mister Rawlinson will be detained until he provides a negative breath test. He will then be charged, but unlike you Miss Lofthouse, I'm afraid that Mister Rawlinson will not be granted bail. He will be staying with us."

Her huge shoulders drooped. "Ow long? yer can't just fuckin' keep 'im." she howled.

"I'm afraid that is most certainly the case Miss Lofthouse…Any response to the charge before we touch on the subject of your bail?...And take heed before you impawn our person, how you awake our sleeping sword of wa…"

"Yeah, I fuckin' 'ave." Tina shouted. "I want 'er doin' for assault."

Tina pointed vexatiously at Matron, who lounged unconcernedly in one of the threadbare swivel chairs at the rear of the charge area, not even bothering to look up from her copy of 'Woman' magazine.

"Methink'st thou art a general offence and every man should beat thee." Mr Cawthorne quoted gleefully.

The suffering Sergeant Makepeace, was growing weary of his Inspector's theatrical rantings and shook his head in desperation. The month previous, it had been Ayckbourne. No doubt Pinter or Orton would get an airing at some stage in the future. Best just to let it ride itself out, but there was no point in winding prisoners up, sooner or later there'd be a complaint.

Tina looked genuinely shocked. "What the fu…"

"Miss Lofthouse." Sergeant Makepeace quickly interceded. "You need to sign here for your bail."

The telephone on the charge desk rang; the handset was casually picked up by the Inspector.

"Bridewell, Inspector Cawthorne."

Alan could just hear the muted metallic voice echoing through the black plastic of the earpiece.

"They are indeed." Mr Cawthorne said, nodding as if the caller could see as well as hear him. "Just one moment." He held the handset out over the top of the charge desk and looked directly toward Alan and Charlie.

"The good operator at Force Control would have converse with either of thee."

Alan glanced across at his crew mate, then lurched himself from the wall and took the handset.

"Pc Pendle."

"Crew of Papa Yankee One Four?"

"'firmative."

"Division are requesting assistance with a 10/9 on eleven beat, Melville Road. Single vehicle versus pedestrian. It looks to have proved, Studio and AIB are en route."

Alan glanced at his watch and sighed; he covered the mouthpiece of the handset with the palm of his hand and looked across to his crew mate, who stood with an apprehensive look about his face.

"Fatal running in the Melvilles Charlie."

Charlie looked despondent. He looked across to the clock on the charge room wall and slumped. "Bollocks! we'll be on duty all day as well…"

Alan returned his attention to the caller. "One Four. Roger that, can you ensure that the Divisional Inspector of the day is aware and that we've got some uniformed support, given last night's incident on eleven beat."

"That's received One Four. I'll note your request on the log. What's your eta?"

Alan put his hand back across the mouthpiece and looked across to the Inspector.

"Mr Cawthorne. Can we be released? There's a 10/9 running. Division wants Traffic."

"Then get thee henceforth from this place and be about your lawful occasion gentlemen." the Inspector said and nodded.

Sergeant Makepeace reached across the charge desk and pressed the door release button.

"Be five minutes. Travelling time from the Bridewell." Alan advised the control room operator and offered the handset back to the Inspector.

There was resonant buzzing and a sharp click as Charlie pulled at the inner door handle.

Alan grabbed for his cap and stuffed his green notebook back into the top pocket of his jacket.

"Could you charge silly bollocks for us Sarge and send the paperwork up to Moorwood?" Sergeant Makepeace sighed resignedly and gave a single sullen nod.

Alan and his crew mate turned to walk briskly up the corridor toward the outer door.

*****

Alan sucked the fresh air deep into his lungs as he walked across the frontage of the Town Hall to where he had left the patroller. It tasted crisp and clean after the thick, overbearing urine and disinfectant laden atmosphere of the Bridewell.

"Fancy pushing for a while Charlie?" Alan asked, reaching into the pocket of his jacket for the car keys. Charlie nodded and deftly caught the bunch of keys as Alan tossed them over the roof of the Rover.

Alan reached for the radio handset as he flopped down into the passenger seat, instinctively reaching for his seatbelt clasp as he keyed the handset.

"Papa Yankee One Four."

"One Four." the operator replied immediately.

"We are 10/16 from the Bridewell and en route to the 10/9. Any further details? Over."

There was a brief pause as the operator searched through the incident log and Alan winced as his crew mate started the patrol car and immediately revved the cold engine which rattled in protest.

"Your patroller's fucked Al, time you got rid." Charlie said, as he dipped the clutch pedal and wrenched the gear lever across to engage reverse.

As the revs died off a little, the synchromesh finally surrendered to Charlie's lack of vehicle sympathy. With a worrying grinding noise followed by a sharp reluctant clunk, his crew mate reversed the Rover across the frontage.

"Hundred and eighteen thousand on the clock! Christ mate, time you 'ad a Granada 28, ours would show this old boat the way to go home."

Alan winced again as the gearbox again protested at Charlie's demand for a forward gear whilst the vehicle was still reversing.

"Easy Charlie." Alan said, with just sufficient dissension in his tone to let his crew mate know that he wasn't impressed with his system of car control.

"This is a three and a half V8 Charlie. None of your V6 'Cologne' shit. It's just nicely run in. She'll still touch one thirty five with a following wind, your two eight will do what…120?"

"Papa Yankee One Four." the radio operator interrupted. Alan depressed the transmit paddle on the handset. "One Four go."

"From the log which is 28 of today…The caller…unidentified via 999, reported one vehicle at the scene. Described as a small brown saloon, no number available at that time. Log further states…Hotel Bravo Two arrives…10/17 on Charlie Bravo Whiskey Eight Eight Three Victor…shows previous keeper informed DVLA no longer the keeper…that was in February last…Hotel Bravo Two reports further…Vehicle appears to be stolen, pedestrian still at scene, appears to have proved…Requests Traffic…Ambulance is en route as are beat Supervision."

"Received. Show us attending on the log please."

Alan dropped the handset back into its cradle and settled himself into his seat as his crew mate dropped down onto the inner Ring Road and accelerated hard toward the 'Badlands'.

\*\*\*\*\*

An ambulance and a single beat patrol car, both positioned at acute angles across the road with their blue lights flashing identified the scene; Alan reached across for the radio handset.

"Papa Yankee One Four, 10/6 Melville Road. Ambulance is in attendance. Any news on Studio yet?"

"One Four, he's still at a burglary on nine beat. He is aware, you're next on his list over."

"Roger that."

Alan walked across to where one of the beat patrol Officers was standing facing the Allegro, which had rolled partially back onto the road surface. Charlie busied himself removing cones from the boot of their patrol car.

The uniformed patrol Officer turned as Alan approached. He nodded a greeting, thumbing the button on the top of his 'Burndept'.

"Traffic's arrived John. We'll hang around for a bit, there's a bit of a crowd gathered but nothing to write home about."

Alan stood motionless, surveying the scene with a practiced eye.

The two crew members from the ambulance were waiting on the pavement to the side of what was clearly the deceased, a blanket from the boot of the panda had been thrown hastily over the body. Alan saw that the blanket had been pulled fully up so that the victim's face had been completely covered which was never a good sign. He noted the river of congealed blood emanating from beneath the folds of the blanket. It pooled out over the pavement to where it dripped, viscous in globules over the kerb edge and onto the street, mixing with the oil and brackish brown coolant from the fractured radiator.

Only the driver's door of the Allegro was open, single occupant then he thought, knowing from experience that joy riders rarely stopped to close doors after dumping their stolen motors.

"What do we know?" Alan asked the beat Officer, who now sauntered up to where Alan stood in the center of the road still taking in the scene.

"Seems somebody killed Huggy Bear mate." he said glibly, pointing to the upturned, wide brimmed fedora lying on the pavement. "Glad you boys are here, I've got a lock up to deal with. Ok if we get off?"

"Any witnesses?" Alan asked, nodding toward the small group of onlookers gathered on the pavement.

"Joking aren't you." His colleague from beat patrol snorted, casting his gaze toward the onlookers. "Hookers, dealers and pimps…apart from old Miss Kizzy there in the Oxfam dressing gown."

"Your Supervision turning up?" Alan asked.

"Bob Allinson's on his way, but don't hold yer breath, he was at a domestic so your guess at an eta is as good as mine. Look, if there's nothing else you need us for…" the beat man said expectantly.

"No…Thanks for turning up." Alan said and then with an afterthought, asked. "How long after the call did you arrive?"

The beat man dug out his green supplementary notebook. He flicked through the dog eared pages. "We got it at three thirty seven from the control room and…we went 10/6 at three fifty four."

Alan did a quick mental calculation. "Seventeen minutes." he muttered to himself as he surveyed the group of seven or eight people, who out of morbid curiosity, had come to view the carnage.

His beat colleague was right, mostly working girls and a few youngbloods, but no colours to be seen.

"All this lot already here when you arrived?" Alan asked, nodding toward the onlookers.

The beat Officer nodded. "Yeah, in fact, I think a few more have turned up since. Boredom must be a wonderful thing. Or business isn't so good eh."

Alan noticed Evie standing to the front of the group; she acknowledged his glance with an almost indiscernible nod.

"What's happening Officer?" one of the ambulance crew called out impatiently.

Alan looked back as he walked toward the group of sightseers. "Two minutes, I'll be with you."

He made an issue of moving the gathered group further back from the scene, holding his arms out wide, he began ushering them away. "Come on, nothing to see here. Can we have you all back a bit."

Evie made a point of refusing to move, standing her ground defiantly and as Alan gently touched her on the shoulder with the tips of his fingers, she hissed loudly for effect. "Who you be pushin' motherfucker?"

Alan quickly withdrew his hand and raised it apologetically. "We just want some room to be able to do our job that's all. Just move back a little, unless of course you want to be in the photographs." Alan nodded toward the plain white Studio van which was approaching.

At the prospect of having their images captured on official Police photographs, a number of the small group quickly backed off, mouthing the usual expected obscenities.

In an instant, as the others turned away, Evie leaned forwards, her lips almost brushing against Alan's ear. "Fastener be down." she whispered, before making a further show of reluctance at being moved along by the law.

"Awright, motherfucker, don't be touchin' the goods an' shit." she shouted loudly, before slouching away up the street, along with the rest of the gathered motley group.

Alan took out his green notebook and hurriedly scribbled a note as he walked up to the waiting ambulance.

Charlie he noted, had started preparing a sketch plan of the scene and had marked the position of the four wheels of the Allegro in bright yellow crayon.

"Sorry 'bout the wait." Alan said to the waiting ambulance crew, as he took out his pen.

The ambulance man pulled away the blanket as his partner completed paperwork on a clipboard; Alan winced at the sight of the man's injuries. Even after attending so many fatals, the damage caused to the human body as a result of traumatic contact with motor vehicles, still shocked him.

The ambulance man continued in a droning monotone voice. "Black male, late thirties, perhaps early forties. Massive, complicated fractures to both legs, tibia and fibula, full exit through soft tissue, which also appears, due to the amount of exsanguination present, to have also disrupted the anterior tibial and posterior tibial arteries. There also looks…"

"Whoa…hang on mate." Alan said, scribbling in his notebook desperately. "Like you'd talk to an eight year old, eh?"

The ambulance man smiled. "Ok, both his legs are broken, the bones have come through the back of his legs and torn through his arteries and major blood vessels on the way out. Looks like he bled to death. His chest cavity is seriously compressed, looks like his ribs have caved all the way in, probably punctured his lungs. His neck is distorted, probably broken and there are no vital signs. Life is extinct."

Alan glanced at his watch and noted the time of pronouncement in his green notebook. "Could I take your name please, just for my report?" Alan asked.

The ambulance man nodded. "Van Buran…Jonathan. I'm the technician, my colleague there is Susan Pellows. He'll be going to the mortuary at the Infirmary. You dealing?"

Alan nodded, "Seems so." looking back to where Charlie was still busying himself with the sketch plan, "Nothing on him, no ID?" Alan asked.

The ambulance man pursed his lips and shook his head. "No wallet. Nothing I'm afraid."

"Ok with you if I sign him for continuity. His face is trashed?" Alan asked.

The ambulance man shrugged disinterestedly. "Yeah, not a problem."

Alan knelt and tentatively lifted one of the dead man's hands, turning it gently by the fingers, so that the palm was face up. The fingers felt cool and strangely waxy and Alan hurriedly scrawled his collar number across the center of the palm and carefully laid it back. He would have to identify the body to the Coroner's Officer as being the same one that he had seen at the scene of the collision.

"He's not wearing any shoes." Alan said, looking puzzled.

The technician shrugged again.

"Pulled clean out of them during the bump?" Alan said, more to himself than the hovering technician.

Again the technician shrugged. "That would be your area of expertise I reckon. We certainly haven't removed any."

Alan scanned the immediate scene. Standing, he walked all the way around the Allegro. He knelt to peer beneath the floor pan...nothing.

"Charlie" he called out. "You seen any shoes?"

His crew mate looked up from his drawing and shook his head. "Why...what's up?"

"Our man's not wearing any." Alan replied, a puzzled tone in his voice.

Unbeknown to Alan, the expensive Italian shoes were missing because well before the Police had been called, the jackals had been at the cadaver. The shoes had gone the same way as the gold identity bracelet and the heavy gold rings, which 'Midnight' in his panic had not had time to take. The genuine snake skin belt with its solid silver buckle, had been undone and whipped out through the trouser loops and squirelled away with equal dexterity.

"Good to take him now?" the technician asked.

Alan nodded, then called out to his crew mate. "Charlie…just chalk his position head and foot before he disappears would you."

A collapsible steel gurney was rattled out from the rear of the ambulance and the technician and his partner collapsed it, before lifting the victim from the pavement.

"Do you want the blanket back?"

Alan shook his head and grimaced. "It's had it mate. Can you chuck it in contaminated for us?"

"Can do…Ready Susan?" His crew mate called out to his partner.

"Thanks for that." Alan said, as the technician and his crew mate wheeled the gurney back toward the rear of the ambulance.

Alan stood and gazed at the scene. The road surface, the collapsed front offside wheel and the twisted ignition wires. He rubbed his chin with his fingertips, feeling the uncomfortable stubble as he soaked in all the information which a crash scene would offer, to those who knew where to look and what to look for.

The Studio man approached holding his camera and tripod. "Am I good to get on now Officer, I've three other jobs to go to."

Alan pondered the scene for a moment. He felt uneasy, something not quite right. "Yes, look…er, could you get shots of the ignition barrel and dust the interior for prints. It's a knock off…Also, I want to roll the car back so that you can photograph the complete tread pattern of the front tyres. Both if you will."

The Studio man sighed dejectedly. "It's a straight pedestrian knock down isn't it? That's what I have on my request form. Anyway, if it's stolen, it can be printed later. I'd normally only take images of the immediate scene and the position of the vehicle. We don't nor…"

Alan interrupted the Studio man's flow. "Look, I'm not trying to tell you how to do your job mate, but I'm the Officer in the case. At a fatal, that makes me the Coroner's Officer and I want the scene and the vehicle properly examined. Oh...and there's a tool roll on the back seat, I'd like that tagged, bagged...and printed...ok?"

The Studio man threw up his arms in despair, then busied himself setting up his equipment.

Charlie walked over and put a calming hand on Alan's shoulder.

"Wassup, mate?"

Alan took hold of Charlie's arm and led him to the far side of the vehicle, out of the hearing range of the disgruntled Studio man, who muttered to himself whilst extending the telescopic legs of his tripod.

"Charlie. Stop a minute, take a look...What's wrong with this picture?"

His crew mate looked puzzled. "It's a knock down Al, driver of stolen motor loses control whilst tearing the arse off it, ends up on the pavement and...Leroy there just happens to be in the wrong place at the wrong time...I don't see the problem."

Alan shook his head. "No...Come on Charlie..think. When's the last time any of the youngbloods on eleven beat stole a fucking Austin Allegro for Christ's sake, and look..." Alan pointed into the vehicle and the conjoined wiring protruding from the base of the steering column. "Whoever nicked this motor didn't know how to 'box' an ignition. He ripped the whole thing apart to get at the wiring, why?...'Cos that's how *he* remembers how to do it. How many 'twocers' do you know would know how to hot wire a motor Charlie? Our man is old school, I bet he's in his late twenties or even thirties. He wanted that motor for a purpose, not to go cruising around in. Where's the street 'cred' in being seen in a shitbox Allegro? You can't even do doughnuts 'cos it's front wheel drive."

Charlie mused for a while and scratched at his nose.

"Look." Alan made a sweeping gesture across the scene with his hands. "Where's the skid marks....there aren't any mate, why?...'Cos there was no braking that's why. That vehicle was under hard acceleration, it's still in first gear. Look how the tyre and wheel rim have been destroyed, it was steered up onto the pavement Charlie, at speed, on purpose..."

"Whoa...hang on Al..."

"No...Charlie, I'm telling you mate. Look...Think back to any of the chases you've been in where the thieving little shit has finally lost control. What's the last thing they do before the motor runs off the road, or ploughs into a tree or a wall?...What's the last thing you always get to see?...Brakelights, 'cos even a 'twocer' with the I.Q. of a rockin' horse can't help it. It's an unconscious act Charlie, self-preservation. You know you're gonna stuff it an' it's probably gonna hurt, so you hit the brakes...So where's the skid marks?"

Charlie pondered for a moment. "Yeah. you're right but, same thing would apply if the driver had say...passed out through drink or drugs. His foot would stay on the accelerator and the motor might naturally swerve onto the pavement...same result. Uncle Tom was just unlucky to be there when it did."

"So where is he then, this unconscious driver of yours?"

"Came round again after the bump, saw what had 'appened and legged it."

Alan smiled and shook his head slowly.

Charlie smirked. "It's as plausible as your murder on Melville Road theory Al."

"You don't just pass out Charlie...It's not instantaneous, unless you have a massive stroke, or a brain seizure or something. In which case, I suspect that legging it after the bump wouldn't be on the cards. An' if he was so pissed he fell asleep at the wheel, his seat belt would have slowly run out with his forward body weight and he'd have trashed his face on the steering wheel.

There'd be blood at least…and look at this." Alan reached into the car and slowly pulled the seat belt out to its full extent.

"Where's the stretch mark? If a driver brakes hard or when a vehicle collides with something solid, the belt will run out for at least an inch or so before the inertia gear kicks in and locks it solid and that's what causes the stretch mark. It's where the weave in the webbing separates slightly because of the sudden jerk. None to be seen here Charlie and that's 'cos our man locked the inertia first to protect himself. He knew he was going to stuff it, so he pre-tensioned it. He froze the belt first Charlie."

"AIB course?" Charlie asked, suitably impressed.

"AIB course." Alan nodded.

Charlie was silent for a while as if considering Alan's explanation. The VHF radio cackling from within their patrol car, broke the silence.

"Papa Yankee One Four."

As Alan walked back to the patrol car, Charlie called after him. "Oi! Al. Never mind the bump, did you see the tits on that ambulance driver?..faaaackin' 'ell."

Alan opened the passenger door and reached for the handset.

"Papa Yankee One Four, go ahead."

"Any update from the scene over?"

Charlie whistled through his teeth, Alan looked back to see a panda approaching. Charlie held three fingers across the upper arm of his yellow jacket, warning him of the imminent arrival of the beat Sergeant.

"One Four. Life extinct pronounced at the scene. Deceased has been removed by ambulance to the Infirmary. Pc 868 will provide continuity to the Coroners Officer. 868 Moorwood Road Traffic will be dealing. Studio is on scene, still no sign of AIB but…I think beat Supervision has just turned up."

"One Four thanks for that. What do you want to do about recovery for the vehicle…and can you confirm the registered number?"

"'firmative. As per your previous. It appears to be stolen…Further, if you could get Nolan's out to do the recovery and make sure that they are aware that to preserve evidence. I want the vehicle recovered with a webbing hoist lift, not dragged onto the back of a flat bed with chains, also, that it should be kept under cover."

"Roger that One Four…Further, there is a note on the log from Mr Samuelson. He is the on-call AIB Officer. He states, will not be turning out to attend at the scene of a pedestrian knock down unless there is a likelihood that evidence will be lost. Usual thing, vehicle will be examined for defects at garage tasked with recovery and scene to be later visited if necessary."

Alan scratched the side of his head with the edge of the handset. "Scared shitless at the thought of attending to a job on eleven beat you mean." he thought.

"One Four received. In that case, can you contact the Council and get street cleansing out for me, the pavement is heavily contaminated, I'll say no more."

"Understood One Four."

Alan checked the handset back into its holder and closed the patrol car door.

*****

"Midnight' heaved himself from the floor where he had been sitting with his back against the door whilst he waited for his breathing to return to normal. The trip hammer pounding in his chest slowly subsided and after taking a final deep breath, he stood and walked to the window. He slipped his middle finger between the gap in the curtains and cautiously parted them. The streets below were quiet, normal. No Police cars skidding to a stop outside his crib, no torch beams arcing through the darkness or Police dogs barking wildly, as they conducted a search for him. He let the curtain fall back into place and sucked in a deep lungful of air.

Crossing to his bed, he picked up the small revolver. It was still warm from where it had laid against his flesh. Even in the dim light, the burnished chromium plated steel reflected, but distorted his facial features.

His fingers moved purposefully around the grip, feeling how they fell pleasingly and automatically into place. He twisted his hand from side to side, inspecting the small handgun from all angles as he sat on the side of the bed.

As if of lesser importance for the moment, he pushed the thick wad of banknotes and the watch casually to one side; he was fascinated and captivated by the sheer feel and presence of the gun.

'Midnight' ran a finger along the length of its barrel and up over the ribbing on the short raised foresight. His finger nail etched slowly across the lettering engraved into the side of the barrel. 'Smith and Wesson'.

Holding the gun in both hands, he carefully pushed the knurled chamber release on the left hand side of the frame forward. The chamber dropped smoothly open and 'Midnight' was presented with a perfect concentric circle of ten small brass cap ends. He had fully expected the revolver to have been empty and his heart skipped a beat.

He inspected the workings of the chamber and pushed the spring loaded release rod, which ran out from its center. The ten rounds were raised from within their chamber housings, held in place by the beautifully machined breach claw.

'Midnight' tipped the revolver backwards and the ten small bullets tumbled out onto the blanket covering his bed. He carefully placed the open revolver down and inspected the bullets, scooping them up into the palm of his hand, noting how the dull grey tips contrasted with the bright sheen of the brass casings.

He knew enough about guns to know that if the bullets had been fired, the end caps would have a small telltale indentation either in the center, or around the rim edge where the firing pin had struck. All the bullets were flawless and 'Midnight' nodded slowly. He smiled to himself as he carefully, one by one, replaced the bullets back within the chamber and closed it.

The wad of notes he estimated to be at least three inches thick. Tens and twenties for the most part. 'Midnight' whistled slowly through his teeth. Cocaine and heroin were the money makers sure enough. There were a few five pound notes and he guessed that these would have changed hands for the small bags of cannabis bush or small blocks of the dark resin. Even so, there must be three or four grand, not bad for a weekend's takings.

The watch which he had fumbled from the 'Fastener's' wrist had been his last consideration. Sheer greed, it had been the money which had first caught his eye. The revolver had been a bonus, a secondary prize. Taking the watch had been an afterthought, its theft a final degrading act after the brutal killing.

He lifted it from the blanket and weighed it in the palm of his hand. It was heavy. The dim light from the naked bulb hanging from his ceiling, danced across the thick links and was reflected in the luster of the dull gold. 'Midnight' identified the famous five pronged crown above the Rolex logo on the upper part of its face, but in the dim light, he could not quite make out the model name. He stood up and tilted the face so that it was nearer to the light bulb. Now he could make out the word 'Perpetual' beneath the Rolex trademark and beneath the center bezel, 'Submariner'.

"The man had style, give him that." 'Midnight' muttered to himself.

He accepted that the watch would have to go, much as he would have loved to keep it.

Although 'Midnight' was unaware that 'Fastener's' body had been hastily searched and stripped of anything of value and stolen before the Police had even been called, he knew that the watch would be readily identified by those who had known or worked for him. Keeping it, flaunting it on his wrist, much as it was tempting, would identify him as having been at the scene at least, or worse, actually involved in the murder.

Again he moved to the window and parted the curtain; the streets were still quiet, even the hookers had given it up for the night. Fatigue swept over him and his chest and shoulders ached where the seatbelt had snatched. He crossed to the bed, gathering up the money and the watch, he opened the drawer of his bedside table and placed them carefully inside. The cash he would enjoy counting later. He was unsure what to do with the watch, but the revolver he would keep.

'Midnight' eased himself down onto his bed, wincing at the sharp stabbing pain which arced across his right shoulder. Still holding the grip of the revolver lightly, he felt remorseless sleep washing over him.

*****

"Yer can't have WANK Derek."

"Course I can, it's an adjective."

"'How do you make that out?"

"It's descriptive, describes working nights…an' it's on a double word score."

The radio operator shook his head in disbelief. Alan stood behind the clerk from the front office and peered down at the battered Scrabble board which sat on the desk between them.

"Walk Del."

The Clerk looked up. "What?"

"You've got an L. Put WALK instead." Alan offered.

The Clerk thought for a moment, then smiled and substituted the letter. "'Appy now?" he looked across at his opponent and grinned inanely. "Eleven on a double word score, is…twenty two to me…Cheers Al."

"What's the score with the fatal in the 'Badlands' Al?" The radio operator asked.

"It's…complicated John. Who's the night D.C.?

The radio operator reached across for the duties and disposition board and glanced across at the clerk.

"Derek...for fucks sake! You don't take four, you only laid three down. The K was already there...and you don't look at them before you pick up. Jesus, it's like playing with a four year old."

Alan looked down at the board. "I can see from the plethora of single syllable words that tonight's effort hasn't been particularly taxing...Oh, and I don't think you'll find ARSE in the dictionary Del."

"What makes you think that was me?" the clerk asked enquiringly, looking up over his shoulder whilst jealously guarding his strip of pale yellow tiles with the palm of his hand.

"Just a wild guess Derek." Alan said sarcastically and smiled across to the radio man.

"It's Bernie Foster Al. Why what's up?"

"Just want a word, 'bout the bump on eleven. Got a number?"

"Yeah, but 'e won't be there. At this time of the morning 'e'll be over at Millbeck...try extension 5037."

"Something else running?" Alan asked.

"Nah, Fiona Pickard's on nights in the front office...need I say more? The radio operator said, tossing the clipboard back onto the desk and scowling at his opponent. "Oi! it's my fucking go Derek...an' you can't have TWAT anyway."

Alan shook his head. He left the radio room and walked down the corridor, passed the deserted front office. He laughed as their voices faded.

"It's a pregnant fish."

"Is it bollocks!"

*****

Alan yawned as he entered the Traffic Office. He felt lethargic and flopped down into one of the swivel chairs. His eyelids felt heavy and there was an unpleasant coppery, taste in his mouth. It had been a long week. Charlie was seated behind the Sergeant's desk, putting the final touches to his sketch plan; he paused and looked up pensively.

"Been to see the Inspector?"

Alan shook his head and reached for the telephone.

Charlie help up a cautionary hand. "Whoa…Al, tell me you're not considerin' puttin' pen to paper with your murder in the 'Badlands' theory."

Alan shook his head. "Just going to have a word with the night D.C., its Bernie Foster. Apparently, he's in at Millbeck doing his best to get inside Fiona Pickard's pants."

Charlie raised a cautionary eyebrow. "Before you share your personal 'grassy knoll' theory with anyone outside this office Al, have you considered what the reaction will be from the senior management team. If you put pen to paper, the D.I. will have your balls off with a rusty spoon. An undetectable murder instead of a pedestrian knock down?"

"Who says it's undetectable?" Alan said defensively.

"Leave it out Al." Charlie's tone was slightly aggressive and Alan was slightly taken aback. It obviously showed and Charlie softened his attitude. "Alright…alright. Look mate, all I'm sayin' is, your theory's plausible. I'm not sayin' it isn't, but that's all it is. You know what they're like over monthly crime figures, if you officially record it as a non-accident…"

"Murder Charlie. That's what it's called when you run somebody over and kill them on purpose."

Charlie became agitated and sighed in exasperation. "You even hint to the Coroner in your report that it might be an unlawful killing and the shit will hit the fan that's all. If it turns out it was just some piss artist…"

"It's on me Charlie, you don't have to sign up to it. I know you're on a 'tick' for promotion an…"

Charlie tossed his pen onto the table top and leaned purposefully back in his seat. "Its fuck all to do with that

Al...Traffic's not exactly top of the Divisional Commander's popularity poll an' rackin' up his crime stats with another murder..." He shrugged and raised his eyebrows suggestively, intimating some form of disastrous outcome. Alan considered his crew mate's advice. His fingers tapped out a random beat on the telephone handset which lay expectantly on its cradle.

"Think about your firearms course Al. How long've you waited, a year, eighteen months?" Charlie threw in casually, hoping to sway his crew mate from being the harbinger of a plague of frogs/boils/locusts being visited upon the Traffic Department.

Alan looked across to where Charlie sat, eyebrows still raised pensively.

"Shit rolls downhill mate, you of all people know that. You've less than a week to wait, why make waves for Christ's sake. I wouldn't put it passed the bastards to take you off it...due to an unforeseen lack of divisional resources." Charlie said, imitating the dry tones of the shift Inspector. "Mate...go down the mortuary. Do the I.D. to the Corner's Officer whoever he is, I'll do a quick report for the Chief's log, enquiries and investigations are still ongoin' etc. By the time we've had our days off and you've been on yer course, it'll have been filed...job's a good'un. Nobody gives a fuck 'bout some nigger pimp run over in the 'Badlands' anyway mate." Charlie stood up, happy that he had steered Alan back to the paths of righteousness. "I'll make a brew eh?" He patted Alan's shoulder as he picked up two mugs from the table top and disappeared from the office.

*****

"Millbeck, Pc Pickard."

"Fiona, its Alan Pendle Moorwood Traffic. Is Bernie Foster about?"

"Hang on a sec."

Alan unconsciously tapped his fingers against the table top as he waited. He could hear a muted voice repeating his name and the sound of a chair scraping against the floor surface as it was pushed backwards.

"D.C. Foster."

"Bernie, its Al Pendle, Traffic at Moorwood."

"Alright Alan. What can I do for you?"

"I was hoping you might be able to tell me something about a black male, resident of our eleven beat, goes by the street name 'Fastener'."

"Mmm." There was a short pause, "That would be one Abby Zippleman. I think its Abdiel, some Hebrew shit or something, you'll have to check. He's on on PNC and local, one of our most wanted. He's a dealer. Pimp, big time. Excellent catch mate, what's he in for?"

"Road collision in the Melville's."

"Can't be your man then, Zippleman doesn't drive, never has, well known for it."

"He doesn't walk too well now either." Alan said matter of factly.

The Detective's tone softened. "Look, er…If you have got Zippleman in, I wouldn't mind assisting…get my name on the charge sheet, second jockey if you like."

Alan frowned. He had been pleasantly surprised to find the night Detective actually sober and now he was puzzled by the sudden and uncommon interest shown once he had mentioned the name 'Fastener'. Alan considered that this Zippleman must be some sort of high value 'nominal', which only reinforced Alan's suspicions that the collision had been part of a turf war thing. Retaliation maybe, some sort of drugs deal gone bad.

"I'd be grateful for any assistance you might be able to come up with Bernie."

Alan heard the chair scrape against the floor again. Clearly the Detectives feet had now come off the table top and he was scrambling to find a pen and a scrap piece of paper.

"No problem. Is he fit for interview?"

"Look Bernie, he might even test *your* interview skills a bit...he's not saying much. The fact is mate..." Alan heard the Detective chortle.

"Crackin' the silent routine is my trademark mate. I was three years on th..."

"Bernie." Alan quickly interrupted. "I...er, might have misled you slightly. He's not saying much...'cos he's dead."

There was a long, pregnant pause. "I don't assist with fatals mate. That's your department isn't it?"

Alan sighed. "Look Bernie, I wouldn't be ringing you if it was a straight fatal. This "Fastener bloke, Zippler or whatever..."

The night Detective abruptly cut him short. "If it's an accident, it's yours mate, end of..."

"Hold on a sec' Bernie." Alan persisted. "That's my point. An accident is defined as being an unforeseen series of events having an adverse effect on persons or property."

Alan could hear the Detective sighing dejectedly into the mouthpiece. "It's a little early for a lecture on traffic law, I'm sure it's all very interesting to you shiny arsed petrol wasters, but I'm tired and all of a sudden, experiencing a very low bullshit tolerance level so..."

Alan butted in. "The adverse inference bit is real enough Bernie...it's the unforeseen part I'm struggling with. This 'Fastener'' bloke...I think it's a murder."

## Nineteen

Alan reached across and pressed the mute button on the television remote and heaved himself up from the settee, his coffee mug left precariously on the armrest as he loped across to the telephone. He quickly lifted the handset to silence the annoying warbling and taking a deep breath, rubbed his face with his free hand to waken himself.

"Hello."

"Oi!..Rearrange this famous phrase or saying…Pidgeon, amongst, in, cat, thrown."

Alan instantly recognised his Sergeant's gravelly voice and instinctively glanced across to the clock above the fireplace. 10.03.

"Hey Sarge, I'm guessing this is about the fatal…"

"You guess right in a manner of speaking. Actually…I was wonderin' if you 'ad a large stockpile of 'Sudocrem', My arsehole feels like the openin' sequence to Bonanza after the reamin' it's just 'ad from Divisional Chief Inspector 'praise the lord' Forrester who by the way, requests your attendance in his office at noon. Your accident report has made its way to 'is desk and is the cause of some concern. Best get in early Al, I'll see you before we go in."

"We?" Alan asked, puzzled.

"Oh yes, we are both summonsed. I'm there, presumably to hold your arse cheeks apart whilst the good Chief Inspector shows you some love as well. It would be considered to be good manners, and might be a good idea to bring some condoms. I use the plural, 'cos I 'spect D.S. Mitchell may also want a piece of your arse."

Alan could hear his Sergeant sucking repeatedly on his cigar which had presumably gone out. There was a short pause and the sound of a faint click from his lighter. "Read your report…quite compelling stuff. Good bit of deductive investigation Al, not that it'll count for fuck all…Needless to say, it's not gone down very well an' I'm guessin' you don't need me to tell you why. Apparently Bernie Foster rang his D.S. at five in the mornin' to warn 'im that some Moorwood Traffic man had lost the plot and was goin' to crime a bump as murder."

Alan sighed. "I only wanted a bit of 'intel' about the victim."

"Thought there was no I.D." his Sergeant said.

"There isn't really Sarge. I saw this hooker I know called Evie, she was at the scene an…"

"Whoa… whoa. You saw a hooker you *know*?"

Alan sighed resignedly, realising how it had sounded. "When I say *know* Sarge, it's a professional thing, I get…"

His Sergeant butted in. "I'd rather not know Al. What you get up to on yer days off is up to you, don't get caught is all."

"I was going to say…" Alan continued. "Is that I get the odd snippet of information from her, she's old school, good as gold Sarge…As long as Vice cuts her a little slack in return. Anyway, she drops the name 'Fastener', covert like. I just wanted to know who he was, being as how he didn't have so much as a library card on him…Trust Fozzie to cover his arse."

"Never trust a fuckin' Detective Al, 'ow many times do I 'ave to tell you?"

"Yeah…well." Alan said knowingly.

His Sergeant paused…" I noticed on the report, that Charlie's name was conspicuous by its absence…'is sketch plan wasn't bad though."

"Charlie doesn't subscribe to my criminal intent theory and to be fair, he did warn me off."

His Sergeant interrupted him. "Look Alan, yer deductions were sound enough an' at the end of the day, yer entitled to yer opinion as the Officer in the case. You wrote it up as you saw it."

"What's your thoughts on it Sarge?" Alan asked pensively.

"'Avn't got any. I'm only a twenty nine year Traffic Sergeant after all, and as I was succinctly reminded by the good Chief Inspector this morning, I'm not paid to think. I signed your report and added that you were an experienced collision investigator and that the evidence from the scene tended to support your conclusions…They just don't want to hear it Alan. Anyway, forewarned is forearmed as they say. See you at about half eleven. Its not as if you were doin' anything else on yer day off, other than engagin' in furious self-abuse eh?"

"I'd planned on going round to see Sully, see how he's getting on. Is it uniform today then Sarge or what?"

"Nah, you'll be alright in civvies, least you won't 'ave to salute the twat. I'd probably avoid wearin' that *'whale oil beef hooked'* 'T' shirt you 'ad on at the Christmas do…an' you might want to save yerself some time. I'd go commando, an' wear yer trousers back to front."

Alan chuckled. "See you at about half eleven…oh, and thanks for the support Sarge."

*****

"Enter."

Alan glanced at his watch, exactly one minute past twelve; the Chief Inspector had kept them waiting for the statutory sixty seconds since the Traffic Sergeant had knocked on the door.

They dutifully entered the office and Alan noticed that no chairs had been placed in front of the desk; clearly this was to be a stand up meeting 'without coffee'.

Alan stood facing the Divisional Chief Inspector's desk, his Sergeant stood to his immediate right. They both waited whilst he asserted his 'power position' by ignoring their presence and continued to read Alan's report. This was purely for show Alan surmised. The fact that he was standing before the man was self-evident that he had already read the damn thing and Alan also noticed that it had been removed from where he had stapled it to the front of the accident booklet.

Whilst waiting for the ritual disemboweling to begin. Alan let his eyes wander over the contents of the Chief Inspector's desk.

A Newton's cradle in a shiny aluminum tubed frame, sat enticingly close to the edge. The five chromium plated balls hanging from their nylon chords, sat motionless and the temptation to reach across, pull just one back, let it go and prove Newton's third law and allow the rhythmic clacking to break the embarrassing silence, was almost unbearable.

A framed photograph of what Alan took to be the Chief Inspector's unfortunate offspring, sat at an angle across the corner of the desk. The two boys, possibly ten or twelve years of age, had posed for the photograph wearing matching dark blue pullovers emblazoned with the local grammar school crest. Alan noted with a sense of satisfaction, that both were doubly blighted, with bright ginger hair *and* a 'cowlick' hairline, clearly inherited from their Father.

Both were seriously overweight, again much like their Father and Alan mused that both boys would no doubt be in the 'high performance' stream, members of the school chess and poetry appreciation clubs, which they would hope to attend, whilst attempting to avoid endless repetitive sessions of having their heads pushed down the school toilets and the backs of their underpants violently wrenched up between the cracks of their arses, by the school bullies.

They both looked as if they had just woken from a very long coma; there was not the slightest hint of adolescent mischief behind their dead eyes.

No photograph of his Wife though, and whilst Alan waited, he allowed his imagination to wander. He tried to decide whether it was because she was either so stunningly beautiful, that the Chief Inspector's concentration would be constantly diverted, or alternatively, that she was vomitously ugly, grossly overweight, with a face infested with moles sprouting thick dark hairs and if her image were to be viewed, even on a photograph, it would turn the unwitting observer to stone. Considering the genetic throwback visibly evident in the fruit of his loins, Alan considered that the latter was the most likely.

The plain painted wall behind the Chief Inspector's desk was festooned with his personal accolades and achievements. The blue shield logo of the Open University declared to all, that Alan Forrester held a BSc (Hons) in Business Management. A second certificate sitting directly to its left and in an identical dark wood frame, confirmed that four years later, he also had secured a BA in Business Studies.

Chief Inspector Forrester, also displayed the commendations he had received from both the Divisional Commander and the Chairman of the Police Authority, for his tireless efforts resulting in a drastic reduction in recorded crime within the Division. There was also a rather drab certificate confirming Mr Forrester's ascendancy to the office of General Secretary of the Christian Police Association.

Alan had always been of the opinion, that any person who felt the need to outwardly display confirmation that their lives hadn't been totally without success, suffered from a serious confidence deficiency, probably borne out of some significant degrading incident during their formative years, possibly having their heads pushed down the school toilets.

Those who are bullied, invariably become bullies.

The Chief Inspector looked up, noticed that Alan was not in uniform. He cast a disapproving glance at the Van Halen 'T' shirt he was wearing.

The report was placed face up on the table top and purposefully turned 180 degrees so that Alan could read it.

The Chief Inspector leaned back in his padded leather swivel chair and placed his fingertips together steeple like. Alan noticed that the Chief Inspector suffered from psoriasis, the almost translucent skin of his inner forearms, was mottled with red, angry eruptions of dried skin. He stared intently at Alan for a moment, before leaning forwards and tapping the report with a fingertip. "I presume that you were driven toward your conclusions as a result of reliable independent witness evidence?"

Alan shifted uncomfortably on his feet. "No Sir, actually there weren't any wit…"

The Chief Inspector held up a hand to stop him in mid speech. "Informant evidence perhaps? Forensics?…*Anything?*"

"No Sir. I've mentioned in my report that the…"

Again the palm of the hand was held up. "Do you have any tangible evidence Pc Pendle and by which I mean, that I am looking for anything other than your unsupported suppositions, to suggest that this is anything other than a fail to stop pedestrian knock down?"

Before Alan could reply, The Chief Inspector snatched up the accident booklet from where it lay on his desk. "You completed this, yes?"

Alan nodded. "Yes Sir."

"Well. Let's look at what we've got shall we?" The Chief Inspector flicked through the small pages of the booklet and read from Alan's original notes in the investigating Officer's report section at the rear. "Single vehicle leaves carriageway to its offside and collides with unidentified male on pavement…Anything to suggest a crime there?" The Chief Inspector looked up expectantly.

"That's just the basic descriptor code for the collision Sir yes. But if you look at all the attendant evidence, the type of vehicle, the lack of skid marks or flat spotting on the tyres, the…"

The Chief Inspector shook his head. "Did you liaise with the Accident Investigation Officer?"

Alan shook his head. "AIB didn't come to the sce…"

"I'm aware of that. I mean, prior to the submission of this report?" The Chief Inspector snapped back, pounding the report with the tip of his index finger.

"No Sir…I have completed an AIB course and in my opinion…"

"I've read your opinions Pc Pendle. I consider them to be totally without foundation and wildly speculative." He paused. "Where was the vehicle stolen from?"

"Its previous keeper details only on PNC Sir."

Alan looked across enquiringly to his Sergeant.

"It was reported stolen from a used car lot on Wellington Street just after nine this morning Sir. That information only came to light after Pc Pendle had actually retired from duty. It's been logged as theft of motor vehicle, but it's a Millbeck crime."

The Chief Inspector looked back to Alan. "Well, I suppose we should be thankful for small mercies...You carried out the identification to the Coroner's Officer at the Mortuary?"

Alan nodded. "Yes Sir, we think that the deceased is..." Alan flicked over the first page of his report and read the name which he had added in bold print "Abdiel Adebowale Zippleman Sir..."

"We *think!*" The Chief Inspector added with an over exaggerated hint of incredulity.

Alan sighed; his obvious sign of exasperation was not lost on the Chief Inspector. "You have something to add Constable?"

Alan felt a cautionary tap against the side of his right foot. His Sergeant continued to look straight ahead. Alan identified his Sergeant's warning and composed himself.

"We're having to wait for fingerprints Sir...If it is this bloke Zippleman, he's known to be of high value. The crime intelligence system has eight pages on him. He's got form for drugs, weapons and living off immoral earnings. Regional Crime Squad have an interest marker on him, yet his last known address is over two years old, I just think..."

The Chief Inspector shook his head. "I have no doubt that the unfortunate deceased may well have been an active member of the criminal fraternity. But you've just described the previous convictions and interest markers of over seventy five percent of the residents on eleven beat...Yes?"

Alan stared straight ahead, gently biting down on his tongue.

"*Yes?*" the Chief Inspector emphasised and waited.

"Yes Sir." Alan acquiesced.

The Chief Inspector turned his attentions to the Traffic Sergeant. "Why was this report submitted unchallenged? Why did *you* as this Officer's supervisor, not make enquiries as to the validity of one of *your* Traffic Officer's, quite frankly, ridiculous assumptions, before it was committed to paper...If this had got as far as the Coroner, we would have looked foolish beyond words…"

"Hang on a moment Si…"

The Chief Inspector slapped the flat of his hand onto the table top to cut him short. "I'm not finished Sergeant." he said, glowering.

"If this had not been retrieved from the outgoing mail by Detective Sergeant Mitchell and brought to my attention…Well…it doesn't bear thinking about. There is no evidence, I repeat, no evidence whatsoever to suggest that this is anything other than an unfortunate knock down, involving a stolen vehicle and that is how it *will* be recorded. There will be no crime submitted." The Chief Inspector took a deep breath and offered the accident booklet up to the Traffic Sergeant.

"Pc Morrisey will be the allocated investigating Officer in this case Sergeant. Once Pc Pendle has had his allocated rest days, he can be deployed on day shifts to clear any outstanding clerical prior to attending his basic firearms course. He is to have nothing further to do with the investigation…Clear?"

"Clear Sir." The Traffic Sergeant said, taking the booklet.

The report was held out across the table top. Alan waited momentarily before accepting it, just to let the Chief Inspector know that he objected to its casual dismissal.

"The content of your report is duly noted Pc Pendle. It is deemed to be of no significant value to the investigation and it will be deposited in the secure waste immediately, and…from this day forth, all reports relating to fatal and potentially fatal road collisions, will be submitted in the first instant to your group Inspector…Do I make myself perfectly clear?"

"Clear Sir." Alan said without emotion.

"That will be all." The Chief Inspector said, waving them away like so many annoying flies. Without a further glance toward either Alan or his Sergeant, he busied himself, unnecessarily shuffling a small pile of papers into some semblance of order.

*****

Sullivan sipped on his glass of Glenfiddich as he read Alan's report.

"That's definitely gonna scar Sully." Alan said, as he inspected the angry wound above his partner's eye. The black sutures protruded like thin quills, where they gathered together the puckered swollen flesh. His partner continued to read.

"You know they've written 'Cyclops' across your tray in the office."

Sullivan paused and peered at Alan over the top of the report. "Do you want me to read this or what?"

Alan nodded. "Course...I was just thinking perhaps you could grow your eyebrows like Denis Healey and do like a comb over or something."

His partner returned his gaze to the pages and after a few moments, passed them back to Alan.

"Well?" Alan asked impatiently.

Sullivan shrugged. "There's a few typos."

"Apart from that." Alan retorted, exasperated at his attempts to tease some support from his partner.

"It's plausible Al, but they're never going to buy it. Not unless Studio come up with prints an' you end up with a collar...*and* if you could get those lame bastards in C.I.D. interested enough to put some real effort into an interview, then...maybe, you might get a cause death by reckless, but murder..?" His partner shook his head and pursed his lips. "Not a price mate...Thinkin' it's one thing...getting' it 'ome's different altogether...Hadn't crimed it 'ad you?"

Alan quickly shook his head. "Charlie wasn't as supportive as I would have hoped..."

His partner snorted with derision. "Oh surely you don't mean Charlie...'What's that you say Sir, there's no paper in the senior officer's toilet...here Sir...please Sir...use my shirt'... Morrisey."

Alan laughed as his partner mimicked their colleague's trademark high pitched voice perfectly.

"The same...Nah, no crime, I just wrote it up as I saw it...I mean, if it was what I reckon it was, somebody's just got away with the perfect crime. Think about it Pete, look at what's happened at Division 'cos of that report. If this Zippleman bloke had been found with a knife in his back, there'd have been an incident room set up by now an' a queue of Detectives clutching overtime cards all the way passed the canteen. It's perfect Pete, 'top' someone with a stolen motor an' the chances of getting your collar felt are virtually nil."

Sullivan sat as if deep in thought and stared into his whiskey. He took a sip from the heavy cut glass and sluiced the liquid around his mouth before swallowing.

"Its *chance* you can't rely on though Al." Sullivan said, shaking his head decisively. "You just can't build chance into a plan."

"Like?" Alan asked enquiringly.

"Like Lloyd Freeman f'rinstance...What was the chance of us comin' across that shit box van on Louise Street, an' wonder what the fuck the 'Eggman' was doin' at three in the mornin' in the Badlands? Five minutes longer chattin' to what'sername in the garage, we'd 'ave missed it an' 'e'd 'ave got away with a murder. I mean, who else but you an' me would've recognized that motor for one thing? It's only 'cos we donked it off goin' for ice cream..."

Alan smiled and nodded slowly as he remembered the 'Eggman murder'.

*****

The sun was already bathing the red brickwork on the front of the Police station as Alan paraded for early turn. That July was proving to be reminiscent of the record summer of '76. The days hot, still and cloudless, the nights humid and sticky with little relief from the heat.

Sullivan was already in the Traffic office as Alan entered, his partner was seated in the Sergeant's chair reading, his feet up on the desk top. Two mugs of coffee steamed invitingly on the table beneath the window.

Alan nodded, yawned and flopped down into one of the swivel chairs, grunting as he reached across for one of the mugs.

"I've managed about an hours sleep, sweating my nuts off all night."

His partner nodded in agreement and returned his gaze to the Chief Constable's incident report.

"To sleep, perchance to dream, aye, there's the rub." Alan sighed.

His partner looked up over the top of the sheet of paper. "Well, if you've bin rubbin' yerself all night, what d'you expect...No sympathy."

Alan smiled. "It's from Hamlet Sully and it's got nothing to do with self-abuse."

Sullivan looked across, his face a picture of disinterest. "Yeah, course...Hamlet....You've been spendin' too much time down at the Bridewell with that idiot Cawthorne. Speakin' of Hamlet, I'm out of smokes, so first stop garage...Oh, an' we're in the 'pig' today."

"He's alright is Mr Cawthorne. He's a character Pete, something the job's woefully short of these days."

"He's not a character Al, he's not right in the head. I couldn't work with 'im. 'E's a fuckin' embarrassment with all his Shakespeare crap."

Alan glanced up to the remarks column on the vehicle disposition board. Next to the registration number of the Supervision Range Rover, their Sergeant had written 'Early turn to use pls, needs running'.

"You know, if Roger actually went out every now and then...I bet the chuffing battery's flat." Alan said despondently as he reached up for the keys.

"Fuck all of note on the Chief's log." Peter said, tossing the night incident sheet across to Alan. "Couple of lock ups for TWOC, an' a street robbery in the Badlands, there's a surprise."

Alan glanced with little interest at the Chief's log as he sipped on his coffee.

"You comin' down?" His partner asked, tapping the face of his watch.

Alan shrugged himself free of the chair. "I shall attend the Divisional early turn parade Peter, because I...fully embrace the integration of Road Traffic personnel with our colleagues on uniformed beat patrol, to further and promote the efficiency of the Division as a whole."

His partner smirked at Alan's sarcastic rendition of the latest Divisional Order in respect of Traffic's role as they walked down the stairs to the parade room on the bottom corridor.

*****

The Range Rover's engine cranked over with tortuous hesitation and Alan looked woefully across to his partner. "What'd I tell you?"

His partner reached across for the radio handset.

Alan held up a cautionary hand. "Don't turn the radio on yet for Christ's sake Pete, there's hardly enough juice as it is."

The heavy engine churned over, coughed and fired moments before the battery finally lost the will to live. As the engine roared into life, a huge pall of blue grey smoke was emitted from the exhaust and drifted slowly across the car park.

Alan tickled at the accelerator pedal. "Keep it runnin' Al, I'm not pushing this bleedin' thing." his partner said, punching the power button on front of the radio. "What's the scores on the doors?"

Alan glanced at the odometer. "Eight two, four two four mate."

Sullivan held his pen between his teeth as he opened the vehicle's log book.

"It's done a hundred and nineteen miles since the twelfth of June. No wonder Roger wants it runnin'…Time it went anyway, that looks terminal." he said, nodding his head toward the oil laden smoke slowly dissipating in the motionless warm air as it drifted across the rear yard.

The rather worrying rattle emanating from the top end of the engine, gradually subsided as the oil circulated around the block and filled the hydraulic lifters.

"Papa Yankee One Zero."

"One Zero." the operator responded.

"We are 10/1 crew is 868 and 418, 10/7 over."

"Nothing at this time One Zero."

The big V8 smoothed out as it slowly warmed and as Alan eased out of the parking space. Sullivan hung the radio handset back in its cradle and activated the electric windows, to catch what little relief there was from the marginally cooler outside air as they commenced patrol.

"Fancy a run out to Thorsby, see if we can snag an ice cream at Brierley's farm?" Alan asked, two hours into their shift.

Sullivan glanced at his watch. "Yeah, why not, I could do with a walkabout…these leather seats are drawing my arse."

Alan grimaced at his partner as he engaged first gear and after quickly checking left and right, he powered the Range Rover out from their parking spot and onto the Ring Road.

*****

Out of the city and on toward the Harrowford Road. The further out from the City they went, the more the landscape gradually changed. From row upon row of dismal council houses, working men's clubs and small run down industrial estates, to the privately owned houses of the more affluent, with their well-kept gardens and manicured lawns.

Once out through the City boundary gates, the dull grey urban vision disappeared in their rear view mirrors. The view ahead was now all vividly green, lush farmland with rolling open fields and woodland. The pavements of the City gave way to grass verges and dense Hawthorne hedgerows. Dry stone walling marked out patchwork like acres, where herds of Charolaise and Friesian grazed lazily in the summer heat.

The sky was now a wonderful azure blue. Brilliant white cumulus slowly shape-changed as their gargantuan masses moved lazily in the upper air.

The exhaust note from the Range Rover sang wonderfully as Alan gave the V8 its head through the open sweeping bends along the minor roads. The sun filtered through the leaves and overhanging branches of the trees on either side of the road. It flickered strobe like up over the bonnet and across the windscreen. The road surface ahead shimmered mirage like in the heat.

All was peaceful, all was good.

After a dozen miles or so, Allan pulled off the Harrowford Road and made a left turn toward the outlying village of Thorsby. Here the road drastically reduced in width and the views were restricted as the bends became more severe. He slowed their vehicle as he noted the slick, dark green evidence of recent livestock movement, splattered across the road surface and the wide tyre tracks left by agricultural machinery.

Up passed the small Wesleyan Chapel with its ancient graveyard of weathered and lichen covered stones. The Post Office, still bearing the Crown flanked by the letters V and R above its cracked oak door lintel and the two wyverns of the coat of arms of Henry Lord Clifford, hanging from a rustic wooden frame above the door of the Craven Arms.

Alan swung the Range Rover off the village road and onto the loose gravel track leading up to Brierley's Farm.

The farm had been devastated by the previous outbreak of foot and mouth disease and the Brierley's had never recovered.

Turning their backs on livestock farming, they had concentrated on an alternative business venture; the top fields now housed a large static caravan park, with a play area for children. The milking stalls had been removed to make way for showers and laundry facilities and the farm house had been extended to include a modern shop where the Brierley's sold homemade bread, scones, jams and if the hand painted board at the side of the door was to be believed, the best ice cream in the County.

Sullivan unclipped his seat belt and glanced over to his partner. "Vanilla is it?"

Alan nodded and as his partner disappeared into the shop, he drove across the rough gravel surface and parked the Range Rover at the top of the car park overlooking the fields, which dropped gently down toward the river which glistened like a bright steel band, as it meandered its way toward the reservoir at the head of the valley.

It was still early and there were only a few vehicles dotted about, mostly parked near to the farm shop entrance from where, by the time Alan had set the handbrake and turned off the ignition, his partner appeared, carrying two large double scoop cones.

Unclipping his tie and securing it on one of his epaulettes, Alan undid the top button of his shirt and breathed the warm countrified air deep into his lungs. The shrill warbling shriek of a Curlew passing overhead caught his attention and he looked upwards, to watch its long curved beak slowly sweeping from side to side, as it winged its way over the top of the patrol car and down across the fields and into the bottom of the valley.

Leaving the vehicle to meet his approaching partner, Alan felt his shirt sticking to his back. He silently uttered an offering of thanks to Chief Mayhew, who had decided that the blue nylon shirts previously worn by male Officers below the rank of Inspector, would be replaced by white cotton for all ranks.

"I'm thinkin' of shavin' my bollocks if this heat keeps up." his partner said out of the blue.

Alan paused; licking the two large, spherical mounds of rapidly melting vanilla, all of a sudden seemed rather less enticing. "Oh…thanks for sharing that very personal thought with me at this particular juncture Pete, it'll probably take me the rest of the day to rid myself of that rather grotesque image."

His partner chuckled as they leaned back against the bonnet of the Range Rover, enjoying the lush, rural vista stretched out in front of them.

"See…I reckon we'd be better off wearing skirts in summer." his partner said. "Get some air round yer nadgers."

Alan looked slowly across at his partner. "Pete, I'm actually worried now…You're frightening me…You don't like…go through Linda's kit and wear her stuff while she's at work do you?…I mean…not that I'd think any less of you or anything…Each to their own."

Sullivan ignored Alan's lurid insinuations and looked genuinely deep in thought.

"No…I mean, think about it, the Scottish cops won't have this problem will they? Just waft the old kilt about a bit and Jock's yer uncle innit?"

Alan looked puzzled. "Pete, I hate to dispel your north of the border genital air conditioning theory, but the Scottish Police don't wear the kilt. Didn't you see 'The Wicker Man'?"

Sullivan pushed the last remnants of cone into his mouth. "He's not a Jock, that's him with the moustache that goes all over the world reportin' on stuff."

Alan sighed, Sully, that's 'Wicker's World'…The 'Wicker Man's' got Edward Woodward in it. You know, that bloke in The Equalizer…He plays a Scottish Police Sergeant who turns up in this isolated village to look for a missing girl…Come on Pete…it's the one where Britt Eckland gets all her kit off an' starts dancing round in the hotel room next to his, bangin' on the walls. He can't get to sleep, probably 'cos he's got a ragin' hard on thinking 'bout Britt Eckland's tits…and the fact that she's banging on the walls half the night I 'spose. Anyway…all the villagers are part of some weird coven or something. He ends up getting' burned alive inside this huge wicker statue an…"

Sullivan shook his head slowly and looked bewildered. "I haven't the faintest idea what you're talking about."

"Have you seen the film Sully?" Alan asked flatly.

"Clearly not Al, or I would have remembered…at least the bit with Britt Eckland showin' 'er tits."

Alan paused. "The point I'm making Sully, is that Scottish Policemen don't wear kilts. In the film, Edward Woodward wears the same uniform as us…with trousers."

"Ok." his partner said with just a hint of boredom. "We off?"

Alan nodded, and pointed to the front of his partner's shirt which bore incriminating evidence of ice cream consumption whilst on duty.

Sullivan swore under his breath.

*****

"Here's today's sinner mate." his partner said, nodding toward an ancient looking van travelling toward them. "It's on its knees."

Alan slowed the Range Rover and watched as the van drove passed them. It seemed to be struggling up the slight incline and leaving a thin plume of blue smoke in its wake.

Alan quickly checked his rear view mirror, he did a shoulder check before doubling the clutch and taking a second gear. He swung the steering wheel of the cumbersome Range Rover hard over. The body characteristically rolled ominously on its suspension as he accelerated after the obvious 'weigher'.

At the first rotation of the blue lights, the van now directly in front of them, moved in toward the nearside grass verge and shuddered to a halt.

Alan set the flashing rear red lights and glanced in his rear view mirror before opening his door. He noticed that the driver's door of the van had also swung open and although the vehicle was brown, the inner edges of the door and the hinge posts were bright Post Office red.

"I'll run it." his partner said, reaching for the radio handset.

Alan walked up to the van driver's door. "Morning driver." he managed to say before immediately taking a step backward and turning his head away from the gagging odour, emanating from within the vehicle.

The driver, who looked to be in his late seventies, wore faded blue full length overalls and green wellingtons, both of which looked to be spattered liberally with some form of animal effluent. He was fat and rivulets of sweat ran down across the fine red capillary lines, chasing across his cheeks and stood out in small droplets across his bald scalp.

His overalls were dark blue. There were concentric expanding salt circles around his armpits, evidence of their constant use and Alan considered that this, along with the state of his wellingtons, was the source of the putrid smell.

The driver put both hands underneath his right thigh and grunted with effort as he heaved upwards, swinging a seemingly useless leg, out over the kickplate onto the road surface.

He shuffled himself across his seat and placed a filthy hand on the top of the steering wheel to assist in hauling the remainder of his bulk out from the vehicle.

Alan was still unsure as to the exact source of the odour, which was making his eyes water and the bile rise up into the back of his throat. He dearly wished he had only had one scoop, whilst at Brierley's farm.

"Sorry lad, takes a bit of effort when I've bin sat for a while." The driver grunted.

"That's alright driver, take your time…You injured? You seem to be struggling" Alan said with a concerned look. The driver smiled and thumped the side of his right leg with his fist. Alan heard a loud hollow thud. "Left it on 235 lad."

Alan looked puzzled.

"Hill 235...Imjin. April of '51. Before your time I 'spose." The driver said.

"Just a bit." Alan replied with a smile. "Korea?"

"That's the one lad, you've got it." The driver said, smiling and exposing remarkably white, even teeth, which belied the rest of his seemingly neglected appearance.

"That would be the 'Gloucesters' then."

"First Battalion. You know your stuff lad...Served have you?"

Alan nodded. "For a while...a spell in Ireland, Oman, you know. Nothing like your lot had to put up with."

"We left over six hundred on that hill. I was lucky I 'spose...Anyway, nowt more boring than old soldiers tales eh. What can I do for you?"

Alan's partner approached carrying his clipboard. "Mr Graveley?" he said, immediately wrinkling his nose as it was suddenly assailed by the sickening smell as he came to stand at the side of the van.

"That's me. Ernest Graveley, how d'you know that?"

"It's on our computer. Checked your van number...over the radio...Comes back as owned by you. You still at Morton Drive?"

The driver shook his head as if in wonderment. "By eck! You've got some kit nowadays you lads...It is. Number thirty seven."

"That's the one." Peter nodded and slowly stepped back a half pace.

"If you don't mind me asking Mr Graveley. What's that God awful smell?" Alan asked.

The driver chuckled and rubbed his grubby hands down the front of his overalls.

"Eggs lad."

"Eggs?"

"Aye, eggs…You get used to the smell after thirty years or so."

The driver limped awkwardly toward the rear of the van and threw open the twin rear doors. The van, which was hand painted a drab shade of brown had obviously once belonged to the Post Office. The faint outline of the Royal Mail lettering and the shape of the Crown below, were still evident beneath the brush marks. The vehicle sagged on its rear suspension, the reason becoming immediately obvious as Alan and his partner gazed into the rear compartment. Rack upon rack of eggs, stacked from floor pan to roof and seemingly, all the way down to the rear of the seats at the front.

"Eggs." the driver beamed. "Take a few for your breakfast's lads." he offered, "You'll not get much fresher. Those there at the back have only been out of the crack an hour."

Alan let his eyes wander across the rows of eggs, many still slicked with feces to which had adhered small particles of straw and feathers. "They just need washing is all. Take a couple apiece."

Alan held up a hand. "No…no thank you Mr Graveley, we're…er, not allowed. Gratuities…you understand."

"Ah." the driver tapped the side of his nose knowingly with his finger and winked. "Can't be seen to be bribing an Officer of the law eh?"

"How many are you carrying?" Alan's partner asked.

The driver scratched the side of his head. "Well, let's see…There's thirty eggs to a tray and ten trays to a plate, you can only load ten trays 'cos of the weight do you see, risk of crackin' the shells…I've fifty trays so…"

"Fifteen thousand." Sullivan said, cutting him short.

The driver looked across to Alan. "By eck! He's sharp as a razor your mate eh?"

Alan smiled. "He's pretty good with figures."

"I'll say." The driver nodded appreciatively.

"What's a tray weigh then?" Peter asked.

The driver pursed his lips and transferred his body weight onto his left leg.

"You could reckon on an average egg weighing two to two and a half ounces maybe, thirty to a tray so…"

"Nearly five pounds a tray. Ten trays to a plate an' you've fifty plates. Best part of two thousand five hundred pounds…You've over a ton of eggs on board driver. It's a seven hundredweight van, no wonder it's on its knees." Peter said, stunning the driver with his lightening calculations. Even Alan raised an eyebrow.

The driver shuffled his weight again. "Well, she does all right Officer, you know…You have to keep your speed down anyway. Eggs is fragile like, an' I only do the one journey do you see, all round the farms…Up at four of a morning, collect me stock, rack 'em all up and take 'em to the wholesale market. I don't wash 'em or owt, they've got lads to do all that. I just get so much a tray see…"

"You might consider getting yourself a bigger vehicle Mr Graveley, one that can take the weight. This one's overloaded…and your springs have seen better days." Peter said, pointing to the rear wheels which were somewhat splayed outward and tucked well up into the arches.

"Aye, well." the driver said, as he scratched his head again. "Its cost do you see, I don't make much, I've got my disability but…"

"Do you get that from the army?" Alan asked.

"Well, I would have normally I 'spose but…I was listed as killed in action you see."

"How so?" Alan asked, looking puzzled.

"Well." The driver paused. He squinted and looked up to the sky.

Alan noticed that his eyes had moistened.

"There were eight hundred and sixty six of us 'Gloucesters' dug in on that hill. Three days we held 'em as they came across the

Imjin. Day after day an' no rest at night. No end to 'em, wave after wave. No artillery support either, all that were used up. In the end, it was just as bad for us with our ammo...A few of the lads got away...I got one in the leg an' I got taken prisoner. Ended up spendin' two years in Chongsong prison camp up the Yalu river." He paused and took a deep breath. "Came home on the 'Empire Orwell', October of '53 we got back. I'd been listed as killed back in '51. My old Mum nearly had a heart attack when she saw me at the door...The leg had gone to gangrene...anyway."

His eyes had misted over. "You don't want to hear all that...Am I to be summonsed then lad?"

Alan shook his head. "One of the 'Glorious Gloucesters'...No I don't think so Mr Graveley, you've paid your dues I reckon...Take less on board eh, or as my partner says, get a bigger van."

"'bliged to you lads." he said, closing the rear doors of the van.

As Alan watched him drive away, his partner lit a cigar and filled the Range Rover with acrid smoke. "Christ Pete, I don't know which is worse, his eggs or your cigar."

"He's full of shit. He'll pull that old war story out of the hat every time 'e gets a tug. Yer a soft touch Al."

"I'll put him in for a verbal caution, we'll get the tick anyway. He was at Imjin Pete, he's a hero, one of the Glorious Glouces..."

His partner snorted. "You didn't actually buy into all that shit did you? The old fart probably lost 'is leg in a 10/9 twenty years ago. All that bollocks about the Ingram river" his partner laughed loudly. "You've been well fucked over mate."

"It's Imjin Pete. It's in Korea, an' it really happened."

"Yeah...right." His partner scoffed. "'E probably saw it all in a film or something..."

Alan shook his head in disbelief.

"It was your call mate…Come on lads, I were a prisoner of war." Peter mimicked the driver by lifting his right leg from his seat and panting loudly.

Alan laughed. "He deserves a caution for puttin' up with that rancid stink every day. Christ that was bad."

Sullivan glanced at his watch. "Oi, meal time. Get a grip Al, I'm starvin'."

"A couple of Edie's poached eggs on toast is it?" Alan asked, with a hint of sarcasm.

"No chance…I'll never eat eggs again after seein' that lot."

*****

The summer didn't prove to be as lasting as the one in '76, but there were further trips out to Brierley's on early turns, and on occasions, the old hand painted ex-Post Office van would get a flash from their headlights or a flick of the blue lights as they passed each other on the Harrowford Road.

A clear moonlit night the following December had ensured that all the windows of their patrol car were closed up tight and kept the heater on full blast, bathing their feet with hot air. The roads glistened with an iron frost and there had been some windscreen scraping to do before they'd started patrol.

"What you got me for Christmas then Sully?" Alan asked as they cruised the deserted streets of eleven beat.

"Same as last year pal, fuck all. What you got me?"

"Same same." Alan replied with a chuckle.

"I'm into Christmas." his partner said purposefully, "I come over all sort of…"

"Hey!" Alan interrupted and pointed out through the windscreen.

His partner looked and turned to Alan with a questioning look on his face; they paused and then said in unison "The Eggman!"

Even under the dull yellow glow of the street lights, the old hand painted Austin 1000 van stood out like a sore thumb, as it trundled out onto the main road from one of the side streets ahead of them. Alan accelerated slightly and as their headlights reached out to the rear of the vehicle, he could make out the back of two heads through the small windows in the rear doors.

"What's your Vietnam war 'ero doin' out in the 'Badlands' at half three in the mornin'?"

Alan smirked. "It was Korea Pete, but your right...Worth a look?"

"Worth a look." his partner agreed and reached forward, flicking the switch for the blue lights.

The interior of the ancient van was heavy with condensation. Alan knocked lightly on the opaque glass of the driver's door, which eventually, was wound down.

The ugliest Negro Alan had ever seen, was seated where the one legged 'Hero of Imjin' should have been.

Across in the passenger seat, sat a female, marginally better looking, but not by much. Her probable forty plus years, were poorly disguised by gaudy, heavily applied makeup and her attempts at belying her age, by bleaching her hair were thwarted by the tell-tale grey roots sprouting from her scalp. She wore a short white skirt which exposed naked thighs, dimpled with cellulite. Dark engorged varicose veins stood out starkly beneath her knees and calves, the by-product of a life on her feet no doubt.

She wore her blouse open at the neck to show an initially inviting cleavage, but the 'crow's feet' wrinkling which started at the folds of slack skin at the base of her throat, descended to where her breasts were bunched together at the open 'V' of her blouse. Evidence that her body had long since unconditionally surrendered to the inevitable effects of age and gravity.

The woolen cardigan she wore open and draped around her shoulders, she now pulled together across her chest as the freezing air swept in through the open window. The well-worn heels of her bright red patent leather shoes were evidence of her walking trade.

She wore no watch, no jewelry to get lost or stolen and the small clutch bag she gripped in her left hand, Alan guessed was just large enough to contain the minimal tools of her trade, condoms and a sleeve of moist wipes.

Alan returned his gaze to the driver who squinted and held up his hand to shield his eyes against the dazzling glare of the torch beam. The hooker turned her head to look out from the opposite window, and as she pulled down the hem of her skirt and shuffled uncomfortably, Alan happened to notice that her right hand was missing its thumb.

The interior of the van no longer smelled of eggs. Now it was the sweet pungent aroma of cannabis which wafted out into the still air. Alan glanced back to the patrol car and saw that Peter was holding the VHF radio handset to his ear.

"Morning driver." Alan said, opened the proceedings with his normal gambit.

Any response would normally be sufficient for Alan to detect alcohol on the driver's breath.

"Wha' be wrang...can a black man not go about his bi'ness widout p'lice 'arrasmen'?"

Alan became defensive; to be met with this immediate aggressive attitude was nothing new in the 'Badlands', but he also knew that the referral to skin colour was being used as a deterrent. The indigenous population of eleven beat knew, that if uniforms saw a public complaint of racial harassment on the horizon, they would back off, not dig too deep, let a 'brother' be on his way. The 'tick' for a minor road traffic offence, was not worth the anguish of an interview with Discipline and Complaints, especially one with racial overtones, not these days. That is, if you were young in service and still gave a shit, or perhaps single crewed, but Alan had plenty of 'time in' and he had his partner to back him up.

"You're not being harassed driver, you're being stopped because it's the early hours of the morning and I'm paid to be curious." Alan responded, with a note of authority in his voice.

"How do you suppose we could tell you were black before we stopped you? Having pulled you from behind?" Alan purposefully used the term 'we', just to let the driver know that there was another uniform present. The driver wrinkled his nose as if bothered by a distasteful smell.

"Do you have your driving licence with you?"

Alan was somewhat taken aback, as the driver fumbled in the inside pocket of his jacket and produced a dog eared licence which he handed out through the open window without diverting his forward gaze.

Alan unfolded the weathered green document and tucked his torch under his armpit, so that the beam illuminated the typed details.

"Mr Lloyd Freeman?" Alan asked.

The driver simply nodded. Alan scrutinized the driver number. "What's your date of birth Mr Freeman?" he asked, having already worked it out from the series of sixteen letters and numbers at the top left hand side of the ragged document.

The driver sighed. "Feb'ry tree a' farty."

His response was purposefully heavily laced with guttural Jamaican 'street speak', but Alan didn't bite.

"Third of February nineteen forty, thank you Mr Freeman…What's your current address?"

The driver scowled, distorting his already intense facial features into an ugly threatening mask. Alan had a mild feeling of foreboding and was relieved to see his partner joining him at the side of the van.

"We just want to make sure you're still at the address shown on your licence Mr Freeman, no big deal." The driver glanced up at the six foot four frame of Alan's partner and complied.

"10/17 shows previous keeper details only. Vehicle excise licence refund applied for end of September of this year. Who've we got?" Sullivan asked.

Alan tilted the licence so that his partner could read the holder's name and address.

Peter nodded and stepping back from the van pressed the red transmit button on the top of his Burndept.

"418"

"Go ahead Pete."

"John, do us a 10/11"

"Pass it."

"Lloyd Garfield Freeman. I.C.3. Male, born three two forty, back Sanderson Terrace."

"Stand by." The operator responded.

Alan leaned slightly into the driver's window and looked across to the female passenger. "Won't keep you long love. You alright?"

She glanced his way, and nodded once before nervously returning her gaze to the passenger window.

"418." Sullivan's radio broke the silence.

"Go ahead."

"Can you speak Pete?"

Alan's partner hurriedly walked away from the vehicle.

"Yeah, go on."

Alan glanced across the windscreen of the Austin. "No road tax Mr Freeman?"

The driver continued to stare directly out of the windscreen.

"Ah bart the car a'Freyday, from the auctions. Ah g'win tax it Monday marnin' firs' ting…a'right?"

"Insurance?" Alan asked, allowing more than a slight hint of cynicism to show in his tone.

"Ah gots the insurance. Don' aks me far it now, ah don' carry it wid I....Who do?"

Peter returned and showed Alan the open page of his green notebook: CRO number from '60, burglary/going equipped, pre-cons for no insurance, drive whilst disq, drugs, no warrants local/national.

Alan nodded, and his partner pushed his notebook back into the top pocket of his yellow jacket.

"Is that cannabis I can smell Mr Freeman?"

The driver shook his head despondently. "I give a fren' a ri' today, 'im be smarkin'…maybe 'im lef' it."

"I'm going to give you a producer for your insurance Mr Freeman and I'd like to see some tax up on that screen should we ever see you again, ok."

*****

During the night parade the following shift, the Inspector had produced a black and white Studio photograph from his briefing sheet and asked for it to be passed around; there were grimaces and groans of disgust from the uniforms as it was viewed.

"Detective Inspector Ellis has asked that this photograph be shown to all Officers during parades." The Inspector then read from the briefing and disposition sheet.

"The body of the so far unidentified female was discovered this morning by Council workers. It had been deposited behind a wall on Morritt Avenue on eleven beat. You will see that the victim has suffered extensive injuries through burning. An initial forensic examination suggests that an accelerant, evidently petrol, was used by the suspect in an effort to hinder identification, however, the deceased's neck was broken and the burning was certainly carried out post mortem. It is now a murder investigation and Officers are asked to view the image to see if they can assist C.I.D. with identification in respect of clothing or any other distinguishing features etc etc…I know there aren't many of either remaining, but it could be that she was a local prostitute you may have come across."

"Excuse the pun." the beat Sergeant threw in, much to the obvious annoyance of the Inspector.

Alan gazed at the photograph, "Jesus Christ!" he gasped.

The victim's charred body had been photographed in situ and was laid on its back in the middle of a large circle of scorched grass. The left side of the body was so badly burned that the flesh had completely disappeared. The grotesque charcoal like skeletal remains, reminded Alan of the photographs he had seen of the residents of Pompeii, caught, baked forever in time by the pyroclastic flow blast from the exploding Vesuvius as they had blissfully gone about their daily business.

The petrol had evidently burned out before the body had been completely destroyed and parts of the right hand side of her body and even portions of her face although blistered and badly scorched, were still visible.

The photograph was in black and white, so Alan failed to identify the red patent leather shoes, one of which had survived the heat, but the hairs on the back of his neck suddenly stood up as he looked at the blackened remains of the victim's right hand.

The thumb was missing.

"Pass it back when you've all seen it gents, thank you…Right, other crimes for today…"

*****

I'm tellin' you Pete that was her; she was with that ugly bastard in the Eggman's van on Louis Street last night." Alan said emphatically.

His partner shrugged and held his hands out as if in confusion. "I didn't see 'er Al….There was a woman in the van, yeah, but..."

"You saw the photograph; the thumb was missing from her right hand. It was obvious last night she was a hooker, I'll tell you…"

Alan quickly thumbed through the self-carbonating copies remaining in his pad of HORT/1's. "Lloyd Freeman. I issued this at three forty two; she was with him then Pete, the same morning…in fact, a few *hours* later, she's found dead behind a wall in the Morritt's…Come on!"

"You're sure about the thumb?…I don't mean in the photograph. What you saw while she was in the van?"

"The thumb was missing Pete…I was gonna make some joke about how she'd ever manage to give a decent handjob…"

His partner smirked. "P'raps she was left handed."

"Freeman topped her Pete. Did you see his eyes, he was like Charlie fucking Manson. Eyes like mad dog's bollocks. He took 'er to…wherever, shagged 'er…argued about money or something and 'e strangled her and broke 'er neck in the process. Find the Eggman's van again an' it'll have 'frensics all over it."

"Where'd 'e get the petrol from?" Peter asked.

"How the fuck should I know…What does it matter?…'E had a can in the back maybe. I don't know…Freeman must be good for it Pete…"

His partner scratched his ear thoughtfully and nodded. "Alright, I'll go along with Freeman bein' a prime suspect…but look, it's quarter past ten…Before we go rushin' off to the Old Bank Club to see if we can find the night D.C. why not 'ave a quiet word with old Ron Dennison, least 'e won't let us make twats of ourselves."

Alan considered the proposal for a moment, then realised that his partner was talking sense. He nodded and they both went looking for the aged Station Sergeant.

\*\*\*\*\*

"D'you fancy another brew or what?"

Alan looked at his watch. "No, cheers anyway Pete, I'll get off, thanks for looking it over."

"I'd ditch it if I were you." his partner said, handing back the report.

Alan folded it and pushed it into the back pocket of his jeans. "When you coming back?"

His partner stretched in his chair. "Stitches come out next Friday. The blurrin's almost gone, just have a bit of a problem focusing…When you off to Stretham?"

"Start next Monday…I'm dropped back to days. I get the weekend off then away for five days, you'll be back by then mate, think positive."

His partner nodded. "Three day shifts…that Forrester's idea of punishment?"

Alan shrugged. "I'm not complaining. I should be able to clear my tray at least."

"Ring me if you need anything." Alan said, as he tossed his car keys in his hand and made for the door.

## **Twenty**

Michael wandered purposefully across the rubble strewn site where the old red bricked terraced housing estate was slowly being demolished. His eyes swept over the broken window frames, which lay shattered and distorted amongst the bricks and cast iron guttering, now crushed and crumbled under the weight of the heavy demolition machinery.

He walked tentatively, carefully, yet stumbled through the churned up mud as the wafer thin soles of his shoes slipped on the wet mildewed coating on the broken paving slabs. Michael paused and bent down to inspect a twisted transom window frame. Brushing away the brick dust and decaying leaves with his grimy fingers, he cocked his head almost comically and pondered over the blistered paint on the window latch he had discovered.

As if suddenly disturbed from a trance, he dropped to his knees, ignoring the mud and the sharp shards of broken brick and glass, he grasped at a small stone and clenched it tightly. He scraped at the painted surface of the latch, uttering a sharp cry of joy as he saw the bright yellow metal exposed beneath. He tugged at the latch feverishly and stood legs apart, whilst he shook the transom like a worrying Terrier.

The latch resisted and remained stubbornly attached to the wooden frame. A puzzled scowl distorted his features; he saw the screw heads yet didn't understand why he could not liberate his prize. Michael only knew that he had found yellow metal and that Mr Dickinson liked yellow metal, almost as much as the dull grey pieces that were much heavier to carry.

Michael dropped the latch and the frame to which it remained attached; his eyes skipped quickly over the pile of rubble on which he stood. Panic seeped into him and he uttered a low guttural moan as if to calm himself. He noticed a large rock which was half submerged in the mud and forcing both his hands into the mud on either side of the rock, he pulled at it. The rock was unmoving; the wet mud refusing to release its grip on the smooth surface.

Michael did not understand the principle of hydraulics. He had seen the rock he wanted and although there were many others strewn across the demolition site which would fit its intended purpose, he did not consider an alternative option. That would require a logical thought process and Michael was only capable of forming basic singular thought processes. He had seen the rock, he needed it and he was intent on freeing it. His cracked fingernails screeched against the smooth sides of the rock as he forced it from side to side, trying to break the vacuum between the wet bed of clay which held it tightly. He pushed and pulled until his fingers ached, slowly, the ground begrudgingly gave it up and with a loud sucking sound the rock was released.

Michael snorted loudly. "Hah."

He lifted the rock and he felt its weight as he balanced it in the palm of his hand. He examined it with a measured eye before he lifted it to chest height and slammed it down onto the frame where the latch was secured. The wood splintered, Michael dropped the rock and grasped the latch again, pulling it with his slimy hands, it had loosened, yet it remained in place.

Again he raised the rock. He made a further assault on the broken woodwork. He stopped mid stroke as if something had disturbed him, something to be afraid of. He looked about him across the clearance area, his breath coming in short bursts due to exertion and now from fear of the unseen thing. A few moments passed, the frightening unseen presence of whatever had disturbed him was blown away with the light breeze.

His limited concentration returned to the task in hand and he struck at the window frame until the latch was finally released. Michael held it up to the sky and admired the shiny metal which was exposed beneath the paint, where the dull edge of the rock had scoured across its surface. He let out an inane shriek of laughter and danced for a moment, before he tossed the brass latch into his battered pram along with the various pieces of metal flotsam he had gathered.

Michael is unfortunate. He is twenty five, yet through some cruel joke, whilst his body entered puberty, his brain decided not to follow suit. His speech is thick, viscous, hindered on its exit from his mouth, by some cloying barrier somewhere between his brain and his vocal chords. The words finally emitted are those of a retard, a simpleton. That he may be, yet he has the joyful exuberance of a carefree child and because of his innocence, he is ridiculed, as is the wont of those who regard themselves as being normal.

Michael is 'not wrapped too tight'. He is 'a card short of a full deck'. He is called 'Looneytunes' and 'Dumbo', yet happily, Michael fails to make the connection between the nicknames and the laughter that follows. So he smiles, thinking all the while that he is lucky to have so many friends.

If the Lord withheld a few brain cells from Michael, he also did him no favours physically; he is a Friday afternoon job. His speech impediment is due to a cleft palate, one which, if anyone could have been bothered, could have been corrected by simple surgery shortly after his birth.

But Michael was born at home, a concealed birth. His Mother's animal panting's, watched only by a reformed prostitute, who had knowledge enough to assist with such clandestine deliveries and the prevention of same, if the unfortunate girl had come to see her early enough.

So Michael entered his world the product of an incestuous relationship between his Mother and her Brother. His world was one of unemployment, poverty and drunkenness.

As he was ejected from the womb, the 'mid wife's' raw hands gathered up his body, undersized and underweight due to his Mother's excessive alcohol intake, blue gray and slicked with blood. Michael was already addicted to nicotine as he was laid out on the grimy living room carpet of his unmarried Mother's terraced house.

Michael has rotting twisted teeth; the upper jaw is crooked and so the teeth have emerged at an acute angle which pushed his cheeks out hamster like. This combined with a nervous twitch, affecting the facial muscles down the right side of his face, give Michael the nonsensical manner of a fool. His body is thin, bordering on skeletal.

Wracked by tuberculosis as a child, his body fought the virus and miraculously won, but he paid a terrible price. His chest is sunken and weak, and he finds his breath hard to come by in the colder months.

Michael has a 'club foot'; this again could have been treated within a week or two of his birth, but along with his defective palate, was ignored. It causes him to drop his shoulder and limp, he drags the foot sideways, quickly wearing out the side of his shoe.

His peers laugh as they follow Michael down the street, imitating his clumsy gait. Michael twitches and hurries his pace to be rid of them.

He is unemployed and for the most part, unemployable, therefore of little or no use to his family. His Mother tolerates his adolescent tantrums and ejects him from the family hovel, rain or shine; the main objective being so that she can be left alone to entertain one of Michael's many 'Uncles', who appear with monotonous regularity. A family has to live after all.

Michael considers himself lucky to have so many 'Uncles'. The sly winks and innuendos are a mystery to him, as are the jeers and calls of "'Ow's yer Uncle Billy today?" from the groups of equally unemployable youths who hang around on Michael's street.

As he pulls the squeaking pram behind him, Michael turns and smiles showing his putrid teeth and with a sudden twitch of his head, professes with an upraised finger to help him form his words, "'E…awrigh'…an'…gi'..mmm…me fif'y pen'…"

He hurriedly stuffs his hand into his trouser pocket, panicking in case he cannot find the prize quickly enough and that his friends will not believe him. His face breaks out into a twisted smile as his grimy fingers clutch at the seven sided coin, he withdraws it and gleefully holds it aloft.

"'E can't be alright Dumbo." a voice shouts. "Yer Mam's puttin' 'im to bed."

Laughter from the gathered group erupts spontaneously. Michael's face stiffens and a frown appears, he cannot understand why they are all so happy, he has the fifty pence after all.

Fingers point to the upstairs window of Michael's house and the innuendo laden remarks continue. They are still a puzzle to Michael although he does wonder why his Mothers bedroom curtains are being drawn at this time of day.

Michael smiles again and twitches; he waves to his friends and turns his back on them. With his right arm outstretched behind him, he pulls the pram across the cobbles.

*****

A light drizzle was falling yet Michael didn't notice. The length of broken cast iron fall pipe had caught his eye. He scurried across to where it lay and again his eyes darted around the rubble for a tool of some kind. He had already forgotten the rock which he had discarded earlier; Michael is unable to retain information.

He frantically heaved at the length of pipe and lost his balance as it moved far easier than he had expected. He couldn't believe his luck, the pipe was cracked in a number of places along its calloused length and as he pulled it sideways to free it from the glutinous quagmire, it fell apart into three manageable pieces. Michael sang out with glee, almost unable to contain himself.

The pieces of pipe are neatly positioned in his pram along with the twisted hinges, the window latches and the odd brass door handle. He rocked the pram back and forth, feeling its weight, calculating its worth with a practiced, critical eye. A vestige of thought flitted through his disorganized brain, he paused for a moment, then nodded in determined self-agreement and snatching at the cracked crossbar, he pulled the pram over the rough ground toward the main road.

*****

Alan's patrol car sat neatly tucked away on the disused garage forecourt facing the main road. The driver's window was fully down and he rested his arm casually across the top of the door.

He looked up and down the main road before taking a long drag from the cigarette concealed in the cup of his hand. He exhaled the smoke out quickly through the window aperture in between the passage of vehicles traveling across the front of his vehicle. No point in inviting a Public complaint.

Alan's attention is focused on Michael, who is struggling with the pram as he negotiated a steep grassed embankment on the opposite side of the road. Michael is leant backwards at almost a forty five degree angle, attempting to keep his footing on the damp grass and maintain his grip on the crossbar of the pram. Sheer panic is etched across his face and he is sweating with effort. Alan chuckled to himself as he watched.

Michael was something of a local celebrity and the local uniforms would often try to engage him in conversation, and give him the odd cigarette if they were in a benevolent mood.

No matter how bad your day was, ten minutes with Michael would guarantee an acceptance that actually, things could be a lot worse.

The pram seemed to be getting the better of him. Michael didn't understand about inertia, momentum or gravity for that matter. The pram and its contents far exceeded his body weight and the steep descent of the embankment, coupled with the damp grass, made for a foregone conclusion.

"Watch yourself Michael." Alan called out, trying to control his laughter.

Michael snatched his head toward the direction of the voice and on seeing the patrol car, instinctively panicked and relinquished his grasp on the pram's crossbar. Gravity immediately had its way. The ancient pram raced down the embankment towards the main road gaining momentum with each yard.

It bounced on the uneven grass surface and its load spewed out, as the small wheels were buffeted and tossed as it hurtled down toward the kerb edge. Michael slipped on the damp grass underfoot and he fell heavily on his backside, crying out in despair at the apparent loss of his prize.

Alan's mirth suddenly turned to horror at the inevitable outcome; vehicles were travelling along both carriageways of the main road, the drivers blissfully unaware of the pram hurtling towards them like a rogue Exocet.

Indeed, their attention more drawn toward the Traffic car tucked surreptitiously away in the garage at the side of the road. The outcome was as obvious as it was unpreventable; Alan closed his eyes and turned away from the imminent vehicular carnage.

There was a howling of tortured tyres as vehicles braked and slewed sideways to avoid the pram which was now gliding unconcernedly across both carriageways.

Alan waited for the crump of pram against metal or the dull thump of imploding headlight units.

Miraculously, the pram survived its journey and collided with the opposite kerb edge, spilling the remainder of its load across the pavement as it upended.

Alan realized that he had been holding his breath and as the pram finally came to a standstill, he breathed out with relief and left the patrol car to placate the drivers, who had avoided the near death experience. "Officer, please tell me there isn't a baby in that pram." the female driver of a rather sporty Ford Capri asked.

Her vehicle was at forty five degrees across the carriageway and her face was a picture of anguish.

Alan smiled. "No, Ma'am, there isn't. There was one in charge of it and I *will* be having words." He glared across to the opposite pavement to where Michael stood with hands now dancing feverishly at his sides, his face a torrent of uncontrollable twitches.

"Oh, thank God." The woman pressed the palms of her hands against her cheeks. "I would never have forgiven myself."

"As long as you're ok." Alan said.

"Yes, thank you Officer." the woman said, fumbling at the ignition key with a hand that was visibly shaking.

The second driver was a little less concerned over the health, safety and wellbeing of the pram's occupant. His Jaguar was also slewed across the carriageway at an acute angle; thankfully, the driver had managed to miss the rear of the Capri by inches.

His sudden influx of adrenalin was released in rather less gracious terms. He activated the electric window which slid down silently. He pointed threateningly at Michael, who still danced nervously at the side of the road. "You fucking idiot…You want locking up."

The driver glowered at Alan, who was walking toward him. He revved his engine and having said his piece, set off with a screeching of his rear tyres.

Alan walked toward Michael, an admonishing look on his face. A dark, damp stain appeared across the front of Michael's trousers and he danced fitfully, apoplectic with anxiety.

"Jesus Christ Michael." Alan said and motioned toward the pram, still upended on the opposite pavement.

Michael's mouth hung slackly open, a thin sliver of saliva ran from his quivering bottom lip and onto his chin. "Ah…wa'..ah.. wa' jus'…"

Alan nodded. "I know Michael, you were just trying to…what for Christ's sake? You could have caused a serious accident and what's worse, I would have had to deal with it…I'm on days, I'm supposed to be resting!"

Tears welled up in Michaels eyes. His gaze dropped to the ground and he dragged the toe of his prematurely worn out shoe, childishly across the pavement.

Alan's anger melted. "Alright, it's alright Michael, no harm done." He considered giving him a comforting pat on the shoulder but then noticed the state of his clothing and decided that a kindly word would suffice.

Michael seemed to sense the change in Alan's mood and his facial twitching calmed, as he wiped at the tears which left pale streaks in the grime on his face.

Alan looked across to the debris scattered across the pavement. "Where were you goin' with this lot then Michael?"

"Di…ckin..sons." he stuttered, pointing down the road toward the scrap metal dealers.

"Not nicked is it?" Alan asked, an exaggerated accusatory tone in his voice.

Michael looked horrified, "N..n..no…ah..foun' it…all."

"Alright Michael, I believe you. Go pick all that shit up and get yourself sorted, ok?"

"Ha!" Michael snorted and beamed widely.

Alan grimaced inwardly at the blackened stumps of his teeth and the waft of fetid breath. "Off you go then, he said, nodding down the road toward the oil soaked wooden gates of Dickinson's scrap yard.

Michael loped across the road and set the pram back on its wheels. "Ah jus' ge…" he pointed back toward the grass embankment.

Alan nodded knowingly. "Alright, just don't get run over crossing the road Michael. You've caused enough mayhem for one morning."

Michael nodded feverishly and making an over exaggerated effort in checking the carriageways, scampered back toward the embankment to collect the jetsam ejected from the pram during its plummet toward the road.

Alan took his seat in the patrol car and watched as Michael rummaged around in the grass for the old discarded pieces of brass and cast iron. Satisfied that he had gathered up all the missing pieces, Michael arranged them all carefully in the bed of the pram and smiling at Alan, he sauntered off along the pavement.

Alan lit a cigarette and relaxed. Ten six days were a breeze.

The early turn crews picked up all the calls. There was only the cross over period of an hour or so between one o'clock, when the six a.m. crews went in, and two thirty, when the late turn crews turned out when he might get a shout.

The radio was quiet and he reached across to the back seats and dug deep into his briefcase for his copy of Colin Greenwood's 'Police Tactics In Armed Operations'. Alan had forked out for a copy of the book as he had been told that the instructors on the basic firearms course considered it to be the 'bible' and font of all knowledge for those aspiring to become authorized firearms Officers. He settled down in his seat to do a little course preparation in the Firm's time.

His studies were interrupted after a few minutes as Michael appeared at the side of the patrol car.

Alan sighed, but tried not to let his irritation show. "How'd you go on then Michael?"

"Th…thirty…pen." Michael beamed and opened his clenched fist to show Alan the three silver coins, brilliant against the dirt engrained into the palm of his hand.

"That much eh." Alan exclaimed. "Off for some more then is it?"

"If a can..f..f..fin' some." Michael stuttered.

Alan backed away from the open window a little to avoid a fine spray of spittle and the retching smell of Michael's fetid breath.

"See you later then Michael…and try and control that bleedin' pram." he shouted, as he watched Michael lurching across the road, back toward the embankment.

"Thirty fuckin' pence…You miserable bastard Dickinson." Alan muttered to himself.

Closing his book, he decided to do his good deed for the day and started the engine of the patroller.

\*\*\*\*\*

As the Police car entered the scrap dealer's yard, a labourer noticed Alan's presence and issued a shrill warning whistle through his teeth.

A large Rottweiler, its black and tan fur, matted with old engine oil, sprang to its feet. It launched itself forward from a kennel amongst the piles of corroding engines stacked in the corner of the yard. Alan quickly calculated the length of the heavy chain which hopefully secured the beast to a metal ring cemented into the high brick wall surrounding the yard. He took a couple of precautionary paces to the left.

The Rottweiler yelped as it was jerked completely off its feet when the chain reached the extent of its travel and snapped tight around its neck.

Almost immediately, Dickinson appeared from within an old caravan which served as the site office.

"Mr Pendle." he beamed with a smile as false as his grandmother's teeth. "To what do I owe this 'onour?"

Alan glanced around the yard. The labourer, probably wanted on a dozen warrants, quickly turned away and busied himself with the pile of ferrous and non-ferrous scrap he was sorting through.

"You can get your junk yard dog under control for starters." Alan said, nodding toward the beast, now slavering at the mouth and dancing at the end of the taut chain.

Dickinson gave a single word of command and the ten stone monster slunk silently back to its lair.

Dickinson was just as fat as Alan remembered. In fact, he was now bordering on the morbidly obese. The only evidence that his oil engrained lumberjack shirt had ever been off his back, were the deep oil stains around the buttonholes. Its continued daily use could be calculated by the dried sweat rings which emanated in differing radii from beneath his armpits. The tail of the shirt hung out from beneath the wide oil stained leather belt, which held up his jeans. The fat on his back was exposed, it protruded disgustingly over the top of the straining belt, mottled and milky white.

The bottom button from the front of his shirt was missing, probably due to the constant pressure of his stomach, which was covered with a thick mat of coarse black hair. It hung in a large fold, spilling out over the top of the polished buckle.

Dickinson it was reputed, bathed twice a year, whether he needed to or not. The smell which hung about him like an aurora, was odious and sickening, as was Dickinson himself.

"Had a visit from young Michael today Mr Dickinson?" Alan asked.

Dickinson scratched his filthy bald pate with an equally filthy finger.

"'E 'as bin in as 'ow you should mention it Mr Pendle. Why? What's the problem?"

Alan casually looked around the yard. "Where's the stuff he brought in?"

Dickinson scratched himself vigorously beneath his armpit and looked around the yard.

"Sorted by now I reckon, our Frank there doesn't hang around." Dickinson nodded toward where his labourer was rummaging around amongst the metal detritus in the yard. "Good lad is our Frank, all this will be 'is one day of course. We're none of us getting' any younger eh, Mr Pendle?"

Alan nodded, ignoring Dickinson's platitudes.

"I'll come straight to the point Mr Dickinson... Young Michael must make two or three trips a day to this yard. He spends half his day wandering around on that demolition site and I personally have seen him come up with sizeable amounts of brass and scraps of lead. Having delivered said amounts of non-ferrous metals to your establishment, he comes away with twenty or thirty pence in his sweaty palm."

Dickinson wiped the top of his bald pate with a calloused hand and fidgeted nervously.

"Now...I'm not suggesting for one moment that a man of your good standing in the community would take unfair advantage over young Michael, just because he's shall we say...a brick short of a full load...Heaven forbid. Strange though..." Alan paused to let the moment hover a little. "I've never seen him with any form of receipt. Perhaps he throws them away, eh?"

Dickinson started to intercede. Alan held up a hand to stop him. "Now I know that over the years, we have built up a good professional relationship Mr Dickinson. I am ever mindful of the odd stolen vehicle which has been turned in...We, the Police on the other hand, may well deserve a smattering of criticism for failing to enforce the laws in relation to the keeping of records and receipts in respect of non-ferrous metals...yours in particular. Getting my drift Mr Dickinson?"

"Well, look...I....er..." Dickinson murmured and looked sheepishly to the ground. He pushed a grimy finger into his ear and jiggled it around energetically, no doubt disturbing the offending family of lice resident within.

Alan continued. "As it's not local knowledge, you could be forgiven for not knowing...that today is Michael's birthday. It would be a nice gesture if that special day were to be recognized, what do you say Mr Dickinson?"

Dickinson knew he was being raped, but managed to smile weakly as he removed the probing finger and inspected a large yellow wad of wax which he hastily wiped across the front of his shirt.

"'E's a good lad is Michael, like you say Mr Pendle, one of my reg'lars...I'll bung 'im a fiver."

Alan remained silent but raised a questioning eyebrow.

"A tenner I mean." Dickinson snapped, his voice breaking slightly.

Alan smiled knowingly. "I'm sure that you will make Michael's birthday very special Mr Dickinson."

He glanced at his watch. "Gosh, is that the time, I'd best be on my way, crime to fight. Communities to protect eh."

Dickinson chewed at the inside of his cheek as he watched the stalwart keeper of the Queen's peace walk back to his patroller.

"Bastard." he muttered under his breath.

*****

Michael looked stupefied at the oil stained ten pound note, Mr. Dickinson had given him.

He frowned as if confused and wondered why Mr Dickinson had slapped him across the side of his head and said "Happy birthday Michael, now fuck off."

Perhaps he had found something very special this time, something that Mr Dickinson wanted very badly. Anyway, he'd be able to have a drink tonight; sure he would, thanks to Mr Dickinson. It must be his birthday, Mr Dickinson had said so. He wouldn't tell his Mum about the money though. No, he mustn't do that; she'd take it off him, like she took the money from the unemployment people.

A secret…That's what it would be…a birthday secret.

## **Twenty One**

Alan's concentration was abruptly broken by a sudden static laden message over the Burndept radio, suspended within the webbing harness which was hung around his neck.

"Papa Yankee One Two."

Without taking his eyes from his book, Alan depressed the small red button on the radio slung beneath his chin.

"One Two. Go ahead."

"One Two, could you cover a 10/15 for us please. Female occupant of seventeen Elsie Terrace reports hearing noises in her loft."

"Noises?"

"Footfalls, apparently there's someone in her loft; it's down as a suspect on premises."

Alan sighed and thumbed the transmit button again. "One Two 10/4, show me attending. Any other units en route?"

"Negative One Two, you're all we've got at the moment. I'll see if there's a dog about."

Consigning Mr Greenwood's instructional masterpiece on Police firearms tactics to his briefcase, Alan started the engine of his patroller and thumbed the rocker switch to activate the blue lights.

*****

Evie sipped her coffee and looked across the chipped Formica topped table at her friend slumped in her seat opposite. It had been a quiet night for both of them and as usual, around noon, the two of them would meet at Della's Soul Food for coffee and a catch up.

Her friend looked worried, her face more drawn than usual after a night on the streets and Evie noticed that her hands trembled as she raised the coffee cup to her lips.

"He did it Eve. He said he was goin' to do it, an' he fuckin' did it."

Evie stretched back in her chair, allowing the hard curved surface of the back rest to force her shoulders backward. It eased the dull ache in the small of her back, but she winced as her muscles protested. She breathed out slowly to ease the pressure.

Evie looked puzzled. "Why 'im tell you 'bout dis?...why 'im not jus' do the fuckin' deed widout?"

Her friend chewed at her bottom lip and gripped her cup tightly, as if she were trying to stop herself from crying. "'Cos 'e wanted to know stuff first...'E frightens me Eve...what 'e did to Mai Long, that fuckin' razor." she paused. "I tol' him 'bout Fastener."

Evie raised a questioning eyebrow.

Her friend sighed with exasperation and her tone became desperate. "I fuckin' know..He got me in his car Evie, drove out to some car park in the middle of nowhere....He wanted to know stuff...He had that look...He would have cut me Evie, I jus' know it...So I tol' him stuff."

"Tol' 'im what?" Evie asked pensively.

Her friend shuffled uncomfortably in her chair and stared down at her hands. "Like...when 'e did 'is collections an' where 'e went after, you know. 'O'w 'e always walks to that same taxi rank on Frazer Road if 'e's goin' gamblin' down town...'E said 'e was gonna see 'im off Evie.....an' look what's 'appened."

"Fast'ner be dead sure 'nough." Evie said quietly. "Seen it...That motherfucker was busted up bad. Truth is, dat nigger fucked up girl. Run down wid dat car an' all, his legs an' face all...Jesus." she said shuddering.

Her friend sat in silence and gazed out through the large window to the street beyond. She fumbled in her grip bag and shuffled her fingers between the packets of condoms to reach down to her cigarettes. Flipping the top of the pack open with her thumb, she offered it across the table top. Evie gripped the edge of one of the filter tips between her long fingernails and drew one out. The packet shook, as her friend placed it against her lips and pulled out one of the cigarettes with her lips.

"Lookit you girl." Evie said pointedly in her singing Patois, a frown creeping across her forehead. "You be a mess, you needs to gweh, wuk someplace else fa'while."

"He's crazy Evie, you can see it in his eyes...He'd find me an' I'd end up like Mai Long."

Evie toyed with her empty cup, turning it slowly on the saucer between her fingertips. Her friend looked dejected and wiped at her eyes with the back of her hand as they sat in silence, watching the morning sky darken. A portent of rain.

*****

Alan killed the sirens half a mile or so from the location of the call, and not particularly looking forward to scrambling around in someone's filthy loft, he keyed his radio.

"Papa Yankee One Two."

"One Two go ahead."

"From One Two, I'm almost 10/6 in the Elsie's. Any news on a dog over?"

The sound of a Police Dog barking, coupled with a verbal threat from its handler of the certainty of forthcoming pain and suffering if the dog were to be released, would usually be sufficient to convince the secreted suspect to capitulate and produce himself voluntarily, whilst the dog was still under the relative control of its handler.

"One Two. Whiskey Delta Three has just gone 10/6 on scene."

Alan smiled to himself and scanned the street names as he passed the seemingly endless rows of back to back terraced houses. The white Ford Escort Dog van half way up the cobbled street caught his eye and Alan swung his patroller from the main road.

"One Two. Show me 10/6."

Alan did not wait for a response from the radio operator, but flicked the switch to kill his blue lights.

He pulled up to the rear of the dog van which was rocking on its suspension, as the excited German shepherd barked and bounced around within its cage. The Dog Handler was standing by the front door of the premises; the female occupant who had a nervous grip on his uniform jacket was pointing up toward the roof area of her house.

The Elsie's had been built just after the First World War, to service the workers at the local Foundry. They were 'two up two down' and the whole terrace, shared a joint loft space. Breaking into just one of the dank, decrepit premises, allowed a burglar with a minimum of effort, to negotiate the various loft panels and gain access to the whole terrace. Although, what any of the occupant's might possess that was actually worth stealing was debatable. The vast majority of the occupants of these rundown Council owned properties, were active members of the 'criminal fraternity' and had a propensity for burgling each other's property. It was simply a matter of time and the law of averages, before the tape deck or television stolen during a burglary, was actually the one which had previously been burgled from the burglar's house. It was simply 'redistribution of wealth' in its basest format.

"Hey Laurie." Alan called out to the Dog Handler as he approached.

The Dog Handler nodded in response. "Casement window's been cracked open down at number one, forcible entry, looks like a screwdriver job or something, Mrs…?"

"Hennigan." the nervous occupant added quickly.

"Mrs Hennigan here says she can hear someone plodding around in her loft. She's scared to go back in. Anyone else turning up?"

Alan shook his head. "I'm it mate. Shift change."

The Dog Handler sighed and turned to the occupant who had stepped out onto the flagstones to peer up at the roof of her premises.

"Is there a loft ladder love?"

She shook her head. "There's nowt up there, 'cept for some of our Michael's old stuff. There's a chair on't landin', yer can reach up from that."

The Dog Handler sighed again and walked to the rear of his van. As the rear doors were thrown open, the beast within reacted frantically at the prospect of some form of action and the van rocked violently as the Dog man opened the inner steel cage door.

He reached in to clip the end of his thick plaited leather leash onto the dog's collar. The polished brass plate, riveted to the upper cross frame of the inner cage was engraved with the name 'Bren'.

The moment the leash was secured, the Police dog leapt from the rear of the van and immediately sat by the heels of his handler. Huge brown eyes, gazed expectantly up toward his master.

Alan cautiously stepped back from the rear of the van, his hands involuntarily crossing over the front of his trousers. Police Dogs, would normally recognise the bright yellow of a Traffic Man's jacket, but a Police dog's 'friend or foe' recognition skills weren't to be wholly relied upon.

Police Dog 'Bren' was a long haired Shepherd. His black and tan coat shimmered as he danced expectantly. His dark, alert eyes darted about the street.

"Do the street Alan. I'll let him hear the pup."

"Works for me." Alan said. He walked across to the pavement on the other side of the cobbled street, to obtain a good view of the entire row of houses.

"Warrabout me?" the occupant asked expectantly.

"You'll be alright if you stay in your front room love. Keep your door closed. I'll take some details from you in a bit, ok. Just let the dog do its thing." Alan said.

The Dog Handler entered the premises and 'Bren' scampered up the wooden staircase toward the upper landing, the leash creaking as the plaited leather was stretched taut.

Alan stood with his hands in the pockets of his jacket, looking up at the upper floor windows along the row of houses. He heard the Dog Handler issue his challenge that there was some 'pain to be had' if the dog had to come up. He looked expectantly at each individual window for the first signs of movement.

'Bren' barked when told to speak, but there was no sign of an escape attempt.

Alan heard the crisp sound of an order. "Stay." followed by the clump of the Dog Handler's boots on the bare wooden stairs as he descended.

"Give us a hand Alan." he shouted across the street from the open front door.

"Sorry?" Alan shouted back, looking slightly alarmed.

"Give us a hand. He's gonna have to go up."

Alan's face took on a disconsolate expression as he walked slowly across the cobbles to the waiting Dog man. "Which entails what exactly Laurie?" Alan asked inquisitively, his tone liberally laced with caution.

The Dog man nodded toward the top of the stairs. "He's indicated, so there's someone up there. There's only a fuckin' chair to stand on, I can't lift 'im on my own."

"Lift him?.. You mean physically? Alan responded quizzically.

The Dog man nodded as if confused by Alan's concern.

"How much does 'Bren' weigh Laurie?...and before you astound me, 'cos I'm already guessing around six or seven stones…in his obvious excited state, how is he going to react to me, essentially a complete stranger, grabbing him and shoving him up through a loft hatch?"

The Dog man chuckled at Alan's obvious hesitancy. "You'll be sound mate, 'e's used to it. You just stand on the chair, push the fuckin' trap door open, kneel down on the chair an' let the boy run up yer back an' 'e'll be up in the loft like a rocket."

"Ignoring my exposed arse in the process I hope Laurie…You'll forgive my natural tendency toward self-preservation…but I haven't had the pleasure of siring any children yet."

"Come on." the Dog man said, grabbing Alan by the arm.

'Bren' sat up as Alan approached up the staircase; his eyes darted backward and forward from Alan to his handler as if seeking advice.

Alan halted halfway up the stairs. "Have a word with him Laurie, for fuck's sake."

"What's up with yer, get up to the landin'…Bren, get down 'ere lad."

'Bren' rushed passed to be with his Handler, almost taking Alan off his feet.

There was indeed a wooden framed chair up against the bare plaster wall of the landing area, Alan pulled it underneath the loft aperture and climbed onto the seat base, feeling the dog's hot breath now wafting up around his ankles.

With a hefty push, the loft cover was freed from its drop fitting and Alan was rewarded with a thick fall of dust. He could hear the Police Dog at his heels squirming and moaning excitedly in the back of its throat.

Alan knelt on the seat and gripped the cross rail on the backrest of the rickety chair.

"Last chance…" the Dog Handler shouted loudly. "Show yerself."

No response.

"Lean for'ard Alan, give 'im something to climb onto." the handler said quietly and pushed Alan forwards so that his head and shoulders were forced down against the wooden cross rail.

"Get up lad, go on."

With a howl, 'Bren' leapt from the floor and in what seemed to be a single movement; up onto Alan's back and in an instant, disappeared into the pitch blackness of the loft.

"'E'll flush the twat out Alan, I'd get back downstairs if I wa…"

From somewhere further along the loft space, over the sound of frantic barking, there was the sound of shattering plasterboard followed by the dull thump of a body dropping onto floorboards below. "'E's out Alan." the dog man shouted.

Alan leapt down to make room for the Dog man who pushed passed him to stand on the chair. He shone his torch beam straight up into the loft like a homing beacon. "BREN! out…Out lad." he shouted.

Alan rushed back down the stairs, out through the front door and onto the cobbles in time to see a young black male, clambering out through an open upstairs window and leaping for the nearby fall pipe.

As the burglar slithered down the pipe toward the pavement, Alan commenced his run, already reaching for the leather pouch containing his handcuffs.

"STAND STILL!" The dog man shouted from the door.

Alan froze and instinctively cupped his hands around his testicles.

There was the sound of skittering claws against flagstones as 'Bren' tried to gain traction. He swept passed Alan and on toward where the young black had now dropped to the pavement and was taking flight. "It's fuckin' Audsley Wickens, the thievin' little bastard." the handler called back over his shoulder, as he set off in pursuit of his dog.

Alan watched as Police dog 'Bren' hurtled down the pavement after the burglar. His long fur rippled like long grass caught in a summer breeze, his ears were laid flat against the side of his head and his eyes were set, fixed on his quarry who pointlessly zig-zagged from side to side, slipping on the cobbles and scrambling to his feet. Desperate to find somewhere out of the reach of almost eight stones of oncoming Police dog and the inevitable pain of its teeth sinking into his flesh, he ran.

"WICKENS…STAND STILL!" Alan heard the dog man shout loudly, as he ran down the street after him. He clutched his handcuffs in readiness.

The dog was almost upon his quarry. Ignoring the dog handler's instructions; frantically the young black searched the street, an open doorway, a bin to climb on, a fall pipe to clamber up, anything.

Across the street, precariously balanced on breeze blocks, bereft of its rear axle and both front wheels, was a rusting Ford Transit. Across the much dented side panels, a hand painted sign declared that it was owned by Murphy's roofers along with a local telephone number. Looking altogether like an abandoned project, its front offside wing still sported its dark brown protective delivery paint and the bonnet was propped open with a length of wood.

The burglar ran for sanctuary. He threw himself to the cobbles and slithered beneath the Transit, ignoring the lake of thick oil which had seeped from the back of the gearbox, he slewed himself around so that he could see the approaching dog.

'Bren' skittered to a halt at the front of the vehicle and peered beneath the front bumper at the breathless heaving body. Down the side of the vehicle, crouched down on his front legs, he moved, barking and twisting his head sideways, pushing his snout under the vehicle to get nearer to the prize.

The burglar maneuvered himself around so that he still faced the dog, shuffling himself further away beneath the vehicle as the dog attempted to reach him.

"SET BREN!" the Dog man shouted as he ran up to the Transit.

Alan joined him after a few seconds, his chest heaving and his breath coming in short gasps. The stitch in his side was painful and his legs shook from the exertion, and for the thousandth time, Alan swore to himself that he would stop smoking.

The Police dog immediately sat by his handler's feet, his head bobbing down between his shoulders to maintain his view of the petrified burglar.

The Dog man squatted down on his haunches and peered beneath the Transit.

"Wickens you burgling little shit..Out..NOW!

Alan fought to bring his breathing under control and leaned with one hand against the rear door of the Transit, feeling slightly dizzy.

The burglar remained quivering in the shallow space between the floorpan and the cobbles, his eyes wide open and fixed on the returned victorious gaze, from the dark brown eyes of the panting Shepherd.

"Wickens, come out...NOW. I won't ask again." the Dog handler again called out to the panicking burglar, quaking beneath the Transit.

Waiting only a moment, he rose to his feet and looked down at his dog. 'Bren' looked up at his handler expectantly, waiting for an order, his tongue lolling out from the side of his mouth.

"Fetch him out Bren." The Dog man said, nodding toward the vehicle.

As if a switch had been flicked, the dog launched itself at the side of the Transit, prancing joyously from side to side, then splaying out its front legs in order to squeeze its large bulk beneath the vehicle's rusting sill.

As the burglar squirmed away from the snapping jaws of the Shepherd, he screamed in abject terror, which only seemed to excite the dog further.

"Fetch him out then lad." the handler urged. "Bastards Bren, get them bastards for me."

The dog howled and squirmed in frustration. The burglar's screams intensified and Alan looked up and down the street, concerned that the incident might be attracting unwanted attention. The barking of the Police dog had been sufficient to ensure that those residents not drinking away their dole money at the pub, stayed inside their squalid hovels. Even Mrs Hennigan had closed her door and Alan noticed that her face was absent from the window.

"I could probably get a cuff on him now Laurie. I could pull him out." Alan offered, growing slightly concerned as he watched the dog splay all four legs and begin to 'limbo' underneath the vehicle.

The dog handler shook his head, unconcerned. "Nah... Let 'im 'ave a taste first Alan, doesn't do 'em any good to pull 'em off once they've bin set to. Confuses 'em see."

There was a deep guttural growling and a thrashing sound from beneath the Transit. The frantic screams ceased and there was a single chilling shriek of pain.

Alan rushed to the pavement side of the Transit and dropping to one knee, grabbed hold of the burglar's right arm which had appeared from beneath the vehicle. Taking his handcuffs, he slapped the ratchet bar down against the wrist bone and the cuff swung completely around and snapped shut.

"I have him Laurie." Alan called out loudly, pulling his prisoner out from beneath the Transit. "He's nicked." Alan knelt down and stared at the shaking, petrified burglar as he eased him out and onto the pavement.

There was the foul smell of human excrement, and the front of his jeans bore the dark indication that he had also lost control of his bladder. To the far side of the Transit, Alan could hear the handler enthusiastically praising his dog. "He's a good boy. Bren's a good boy." There was the sound of patting and the ruffling of fur, which was followed by joyful barking as the Shepherd was lead prancing back to the Police van.

The sobbing burglar was dragged to his knees. Alan secured his hands behind his back with the other cuff before raising him to his feet. He grimaced with pain and cried out, shifting all his weight to his left leg. Alan glanced down to the side of his prisoner's right calf. Neat holes had been punched through the denim and blood was flowing freely from beneath the material and onto the side of his tattered trainers.

"You're not obliged to say anything but anything you do say may be given in evidence, you're under arrest on suspicion of burglary." Alan said, as he led his hobbling prisoner back toward his patrol car.

Job done, 'Bren' leapt back into his cage and the dog handler closed the steel mesh door.

"Do us a favour Laurie, get us an accident sign out of the boot, he's shit himself. I don't want it all over the seats." Alan said as he opened the rear door of the patroller. He pushed the prisoner up tight against the roof gutter, as the dog man unrolled the large blue and white plastic roadside 'Police Accident' sign and laid it out across the back seats.

"Keep your feet on the rubber mats; I don't want you bleedin' all over my carpets." Alan said as he forced his prisoner's head down and eased him into the vehicle after making sure that the plastic sign was placed squarely beneath his backside.

"Where's 'e goin' Alan?" the dog handler asked, as Alan closed the rear passenger door.

"Bridewell Laurie…Custody Sergeant at Moorwood'll go ballistic if I turn up with him in this state."

The dog handler frowned. "They'll get the Force Surgeon out to 'im. Christ, 'e only needs a plaster."

"I'm not talking about his fucking leg Laurie. Have you smelled him? It's enough to make you gag. Custody'll go ape shit. He'll be to strip off. His kit to tag and bag, shower him down an' give him some of Custody's 'tracky' bottoms. I'm not exactly flavour of the month at Moorwood at the moment mate. No…he can go to the Bridewell."

The dog man nodded. "I'll see Mrs Hennigan then, get some details. D'you want me to call it in?"

"If you don't mind Laurie, sooner I get him stowed away the better. I'll see you up at Moorwood Traffic to do our books. You on earlies?"

The dog man shook his head. "Days…I'm off at five."

Alan took his seat, grimacing at the bitter, fetid stench. He quickly started the engine to provide power for the electric windows. Depressing the rocker switches, both front windows slid down silently and he turned the blower up full to circulate some fresh air into the cab. He nosed the patroller out from behind the dog van and accelerated away towards the City.

*****

The shop smelled musty, like an old church hall. It was brightly lit, almost garish with large star shaped price tags in fluorescent pink, yellow and lime green, attached to the numerous articles offered for sale.

Both electric and acoustic guitars were stacked in racks around the side walls, all tilting uniformly and gathering dust. Amplifiers and microphones were heaped beneath.
Televisions and VHS recorders stacked on plinths rising from floor to ceiling, all bore similarly colourful notices guaranteeing their full working order. Their remote controllers taped to their side cases. Tape decks, turntables and full stereo systems, all individually priced in dazzling fluorescence, were all neatly stacked to catch the eye.

All the detritus of society was here. Racks of clothing, suits and a myriad of leather jackets, all sorted by size and quality. Golf clubs and sports equipment, air pistols, rifles and telescopic sights, all similarly stacked or racked.

The sturdy counter top was glass, frosted almost to opaqueness from the constant passage of relinquished or abandoned articles passed across its surface. Beneath, black velvet cushions cosseted watches, rings and jewellery. Necklaces and brooches in profusion, all glittering, polished to tempt the prospective purchaser.

'Midnight' stood before the counter, his hands pushed deep into the side pockets of his jacket; he gazed around the shop as the proprietor peered through his eyepiece.

The watch was carefully weighed and the heavy gold bracelet scrutinized for scratches or blemishes. He gently twisted the knurled bezel to check for correct tautness. The broker tilted the watch to check that the small 'cyclops eye' panel positioned over the date window, was genuinely magnifying the small number to two and a half times its actual size. He held the piece to his ear, the second hand swept silently and near seamlessly around the face. Eight almost indiscernible movements to each second, giving the impression of perpetual movement.

The broker inserted one end of what looked like a dentist's stainless steel tool into the side lugs of the watch and expertly removed the heavy gold bracelet.

Using his eyepiece which he gripped tightly between his eyebrow and the muscle at the top of his cheek, he checked between the lugs for numbers. At the six o'clock position, the serial number, the model number at twelve.

He nodded to himself and with impressive dexterity, replaced the bracelet. With a gentle tug to ensure its security, he turned his attention to the triple-lock crown seal. Again he used his eyepiece to check for the three miniscule raised dots positioned beneath the trademark Rolex crown on the head of the mechanism.

'Midnight' watched intently as with practiced fingers and a half moon shaped implement, the smooth back plate was removed. The broker nodded, satisfied to see that the inner movement appeared to be genuine. All the gear wheels and cogs were indeed different colours.

He used his magnifier to check the four figure number stamped into a tiny gold plate, pressed into the stainless steel chassis. The numbers were evenly spaced and their depths of impression were equal. Lastly, with the back plate replaced, he turned the watch and lowering his eyepiece to within half an inch of the face, closely examined the writing. It was as it should be, slightly convex and perfectly spaced.

Slowly, he placed the watch onto a thin velvet cushion on the counter top, withdrew his eyepiece and rubbed his eyes with his knuckles. He looked up at the tall, muscular Negro behind the counter, their eyes met.

"This is a fine timepiece my dear. Are you wanting to sell it or raise funds against it?"

'Midnight' shrugged. "What's the difference?"

The broker smiled.

"If you require a loan against its value, this would entail you relinquishing the item to me, against receipt of course... and for an agreed period, you will pay me five per cent interest per month over however long you require the loan." He paused purposefully to drop the eyepiece into the middle pocket of his smock and replace his normal glasses across the bridge of his nose. "Or...if you have no further need for the item, I am prepared to make you an offer on it. If you accept the figure, the item becomes my property to dispose of as and when I see fit."

"It's the real thing then?" 'Midnight' asked.

The broker looked slightly confused.

"You need to ask?...The watch is not yours?" he asked, in hushed tones as if gently interrogating him.

"I won it at poker." 'Midnight' said and shrugged again. "I might have been fucked over."

The broker raised an eyebrow. "Eloquently put my dear...The table stakes must have been incredibly high." He paused again. "What took the pot?"

'Midnight' quickly thought back to the endless games he had played in prison, the stakes there, nothing more than cigarettes or someone's dessert after mid-day meal.

"Straight flush, nines through fives. He was into me for over six grand." He nodded down toward the watch. "That cover it?"

The broker chortled. "With change. In fact, you seem to have come out the better side of the debt my dear." He picked up the watch and smoothed his thumb across the flawless glass face.

"It's eighteen carat, a hundred and fifty grams, which is a little over five ounces. Personally, because of its weight, I would find it a little cumbersome to wear, but as with most things in life, it is a matter of choice."

"What's it worth?" 'Midnight' asked. He was becoming weary with the broker's Jewish singsong bullshit.

The broker looked down again at the watch in the palm of his hand. "The black face and bezel on the 'Submariner' is not as popular as the blue. To find a green would be quite rare…it is however relatively unmarked…"

"How much man?" 'Midnight' urged.

The broker slowly shrugged his shoulders. "On such a watch as this…I could go to seven thousand."

'Midnight's' heart thudded in his chest; he fought to keep his facial expression under control. "That's a sixteen grand watch if it's real."

"Perhaps more." the broker acceded with a wry smile. "When new and with the proper certification, but this watch…." he shook his head ponderously. "It has no provenance. Its true worth is in its integrity. You may well have come into its possession lawfully, who am I to say? But the loser….well my dear…" he shrugged. "Who knows? You understand my predicament my dear, the risk is all mine…"

'Midnight' looked directly into the broker's eyes. He fixed his gaze, there was no sign of bluff. "I'd take eight on it."

The broker raised the palms of his hands. "I thought you said that the pot was only worth six thousand. I offer you a thousand more than the debt and this is not enough?"

"That's the gamble man. If he'd topped my flush, he'd have kept his watch and the six grand. Like you said old man, it's a matter of choice."

The broker chortled. "I'll tell you what, I'll meet you in the middle, seven and a half and my children won't eat for a week."

'Midnight' nodded slowly. Seven and a half thousand pounds, just for the extra ten seconds it had taken to snatch it. He'd considered the four grand wad to have been a bonus. He'd got rid of the competition and gotten nearly twelve grand into the bargain.

"Ok, deal."

The pawnbroker smiled. "Come back in an hour my dear, I don't keep that kind of cash on the premises." He shrugged and raised the palms of his hands in the way of the Hebrew. "Such a world we live in."

*****

Alan drove around the perimeter drive of the Police station and into the back yard. As he reverse parked his patrol car he noticed the Police flatback recovery wagon in his rear view mirror.

"Another suffering panda consigned to the workshops no doubt." he thought and instinctively cast a glance toward the petrol pump. Unusually, it appeared to be unscathed.

Grabbing his briefcase from the rear seats he checked his watch, two hours to go. He weighed up the chances of getting a further call and decided that they were slim enough now that the late turn crews were on. He decided to risk it and pulled the vehicle's log book out from where it was wedged between the front passenger seat and the center console and added the end of shift mileage, one hundred and eighteen thousand, two hundred and forty two.

Alan patted the top of the dashboard fascia lovingly and pushed the dog-eared log book back down the side of the seat.

The late turn crew was still in the Traffic office, Oldfield and 'Barney' his 'Aide' were seemingly busy with clerical. They both ignored Alan as he entered.

The Sergeant, as usual, omnipresent behind his desk grinned knowingly, his cigar clenched firmly between his teeth.

Pc Oldfield stretched theatrically, "E're Barney, I could *murder* a brew, go make us one."

"What....go all the way downstairs, leave it out, climbing them stairs is *murder* on my legs."

The 'Aide' tittered like an eight year old hearing the word penis for the first time.

The Sergeant chuckled, Alan stood nodding knowingly. Clearly the inter office 'banter' had started.

Oldfield swung round in his chair and slapped Alan playfully across the shoulder. "Here, Al, let's 'ave a read of yer report."

Alan dropped his briefcase by the side of the desk and carefully placed his white topped cap on top of the stationary drawers. "It's gone mate. Made to disappear on the orders of the very reverend Mr Forrester."

Oldfield snorted in disdain. "Huh…fuckin' typical, God botherin' twat, more concerned 'bout 'is fuckin' crime stats than a good bit of collision investigation…You 'ad Charlie half convinced mate."

Alan shrugged his shoulders. "Not enough to go along with it. My arse is still smarting, how's it finally gone in Roger?"

"Nothin' like your epic whodunit fail to stop 10/9. Stolen vehicle involved, enquiries to trace driver as yet without gain. 'Bout three lines, Charlie's usual spiel." The Sergeant said, reaching across the desk for the 'Team' lighter and setting fire to his cigar stub.

"I'd 'ave told 'im to go fuck 'imself. Monday to Friday twat, when did 'e ever deal with a 10/9." Oldfield's 'Aide' offered with false bravado.

The Sergeant leaned back in his chair and drew on his cigar. "And I reckon your aideship would have gone down as the shortest in the annals of Traffic history young Barney. Forrester might well be an arsehole, but unfortunately, not only has 'e got a direct line to God, he also runs the Division, which reminds me, you'd best chuck us the keys to 816."

"Why, what's up Sarge, the 'pig' got a flat battery again?" Alan asked.

"Yer'd best prep yerself for some bad news Alan lad. 'Cos secondary to the reaming you 'ad from the Reverend Forrester over yer Agatha Christie's 'Murder on Melville Road' saga…Yer allocated motor's history."

Alan frowned. "What do you mean history?"

"We've all 'ad us bollocks clipped." Oldfield spat.

The Sergeant shrugged resignedly. "Replaced mate. Yer beloved SD1 is goin' to that great auction in the sky. Central garage is here for it. They're out back with the flatback."

"It's running as sweet as a nut Roger." Alan protested.

The Traffic Sergeant picked up the minute sheet from the Divisional Chief Inspector. "It would appear that 816 is returning just eighteen miles to the gallon, an' its bin to workshops nine times in the last twelve months. Forrester has decided in his infinite wisdom, that it is no longer economically viable, an' it's a drain on Divisional resources…The V8's 'ave 'ad their day Al. The only reason I've managed to keep hold of the 'pig' is 'cos it's got a stem light an' I managed to convince 'im we needed it for 10/9's out in the sticks." the Sergeant said, before tossing the minute sheet back into his tray.

Alan looked dumbfounded. His Sergeant shrugged, resigned to the further emasculation of his Department.

"Charlie's 'Granny' will be gone by the end of the month." he said.

"What we getting?" Alan asked cautiously.

"Got." his Sergeant corrected him. "They're already here, well two of 'em anyway. Mick the handyman's swapping all the kit over and cuttin' rubber floor mats to fit."

"Fit what?" Alan said expectantly.

"Cavaliers Al." Oldfield said despondently. "The final fuckin' humiliation, we'll be a laughin' stock."

"Tell me it's not true Roger." Alan said, horrified.

The Sergeant sighed. "'fraid so."

Alan looked aghast. "Cavaliers...fucking Vauxhall Cavaliers...for Traffic...SRI's at least?"

The Traffic Sergeant shook his head slowly. "We might get one, but the rest are 1600's. Forrester reckons he can run two Cav's for the price of one Rover or a 'Granny'."

"What's the top end of a 1600 Cavalier?" Alan asked.

Oldfield sighed. "Ninety downhill with a followin' wind...maybe."

"About as much use as a chocolate fireguard in a chase then." Alan said. "How are we supposed to keep up with a 'Cossie'?...Or one of those new XR3i's?"

The Sergeant raised a cautionary hand. "Ah...that might become something of a 'moot' point actually. The Chief has decided on a non-pursuit policy...Read the 'weeklies' lads, you need to be aware. The Force is goin' all fluffy an' pink...We will no longer engage in the pursuit of stolen motors...Chief Mayhew reckons that stats show, that most 'knock offs' are dumped within five minutes of a chase commencin'....so, the operator at Force Control will now decide when the chase gets pulled. Once yer told to abort, that's it lads, game over. Give it five minutes or so, do an area search, find the motor an' call for recovery."

"Five minutes is a bit optimistic Sarge. Cavalier versus Cosworth or SRI." Oldfield said decidedly. "We'll be blown out of the water in less than a minute."

The Trafic 'Aide; piped up. "An' what about the 'twocer' Sarge? Forrester's detection figures are gonna take a nose dive".

The Traffic Sergeant shook his head. "Woe betide yer if yer carry on after you've bin aborted, 'specially if the fuckin' wheel comes off an' there's a bump. New rule Barney lad, it's all about budgets now. No one gives a flying fuck about crime bein' detected, it's about balancin' the Divisional budget. Financial restraint is the new key word....Oh, an' while we're on the subject of budgets, don't expect the clothin' van to turn up any more. Shirts, trousers, yellow jackets an' stuff will now only be replaced when necessary, an' you'll 'ave to put a minute sheet in sayin' why it needs replacin'…I'm glad I'm down to months now. You lads 'ave got it all to come…Barney, make a brew, there's a good lad."

"Have you had a go in one yet Sarge?" Alan asked.

"Yeah, did an evaluation this mornin'. Pathetic, wouldn't pull a fuckin' hen off its nest. No bollocks at all, naught to sixty in three days."

Alan sighed and turned to pull open his clerical tray. There was still no sign of the paperwork from the lock up on nights. "Anything come from the Bridewell on Rawlinson and Lofthouse Sarge?"

"Not unless it's languishin' in yer tray Pendle lad, best give 'em a ring. Oh, an' while I think on, what's the score on the lock up this mornin' in the Elsie's? Yer s'posed to be clearin' yer backlog, not addin' to it."

"Laurie Carswell's on his way up Sarge. I think he wants the collar, being as how his dog had a nibble."

*****

Police dog 'Bren' slunk stealthily along the top corridor, his head hung low, as if following an invisible trail. His huge paws padded rhythmically, silent on the carpeted surface, his eyes darting from side to side as he passed by the various open office doors.

Pc Carswell his handler walked a few paces behind, the leather braided lead held loosely in his hand. 'Bren' paused and looked back, but satisfied with the near presence of his handler, continued to pad down the long corridor.

A typist emerged from the typing pool carrying a large bundle of papers. She shrieked with terror as she saw the beast skulking toward her. Bren's bulging shoulder blades rippled beneath the long fur, his eyes glinted deep red in the glare from overhead fluorescent strip lights. His tongue lolled out from between his teeth. The bundle of typing was discarded in panic and the pages scattered across the corridor floor. 'Bren' stopped to sniff at them as the typist fled, slamming the typing pool door behind her.

Pausing at the open door to the Duties Clerk office, his head slowly swiveled. His gaze fell on the occupant, who jumped in horror and slopped coffee down the front of his trousers. Ignoring his scalded testicles, he leapt from his chair and onto his desk. "What the hell!"

'Bren' moved on, sniffing as he went.

Pc Carswell paused at the door to the Traffic office, his hand resting on the handle. "Bren" he called out softly. The dog stopped and looked back. "I'm in here lad, don't wander off."

"Hey up Laurie, I was wondering when you'd show." Alan said, as he tipped his chair back and reached out to press the switch on the side of the kettle.

The Dog man nodded to everyone. "Usual hive of industry in Traffic I see…Hey Sarge, how's it going?"

"Bad to worse Laurie." The Sergeant said decidedly and leaned back in his chair plaiting his fingers behind his head. "Way things are goin' you'll be getting' a push bike with a sidecar for yer pup."

A further fearful scream echoed from somewhere down the corridor accompanied by the sound of shattering crockery. 'Bren' 'avin' a smooch round is 'e?" the Traffic Sergeant asked.

The Dog man nodded. "He gets bored sittin' in the van, he'll be along in a minute. He knows where to find me. Not done yer book yet have you Al?"

Alan shook his head. "Nah, waiting for you mate, didn't know how you wanted to wor…"

The door to the Traffic office was suddenly thrown open and the Detective Sergeant peered in. "Laurie for fuck's sake…your dog's humpin' the D.I.'s leg, everybody's abandoning ship…call him off eh…*please*."

The Traffic Sergeant chuckled and almost choked on his cigar smoke.

"CARSWELL…GET IN HERE *NOW*" a wavering yet forceful voice called out from the Burglary Squad office.

The Dog man smiled. "Tell the D.I. 'e won't be long, an' it'll brush off once it dries..I wouldn't interrupt 'im if 'e's got to the vinegar stroke mind…Could turn nasty."

The Traffic men's laughter erupted.

"Laurie." the D.S. hissed forcefully. "Get the Hound of the fucking Baskervilles off the D.I.'s leg and out the Squad office…This is NOT a request."

Pc Carswell winked at the Traffic Sergeant who was by now, beside himself with laughter and wiping tears from his eyes.

The Dog man poked his head around the office door frame and gave a short shrill whistle through his teeth.

There was the sound of claws snagging against carpet fibers and almost instantly, the Shepherd was at the Traffic office door, panting and prancing to nuzzle his handler's outstretched hand.

"Sit Bren." his handler said, pointing down toward the corner of the office. Instantly 'Bren' dropped to the floor and rested his huge head on his front paws.

"See if you're 'appy with that Alan?" the Dog man said, handing Alan a typed copy of his incident report.

"Any biscuits around?" he said to no one in particular.

"I've got a Mars bar in my snap box." the Traffic 'Aide' offered.

The Dog man shook his head. "Nah…Thanks anyway Barney, chocolate makes 'im throw up."

Alan looked up from the incident report, a quizzical look about his face. "Didn't seem to bother him when he took a chunk out of young Wickens."

## **Twenty Two**

The thought nagged at him, nattered like an insatiable itch, constant, distracting and unreachable.  She knew. She was the only one who did. She was the solitary fly in the ointment and he knew that in the end, it would have to be picked out carefully, to leave the salve once again virgin and unblemished.

He had been a fool to confide in her and for that he berated himself. But what was done was done. He had needed information and she had been quick enough to offer it up, out of fear of him probably, but still offered up all the same. She had been the one who had known his habits, routine and weaknesses.

'Fastener's' death had triggered a confused panic amongst his soldiers. The 'blues' had been locked down. The 'Manager', fearing a coup by an outside faction, had issued orders to the street 'lieutenants' to distribute the 'product' to a number of 'safe' houses for security. The heavy bolts on the Louis Street 'blues' were slammed home.

The 'Manager' waited for the approach which would certainly be made.

'Midnight' lay on his bed pondering. He fondled the small handgun, slowly turning the cylinder, listening to the metallic clicks as it rotated. The ten small bullets lay scattered across his blanket; he lay the revolver down and picked up one of the rounds, rolling it between his index finger and thumb as he considered his next move. He sucked pensively on his teeth, his forehead screwed up into an intense frown as he remained deep in thought. If she got lifted by 'Vice', he knew that she'd sing to save her own ass. She'd offer information on him in exchange for a walkout, she'd 'squeal for a deal' sure enough, and the information she had, was worth far more to the Vice cops than a prosecution for 'common prostitute'.

Financially he was ready to re-assert himself, to recover his losses and to make his mark again. He had a little over twelve thousand and change in a tattered rucksack, which he had pushed into the bottom of his wardrobe. He could now afford to leave his squalid bedsit and rent a decent flat, somewhere away from the dreary greyness of the Melbourne's, somewhere modern, bright with central heating and a TV, somewhere anonymous, a bolt hole where nobody knew him.

He also had enough to buy two 'keys' of good quality Manchester 'blow'. By the time he had cut it with corn starch, baby powder or flour, it would weigh in at four or five times its original weight. But first, he had to be safe.

'Midnight' pushed the knurled release on the side of the revolver's frame. The cylinder swung out easily revealing the ten empty chambers. One by one, he fed the rounds back into place, checking again that the rim edges of all ten bullets were unblemished. He spun the cylinder slowly with his thumb one last time before snapping it shut. Ten shots, that's all he had. 'Midnight' had no idea where he could source more and if he made enquiries locally, everyone would know that he had come by 'Fastener's' piece. It would be as good as a hanging a sign around his neck, that he had at least been there, or maybe, had been causal to his demise.

It would have to be Manchester or down to the 'Smoke' if necessary. He still had contact with some of the old poker school from Holdthorpe. They would hook him up with what he needed for old times' sake, but for now, ten rounds would have to do.

Word on the street was that 'Fastener's' corpse had been plundered long before 'Babylon' had arrived and the older brothers had voiced their disgust at the act. "Young blood mo'fuckers got no goddam respec', rippin' into a nigger when 'e down. Dat 'Fas'ner' still be live I heard it when they bloods strip dat nigger. Even took dat nigger's shoes…motherfuckers."

'Midnight' took a deep breath and nodded slowly, as if all of a sudden, all his doubts were exorcised and his mind was made up.

Launching himself from the bed, he grabbed his jacket from where it hung on the back of the chair and patted the pockets to make sure he had his keys. Closing the door to the bedsit firmly behind him, he walked out into the night. He had learned a lot more than just how to play poker during his five years in Holdthorpe.

*****

A cloying damp mist hung low around the grey slate roofs of the houses, it whispered across his face as he walked and the sound of his footsteps were dulled in the still dead air. The street lights glowed with an ethereal yellow halo which surrounded their warm sodium filled bowls. The miniscule water droplets captured the emitted light and refracted it to form a fine circular shroud, leaving the streets and pavements in only half light.

As he walked, 'Midnight' mentally prepared himself, working out the minutia of his plan. The streets were all but deserted; it was a night to be inside.

At the junction with the main road, he walked across the carriageways and onto the forecourt of the all night garage. He pushed the glass shop door open with his jacketed forearm.

After his purchases, from the relatively bright lights of the garage forecourt, he walked quickly back into the dimly lit side streets and made his way home. The thin plastic bag containing his goods banging lightly against the side of his leg.

*****

She huddled down into the raised collar of her thin coat, pulling the lapels together across her throat. Her craving was now intense, gone was the energy and euphoric excitement she had felt after her last 'fix'. Now she fidgeted with anxiety, she felt exhausted and chilled to the bone.

Perhaps, she fooled herself, it was the cold, the descending mist, seeping through her sparse clothing which was causing the tremors in her arms and legs.

Above her the mist now blew gently in a slight breeze. It wafted across the glowing hood of the street light above her. It condensed as it touched the warm sodium filled glass and dripped in large droplets onto the pavement.

The headlights of a car cut through the eerie haze. The fine water vapour suspended in the air, muffling the sound of its engine as it approached.

She opened the neck of her coat again to expose the plunging neckline of her blouse and hitched up her skirt slightly. Adopting a forced smile, she moved toward the pavement edge in expectation.

The large Mercedes slowed and as the windscreen wiper cleared the fine damp haze from the screen, she could see the middle aged driver nervously peering out toward the pavement. The Mercedes slowed further, perceptibly. She stepped further toward the kerb edge, expecting the front passenger window to slide down.

The driver inspected her.

Perhaps it was the periorbital dark circles around her eyes or the way he had seen her fidgeting on his approach. Maybe her stick thin arms and legs had compounded his suspicions, that she was nothing more than a 'crack whore', but in any case, the Mercedes accelerated away, the red glow from its tail lights quickly swallowed up by the thickening mist. She shouted 'Fuck you." after the disappearing vehicle and stamped her foot in exasperation.

A 'ten spot' was all she had managed so far, picked up by the driver of a battered Ford Transit and driven to the unlit back streets. The vapours from the tile adhesive, smeared across the front of his overalls, had made her gag and her eyes water as she had taken him in her mouth. His hand had pressed down hard on the back of her head, preventing her from lifting away whilst his other had pulled up the back of her skirt and had been forced down the back of her knickers. As he had suddenly stiffened and released his hot seed against the back of her throat, she had felt a calloused finger roughly forcing its way into her anus. That had been over two hours ago and what she had earned, wouldn't take care of her craving.

*****

'Midnight' emptied the chambers of the revolver, letting the dull brass rounds fall once again onto the blanket across his bed. He walked through into the small kitchenette area and lit the gas on the single ring of the small propane gas cooker, adjusting the flickering blue flame down to its lowest setting.

Tearing off a six inch length of tin foil, he wrapped it around the end of the revolver's barrel, squeezing and smoothing it so that it perfectly formed a tight sheath across the raised stubby foresight and along the first two inches of the barrel.

Laying the revolver down on the small fold-away breakfast table, 'Midnight' twisted the top off the plastic bottle and tipped the contents of the soft drink he had bought into the sink. As the brown carbonated liquid gurgled away, he ran the cold tap and rinsed the inside of the bottle clear of the sticky sugary contents before wiping it dry with a towel.

Reaching again for the revolver, he held it in his left hand. With his right, he played the neck of the bottle over the gas flame until he could see that the polypropylene plastic was becoming soft. Quickly withdrawing it from the heat, 'Midnight' gently pushed the tin foil covered barrel end into the neck.

The hot plastic, softened by the heat, expanded with the pressure and distorted to allow the foresight and the first inch or so of the barrel to enter.

He waited, holding the bottle perfectly in line with the barrel until he was satisfied that the plastic had hardened sufficiently to retain its newly formed shape. As he gently withdrew the revolver's barrel, the tin foil slipped from the chromed surface of the stainless steel and remained heat welded within the neck of the now fully hardened bottle neck.

'Midnight' inspected his handiwork and satisfied that the barrel now slipped easily into the neck of the bottle, he pulled away the remnants of tin foil where they protruded from the open top and laid the bottle upside down in the sink, allowing time for the last of any water remaining inside, to drain away. He left it to dry out completely.

While he waited, 'Midnight' flicked through the glossy pages of the 'Men Only' magazine he had purchased from the garage before tearing six inch strips from the pages.

The paper was good quality and of a reasonable thickness, thick enough, in fact, that when he rolled the strips into a tight tube and placed them on the table top, they quickly unraveled and after a few moments, had lain almost flat.

More of the strips were prepared and retrieving the bottle from the sink. 'Midnight' flicked it sharply; neck downwards to eject any remaining droplets of water which might have lingered.

He rolled the first strips of paper into a tight tube and pushed them down into the bottle.

Once passed the restriction of the neck and fully inside the body of the bottle, the strips unraveled, forming a thin skin on the inside. More strips were rolled tight and similarly added until the inner wall of the plastic bottle was loosely lined with almost an inch of paper.

'Midnight' slotted the barrel of the revolver into the neck of the bottle and pulling off a foot or so of the black electrical tape he had purchased, wound it tightly around the joint and sealed the gap between plastic and steel until he was satisfied that the 'silencer' was securely fixed in place. Another worthwhile skill learned whilst at her Majesty's establishment Holdthorpe.

He dry fired the Smith and Wesson once to familiarize himself with the trigger pressure required to bring back the hammer and activate the action. Then he carefully re-chambered all ten rounds and placed the revolver within the thin plastic bag he had been given to carry his purchases from the garage.

*****

The mist was swirling now and the miniscule droplets had seeped into the fibers of her short coat. She could feel the cold dampness against her bare legs and her hair now hung in lank strands across her forehead. She shivered uncontrollably both with the plunging temperature and the symptoms of her cocaine withdrawal. Her anxiety levels rose, if she didn't get a 'punter' in the next half an hour, she knew that she would have to go and beg Sylvester for a gram of the 'paradise white', just a line on account. Perhaps if he was in a giving mood, he might accept a blow job in exchange for a grain or two of the Mexican black, just a few specks on a spoon, a few drops of water then held over the flame until it melted.

She pictured the bubbling light brown liquid as it danced in the bowl of the heat blackened spoon held over the flame, Imagined the sharp sting as the needle found a vein in her arm not yet hardened and narrowed by sclerosis. She remembered the immediate ecstatic 'rush' as the tourniquet wrapped tight around the bottom of her wasted bicep, was released and the drug shot up into her brain.

The heroin would rush through the blood-brain barrier and be converted to morphine; she would feel a warm pleasurable flush on her skin before falling into a semi-conscious dream like state.

The craving pulled at her and she moaned pitifully as she tried desperately to force the thoughts from her mind. In ten more minutes she knew that she would be climbing the steps to his flat, banging on his door and pleading with her man Sylvester to help her out, just this one time.

*****

'Midnight' sat in the Cortina with the engine running, waiting until it had warmed through. The windscreen wipers juddered noisily across the glass, clearing away the tiny mist droplets as the rubber blades arced backwards and forwards.

The revolver lay on the front passenger seat, still within the plastic bag. His heart thudded in his chest and he could feel it pounding in his temples as he gazed down at it.

He had considered using some of the black tape to slightly alter the registration number of his car, or disabling the small number plate lights on the rear bumper, but decided that the effort was unnecessary. The night was perfect; the mist was heavier now and swirling wraith like across the beams of his headlights. The lights glared back at him, reflected in the billions of water droplets suspended in the cold air.

He drove. The engine was now warm enough to feed hot air onto the inside of the windscreen and keep it clear of condensation.

'Midnight' turned and drove slowly into the street, his eyes scanning the alleyways and cobbled side streets for any signs of life. He flicked the headlights onto main beam, the reflective glare intensified, but it would serve a purpose, she would not be able to recognise his car until it was upon her.

As 'Midnight' drew nearer, he saw her. There was her lamp post, her 'turf', if she was working; he knew that this was where she would be.

He released his seat belt, he didn't want it snagging at the last moment. He gently slipped the car into first gear and reaching across the front passenger seat, he wound the window completely down.

Easing the car over toward the nearside kerb edge, he reached into the plastic bag with his left hand. His fingers curled around the molded grip. With a flick of the wrist, he shook the bag away into the footwell.

She squinted against the harsh glare of the oncoming headlights and half turned her head away as she walked toward the kerb edge.

'Midnight' glanced one last time into the rear view mirror, searching for the tell-tale sign of headlights. He saw nothing in the reflection but the dark grey veil across the road. His eyes flitted from where she was approaching, one hand now held up, to shield her eyes against the glare of his headlights. He searched down the road to where his view of it quickly disappeared into the mist. He dipped the clutch and felt the tyres rub gently against the kerb edge as he stopped momentarily.

She bent down to speak. As her head entered the warm interior of the vehicle, she recognised his eyes and the fixed, professional smile dropped from her face. His outstretched arm was holding something, a strange shape.

In the fraction of a second it took her to realise what it was, she saw the plastic bottle suddenly glow bright red, followed in a thousandth of a second, by a brilliant white light, not two inches from her face.

The forty grain, three and a half gram lead round, exited the barrel at almost eight hundred feet per second. Even insulated by the thick paper padding, the plastic bottle immediately swelled to almost twice its original size. The super-heated propellant gasses exited the barrel and expanded behind the bullet, which punched its way out through the thin polypropylene skin and struck the cornea of her left eye.

The bullet tore through her iris and the glutinous vitreous body of her eyeball before severing the optic nerve. Not yet distorted, the small lead projectile passed into the cerebral cortex and cerebellum area of her brain. Her thinking and perceptive abilities were immediately destroyed along with all thought processes from her brain back to her muscles. Her body remained standing by reflex action alone; she had not yet started to fall.

Through the soft tissue it continued, unopposed and undeflected until it impacted with the inner surface of the parietal cap of her skull. Kinetic energy was transferred back to the soft lead of the bullet which was still travelling at well over eight hundred feet per second. In a nanosecond, on first contact with bone, the nose of the soft lead round first flattened, then 'mushroomed'. Her head was suddenly and violently snapped backwards as the round exited through the back of her skull, along with minute splinters of bone fragment, brain matter and the soft flesh of her scalp.

In the darkness, 'Midnight' had been momentarily blinded by the primary muzzle flash escaping between the cylinder and the revolver's barrel as the hammer had fallen against the outer rim of the bullet casing. He had squinted, half expecting the home made 'silencer' to explode. It had held, and in fact, had worked with a modicum of success as his cell mate had assured him it would.

There had been a metallic click as the cylinder rotated and the hammer had fallen. The revolver had twitched slightly in his hand and there had been a sharp crack, but the sound produced by the muzzle flash, had been vastly reduced by the thick sheets of paper within the plastic bottle, and the dense mist had ensured the report had not travelled far enough to echo around the walls of the surrounding houses.

The bullet had travelled at twice the speed of sound, so Trina McKnight had heard nothing.
She may have momentarily felt the molten particles of plastic spattering against the side of her face, or the searing heat from the burning gasses and flakes of scorched paper as they were expelled and blasted against her cheek. There may have even been a brief instant of pain as the bullet first made contact with her eye, but no more than that. Her body had frozen for the

briefest of moments and then fallen to the pavement as if poleaxed.

'Midnight' had released the clutch and accelerated away into the mist the moment he had squeezed the trigger. Not waiting to see her fall, and not caring to see her leg twitching violently as the last confused electrical signals from her devastated brain, caused the nerves in her muscles to spasm, before finally accepting that she was dead.

*****

'Midnight' drove; he pushed the Cortina as hard as he dare in the poor visibility. A strange pungent smell filled the interior of the vehicle. Cordite and scorched paper, mixed with that of molten plastic. It stung his throat, and his eyes watered from the fumes. He quickly wound down his window to allow a through draft to dissipate the acrid smell.

He felt strangely calm and focused his concentration on his driving as well as how to tie up all the loose ends. Shooting the McKnight woman had been unbelievably easy and all over in a split second. He realised that he hadn't suffered from any of the nervous sweating or shuddering muscles as he had with 'Fastener'.

He again recalled the words of his cell mate, a man destined to spend the rest of his life in a space measuring eight feet by six. *"The first's the 'ardest Jimmy…after that they're all jus' fuckin' meat."*

The revolver was where he had dropped it immediately after taking the shot.

He cast a fleeting glance down into the passenger footwell. The end of the plastic bottle was blackened and distorted and a thin wisp of smoke still spilled from the exit hole, where the bullet had punched through. The inner paper cladding looked to be still smoldering slightly and getting rid of the 'silencer' became his primary objective.

Out onto the main road and towards the City, where the bright lights cut through the mist. 'Midnight' took extra care with his driving, he needed time to disassemble the silencer and a pull by the Traffic cops after a stupid mistake, would mean game over. He stayed on the main road, the Cortina becoming anonymous amongst the other traffic braving the foul weather.

Further out of the City and out onto the Ring Road. The mist slowly cleared as he drove out through the City gates and onto the unlit single carriageway roads, with rolling fields on either side.

After a mile or so, a small side road caught his eye. 'Midnight' glanced up into his rear view mirror and seeing that the road both ahead and behind was clear of any traffic, he quickly braked and swung the Cortina into the mouth of the single track road.

He drove carefully over the rough surface between the overgrown grass verges and noting a break in the dry stone walling, decided that the open gateway to the field, was wide enough to allow him to turn and it was far enough away from the main road to hide his presence. He turned off his lights and the ignition, sitting in silence, other than the ticking of the Cortina's engine as it cooled.

'Midnight' retrieved the Smith and Wesson from the floorwell and tore away at the black plastic tape securing the bottle to the barrel end. It had softened with the heat from the muzzle blast and the adhesive backing formed fine silk like strings and left a sticky residue on the barrel as he pulled it away.

He rolled the length of stretched and rippled tape into a tight ball between the palms of his hands. Pulling the bottle free, he pushed the ball of tape in through the open neck and after carefully sliding the revolver beneath his seat; he left the vehicle and knelt by the grass verge.

Playing the flame from his lighter against the thin shell of the plastic, it first sagged before falling into an ever widening hole. The polypropylene blackened, then dripped in molten globules onto the damp grass. The paper within finally caught hold, and 'Midnight' laid the bottle on the verge and stood watching as the 'silencer', along with any incriminating fingerprints burned.

*****

"Emergency, which service do you require?"

"Look…you'd better send the Police and an ambulance…Lawrence Place just off Porter Street, there's a girl laid out on the pavement."

"Are you with her now caller?"

"No…I…er just noticed her…as I were passing… you know. She looks to 'ave collapsed like."

"Where are you calling from sir?"

"I'm at a call box…Look, just send an ambulance…ok?"

"Can I take your name caller?....Hello…hello…Are you there caller?

## **Twenty Three**

The front face of the radio alarm suddenly illuminated and the dulcet tones of Mike Read advised all his breakfast show listeners that it was eight am. Alan opened his eyes and rolled over onto his back, reaching out to touch the 'snooze' button on the top of the Panasonic. The split flap display clicked quietly over to 8.01 as he rolled back and slipped his arm back under the duvet and curled it around her waist feeling the 'bed warmth' of her. She stirred and snuggled back against him. "Time is it?" she asked dozily, pulling his arm tighter around her waist.

"Just gone eight." Alan whispered into her ear, moving his hand up the front of her 'T' shirt and gently cupping one of her breasts. The warm, spicy fragrance of her lingering 'Obsession' and the fresh smell of her tousled hair aroused him as he kissed her neck.

She groaned with mock annoyance and pulled the duvet up around her ears.

Alan stretched and pressed himself up against her, feeling the heat from her nakedness where the 'T' shirt had ridden up over her buttocks.

"You'll be late." she warned, giggling sensually as she felt his hardness against her.

"Worth it." Alan said, but knowing she was right, he quickly kissed her again beneath her ear and leaping into action, threw off the duvet.

She grunted her disapproval as the warmth of the bed fled into the expanse of the room. She quickly gathered the duvet around her. Fully awake now, she sat up and stretched, leaning back against the headboard, she watched Alan as he loped toward the bathroom.

He paused at the door looking back at her. "You coming round after lates San'?"

She nestled further down into the bed. "All depends." she said smiling coyly.

"On?" Alan asked her enquiringly.

"Whether you're actually considering making an honest woman of me at some stage." she said smiling alluringly and allowing the duvet to fall down below the swell of her breasts.

Alan sighed. "I've been there San', didn't work out too well."

She looked despondent. "I'm nearly thirty Al, I just want to know where this is going. A little commitment on your part…you know."

Alan shrugged. "What's wrong with the way things are?"

She looked away, out through the half closed wooden slats of the window blind. Her eyes misted over.

Alan recognised the approaching sulk; he sighed and returned to the bed. He gently tucked her hair behind her ear and stroked her cheek. "Come on San', don't be like this, we're doing ok."

"*You're* doing ok Alan." she replied quickly, her tone changing as she turned back to him, looking him directly into his eyes. "I'm here for you whenever you want me…I just feel a bit like your 'Martini girl' Alan, you know…anytime, anyplace, anywhere…"

Alan glanced guiltily across at the radio alarm clock. The stark white numbers warned him it was 8.12.

He sighed. "Look, I'm gonna be late, we'll talk tonight ok? Ring me in the Traffic office if you end up working over…yeah?"

She nodded once, her face expressionless as she returned her gaze to the window.

*****

Despite being one of the most stolen vehicles in the Country, Alan's 2.8 Capri was still parked on his drive where he had left it. The six cylinder 'Cologne' fired up instantly and glancing up to the bedroom window, he noted with a little disappointment that she couldn't even be bothered to get out of his bed to wave him off.

Still mulling over what she had said, Alan made his way through the remaining dregs of rush hour traffic and eventually drove onto the perimeter drive of the Police station.

The only drawback to working a day shift was the perennial problem of parking. Early turn got all the prime positions and the 'nine to fivers' had their pick of the rest. Officers the rank of Inspector and above, however, got to park their vehicles in the heated garage which was actually intended for the Traffic response vehicles. Made perfect sense Alan supposed, having to waste five minutes, scraping the ice from the windscreen before being able to set off to an emergency call and accelerating a stone cold engine. This paled into insignificance alongside the importance of having one's personal vehicle conveniently placed, so that Mick the Handyman could busy himself washing and valeting it, whilst the Inspectors and above, toiled in their offices manipulating endless crime 'stats' and returns.

Strange how the patrol vehicles were suddenly to be found housed in the garage during the annual visit by Her Majesty's Inspectorate of Constabulary.

The parking stakes were truly desperate, not a free space was to be seen. Alan noted that there was even a plain C.I.D. car abandoned in the automated car wash bay and that particular offence was normally punishable by public flogging.

Resorting to abandoning his Capri on the grass by the side of the gymnasium, he winced as his tyres slowly clawed their way over the raised kerb edge and Alan once again cursed the City planners for not pre-supposing that by the '80's, most cops would actually own their own cars and would need somewhere to park them.

Alan walked to the rear entrance of the station and punched the five figure code into the door lock. He walked the length of the short corridor to the front office desk to sign the duties sheet. Nodding to the clerk, he was handed a 'Burndept' radio, trusting to luck that it would have had a fully charged battery attached.

Sergeant Dennison ensconced comfortably in his office opposite, looked up from his newspaper and winked.

"Page three again Sarge? You'll go blind." Alan called out.

The old sage chuckled. "At my age, I'll risk one eye Pendle lad…Anyway; I thought you were away shooting or something equally ridiculous."

"Next week Sarge, start Monday…Parking's a bit tight today, something on?"

The Station Sergeant placed his newspaper down on the desk.

Sam Fox's breasts looked just as magnificent upside down, but Alan tilted his head and shuffled around to the side of the desk for a better look anyway. The Sergeant quickly closed and folded the paper. "Belay that inappropriate behavior, Pendle, you'll only upset yerself for the rest of the day an' you might 'ave a bit of runnin' round to do."

Alan looked puzzled; the old Sergeant leaned back in his long suffering chair. "If you 'adn't noticed Alan lad, my station's full of grim faced Detectives. Upsettin' the tranquility and equilibrium of the place. All rushin' round clutchin' overtime cards and cloggin' up the bleedin' canteen. Our Edie's 'avin' a job copin', she's never had to burn as much toast…Can't get near the 'bandit' in the bar area, an' I've fed the bastard all week, must be ready to drop…Some bleedin' visitor'll put one ten pence in and drop my fuckin' jackpot."

Alan adopted a suitable sympathetic expression. "Sarge, I must admit to being slightly disappointed…I would have thought a man of your experience and ingenuity would have the 'nouse' to remove the fuse from the plug and place an anonymous yet convincing 'out of order' sign on said gaming machine…just to protect your investment as it were."

The Sergeant adopted a stern, accusatory expression. "I'm surprised at you Pendle lad. Why, that would be a totally scurrilous act of selfishness, borderin' on criminal deception…an' I wish I'd fuckin' thought of it…You don't suppose it's too late?"

Alan shook his head. "Nah…You'd know if some 'tec had dropped the big one Sarge, they'd order the bar opened. Anyway, I've clearly missed something…."

"Shootin' incident on Lawrence Place last night. Well, early hours of this mornin'…One of your lads first to the scene, young Charlie Morrisey I hear…Thankfully, all over by the time 'e got there a'course…Anyway, it's all 'ell let loose upstairs. More Detectives than it takes to change a light bulb. I'd stay anonymous if I were you…Now bugger off, there's a good lad, I've a sign to manufacture."

*****

The four electric extraction fans hummed. The Detective pressed his handkerchief hard up against his nose. The 'Vicks' vapour rub he had smeared it with in preparation for his attendance at the post mortem, barely masked the invasive smell of formaldehyde and disinfecting agents which pervaded.

Although bemoaning his fate at being delegated Coroner's Officer by the Detective Superintendent brought in to head up the murder enquiry, he considered his 'voluntary' attendance at the P.M. was a small price to pay to avoid the odious witness canvassing tasks his colleagues would have to endure doing thankless house to house enquiries in the 'Badlands'.

The Task Force lads would be on their hands and knees doing a fingertip search for evidence. There'd be a six pack for the Officer who found the murder weapon if it had been ditched.

Chance of finding a witness willing to put pen to paper in the 'Badlands'?....Nil he mused.

The post mortem examination room was harshly lit. The large bank of overhead lights above the examination table reflected back from the polished white tiled walls and glinted from the stainless steel sinks and instrument trolleys. The Detective gagged and breathed in through his mouth, willing himself not to throw up.

The 'deceased' was laid out on a raised edge stainless steel table positioned in the center of the room. The table bed was slightly concaved and had a five degree tilt toward a draining aperture at the lower end. This ensured that blood and bodily fluids would flow away into a large stainless tube, positioned above a drain hole in the green anti-slip surface of the floor.

Rows of medical instruments had been neatly arrayed in preparation for the autopsy and the Detective grimaced at the sight of the small hand held circular skull saw, the rows of scalpels, hammers, the clawed forceps and various cutting and hacking instruments the Inquisitor General Torquemada could only have dreamed of having at his disposal.

The twin plastic flap doors suddenly burst apart and the Pathologist already clad from head to toe in faded greens, entered. He nodded briefly at the Detective and approached the examination table.

Looking about the room to ensure that all had been properly prepared, he reached up to a microphone suspended from a drawdown wire attached to a pulley block on the ceiling. He flicked a small switch and glanced at the clock on the wall opposite as he pulled on gossamer thin rubber gloves. Clearly unperturbed by the sight of the slaughtered body presented before him, he cleared his throat and commenced proceedings.

"The time is ten o'clock in the forenoon, the date is Friday the 28th of March 1985, I am Mr Godfrey Forbes-Wright, consultant Home Office forensic pathologist, carrying out a post mortem examination on the body of a female decedent at the behest of the Police, in what has described as being a 'suspicious' death. If you would fully identify yourself for the purpose of the tape Detective and provide evidence of continuity."

The Pathologist nodded expectantly. "You may need to remove your 'kerchief Detective." He said and pointed upward toward the microphone.

The Detective sucked in a last deep breath through the eucalyptus sodden fibers. "Sir, Detective Constable 113 Simon Wiggins, Moorwood C.I.D. exhibits and Coroner's Officer. The deceased was pronounced 'life extinct' at 02.37 hours this date by Doctor Alvin Porter, at the City Infirmary." The Detective sucked air through his handkerchief again, even though the stringent fumes were now making his eyes water.

"The deceased is one Trina Louise McKnight, a white female, twenty eight years, registered unemployed; however, she is known to be a common prostitute with an address of Flat 3b Lawrence Place in the Crossflats housing projects Sir. Continuity identification was provided by Road Traffic Constable 1172 Charles Morrisey, who was the first attendant Officer. Whilst at the scene, he marked the left palm of the deceased with his collar number and further identified the deceased to me at the Infirmary mortuary at 8.05 hours this date. The body here present is that of the female Trina Louise McKnight, identified to me by said Police Constable Morrisey sir."

The Pathologist nodded. "I am grateful Detective. Right, I think we will make a start…The body presented is that of a mature female, subject of what appears to be a violent intrusive trauma to the left side of the face. There are signs of a small entry wound at the left corneal orbital and an enlarged exit wound determined by expressed internal matter from the rear area of the skull".

The Detective grimaced as the Pathologist twisted the deceased's head around to fully expose the extent of the damage caused by the exiting round and shattered skull fragments. He felt his breakfast rising as the Pathologist peeled back a large flap of her scalp, exposing the stark blood flecked whiteness of her skull and the mottled grey porridge like mess beneath.

Totally undeterred by the nightmare scene laid out before him, the Pathologist continued.

"As death appears at first blush to be a result of gunshot trauma, either as a result of a criminal act, an accident, or self-induced, it will therefore necessitate a second post mortem examination to be carried out…The second examiner has not yet been determined…Now, the body although mature, appears to be under nourished, the weight has been determined at…" He quickly glanced at the mortuary assistant's notes. "One hundred and four pounds, there is visual evidence of substance abuse with sanguineous crusting in both the lower bicep extensions and forearm hollows…This is consistent with habitual hypodermic intrusion, so a toxicology report will be required."

The Pathologist paused and raised his eyes toward the suspended microphone.

"Note to self...Given the deceased' implied profession and the evidence of substance abuse, there may be a potential risk of human immunodeficiency virus, acquired immunodeficiency syndrome, hepatitis and other communicable diseases. A bio-hazard symbol is to be placed on the front of the notes please."

The Pathologist reached for a scalpel and placed the tip carefully at the pubic bone. In a swift, well-practiced motion, he swept the blade upwards to the sternum. The flesh of her stomach fell slackly apart exposing a thin yellow lining of subcutaneous fat.

The room was immediately filled with a fetid, sickening odour.

The Detective swallowed hard as his stomach churned, even in the artificially chilled examination room, he felt small beads of sweat developing on his forehead. His legs felt strangely weak and a dark veil was encroaching into his peripheral vision.

The Pathologist paused, concerned at the Detective's swaying motion. "Are you feeling unwell Detective?...Your pallor is decidedly pale, perhaps a little fresh air?"

*****

The Traffic office was empty. Alan checked his clerical tray with a casual air of disinterest and glanced up to the vehicle disposition board. No vehicle allocated for him and the board was devoid of keys. Everyone was out; even the keys for the Sergeant's Range Rover were missing.
All engaged on Charlie's shooting incident no doubt, Alan thought.

Opening Morrisey's clerical tray for a 'nose' about, he saw a copy of Charlie's initial witness statement which he had prepared for the Coroner.

Clicking the switch on the bottom of the kettle, Alan settled back in a chair to read it. "Witness statement of Constable 1172 Charles Watson Morrisey...'*Watson*'...fuck me, Charlie, you kept that quiet…Two thirty three a.m. anonymous three nines…blah…blah…area search with beat units…Lawrence Place…blah…blah…" Alan quickly skimmed over the preamble of the statement. "Female found in a collapsed state on nearside pavement when facing Porter Street…blah…blah…serious head injury consistent with gunshot…ambulance and supervision requested…blah…blah, scene preserved…"

Alan was interrupted by the appearance of the front office clerk who was clutching a small scrap of paper.

"Al, sorry mate, meant to give you this when you came in…This woman called at just after eight wanting to speak to you personal like, wouldn't tell me what it was about…Sounded foreign."

"Foreign?" Alan asked. "What, like Chinese?…French?…Serb Croat?…What?"

The clerk shrugged. "Hard to tell over the 'phone mate, it wasn't a good line…Just not English, you know."

"Not that epitome of beauty Miss Selina Scott calling from the BBC for an update on Charlie's job then?" Alan said with mock despondency, as he reached out to take the offered note.

"Don't think so Al, maybe a bit afro-Carribean if memory serves." The clerk replied.

"Afro-Carribean….very politically correct." Alan raised a sceptical eyebrow. "Given up using your usual racial epithets for lent 'ave we?…Racial Harmony Unit got to you at last Derek?"

The Clerk smiled. "I know I 'ave in the past, bin known to call a spade a spade Al, but these days, you never know who's gonna grass you to D n' C…Not the likes of you I 'asten to 'ad…but. Well…you know what I mean."

Alan glanced at the name and telephone number, frowned and called out as the clerk turned to leave. "Ere, hang on Del, this 'as got an 01 prefix. That's London, an' I don't know anyone called Mrs Garretty. You sure this is for me?"

The Clerk shrugged. "I just took the call Al, but she specifically asked for you an' you're the only Pendle I know in Traffic at Moorwood. Sorry mate, I am *sans* further knowledge."

Alan looked puzzled. "Ok. Cheers anyway Del."

Coffee first, 'phone call second he decided and as he stirred the steaming brew, he racked his brain trying to think of a 'Londoner' he might have recently dealt with. Nothing came to mind and as he took his first sip, curiosity got the better of him and he reached for the telephone handset.

\*\*\*\*\*

The Detective tossed away his cigarette as the mortuary assistant poked his head around the rear door of the mortuary and beckoned him with a crooked finger. "Mr Forbes-Wright has finished, he'll have a quick word with you if you like."

The Detective nodded, stepped on the smoldering cigarette and followed the mortuary assistant back into the reception area.

He noticed that the attendant, who bore a striking resemblance to the comic actor Marty Feldman in the film 'Young Frankenstein', dragged his left leg awkwardly and was slightly 'hunch backed'. The left hand side of his mouth hung loosely away from his bottom jaw as if the facial muscles had failed and a thin, glistening sliver of saliva oozed over the top of the slack lip and dripped down onto his stubble covered chin. He personified the Detective's expectations of a ghoulish mortuary assistant and simply added to the depressing, pervasive atmosphere. The Detective shuddered and searched his jacket pocket for the 'Vicks' impregnated handkerchief.

The Pathologist was by now thankfully, seated on one of the long wooden benches in the main reception area and was busily making up his notes. He looked up as the Detective approached.

"Ah, there you are…Well, Detective Wiggins. My preliminary examination will, as I am sure you expect, show that the deceased suffered a traumatic intrusion of the upper quadrant of the cerebrum and parietal lobe with devastation of the major blood vessels. There is evidence of massive exsanguination and exfiltration of a blunt object through the parietal cap."

The Detective looked dumbfounded. "Pretend I'm still in primary school Sir?"

The Pathologist smiled. "She was shot through the head Detective, through the left eye to be precise. The bullet, from a small caliber weapon by the way, point two-two perhaps, passed through her brain and exited through the back of her head; not survivable under any circumstances I'm afraid…There is also evidence of prolonged drug abuse, recent tearing of the soft tissue around the vagina and cervix as well as a recent intrusion into the anal passage…"

The Detective shot a suspicious glance toward 'Igor' the mortuary assistant who quickly averted his gaze, sniffed and shuffled away quickly.

"However, given her alleged profession …The Pathologist continued…no surprises there. The 'tox' and tissue results will be some time I'm afraid, there is something of a backlog, but for the purpose of your investigation, I can confidently state that there is little doubt that the primary cause of death was due to the gunshot wound and unless there is evidence to suggest suicide or an accidental discharge, I believe you have your murder Detective."

\*\*\*\*\*

Alan drummed his fingers against the table top as he waited. The purring of the ringtone in the earpiece was suddenly interrupted by a distant and faint "Hello."

"Oh, hello, this is Constable Alan Pendle; I've got a message to contact a Miss Garretty on this number?" Alan could faintly hear the female's voice calling out. "Evelynne, it's for you."

Alan frowned…*Evelynne?* The sound of the handset being set down onto a hard surface resonated through the earpiece. Alan waited…puzzled.

"Mr Pendle?" a voice said softly.

"Yes, who is this?"

"It's me Mr 'P'…Evie."

Alan felt suddenly cold and the hairs on the back of his neck immediately stood on end.

"Evie !…What the…"

"Jus' listen up Mr 'P'." Her voice was wavering, hushed and hesitant. "You always bin a gent…never put a workin' gal down…You be needin' dis…Trina McKnight be dayd an' that mo'fucker 'Midnight' be down fo' it."

Alan took a very deep breath. "Whoa…whoa. Evie, what the fu…Jesus! Where's this coming from?"

Other than the sound of laboured breathing, the line went silent for a moment. "You do wid dis what's you needs to do wid it Mr 'P'. My girl Trina knew dat mo'fucker Lyburn done for 'Fastener'. She tol' me how he plan out all dat shit an' she be scared, she be real scared Mr 'P'. She tol' me so, an' when I seen her, dat girl be shakin'…You knows me Mr 'P' an' I trus' you wid dis an' only you…Don't be axin' me where I be at, 'cept I be safe wid my sistren till dat mo'fucker be caught, you be…"

"Evie…Evie. Hang on a minute…Look…" Alan's voice was hushed, his tone incredulous. "You're telling me that it was some bloke called Lyburn that murdered 'Fastener' and then…"

"Dat be right Mr 'P', an' dat girl Trina knew why it needed to be done. Listen up. Lyburn be a nigger by way of 'Midnight'. He be runnin' Trina…He be runnin' the 'Chinese' till he near kilt her wid dat mo'fuckin' razor he done totes. Trina tol' me 'bout the car shit an' all…You seen it, Mr 'P', you be deyr dat night, you seen what that mo'fucker done. 'Midnight' done murdered his black ass firs' an' now Trina be dayd 'cos she be knowin'…I aint comin' back for shit, else I be nex'."

"The McKnight girl was shot Evie, different altogether."

"Sheeeeet Mr 'P'" she drawled. "Everybody be knowin' 'Fastener' carry a piece…Dat mo'fucker 'Midnight' done snatch it up is all…Local youngbloods strip dat nigger for the res' of his fancy duds long 'fo you gits deyr."

Alan's heart was pounding, his mind raced as he continued to listen to her ramblings.

"You do what need be done Mr 'P', an' do what right by my girl Trina."

Before Alan could ask any of the searching questions he had swirling around in his mind, he was rewarded with a faint click and the sound of the dialing tone.

Alan blew out his cheeks and exhaled slowly through tightly pursed lips. He sat for a moment, holding on to the faintly buzzing handset before whispering to himself.

"Fuuuuuuck me."

*****

Clutching the hastily scribbled note, Alan returned to the front office and leaned against the counter top waiting for the clerk to finish on the telephone. The clerk was slumped in his chair, clearly bored, his pencil poised over a partially completed crossword.

"What makes you think your cat has been stolen Mrs Petrovich?…I am aware that…yes, but it is very rare for vivisectionists to abduct cats, its norm…I'm sure *your* cat is very special Mrs Petrovich, but…" The clerk held the handset away from his ear and looked apologetically to where Alan waited at the counter, slowly wafting the scrap of paper.

"Mrs Petrovich, I can tell you're upset, but I'm not prepared to record a crime at this stage…No, I'm not neglecting my duty Mrs Petrovich…I'll make a note…" The clerk rolled his eyes up toward the ceiling and sighed. "I tell you what I will do…No…look, it's not a theft Mrs Petrovich. I appreciate what you're telling me and I'm sure that Albert was it?.Yes…What?…really…reincarnation of your late Husband…You put him out for the night and now he's missing…Well, look…I'm sure he's probably still out somewhere 'tomming' next door's Siamese and whe…Well, I'm sorry you feel that way Mrs Petrovich, I'm only trying to make light of th..."

The clerk looked puzzled at the handset now dead in his hand. He shook his head slowly and looked across to Alan.

"There's just no helping some people Al. What was it you wanted?"

"You handled that particularly well Derek, very sensitively done mate…Anyway, about this telephone call you took." Alan said, holding the scrap of paper aloft.

"Go on." The clerk looked apprehensive.

"Need you to sign it on the back Del."

"Because?" The clerk replied warily, his apprehension increasing.

"'Cos it might become an exhibit. You need to sign it as having taken the call, an' I could do with a line or two in a witness statement, just to say what time and date you took it. Oh, an' if you've got a spare exhibit bag kicking around …"

The clerk got up from his chair and approached the counter. "What's the…"

"It's… *complicated* Del." Alan said hesitantly. "Nothing for you to worry about, its more to cover my arse, so just put yer moniker on the back and I'll let you get back to your crossword."

The clerk hesitated, pen poised over the back of the note. He looked at Alan suspiciously. "If this is one of your trademark 'snaggy' jobs Al." he said, with a cautionary tone as he reluctantly scrawled his signature. He reached beneath the counter and tossed Alan a thin, self-sealing exhibit bag.

"Statement?" Alan asked expectantly.

"What now?" The clerk said despondently.

"Derek. I can see you're rushed of yer feet." Alan replied with a hint of sarcasm. "It'll take you two minutes…Just do it while it's fresh in yer mind, then you can forget all about it." Alan said reassuringly.

The clerk sighed and returned to his desk, unable to disguise the look of foreboding now etched across his face, as he reached for a blank witness statement form.

"Oi!" A voice called out from behind.

Alan turned from the counter and peered into the Station Sergeant's office.

"What you doin' upsettin' the natural tranquility of my office staff young Pendle?"

Alan walked to the open door and leaned against the frame. "Might be something or nothing Sarge, but…"

Sergeant Dennison folded his newspaper. "Enlighten me." he said, motioning Alan into his office. Alan closed the Station Sergeant's door behind him and took a seat.

The veteran Sergeant listened intently as Alan told his tale, nodding slowly in agreement as he considered Alan's suspicions regarding the 'knock down' and smiling knowingly as he went on to describe the Chief Inspector's reaction to his report.

"I'm safe in assumin' that you didn't actually get rid of it?"

"In my locker Sarge."

The old Sergeant nodded his approval at Alan's total disregard for the Chief Inspector's instructions. "Here's the 'crippler' though Sarge." Alan said and held up the scrap of paper now sealed within the exhibit bag. Alan relayed the information he had received from Evie, careful not to embellish the tale or to leave anything out.

Ron Dennison was a man to be trusted. The Sergeant's eyes widened as the tale progressed; he tapped the end of his pencil against the edge of his desk whilst he considered his response.

"Who else knows?..About this latest info?" the old sage asked, pointing to the exhibit bag.

"You Sarge…that's it."

The Sergeant nodded slowly. "Well, yer can't sit on it Alan lad, I know you wouldn't anyway…an' if it's right, if this hooker Evie is to be believed, then it's a double homicide, same suspect. If memory serves, this isn't the first time Traffic've come up trumps with info leadin' to a murder detection, you an' Sully wasn't it?…That old hooker what got 'erself barbequed in the Morritts'…?"

Alan nodded. "Stroke of luck that one Sarge."

The Station Sergeant shook his head. "Luck had fuck all to do with it Alan lad, good copperin' was what that was. Most villains end up gettin' their collar felt 'cos some young copper on the beat notices some small detail an' 'as the balls to put pen to paper."

"Didn't do me much good earlier this week Sarge, my arse is still singin'…"

The old Sergeant chuckled; his voice then adopted a more somber tone. "Look…Alan, take my advice, get yerself ensconced in yer office, get typin'…Full report…No holds barred, make sure you mention everything you can remember about the 'phone call from yer pet hooker…Where's yer Sergeant today?"

"Day off Sarge, he's…"

"Find 'im." The Sergeant interrupted, "Once you've put pen to paper, find 'im, make sure Roger's aware. The sooner 'e knows the better. He's a good man, he'll watch yer back."

The old Sergeant lowered his voice. "Get yer arse covered Alan lad." he cautioned. "There might just be a shit storm on the way, an' the reverend Forrester might just 'ave to dodge a few awkward questions if it turns out as you was right all along."

Alan looked puzzled.

"What difference does it make, even if I am proved right?"

"Think Alan." The Sergeant raised his eyebrows inviting further consideration. "If the 10/9 had been investigated as a murder,

Vice would have been tasked to do street enquiries…Who else is about at that time of the mornin'?…There'd 'ave been a blanket sweep of all the hookers workin' the 'Badlands'. Moorwood cells would 'ave looked like a CID 'stag night'…Someone would've squealed, bit of info for a walkout…maybe even this McKnight woman, lay it on a bit thick an' she might 'ave come across. Would she still be alive?…witness protection, protective custody job, who knows? But I bet Forrester's arse will be twitchin' sixpence halfcrown if it leaks to the press, an' it will if the 'Moorwood mole' gets wind of it. Forrester 'as upset plenty of 'is parishioners durin' his meteoric ascendency…Might just be one or two who reckon it's time for a little pay back."

Alan sighed dejectedly. "Where would that leave me though Ron? A 'purple peril' for neglect of duty…What?"

The Station Sergeant shook his head. "Nah…but you're gonna have to be straight 'bout what Forrester ordered you to do…You could sit on it an' do fuck all, but if the shit hits the fan…an' it will…yer long enough in the tooth to know 'ow it works Alan. There'll be more arse coverin' than a Traffic 'do' in a queer's bar. Bernie Foster gave 'is D.S. the heads up quick enough didn't 'e? You can bet there'll be some duckin' an' divin' in the C.I.D. office if D 'n C gets called in…You might 'ave some explainin' to do 'bout yer relationship with this Evie woman mind."

"I haven't got a *relationship* Sarge. She dobs in a bit of useful info from time to time is all."

"D 'n C'll want to see some evidence." The Sergeant cautioned.

Alan shrugged nonchalantly. "Me and Sully can show a couple of good lock ups on the strength of Evie's say so, and so have Vice when we've passed it on."

The Sergeant drummed his fingers on the table top, deep in thought. "Look lad, I'll make a note of our conversation, so there's no question you just sat on it…Make a note of that telephone number down in the 'smoke', then we'll lock that evidence bag in my safe so it can't go 'walkabout' from yer clerical tray. Get the whole thing down in a witness statement, then go find Roger."

Alan nodded and handed the signed and sealed evidence bag to his old mentor. "I'll crack on. Thanks for that Sarge, 'preciate your help."

"Told you years ago, doin' the right thing'll never do you wrong Alan lad…Oh! 'fore you disappear." The Sergeant slipped on his reading glasses and reached across for his newspaper. "Thirteen down…'Tales you can read backwards'. Something 'a, somethin' 'a'…five letters."

Alan thought for a moment and then smiled.

"Bit like my accident reports Sarge."

His old mentor shook his head. He looked up, puzzled.

"sagas" Sarge.

*****

Alan fed the witness statement form down into the typewriter and squared the page up between the rubber rollers. He stared long and hard at the pre-printed cautionary heading.

*'This statement (consisting of   pages each signed by me) is true to the best of my knowledge and belief and I make it knowing that, if it is introduced in evidence, I shall be liable to prosecution, if I have wilfully stated in it anything which I know to be false or do not believe to be true'.*

The Traffic office was quiet. Alan sat back in his chair and reached for his cigarettes, he considered with a little trepidation the effect that submitting a statement would have. There'd be more than a few ructions, ditching a written report was one thing, a sworn witness statement was not so easily disregarded.

'Archbishop' Forrester would certainly have him excommunicated, boiled in oil maybe, flayed, or whatever abominations 'lay' preachers were actually allowed to visit upon heretics these days. However, this was his last working day before weekend off, then five days away from Division at

Stretham. Even Forrester couldn't mix him a powder that quickly...could he?

Alan's fingers hovered hesitantly over the keys...Sergeant Dennison's words echoed back. *"Yer can't sit on it Alan lad."*

He took a long pull from his cigarette and inhaled deeply. Recalling one of his Sergeant's favourite sayings: "Faint heart never fucked a pig." he began to type, his mind flitting back to the last time the good Sergeant Dennison had 'secured' evidence for him and his partner in his office safe.

*****

A warm summer's evening the year before, Alan and his partner had sat in their patrol car, tucked neatly away up a side street off the main Harrowford Road, watching the early evening traffic meandering in and out of the City.

The radio was quiet and Sullivan slouched down into his seat and lit a cigar. Alan grimaced as the pungent aroma immediately filled the interior of the patroller.

"Jesus Sully!...Open a window for Christ's sake, it smells like old wino's socks."

Sullivan chuckled and tipped the switch on the centre console. With a faint whine, the glass slipped effortlessly down into the door panel and tendrils of blue, grey smoke were whipped away in the warm breeze.

"This mate...is a 'Swisher Sweets'." his partner advised emphatically, as he rotated the long fat cigar slowly between his lips. "Nearly three quid a throw."

"How much!" Alan exclaimed with a look of disbelief.

"See..I wouldn't expect you to understand Al'. You've got more of a...'ow can I put it without upsetin' yer sensibilities...more of a Benson an' 'edges mentality. Fags for the masses...It's like Winston Churchill said, 'A woman is just a woman, but a good cigar is a smoke'..."

"Kipling Sully." Alan replied dryly.

"Who?" his partner asked.

Alan shook his head in disbelief. "It wasn't Winston Sully, it was Rudyard Kipling. Literary genius. 'The Man who would be King'…'If'…ringing any bells yet?"

Sullivan shook his head, a blank expression on his face.

"The Jungle Book then…Even you must have heard of that." Alan said.

"Thought that was Walt Disney." his partner replied.

"No mate…Disney just made…Jesus Pete…the literary world actually consists of more than 'Fishin' World' an' 'Mayfair'…Ever thought of getting yerself a library card?"

His partner shrugged. Alan threw up his hands in exasperation. "Sully, 'a woman is only a woman, but a good cigar is a smoke' is definitely Rudyard Kipling, not Winston…Churchill certainly smoked cigars, you're right there, I also agree with the popular opinion that he was the best prime minister we've ever had and, that he was probably the last white man to be called Winston…but that aint his quote."

The evening traffic continued to drone past. Sullivan drew on the cigar which hissed quietly as the short stub of light grey ash glowed bright red and ate away a fraction more of the dark brown outer leaf. His partner slowly and purposefully exhaled the smoke, as if savouring the moment; he shrugged his shoulders as he pursed his lips and blew out a perfectly formed shimmering ring of blue smoke. "Whatever, anyway, enough borin' history shit, how'd it go last night?"

"With?"

Sullivan sighed heavily to emphasise his impatience. "Yer first date with the lovely Sandra Prestwick."

Alan smiled. "I *knew* you wouldn't be able to help yourself, I bet you've bin edgin' to ask since we came on."

His partner shrugged and feigning disinterest, casually extending his arm out through the open window and tapped the ash from the end of his cigar. "Just got your domestic interests at 'eart Al'...What's she like then?"

"At what exactly?" Alan teased.

His partner nudged him playfully in the ribs. "Come on Al, don't be shy, I'm yer partner, is she a screamer or a moaner or what?"

Alan smiled sardonically and shook his head slowly. "Oh, that's you isn't it Sully, everything reduced to the sordid and base...Here am I seeking to enter into a meaningful relationship with Officer Prestwick, based on mutual trust and respe..."

His partner burst into laughter. "Fuck off Al, this is me yer talkin' to not 'er Mum...Mutual trust an' respect" he mimicked. "Yeah, right...'course...You forget mate, I *know* you."

Alan chuckled at his partner's easy banter. "As it happens Peter, I took her out for a very nice meal at La Policelli in Harrowford."

His partner chortled. "Durin' which no doubt, you gazed into her limpid pool like eyes an' discussed the appalin' famine situation in Ethiopia and 'ow you raised three fuckin' quid for 'Live Aid'....See 'ow carin' and considerate I am Sandra...Now, get yer kit of."

Sullivan's laughter was infectious and Alan struggled to maintain a straight face.

"Great tits though." Sullivan said decidedly.

"Oi!...have a little respect." Alan retorted with mock annoyance.

His partner shrugged. "I'm only statin' the obvious Al...She's sex on a stick...fantastic set of top bollocks, nipples like blind cobbler's thumbs. Bet you can't wait to get yer 'ands..."

Their reveries were interrupted by a harsh static hissing from the VHF radio.

"Any Traffic unit to assist Division with a fail to stop Meagers Lane?"

Alan snatched up the handset as his partner fired up the engine. "Papa Yankee One Five."

"One Five, Division are in pursuit of a Ford Escort in brown, Lima Uniform Uniform One Zero Three Papa, last known location Meagers Lane towards Crossflats Avenue. Go to channel two to assist."

Alan keyed the radio handset. "One Five, roger that, reverting to channel two."

The big V8 growled pleasingly, as Alan's partner accelerated the Rover out onto the main road and toward the location of the pursuit. Alan clicked through the channels on the VHF set and was rewarded with a frantic, almost incoherent babble as the beat patrol Officer attempted to update the local Control Room operator with their location.

"We're still on Crossflats…He's swerving…Wrong side of the road at…"

Alan winced as he listened to the panicked commentary, which could barely be heard through the background howling of sirens.

"Must be a Divisional van Al…if 'es usin' VHF." Sullivan said, as he hurriedly checked over his shoulder before powering the Rover out from a minor junction.

Alan nodded and keyed the handset. "Channel two control…This is Papa Yankee One Five, can you put us on talkthrough please."

"Last unit, talkthrough is on." The controller responded.

"Break, break, break." Alan transmitted, taking control of the airwaves. "Unit engaged in pursuit on Crossflats, this is Papa Yankee One Five Moorwood Traffic, what's your callsign over."

Through the static, the wail of the sirens and the directions being shouted out in the background by the van driver, Alan could barely make out the almost incomprehensible transmission. "Hotel Echo Three."

Peter nodded and eased his foot down onto the accelerator pedal to push the SD1 a little harder.

"Divisional Van. It'll be a shagged out Transit, no wonder they're panickin'."

Alan nodded in agreement and squirming at the screeching of the sirens through the earpiece, keyed the handset again. "Hotel Echo Three from One Five, just give street names and direction of travel and 'can off' your sirens when transmitting."

The airwaves suddenly became awash with various callsigns offering assistance. The units declaring their current locations and where they would lay in wait.

The Control Room operator advised all the units in attendance. "Lima Uniform Uniform One Zero Three Papa shown on PNC as a Ford Escort in brown. No lost or stolen reports, previous keeper details only."

Alan keyed the radio handset again. "Roger that control, Echo Three what's your location?" The airwaves remained silent and with a knowing nod, Sullivan looked across to his partner. "Sounds like they've lost it."

"Er…from Hotel Echo Three, the vehicle was last seen on Crossflats Avenue towards the City…We've.. er…lost sight of it."

"Any further details Echo Three, occupants, offences over." Alan asked.

"From Echo Three, it's one up, white male, no seat belt. When we lit him up, he made off, he was throwing stuff out the driver's window on Meagers Lane."

"Chucked 'is stash." Peter said decidedly.

Alan nodded and flicked off the blue lights as the speed of the Rover decreased and his partner continued toward the general area to conduct a search.

Alan transmitted again. "Echo Three, it might be worth a trip back to the Meagers to retrieve whatever he was ditching, you never know your luck. Papa Yankee One Five is resuming to area search."

"All units Channel two control, talkthrough is off." The operator at the control room advised all units.

Alan replaced the handset and returned the VHF radio to the Force Control channel and settled back in his seat. "Not much chance in a Divisional Transit to be fair, Pete…What about having a float up to…"

Alan was thrown back in his seat as his partner suddenly accelerated the Rover hard.

Glancing across to the main road, he laughed loudly and instinctively reached once again for the radio handset and threw down the switch to activate the blue lights.

"What's the fuckin' chances eh mate?"

His partner smiled and settled himself squarely into his seat. "Told you before Al, God definitely wears a yellow jacket."

The rotating bank of blue lights whirred and lances of blinding blue light raked and danced across the carriageway and reflected back from the glass frontages of the shops on either side of the road. Alan's partner touched the small red button on the front of the public address handset clipped to the dashboard facia, a single deafening 'whoop' from the sirens alerted any pedestrians to their presence, as the patrol car emerged out of the junction mouth and onto the main road.

The driver of the Ford Escort, suddenly alerted by the dazzling array of blue lights, shot a panicked glance across his right shoulder as the powerful V8 Rover surged out from the side street.

Sullivan feathered the accelerator pedal and felt the rear end of their patroller skitter on the damp road surface. As the vehicle straightened, he accelerated hard and drew up directly to the rear of the Escort. In response to their unexpected presence, a small puff of blue smoke from the exhaust of the Ford was sufficient to convince Alan that the 'game' was on.

His partner flicked the headlights onto main beam to blind the panicked driver. As the interior of the Escort was suddenly flooded with light, the driver quickly reached up and slapped the rear view mirror aside.

Sullivan nodded knowingly. "Not his first time at the dance by the look of it mate."

Full beam directly into the rear view mirror would usually cause the driver of a stolen vehicle to push it to one side to prevent being dazzled. It also of course, denied him any rearward view of the pursuing patrol car which was exactly why the Traffic men did it. The driver would expend half his limited concentration abilities wondering where the patrol car actually was, whether he was going to be overtaken or if the Traffic men were positioning themselves in preparation for a timely 'nudge' into the nearest lamp post.

Alan keyed the radio handset. "Papa Yankee One Five."

"Go ahead One Five." The Force Control Room operator's response was immediate.

"One Five, be advised, we are in pursuit of a Ford Escort saloon in brown, Lima Uniform Uniform One Zero Three Papa. Vehicle has single male occupant. Merrill Avenue towards Town Street North. Vehicle previously failed to stop for Divisional unit on Meagers Lane, speed is fifty and rising, traffic conditions are light."

The control room operator responded immediately. "Received One Five, maintain your commentary, talkthrough is on…Any Traffic unit able to assist Papa Yankee One Five on Merrill Avenue with a fail to stop."

The airwaves were immediately filled with the controlled responses from Traffic men coming to assist. Not the wild, almost hysterical babble from the beat patrol Officers, but from those who engage in pursuits in some area of the City on a daily, sometimes hourly basis.

The various callsigns were transmitted sharply and succinctly, with the last numbers of their callsigns and locations only. Alan responded with equal brevity. Speed, location and direction of travel, along with any offences committed by the fleeing driver, all the information recorded on the incident 'log' now being kept by the operator at Force Control, to assist in the preparation of the charges which would follow, once the errant driver was 'in the bag'.

The Ford Escort was struggling. The aging Divisional Ford Transit might not have been too much of a challenge, but the V8 Rover was a different matter. It simply 'toyed' with the worn out Ford, like a cat pawing at an injured bird.

Sullivan was calm, his concentration intense. His eyes flitting from the numerous emergent junctions along the route, back to the rear of the Escort, the brake lights and false indications from the panicked driver as he tried to throw them off his tail.

Between his brief spells of commentary, Alan activated the sirens to warn other motorists and pedestrians of their approach. The strident 'yelping' of the sirens coupled with the intensity of the blue lights raking across the rear of the vehicle, simply adding to the Escort driver's psychological stress.

"One Five. Vehicle is still Merrill Avenue, speed is sixty plus, traffic conditions are moderate, no danger to pedestrians at this time, still toward junction with Town Street".

The pace of the pursuit now quickened. The fleeing driver knew that the Traffic cops would have been on their radio and that their colleagues would now be streaming in from all over the City and closing in on him.

His eyes flitted from left to right, searching for a side street or a snicket, any avenue of escape, any opportunity to gain a little ground on the Traffic car, just enough so that they would lose sight of him, just for a moment, just enough time for him to disappear up one of the cobbled side streets, dump the Escort and run, run and then brazen it out, to stand at the side of the road and watch the howling Traffic cars converging on the abandoned motor, just the usual interested bystander.

He is oblivious to the flashing headlights and horn blasts from the oncoming vehicles as they are forced to swerve or mount the kerb to avoid him. He holds his breath and maintains his speed on the approach to a crossroads. He ignores the red traffic light, his heart missing a beat and his sphincter tightening as he twitches the steering wheel sharply to the right, to avoid the front end of a car emerging into the junction from his left.

There is a blaring of a horn and a screech of tyres. His head whips around, searching for the Traffic car, hoping that they've been forced to stop at the junction.

Sullivan braked and the front of the heavy SD1 dipped as the pads bit hard into the front brake discs. A quick flick of the gear lever with his open palm and second gear was selected.

Alan nodded his thanks to the driver of the vehicle, now stationary in the middle of the junction, his hands thrown up in shock and disbelief at his 'near death' experience.

"Yes, yes." Alan shouted and Sullivan was back on the accelerator. The V8 growled and their Traffic car quickly made up the lost ground on the Escort.

"One Five. He's through the Town Street lights at red, now towards the…" Alan paused as without warning, the front of the Escort dipped sharply. Its rear end slewed wildly out to the left, the rear tyres spinning, howling in protest as they struggled to maintain a grip on the road surface as the driver suddenly swerved from the main road and up into one of the many cobbled side streets.

"It's a left, left into Mafeking Avenue." Alan immediately transmitted.

The Escort bounced crazily on the raised cobbles as it accelerated up the long incline between the rows of corporation terraced houses. A wooden clothes prop is ignored, shattering against the front bumper of the Escort and the washing line, stretched between the opposing cast iron guttering fall pipes, whipped wildly upwards and then, heavily laden with faded, threadbare bed sheets and pillowcases, descended rapidly, to fall across the bonnet of the following Rover.

For a brief moment, the front of the SD1 was festooned with damp washing before the sagging clothesline rolled up the windscreen and was stretched like a bowstring. With a sharp whip like crack, it snapped, strewing the washing out across the filthy weed infested cobbles.

"Mrs Miggins' aint gonna be best pleased." Sullivan said and chuckled as he powered the Rover up the street.

Alan smiled. "Yeah, the one day of the year her bed sheets get changed, matey boy here decides to…Whoa!…whoa"…" he shouted frantically as he saw a Police Ford Transit skidding to a halt across the top of the street completely blocking the Escort's escape route.

The front wheels of the Escort suddenly locked up and the vehicle came to a juddering halt.

"It's game over Sully." Alan said, instinctively reaching down for the seat belt release button with his left hand and the door handle with his right.

Two helmetless uniformed Officers leapt from the Ford Transit and ran toward the front of the Escort. There was a savage grinding of gears, followed by a loud crunch and the Ford lurched backwards colliding with the front of the Rover.

Alan threw open the door of the patrol car and quickly ran to the driver's door of the Escort. The driver was still frantically revving the rattling engine in an effort to push the Rover backwards. Alan snatched at the chromed door handle. The engine of the Escort was still screaming in protest and the driver wildly fumbling with the gear lever.

The driver's door was locked, yet for some strange reason, the window was wound fully down. Alan reached in and fumbled for the ignition key.

"Enough." he shouted at the driver. "You're nicked."

Alan twisted the key. The engine revs immediately died off and the engine gave out with a final deathlike rattle.

The driver stared up at Alan, beads of sweat stood out on his forehead and he was breathing in short, shallow gasps. He gripped the steering wheel, his knuckles white with the pressure, his legs shaking as the adrenalin flowed.

The uniforms from the Transit were at the front passenger side of the Escort. The door was locked and as one tried the rear door, the other withdrew his truncheon and there was a sharp hollow sounding thud as the glass was assaulted.

Alan leaned further into the interior of the car, forcing his left arm across the driver's chest and pushed him back into his seat to give the seatbelt a little slack. With his right hand, he reached down to release his belt. "I said out…you're fucking nicked."

The seat belt clasp sprung free from the retaining stalk and Alan gripped the drivers left wrist and pulled. The driver's grip on the steering wheel was vice like and even using all his body weight, Alan could not break the fingers free of the wheel.

There was another sharp crack as the uniform's truncheon again struck the passenger side glass. Alan released his hold on the driver who sat rigid, gripping the steering wheel, panting and staring down at his feet, his eyes wide with fear. Alan quickly glanced across to the front passenger door to locate the position of the door handles. His left hand fumbled across the inside of the driver's door, finding the release handle, he pulled it and wrenched the door open.

Sullivan was now at his side. "Grab 'is right wrist Sully." Alan shouted.

His partner quickly moved to one side and pulled the driver's door fully open. He reached in to prize the driver's fingers from where they were wrapped like steel rings around the time polished plastic rim of the steering wheel.

"Give it up you fuckin' idiot." Alan shouted as he reached fully across the driver to get both hands around the driver's left wrist.

Traffic cars screeched to a halt and yellow jacketed Officers ran from their vehicles to assist with the arrest.

The wailing and yelping sirens and the sound of the commotion in the street provided the unemployed residents with a brief respite from their daily monotony. The plates of Spam and chips and the patronising dulcet tones of Nicholas Parsons and his 'Sale of the Century' were temporarily ignored, as the game show on their televisions was abandoned in favour of the 'real life' drama unfolding out on the street.

As Alan and his partner struggled with the rigid driver. There was a dull crump and he felt a sharp stinging sensation across his face as shards of glass from the shattered passenger window burst inwards.

He instinctively closed his eyes and turned his head away. Scrambling fingers pulled at the door handle and the uniform was in, kneeling on the front passenger seat. His truncheon swept down, the heavy wood impacted with the back of the driver's head, with a sickening, dull thud.

Alan felt the miniscule particles of glass scratching his eyes and he shook his head and blinked to get rid of them. Again and again the truncheon fell. Alan heard the driver screaming and then felt the sting from a sharp blow to the side of his face. He released his grip and instinctively withdrew from the vehicle, putting his hand up to where he had felt the blow land; his fingers came away with blood smeared across the tips.

The driver was limp, slumped forwards over the steering wheel. Rich oxygenated blood gushed from a vicious wound on the back of his head and ran down through his hair and onto the collar of his leather jacket.

"What the fuck…" Alan shouted and leaned back into the Escort. He pulled the moaning driver back away from the steering wheel. His head lolled sideways and the blood from his head wound now spattered onto the headrest and across the sleeve of Alan's yellow jacket.

The uniform was still kneeling on the front passenger seat, his truncheon still gripped hard. His hands were shaking, he was breathing hard and his eyes were wide with wild excitement.

"Get the fuck off my prisoner." Alan spat, casting a worrying glancing back at the now semi-conscious driver. Alan angrily pushed the uniform away, the palm of his hand slamming hard against his chest. The uniform fell backwards from the vehicle and out onto the street. His boots slipped on the damp cobbles. His arms flailed wildly as he struggled to regain his balance, the truncheon still gripped tightly in his right hand.

Sullivan peered into the interior of the vehicle and seeing the extent of the injury to the driver, sighed heavily. "Jesus Christ…" he whispered to himself.

He looked over the roof of the Escort to where the uniform, assisted by his beat colleague, was now scrambling to his feet, wiping away the dirt from the back of his trousers.

"Don't just fucking stand there you moron, get a field dressing…Look at the state of 'im." Sullivan shouted at the uniform, whilst making a mental note of the three chromed numbers on his epaulettes. He was acutely aware that the small crowd of interested bystanders which had now gathered on the street, were becoming increasingly hostile.

A 'slapping' after a chase was expected, an acceptable occupational hazard for those who chose to take a vehicle without the owner's consent, but a 'staffing' was historically reserved for those who chose to fight back or who had produced a weapon of some description.

Rising howls of dissent and derision arose from the gathered locals, as the driver of the Escort was hastily pulled from his vehicle and the extent of his injury became visible. He was quickly bundled into the back seat of their patroller, his hand pressing a blood saturated dressing against his scalp.

Sullivan looked across at Alan as he quickly took his seat. His eyebrows lifted in a silent questioning gesture and he leaned forwards and squinted as he examined the small weeping cut on the side of Alan's face.

"That could've been nasty mate. Another half inch and it'd've been yer eye…" Sullivan said as he slipped the Rover into reverse…and what the *fuck* was that all about?" he said, nodding toward the rear seats.

Alan shook his head in bewilderment and pulled down the sun visor to examine the side of his face in the vanity mirror. "I have no idea Pete." he replied, slowly shaking his head in disbelief. "Beat lad just lost it. Did you see his eyes mate? Like mad dog's bollocks."

"I saw our prisoner gettin' a right royal arseholin' is what I saw Al." Sullivan whispered emphatically. "As did all the other malcontents out on the street…There's a shit storm on the 'orizon…'ave you seen the back of 'is 'ead?…You can see 'is fuckin' skull."

Alan half turned in his seat and looked across to where the Escort driver sat bleeding in silence, resigned to his fate.

"Why'd'you run?" Alan asked, purposefully ignoring the discomfort on the driver's face, wincing as he pulled the sodden pad away from his head to inspect the damage.

"No insurance." The Escort driver replied quietly as he replaced the dressing against the back of his head.

"And…? Alan asked tentatively.

"No licence…at the moment." The driver responded.

"I think disqualified is the term you're searching for." Alan said and sighed despondently as he slowly shook his head. "That van at the top of the street, was it the same one that had a go at you on Meagers Lane?"

The driver shrugged, but remained silent.

"What was it they saw you getting rid of?" Alan asked expectantly.

The driver ignored Alan's questions and turned his face away to gaze out of the window as the Rover sped toward the City.

*****

Their reception at the Bridewell had been less than cordial. The Inspector casting an accusatory eye, firstly, at the state of their prisoner, still clasping the sodden field dressing to his head and secondly, at the blood spattered across Alan's yellow jacket and the small cut on the side of his face.

The Inspector's voice was like thunder. "Infirmary…NOW!…and don't ever bring a prisoner to my Bridewell in that state again."

"Sir." Alan immediately acquiesced, not bothering to protest his innocence in the matter.

The electric solenoid buzzed as the Inspector thumbed the button to release the inner door and Alan gripped his prisoner by his arm and led him back out into the outer corridor.

*****

"He might not Sully, he might just suck it up." Alan said hopefully.

"You've more chance of fingerin' Maggie Thatcher in the back seats of yer motor." Sullivan retorted flatly. "He's 'ad a right strokin'. Spent two joy filled hours in the Infirmary, 'ad eleven stitches an' 'e's gonna 'ave a mammoth 'eadache for a week…All 'e'll be able to see is fuckin' pound signs…a'course 'e'll complain…an' I aint getting' locked up 'cos some fuckin' plod from Division can't control 'imself."

"Nobody's getting locked up Pete…" Alan said dismissively.

His partner snorted derisively. "You're fuckin' jokin'…Look…getting' a smack after a chase is one thing…this kid's got a two inch hole in 'is scalp…It's a wounding Al, straight up section 18 an' if it comes on top…that's prison time, eighteen months starters…We'll 'ave to put pen to paper mate."

"Jesus Pete." Alan blew his cheeks out and exhaled slowly through pursed lips.

"What's to think about Al?" His partner asked, an incredulous tone in his voice.

Alan shrugged. "Doin' statements is a bit strong Pete…against a cop…"

His partner shook his head. "Don't give me that 'code' shit Al'. That was ten…fifteen years ago, those days are gone. There is no 'code', it doesn't exist anymore, an' it doesn't pay my mortgage or put food on the table." Sullivan didn't wait for a response; he snatched for the telephone handset and punched in the four figure extension for the radio room. "John, its Sully upstairs….'ave a squint at the Force nominal role an' tell us who 707 is."

Alan lit a cigarette. His partner held the handset to his ear and reached across the table for a scrap of paper, pulling off the top of his pen with his teeth.

"Bainbridge, Kevin…where's he at John?" Sullivan asked, as he held the paper in place with his elbow and scribbled down the details.

"Thanks John, can you show me an' Al' 10/5 clerical." Sullivan dropped the handset back onto its cradle.

"Our hero of the day is Constable Kevin Bainbridge, Millbeck, uniform beat patrol."

Alan flicked the ash from the end of his cigarette and pondered as he looked across to his partner.

"Was he part crew of Echo Three?" Alan asked.

"Soon find out." Sullivan replied, reaching again for the handset. "What's Force Control's extension?"

Alan shrugged and hauled himself out of his chair, suddenly feeling extremely fatigued. He gathered up the mugs abandoned on the windowsill and table top and left his partner to his enquiries while he went to the night kitchen to do the washing up.

*****

Sergeant Ronald Dennison sucked on the much chewed stem of his pipe as he read through their signed witness statements.

"Didn't know who else we could come to Sarge…You've always steered us right…what do you reckon?" The old Sergeant shuffled the pages of the statements into some semblance of order and placed them carefully on his desk top.

"'as 'e made a complaint?"

"Not that we know of Sarge…but I've got a bad feelin' about it." Sullivan said, sinking further down into his chair.

The Sergeant withdrew the pipe from between his teeth and placed the smouldering brier root bowl in the glass ash tray on his desk. The mouthpiece glistened with brown stained saliva and a thin tendril of blue smoke seeped from the end of the stem and floated wraithlike toward the ceiling.

"What's 'e gonna be charged with?"

"It'll be drive whilst disqualified, no insurance an' reckless drivin' Sarge. We've done statements to prove the motorin' offences, just not sure what to do 'bout what 'appened after."

"Witnesses?" the old sage asked questioningly.

Sullivan sighed. "Apart from the injured party…*if* D n' C care to go lookin'…The Inspector and Sergeant at the Bridewell…the A n' E nurse what stitched 'im up, if you'll pardon the expression…an' not forgettin' 'alf the residents of Mafeking Avenue."

The old Sergeant raised his eyebrows. "Not good lads." he said, quietly reaching for his pipe. Sealing his lips around the scarred end of the stem; he sucked gently and while pondering, stroked his chin with his fingertips.

"Right…these." he tapped the statements with the end of his pipe. "Need to go in an envelope… I'll date an' sign the seal and shove 'em in my safe…*If* he makes a complaint, you've covered yer arses an' if 'D n' C' do come a'knockin'… I know it goes against the grain lads, but you'll 'ave to submit these and young Bainbridge will 'ave to suck the 'ammer for it. *If* 'D n' C' stay none the wiser…well, yer laughin'." He leaned back in his chair and folded his arms across his stomach. "That…is the best I can come up with lads."

Alan looked across to his partner and nodded his agreement to the proposal.

*****

Sullivan's earlier prophetic opinions were soon to be proved correct.

An offer from the Prime Minister to have her snatch fondled in the back of Alan's Ford Capri was clearly *not* on the cards and he was rudely awakened by the impatient and repeated ringing of his front door bell, less than two hours after he had finished his shift.

Alan threw back the duvet and reached for a pair of faded track suit bottoms, from the chair at the side of his bed.

After making himself half decent, wearily Alan dragged himself from the bedroom and padded barefoot across the living room.

Yawning, he approached the front door to see two dark shadows of impending doom. The shapes, even distorted through the small panel of rippled glass, were readily identifiable as the be-suited forms of Detective Superintendent Ronald Allenby, standing six feet five inches in his stocking feet, accompanied by his omnipresent 'bag man' Detective Inspector Francis Harriman, at just five feet four in platform shoes.

Colloquially known throughout the Force as 'Little and Large'…Allenby and Harriman were investigators from Discipline and Complaints, the 'Inquisitors' from D n' C…The 'Rubber Heel Squad'.

Alan's heart rate suddenly rose, not quite sufficient to bring about a myocardial infarction, but certainly enough to dissipate any residual 'just woken after less than two hours sleep' syndrome and to cause an immediate and distinct shrivelling of the testicle sac, coupled with a sharp puckering of the anus.

"Here it comes." Alan thought to himself as he fumbled with the door keys.

As the door was opened, Alan was greeted by a blast of chilled air, either due to the fact that the warm air from within his flat had suddenly rushed out, or, if the urban legend was to be believed, the presence of 'The Black Rats', was always accompanied by a noticeable lowering of the ambient air temperature.

Detective Superintendent Allenby appeared stony faced, emotionless. He was clutching an A4 sized form which he immediately thrust forward into Alan's face. His six feet five frame towering over his subordinate, who appeared almost comically shorter, now standing obediently to the side of his liege Lord, but on the lower step.

"Recognise this Constable Pendle?" Detective Superintendent Allenby said flatly, wafting the sheet across the front of Alan's face. Clearly the two investigators had decided to dispense with offering Alan the conventional compliments of the day.

Alan scratched the side of his face and squinted at the wording on the form. "It's a caution and charge form Sir."

Allenby nodded. "Very perceptive Constable Pendle, it *is* a caution and charge form and you will note that the top portion…" He paused and with his left forefinger pointed to the upper part of the form where the accused's details would normally be found. "Has been intentionally left blank…but I guarantee that before this day is out…someone's name will be suitably appended." Alan was then rudely nudged aside as the two investigators entered.

"You know who I am." Allenby stated matter of factly. "This…he nodded down toward his sidekick…"As you know, is Inspector Harriman, who will be taking contemporaneous notes during our conversation."

Alan adopted a quizzical expression. "I don't want to appear at all pedantic Sir, but isn't there a small matter of a warrant to enter premises?"

Allenby smiled. "I know about you Pendle…You're a fucking smart arse by all accounts, bit of a barrack room lawyer, but before you mistakenly draw on your very limited knowledge of my powers of entry, you're in receipt of rent allowance from the Force in respect of this property…Yes?"

Alan nodded.

"Well then." Allenby said and smiled sickeningly. "I represent the Force and the Force having shall we say…a 'vested' financial interest in this property, gives me the right of entry…agreed?"

Alan nodded again, knowing that what the Force provided could just as easily be rescinded… with a simple stroke of Mr Allenby's pen.

Allenby pointed to the pre-typed offence section on the form. "On 14th of July in Mafeking Avenue at Moorwood, did with intent, unlawfully and maliciously, cause grievous bodily harm to one Liam Francis O'Donnell, contrary to section 18 of the Offences Against the Person Act 1861." He paused as if to allow the gravity of the matter to fully sink in. "This offence as you well know Constable Pendle, is indictable only, which means the Crown Court and…it carries a maximum penalty of imprisonment for life." Again he paused, giving Alan a second or two to think.

Allenby shrugged nonchalantly. "Personally Pendle, I don't give a flying fuck who's name ends up getting typed on the top of this form…but there's only one bus coming…You're either getting on it or not…There won't be another chance…so think on."

His pet dwarf hovered, pen poised over the page of his dog-eared notebook.

In the nanosecond it took for Alan to realise that if the 'Inquisitor General' had any actual evidence of wrongdoing on his part, he would have had his collar felt and be half way to the Bridewell by now...Allenby was 'fishing'.

"The bus is coming Constable." Inspector Harriman said temptingly.

Alan looked down at the simpering Inspector. He felt almost sorry for him. Harriman had to look up to everyone. Back in the day; Harriman wouldn't even have made the height restriction for a City Officer.

"I'm a Traffic Man Mr Harriman; we tend to avoid public transport. Buses are for poor people and disqualified drivers."

The Inspector's patronising grin dropped from his face like a wet flannel.

In his peripheral vision, Alan noticed the corners of Allenby's mouth lift, with just a hint of a smile.

The game was obviously afoot and Alan instinctively decided that it was time to dive out from between the rock and the hard place; in fact the decision to grass up a fellow Officer had been reached far more easily than he would have expected.

Sullivan was right...There was no 'code' and he already knew that in making his statement, he'd willingly 'given up' Bainbridge. Not out of any self-preservation considerations, not because he'd also felt the blunt end of his truncheon and had the swelling to prove it, but simply because Bainbridge had pissed him off. O'Donnell would probably get a walk out on all charges; their efforts had been for nothing.

Bainbridge was history...c'est la vie.

Alan made eye contact with the towering Superintendent. "Neither me or Pc Sullivan are guilty of any offence Sir. O'Donnell's was a righteous arrest, an' I didn't use any force in effecting it... neither did my partner. Sullivan and me witnessed the assault and we've already made our statements. Sergeant Dennison has them."

Superintendent Allenby's eyes tightened. "Dennison?" he asked suspiciously.

"Station Sergeant at Moorwood Sir." Alan replied.

Allenby paused and stared at Alan before he carefully folded the charge sheet and slipped it into the inside pocket of his jacket. He glanced disapprovingly at Alan's crumpled 'T' shirt and the tattered tracksuit bottoms.

"Get yourself properly dressed. If you're not out of your house out and sat in the back of our car in five minutes, you're locked up on suspicion…kapeesh?"

## **Twenty Four**

Alan toyed with the frayed piping along the armrest of the easy chair in his Sergeant's front room. Roger's black Labrador 'Bella' lay at his feet, asleep now and breathing softly, her head resting across one of his shoes. She wasn't going to allow Alan to escape without waking her for some more serious fussing.

The high backed chair was one of a matching pair. The coarse tapestry weave now worn through to string like threads along the tops of the arm rests. The sofa, the third piece in the set, bore evidence that Bella had at some stage, amused herself chewing the braided rope of knotted tassels, which now sagged sadly, torn away along the length of the base.

The heavy turned potbowl legs had not escaped her attention either; the wood beneath the glossy varnished surface was now exposed, scarred and torn, showing stark white beneath the dark brown polished surface.

On the wall above the sofa, within a large intricately moulded gilt frame, hung a copy of Turner's 'The Fighting Temeraire'. The 'heroine' of Trafalgar appearing out of the mist, ethereal and ghost like beneath a glorious sunset, now being tugged to her last berth to be broken up.

Alan stared at the classic painting and wondered if Turner had intended to evoke such a sense of loss, sadness at the famous old 'bark' being so casually discarded. Now only fit for the breakers yard, the Temeraire's naked, skeletal masts were almost shrouded by the greasy billowing smoke, spewing out from the high stack of the 'modern' coal powered tug.

Out with the old and in with the new. The way of the world, Alan thought.

His Sergeant flicked the ash from the end of his cigar into a large polished brass coal scuttle which languished at the side of his easy chair, then returned his gaze to the typed pages.

While he waited, Alan looked around the room. It was dark and slightly oppressive. The walls were papered in a deep maroon flock, emblazoned with a white 'fleur-de-lys' pattern, which fell from the nicotine stained ceiling, to a brown stained wooden dado rail, encircling the room.

Heavy brown velvet curtains, supported by a brass rail and gathered at the waist with gold braided ropes, hung from large wooden rings. These were drawn aside now and secured to brass fittings at either side of the French windows which provided a meagre source of light across the dark brown patterned carpet. There was an all pervading smell of stale cigar smoke, rancid, permeating from every fibre and surface.

A long row of imitation leather video cassette tape storage boxes, dark green and richly embossed with equally imitation gold leaf, sat atop a stained and varnished slab of plywood. To the casual observer looking every inch the complete works of Dickens.

A rustic stone fireplace housed a flickering imitation coal effect electric fire. Within the small alcoves in the stonework were various items of bric-a-brac and a number of brass framed photographs. Bella as a pup, Roger and his Wife Sally posing as they fed the Barbary apes on Gibraltar's rocky outcrop. There was also a faded sepia image of a heavily jowled lady wearing a black shawl and what looked like a white cotton shower cap. Her fierce scowling countenance looked as if it could've stopped a clock. She reminded Alan of a picture he'd once seen of Queen Victoria, but on a *really* bad day. Roger or Sally's Grandmother perhaps, Alan wondered.

To either side of the video storage boxes and holding them securely to attention, was a pair of small wooden box speakers. To the side, exposing a raft of twisted wires, sat a bulky 'Amstrad' music center, the top turntable protected by a smoked grey plastic cover. Its brushed aluminium face sported twin cassette decks along with a tuner amplifier, adorned with a myriad of switches and buttons. A small plastic, wood effect stacking system filled with cassette tapes provided the fulcrum point for Roger's collection of LP's which leant at an angle, wedged between it and the side of the stereo. From the glossy cover of his first solo album 'Being With You', Smokey Robinson smiled across at Alan as if they'd been friends forever.

On the screen of the large colour television, tucked away in the far corner of the room, Joe Montana, the quarterback for the San Francisco 49ers was frozen in mid pass.

Grainy white lines flickered across the bottom half of the screen and Alan guessed that either the tracking needed adjusting on his Sergeant's VHS recorder, or that he had watched the Super Bowl play off so many times since he had captured it in January, that the tape was almost worn out.

At the time Alan had interrupted his Sergeant's day off, the Miami Dolphins in their turquoise and white livery, were holding off the '49ers' 10 to 7 in the first quarter. Alan also knew that the maroon and gold clad gladiators from San Francisco, soundly defeated the Dolphins by 38 to 16 to take the championship and their second Super Bowl title.

Alan had next to no interest in American football, but his Sergeant lived for it and Alan, like the rest of the lads, feigned interest as Roger sat at his desk and constantly waxed lyrical about the various games during the 'play offs'.

The members of the Traffic office could by now, reel off the names of the various teams and quite a few of the players and each year, come January, Roger would throw a Super Bowl party at his house.

Sally, his suffering Wife would prepare copious amounts of sandwiches and make sure that the cans of Budweiser had been in the fridge for at least two hours before 'her boys' turned up.

Bella's leg twitched rapidly and she whimpered. She was obviously off somewhere chasing rabbits and Alan leaned over and ran his hand gently across the top of her head and onto the soft silky hair behind her ears.

He could hear Sally humming as she busied herself in the kitchen, and there was the tinkling sound of a spoon stirring coffee.

His Sergeant finally looked up from the pages. "This Evie woman." Roger said, glancing cautiously toward the living room door and dropping his voice to a whisper. "She's a hooker at the end of the day Al, hardly what could be described as a credible witness. She got much form?"

Alan shrugged. "Common prostitute, a bit for shoplifting a while back. A caution for cannabis…It is what it is Sarge."

His Sergeant stared back down at the pages of Alan's statement, he scratched his forehead nervously.

"If it's right, we've got a double murderer runnin' loose in the Division an' 'avin' identified the prime suspect, you've just deprived twenty odd grim faced Detectives of enough overtime to keep 'em in beer money for a month of Sundays…Don't be thinkin' of applyin' for C.I.D. anytime in the next decade."

Alan sighed heavily and shrugged his shoulders. "Evie's info's always been good Roger…It might all be bollocks but you must admit, it's got a ring of truth about it. I'll always be convinced that fatal in the Melville's was no accident, an' I know Evie was there, 'cos I saw 'er…Just how tight she was with this other hooker McKnight I don't know, but McKnight's laid on a slab at the mortuary with a hole in her face, an' Evie's done a runner down to the 'smoke'…She sounded scared shitless on the phone."

His Sergeant sucked on the wet stub of his cigar whilst he pondered for a moment.

"Who knows about this?"

"Just you and Ron Dennison Sarge…Derek Bentley took the call, but it was only the number an' a message askin' me to call back. I didn't twig at first…The name Evelynne Garretty didn't mean a thing."

His Sergeant maintained eye contact. "It's your statement at the end of the day Alan. Once it's in, it's in. No goin' back an' there'll be hell to pay if you're wrong. Frank Ellis is likely to tear into Forrester for shit cannin' yer original report, an' if this turns out to be bollocks after all, spreadin' yer arse cheeks for another reamin' is the best you can 'ope for."

Alan thought for a moment. "I'll take it under advisement Roger but I reckon I've got to run with it. If it's right an' this sooty Lyburn ends up getting his collar felt, it'd be a hell of a coup for Traffic an' even Forrester won't be able to bitch…Two detected murders?"

His Sergeant pursed his lips. He nodded slowly and smiled. "Better pick up some KY jelly on the way in then, just in case."

The living room door was shouldered open and Roger's Wife entered carrying a small metal tray on which sat two mugs of coffee and a plate of assorted biscuits.

She smiled at Alan. "And how's it going with you and that girlfriend of yours Alan?…Sandra Prestwick isn't it?…Lovely girl…such friendly eyes…She came to take a report when our garden shed got broken into you know."

Alan nodded. "She told me about it…Still undetected?"

"It is I'm afraid." Sally replied pensively. "Although you know…" she continued in hushed tones. "I always suspected it was one of those foreigners from across the road. They're from Rumania or out that way somewhere…They live like gypsies you know Alan…hardly speak a word of English any of them…That Enoch Powell was right, we'll live to regret opening our doors to all and sundry. There's hardly a white face to be seen down at the shopping center…I just don't know where it will all end."

Alan adopted his genuinely concerned look and reached for one of the Bourbons, much to the immediate chagrin of his Sergeant who frowned threateningly.

Alan's fingers hovered over the plate and he diverted toward a custard cream. His Sergeant smiled and nodded his approval.

"I'm gonna 'ave to go in Sal." Roger said decidedly, shuffling himself forward to liberate the two Bourbon creams.

It was his Wife's turn to frown. She sighed despondently. "Oh Roger…You promised you'd get the lawns cut today…"

"Needs must I'm afraid dear…Our Alan here has come up with some very interestin' info an' Frank Ellis is gonna want it ASAP."

\*\*\*\*\*

"When did you come by this information?" Detective Inspector Ellis asked, placing Alan's statement face down on his desk. Alan shuffled uncomfortably in his seat.

The D.I. was wearing his trademark tweed hacking jacket, with scuffed brown leather patches at the elbows. His shirt collar was frayed and open at the neck. His tie, D.I. Ellis's one concession to the Force dress code policy, was loosened; it hung slackly against the front of his shirt. Alan noticed that it bore the relatively recent evidence of curry or brown sauce.

His heavily jowled face featured at least a day's growth and he looked as if he hadn't slept in a week. His piercing blue eyes were alert enough though, and now they seemed to bore questioningly into Alan from where the D.I. slouched in his swivel chair, at the other side of the paper strewn desk.

"Just after ten, when I came on this morning sir. I got the note from Derek in the front office; I rang the number an' spoke with Evi…Miss Garretty."

The D.I. glanced at his watch and scowled. "Over four hours ago?"

Alan sighed. "Sir…I took a severe rectum probing from Chief Inspector Forrester over the report I submitted about the fatal in the Melvilles, so I admit…I was slightly hesitant to put pen to paper again until I'd seen my own Supervision."

D.I. Ellis diverted his gaze toward Alan's Sergeant, who was leaning casually against the door frame. He smirked. "You look like shit Roger, fancy a pick me up?" he said, opening the bottom drawer of his desk and offering up a half empty bottle of 'Ballantines'. Roger dismissed the offer with a quick shake of his head. "Regarding my dishevelled appearance Frank, I'm day off, what's your excuse?…I'll pass on the drink thanks unless you can get the cast of Miami Vice out there to rustle up some coffee."

The D.I. chuckled. "We don't do coffee Roger, that's for you shiny arsed petrol wasters. This is C.I.D.…Now, before I put my arse on the line an' kick that lot into action." he motioned out toward the plethora of Murder Squad Detectives lounging in the spacious C.I.D. office. Ellis stared across at Alan and pointed a cautionary finger. "What's the strength of this info?…How well do you know this hooker Garretty before I bother my Detective Chief Superintendent?"

He pointed down to the statement. "Think carefully; convince me that this isn't just a crock of shit."

Alan took a deep breath. "From the beginning?"

"From the beginning." The D.I. nodded and turned to wink slyly at Alan's Sergeant. "An' don't miss out the juicy bits if you've bin gettin' freebies." he added.

*****

Detective Inspector Frank Ellis was a patient man, he was known for it, a deep thinker with the analytical mind of a veteran Detective. There was no interruption as Alan told his tale; Ellis leaned casually back in his chair, his legs crossed, feet up on the table top. His fingers caressed the rim of the heavy cut glass tumbler. The remains of the two fingers of 'Balantines' he had poured himself glowed with rich amber in the fluorescence from the overhead strip light.

Almost twenty minutes it took. Ellis listened, nodding thoughtfully as he considered Alan's theories and conclusions regarding the Melvilles fatal. Other than a knowing frown when Alan described how they had been disregarded by the Divisional Chief Inspector, his face remained passive. At the conclusion, Alan sat back in his chair and waited for a response.

Ellis looked across to his old friend the Traffic Sergeant. He raised his eyebrows questioningly. "Roger?"

"It's your call Frank, you're the Detective, but I'm satisfied 'is theories about the bump are sound. Whether this Garretty woman is pullin' 'is pisser about this Lyburn fella seein' off 'er mate as well…Who can say?"

D.I. Ellis paused for a second as he stared at Alan intently from across his desk.

He sucked on his teeth as if weighing up all his options. Suddenly, he tossed back the remains of his whiskey and as if electrified, with alarming alacrity, he leapt from his chair and strode purposefully across to the office door.

"Harry." he called out across the floor of the C.I.D. office.
"Boss?"

"Get off yer arse an' get me everything known about an IC3 name of Lyburn. Street name 'Midnight'. Do national an' local an' while yer at it, get me the name of a reliable 'suit' down in the Met…I want somebody findin'…"

"Got it Boss."

"Dennis."

"Boss?"

"Smarten yerself up for Christ's sake, borrow a fuckin' tie. Grab a motor an' go pick up John Sommerville from H.Q…Tell 'im it looks like we might just 'ave a suspect for the shootin', an' we're up an' runnin'…"

"On it boss."

"Joan."

"Yes Boss?"

"See if you can drum up some coffee for our illustrious guests from the Traffic Department."

D.I. Ellis returned to his desk and made hard eye contact with Alan. "Right lad, we'll run with it…Retrieve that exhibit bag for me. 1 want that telephone number tracing so I can get the Met to go visit this Garretty woman an' get 'er to commit to a statement, take 'er into protective custody if necessary… an' I'll want that original accident report…I presume you kept it?"

Alan nodded. "Yes sir…But the thing is…" Alan shot a concerned glance across to his Sergeant who interceded. "The thing is Frank, Alan here was ordered not to have anything else to do with the job in the Melvilles. Alan Forrester took 'im off the case and dropped it on Charlie Morrisey's toes. Fact is…that original report should have bin destroyed as ordered. Comin' to you with this might be seen…"

The D.I. glowered. "You let me worry about the self-righteous Mr Forrester Roger. When John Sommerville finds out that we could 'ave known about this Lyburn character over a week ago, he might 'ave a few 'arsh words…Bernie Foster an' Dave Mitchell might not escape an arseholin' either. More concerned with brown nosin' up to Alan Forrester an' protectin' 'is fuckin' crime 'stats' than showin' any interest in what your boy 'ad to say…"

The Traffic Sergeant nodded toward Alan. "'E's away shooting at Stretham all next week Frank.."

The D.I. shrugged nonchalantly. "Not a problem Roger…'E's better off out of it for the time being anyway. But get young Morrisey in 'ere. I want all the paperwork 'e's got on that fatal in the Melvilles. Let's see if there's anything that ties it to the shooting. It's all a bit 'Jackanory' at the moment. If what this Garretty woman says is right, an' after Lyburn 'topped' this Zippleman bloke with the stolen motor, he stopped off just long enough to souvenir the gun which said Zippleman was reputed to carry an' with it, sees off the McKnight woman, it's a corkin' job…We've just got to get it 'ome is all."

He looked back to Alan and nodded toward the main office. "You just make sure one of those suits out there's got a number we can contact you on. Detective Chief Superintendent John Sommerville's comin' in…'E's not a man to be fucked with, an' 'e'll no doubt want a word before you disappear for a week, so make yerself available."

*****

'Midnight's' eyes fluttered and opened, for a brief moment he was disorientated, not used to waking to the warmth of central heating or the spacious, modern surroundings of the newly rented flat. A hundred and fifty per calendar month was expensive, but he was away from the dismal dreariness of the 'Badlands' and here at least, he was unknown. He had secured the self-contained flat on the outskirts of the City, through a local letting agent. It had eaten into his ill-gotten gains as he had paid six months in advance, cash, with a receipt made out for the purposes of the letting agent's files and 'Midnight's' anonymity, in the name of Mr Lester Williams.

The bedroom, separated from the main living room, had been recently painted and the lingering aroma of emulsion smelled fresh and somehow clinical.

Across from the double bed and extending across the entire width of the far wall, were fitted wardrobes with mirrored doors, creating the illusion that the room was actually twice the size. The room was modern, light and airy.

'Midnight' sat up and stared at his reflection. For a brief moment, he panicked at the enormity of the road he had taken. If they took him, this time, it would be a double life sentence. Thirty years in Belmarsh or Wakefield. Even with time off for good behaviour and that wasn't his style, he'd be almost seventy before he saw the streets again.

The five stretch he'd done in Holdsworth would seem like a long week-end. His cell mates words *"The first's the 'ardest Jimmy...after that they're all jus' fuckin' meat."* echoed in the back of his mind over and over.

'Fastener' had been his first, but he hadn't found it that hard. Sure, he'd been nervous whilst he had been waiting and whilst picking just the right place to mount the pavement, but taking his life...Nothing.

McKnight was the one that came back to him. Each time he closed his eyes she appeared, ethereal, spectral and accusing. The vision of her head being snapped violently back over and over, the eyeball disintegrating. The explosion of blood and brain matter bursting from the back of her head. The way she had remained standing, just for an instant, staring at him with disbelief. The muzzle flash still reflected in her one remaining eye, the right side of her face blackened and burned, until her brain realised that she was dead and allowed her legs to fold.

He shuddered briefly and threw off the duvet; his body glistened with a thin sheen of sweat. It was the heat he lied to himself, not used to it after the cold and damp of his bedsit.

But it wasn't the heat that had woken him twice during the night, sitting bolt upright with a loud grunt, it was when the ghostly apparition of the McKnight woman had appeared.

'Midnight' swung his legs out from beneath the cover and allowed his toes to revel in the caress of the thick carpeting. Padding silently to the small en-suite bathroom, he stretched as he urinated, flexing his shoulders and arching his back to ease the night's stiffness.

Today he would go back to his old bedsit and gather up the rest of his meagre belongings. There wasn't much, some of his clothes he wanted, but the rest, what there was of it, could stay. He could afford to buy new.

The money and the revolver were safely ensconced in a left luggage locker at the City railway station. The twelve grand wouldn't last forever and he would need another car, newer and road legal, one that would go unnoticed. He was out of the 'Badlands' now, and the battered old Cortina looked out of place amongst the shiny modern Sierra's and Golf's parked on the street.  He needed a big score, a 'one off', one that would net him enough to live anonymously for a year or so, here in the land of the gainfully employed.

Enough time for the dust to settle. Time to think.

*****

Alan walked with his Sergeant down the corridor from the CID office. As they passed the front desk, his Sergeant placed a fatherly hand on his shoulder. "I'm getting' off Alan, still got time to get the lawns cut, or it'll be porridge for tea."

Alan chuckled. "Thanks for coming in Sarge, 'preciate your support."

"Not a problem Al, look…." his Sergeant glanced at his watch. "It's gone three, make sure yer dockets clear an' get yerself off…Go see that malingerin' twat Sullivan on yer way 'ome, an' I'll see you after you've finished at Stretham, alright?"

"Cheers Sarge, I'll ring in during the week and let you know how it's going."

As Alan turned to head up the stairs toward the top corridor, the front office clerk called out to him from behind the counter. "Oi! Al, you goin' back to yer office?"

Alan nodded, "Yeah, why. What's up Derek?"

"You've a surprise visitor mate."

Alan sighed. "Del, I've had enough surprises for one day thanks, enlighten me."

The clerk held up the fire register. "The 'Muppet' has returned…an' 'e's signed in as *Inspector* Goodwill."

Alan's face dropped in disbelief. "You are fuckin' joking Del."

"'fraid not mate, here it is in graphic detail." the clerk replied as he held up the register. "The book doesn't lie Alan. Inspector A.M. Goodwill, Discipline and Complaints to see Constable 868 Pendle. 'E signed in twenty minutes ago…'E's ensconced 'imself in yer office mate, probably rootin' through yer docket, plantin' 'alf an ounce of cannabis as we speak."

Alan shook his head slowly. "I'd hoped we'd seen the last of him after the twat left for Bramshill…Thanks for the heads up Del."

With a certain amount of trepidation, Alan mounted the stairs. Whatever the reason for Goodwill's appearance, it was certain to put a dampener on the day.

*****

Archibald Marcus Goodwill, known previously to his suffering uniformed colleagues as the 'Muppet'. 'Most Useless Police Probationer Ever Trained'.

Goodwill was limp wristed, overtly effeminate and if the rumours were to be believed, 'batted for the other side'. He was known as 'Archie' on a good day and 'Santa' behind his back.

The analogy being, 'Santa'...Christmas...*goodwill* to all men.

He had arrived at Moorwood Division direct from Durham University, armed with a degree in some spurious 'ology' or other, and had the annoyingly pretentious habit of adding B.A. after his signature. This, his fellow Constables quickly decreed stood for 'Backside Available'.

As a graduate entrant, he had been quickly earmarked for the accelerated promotion scheme. After his two year probationary period, he (naturally) breezed the Sergeant's exam. He was then whisked off, to the Police Staff College at Bramshill in Hampshire for twelve months, much to the relief of his colleagues, all of whom hoped when he returned as a newly promoted Inspector, he would be 'salted away' to some anonymous non-operational Department at Headquarters, to quietly await the arrival of his third 'pip'.

Archie's one saving grace was that he had never made any pretence about his career aspirations. Never attempting to endear himself to his fellow uniformed Officers, who he considered to be lower forms of life, he wallowed unashamedly in his upper class status and numerous academic qualifications.

He would state categorically that he had no intentions of remaining at the rank of Constable for a solitary day longer than required during his two year probationary period. That dismal accolade he would leave to those who due to either their personal academic failings or working class backgrounds were best suited to the rank and file.

Archie's sights were set fairly and squarely at the rank of Chief Constable and there was little doubt in anyone's mind that within a relatively short period of time, he would attain it. It also quickly became apparent that he'd step on anyone to achieve his goal.

Fortunate to actually make it as far as 'independent foot patrol', Goodwill had been discarded by a number of Tutor Constables. He was literally passed from 'pillar to post' by the exasperated shift Inspector, who was under orders from Headquarters to ensure that the star in the Force's firmament made it through his probation.

The weekly reports compiled by his numerous Tutors showed his progress to be painfully slow and bore comments alluding to his 'aloof attitude' and that 'Pc Goodwill displays a worrying lack of communication skills when dealing with members of the general public. His only consistency is that he shows a total disregard and a marked disdain for any advice or guidance provided by his uniformed colleagues'.

There were more colourful comments, usually aired in person by the retiring Tutor to the shift Inspector. "He might have a degree boss but he couldn't open a bleedin' umbrella." "If he makes it sir, I'll show my arse in Burton's window."

The Divisional Commander persevered and Archie's weekly reports were 'doctored' accordingly.

From Alan's point of view, the 'Muppet' had nailed his colours to the mast at an early stage of his ascendency.

*****

"We 'ad Chinese yesterday Sully…and Monday, I'm getting slanty eyes. What about having a float up to that Greek place on Delph Lane, they're supposed to be good to us?"
Sullivan grimaced. "They eat snails an' shit Al…Stick to what we know eh."

Alan glanced across to his partner and sighed heavily. "That would be the French Sully…the French eat snails. The Greeks on the other hand, as you should recall from your previous holidays, are famous for their exquisite meat dishes such as moussaka, stuffed olive leaves and kleftico …I'm just saying, it wouldn't hurt to extend our culinary horizons passed chicken fried rice for once."

The decision as to which food outlet they should descend upon, was interrupted by the Divisional radio operator.

"Moorwood patrols, especially Traffic. Observations please for a Honda 125 solo motorcycle in red. Oscar Romeo Whiskey Seven Five Six Sierra, just stolen from the drive of 36 Denholm Avenue no direction of travel."

Alan depressed the button on the top of his 'Burndept'.

"John, me an' Sully are on East Morton Road. Was it ridden away?"

"Looks like it Al" the radio operator replied. "The complainant says 'e was workin' on it, left the engine runnin' while he went inside to make a pot of tea. He heard it revvin'…He ran out to see it dissapearin' at a rapid rate of knots down Denholme Avenue towards the Edward's…Looks like an opportunist theft…White lad, no helmet, wearin' a denim jacket."

Alan pressed the transmit button on his Burndept. "Show Papa Yankee One Three on area search then John."

"Roger that Al."

Sullivan snorted with derision. "Fuckin' idiot, what's 'e expect leavin' it runnin' unattended in the Denholme's?…'E'll 'ave a job getting' that one passed 'is insurance company. Might as well 'ave 'ung a sign on it…Free to good 'ome."

Alan chuckled. "As caring as ever Pete …Oh, and whilst we're on the subject of fucking idiots." Alan said nodding up the road. "Isn't that Officer Goodwill I see going lawfully about his constabulary duties?"

As Sullivan peered up the incline of the road to where the hapless 'Muppet' was walking his beat, his attention was diverted to a small motorcycle which suddenly came into view over the brow of the hill.

Goodwill stopped mid stride on seeing the oncoming machine and noting that the rider was helmetless and therefore committing a reportable road traffic offence, stepped out into the middle of the road directly into its path. He raised his right hand, palm facing forwards in the Home Office approved 'number one' stop signal.

The rider's field of vision was seriously reduced due to the 40 mile per hour blast of air in his face. This caused him to squeeze his eyes down to slits. He had not had the time, given that he had stolen the machine only moments previously, to fully acquaint himself with the controls of the machine. Through his watering slits, at the last moment, he saw the 'Muppet' standing rigidly to attention in the middle of the road barely thirty feet away.

Instinctively stamping down hard on the pedal beneath his right foot, had the effect of causing the rear wheel of the Honda to lock solid.

Goodwill to his credit, looking to all intents and purposes like Gonville Bromhead facing the Zulu hordes at Rorke's drift, unflinchingly stood his ground. However, as his degree was in entomology and that particular subject not concerned one iota with the general law of physics, he was blissfully unaware that at 40 miles per hour, the motorcycle was hurtling towards him at almost sixty feet per second.

The 'Muppet' had stepped into the road a little over ten yards in front of the oncoming Honda. In so doing, he had provided the rider with considerably less than the required 120 feet it would take even a person capable of cogent thought, to have brought the machine to a halt. The outcome was inevitable and eventually, hilarious.

Had the dim-witted rider simply accelerated, with a simple shifting of his bodyweight, he could have weaved the Honda around Officer Goodwill and continued on its way down the road (albeit towards Alan and Sullivan's approaching Traffic car), leaving Goodwill frustrated.

An unfortunate amalgam of panic and confusion was the rider's downfall. Stamping on the rear brake pedal and at the same time snatching at the *clutch* lever whilst attempting to avoid the 'Muppet' had the effect of causing the screaming rear wheel to slew wildly out to the offside.

The rider fought valiantly with the handlebars to no avail. Control of the Honda was now irretrievably lost.

The law of physics simply cannot be defeated, every action having an equal and opposite reaction. The rider, his legs now fully outstretched winglike to either side of the machine, careered from the carriageway, mounted the nearside kerb, skidded across the pavement and ploughed through a seven foot hedge.

In a flurry of privet leaves, the machine and rider disappeared into the front garden of one of the adjacent Council owned semis.

Alan and his partner were stricken with uncontrollable laughter and Sullivan was hard pressed to control their patrol vehicle, as he accelerated up to where the 'Muppet' was now clawing his way through the newly improvised gap in the hedge.

Sullivan wrenched on the handbrake. He snatched the keys from the ignition barrel, before hurriedly following Alan through the gate kindly erected by the Council, which provided access to the garden where Officer Goodwill was found kneeling by the side of the rider.

The premises had recently become unoccupied and the windows and doors had been hastily boarded up by the Council.

The front garden contained the normal Council tenant detritus. Empty beer cans in profusion, numerous plastic bags filled with household rubbish, a manually operated lawnmower which clearly had not seen action in over a decade, a plethora of soiled disposable nappies left out to soak up the rain and now swollen to bursting point and of course, the omnipresent Ford engine block and accompanying rear axle, both now corroded beyond redemption.

The 'Muppet' had lost his helmet as he had forced his way through the overgrown privet hedge. It now lay with its chromed top comb firmly implanted in one of the large mounds of dog excreta which had been deposited at random intervals across the neglected overgrown lawn.

Cautiously negotiating the veritable minefield of slowly bio-degrading dog shit, Alan and his partner approached and stood over the 'Muppet', who was feverishly tending to the rider.

Certainly the adage that 'crime does not pay', was clearly pertinent in this case.

The rider was lying on his back, wailing like a banshee and bleeding profusely from an angry gaping wound in his upper thigh.

As the Honda and rider had exploded through the dense foliage, the thick branches of the privet hedge had snapped and a splintered end had torn into one of his flailing, outstretched legs. Goodwill had a clenched fist pressed into the rider's inner thigh; applying pressure on the femoral artery just above the ragged tear which Alan noted was still effusing copious amounts of blood which seeped from beneath the ripped denim material of his jeans.

Alan leaned over and examined the rider's face, which was twisted in agony.

"Well, well, well…Check this out Sully…Thomas Henry Pratt…prat by name and prat by nature."

Sullivan peered over Alan's shoulder and beamed. "Fuck me sideways so it is…Its divine intervention Al…'Ere Archie what you doin' son?"

The 'Muppet' looked up, bewildered at the apparent callousness of his fellow Officers.

"He's bleeding badly; I think it's his main artery, got to keep pressure on it…He needs an ambulance quickly."

Alan made a point of looking across to the adjacent houses, all of which were similarly boarded up. "Don't be so hasty Archie, know who that is?"

The 'Muppet' looked up, now totally bewildered. "Wha…?"

"That, Archie"…Sullivan said, pointing down to the hapless rider whose face had taken on a rather waxy paleness. "Is Thomas Henry Pratt…Thievin' toe rag of this City. Don't you read yer crime reports?"

Alan squatted down on his haunches and casually placed two fingers on the side of the rider's neck feeling for a pulse. "Hmmm…its weak Tommy, very weak, not good at all…Moments away from shrugging off your mortal coil I should say…What do you reckon Sully?"

Sullivan adopted a concerned expression and reached into the pocket of his jacket for his cigars. "I'm no doctor Al…but its not looking good."

The 'Muppet' was dumbfounded. He stared up at the two Traffic men. "I need help with him… Haven't you got a tourniquet in your car or something?" he shrieked as the blood now seeped up between his fingers.

Alan placed a fatherly hand on Goodwill's shoulder. "Archie." he said softly. "This is Tommy Pratt, prolific burglar, thief and general arsehole an' you would be doing the civilised world, not to mention Mr Forrester's crime figures a huge favour, if you were to just take yer hand away an' let him bleed out quietly…There's no one around…Look, the whole street's boarded up…Only the three of us will ever know an' me an' Sully won't say nothing."

Goodwill unable to believe his own ears, looked pleadingly up to Sullivan for support.

Sullivan took his time lighting his cigar. "Secret's safe with me Archie." he added, winking slyly.

The 'Muppet' shifted his weight and placed a second hand onto the rider's leg and pressed down harder.

The rider moaned; the pupils of his eyes, now dilated to pinpricks, slowly disappeared under his drooping eyelids. Goodwill's eyes filled with tears and he started to shake with fear and frustration.

"Protection of life and property!" he screamed at them, his voice cracking with emotion.

Alan patted him gently on the shoulder. "You're right, of course Archie." Alan said patronisingly. "But with shitheads like Pratt here, you can skip the protection of life bit an' move straight to protection of property…You'd actually be keepin' to that part of yer oath by allowin' Tommy the burglar 'ere to slip away unnoticed"

Goodwill started to sob with frustration, his head dropped in despair. "How could you…"

He froze as he heard the unmistakable sound of sirens approaching. He looked up at Alan, now more confused than ever.

Alan patted him gently on the back and smiled. "Called it in before I left the patroller Archie." he whispered, before standing up to walk out to the street to guide the Ambulance crew to their location.

Sullivan leant over, he ruffled the 'Muppet's' hair and chuckled. "You did good Archie…I bet there's a 'commend' in it…Me an' Al'll put in a good word to yer Inspector."

*****

Alan opened the door to the Traffic office to be greeted by a rather wolfish smile from the smartly dressed figure seated behind his Sergeant's desk.

"Mr Goodwill, what an unexpected pleasure." Alan said, with just the merest hint of sarcasm.

"That would be Inspector now Pendle…or sir." Goodwill replied sardonically.

Alan raised a disinterested eyebrow, unimpressed by the 'Muppet's attempt at an assertion of seniority and pulled one of the swivel chairs out from beneath the desk opposite.

Seating himself, he swung around to face the Inspector. The icy reception had set the tone of the meeting and although it had been over eighteen months since Archie had left the Division to go to Bramshill, clearly there was to be no playful banter or joyful reminiscing.

"I noticed you signed in as D n'C...Mr Allenby's new 'bag man' is it sir?" Alan asked.

"Investigating Inspector is the correct title Pendle."

Alan stared back at Goodwill and smiled mischievously. "That would be Constable Pendle sir...or Alan, I don't mind."

"Touche." Goodwill said, allowing himself a wry smile.

"I presume you're not here to swap pleasantries sir?" Alan said.

"As astute as ever...You are of course correct." The Inspector replied, reaching down into his briefcase.

"I am here to serve you with this." Goodwill said, sliding a document across the table. "I presume that it doesn't come as a complete surprise?"

Alan immediately identified it as a Form 147 an official notification of a public complaint. A 'purple peril'.

Goodwill read aloud from his copy. Alan scanned down the form and followed the Inspector's words disinterestedly.

"This is to notify you, Constable 868 Pendle Moorwood Divisional Road Traffic, that a complaint has been laid by Mr Edward Rawlinson of 18 Harold Square, who states that during his arrest for motoring offences, he was unlawfully assaulted. He...Mr Rawlinson, complains that you kneed him in the small of his back, this caused bruising and discomfort and he further alleges that the amount of force used to effect his arrest was excessive and unjustified...Mr Rawlinson states that his complaint of assault is supported by witness evidence. The injury sustained by Mr Rawlinson constitutes a criminal offence, that being one of common assault, which is contrary to Common law." Inspector Goodwill raised his eyes from the document. "Any response to the allegation?"

Alan sucked at his teeth for a moment as he looked across at the child prodigy.

"I think I'll reserve my position for the time being sir."

"Very good, I'll note your response." Goodwill said, hastily scrawling something on the bottom of his copy before folding it and dropping it into his briefcase.

Alan leaned backwards in his chair and seeing that there appeared to be sufficient water in the kettle, clicked the small switch at its base.

"Care to stay for a brew Mr Goodwill?"

The Inspector was clearly taken aback. "Very magnanimous of you under the circumstances. I will yes…as long as I can observe as you prepare it." he said sardonically.

Alan chortled. "I'm fresh out of strychnine at the moment Arch…I mean Sir, so you're safe."

*****

As Alan returned to the Traffic office carrying two steaming mugs of coffee, Inspector Goodwill contemplated his relaxed demeanour. "You seem to be somewhat complacent about Mr Rawlinson's complaint. It's quite a serious allegation you know."

Alan slid one of the mugs across the desk toward the Inspector and took his seat. "Are we 'hats off' Mr Goodwill?"

The Inspector recognised the term and nodded. "Up to a certain point…yes, why not."

Alan nodded his gratitude. "You see, Mr Goodwill, I am not only complacent as you so eloquently put it…Actually, I couldn't care less. Suffice to say, I won't lose a moments sleep over it. The Police Complaints Authority will take one look at Rawlinson's 'previous' an' determine that he's a lying shithead with more 'form' than Red Rum. That, coupled with a fully supportive statement from Pc Morrisey my partner on that particular day, should see his half arsed complaint safely written off as vexatious and unfounded sir. As for his complaint bein' corroborated by witness evidence. I suspect that this would be from his 'in house' slag Tina Lofthouse, who coincidentally sir, just happens to be his co-accused."

Inspector Goodwill shook his head slowly. "Times are changing Alan…Your somewhat 'Neanderthal' style of policing is over. Remonstrative justice meted out on the street is no longer acceptable and Officers will be held to account."

"Remonstrative justice…well put Mr Goodwill." Alan said with a smile. "I can see why you opted for D n' C…Your chosen career path is it now sir? The police that police the police?"

Mr Goodwill smiled and shook his head. "A temporary position I assure you…Actually, I've already got my third pip. I've got 'D' Division. I take over from Chief Inspector Spencer within the month…So you see, I seem to have stayed the course…contrary to the general consensus of opinion amongst my peers that I would never make a Police Officer whilst I had a hole in my backside."

Alan winced a little.

The Inspector smiled knowingly. "Oh yes Alan, I heard it said on numerous occasions. I believe that you also voiced similar opinions, but as you can see, I have made it and not without a modicum of success so far. You still appear to be in the starting gates Constable, whereas I am halfway down the second furlong." Inspector Goodwill sipped at his coffee and there was something of an awkward silence.

Alan opened his mouth as if to speak and then thought better of it.

The 'Muppet' frowned. "Hesitancy not normally associated with your trademark verbosity Alan…we are 'hats off' as agreed."

Alan paused for a second and then swung his chair around so that he fully faced the boy wonder. "See, the thing of it is sir…There's cops and there's *cops*…Getting through your probation, your time at Bramshill and your promotion to Inspector in Discipline and Complaints doesn't make you a cop Mr Goodwill. Don't get me wrong, I'm actually very pleased to see that you're doing well and I'm sure that you'll go all the way to the top, but you'll never be a *cop* Mr Goodwill."

The 'Muppet' suddenly felt a little uncomfortable and squirmed in his seat. His face became taut and was on the point of remonstrating with Alan about his lack of respect, but realised that he had invited him to speak freely and was now reaping the rewards of his rather reckless tolerance.

Alan smiled mischievously, enjoying the moment. "You're promoted because you're smart Mr Goodwill…no denying it…You're a degree entrant, an' it doesn't matter what subject your degree is in. Just gettin' it proves that you have the tenacity to study and the capacity to retain the information…that you can pass exams. You obviously listened while you were at your exclusive public school…Where was it…Sherwell or something?"

"Sherbourne…in Dorset." Goodwill prompted.

"That's the badger." Alan quipped. "Anyway, you earned your place at University an' I genuinely take my hat off to you.

The 'Muppet' nodded appreciatively.

"I on the other hand." Alan continued, "Having failed the eleven plus spectacularly, went to a secondary modern in the City. While you were being fed a diet of latin, chemistry an' all that sines and cosines bullshit, I spent most of my time trying to see up Miss Godden's pleated skirt for a glimpse of creamy white thigh above her stocking tops, or if she got really careless, a view of her pantie covered magic triangle…I left school at fifteen without a single 'O' level to my name. For me Mr Goodwill, it was the choice of either a lifetime of drudgery in the local wool mill or taking the Queen's shilling…I don't begrudge you your success sir…not for a moment believe it or not. I remain at the rank of Constable through personal choice Mr

Goodwill, not for want of trying…I love working the streets with my partner, smashin' down doors in the Elsie's at three in the mornin', the chases and the arrests. I still get a kick out of outsmarting villains, I'm a street cop sir…you're an academic, an office wallah. We're chalk an' cheese, oil an' water. I couldn't do your job, I accept that, but you should equally accept that you wouldn't last a day working the 'Badlands'. That's the difference between us…It's horses for courses Mr Goodwill, we just chose different career paths."

The 'Muppet' squirmed uncomfortably and averted further eye contact. He placed his mug carefully on the desk top. He was somewhat pan faced as he reached down for his briefcase.

"I think before this conversation degenerates further, I'll take my leave. Thank you for the coffee Pc Pendle. I've no doubt I'll see you at your interview." Goodwill said tersely as without further ado, he swept out of the office.

"You're welcome sir…You'll give Mr Allenby my regards?" Alan called after him, his voice trailing off as the office door closed.

*****

Alan turned the ignition key and the 'Cologne' V6 fired up instantaneously and quickly settled down to a satisfying purr. Slipping the clutch, he eased the Capri slowly off the grassed area at the side of the gymnasium, allowing the tyres to slowly creep over the raised kerb edge and onto the tarmac surface of the car park before accelerating. Having the weekend off before he started at Stretham was a bonus and Alan decided to call in and see Sullivan on his way home, and give him all the news. He drove slowly around the Police station perimeter drive toward the Ring Road savouring the thought of two days off, then five whole days away from Division.

Once out onto the dual carriageway Alan eased down on the accelerator pedal and the Capri surged forwards, rewarding him with a satisfying growl from the twin exhausts.

Alan opened the centre console and scanned through his collection of music, choosing Whitesnake's 'Saints and Sinners'. Whilst keeping his eyes on the road, he shook the cassette from its plastic box and slipped it into the head unit of the player in the dashboard. The interior of the vehicle was suddenly filled with David Coverdale's distinctive gravelly voice.

Alan smiled to himself. The murder enquiry was down to the 'suits' in C.I.D. now and Pope Forrester the third could howl about his crime figures all he wanted.

Detective Chief Superintendent Sommerville was the Senior Investigating Officer and according to D.I. Ellis, he was 'not a man to be fucked with'. There may well be retribution. Forrester would no doubt want to know why his explicit instructions in respect of the original accident report had not been complied with, but that would be *after* Stretham, and if Lyburn had had his collar felt by then…well, how bad could it be?

Confident that all was good with the world, Alan turned up the volume and began to sing loudly… *"Here I go again on my own…going down the only road I've ever known…"*

*****

Blissfully unaware that he was now 'C' Divisions 'most wanted', or that a team of Murder Squad Detectives were at that very moment, being briefed on the Zippleman and McKnight cases, 'Midnight' drove onto the Ring Road and headed back towards the 'Badlands' and his bed sit.

There were just a few clothes he wanted along with his tape deck, his collection of Bob Marley and Motown albums and the ivory handled razor which was still in the top drawer of his bedside cabinet, along with an ounce or two of good quality 'bush'.

Once the place was seen to have been deserted, the alcoholics and drug addicts would quickly take up occupancy, that is, until the Council realised that no rent was being paid. After a raft of unanswered letters and demands lay unopened on the floor beneath the letterbox, enquiries would show that Mr James Frederick Lyburn was no longer drawing benefit and that strangely, Mr Lyburn had not seen fit to provide the unemployment benefit office with a forwarding address and as such, they had no knowledge of his whereabouts and could not assist. Only then would the Housing Clearance Department attend. The bedsit would be stripped of its furniture and fittings and the door and windows would be boarded up. Mr James Frederick Lyburn had, to all intents and purposes, simply disappeared from the face of the earth.

*****

'Midnight' sat in the outside lane of the dual carriageway and noted the set of traffic lights ahead, which were turning through the amber sequence to red. Easing off the accelerator, he allowed the Cortina to cruise up to the stop line. He braked to a halt and set the hand brake, he became aware in his rear view mirror, of the approach of a sporty looking black Ford Capri which pulled up and stopped alongside him in the nearside lane.

From within his own vehicle, 'Midnight' could hear the deep reverberating sounds of rock music emanating from within the Capri. He looked across at the driver. Some white dude with short hair and a big moustache, singin' like a mo'fucker. His senses immediately prickled and relying on his 'street' instincts which screamed 'Babylon', he quickly looked away, turning his face toward the traffic light to his right.

Alan casually glanced across to the Cortina and realised that singing at the top of his voice, he must have looked like a madman. Slightly embarrassed, he turned down the volume and was relieved to see that he didn't seem to drawing any attention from the driver of the battered Ford, who seemed to be watching the traffic light to his right intently.

As the driver was black, Alan's gaze instinctively fell to the tax disc in the bottom corner of the Cortina's windscreen. Not quite able to see the expiry date; he eased the Capri forwards slightly, the front wheels crossing over the stop line.

The traffic lights were taking an interminable time to change; 'Midnight' saw the movement in his peripheral vision. The lights were still at red and the Capri moving forwards, caught him unawares and he unconsciously looked across to the driver.

At the same moment, Alan became aware that the driver of the Cortina was looking across at him. He quickly diverted his gaze from the excise licence, which much to his surprise, given the ethnic origin of the driver, for once, appeared to be valid.

For the briefest of moments, their eyes met. Alan noted the trademark yellow tinge to the sclera of his eyes and the broad spread of his nose. The face was somehow disturbing and for some unknown reason, Alan felt strangely uneasy and for a moment, he felt that he recognised the face from somewhere. His sixth sense bristled, it wasn't right, *he* wasn't right. It wasn't just the fact that he was black and driving a Ford Cortina, it was more than that, it was an intuitive sense that couldn't be explained. Cops just *knew*.

Many a probationary Officer had wondered what it was, that had caused the Traffic man he was in company with, to suddenly slew his SD1 around in a handbrake turn and accelerate off after what had been to him, an innocuous driver.

*****

Fortunately, all a Police Officer needed to show was that he had a 'suspicion' that an offence had, or was being committed in order to cause a vehicle to stop.

Defence 'brief's' made a point of challenging the Officer at Court as to why his 'Client' had been stopped. The 'rule of thumb' being, where the evidence of guilt is overwhelming…attack the Officer's integrity.

"It is true, isn't it Officer that the alleged offence for which my client appears before the Magistrate today, was not discovered until his vehicle was actually stopped?"

The Officer nods to the Magistrate. "That's correct Your Worship."

"Then what was it that caused you to stop my client in the first place?"

The Officer pauses for a second. "It just wasn't *right* Your Worship."

The 'brief' throws up his hands in a theatrical gesture of despair. "Perhaps you will do the Court the service of enlightening us Officer, what was it that wasn't *right*? Did my client appear furtive; perhaps he attempted to evade your attention by looking askance…There would surely be some reason as to why my client's vehicle was singled out from amongst the many others on the road at that time…Or Officer, could it be simply because my client is black?"

The 'brief' waits smugly. The Courtroom is hushed. The Magistrate looks across to the witness box and peers expectantly at the Officer over the top of his glasses. The Officer ignores the 'brief's' attempts at goading him with scantily veiled allegations of racism and looks to the Magistrate. "Your Worship…Firstly, I take great exception to Mr Samuelson's allegations that it was simply his client's colour that was in any way causal to him being stopped. Mr Samuelson is asking the impossible… *knowing* is just something that an experienced Police Officer inherits. Trying to explain how I knew that there was something not quite right would be like…trying to describe pain to someone who had never experienced it, or colour to a blind person. Cops just know when something's not quite right Your Worship, but it can't be explained."

The Magistrate nods slowly and rubs his chin with his fingers. He turns to the frustrated 'brief'. "Well, there you have it Mr Samuelson…That I think, is the best you are going to get…Perhaps we can move on?"

*****

The Cortina suddenly lurched forwards and immediately made a right turn, Alan glanced up at the green light, he shrugged off the feeling of déjà vu and committed the registered number of the Cortina to memory for future reference.

"Jesus…That was one ugly nigger." he muttered to himself as he released the clutch.

The bonnet of the Capri rose gently to the occasion as Alan accelerated away along the Ring Road.

### **Twenty Five**

"Gentlemen, welcome to Stretham and the basic firearms course."
The Sergeant walked slowly between the evenly spaced desks. He glanced at each of the pensive hopefuls as he dropped dog-eared copies of Superintendent Greenwood's manual on 'Police Tactics in Armed Situations' before each of them. Alan toyed with his 'Maxpax' coffee, swirling the insipid liquid around to fully dissolve the remaining dregs which had cloyed into a congealed mass at the bottom of the plastic cup.

"For those of you who don't know me, I am Sergeant Chris Forbes. I'm the senior firearms instructor and you either leave here with a permit to carry firearms or not, purely on my say so."

He sat casually on the edge of the desk at the front of the briefing room and faced the six Officers. His eyes scanned across the faces, scrutinising each of them in turn as he spoke.

"Gentlemen, I'll go through the basic housekeeping rules first then we can get down to business."

The Sergeant was tall and rail thin. He had a shock of short blond hair parted in the center and plastered flat to his scalp with Brylcreem, the back and sides of his head were shaved 'down to the bone' to a point two inches above his ears. He had brilliant blue eyes and coupled with his aquiline nose and square Nordic jaw, he bore a disturbing resemblance to Reinhard Heydrich the 'Butcher of Prague'. Alan imagined that he would not look out of place wearing SS runes on the collar of his black single piece boiler suit.

His overalls were pulled in at the waist with a wide black leather belt, the right hand side of which sported an empty black leather holster. Its securing overstrap appeared to be badly perished and looked to have lost all elasticity; it drooped limply down the side of the scratched and scuffed leather. Alan noticed with a little amusement, that the Sergeant's chromium plated chevrons and collar numbers, which he wore on a black sleeve slipped over the epaulettes at his shoulders, had been painted 'tactical' matt black. Alan considered it to be a bit 'over the top' and wondered what *that* said about the Sergeant's behavioural profile.

"Any infringements of range safety rules, or failure to comply with my instructions, or those of the other course instructors will result in you immediately failing the course and being returned to your respective Divisions. If at any time, I or any of the instructors feel that for whatever reason, you are not suitable to become authorised firearms Officers, you will similarly be sent packing. There is no tolerance here Gentlemen. There is no appeal process, my word is final."

He paused for a moment to allow the student Officers to fully digest his warning.

"Daily appraisals on your performance will be handed to you and you will be invited to read and sign them. You will note that there are no spaces provided for *your* comments, frankly, we are not interested in what you think. Do as you are told; perform well on the range, if you are successful in passing both the written and practical exams and if you attain the required scores on the final shoot, you will pass the course. All three disciplines must be passed Gents, if you attain one hundred percent on the written, but get less than forty out of forty eight on the final shoot, it's a fail, similarly, even if you can shoot the bollocks off a wasp at twenty five yards, but show a lack of reasoning or sound judgement during the practical's, you'll be on your way…Questions so far?" His eyes flitted enquiringly across the faces of each of the students. "No?…Good, let's get on."

The Sergeant flipped open the top cover of an olive green metal ammunition box on the side of the table. He reached in and withdrew a revolver, its cylinder already released to reveal the six empty chambers. The revolver's original blued finish was worn almost to translucency. He held it aloft.

"This, gentlemen, is the ubiquitous Smith and Wesson .38 Police Special, 'tres ocho especial'. You may also have heard it referred to as the 'Saturday night special', it actually dates back to 1898, not this particular piece I hasten to add…" His effort at classroom humour was rewarded with a brief ripple of laughter. "You will note gents, that I hold the weapon up for you to observe, with the cylinder open to show you that all six chambers are empty. This is called proving the weapon. Whenever you are asked to relinquish your firearm to me or any of your instructors, you will prove the firearm prior to handing it over. *Any* infringement of this rule will result in your immediate removal from the course. No mercy will be shown. Get used to carrying out this simple task from the outset. Along with keeping the weapon pointing downrange at all times, proving is a basic safety drill. I cannot stress this point strongly enough gents. As authorised firearms Officers, you may be called upon to attend at various crime scenes where firearms may have been used; these will be required to be proved prior to tagging and bagging as evidence. Firearms of all types, ages and descriptions will be handed in at your Police stations during amnesties or when Grandma Miggins clears out her loft and finds the Luger which her Husband took off some German officer in the war." There were smiles and a brief ripple of laughter from the students.

The Sergeant continued in a cautionary tone. "It's a serious business gents. During the five day course, we will familiarise you with as many types of firearm as possible so that you will be able to carry out safe proving procedures during the course of your duties. You would be amazed at the amount of unregistered firearms out there. At Fell Road Police station last year, a Bren gun and almost a hundred rounds of 7.62 ammunition were handed in, much to the chagrin of the Officer in the front office, who hadn't a clue what to do with it. As an authorised firearms Officer, you will get the shout to attend and make the weapon safe. Don't embarrass yourselves; do not place yourself or any of your colleagues in danger. If you are unfamiliar with the workings of the weapon in question, contact us and one of us will attend. If it's while you are on nights, simply seize the thing and secure it in the station armoury. You're not expected to be expert in all types...We will touch on this important subject later on during the course. Any questions so far?"

The Sergeant peered across the room and made eye contact with each of the hopefuls.

"No...Right. We've a lot to get through gents, so returning our attentions to the Home Office approved issue sidearm." The Sergeant again lifted the revolver and passed it slowly across the front of the desks so that all could see it clearly. "The 38 Police Special has a muzzle velocity of 940 feet per second and for

Police purposes, fires a 158 grain, semi wadcutter round." He leaned across the table and peered into the metal box. Reaching in, he withdrew a single round and held it up, gripping it between his thumb and forefinger.

"This Gents, is actually a .357 round. The .38 caliber size actually relates to the diameter of the brass case. It's a rimmed center fire cartridge and you will see when I pass it round, that the 'business end' is coated with molybdenum disulphide…Teflon to you lot, same as your Mum's frying pan." A few chuckles rippled around the room. The Sergeant continued. "This coating prevents premature barrel wear and because we will be using the indoor range, it helps to keep the lead displacement down to an acceptable health level."

The Sergeant casually tossed the round across to the one of the students seated on the front row. It was caught deftly and examined before it was passed across to his neighbour. "To successfully complete the course, you will also have to show that you are proficient with the Remington 870. This is a 12 bore pump action, fixed choke shotgun. It's a bottom loader, holds eight cartridges…actually, nine if you rack one up first then reload…We use triple 'A' as well as the rifled slug which is a solid ounce of lead and reasonably accurate up to forty or fifty yards…although some of your instructors have successfully targeted rounds at seventy five yards. You will also be instructed in the use of the CS gas 'ferret' which is also a 12 gauge cartridge delivered from the Remington, excellent for room clearance, as you will come to fully appreciate when you sample a small dose of gas during the course…"

 One of the students tentatively raised a hand, curiosity etched across his face. The Sergeant nodded toward him.

"Sarge, when would we use rifled slugs?"

The Sergeant rummaged through the ammunition box again and withdrew a bright green shotgun cartridge, which he held aloft, gripping the brass end cap between thumb and forefinger.

"This...is a rifled slug cartridge, you will note that its jacket is green, triple 'A' cartridges are red so that even in poor lighting conditions, you will be able to tell the difference...In the colour spectrum, red is the opposite of green...To answer your question, you would only use a rifled slug to destroy beasts such as horses or cattle. A .38 round may not penetrate the skull of a large beast even if up close, but a single rifled slug to the forehead will ensure that the beast is put down as swiftly and humanely as possible...We have had instances where 'rogue' beasts have escaped from the City abattoir on Wray Street. They smell the blood and just go crackers. We've had 'em leaping straight out of the captive pens and ending up on the Motorway...There's no coaxing 'em back once they've lost it...They just stand there bellowin', shittin' and pissin', foaming at the mouth and you can tell by their eyes that they've gone mad...A rifled slug delivered either here..." he tapped himself once on the centre of his forehead with his fingertip. "Or here." pointing at his chest. "The ounce of lead will enter into the body, kill the beast instantly and completely fragment so that there's no risk of it exiting and killing some random member of the public...ok?"

The student nodded, a rather pensive expression on his face, inwardly squirming at the thought of being called upon to slaughter an innocent beast.

The Sergeant dropped the cartridge back into the box and shuffled himself further back onto the table top. "Ex forces lads?" he enquired.

Alan raised a hand and looked expectantly around the room. His was the only one raised.

The Sergeant made eye contact. "Pc?"

"Alan Pendle Sarge. Moorwood Traffic...Sixty nine to seventy five...army."

"With?" the Sergeant asked quizzically.

"Para's Sarge."

The Sergeant stared at him and pointed a cautionary finger. "Forget *everything* they ever taught you. The tactics and rules of engagement in the Police are completely different…ok?

Alan nodded, slightly confused.

"The years you've mentioned would suggest you probably served in Northern Ireland?" the black clad Sergeant said.

Alan nodded again. "It's a fair while ago now Sarge."

"Nonetheless, forget how you did things back in the day. The Police won't close ranks if you fuck up…ok?"

The Sergeant gazed around the room. "Any of you have any previous experience with firearms…other than Colonel Pendle here?" There were no takers. He heaved himself from the table top and walked slowly between the desks.

"The use of lethal force will only be used when all other avenues to resolve a situation have been exhausted. There are no time limits on containment. You will negotiate, cajole, lie and deceive in order that the incident can be resolved without the use of firearms…Note this well gentlemen…..*only* if there is an immediate threat to your life, or to anyone else's….or, to prevent an atrocious crime, may you lawfully or indeed morally discharge your weapon…We do not shoot to kill Gents, we shoot simply to stop the suspect from taking our life or that of another. We aim for the largest part of the body…that usually means the chest area…Shoot a man in the stomach, leg or shoulder, he may well go down, but he'll still be capable of returning fire and having been shot, he'll be seriously pissed off, so probably will…You will soon find out that it is impossible to shoot a weapon out of someone's hand with a revolver…that Gentlemen…only happens in Hollywood. You will see when we get out onto the ranges that although you may be able to actually hit the targets at twenty five yards…and some of you may even achieve reasonable groupings, Mr Greenwood will tell you…" the Sergeant pointed down to the well-thumbed manual on the desk in front of him. "That most tactical firearms situations are resolved one way or another, at a distance of ten yards or less, up close and personal as they say…A semi or full wadcutter round delivered to the upper chest area will invariably put the suspect down. The round will mushroom on impact, enter the chest cavity and fragment so that it remains within the suspect…we do not want the round exiting the suspect, 'winging' its way across the street and dropping some innocent bystander. If it comes to the point where you are forced to discharge your weapon, believe me…you'll be shakin' like a shitin' dog, and panting like a newlywed and your arsehole will be giving it 'sixpence half-crown'. You'll be lucky to get an aimed shot home, even at ten yards."

The Sergeant continued to wander between the desks as he continued with his oratory.

"We do not fire warning shots. We never 'threaten' to shoot, the suspect may just call your bluff and invite you to get on with it…Section three of the Criminal Law Act 1967 states that a person may use such force as is reasonable in the circumstances in the prevention of crime, or in effecting or assisting in the lawful arrest of offenders or suspected offenders or of persons unlawfully at large…The key word here gentlemen is 'reasonable'. If you discharge your firearm…" he took his place back at the front of the room, paused and again pointed a cautionary finger toward them. "You will have to show that your use of deadly force was reasonable, justified, necessary and appropriate under the circumstances. Otherwise, you'll be looking for Rumpole's telephone number."

The Sergeant leant back against the table and allowed his words of wisdom to sink in.

"Now, if you would now all go to the table at the rear of the room, you will find that there is a pair of overalls, a belt, holster and revolver for each of you. Gentlemen, you will note that the weapons are laid out in a proved state, that is to say with their cylinders open and the chambers empty…Whenever you are asked to hand over your weapon to me or any of the instructors, you will point the weapon down range and open the cylinder. Even if you have discharged all six rounds, the spent cases must be removed from their chambers for the weapon to be deemed proved. "If you leave the range for any reason, to go for a piss or to change your underwear having frightened yourself, you will leave your weapon in a proved state. Any infringement of this safety rule…no excuses Gentlemen…you're back to Division, is that perfectly clear?"

The student Officers nodded.

The Sergeant shook his head. "Not good enough chaps…is that clear?"

"Yes Sergeant." the room responded loudly in unison.

"Better." He nodded. Confident that they had all been made fully aware of the stringent range rules, he continued. "Right, get yourselves kitted up and we'll move out to the range."

The chair legs screeched against the painted surface of the floor as the Officers left their desks and sauntered to the rear of the briefing room.

The six .38's had been placed atop neatly folded overalls. The leather belts had been rolled and were positioned to one side of the open chambered weapons, the holsters directly opposite.

"They are all the same Gentlemen." The Sergeant called out. "Doesn't make any difference which one you choose. Some are shinier than others, but that doesn't mean they'll shoot any straighter…Pc Pendle."

Alan looked around. "Sarge?"

"You're first up…See the Chief Inspector in the top office."

*****

Alan sat across from the Chief Inspector in a small, windowless room at the rear of the fifty yard indoor range. During a brief respite from the constant resonating cracks from the within the partitioned practice booths at the head of the range and the orders barked by the instructors, the massive overhead extractor fans hummed loudly, barely clearing the air of the acrid stench of cordite, which even within the closed confines of the interview room, stung the back of Alan's nasal passage.

The instructors paced between the six booths, pausing as they dispassionately observed the style and performance of those Officers hoping to become proficient in the use of the .38 revolver.

Alan rested his hands on the scarred surface of a steel topped table. Its original dark brown vinyl covering, the remnants of which could just be made out beneath the crimped edging plates, had obviously long since ripped or worn beyond repair and had now been completely removed.

The painted plasterboard walls were bare and added to the cold, clinical austerity of the room. A bulkhead light in the center of the ceiling provided a dim, single point of light, causing the Chief Inspector to hunch down over the desk top and peer intently through his bifocals as he silently pored over Alan's personnel file.

There being nothing else to divert his attention, Alan watched as the Chief Inspector leafed through the contents of the buff coloured folder.

A fresh period of shooting began after his five fellow students had reloaded. Alan could hear one of the range safety Officers, shouting abuse to one who had failed to keep the muzzle of his revolver facing down range. He smiled to himself at the 'choice' phrases used to describe the student's failings; the course only available to male Officers, the language used was coarse, abrasive and satisfyingly industrial.

The Chief Inspector looked up over the top of his rimless glasses, his face was emotionless, nothing given away, no clues in his facial expression; Alan considered that he would probably make an excellent poker player.

"You know what this is about?" he enquired softly. Alan nodded. "Behavioural profiling Sir…Am I a fit person to be trusted with a firearm."

The Chief Inspector hinted at a smile. "It's not about trust Pendle, it's about suitability. There is a definite and important distinction. What is it about strapping on a .38 Special that turns normally mild mannered Police Officers into John Wayne? …You've heard of the John Wayne syndrome?"

Alan nodded again. "Yes Sir, I have…Not something I've ever suffered from. I'm comfortable around firearms Sir, I…"

The Chief Inspector held up a solitary finger, stopping Alan mid-sentence. He flipped back through the sheets in the personnel folder.

"Six years military service…Ireland, two tours. Oman, Cyprus, see any action?" he asked casually.

Alan cautiously raised his eyebrows, not quite sure what direction the line of questioning was taking, or what would be an 'acceptable' response.

"The odd angry shot Sir. Nothing to write home about."

The Chief returned his gaze to the contents of the folder and as he read on, nodded appreciatively.

"I see you were decorated and mentioned in dispatches."

Alan shrugged nonchalantly. "Everyone got the campaign medal Sir and the dispatches thing… I actually tripped up over an old toilet door used to cover an arms cache…just over the border in Muff."

"Muff?"

"County Donegal Sir…The 'boyos' had forgotten to take the door handle off. I got a twisted ankle and the regiment won a few rusty old Lee Enfield's and a hundred or so rounds of .303 …It got written up right that's all."

The Chief Inspector eased himself back in his chair and intertwined his fingers behind his head.

"Hard was it...Ireland?" he asked, with an inquisitive tone. The Chief Inspector maintained hard eye contact as if searching for any giveaway behavioural deficiencies.

Alan met his stare. "I was away from Derry before the '72 thing, if that's what you mean Sir; I was in Ghallah by then."

"Ghallah?"

"That was the Oman tour Sir. I was... seconded...Sultan's armed forces, a training role is all."

"Any action?" The Chief Inspector asked enquiringly.

"I worried a few camels and came down with heat stroke sir."

The Chief Inspector cracked a smile which he allowed to flit across his face momentarily.

He paused and searched Alan's face. "You seem somewhat...hesitant to talk about your military service Pendle. Most old soldiers love to tell war stories."

Alan met his inquisitive gaze and shrugged his shoulders. "I'd never planned to be a career soldier. I was never very good at it to be honest with you Sir. The truth is, while I was in Cyprus, after the Turkish thing in '74 had calmed down, I bought myself out so I wouldn't have to do another tour in Ireland. After '72, my regiment weren't exactly 'flavour of the month' with the indigenous population...The Police force seemed a far safer option."

"Scary place, Ireland eh?" The Chief Inspector said.

Alan looked down at the gouge marks on the dull grey metal table top while he carefully considered his response.

"It had its moments Sir, yes."

The Chief Inspector's eyes narrowed almost imperceptibly, but he seemed satisfied with Alan's explanation and returned his gaze to the buff folder and slowly flicked through the contents.

While he waited, Alan's thoughts returned to a cold November evening in Derry's Bogside.

He could once again smell the fetid stench wafting up from the muddy waters of the river Foyle, as it flowed slowly beneath the twin decks of the Craigavon Bridge. He remembered the damp air seeping through his smock, chilling him to numbness and the dull ache in his forearms from the weight of the 7.62 self-loading rifle.

He leaned back against the cold grey stone, grateful at least that the upper deck of the bridge was sheltering them from the rain.

The incessant bloody rain.

His Corporal chewed gum and hummed quietly to himself. The collar of his smock turned up against the cold, he rocked slowly from side to side to ease the aching in his ankles and for the umpteenth time, checked his watch.

"Where's our fucking relief." he muttered impatiently, peering across the bridge span across to the Waterside, searching for the eagerly awaited Land Rover which would take them back to Barracks.

Alan eased his forearm out from beneath the ventilated forward grip of his rifle and glanced at his watch. "It's only twenty to Corp, bit early yet."

His Corporal turned to him. "I know what fucking time it is private Pendle, but I have an arrangement with Corporal West see…I am away to the Embassy Ballroom on Strand Road the night. Might just be the night I finally crack the pants off a certain Colleen from De Burgh Terrace, by the name of Siobhan O'Donoghue, which would be a singular and welcome respite from the abject fucking boredom, which has been my daily lot in this fucking joke of a Country."

Alan shrank down into his damp smock. His Corporal was clearly not in the best of moods and the last four hours spent in his company on the checkpoint, had been somewhat strained. Corporal McBurney was a dour man, not the easiest to get on with, or to understand for that matter. His northern Scots accent was course, and so broad so as to be almost unintelligible.

Alan attempted to lighten his Corporal's mood. "It's not so bad here Corp, I don't really mind it, reminds me a bit of York with the river runnin' through it an' all…'cept for the accents a'course."

His Corporal snorted derisively. "How long you been here now Pendle, two months?"

"Seven weeks Corp." Alan replied meekly.

"Ex…fuckin'…actly, I'm nine months in." Corporal McBurney said with a bitter tone in his voice. He sighed and looked out across the Foyle and continued to speak, not directly to Alan but seemingly to the world in general.

"I hate this fucking City; in fact, I hate this whole fucking Country. I hate the people and their constant bitchin' 'bout the Brits and how we've fucked over them since King Billy came up the Boyne. I hate their fucked up moronic accents, Irish stew an' soda bread. I dinna like Guinness, an' I've been pissed wet through ever since I got here in Feb'ry. Three more weeks an' I'm away. Back to Aldershot…canny come soon enough." He snorted back and spat a huge wad of phlegm out across onto the road surface, as if to express his utter contempt either for Londonderry or Northern Ireland in general. "Where's that scouse shite West?" he muttered, glancing again at his watch.

Alan swung the ten pound weight of the S.L.R. across his body and let it drop into the crook of his right arm, to ease the dull ache in the joint of his left elbow.

"Could be worse Corp, least we're not hoofing it around the Creggan estate." Alan offered.

The Corporal ignored Alan's attempt at pleasantries and walked a pace or two away toward the bridge end. He leaned against the huge sandstone support blocks under the metal upper deck and peered expectantly across the arching roadway to the Waterside.

Uncomfortable with the somewhat strained communication between them, Alan busied himself wiping away a thin film of condensation, which had formed on the lightly oiled surface of his rifle barrel. He toyed with the gas regulator to the rear of the forward sight base, whilst his left thumb unconsciously stroked the safety catch to ensure for the hundredth time, that it was on.

Headlights approached from the Waterside and his Corporal shrugged himself away from the wall in expectation. It certainly wasn't a soft cover Land Rover. One of the headlights was seriously dimmed, an earthing fault perhaps and anyway, they were set too far apart for it to be a 'Landy'.

The car emerged from the gloom beneath the upper deck, a Cortina estate, slowing as it approached the 'T' junction with Foyle Road.

Corporal McBurney sighed dejectedly and slumped back against the wall. Alan frowned as the old estate car continued toward them and passed between the stout metal stations supporting the upper deck of the bridge. Both front sun visors were down and the rear nearside passenger window was wide open.

The Cortina swung slowly to the right, its one good headlight beam sweeping across the arched door of the old Londonderry Corporation Electrical Works building. The car slowed further, almost to a stop and Alan stared in disbelief, as a gloved hand holding an old Webley revolver emerged from the open rear window, its trademark slab sided barrel easily identifiable even in the dim light beneath the bridge.

Alan opened his mouth to scream a warning. He felt the immediate fear fuelled rush of adrenalin as he tried to dive for cover, but his legs refused to move and the words wouldn't come.

Blinded by the muzzle flash and deafened by the loud report which echoed and reverberated back from the overhead canopy, he froze, rigid with shock and fear, unable to bring his rifle to bear.

Something warm and moist slapped into his face, and he was suddenly aware of a coppery, salt taste in his open mouth.

Then Corporal McBurney was falling, his rifle clattering to the pavement. Alan was snatching at his breath in short spasms, a loud roaring in his ears, drowning out the sound of the accelerating car, its tyres screaming as it sped away. Specks of light grey porridge like matter, flecked with blood, spattered across Alan's face and neck and down the front of his smock. He retched, and began spitting out the foulness in his mouth.

Corporal McBurney now fallen to the damp pavement, his right leg twitching grotesquely, dark blood pooling out across the paving slabs from the hideous wound, where the heavy .455 round had exited and taken away the side of his head.

*****

Corporal McBurney, encased in an oak casket draped with the Colours, carried slowly by the six, all as smart as ninepence in their number two's. Up the ramp and into the cavernous cargo bay of the 'Hercules'. Then the short flight from Ballykelly to Lossiemouth, greeted by an iron grey morning sky over Nairn, a biting wind howling in from the Moray Firth and the rain whispering in the trees.

The six of the carrying party, standing three either side of the grave, their maroon covered heads bowed as they sorrowfully watched Corporal Francis Ewan McBurney being lowered into the rich, dark soil of his birthplace.

His Mother wept quietly, her face buried in her 'kerchief.

His Father, heavily bearded, stoic, an arm around his Wife's shoulder, looked ashen and broken, his face blank, expressionless, the pleats of his kilt feathered by the wind.

The priest intoned as a lone piper played.

'Flowers of the Forest'. The strident strains of the ancient lament were whipped away in the wind, out between the ageless, tilted gravestones. The identities of those interred beneath, almost illegible through centuries of erosion and a thick covering of wind born lichen.

A handful of earth was cast. There was a hollow thud as it struck the polished brass plate on the coffin and the priest's monotone incantations continued.

"In the sure and certain hope of resurrection to eternal life..." and Alan's inward shame as the stinging hot tears, thankfully disguised by the rain, fell onto hallowed ground.

Tears of grief for what had been done and tears of guilt for what had not.

*****

Alan looked up, realising that he had been daydreaming and staring blankly at the table top.

The Chief Inspector fortunately, was still studying the contents of the file and when a moment later, he again looked up, Alan was ready to meet his gaze.

"Your Mr Forrester seems to consider you to be 'somewhat impetuous and prone to jumping to fanciful conclusions' or so it says here." An enquiring glance from the Chief Inspector was accompanied by a wry smile. Alan gave an inward sigh. "So, the God bothering twat managed to mix me a powder after all." he thought.

"We don't always see eye to eye Sir...mostly on operationa..."

Again a raised finger from the Chief Inspector cut him short. "Your Sergeant on the other hand, has provided a glowing testimonial...Self-motivated and disciplined, a mature Officer who constantly strives to excel. Pc Pendle displays a terrier like quality in respect of his investigative skills." The Chief Inspector looked up. "Impetuous, fanciful, yet disciplined and mature. Rather diverse opinions." he said questioningly.

Alan considered his options and decided that an ounce or two of discretion would possibly serve him best. Chief Inspector

Forrester was a back stabbing office bound arsehole, but it might not be prudent, or productive to actually say so.

Choosing discretion over honesty, Alan decided on his response. "I believe that my Sergeant is better qualified to provide a continuous assessment of my abilities and attitudes Sir…What I mean is Sir, I work alongside my Sergeant every day. I very rarely get to see Mr Forrester."

The Chief Inspector smiled. "I don't miss much Pc Pendle. I am aware of the…shall we use the term…'strained' relationships which have recently developed between yourself and Chief Inspector Forrester over an ongoing murder investigation. For the record, I joined with Alan Forrester, he can be…somewhat single minded. Detective Inspector Frank Ellis more your cup of tea I suspect?"

Alan allowed a giveaway smile, knowing that it would declare more to the Chief Inspector than any verbal confirmation.

The Chief instructor nodded knowingly. "Well, enough about that matter. All will come out in the wash as they say and I have no doubt that if your latest 'impetuous' conclusions bear fruit…" he smiled. "There will be an addition to the numerous commendations which I note in your personnel file. Now, what can you tell me about section three of the Criminal Law Act?"

Alan took a deep breath and quoted the definition verbatim.

The Chief Inspector nodded, clearly impressed with Alan's precise rendition of the definition. "And how would you relate that to the Police use of firearms?"

Alan considered his response carefully. "I think we would have to go a little further Sir, section three is self-defining but for our purposes…If the situation necessitated the use of firearms, we would have to show that the use of what could prove to be deadly force was justified, necessary *and* that we had exhausted all other avenues."

The Chief Inspector smiled. "I see you've read your Greenwood…but I note that you used the term 'we'…I presume, meaning the Police collectively. If you're confronted with a spontaneous incident…If you manage to weigh up all your options and convince yourself that you're covered under section three…all in a split second." The Chief Inspector paused and pointed a cautionary finger. "and that might be all your given to make what is I guarantee you, a life changing decision… If you discharge your firearm, it's you Constable, you alone who will have to justify your actions…understand?"

Alan nodded sombrely. The Chief sat back. "Still want your ticket?"

Alan smiled and nodded again. "Yes Sir. I wouldn't have applied for the course if I'd had any doubts."

"Good lad…we'll talk again as you progress through the course and I've had the chance to read your instructor's daily appraisals. Get yourself off. Five minute smoke break, then back on the range."

Alan ignored the opportunity to have a much needed cigarette and returned to the rear of the range, eager to start practising with the .38.

One of his fellow students was sullenly removing his overalls, dropping them in a heap on the long bench and shaking his head slowly.

"I'm what's called 'gun-shy' by all accounts." he said without looking up. "I close both my eyes just before the fucking thing goes off. 'Forbsy' says its common ailment an' there's fuck all you can do about it, so it's me back to pushin' a 'panda'."

Not bothering to slide the holster from the leather belt, it was dropped unceremoniously onto the long wooden bench to join the crumpled overalls. "G'luck to you anyway mate."

"Yeah…. cheers." Alan replied hesitantly as he watched the first 'wash-out' grabbing for his coat and walking toward the exit door.

"Pc Pendle, bay three…*NOW*." a voice behind him called out.

Alan turned; Sergeant Forbes was standing at the head of the empty bay, his arms folded across his chest.

"Come on then Colonel. Chop chop; let's see what you've got."

After involuntarily tightening the belt around his waist and making sure that the holster was correctly positioned, Alan reached for the revolver which was resting on the wooden shelf at the front of the segregated bay.

The Sergeant stood directly behind him and slightly to his left, watching as Alan took the revolver in his right hand and whilst directing the barrel downrange, he pushed the well-worn crosshatched thumb piece forward. Tipping the revolver to the left, the cylinder fell open to reveal six empty chambers.

"Weapon is clear Sergeant." Alan called out, holding the revolver up to shoulder height.

"Proved." the Sergeant responded. "Load the weapon."

Alan laid the .38 revolver in the palm of his left hand, ensuring that the 'business end' remained facing down range.

With slightly shaking fingers; he prized a bullet from its grip rail in the plastic box to his right and with the middle finger of his left hand poking through the cylinder gap, he gently turned the cylinder. One by one, he fed six rounds into their respective chambers. "Six rounds loaded Sergeant." Alan called out.

He dropped the barrel end slightly to ensure that all the rounds remained fully seated and whilst wrapping his fingers around the polished wood grip, with the palm of his left hand, he gently closed the cylinder.

The Sergeant took a half step backward and moved further to the left to watch Alan's eyes. "Identify your target, and with six rounds, double action, in your own time, fire the weapon."

Alan stood with his feet a yard apart, and allowed his knees to sag slightly to steady himself. With the palm of his left hand supporting the base of the wooden grip, he raised the nineteen ounce revolver to eye height.

He sighted along the barrel and keeping both eyes open, he focused on the centre of the upper body shaped target which seemed alarmingly miniscule, even at twenty five yards. He held his breath and gently squeezed the trigger.

The revolver twitched only slightly as the first round was discharged. He paused fractionally, steadying himself before firing again. He allowed the raised front sights of the revolver to become a blur, it was the target which he held in focus, willing the bullets toward the center of the cardboard target.

All six fired, Alan remained facing downrange. Remembering his 'Greenwood', he lowered the revolver before thumbing the cylinder release and holding the weapon over the open metal ammunition box on the shelf to his left, he pressed the extractor rod with the tip of his forefinger and the spent cartridge cases clattered noisily into the bottom of the box.

Leaving the cylinder open, he again raised the revolver to shoulder height and shouted. "Weapon is clear Sergeant."

The Sergeant leaned over Alan's left shoulder. "Good stance…confident shoot and correct procedures. Well done Pendle." Again he took a step back and shouted. "With six rounds…reload."

To his left and right, in his peripheral vision, Alan could see the barrel ends of the revolvers protruding out from behind the grey painted breeze block bay walls. He heard the sharp staccato bark of the weapons as they were discharged and the shouts from the instructors.

Each Officer fired their quota of eighteen rounds and the air in the indoor range quickly became heavily laden with the acrid stench of cordite.

"Clear your weapons gentlemen and step out of the bays." The Sergeant shouted when all the firing had ceased. "We'll see how you've done."

Alan, along with the rest of the students stepped back out of his bay. The assisting instructors entered and checked that all the weapons had been proved and placed back on the shelves at the front of each cubicle.

There were five shouts of "Clear." before the Sergeant beckoned them all to join him on the short walk to the far end of the range to check their results.

"Stand facing your respective targets gentlemen. Time to read 'em and weep."

Alan peered at the black representation of the male upper torso. It was peppered with holes, but Alan couldn't make out the number.

The instructors carefully examined the various targets and called out the results. "Bay one Sergeant." The Sergeant glanced at the sheet on his clipboard. "Robinson."

"Thirteen, wide spread Sarge".

"Bay two…"

"Mellors."

"Eight on target Sergeant…wide spread."

Alan heard Mellors, immediately to his left sigh dejectedly.

"Bay three…"

"Pendle."

Alan held his breath.

"Eighteen on target, good close grouping."

The Sergeant lowered his clipboard. "Tell it."

The range assistant replied. "I count four in the middle X Sarge, ten in the upper left eight and nine rings and four in the lower right nine ring…'bout a ten inch group Sarge."

Alan beamed inwardly; the Sergeant closed in and whispered in his ear. "Don't get fucking cocky Pendle; accurate shooting on its own won't get you a ticket…alright?"

Alan kept his eyes straight ahead. "Yes Sarge."

"Bay four…"

*****

The five days were exhausting and they lost one more from their group, Mellors the Detective from the Burglary Squad. He just couldn't shoot straight.

"Practice doesn't always make perfect." Sergeant Forbes had told him, shaking his hand before he left.

Alan's scores remained consistent; he was confident during house searching and showed good command skills when he took the lead during the vehicle 'hard stop' practicals.

He had also proved to be equally proficient with the shotgun; the foot square heavy metal plate ringing out to confirm each strike. The heavy rifled slugs had swung the much dented plate crazily on its suspending chains as they slammed home.

His daily assessments showed that he exercised restraint and sound judgement during the hostage exercises. He attained a passable score on the written exam and at the end of the fourth day, Sergeant Forbes had written. "I am confident that Pc Pendle will successfully complete the Basic Firearms Course (dependant on the results of the final revolver shoot) and that he is suitable to become an authorised firearms Officer."

Handing him his final assessment sheet for signing, The Sergeant had offered an unexpected word of advice.

"Pendle. Tomorrow, just treat it as a normal shoot. Don't fuck up your concentration, thinking about attaining the required score, we both *know* you can hit the target. I've seen loads of lads come here and do just as well as you during the course, then they 'dip' on the final shoot. Shoot to hit the target, not to pass the course…ok?"

Alan nodded and handed back the signed form. "Thanks Sarge, 'preciate that."

*****

"You're a very interesting man Pendle." The Chief Inspector said as he eased himself back in his chair. He looked over the Senior Sergeant's final report. "You only dropped two shots during the final .38 shoot and none with the shotgun. Sergeant Forbes describes you as being 'quiet the most competent Officer he has ever trained'. 'Instinctive'…'Confident' and 'Decisive' yet restrained." The Chief Inspector adopted a wry smile. "I think you're something of a dark horse Mr Pendle."

Chief Inspector Hall looked enquiringly across at Alan; there was a pregnant pause as he invited a response. He had been chosen as the head of firearms training because of his renowned interview techniques and an uncanny skill as the judge of a man's character, able to weedle out weaknesses and identify underlying deficiencies, any minute cracks in the temple walls which might eventually crumble under pressure. Mr Hall would identify those Officers who might act too readily…or conversely but of equal concern…not at all.

Alan breathed in deeply and exhaled slowly through his nose. He waited for a moment whilst he wondered if he had weighed this Chief Inspector up correctly. It went against the grain to trust anyone above the rank of Sergeant and even then, not always.

They continued to look at each other across the metal table top, the Chief Inspector furrowed his brow. There was perhaps something troubling this Officer, something in his past which he had not let slip, something ancient, nagging at his conscience.

Alan broke the stalemate. "Did you ever wonder if your indecision or inaction might have been the cause of someone's death sir?…Or, if you'd been quicker off the mark, perhaps it could have been avoided?"

The Chief Inspector didn't reply. He knew there was more to come.

"Or if there was some act that you were…not ashamed of exactly, but if you could turn the clock back, perhaps you would deal with it differently or take a different course of action?"

The Chief Inspector nodded. "On many occasions…Too many to remember if truth be told, but turning the clock back isn't an option available to us lad."

Alan sighed. "Yeah, I know sir…Perhaps I want to be a firearms Officer because I want to prove to myself that I will be able to do the right thing at the moment of truth, should it ever arise…That I'll make the right choice sir."

"I'm sure that you will Pendle. I think you're made of the right stuff…I'm signing you off." he said decidedly. "You're hereby authorised to carry the .38 revolver and the Remington 870. Your personal record will be amended accordingly…and, if you should ever tire of speeding round the City persecuting innocent motorists, you might consider applying for an instructor's post here…Think about it." the Chief Inspector said closing the buff folder.

Alan's de-brief was clearly over. Pleasantly shocked and glowing inwardly, Alan stood up and offered his hand. "Thank you sir."

The Chief took his hand and after a brief but firm shake, waved him out of his office. "Tell McPherson to come in will you."

## **Twenty Six**

The transom window in the Traffic office was wide open. Wisps of blue, grey smoke curled out across the painted soffits, up and over the plastic roof guttering to be whipped away in the light breeze. Much like the Royal Standard fluttering above Buckingham Palace, indicative to all who could read the signs, that his Royal Highness the Road Traffic Sergeant was in residence.

A late afternoon sun played through the gently swaying branches of the trees at the far end of the station car park. The rays flitted across the painted office walls and every now and then, glinted brightly against the rows of keys hung on the vehicle disposition board. The offices on the upper floor of the station were closing down for the weekend; the duties clerk stretched the plastic cover over his typewriter and locked his jar of coffee in the drawer beneath his desk. The typists laughed and gossiped as they washed their cups and plates in the night kitchen. It was Friday after all and the non-operational types working nine five days wanted to get a 'flier' to beat the traffic on the Ring Road.

The telephone warbled and the Traffic Sergeant furrowed his brow in annoyance at being disturbed. Without taking his eyes from the article on the Pittsburg Stealers in his copy of 'Gridiron' magazine, he reached out to lift the handset from its cradle.

"Moorwood Road Traffic, Sergeant Kemp."

"Hey Sarge, how's the murder capital of the North?" Alan's Sergeant smiled as he recognised Alan's voice and sucking on fresh air, peered at the end of his cigar and noting that it had temporarily given up the ghost; he set it down in the ashtray and leaned back in his chair.

"You might well ask Pendle lad. Not a moments fuckin' peace since the shit hit the proverbial. Can't get parked, 'ave to queue up for a slice of toast and worst of all, I 'ave to spend most of my day out on patrol to avoid Forrester's wrath…How've you got on?"

"You will be pleasantly surprised to hear that I breezed it Sarge. I only dropped two on the final shoot, passed the written and all the practicals. Chief Inspector Hall's given me my ticket so I'm now an authorised firearms Officer, .38 and shotgun.

"Never doubted it for a moment Alan lad…Where are you now?"

"Still at Stretham Sarge, thought I'd ring in and give you the news."

"Are you done now?"

"Yeah, just finished all the admin. Picked up our tickets and we've been cut away early."

His Sergeant glanced up to the clock above the office door. "It's gone four Alan, by the time you've got yerself sorted and travelled back…call it a day I reckon. 'Ave you spoken with Sully?"

"Not yet Sarge, thought I'd give him a bell later."

The line went quiet for a moment.

"You won't 'ave 'eard then?"

"Heard?" Alan said cautiously.

"He's failed his eyesight test again, can't focus. His right eye's still knackered. He's had his advanced ticket pulled…"

"You're joking Sarge." Alan said, horrified.

"'Fraid not." His Sergeant replied. "He'll be able to come in if 'e wants, but he'll be on restricted duties, clerical an' stuff, but no drivin' till it's sorted…"

"Jesus!…How long Sarge?"

Alan could hear his Sergeant give a long doleful sigh. "Who can say Al, you know what the Force Medical Officer's like, he thinks getting' up in a morning should be fuckin' risk assessed…Looks like you'll be on yer own for a while. You might 'ave to get someone from beat to crew up with you on full nights, unless one of the half night crews will swap."

Alan was silent for a while. The exuberance at passing his firearms course was dampened by the news that his partner's injury might be a long term or even permanent issue.

His Sergeant let Alan ponder for a moment or two, knowing that the news would be devastating then quickly changed the subject. "Look Al, I've put you down for ten six days tomorrow. On the strength of you passing yer course an' bein' our new AFO, Forrester has made a request, I use that term loosely, that you assist the Station Sergeant with an audit of the armoury. It's just 'is way of kickin' you in the bollocks for the arseholin' he took from John Summerville for shit cannin' yer accident report. Anyway to be fair, I know Ron Dennison's ex forces, but the last time he 'ad 'is 'ands on a weapon it was probably a fuckin' longbow at Agincourt. Yer docket's pretty clear so we might as well try and win a few brownie points…Do the ten six tomorrow, get the armoury squared away an' drop back on yer normal rota on Sunday."

Alan focused his thoughts and drew a comparison that if his partner had broken his leg, he'd be on his own for a good while. *But a broken leg would mend wouldn't it...* He shook the thought from his mind. "Yeah, ten six suits me fine Sarge. I'll swap war stories with old Ron for the day…While we're on the subject of Detective Superintendent Summerville, how's the job going?"

The Sergeant retrieved his cigar stub from the ashtray and reached for his lighter. "We are livin' through interestin' days Alan lad. The place is full of grim faced Detectives. There's an incident room runnin' upstairs an' the CID office smells like a distillery. We 'ad the knuckle draggers from Task Force camped out in the gymnasium for a day or so, I think they expected an early arrest, but yer pet hooker 'as gone to ground…"

"What…Evie?"

"Disappeared from the face of the earth mate. Frank Ellis got that telephone number traced to a two up two down in Stepney. He 'ad the Metropolitan Police's finest go round to try and firm up a witness statement. They spoke to 'er Sister who by all accounts told 'em that she'd gone back to some place called Little London. I think the Met lads were a bit confused, till she let on it was a town in Jamaica…Not sure how that avenue of investigation will progress, although I've no doubt that some lucky twat will get a field trip out of it..."

"Well Sarge, given that I can identify said witness, I could do the trip to the Caribbean. You'd have to come along as well a'course in your supervisory capacity…"

His Sergeant snorted. "Hah, dream on Al, you've more chance of wakin' up with a ten inch cock…It'll be John Summerville an' which ever Detective 'appens to be flavour of the month."

Alan chuckled. "Well, I'm not cutting two inches off my cock just to win a few days in the sun Sarge. Anyway…What's the score with Lyburn?"

"Yer main suspect 'as gone to ground as well…They 'ad a full team sat on 'is last known address for a few days. No gain though, seems like he's 'ad it away on 'is toes as well…You can imagine how well 'ouse to 'ouse enquiries went on eleven beat. After the McKnight woman got whacked, none of the hookers are talkin' an' a'course local informants are a bit thin on the ground…So we've no up to date description, no details of a motor or where 'e might 'ave fucked off to…Anyway, you get yerself off 'ome. I'm not in tomorrow, takin' Sally to see 'er Mother. Personally, I'd sooner 'ave wasps shoved up my arse, but anything for a quiet life. Oldfield and Barney are on 'earlies' so you'll be able 'ave a catch up when they come in for meal."

Alan smiled to himself and wondered how long it would take before the mental image of his Sergeant suffering death by anal wasp insertion dissipated.

"See you Sunday then Sarge."

*****

To the casual passer-by, the house on Alma Street was unremarkable enough. Square and imposing, sturdy, in time discoloured weather worn Yorkshire stone.

From the pavement, access to the front of the Georgian style house was gained via a tall wrought iron gate hung between two large stone pillars. Thin wires from a small pressure switch attached to the wooden latch post were well camouflaged, weaved between the branches of the overgrown privet hedge which extended from the high stone wall at the edge of the pavement along the side of the loosely gravelled path to the left of the front door. Buried beneath the path, they emerged to run up the side of the entrance steps and through a small hole drilled in the bottom of the door jamb. Now inside the entrance corridor of the house, the wires snaked their way up the wall and disappeared through the ornate plastered ceiling, up between the floorboards to appear again poking out through the threadbare carpet in a small room on the upper floor. Here the wires ran haphazardly across the floor to the top of a small bedside cabinet where they were connected to a small battery powered bulb holder.

As with all the houses owned by 'Soldier' Garrison, 'watchers' remained ever vigilant. One, seated behind a single pane casement window directly above the front door, would see a small six volt bulb glow dimly should the gate be opened.

Four well-worn stone steps rose from the gravelled path which curved around across the front of the house. The steps were flanked on either side by metal railings, sunk deep into concrete footings at the foot of the steps and rising at a sharp angle, to be bolted securely to the solid wooden Corinthian style columns which supported an indented stone arch above the door.

No identifying numbers, handles or fitments were to be seen adorning the thick oak panelled door. Access was gained only from within.

The upper and ground floor casement windows to the right of the door were in painted stone. Mullion frames within a mock 'keep' protruded a full five feet from the face of the house and were topped with a false castellated parapet.

The small ground floor side casement windows, provided for an extra view of the front door and along the wide wooden window ledges, a second 'watcher' lounged with his back against the wall. Only after parting the heavily stained net curtains and giving a nod to the junior 'soldier' manning the door, would a heavy steel bolt be withdrawn and the 'visitor' allowed access.

Terracotta lattice style air vents beneath the ground floor windows, provided ventilation to the spacious cellar where the 'blues' manager had a large Formica topped table and a battered leather swivel chair. A slim grey metal cabinet stood against the far wall of the cellar. At first glance, a simple piece of obsolete office furniture. The discerning eye however, would notice the double slotted key portal in the left hand side of the door, evidence of a multiple lever asymmetrical double bitted lock.

The body of the cabinet was constructed from a single sheet of pressed steel, no riveted joints or welds were evident. The back of the cabinet sat flush against the wall. Those familiar with gun cabinets would know that it was fixed securely with four thirteen millimetre case hardened bolts within steel expanding rawls, fed deep into the stonework of the cellar wall. The cabinet was immovable and without the large double headed key, virtually impenetrable.

Eight stone steps led up from the cellar to a small door leading to the dimly lit ground floor corridor which ran from the steel sheeted front door, toward the three rooms at the back of the house where the hookers plied their trade.

The furnishings in the back rooms were Spartan. A naked nicotine stained bulb hanging from the centre of a plaster ceiling rose, a metal tube framed bed and a mattress over which was stretched a plastic wipe clean sheet. Purposeful, clinical and austere.

The rear ground floor windows were all painted over from the inside, to provide for confidentiality from the prying binoculars and cameras of the Vice Squad.

The small neglected garden at the rear of the house was isolated from a cobbled side street by a breeze block wall. Ten feet tall, solidly buttressed every six feet along its length and topped with shards of broken glass, intended more as a deterrent to the leather gloved hands of 'Babylon' than would be burglars.

To the side of the house, the cast iron access cover to the main sewer was sealed down tight with cement to frustrate the Officers from the Drugs Squad with their waiting nets and plastic evidence bags.

At the first signs of a raid, pills, bush, small crystalline rocks, resin and powder would all be hurriedly flushed down the toilets to flow freely away beneath the street, unhindered and inaccessible. No evidence… no prosecution.

A veritable fortress, hidden in plain sight amongst similarly grandiose residences, formerly owned and occupied in a bygone age by the wool barons of the City.

*****

'Midnight' glanced furtively over his shoulder to the left and right as he slipped the plastic hooded key into the lock of the small metal left luggage locker. The City railway station was almost deserted. All the retail outlets had long since closed, their roller shutters drawn and padlocked for the night.

In the main concourse, a homeless old man in a tattered trench coat and baggy corduroy trousers, gathered in and tied tight about his ankles with bailing twine, sat on one of the metal slatted seats. He mumbled incoherently to himself in a strangely cultivated voice as he rummaged through the few possessions he kept in a large canvas bag.

An old Negro wearing a faded cap and jacket bearing the British Rail logo pushed a wide headed broom, sweeping up the cigarette ends and discarded ticket stubs. His face was grey and strewn with a web of deep wrinkles, the product of decades of poverty and mundane, unfulfilling employment. He hummed as he wandered listlessly up and down the concourse floor.

Outside the main entrance foyer a few diehard taxi drivers gathered in a small group around the front of the first car in the rank, hoping that the late night train due in from Kings Cross might be worth the wait.

The tannoys were silent. The ticket collector's box at the side of the turnstile was deserted.

With a last glance out across the concourse, 'Midnight' turned the key and opened the locker door.

Wrapped in an old 'T' shirt, the revolver lay where he had left it, tucked away toward the back of the locker behind a rucksack containing his money. Leaving the rucksack within the confines of the locker, 'Midnight' unzipped the center compartment and flicking his thumb across one of the thick wads, he extracted what he thought would be sufficient from beneath the restraining rubber band. With another cautious glance out toward the concourse, he quickly folded the notes and pushed them into the back pocket of his jeans. He secured the rucksack and pushed it to one side. His heart rate quickened as he wrapped his fingers around the soft cotton of the 'T' shirt and felt the hard chromium plated steel within the folds.

'Midnight' moved closer to the bank of lockers and quickly removed the revolver, slipping it quickly down the front of his bomber jacket before zipping it up to his throat. He closed the locker door and after withdrawing the key and ensuring that the door was secured, palmed the key into the front pocket of his jeans. Pushing his hands deep into the side pockets of his jacket, he walked the short distance to the exit doors, gripping the forty four ounces of Smith and Wesson beneath the pocket linings.

*****

'Midnight' felt an uneasy sense of déjà vu as he eased the Cortina into the kerb edge and killed the engine. He sat for a moment and listened to the ticking of the engine as it cooled. He looked across the street to where a certain lamp post cast its pool of yellow light across the pavement and he remembered the 'Chinese'.

She had worked beneath that lampost hour upon hour for him, her tiny frame and childlike looks making him a small fortune. Her hair, so black it had seemed tinged with blue, cascading from beneath her trademark sailor's cap and onto her shoulders. He remembered how it had shimmered even in the dull yellow light as she had fallen. Her almond eyes had squeezed tight shut at the sudden searing pain from his razor as it had slipped deep into her and had then flickered as she had lost consciousness. He could almost feel again the warm blood as it had spurted from her side and out between his fingers to spatter onto the paving stones and the almost weightlessness of her tiny body as she had gone limp. In his mind's eye he saw her ethereal figure, standing again under that very lamp post and for a brief, fleeting moment before the ghostly apparition faded, he experienced a previously unknown sensation…Regret.

'Midnight' frowned at his moment of weakness and glanced at the clock in the center console, almost one o'clock, the Alma Street 'blues' would be well underway.

He reached beneath his seat and after a cursory glance up and down the street, withdrew the revolver and stuffed it quickly into the side pocket of his track suit top.

*****

A veil of smoke hung in a thick pall beneath the flaking paint of the high ceiling in the main bar area. The heady pungent aroma of cannabis pervaded the room, the viscous fumes having seeped into the heavy velvet curtains drawn across the ground floor casements and the threadbare carpet. It permeated into every fibre of his clothing and assailed his nostrils, thick and cloying. Mixed with the rancid smell of the sex sweat from the hookers who danced enticingly in front of prospective punters, 'Midnight' felt that each breath was like drowning in oil.

A makeshift bar had been erected diagonally across the far corner of the room. The barman, heavily bearded with waist length dreadlocks, sprouting from beneath the statutory knitted headgear favoured by the Rastafarians, served cans of cold beer from a large fridge and shots of hard liquor directly from the bottles which stood in rows on a precariously sagging shelf.

Around the walls of the spacious room, sofas and high backed lounge chairs provided support for those slumped in a soporific state, through the effects of either alcohol or drugs. Between the chairs and settees, small glass topped tables, strewn with short tightly rolled tubes of cardboard and thin plastic cards, bore the dusty residue of cocaine.

Opposite the bar area, two gargantuan speakers stood either side of a small folding card table on which was a twin deck record turntable. A young black wearing a pair of headphones, danced behind the table as he fed the separate decks with a constant diet of reggae and Motown hits. The music was deafening, even above the raucous laughter and the hubbub of conversation.

'Midnight' sipped his beer slowly and watched covertly as money was passed over the bar to a young black wearing his colours. He took the wad of notes and without counting, stuffed it into a small canvas sack before weaving his way through the throng of people on the dance floor, toward where the dealers were gathered together in a small group. More notes were handed over.  The 'money mule' nodded appreciatively and after lightly clenched fists were touched together, he stroked the main dealer's outstretched palm with his own.

A tall black hooker returned to the bar area, adjusting her short skirt as she took a seat. She was seized upon immediately by the 'money mule' who held out his hand expectantly. Begrudgingly, she pushed her fingers down the front of her flimsy blouse and withdrew a folded ten pound note from between her pendulous breasts and slapped it down into his open hand.

The 'mule' scowled at her offering. "What the fuck?" he shouted over the din, sneering at her questioningly.

She shrugged her shoulders. "Dude jus'wanted a handjob is all, I offered to suck the mo'fucker fo' twenty. He done cum his load fo' I could talk him roun' to it."

The 'mule' glared dispassionately down at her. "You needs to work on yo' fuckin' bedside manner bitch…'Soldier' be won'erin' if you bein' straight…think on it." the 'mule' said threateningly as he stuffed the note down into the sack.

'Midnight' went through the motions of drinking, although the can he held had been empty for some time. His reactions would need to be keen, not dulled by the effects of the strong lager.

He slumped back into the worn leather of the chair, keeping his right arm across the pocket of his tracksuit top to ensure that even in the dim light, no one would recognise the shape of the revolver. Smiling drunkenly, he shook his head, declining the offer from a hooker and gently but firmly pushed her away as she tried to sit on his lap. Undeterred, she lifted the front of her short skirt and displayed her perfectly shaved vagina. Placing one hand on the back of his chair she leaned across him and straddled his outstretched legs. She looked down at him and ground her hips invitingly. She was rail thin. Her scrawny arms bore the dark telltale scabs of the habitual heroin user and the yellowing bruises beneath almost translucent skin, where her veins were slowly collapsing. The skin was stretched drum tight over her pelvic bones. Her bare legs were bruised and stick thin, her sunken eyes and tired features reminded 'Midnight' of Jews he had once seen in a program about the Nazi death camps.

She dropped the hem of her skirt and smiled at him exposing yellowing teeth and brushed her fingers temptingly across the front of his jeans.

Fearful that she may touch the hard steel within his jacket pocket, he shook his head again and pushed her away using a little more force. The false alluring smile quickly dropped from her face and with a look hovering somewhere between disappointment and distaste, she shuffled away into the crowd.

In his peripheral vision, 'Midnight' kept the 'money mule' in sight, noting as he disappeared from the room clutching the bulging canvas bag.

By the time 'Midnight' had been to the bar and bought himself another can of beer, he was back, the empty bag now hanging limply from the pocket of his sleeveless denim jacket.

The 'blues' was reaching its crescendo. The hard core 'punters' still in attendance were now mostly drunk or slumped in drug induced euphoria. A few still danced as the music thumped out relentlessly and the hookers disappeared with conveyer belt regularity to the rooms at the back of the house with their client's.

'Midnight' eased himself up from the low chair and swayed drunkenly toward the outer corridor, nodding to the soldier on the door as he made his way toward the toilet.

He paused and with an outstretched arm, he supported himself against the wall as if unable to focus and waited for his moment.

*****

As the door to the first floor corridor opened, the volume of the music banging out from the huge speakers in the main bar area increased dramatically, causing the 'Manager' to look up from where he sat behind his desk.

The intense throbbing beat of the music again became muted as the door was closed and he was momentarily startled to see someone other than his 'money mule' entering the cellar.

'Midnight' kept his hands deep within the pockets of his tracksuit top, the waistband cord pulled uncomfortably tight and secured with a knot. The thumb and three fingers of his right hand curled around the grip of the revolver. His index finger remained ready, crooked lightly around the trigger as he descended the steps.

The 'Manager' leaned back into his chair and scowled threateningly. "You got trouble wid readin' nigger?"

"Lookin for the piss stones is all man." 'Midnight' said, continuing down the steps, but withdrawing his left hand from the ruffled folds of his tracksuit top and holding it up apologetically.

The 'Manager' pointed angrily toward the top of the stairs. "Would the mo'fuckin' shithouse have a private sign on the door?..You gots to be stupid or trippin' nigger, get the fuck out my office fo' I kicks yo ass."

'Midnight' strode purposefully toward the front of the desk and produced the revolver from his pocket.

The 'Manager's' face suddenly took on an ashen hue, the confident look on his face wiped clean away.

At the sight of the snub nosed revolver, he forced himself back into his chair and gripped the armrests tightly. He stared at the end of the barrel now hovering only inches from his face and even in the dim cellar lighting, he could see the dull grey ends of the bullets seated within their individual chambers. 'Midnight' stared deep into the 'Manager's' eyes and nodded toward the grey cabinet. "Keys." he demanded.

The 'blues' 'Manager' glanced nervously toward the cellar steps, the pounding reggae beat beat remained muted. None of his soldiers had noticed that his assailant had slipped quickly and quietly through the door from the upper corridor.

"You gots to be out yo fuckin' mind…You know who dis crib be runnin fo'?" the 'Manager' stuttered with false bravado, unable to take his eyes from the barrel end of the revolver.

'Midnight's' heart was racing. He could hear the pounding blood rush in his ears, he knew that it might only be moments before someone came to the cellar. He pushed the barrel end forwards and pressed it hard up against the 'Manager's' forehead. "Keys motherfucker, I aint gonna ask again."

The 'Manager' arched his back in an effort to ease the pressure from the hard steel of the revolver pressed against his skull. With his right hand, he fumbled in the pocket of his trousers and dropped a large brass key onto the desktop. "You bes' be buyin' a ticket to the fuckin' moon nigger…'So'jer' be wearin' yo balls fo' cufflinks."

The threats of certain recrimination were cut short as 'Midnight' rammed the revolver's barrel violently into the 'Manager's' mouth.

His upper left incisor snapped cleanly away at the gum line. The upper right tore itself from its roots and twisted away to the side to make way for the serrated raised foresight as the barrel punched through toward the back of his throat.

*"The first's the 'ardest Jimmy…after that they're all jus' fuckin' meat."*

'Midnight' pulled the trigger.

A metallic resonant bark rang out and bounced back from the close confines of the cellar.

The 'Manager's 'cheeks ballooned in an instant as the hot gasses from the muzzle flash expanded within his mouth, helping to deaden the sound of the shot, but incinerating the soft flesh of his uvula and palate. His head was snapped back violently against the soft cushioned headrest of the chair as the .22 caliber bullet exploded into the muscles in the back of his neck.

It tore through the cervical vertebrae and separated his spinal cord. Not a twitch from his body, no sound was uttered, all impulses to and from his brain ceased instantly.

In the same instant that the bullet fragmented as it struck the wall at the rear of the cellar, small tufts of white fibrous material spat out from the back of the chair, the silken strands swirling momentarily in the hot gas vortex before slowly floating to the floor.

The cellar was immediately filled with the acrid stench of cordite.

'Midnight' stood transfixed for a moment, waiting for the sound of the music to increase as the door from the corridor was opened, fearful that even over the almost deafening reggae beat, the shot had been heard.

The muted wailings of Bob Marley remained constant and 'Midnight' pushed the revolver down the waistband of his jeans and snatched the key from the table top.

He knelt on the floor facing the cabinet. The double headed key entered the shaped portal and passed through three millimetres of hardened steel. 'Midnight's' heart pounded loudly in his temples and his breathing came in short, frantic rasps as he twisted the key clockwise and felt, more than heard the solid metallic 'clunk' through the head of the key as the lock activated. He pulled on the door, but it was unforgiving.

The seconds were ticking by and 'Midnight' knew that his luck wouldn't hold forever. The trusted 'money mule' would soon be entering the cellar to deliver the swathes of notes collected from the bar staff, the hookers and the dealers. Only eight shots left in the revolver now and 'Midnight' now knew that although the small .22 rounds were effective with a shot to the head at point blank range, he was not confident that a shot to the chest or stomach would prevent a soldier, keen to earn his colours, from returning fire with a more deadly nine millimetre pistol.

In a moment of blind inspiration, he twisted the key again. The double bitted lock activated with a satisfying thud and 'Midnight' held his breath as the thick steel rods slid back into the inner body of the door, allowing it to swing open.

A loud high pitched scream from one of the back rooms caused him to freeze; it was followed by a peal of laughter and the heady beat of the music went on.

'Midnight' gasped as he cast his eyes over the neat pile of notes stacked to the left of the cabinet, all segregated into thick wads of fives, tens and twenties and secured with rubber bands. To the right, a small cardboard box contained small dealer sized plastic bags of cannabis. In another, sachets containing powder, some, the recreational white, others the more addictive brown.

'Midnight' quickly pulled down the zip of his tracksuit top and with hands shaking from the adrenalin rush, he grabbed at the piles of notes, two, three, four wads, then five at a time as many as his fingers would hold. Frantically, he stuffed them down into the jacket and manoeuvred them around toward the back and the sides. His heart beat like a trip hammer, any moment he could be discovered. How many seconds had passed?...enough...enough.

His head rushed dizzily as he scrambled to his feet and momentarily, the walls of the cellar swirled drunkenly around him.

'Midnight' squeezed his eyes shut tight and shook his head. His equilibrium slowly returned, although the rushing sound in his ears remained. His legs shook, as with a last glance at the 'Manager's' lifeless body slumped in the chair; he made his way to the foot of the steps.

The tightly tied cord in the waistband of his jacket held the wads of notes in place and in the dimly lit house; the baggy folds would hopefully disguise their presence.

'Midnight' slipped his fingers beneath the waistband at the small of his back and eased it over the grip of the revolver where it protruded from the top of his jeans.

He took the steps two at a time and pausing to take a deep breath, he wrapped his fingers around the brass knob; turning it slowly and cracked the door open an inch or so. 'Midnight' peered out into the corridor and toward the front door. Only eight bullets left now and not wanting to shoot his way out of the house, he waited.

The soldier on the door had his back to him. He was leaning against the door jamb, talking to the first floor 'watcher', who still lounged across the window sill in the room immediately to the left of the front door.

The music was still deafening. Eddy Grant's 'Electric Avenue' was blasting out from the room opposite where the barman continued to serve up cans of 'Red Stripe' and 'Yardy Lager' and shots of 'Coruba' and 'Mount Gay' rum.

A hooker emerged from the bar area, supporting an intoxicated punter by the arm, his eyes glazed and his jeans open at the front where she had fondled him to hardness. Momentarily shielded from the view of the door soldier, 'Midnight' quickly slipped through the door and entered the corridor.

Showing no interest in 'Midnight', the hooker led her 'trick' toward the rooms at the rear. Her large breasts swayed unfettered beneath a flimsy translucent blouse and 'Midnight' felt their softness against his arm as she brushed past him.

Feigning drunkenness, he staggered down the corridor and toward the metal sheeted front door. The soldier casually glanced over his shoulder and shrugged himself away from the door jamb. Without interrupting his conversation with the 'watcher', he palmed the protruding bolt handle and slid it back.

'Midnight' stepped out into the fresh air. Hearing the steel bolt being slammed home behind him, but mindful that he would still be within the view of both 'watchers', he supported himself with a hand on the metal railing and swayed as he descended the steps, faltering as his feet found the loose gravel of the path.

All the way to the gate, he staggered and swayed. As he fumbled with the latch, he expected to hear the soldier's shouts at any moment.

The gate shrieked loudly on its rusty hinges and he stepped out onto the pavement. Only when hidden from view by the hedge, did he start to run.

## **Twenty Seven**

It is not chance, but fate which determines the course and ultimate outcome of life.

Chance is the turn of a card from an unstacked deck. It is the role of an unbiased dice or in the dancing ball as it tumbles into either the red or the black in the true spin of the roulette wheel. Chance is in the simple flip of a coin.

Fate, or to give credence to Edward Lorenz's 'chaos' theory on the unpredictability of the future, more commonly known on the 'butterfly effect', is the debilitating bout of vomiting and diarrhoea, preventing the departure on the holiday flight which subsequently plummets into the mountain side. It is the annoying puncture and the extra half an hour spent replacing the wheel which avoids the multiple fatal collision on the motorway.

Fate is the minute particle of millstone, broken away and baked in the whole wheat bread from which Pc Oldfield made his breakfast toast, on which he cracked a tooth, requiring an emergency visit to the dentist, causing him to call in sick, leaving Pc Barnett his Traffic 'Aide' without a qualified partner for the early turn shift.

*****

Alan breezed into the Traffic office humming to himself. He smiled at the young Traffic 'Aide' who was seated at the Sergeant's desk, a pile of offence reports strewn haphazardly across the table top.

"Hey Barney, how's it going lad?" he asked, as he opened his personal tray in the bank of grey metal drawers and grimaced at the growing mound of paperwork.

Pc Barnett nodded wanly and tossed his ballpoint onto the desk, stretching himself in the chair.

"Yeah, ok thanks Alan…Heard you got your ticket." he replied.

Alan noted that the 'Aide' seemed to lack his usual enthusiasm. "Certainly did mate. You ok? …You sound a bit pissed off…Oldfield gone out without you?"

"Nah…He called in sick. I'm bored to fucking tears."

"What's the malingerin' twat come down with now?" Alan asked, casually leafing through the amount of paperwork in his tray and tutting to himself. "Christ, I've only been away a week, no wonder the Amazon rain forest's so fucked up?"

"Had to go to the dentist." Pc Barnett said to Alan's back.

Alan looked back across to the 'Aide' who was slowly swivelling around in the Sergeant's chair. He frowned. "You don't go sick just to go see the dentist Barney, you go in your own time, Roger'll go ape-shit."

The Traffic 'Aide' shrugged his shoulders. "Broke a tooth apparently. He reckons he's in agony…Says 'e might be in later if 'e gets it sorted…Don't suppose I could crew up with you?"

Alan adopted his best sympathetic expression. "Under normal circumstances, I would deem it a pleasure Barney lad…Unfortunately…I am down to work with the ancient mariner today. Ron Dennison's got to do an audit on the armoury…an' as I'm the newly appointed AFO for Moorwood, it's down to me to assist…proving and logging…shit like that. The very reverend Forrester doesn't want old Ron messing around with firearms. A negligent discharge might well rid us of that lazy twat Bentley in the front office, but it'd look bad on the Chief's log…Sorry all the same."

The 'Aide' smiled dolefully and reached for his pen.

Alan's conscience got the better of him. "Look…If I get finished, I'll give you a shout…We could have a run out to Brierley's farm for an ice cream."

Pc Barnett nodded enthusiastically and beamed. "That'd be great Alan…Cheers."

Alan glanced up at the Traffic Sergeant's scribbled instruction in the remarks column on the vehicle disposition board. "There you go Barney…If you get sick of doing yer paperwork, Charlie's old Granada's got to go to Central garage. There's a new Cavalier to collect, you're allowed to do transport jobs, statement taking, enquiries and stuff aren't you?…As long as you don't get involved in any pursuits or anything, you'll be ok."

"You reckon Roger'd ok it?" the 'Aide' asked cautiously.

Alan nodded confidently. "Barney, you've got a temporary permit, you're authorised to drive the damn thing, you just can't respond to anything till you're advanced…No blues and two's or exceedin' the speed limits, but you could do a transport job. Look…Give Central garage a bell, make sure they're ready for the swap an' 'ave a slow drive downtown…It'd be worth it just to see Charlie's face when he turns up for 'lates' and finds 'is beloved 'Granny's bin' replaced by a sixteen hundred Cavalier."

Pc Barnett looked apprehensive. "Should I ring Roger to check?"

Alan shot the 'Aide' a disparaging glance. "Barney, strap on a pair for fuck's sake, it's only a transport job…Anyway, Roger's gone to see 'is Mother in Law so you've shit out…It's just something for you to do until Oldfield drags his arse into work, or I get finished with the old man of the sea."

The 'Aide' shrugged his shoulders. "If you say it'd be ok"

"Barney…life is nothing without an element of risk." Alan paused and looked up to the ceiling as if deep in thought. "Not sure who said that…but it's true anyway."

He glanced at his watch. "Shit…It's eight bells or whatever…Ron Dennison will be after my arse…an' you know what they say about the 'rum, bum an' baccy boys'."

The 'Aide' looked puzzled.

"The Navy?" Alan asked questioningly.

The 'Aide' shook his head slowly. Clearly confused.

Alan sighed. "Never mind Barney…I'll explain it to you when you're a bit older…Look, if you're gonna take Charlie's Granada downtown, don't get yourself involved in anything. In fact, don't book on with the Control Room, what they don't know won't hurt them an' you'll be there an' back in an hour."

*****

Alan nodded to the front office clerk as he entered the hallowed portals of the non-confrontational. "Hey Derek, how's life in the fast lane?"

The clerk folded his newspaper and placed it in his 'out tray'. "Hectic as always...I know you operational types think that working in the front office is a breeze, but I can tell you..."

Alan held up the palms of his hands in supplication. "Derek...Let me stop you there...You can 'ave yer job in the front office...Personally I wouldn't 'ave it for a gold pig..."

The clerk nodded appreciatively. "Seen the Chief's log?"

Alan shook his head. "I don't do the 'Beano' Derek...Anything of note?"

The clerk reached across his desk and rummaged through the pile of crime complaints and lost property reports in his tray. "Check this." The clerk leaned back in his chair and swivelled round to face Alan. "04.30 hours this date, the body of an afro-Caribbean male, large build, mid to late thirties, was discovered on waste land adjacent to Berrisford Way, eleven beat, Moorwood Division. The male, as yet unidentified, had sustained a single gunshot wound to the head. D.C. Selway, Millbeck CID requests all Officers to view the briefing board photographs to assist in identification, any info to...etc etc...'Badlands' is livin' up to its name eh?...Second shootin' in as many weeks, an' that head honcho pimp of yours, 'topped' in the 10/9 in the Melvilles...I'll tell you, there's a fuckin' vigilante on the loose Al...'E's sendin' a sublinear message.."

Alan smiled and shook his head slowly. "Two or three violent deaths a week in the 'Badlands' is nothing fresh...and its subliminal Derek."

The clerk shrugged. "Whatever...There's definitely a pattern emergin' Al".

Alan smiled cynically. "An' you base this theory on...?"

The clerk snorted. "You need to read more mate...It's a well-documented fact that serial killers actually *want* to get caught...so they leave enticin' messages within their MO's for the investigators...cat an' mouse like...You know, a game."

Alan's face remained passive, quizzical.

The clerk sighed frustratedly. "No wonder you lot in Traffic stick to speeders an' bald tyres…Look Al, think about it…a high profile pimp…sex trade. A hooker…sex trade an' now some unknown Jamaician 'Yardy' bad ass who'll probably turn out to be a drug dealer…I tell you Al, it's a vigilante wot's 'ad the call from God to rid the world of assholes." the clerk said decidedly and tossed the copy of the Chief Constables nightly incident log onto his desktop.

Alan considered the clerk's theory for a moment. "Well Derek…That's all very interesting, but given the equally well documented lack of professional abilities within the ranks of CID, corroborated I might add, by the appalling statistics on undetected crime in Moorwood Division, I suspect that yer vigilante will soon get bored with leaving his hidden messages, abandon all hope of ever getting his collar felt and quench his insatiable thirst for notoriety by giving himself up at yer front counter…If he does Derek…an' it transpires that in fact you were correct and that he is on a divinely ordained mission to rid the world of assholes…Make sure you give him Forrester's home address before you chuck him in the can eh?"

The clerk chuckled and nodded knowingly.

"Oi…Dirty 'arry." A gravelly voice called out.

Alan turned to see the Station Sergeant standing by the open door to the station armoury, impatiently tapping the face of his watch.

"Sorry Sarge." Alan said apologetically. "I got waylaid by Officer Bentley and his 'Angel of Retribution' theory."

"Well waylay yer backside in 'ere an' let's get crackin'…Four bells was fifteen minutes ago."

Alan smiled at his old friend. "That some form of Pavlovian thing Sarge?..The bell rings an' you naval types get rewarded with a mug of grog or a weevil infested biscuit?"

The old Sergeant smiled. "Insubordination's a keelhaulin' offence young Pendle, twenty with the 'cat'…Second offence…flogged around the fleet."

Alan adopted a quizzical expression. "Bit draconian if you don't mind me sayin' Sarge. I mean…I'm sure that bein' 'press ganged' into service and forced to endure the rigorous discipline in the Royal Navy of the sixteenth century must 'ave bin' why Britannia actually ruled the waves an' all that, but…"

The office clerk slouched back into his chair and smirked. "Hey Sarge." he called out. "Must 'ave bin a twat on the 'Bounty'…Fletcher Christian a mate of yours was he?"

The fatherly smile suddenly dropped from the Station Sergeant's face. Witty banter from a fellow time served ex-serviceman and a Traffic man 'to boot' was one thing, but he wasn't about to let the office 'clerk' take the piss.

"Listen up Bentley you trench dodging prat..."

The clerk immediately realized with some visible discomfort that he'd overstepped the mark. "I didn't mean anything disrespe…"

"The likes of you..." The veteran Sergeant growled, interrupting and pointing an accusatory finger at the shrinking office clerk. "Would be volunteerin' to bend over the bow gunwhale to take a peek at the golden rivet…probably on a daily basis."

He directed Alan toward the armoury with a nod and Alan chuckled as he left the office clerk slumped in his chair with a confused frown on his face.

*****

'Midnight' stretched his legs out in front of him, his arms fully extended and resting across the top of the settee. He tapped his fingers gently against the soft brown leather and considered the pile of notes stacked on the small coffee table. Just short of twelve thousand pounds…A year's wage for most law abiding folks, but probably only a month's takings for the 'Soldier' he reckoned.

The morning local news on his TV had reported that a body had been found dumped on waste land. That'd be on Garrison's orders he thought. There would have been a shit storm. His blues 'Manager' had been blown away and his stash 'souvenired' right from under the noses of his soldiers.

He smiled to himself as he imagined 'Soldier's' rage and rantings. *"Get rid o' that dumbass motherfucker...think I want they 'Babylon' rasclart spoonin' roun' my crib wid all dey f'rensic bullshit..."*

'Midnight' chuckled to himself. The 'Manager' had been given a typical 'Yardy' funeral, his body tossed unceremoniously onto some waste land, well away from the 'Soldier's' house on Alma Road.

He took a deep breath and sighed satisfyingly as he gazed at his prize and mulled over his options. Not safe to keep it here and he sure as shit couldn't bank it...No, it would have to go to the left luggage locker with the rest of his cash, along with the revolver.

He considered his priorities. He could afford a better ride now, time the old Ford went anyway. A nigger in a busted up Cortina was beggin' for a pull...Keep a grand or so back for a new set of wheels...Something nondescript, grey and unremarkable, one o' they Volvo's or some other 'old man's' shit.

He pursed his lips and remembered the rush he had felt. Taking down the 'Soldier's' blues had been intoxicating. He stared again at the pile of cash...an hour's work.

His heart beat a little quicker as a crazy idea started to formulate.

*****

The station armoury, accessed via a heavy metal door to the side of the front office, was small, windowless and claustrophobic. A thin layer of dust lay atop two tall grey metal cabinets standing against the far wall.

To the left hand side of the room, a rubber topped table, equally coated in fine dust, stood above two smaller metal cabinets which had been pushed back against the skirting board. A single dim bulkhead light, provided meagre lighting. The air inside was musty, stale and Alan wrinkled his nose up in distaste.

"Christ Ron, it's like Tutankhamun's tomb in 'ere, when was it last cleaned out?"

The Station Sergeant shrugged his shoulders. "Beats me Alan lad, not my normal domain, cleaners aren't allowed in for obvious reasons. It could sit undiscovered for another thousand years for all I care…Forrester wants it auditin' so…"

Alan knelt in front of the first of the olive green cabinets situated beneath the table and twisted the central handle. The double doors opened with a sharp protest from the hinges.

"Jesus…It's not even locked Sarge." Alan said, looking up to where his mentor stood with his back against the steel door jamb.

Sergeant Dennison shrugged disinterestedly. "Outer door's kept locked. I s'pose if they need to get to the guns in a hurry, they don't want to 'ave to find more than one key…an' if by chance the fuckin' Belfast Brigade stormed the buildin' after our firearms, they'd have to get passed 'gunner' Bentley out there."

Alan smiled at his Sergeant's sardonic wit. "Derek not your flavour of the month then Ron?"

"'E's a fuckin' idiot." the Sergeant retorted flatly. "I could forgive 'im that…bein' as 'ow its prob'ly genetic, but 'e's a lazy bastard as well…Hear about 'is last yearly appraisal with 'Geordie' Childs?"

Alan shook his head; he stood up and leaned against the table top, eager to hear the Sergeant's tale.

"Fucknuts out there is up for his yearly staff appraisal. Superintendent Childs calls 'im in and tells 'im to sit down…scans through 'is personnel record, looks up an' says

'Well PC Bentley, you've got twelve years' service in…'
Bentley stops 'im an' says, 'it's fifteen Sir, I've got fifteen years in'…'Geordie' says…You've 'ad three years on the fucken' sick you lazy twat…'

The Station Sergeant's gravelly laughter was infectious and Alan chuckled as he bent down again to inspect the contents of the first cabinet.

A pressed steel rack held five revolvers, all of which were secured with a thin metal rod, fed through each of the five trigger guards and padlocked to a ring on the left hand frame of the cabinet. The open padlock swung gently on the welded ring.

Alan shook his head in despair at the lack of security.

Beneath the rack, scattered haphazardly across the base of the cabinet, were grey plastic snap wallets, each designed to hold six rounds. "Got your pad ready Sarge?" Alan asked, looking up to his old mentor.

"I 'ave Pendle lad…Read 'em an' weep." The old Sergeant said nodding.

Alan thumbed each of the knurled release studs on the revolvers. He noted that all thirty chambers were empty and snapped the cylinders shut. "Right Sarge, five times Police issue Smith and Wesson .38 caliber revolvers, with accompanying leather holsters, which looking at the state of them, were first used during the Balkan Street siege…all weapons proved…Need the serial numbers?"

The old Sergeant scrolled his pipe stem down the list on his clipboard. "Nah…five is says 'ere and five there is…Next."

The laborious task of counting all the rounds within their wallets proved to be too much for the ancient mariner, who looked around impatiently and busied himself fingering strands of rich dark tobacco from a plastic pouch into the bowl of his pipe.

Alan snapped the last of the wallets closed. "Twenty wallets, all containing six rounds of .38 caliber. One hundred and twenty rounds in all Sarge." Alan looked up; his Sergeant was patting his trouser pockets. "My bleedin' lighter's gone walkabout…chuck us yours Alan."

Alan adopted a quizzical look. "It's your station Sarge, and far be it from me to question your obviously superior intellect, but…do you think it's a good idea to stoke up in here?"

The Sergeant considered Alan's advice for a moment, he sighed dejectedly and slipped the pipe back into the top pocket of his shirt. "'ow many bullets?"

Alan smiled as his Sergeants impatience. "One hundred and twenty Sarge all present and correct." The Sergeant glanced down his sheet and nodded.

Alan stood up and brushed the dust from the knees of his trousers. "You still on with that shipbuilding of yours Sarge?...What's it called….the 'Penelope' or something?"

The old Sergeant smiled. "It's not a ship you fuckin' landlubber, it's a boat, a narrow boat to be precise. A ship is something which is big enough to carry a boat…like lifeboats see…an' its not an 'it'…boats are always referred to as 'she'…"

"Yeah, what's that about?" Alan asked.

Sergeant Dennison raised an index finger. "Ah, now you see Pendle lad…its 'istoric…A lot of old matelots will tell you it's 'cos a boat, like a woman is unpredictable….but the truth is….most boats are regarded as being a mother figure to all the matelots servin' on 'er…Back in the day, they even 'ad carved female figureheads and they'd give their oaks female names."

"Yours must be about ready eh?...When's the great launch ceremony…?"

"You've missed it lad, she's sat down at Brammerton on the Broads, an' in exactly sixty six days, I shall be livin' on 'er." The old Sergeant's eyes dropped to the floor and he sighed sorrowfully. "Course…I'll be on my own now our Penny's gone…" He looked up and forced a half smile. "Not 'ow we 'ad it planned out Alan lad…..always reckoned on me an' the Wife enjoyin' my retirement chuggin' about on the Broads. I'll tell you lad, there's nowt certain in life. Here's me, never gave a toss about anything, been on the 'baccy all my life an' no stranger to the rum either…My Penny were a good Methodist, never missed a Sunday service, stayed clear of drink an' never touched a cigarette in 'er life…lung cancer took her in four months…" Alan nodded respectfully and for a moment, there was an awkward silence between them.

He patted his old friend on the shoulder. "I'll finish this Ron, leave us your pad an' pencil, you get yourself off for a smoke, I'll give you a shout if there's any problems."

The Sergeant brightened slightly; he wiped at his eyes with the back of his hand and nodded appreciatively. "You know, Alan lad, when they sent the old 'Illustrious' up for scrap back in fifty five, I knew it was time to get out the Navy…Ten years I'd served on her, man and boy…Somehow you just know when it's the right time to go…This job's fucked now…God botherin' twats like like Forrester runnin' the show…Three days 'e gave me…three days compassionate leave when our Penny died. You're on your own Alan lad, you can't rely on anyone anymore…'cept for your mates. Don't expect this job to form square to protect you…Just get your time in…take the pension an' fuck off …an' don't look back at the yard arm as you walk away."

Alan blew out his cheeks. "Jesus Ron, I've got nearly twenty years to do yet."

The old Sergeant half smiled. "Good luck with that lad."

*****

Pc Barnett slowly rotated his ballpoint between his fingers and looked again at the clock above the Traffic office door. Nearly eleven o'clock and there was still no sign of his Tutor. His eyes wandered across to the vehicle disposition board and the two sets of keys for Pc Morrisey's Ford Granada hanging from the hook. The same hook across from which, was the remarks column, in which Sergeant Kemp had scrawled: '*807W to go to CG...collect new Cav pls*' and as an afterthought, he had added a large asterisk and *'remember to swap equipment'*.

The 'Aide' reached for the telephone and glanced down the list of useful telephone numbers pinned to the wall at the side of the Sergeant's desk.

"Central...David speaking."

"Hello mate, its Pc Barnett from Moorwood Road Traffic. I understand there's a replacement car to collect."

"Where are you from again?"

"Moorwood."

"Traffic you say?"

"Yes." Pc Barnett said, sighing with frustration, but resisting the almost overpowering urge to apologise to the mechanic for his mistake in previously speaking in Swahili.

"Hang on a 'sec."

Pc Barnett heard the muted tones of the mechanic as he shouted out to someone, presumably the garage foreman. A response echoed back in the cavernous garage but was inaudible.

"Hello..."

"Yeah, go on." The 'Aide' replied.

"There's a Granada to come in...807W an' yer new Vauxhall's ready...But think on, it's Sat'day. We're only here while one o'clock."

The 'Aide' thanked the grease monkey for his assistance and dropped the telephone handset back onto its cradle. He slumped back into his chair and pondered on the situation.

Oldfield wouldn't be in. He'd take the whole shift off wouldn't he?...might as well...Once you've called in sick, it's recorded as a full day on your record so might as well make the most of it...and Alan wouldn't get finished any time soon, once him an' old Sergeant Dennison started swapping war stories..."

Launching himself out of his seat, the 'Aide' grabbed his yellow fluorescent jacket from where it hung over the back of his chair. He patted the top pocket to double check that he had at least got a pad of HORT/1's and his pocket note book and reached up, snatching the keys from the hook.

*****

The Ford Granada looked old, box like and worn out. It sat like a behemoth between two of the new modern Vauxhall Cavaliers. Pristine, their fluorescent markings and Force crests, vivid, crisp and bright against unblemished white paintwork.

Charlie Morrisey's 'Granny', appeared somehow out of place, a shire horse amongst stallions. Out of time, and strangely out of place. A throwback to the times when the Road Traffic Department had been the flagship of the Force. A time when most members of the motoring public were lucky enough to be driving an Escort, an Avenger or a Marina, small, economically engined family saloons, no match for the 28S Granada's or the Rover SD1's with their thirsty V8's.

The sight of one of the powerful Traffic cars looming up in a rear view mirror, headlights flashing, sirens yelping and a bank of the new American style roof lights rotating, was sufficient to cause even those drivers rash enough, either through false bravado or the stupefying effects of alcohol or drugs, to come down on the middle pedal, instead of opting for the one on their right.

The paintwork on Charlie's Granada was yellowing. The once gleaming bodywork now dulled with a patina of minute swirls where the plastic flails of the station car wash had whipped the lacquer to an almost matt finish. The old pattern red side stripes had now faded to a dull pink and were slowly releasing their adhesion with the body panels. The Queen's crown above the Force crest in the center of the door panel was missing, although its distinctive shape could still be discerned, where road grime had adhered to the sticky residue left by the self-adhesive backing.

A faint hint of discolouration and a bubbling of the paint along the lower edges of the door skins and wheel arches, was a tell-tale sign of the slow progress of corrosion and another winter patrolling roads sprayed with rock salt, would no doubt see the cancerous bubbles bursting through the wafer thin paint.

Pc Barnett slipped the key into the door lock and with a twist, the central locking system activated with a dull thud. As he opened the driver's door, it dropped slightly on its hinges and his nostrils were immediately assailed by a strangely antique odour. An 'old car' smell, that no amount of air fresheners or valeting would ever eradicate. It was the stale smell of a hundred thousand cigarettes, the fish and chips, the Chinese and Indian takeaways eaten hurriedly by the road side, a rancid hint of sour milk, obtained for the office coffee 'swindle', but spilled during a spontaneous pursuit on the way back in. The smell of hundreds of handcuffed 'passengers', reeking of stale beer, blood and vomit which had permeated into the very fibres of the interior.

The 'Granny' had given good service, worthy of a mention in dispatches as it was retired out to the Central Garage. It would be stripped of all its markings and official electrics and driven ignominiously through the local auction block, where the grommets filling the aerial holes in the roof, would attract knowing nudges from the second hand car dealers.

Pc Barnett twisted the key in the ignition. The dashboard lights illuminated and needle in the fuel gauge crept tentatively up from the red section. The 'Aide' nodded to himself. Almost a quarter of a tank, more than enough to get down to the Central Garage. He twisted the key again and the V6 Cologne fired up immediately.

There was the usual disturbing rattle emanating from the top end of the engine which quickly disappeared as the hydraulic tappet buckets filled with oil. The oil pressure gauge hesitated momentarily, then swung lazily across into the green.

Pulling the log book out from where it was wedged between the front passenger seat and the center console, the 'Aide' checked the last recorded mileage, subconsciously glancing up to the odometer. One hundred and thirty eight thousand, two hundred and forty three. The mileage tallied.

His finger index finger hesitated over the power button for the VHF radio shoehorned into the dashboard facia, but recalling Alan's words, decided that his advice had been sound. What the Force Control Operator didn't know, wouldn't be the cause of any complicated explanations as to why he couldn't attend at an alarm call, or just help out with a few 'immediate's' while the early turn crews were in for meal.

No, eleven miles down to the City and eleven back in one of the new 'Cav's' and his collar number first in the virgin log book.

*****

Fate, whilst organising events surrounding the ultimate demise of all three hundred and twenty nine passengers aboard Air India flight 182 over the Irish Sea, took a moment out. Mindful of the earlier hand played in the 'Aide's' future, it caused a minute fluctuation in the voltage output of a vehicle alternator, just sufficient so as to cause the filament in the rear offside brake light bulb to overheat and burn out. Coincidentally, at the same moment that 'Midnight' Lyburn was applying his brakes for the red traffic light ahead.

Although conscious and very wary of the presence of 'Babylon' in his rear view mirror, he was oblivious to the moving road traffic offence he was now committing, The offence was not lost on the 'Aide' who was following the old Cortina in Pc Morrisey's Granada.

Stopping to the rear of the Ford, the 'Aide' set the handbrake and racked his brain for a moment and whilst waiting for the lights to change, he jotted down the Ford's registration number in his green 'supplementary' pocket notebook...'Road Vehicles Registration and Lighting?...Construction and Use?...The 'Aide' frowned with frustration. Oldfield would have reeled off the Act and Section in an instant.

With a sigh, he dismissed his lack of knowledge as unimportant for the time being, the driver in front wouldn't have a clue anyway, and in any case, he could look up the offence when he got back to the Traffic office. Suffice to say, a defective brake light was an easy addition to his monthly 'blood sheet'.

'Midnight' glanced furtively up at his rear view mirror. His mind raced, 'Babylon' was on his own, but the rucksack containing the cash would take some explaining away if his vehicle was searched. The revolver, wrapped in the old 'T' shirt would be his undoing, it would cost him thirty years, minimum.

His eyes skipped to the other side of the Ring Road junction and the exit slip road leading into a Council housing estate in the process of being demolished.

The traffic lights seemed to take an interminable time to change. 'Midnight' reached across to the front passenger seat and unzipped the rucksack. With a cautious eye on the rear view mirror, he rummaged amongst the wads of notes until his fingers felt the solid shape of the revolver. Quickly he shook it free of the folds of its wrapping and stuffed it into the side pocket of his denim jacket. 'Babylon' might just feel confident enough, even on his own, to carry out a cursory search of his vehicle, but a body search, in public view, not likely. But not worth the risk.

'Midnight' took a deep breath as the lights changed. He slipped the Cortina into gear and indicated a right turn. His foot shook slightly as he released the clutch and slowly moved off into the slip road. He willed the Traffic car to continue along the Ring Road.

The 'Aide' dropped his green unofficial notebook into the side door pocket of the patrol car, glanced in his rear view mirror, he slipped the 'Granny' into first gear and flicked the indicator stalk.

*****

The first of the tall grey cabinets at the rear of the armoury opened with a dry, high pitched complaint from its hinges. Alan became aware of the fragrant smell of Balkan Sobranie pipe tobacco and realised without looking around, that his Sergeant had returned.

Placing the inventory pad down on the table top, his eyes fell on the contents of the cabinet. A pair of Remington pump action shotguns had been correctly stored, their stocks and barrel ends secured within the internal rack and their actions left rearwards to show that their breaches were empty. Alan looked back and nodded to his old mentor and ran a finger down the list on the sheet. 'Remington 870 pump action shotguns x 2'. He glanced back to the shelf on the far right of the cabinet and counted off the cartridge boxes. "Six times boxes of Eley twelve bore triple 'A' and two of rifled slug, you want them opening and counting Ron?"

"Does it just say 'ow many boxes there should be?" The Sergeant asked, pointing his pipe stem at the clipboard.

Alan checked the list and nodded.

"There yer go then, no point in complicatin' things, crack on lad. There's breakfast to be 'ad, I can 'ear Edie scrapin' the toast…an' the one armed bandit's callin' me."

Alan smiled and closed the first of the metal cabinets. He leaned back against the table top. "I get the distinct impression that your heart's not altogether in this task Ron."

The old Sergeant smiled wanly. "My hearts down on the Norfolk Broads Alan lad, along with our Penny's ashes."

Alan nodded slowly and for the first time, noticed how worn out and tired his old friend looked.

"You look pissed off in the extreme Sarge." Alan said, with a concerned tone in his voice.

"To be fair Alan." The Sergeant replied, sighing deeply, "I'd 'ad enough months ago, maybe even for the last couple of years. I'm just seein' the last few days out now and to be honest, much as I've loved the job, when I get to hand in my warrant card, it'll be like havin' a millstone lifted from round my neck".

"That bad eh?" Alan said.

His old friend smiled weakly. "You've got a fair way to go yet Alan, what is it, nineteen, twenty years to do? You can bet by the time you get to my stage of service, the job'll bear no resemblance to what it was when you joined. Cops were sayin' that the job was fucked when I signed up back in fifty five, but now...Look at what we've 'ad to put up with over the last twelve months, this new 'pace' thing, utter bollocks." he snorted, "Brought in by the bleedin' heart liberals in the gov'ment and the likes of that fuckin' idiot Scarman...suckin' up to the blacks...Good old fashioned policin's what we need to get back to, you'll see Alan, you mark my words lad, as soon as they get a few black faces in parliament, then you'll start to feel the squeeze."

Alan furrowed his brow and pursed his lips as if deep in thought. "It's all down to the 'Met' and the race riots in Brixton, that's what brought it all about Sarge, that and the 'Sus' law...Coupled with the fact that we've been caught being somewhat 'economical with the truth' too many times in Court. Noble cause corruption just won't cut it anymore...I mean, I'm not particularly enamoured with the new police and criminal evidence act, but how long did we think we'd get away with just feeling someone's collar, banging him up in a cell while we disappeared up to the Traffic office, had a brew and wrote up his interview in our notebooks? How many times have you taken the oath and given evidence that your notes were a true and accurate recollection of the interview and that they were made up as soon as practicable afterwards and…Swearing blind that he'd never asked for a solicitor…We've all got away with it for years Ron and the Magistrates always came down on our side…This tape recording of interviews was bound to come in. We're all going to have to learn how to actually 'interview' people, which is a bit of a worry when you consider some of the Neanderthals we work with."

"The right people 'ave always got sent down Alan." His Sergeant said decidedly. "Just deserts lad, protectin' the public from the wrongdoer, that's what it's all about." He jabbed his pipe stem back between his teeth and nodded emphatically.

Alan pushed his hands deep into his trouser pockets. "Just between you and me Ron, did you ever feel bad about the way we got Delroy Francis sent down?"

The old Sergeant sucked thoughtfully on the stem of his pipe. "Remind me, I've slept since then."

"Come on Sarge, Delroy Francis was the sooty from Conway Terrace, strongly in the frame for all the rapes in the sheltered housing bungalows down on Cromwell Road. All the victims were old ladies, some in their eighties. He did five or six over a nine month period."

The Sergeant nodded. "I remember it, two, maybe three years ago…Used to beat the shit out of 'em…"

"That's the fella, you were Custody Sergeant then. Our boy Delroy had a penchant for raping wrinklies, some of them were even sodomised. He even used to have a shit on the front room carpet just to add to the humiliation…it was like his calling card…Jemmied his way in through bathroom windows. Masked up, he'd rape them in their own beds."

The Sergeant nodded and hummed his acknowledgment through his teeth. "Big ugly bastard, shaved head…looked like 'im out of Hot Chocolate but not as good lookin'."

"That's the badger...'member how he ended up going down?" Alan asked inquisitively.

The Sergeant shook his head. "Nah...I remember C.I.D. 'ad 'im down as favourite, but they were strugglin' to catch the bastard bang to rights."

Alan smiled knowingly. "That's right Ron, they were struggling because our friend Delroy was a lot smarter than your average nigger. He was careful, never uttered a word so as not to give his accent way. Wore gloves and a ski mask, every time. He even wore a pair of socks over his trainers, no foot or fingerprints and no description of his face from any of his victims. The last one he raped was nearly ninety for Christ's sake. Did you see the hospital photographs? She looked like she'd been hit by a bus, one more punch in the face and it might have ended up being a murder. God knows how, but she managed to pull the emergency cord by the side of her bed and the housing manager raised the alarm. Me and Sully were on half nights, we got the shout, picked up the night Detective from the 'Dog and Gun', it was Davy Jepson as I recall, anyway, we shot straight round to his crib and Delroy gets his collar felt. The bastard hadn't even had time to get a wash, you could still smell the lavender on him. Me and Sully did the transport job back to the nick, and your right, he was an ugly bastard, stared at me in the rear view mirror all the way back to Moorwood, ugliest nigger I've ever seen. His eyes were dead Ron, like piss holes in the snow, made the hairs on the back of my neck stand up."

His old friend smiled weakly and nodded. "Yeah, I remember 'im. Good lock up."

Alan nodded. "Good lock up, but Francis wouldn't have it Ron. I was 'second jockey' on the first interview. Our friend Delroy just sat there with a big shit eating grin on his face all the way through it. He knew we had fuck all."

The Sergeant sucked on his pipe. The solidifying tobacco juice in the bowl gurgled wetly.

Alan raised his eyebrows and nodded knowingly at his old friend. "It was his trainers Ron, remember? Davy Jepson got them out of Francis' property bag, not signed out of course...I drove Jepson back to the scene. We were back there well before the Studio man turned up...Jepson puts Francis' trainers on and leaves perfect imprints in the flower bed under the window and a muddy footprint on the toilet seat in the bathroom. His trainers went back into his property bag, an' no one was any the wiser. 'Course, Delroy howled 'fit up' but he still went down the steps for fifteen."

"Conscience prickin' you a bit, is it?" his old friend asked.

Alan shrugged his shoulders. "Sometimes...I know all the rapes stopped, and we all *knew* that Francis had done them, but of all the stunts I've pulled, and there's been a few over the years Sarge, that job with Francis...That stare he gave us from the dock as they took him down...Davy Jepson winked at him...but I felt...I don't know Ron..." Alan paused, searching for the right word.

The old Sergeant pointed his pipe stem at Alan. "That bastard got what 'e deserved...Look lad, you can do all the soul searchin' you want. Them old biddies...every one of 'em was somebody's granny. I'd 'ave given 'im thirty never mind fifteen, and I'd 'ave 'ad 'is bollocks removed with a blunt spoon....The punishment fitted the crime. 'Ow Francis was written up? Come on Alan," the old Sergeant snorted. "It's no different from you givin' evidence that the driver was stopped 'cos you observed 'is motor wanderin' in the carriageway, when in fact, you an' Sully 'ad prob'ly been 'sat' for an hour waitin' on 'im to come out the pub...You know 'im...You know 'e always drives 'ome pissed...so yer 'avin' 'im. Yer make it fit...Or what about addin' just a few extra miles an 'our onto yer speeder, 'cos 'e's a known travellin' burglar, an' what's the best way to inconvenience 'im?...get the twat twelve points on 'is licence, get 'im disqualified. It's all ways an' means Alan, practical policin', call it what you want. We all 'ave a line we're willin' to cross for what we see as a just cause…The line's closer to some than it is for others that's all…If it feels right in 'ere," the Sergeant said, tapping the area over his heart with his pipe stem, "then it's the right thing to do."

Alan sighed, nodded and reached for the inventory pad. "I'll finish up here Ron, you get off for your breakfast if you want."

The old Sergeant beamed. "That's my boy, I'll be in the bar, feedin' the bandit, give us a shout if yer need me."

*****

'Midnight' cursed under his breath as he watched the Granada following him into the slip road. The second set of lights were at red. He stopped at the white line and as the cars set off from the lights on the opposite dual carriageway. His eyes darted from his rear view mirror to the road leading into the housing estate.

The old estate of back to back terraced houses was being demolished and a work scarred JCB sat at a crazy angle atop a mound of crushed bricks and roof tiles. Rusting lengths of mulch filled guttering and shattered cast iron fall pipes, poked upward like skeletal fingers from the field of devastation.

The pavements flags were cracked and broken and the road surface was covered in a thick film of glutinous mud, deposited by the tyres of the wagons, as they had borne the debris away from the site.

His breathing quickened and he felt his heart pounding in his chest and the blood rushing in his ears. He weighed up his options. He told himself that he was overreacting. 'Babylon' might just be visiting someone in one of the few remaining houses, come to take a statement or a report of theft or burglary, but if 'Babylon' had followed him off the Ring Road to stop him, he knew his choices were limited. He could run, but he knew that his old Cortina would be no match for the more powerful

Granada. He'd be all over him *and* on his radio to summon the rest of his mates. They'd be on him like a pack of hyenas. If he was taken, it'd all be over. The revolver would tie him to the McKnight killing *and* that of 'Soldier' Garrison's 'Manager'. It'd be thirty years, this time, he thought.

He mulled the thought of it over in his mind, thirty years in a cell twelve by eight, slopping out, the overbearing discipline and the beatings. The five stretch in Holdthorpe had been hard enough, but he had tasted freedom again and of late, it tasted good.

No, he decided, if it was for him, he'd brazen it out. He'd make the usual excuses as to why he wasn't carrying his driving licence or any of his 'docs'. He'd take the HORT/1 and agree to produce them within seven days. By the time 'Babylon' realised that he'd failed to produce, the Cortina would be down in Dickinson's scrap yard and the summons would be returned 'Not known at this address'.

He repeated his assumed name to himself and memorised a false address and date of birth. Reason for his journey? Just looking for an old mate Officer, used to live down the bottom end of the estate, hope his crib's still standing.

The lights changed and 'Midnight' set off, across the dual carriageway and onto the mud spattered road leading into the estate.

A single flash of the Granada's headlights in his rear view mirror confirmed his worst fears. His heart sank, but he drove on for a few more yards, taking the Traffic car deeper into the estate and further away from the Ring Road traffic. A second flash, double this time, more demanding.

'Midnight' raised a hand, acknowledging the Traffic man's signal and slowly pulled the Cortina across to the nearside kerb edge, the tyres crunching on the broken glass and pulverised brick. "Be cool mo'fucker" he whispered to himself, as he came to a halt and set the handbrake.

The 'Aide' activated the rear flashing red lights and was surprised to see that the tall Negro driver had already left his vehicle and was walking towards his Traffic car. He was smiling, not displaying the usual threatening scowl he had expected.

The 'Aide' opened his door and stepped out to greet the approaching driver and sighed despondently as his new Russell and Bromley's sank up to their welts in the thick slurry of mud.

"What's the problem Officer?" 'Midnight' asked, maintaining his reassuring smile.

"You've a brake light out driver…offside." The 'Aide' said, pointing to the Cortina's rear light cluster. "Noticed it at the traffic lights."

'Midnight' pushed his hands deeper into the pockets of his denim jacket, his right hand cupped around the frame of the revolver to disguise its shape. He shrugged his shoulders and shook his head slowly.

"Sorry man…Look, I'll get a new one fitted today ok?...sorry 'bout that."

"Is it your car driver?" The 'Aide' asked, dropping into the set routine he had learned from his Tutor.

'Midnight' nodded. "Yeah, only had it a few days though." he said, knowing that if 'Babylon' checked, it would come up with previous keeper details only. "New logbook didn't come through yet." he offered.

The 'Aide' nodded knowingly. "Got any of your documents with you driver?"

'Midnight' shook his head. "All back at my crib." he said, looking down at the fresh face of the young Traffic cop. "Mo'fucker don't even shave yet" he thought to himself.

"Take a seat." The 'Aide' said, opening the rear door of the patrol car.

'Midnight' looked down at his trainers now caked in mud. "You sure you want all this shit on your carpets man?" he asked, nodding down toward the road surface.

The 'Aide' shrugged his shoulders nonchalantly. "Just try and keep your feet on the rubber mats driver, I won't keep you long."

'Midnight' kept his hands in his pockets and slipped in behind the driver's seat. He closed the door himself, but left it just off the latch, knowing that the child locks might be on.

The 'Aide' took his seat and half turned so that he could see the reflection of 'Midnight's' face in the rear view mirror. "It's only a brake light driver, but I'm going to report you for the offence ok?"

'Midnight' sighed theatrically, with the pretence of one who actually gave a shit.

"Under the police and criminal evidence act, I have to tell you, that although you are sat in my vehicle, you're not under arrest, you can leave at any time and you're entitled to free legal advice. However, you are going to be reported for the offence and as such, I require you to provide me with your correct name, address and date of birth, if you ref..."

"Hey...no problem man." 'Midnight' interrupted, "You got your job to do..."

"Let me finish please driver. It's important that you understand the new rules." the 'Aide' said, holding up a cautionary hand. "If you cannot provide me with any form of identity or if you refuse to provide me with your name and address...or, if I believe that the details you provide are false, under section twenty five of pace, you *will* be arrested...do you understand?"

The 'Aide' stared unflinchingly at the reflection in his rear view mirror, awaiting a response

'Midnight' furrowed his brow. "For a busted brake light?"
The 'Aide' reached into the top pocket of his fluorescent jacket for his pad of 'producers'. "It's not about the specific offence driver. The new rules are about making sure I can get a summons served if you fail to produce any of your documents. So, if we can start with your name..."

'Midnight' suddenly realised that he had seriously misjudged the situation. Times, as well as the law, had clearly changed. He'd got no form of identity. If 'Babylon' ran the car through the system, it'd come back with someone else's details.

He was miles away from the 'Badlands', 'Babylon' was on his own turf, he would feel confident and secure. No threat of a brick through his windscreen here, no group of youngbloods to gather around his patroller and rock it violently on its suspension, none to lean against the door trapping 'Babylon' in his seat whilst they set a 'brother' free. No matter what details he gave, this young cop would take him anyway. The prospect of arrest was too much to risk.

In a heartbeat the decision was made.

His eyes flitted across to the demolition site. It was deserted. The young cop's pen was poised over the pad of 'producers' and he was still looking expectantly into the rear view mirror.

Their eyes met.

It was perhaps the coldness he saw in the reflection, the nervous shifting of the driver's gaze to the rear window, a sudden aurora of electricity within the vehicle which made the hairs on the back of the 'Aide's' neck bristle and caused his sixth sense to scream 'assistance required'. He reached out toward the power button on the VHF radio.

With that action and in the same instant, the 'Aide's' fate was sealed.

'Midnight' lunged forwards. With his left hand, he reached over the top of the driver's seat and hooked two fingers down the back of the 'Aide's' shirt collar, wrenching him violently back into his seat. His right hand came free of his jacket pocket, his finger already curled around the trigger of the revolver.

The 'Aide' retched and choked, his mind numbed by the sudden shock of the assault. He arched his back in an attempt to ease the restriction at his throat. His legs flailed as he fought for breath, his mud caked shoes striking the underside of the steering column, spattering the carpets and door panel with the tell-tale signs of a violent struggle.

'Midnight' pushed the barrel end of the revolver hard into the soft cloth covering the back of the driver's seat. He squeezed his eyes tight shut and pulled the trigger twice in quick succession.

In the closed confines of the patrol car, the bark from the revolver was deafening.

He felt the jolt of the 'Aide's' body through his fingers as the two small rounds exploded through the foam rubber of the seat. They passed through the seat backrest and the thin material of the 'Aide's' fluorescent yellow jacket at almost eight hundred feet per second and created a lead snowstorm as they splintered and shattered against his spine.

The distorted particles of lead, some now only the size of shotgun pellets, ricocheted off the 'Aide's' vertebra and tore into his lungs, aorta and heart.

'Midnight' gripped the shirt collar tighter, pulling his victim firmly back into his seat. He felt the 'Aide' convulse.

He shot a panicked glance out through the rear window of the patrol car. The road behind was still clear. The traffic on the Ring Road continued in its never ending flow around the outskirts of the City. The flashing red lights at the rear of the patrol car within the estate might be the source of a little interest, but at best, worthy of perhaps a cursory glance, but nothing more. Simply another suffering motorist being persecuted at the hands of the local Traffic cops.

'Midnight' felt the 'Aide' becoming weaker. His kicking had diminished, his left leg now just twitched and for a moment, thumped loudly against the plastic centre console. His head drooped forwards as his heart palpitated and 'Midnight' could hear the liquid rattle of laboured breathing. The 'Aide' gave a last watery cough and a fine spume of bright red blood misted the instrument panel.

The expelled gasses and burned cordite from the expended rounds filled the interior of the Granada, 'Midnight's' eyes watered and he gagged at the stench.

The 'Aide' was motionless. 'Midnight' released his grip on the collar and frantically scanned the demolition site for movement. The 'Aide's' head slumped forwards, his chin resting on the top of the Burndept radio hanging in its webbing harness around his neck.

With a backward glance through the rear screen, 'Midnight' confirmed that the traffic on the Ring Road continued its unabated flow. He quickly stuffed the revolver back into his jacket pocket and with his elbow, nudged the passenger door open.

*****

Michael grunted with effort as he heaved himself up and out of the deep trench where the old footings had been excavated. The scuffed toe caps of his worn out shoes slipped and scraped along the smooth sides of the trench as he scrambled to gain a foothold in the damp clay walls. As he heaved himself up with muscle wasted arms, he winced as the thin flesh on the inside of his forearms was assailed by the sharp shards of crushed brick and debris at the side of the trench.

He kept a tight grasp on the two short lengths of lead piping he had spotted at the bottom of the trench and with a final effort, hoisted himself clear and tossed his precious find into the battered pram to join the collection of twisted hinges and window latches ignored by the demolition men.

As he stood up to catch his breath, with dismay, he looked down at the front of his trousers and was immediately filled with childlike trepidation at the damp clay and red brick dust which was now deeply engrained into the material. His 'Mam' would shout at him and if he had been drinking, the beating from the latest 'Uncle' to appear on the scene, would be savage, but no more than he had become accustomed to over the years.

Michael panicked and wiped at the front of his trousers with hands that were equally as filthy. His fingernails were torn and broken where he had dug his fingers deep into the rubble to retrieve the discarded scrap metal and the wiping with hands still covered in mud, only made the matter worse.

The berating he would receive from his Mother was suddenly forgotten, as his attention was diverted to the Police car down on the road leading into the estate.

Michael gave out a single grunt of expectant pleasure and he grabbed for the twisted pram handle. He quickly made his way across the site and down toward the main road, the buckled wheels of his pram bouncing wildly over the crushed detritus. He hoped that the Policeman was one that he knew, one of the friendly ones who would sometimes hand him a sandwich or a piece of cake from the plastic boxes they all carried, or a proper cigarette, from a packet, a whole one all to himself instead of one of the squashed tab ends he retrieved from the gutters and pavements.

Michael's inane smile disappeared from his face and was replaced with a confused frown as from the edge of the pavement; he peered cautiously into the patrol car.

## **Twenty Eight**

Sir Angus Mayhew KBE QPM, stood up straight and stretched. He placed his hands on his hips and slowly arched his back to ease the ache from the sciatic nerve which constantly nagged at him whilst gardening.

With his fingertips, he kneaded the small of his back as he surveyed the neatly manicured garden and as the pins and needles down the back of his legs receded and the pain slowly subsided, he withdrew his pipe from the pocket of his moleskins.

The weeds he decided, would never abate their constant assault on his shrubberies and flower beds, but he did his best thinking whilst attempting to hold back the onslaught and the sight of the flower beds in full bloom was well worth the effort. A hot bath and a balloon glass of Courvoisier warmed by heat of his hand would soon put the world to rights.

He reached across to the gloriously flowering Semperfloren and recovered the long handled hoe he had rested gently against the pure white flower heads. Using the hoe to steady himself, he balanced on his right foot and raising his left, he tapped the bowl of his briar against the heel of his favourite gardening brogues. The fine white ash fell way and in the slight breeze, disappeared amongst the Hydrangea and Abelia Grandiflora.

He patted the pocket of his hacking jacket and felt for the outline of his tobacco pouch. Whilst he rubbed the rich dark strands of Borkum Riff between the palms of his hands, he let his eyes roam across the expanse of his lawn. He nodded with satisfaction. It had recovered well from the scarification and vigorous raking it had received that April.

He'd considered that at the time, he might have been a little aggressive, but the new seeds had taken well, the brown patches had filled in nicely and the moss and thatch were for this year at least, eradicated.

Tamping the ball of tobacco down into the bowl of his pipe, he closed his eyes and turned to face the house, letting the early afternoon sun bathe his face.

His wife Elspeth, opened one of the windows in the day room which overlooked the garden; she leaned out and waved to attract his attention. "Off with the fairies again." she thought to herself, seeing him standing with his face toward the heavens.

"Angus dear...Telephone." she called out.

Sir Angus frowned, annoyed that his peace and tranquillity had been rudely interrupted. "If it's that chap from Mercedes again, tell him we haven't come to a decision yet."

His Wife shook her head. "It's Moorwood dear…Chief Superintendent Sommerville."

"John Sommerville…on a Saturday?" he thought to himself, wondering what could have dragged his old friend and latter day partner in CID away from the golf course.

"Two minutes." he called back.

Stabbing the flat blade of the hoe into the freshly turned soil, he walked back toward the house with a gnawing sense of foreboding.

His Wife frowned as she noticed that he had not removed his gardening shoes before entering the house. "Will you take tea now, dear?"

Sir Angus shook his head. "It's a little early Elly, I want to get the lawn borders cut back…What's John want, did he say?"

"No, but he's certainly not his usual jovial self I must say. It's the phone by the bookcase…Do wipe your feet dear, I've just had the carpets cleaned."

*****

"John." Sir Angus said into the mouthpiece, looking out through the French windows to his lawn.

"Angus, there's been another shooting in 'C' Division, Moorwood…"

Sir Angus frowned and sighed heavily. "Christ, John, that's the third in as many we…"

"Angus…It's one of our own."

"Oh dear God." Sir Angus said quietly. He swallowed hard and took a deep breath to compose himself.

He looked across to his Wife who was standing at the doorway. She noticed that the colour had suddenly drained from his face and that his shoulders had slumped.

"Angus?" she said worriedly, approaching him with deep concern etched across her face.

"How bad is it John?" Sir Angus asked.

"As bad as it can be I'm afraid…Constable 338 Anthony Barnett…Traffic 'Aide' at Moorwood…He was shot…twice…Life pronounced extinct at the City Infirmary."

Sir Angus listened in stoic silence as his old friend provided what few details were known.

"Was he a married man, any family?"

"He was twenty two Angus, still lived with his parents; they have a small farm in Coaxley by all accounts. I've had D.I. Frank Ellis brought in, he's running the incident room for the previous murders. All the early turn Officers have been retained on duty and the Officers on late turn have been contacted and warned to parade as soon as possible."

Sir Angus nodded slowly and looked again at his Wife who hovered by his side.

"Has the shooter been identified…taken into custody?"

"No Sir, and no witnesses at present. Apparently, the Officer was still in his patrol car when he was found, engine still running…He was shot through the back seat of his patrol car Angus…"

Sir Angus rubbed at his temple with his fingertips. "His next of kin John?"

"Being warned as we speak Angus…I've taken the liberty of having your car sent round, I thought that you might want to come in."

"Yes, yes of course, thank you John…In the meantime, ten twenty one for all firearms Officers is granted on my authority. Have them all brought in if necessary, let's get them out there, show an armed presence on the streets. I'll inform the Home Secretary…I want this bottomed John and quickly if you please…Full resources brought to bear…I'll be in within the hour."

Sir Angus calmly replaced the handset onto its cradle and turned to face his Wife. "I've lost one of my boys Elspeth

…Traffic man, twenty two years of age for God's sake." He shook his head in despair. "Shot like a dog, in broad daylight."

His Wife held her breath, her hands pressed tightly against the sides of her face, horrified.

He glanced down at his soil stained hands. "I'd better get myself cleaned up, my driver's on his way over."

His Wife nodded. "I'll get your best uniform brushed down dear." She paused. "I am so sorry." she said, placing a tender hand on his shoulder.

As a gleaming black Ford Granada pulled up outside the Chief Constable's residence, a sorrowful Detective Sergeant, accompanied by a uniformed Policewoman, knocked on a farmhouse door in Coaxley.

*****

Alan doused his face with cold water and looked up from the sink to stare at his reflection in the mirror. The redness from his weeping, alone in the Traffic office, was now hardly noticeable and he leaned forwards with his hands gripping the sides of the sink bowl, taking deep breaths to compose himself.

Barney was dead and it was down to him.

The 'Aide' had taken Charlie's 'Granny' out on his advice.

*"Barney, life is nothing without an element of risk."* Those few prophetic words echoed over and over in his mind.

He consoled himself that he had told the 'Aide' not to get involved with anything, there and back, that's all it should have been. "I guess Barney just couldn't resist it." he thought to himself.

He leant again over the sink, cupped his hands and scooped cold water up and onto his face. Shaking his head to clear the guilt, he dried himself.

The station was quiet, subdued. Alan left the toilets and entered the lower corridor, walking toward the incident room, he passed two Policewomen hugging each other, both of them in tears. At the end of the long corridor, he pushed the double doors to the incident room and entered.

All the uniforms from the early turn shift were already seated, all looked crestfallen and deep in shock.

A Policewoman wept unashamedly into a handkerchief and Alan noted that he was not the only male officer with reddening around the eyes.

With a grim face, he nodded to one or two as he went across the room to the windows which overlooked the perimeter drive. He stood and watched as the blue Task Force Transits, the Traffic cars and the 'pandas' poured in from the neighbouring Divisions. All would answer the call, there would be no complaints regarding extended shifts and although it would be authorised, there would be no overtime claims submitted. One of their own was down.

The incident room filled quickly. There was no banter, no quips or laughter, no one spoke. In solemn silence they took their seats, perhaps like Alan, they were only just managing to hold the tears of loss at bay.

There was a knocking from the table at the front of the room. Detective Inspector Frank Ellis brought the room what little order was required. Beside him stood Detective Chief Superintendent John Sommerville, who gave his D.I. a friendly pat on the shoulder before taking a seat.

D.I. Ellis looked out across the sea of disconsolate faces. He identified those who showed anger, those who were sorrowful and those who simply sat in shock, staring at their hands and wondering why.

He'd seen it before, known it before. The 'Aide' wasn't the first, he wouldn't be the last, but now was not a time for mourning, that would come later when the piper would play the lament and the streets of the City would be lined with uniforms.

Now he had to motivate his troops, every hour that was lost would make his job harder, evidence would be disposed of, the initiative would be lost.

He leaned forwards, his knuckles resting on the table top. "Now, listen to me, all of you…I know you're all down, but I want you all to put your personal thoughts aside, we've a cop killer to find, I want…"

The double doors were thrust open and Detective Chief Superintendent Sommerville rose swiftly from his chair. "On your feet for the Chief Constable."

The room rose in unison as Sir Angus Mayhew strode purposefully to the front of the room. The bright silver braiding across his epaulettes and lapels stood out starkly against the darkness of his dress uniform. "Please, please, be seated." he said almost apologetically as he approached the table at the front of the room.

He took the outstretched hand of his old friend and shook it as he nodded to the Detective Inspector. A chair was hurriedly produced and the Chief nodded his thanks. "Please carry on Inspector, I'll address the Officers in a moment."

D.I. Ellis nodded respectfully. "Thank you Sir." Again he turned to face his audience. "This is what we *know*, all else is rumour and speculation."

He paused at the arrival of a second 'serial' of Task Force Officers. "Take a seat where you can gents." There was a general shuffling of chairs and the D.I. continued.

"For the benefit of those Officers from neighbouring Divisions, firstly, thank you for your assistance…I am Detective Inspector Frank Ellis, I'll be running the investigation under the direct supervision of Detective Chief Superintendent Sommerville, who will be the Senior Investigating Officer. This is the incident room for the McKnight and Williams murders, I will come to what we believe may be a link between these shootings and the one claiming the life of our friend and colleague later."

Frank Ellis took a deep breath. "Police Constable 338 Anthony Robert Barnett was murdered at approximately eleven thirty this morning…He was shot…twice whilst conducting what looks to have been a routine vehicular stop on Bollingbrook Street. We say this because the rear 'reds' on his patrol vehicle were still flashing when he was found. The first witness at the scene came across the Officer, at first, thinking that Pc Barnett was asleep at the wheel…until he saw blood. He then ran out into the Ring Road and waved the traffic to a halt. This male has been identified as one Michael Hennigan. Hennigan who lives locally, apparently spends his time foraging for scrap metal. He can best be described as being educationally subnormal. Some of you from this Division may have come across him, always accompanied by a pram by all accounts." There were a few weak smiles and knowing nods around the room. "Hennigan is being interviewed by my Team as we speak, but first indications are that he is simply a witness and will be eliminated from the murder enquiry.

D.I. Ellis took a further deep breath. "The sorrowful facts are that Pc Barnett was shot twice with what appears at this stage, to have been a small calibre round. The shots were fired from the rear of the Ford Granada vehicle Pc Barnett was driving. Scorch marks are evident in the material to the rear of the driver's seat. As Pc Barnett's pad of 'producers' and his pen were found in the front footwell, it would appear that he was in the process of carrying out a routine document check, mud deposits were found on the floor in the rear. The same evidential residue within the front of the vehicle also suggests that Pc Barnett struggled with his assailant before he was shot."

The D.I. picked up a large plastic evidence bag from the table top and held it aloft. "PC Barnett's HORT/1 pad was still blank, but his green supplementary notebook was found in the driver's door pocket. The last page bears the registration number romeo november alpha, two two three romeo, a PNC check shows this to be a Ford Cortina in red, previous keeper details only. The colour is *not* to be relied upon, the vehicle may well be bearing false plates, but what we can say, is that the entry Pc Barnett made, is written in the same blue ink as the pen which was found in the vehicle. I know that it is common practice…"

Alan suddenly went cold and the D.I.'s words became muted.

He raised his hand slowly; the D.I. paused and nodded in his direction.

The occupants of the room turned expectant eyes toward him.

"Sirs." Alan began cautiously, mindful of the presence of his Chief Constable. "I know that vehicle. It is a Cortina and it is red. I saw it only a week or so ago, on the Ring Road, the driver was IC3 male…."

Sir Angus Mayhew raised a finger. "Expand if you would Officer."

Alan rose to his feet. "I was off duty Sir; I was on the Ring Road, on my way home. I was in my personal vehicle and that same Cortina was alongside me at the traffic lights at Kingsway. There was an IC3 driving, he was in the offside lane, the driver made a point of looking away when I pulled forwards to have a look at the excise licence. It was just natural Traffic man's curiosity Sir….habit I suppose, but…"

D.I. Ellis raised a hand. "Description?"

Alan swallowed hard. "IC3 male, late thirties, early forties, clean shaven, short cropped hair, I didn't really pay that mu…"

D.I. Ellis raised a hand, stopping Alan in mid-sentence and turned to look at his Detective Chief Superintendent.

Mr Sommerville rose to his feet and stared hard at Alan. "Officer, have you prior to, or after that date, ever *actually* seen the nominal known as James Frederick Lyburn aka 'Midnight'?"

Alan's heart missed a beat as the shock of realisation unfolded. His shoulders slumped and he closed his eyes for a second. He shook his head slowly, as if in self-recrimination. "No Sir…It never dawned on me…not until today."

"Stay behind after this briefing if you will Alan." D.I. Ellis said, before returning his gaze to the gathered Officers, their faces now showing signs of confusion.

"The scene produced a full set of tyre marks, left in mud deposited by the plant vehicles exiting the demolition site. Until they could no longer be distinguished, the vehicle we are looking for, drove along Bollingbrook Street and further into the estate. Based on the 'intel' we've got, this vehicle may well be local to us…The impressions were quite deep, so there's obviously plenty of tread on his 'boots', it's a dry day, which means that unless he's 'twigged' and had the hose pipe out, we're looking for a Ford Cortina with mud still ingrained into the tread pattern of the tyres. There's a 'snatch' plan in operation, we've got armed Officers situated at all the major road junctions. What I want…what I need from *you* ladies and gents, is a thorough street by street search. Every single street in the Division, every back street, alleyway and car park. Work your search by your normal beat areas so that there is no duplication and nothing gets missed…Use your A to Z's. If the vehicle is housed, note the location and drive on by. Use your personal sets to inform the radio room. Keep your operator informed. Only UHF sets ladies and gents. The press will no doubt be sniffing by now and we know that they scan the VHF Police band, let's keep it tight, keep it in house…If the vehicle is seen whilst mobile…and I cannot stress this strongly enough ladies and gents." DI Ellis paused and stared hard at his audience. "*No* attempt to conduct a physical stop should be made. If the intelligence is correct, the occupant or occupants should be considered to be armed and extremely dangerous and as we have seen this morning, readily prepared to use deadly force against an Officer to evade arrest. Location and direction of travel *only*. Let the AFO's do what they're trained to do…Time is of the essence ladies and gents…Find me that vehicle…If it's found abandoned, it should be regarded as a crime scene and preserved. I don't want to teach granny to suck eggs, but resist the natural temptation to go 'rooting' through it looking for evidence. Once again, leave that to Studio, we don't want any cross contamination problems…ok?...Sir." D.I. Ellis said, nodding respectfully to his Chief Constable.

Sir Angus rose from his chair.

"As D.I. Ellis has stated, you all know the importance of the early harvesting of evidence, so I will not keep you from your duties. During your search for that vital evidence, I reiterate Mr Ellis's words…safety first. Unarmed Officers are under no circumstances to approach the vehicle or occupants. We have lost a valued friend and colleague. This day, we have paid for our commitment to the preservation of law and order with our most cherished blood. Be diligent, be thorough, but above all, be safe…Now, be about your duties."

As one, the attendant Officers rose from their seats and table tops, as Sir Angus turned to his old friend. "Now John." he said, "Exactly what *do* we know?"

\*\*\*\*\*

'Midnight' paused, holding the door to the left luggage locker open. His eyes flitted left and right, his left hand resting on the top of the rucksack he had pushed hurriedly away out of sight. Out in the main concourse, the City railway station was thronging with people.

The hollow sound of the tannoy system echoed in the cavernous hall, the desultory tones of the operator gave out information to those swarming through the turnstiles toward the various platforms. Expectant faces peered up to the information boards. The large black and white split flaps rotated, updating the latest information on arrivals and departures with mechanical applause.

His hand hovered over the rucksack. Undecided, he hesitated as he watched the lunchtime crowds going about their daily routines, ordinary people with ordinary lives, blissfully unaware of the presence of a murderer in their midst. Amongst the crowds, he was inconspicuous, just another black face, lost amongst those rushing toward the platforms or out to the car park and the waiting taxis.

The seconds ticked by. His fingers tapped lightly against the hard steel beneath the canvas of the rucksack as he pondered his choices. Fight or flight, get out now, or risk one more take down...The 'blues' on Rochester Road maybe.

He chewed at the soft flesh on the inside of his cheek as he pensively considered the pros and cons. He knew that the word would be out now...in this City at least...The Alma Road 'blues' had been taken. A brazen, balls out takedown. Security would now be intense, the 'Soldier' had been invaded, in one of his own cribs and how easy had it been.

'Midnight' knew that what he had achieved was unheard of, and there might even be those amongst his peers who would allow themselves an appreciative nod at the sheer audacity of the move, but not in 'Soldier' Garrison's presence.

The cop had been an unforeseen problem, but much like at the Alma Road 'blues', he had left no clues, no witnesses, no fingerprints, nothing to connect him to the crimes, he was clean away.

He slammed the locker door shut, but paused again, the plastic key shroud remained between his fingers.

He leant his forehead against the cold metal. *Fight or flight...fight, or flight.* He scowled, annoyed and frustrated at his own indecisiveness.

The tannoy system continued to blare out information. 'The train standing at platform three, is the twelve fifteen to Manchester Piccadilly, calling at Huddersfield, Stalybridge and...'

The voice of the information clerk suddenly faded into the background as it came to him in an epiphany.

He lifted his forehead away from the locker door, hardly able to believe that he hadn't previously considered what had now become glaringly obvious. Garrison…'Soldier' Garrison. 'Midnight' nodded his head slowly as the realisation solidified. Why risk *taking down* the 'blues' when he could *have* them all.

Glancing back toward the concourse, he swung the locker door open and with fingers that were surprisingly steady, he unzipped the rucksack and withdrew the Smith and Wesson, hastily pushing it deep into the side pocket of his jacket.

Six bullets left…More than enough to secure an empire.

### **Twenty Nine**
*"Culpae poenae par esto"*

Alan's briefing with the Chief Constable and the senior investigating Officers had been less reproachful than anticipated. D.I. Ellis confirming that Alan's initial opinions regarding the road collision involving the 'nominal' Zippleman been ignored, but that he had 'stuck to his guns'. As a result, the dots had eventually been joined, albeit too late to prevent further atrocious crimes.

Sir Angus frowned disappointedly as the full tale unfolded. "I shall want a full report on this Mr Ellis, however, I will deal with Alan Forrester's indecisiveness at a more appropriate juncture."

Alan noted that the Chief looked askance to his Detective Chief Superintendent and guessed that in that one glance, there was a mutual understanding. Forrester was finished at Moorwood, a 'sideways' move to fingerprints perhaps, or if there truly was a God, the Uniform Procurement Department or Statistics and Planning.

"However." Sir Angus continued. "Now is not the time for recriminations, we must act." He turned to D.I. Ellis. "All authorised firearms Officers are granted 10/21 status Mr Ellis, action this day if you please. The Home Secretary has sent his condolences. Mr Hurd will no doubt take a keen interest in how expeditiously we conclude this appalling matter. I shall be in the Force Control Room, I expect regular and reliable updates."

D.I. Ellis nodded. "I'll see to it Sir."

Sir Angus turned his attentions to Alan. He paused for the briefest of moments as if considering his words carefully. "I know how devastated you must be to have lost both a friend and colleague Constable Pendle, and how frustrated you must feel at having your initial investigations thwarted, however, it is at times such as these where we show our stoicism and professionalism. I understand that you are newly qualified as an authorised firearms Officer?"

Alan nodded. "Yes Sir."

The Chief pinched his lips together thoughtfully. "On my express authority then, take up arms and be about your duty…Off you go."

Alan braced up, pulling his heels sharply together. "Sir."

*****

Now he pressed his forehead hard up against the nameplate holder on the front of his locker, welcoming the discomfort as the domed rivet heads dug into the thin flesh above his eyebrows. The dull ache diverting his thoughts away from guilt and despair.

His peers had not been at the briefing with the Chief Constable, they were all out, manning the junctions on the 'snatch plan', or searching the streets.

The tale would sweep through the station like a virus and the mark of Cain would be upon him. It was Alan that had sent him out, on his own and now Barney was dead.

Sergeant Deal's words came flooding back to him. *"If yer save more lives than yer take Alan lad, yer thirty years won't have bin wasted."* How many lives had he taken, or at least been a contributory factor, how many had he saved? Ten years had passed since his Tutor Sergeant had offered those pearls of wisdom during his first days at Broughton. Alan had no idea how the scales would tilt when it was finally reckoned up.

He consoled himself with the knowledge that there had always been 'unauthorised use'. It was accepted practice and the Chief certainly hadn't questioned it. 'Aides' were expected to run errands, cigars for the Traffic Sergeant, milk for the tea fund, the night Detective to run home, too pissed to walk, let alone drive. Alan had done all these things and more whilst in his 'Aideship' at the Central Garage and the truth was, he'd stopped a few motorists whilst en route, donning his Tutor's cap with its pristine white cotton cover, just for a few moments, just to feel the rush.

Alan took a deep breath and exhaled slowly. He unclipped the chromed Carabiner clip securing his handcuff and locker keys to his belt loop and slipped the key he'd marked with 'tippex' into the lower lock. He rummaged about the top shelf, pushing aside the stack of completed pocket notebooks and his copy of 'Hughes' road traffic offences. He nudged aside the distinctive dark green bottle of aftershave, the cans of deodorant and his spare white tops and reached to the back of the shelf where sat the box he sought. An item he had purchased during the week prior to his attendance at Stretham, on the unswerving assumption that he would pass his basic firearms course.

Alan flipped open the lid of the box and carefully drew out the Bianchi holster, custom moulded to form a perfect fit for the Smith and Wesson .38 Police Special.

The holster, of thick, polished leather was marketed as Bianchi's 'High Rise' version, sitting high on the user's belt to facilitate the *'ease of access and comfort demanded by the mobile law enforcement Officer'*

Alan replaced the box and secured his locker before walking between the tall grey rows and out toward the main corridor and the station Sergeant's office. Feeding his belt back through the loops on his trousers, he secured the buckle and adjusted the position of the holster.

The normal hubbub of the station was noticeable by its absence. Only the constant chatter emanating from the radio room broke the mournful silence, the mobile beat units calling in their present positions and negative results of the street by street searches.

The station Sergeant's office door was closed, Alan peered through the slim glass center panel. Sergeant Dennison was seated at his desk. He was slumped forwards in his chair, his elbows on the table top, his huge hands, flat against either side of his face, supporting his head.

Respectfully, Alan knocked once. The old Sergeant looked up and nodded. "Christ, he looks like I feel." thought Alan as he entered.

His old friend glanced at the holster at Alan's side before looking up to meet his gaze. The old man's eyes looked tired and rheumy.

"Not what you expected for your first job, eh Alan?" he said quietly.

Alan shook his head slowly. "No Sarge…No its not.

Sergeant Dennison heaved himself up from his chair wearily, as if the act alone was sapping the last vestige of his strength.

"Come on then lad, let's get you tooled up." he said, patting Alan gently on the shoulder as he left his office and walked toward the armoury.

*****

"Put yer mark on 'ere lad." Sergeant Dennison said, holding out the register.

The .38 revolver, its original blued finish now worn and mottled, sat atop the metal table, its cylinder laying impatiently open.

Alan scrawled his initials and collar number on the inventory sheet before retrieving the revolver. After spinning the cylinder and giving the ejection claws a cursory inspection, he opened the first of the plastic cartridge cases and one by one, checked the fulminate of mercury firing caps on the rounds before feeding them into their chambers. Satisfied that they were all live and properly seated, he slipped the empty plastic case into his trouser pocket.

Sergeant Dennison handed him a second six round holder, placing the grey plastic case on the table top.

Alan snapped the revolver's cylinder closed and holstered the sidearm into the virgin leather, pressing the quick release stud on the cross-strap to secure the hammer.

"'Ere, better safe than sorry." Sergeant Dennison said, tossing a third cartridge case unceremoniously onto the table.

Alan looked up after satisfying himself that the press stud was fully secure. "Jesus Ron!" he said quizzically, "We want to bring him in…not weigh him in."

The old Sergeant's countenance suddenly changed. "Bring 'im in…BRING 'IM IN!" he snorted in disgust. He turned quickly and pushed the heavy armoury door closed. "You listen to me." he said in a hushed growl. "This isn't some nigger pimp or a ten bob hooker laid on the slab, this is one of our own…One of *your* own for Christ's sake…That yardy fuck killed our boy to save 'is own worthless skin." His old friend's face was reddening and the finger he was pointing was shaking. "You get the drop on this bastard, you put two in 'is chest an' don't you think twice about it."

The old Sergeant paused to compose himself. He nodded emphatically as if confirming his convictions, then turned to slam the door to the gun locker shut.

There was an embarrassing silence and Alan slipped the plastic wallet containing the spare six rounds into the top pocket of his shirt.

"You don't think that Barney would prefer it if his killer spent the next thirty years slowly rotting away in a twelve by eight in Parkhurst then Ron?" Alan asked to break the uneasy silence.

His mentor shook his head. "Use yer brain lad, 'e's a cop killer. 'E'd be a fuckin' 'ero in the slammer…No, there's only one way to deal with a rabid dog, an' the answer's tucked away in that fancy new holster o' yours."

Alan pushed the unwanted ammo case back across the table top. The Sergeant sighed and nodded knowingly. "Twelve it says in the book, an' twelve it shall be then." he said, retrieving the unwanted rounds.

Alan lifted his eyes from where he had been staring at the threadbare carpet. "I had him you know Ron." he said, looking directly into his old friend's eyes.

The Sergeant looked puzzled.

Alan glanced across to the armoury door and placed a hand against the cool metal sheeting. Satisfied that it was fully closed, he suddenly felt the almost irresistible urge to sob, to blurt out his feelings of worthlessness, in the sanctity of the confessional to a man who would understand, a man whom he trusted implicitly, to a man who wouldn't judge him.

"I had him…I saw him Ron, over a week ago on the Ring Road, on my way home. He was driving that shitbox Cortina, the same one that Barney just couldn't resist pulling over." Alan said, shaking his head slowly. "I didn't twig it was Lyburn…Should have done, we'd all seen his prison photo on one of the briefings…I should have remembered the face Ron, should've followed the bastard…If I'd got him housed for CID, Barney might…"

"BELAY THAT SHIT…HEAR ME… RIGHT NOW." his old friend shouted, his voice wavering.

Their eyes met and his Sergeant's voice softened. He rested a fatherly hand on Alan's shoulder.

"Put yerself on the other side of that, or it'll fuck you up forever lad…What's done is done, young Barney rolled 'is own dice. God forgive me for sayin' it, but it's true, we both know it."

Alan took a deep breath and nodded.

"You've nothing to beat yerself up over." the old Sergeant said, shaking Alan's shoulder firmly. "Now, listen to me. Get yer mind right, you'll need yer wits about yer if it comes on top…Go on…get yerself out. That bastard's out there somewhere an' there's a reckonin' to be 'ad."

*****

Alan tossed his yellow jacket into the rear seats of the Traffic Sergeant's Range Rover. It was the only vehicle available to him, all the other cars commandeered to man the 'snatch plan' which Detective Chief Superintendent Sommerville had ordered. The Division was covered, a marked Traffic car or a 'panda' stationary at every major junction.

The AFO's would be sitting patiently, waiting for any news of a sighting, listening intently, in silence so as not to miss a word of the chatter on 'talkthrough'.

Alan knew exactly how they would be feeling. Apprehensive, and only too conscious of the heavy revolvers pressing against the sides of their seats. Next to them, their front seat passengers, the wooden stocks of their Remington shotguns resting against their knees, eight cartridges already in the chamber, barrel end resting on the floorpan. Each Officer, no doubt like Alan, wondering how they would measure up if it should come to the 'moment of truth'.

Remembering D.I. Ellis's words, Alan kept his transmission on the vehicle's VHF set to a minimum.

"Papa Yankee One Three to control."

A brief hiss, then the operator responded. "One Three, go."

"Papa Yankee One Three. I am 10/1, crew is 868. Be advised, I am 10/21 on CC's authority, over."

Alan expected there to be a short pause whilst the Control Room duty Inspector confirmed the Chief Constable's authority for armed patrols. The operator, however, responded immediately.

"10/4 One Three. Confirm you are aware 10/99ZZ."

"So advised." Alan replied, before replacing the radio handset into its holder and gently easing the aged Range Rover out of its allocated bay and out onto the station perimeter drive.

*****

'Midnight' spat contemptuously. The fine stream of saliva forced out between his front teeth, sprayed across the pavement.

He tore the fixed penalty ticket out from where it had been lodged beneath the Cortina's windscreen wiper blade.

He glanced up and down the busy thoroughfare outside the City railway station and in the absence of any yellow banded flat caps; he screwed the ticket into a tight ball and tossed it down into the gutter. His mind was set on 'Soldier' Garrison, not on the yellow lines he drove away from.

His lack of concentration and the strident, blaring horn blast from a vehicle he had pulled out in front of, went unacknowledged, as he joined the manic midday traffic swarming around the busy City centre.

His lack of lane discipline and the angry audible admonishment however, attracted the attention of a young Constable, as he stopped to give directions to a small group of Chinese tourists.

Had 'Midnight' glanced up to his rear view mirror, perhaps to note the following driver's gesticulations and silently mouthed obscenities, he may have noticed not only the beat patrol Officer, but that he was now speaking hurriedly into his personal radio.

*****

D.I. Frank Ellis sat in silence, slowly rotating the thick, cut glass tumbler of whiskey between his thumb and forefinger. His desk was as cluttered as always, the crime files for checking, the actions and intelligence reports all forgotten for the time being. Everything relegated to the back burner until the Traffic 'Aide's' killer was brought to book.

His office door for once, remained open. It was normally closed, a shield against the loud, raucous banter, usual for a busy CID office, especially when there was a major incident running.

His Detectives sat quietly at their desks. There was a murmur of conversation, but almost inaudible. The office was hushed, respectful.

Detective Chief Superintendent John Sommerville, stood with one of the Murder Squad Detective Sergeant's. They studied the evidence board which had been placed across the back wall of the spacious CID office. The D.S. pointed to one photograph, then another, Mr Sommerville nodded as the information was passed, he stood with his hands clasped behind his back and rocked on his heels.

D.I. Ellis sighed and gazed at the photograph of his Wife which sat at an angle toward the rear of his desk. He wondered for a moment how she would react to the 'knock'. He pictured her smiling as she opened the door to see the uniforms at her doorstep and the way it would fall from her face, as she saw their telling sorrowful expressions.

He took a sip of his Balantines. "Here's to you Barney lad." he whispered quietly.

One of the telephones in the outer office warbled. A Detective reached across his desk to grab for the handset. As if electrified, he snatched up a pen and began scribbling furiously. Cradling the handset between his chin and shoulder, he held up his hastily scrawled note and shouted toward Mr Sommerville's back.

"Boss…sighting!"

Detective Chief Superintendent Sommerville turned swiftly on his heels.

"Romeo November Alpha Two Two Three Romeo sighted two minutes ago. City Square boss, drove into Kings Street. Red Ford Cortina, IC3 male, almost caused a 10/11 outside the railway station."

Frank Ellis dropped his glass onto his desktop. He leapt from his seat and strode out into the main office. Mr Sommerville, his face expressionless, reached out for the handset.

"Detective Chief Superintendent Sommerville here…has that last been confirmed?…right, get it out over all channels…yes, VHF as well…Is Mr Mayhew aware?...right, thank you."

He handed the telephone back and turned to the expectant faces of his Detectives, now all gathered around the desk.

"We might have the bastard." he said, pounding his fist into the palm of his hand.

He turned to his D.I. "Get someone to jack up a VHF set in here Frank, I want to hear what's going on."

"What's the score boss?" one of the Detectives asked.

"Some foot plod sighted our man in the City Center, red Cortina, the number's right, no driver description though, other than it was an IC3 male."

There was an excited murmur amongst the Squad. Mr Sommerville raised a hand to silence them. "He's a long way from being in the bag gents, don't forget, it might be a 'pool' car, used by all and sundry. It might not be our shooter, but it's a start."

He turned to his D.I. again. "Get me a large scale map of the Division Frank."

*****

The Range Rover's V8 burbled pleasingly as it idled. Alan sat facing the dual carriageways of the Ring Road, the rear wheels of the patrol car raised slightly as he had reversed up the slight incline of the grass banking.

His view down the Ring Road toward the City was strategically excellent, there were no junctions or cut-throughs, nowhere to turn. If the Cortina came into view, the driver would be committed to driving directly across his path.

The operator at the Force Control Room had advised all units regarding the most recent sighting.

"All units, be advised, sightings only, I say again, sightings and direction of travel only at this time. 10/99ZZ."

Alan reached down and adjusted the position of his sidearm, pulling it forwards and away from the seat side squab. He craved a cigarette, but was well aware that he was within public view, he sighed and accepted that he would have to squirm for a while longer.

He tried to think of something else, anything to erase Barney's image from his mind's eye, but there he remained, sat at the desk in the Traffic office, listening to Alan's advice. *"Life is nothing without an element of risk."* How prophetic those words had been. Alan knew that they would haunt him forever.

He reached up to touch his shirt pocket, involuntarily checking that the plastic wallet containing the spare six rounds were still in place. Sergeant Forbes' words echoed in the back of his mind. *"Six rounds chambered gentlemen and six in your top pocket, if you need more than twelve rounds, you're in the wrong business."*

The radios were silent. Alan reached forwards to adjust the volume, although the last transmission had been both loud and clear.

His mind wandered. He thought about Barney's parents, listening in dumb shock as the news was broken. The worst job in the world for a cop…The death warning.

A short static laden hiss as somewhere, a handset was depressed. Alan held his breath.

"Hotel Bravo Three…vehicle sighted Devonshire Road, out of the City, I say again, Devonshire Road, one IC3 male, over."

Alan immediately pictured the route in his mind. He'd come out of the City centre onto Kings Street, passed the GPO sorting office and the Casino and carried straight on. Alan knew that the Devonshire Road would eventually take him to the traffic lights outside the Odeon cinema. There should be a 'panda' or a Traffic car positioned there. If he continued straight on at the lights, it'd bring him towards the Ring Road. "He's heading home." Alan thought to himself.

The operator at Force Control confirmed the sighting by the occupants of the 'panda' and asked for all units to confirm their positions.

One by one, callsigns were transmitted and in return, received advice from the Control Room Inspector as to where they might best position themselves.

Alan's heart rate quickened slightly as a second sighting was confirmed. "He's straight on at the lights. Still on Devonshire Road toward the Ring Road, permission to follow, over."

"Negative, negative. Last unit, confirm instructions, sightings and direction of travel only." The operator responded decisively.

"Hotel Bravo One Four…received." The 'panda' driver replied dejectedly.

"All units, especially 'C' Division…Vehicle is Eastbound, Devonshire Road towards the Ring Road, I say again, Eastbound towards Ring Road, Papa Yankee One Three, confirm your position over."

Alan reached across to the radio handset where he had left it on the front passenger seat and depressed the transmit bar. "One Three, Ring Road, Eastbound, static. Warwick Road roundabout."

"10/4 One Three, remain in situ…All units, 'Gold' commander has now authorised a covert follow by any plain vehicles. Subject is to be housed for containment…Any unmarked vehicles location Ring Road, respond."

Alan listened intently. "Come on…Come on for Christ's sake, where the fuck's CID." he muttered to himself impatiently. He knew however, that few, if any, of the Vauxhall Chevettes and Morris Itals used by CID had VHF radio sets fitted, the aerials were too much of a giveaway. Any messages would have to be re-transmitted from Moorwood's radio room to the Force Control Room.

Alan pressed the button on the top of his 'Burndept' personal radio.

"868"

"Go on Alan."

"Are we still on talkthrough John?"

"'Firmative."

"CID have got local sets with them haven't they?"

"'Firmative, just no response at this time over."

Alan sighed and shook his head in dismay.

*****

"This radio's shagged Mick, I'm getting' fuck all." the Detective said, banging the 'Burndept' against the top of the dashboard.

His partner snatched at the personal radio, momentarily taking his eyes off the road and the red Cortina which was four vehicles ahead of them. He quickly glanced at the channel selector knob on the top of the radio and gave his passenger a disparaging look, before tossing the set back into his lap.

"Its channel two Rodney, yer on four, no wonder we've no fucking comms." he said, shaking his head in disbelief.

His passenger, face reddening, fumbled with the small knurled knob and depressed the transmit button.

"CID a message."

*****

'Midnight' drove cautiously, tentatively, only his mind racing. 'Babylon' was everywhere, stationary at every junction he had passed. In his peripheral vision he had noticed their heads turning, their eyes following his course and he had seen them reaching for their radios.

A chill ran up his spine. They knew…but how?…was it all just a big show because they'd lost one of their own?…Couldn't be looking for him, he'd left nothing at the scene.

It came to him in an instant. It wasn't for the cop. Somehow they'd tied him to that bitch McKnight…her and 'Soldier's' manager. McKnight had blabbed, spilled her guts 'bout the 'Fastener' before he'd wasted her. She'd got herself lifted by Vice an' done a deal.

He paused, then slumped with realization. She'd gone howlin' to that mulatto crack 'ho Evie, they was always tight, an' she was always jawin' with the man, buyin' herself some slack, an'…she'd been missing from her pitch for a while.

The thoughts whirled around in his head, he was confused. If they wanted him…why weren't they taking him?

*****

It was the brief flash from the headlights and the raised hand he caught sight of in his rear view mirror that determined his fate. Puzzled for a second, until he also noticed the dark blue saloon a few cars to his rear, move swiftly back in line from its slightly extended position.

The uniforms in the 'panda' parked up on the approach to the junction hadn't been flashing at him, they'd flashed at their mates…in CID.

*****

"What the fuck are those woodentops playin' at." the Detective shouted. "Jesus Chri…"

"'E's twigged us Mick." his partner blurted. "An' 'e's goin' for it."

'Midnight' stamped on the accelerator. A bluish, grey plume of oil laden smoke billowed from the exhaust and the engine rattled in protest as he raced for the changing traffic lights.

The Detective braked hard, forced to remain behind the cars stopping for the red traffic light. He slammed his fists against the steering wheel in frustration as he watched the Cortina accelerating away and disappearing out of sight. He mouthed a silent obscenity and turned to his partner. "Call it in Rodney." he said with a sigh.

*****

Sir Angus Mayhew paced slowly between the glowing banks of consoles in the Force Control Room. He turned as an operator called out to the duty Inspector, seated on a raised plinth at the head of the room.

"Sir, CID report losing sight of the suspect at the Odeon cinema traffic lights on Devonshire Road. Unit reports suspect appears surveillance conscious and has tactically evaded the covert follow. Subject vehicle last seen at high speed toward the Ring Road."

The duty Inspector looked enquiringly over the top of his master console toward the Chief Constable.

Sir Angus paused for a second. He sighed and ran his fingers thoughtfully across his chin. "We'll not get him housed now Inspector. The die would appear to be cast". He sighed again, deeply this time, well aware of the potentially disastrous consequences of his next order.

"All AFO's to converge to area Inspector. Prosecute a 'hard stop' where possible." he said with trepidation.

*****

Alan reached across with his left hand and pulled the chrome seat belt clasp from where it hung at the central door pillar. He slotted it firmly into the top of the raised stalk to the left of his seat and rocked his body slowly forwards, to test the belt's inertia release.

The VHF radio was suddenly alive with callsigns and locations as the Force Control operator confirmed the Chief's order.

"All Whiskey units, 10/21 is re-affirmed…Romeo November Alpha Two Three Two Romeo…Occupant to be apprehended…10/99ZZ."

*****

As if unavoidably attracted to one another by some irresistible, magnetic force, 'Midnight' sped along the dual carriageway toward where his nemesis waited. As if somehow pre-ordained, Alan would, as he always suspected, be the one to make first contact.

He craned his neck and peered down the Ring Road, watching as the vehicles appeared around the gently sweeping left hand bend.

Wincing, he adjusted the position of the holster to ease the pressure of the revolver's hammer against the flesh at his hip and in the same instant, the Cortina came into view.

His heart suddenly raced at the immediate infusion of adrenalin. Without thinking, he dipped the clutch and slammed the gear lever forwards. The V8 growled as he pressed the accelerator and simultaneously released the handbrake.

*****

'Midnight' cursed as he spotted the brightly liveried Range Rover, its headlights now flashing and blue lights rotating. He slowed momentarily, frantically searching for an avenue of escape, but such was his momentum, he was across its path in an instant, and in a seamless manoeuvre, the dazzling headlights were now directly behind him.

Alan flicked the 'handsfree' stalk attached to the top of the steering column and the red transmit light illuminated on the VHF set. Each activation would give him eight seconds of air time.

"Papa Yankee One Three…Be advised…I am in pursuit of suspect vehicle. One IC3 male."

The operator responded immediately. "Speed and location One Three?"

"Ring Road eastbound from Warwick Road, now sixty plus over."

"Received One Three…All Whiskey units…"

\*\*\*\*\*

'Midnight's' eyes danced between his rear view mirror and the road ahead, he weaved erratically from left to right, passing between vehicles heedless of their close proximity and the angry horn blasts as he forced his way through.

Alan flicked at the stalk. "One Three, Ring Road East, Harrowford roundabout." His mouth was suddenly dry, his commentary clipped and precise.

Without taking his eyes from the road, he quickly reached across and with his index finger, stabbed at the small button on the front of the public address system handpiece. The yelping tones of the siren filled the air with a warning.

The roundabout ahead was festooned with large oblong black and white chevron boards. Mature trees and bushes adorned the domed, grassed central island, all protected by high concrete kerbing around its circumference. No view of the road beyond, or into the first exit for the Harrowford Road.

Alan glanced to his right, his lights and sirens had done their work, the bonnets of the vehicles on the roundabout dipped sharply as brakes were slammed on.

The Cortina remained in the outside lane. Its course to the roundabout cleared as vehicles ahead, dived for the nearside to avoid a collision.

Alan maintained his engine revs. He quickly dipped the clutch and slipped the gear lever forwards. The engine raced, but Alan wanted stability, Range Rovers tended to lean precariously whilst cornering at speed. He drew closer, the heavy steel front bumper now just inches from the rear of his quarry.

"Push a little, not too much. Make him maintain his speed, he'll be panicking. He'll not react in time." Alan whispered to himself.

He drew a little closer. The roundabout loomed and still no sign of brake lights from the Cortina. Thirty yards, twenty…fifteen.

Alan braked hard and felt the throbbing pulse sensation against the sole of his shoe as the anti-lock braking system activated…Off the brakes, in with the clutch and second gear taken for the roundabout…A last glance to the right…Clear…back on the accelerator.

No such car control from his target. The Cortina barrelled on and into the roundabout. The tyres howled in protest as traction was lost and the rear of the vehicle first slewed wildly out to the right and then left as his target fought to retain control.

"Wrong gear…wrong position…wrong speed." Alan thought, allowing himself a brief satisfied smile.

The rear nearside wheel of the Cortina impacted hard against the raised kerb as it snaked across the carriageways. There was a shriek of tortured metal and a flurry of sparks as the steel wheel rim, bit into the concrete. Somehow, his target regained control and the Cortina accelerated again.

Alan flicked the 'handsfree' stalk. "It's a left, left, left, Harrowford Road out of the City."

"Received One Three, maintain your commentary."

*****

The duty Control Room Inspector called out to his operator. "Sterilise that roundabout."

The operator nodded and glanced up to her disposition board. "Hotel Bravo Four, go to static road block Harrowford Road."

The 'panda' driver, waiting at the blind side of the roundabout, flicked on his blue roof light and headlights. He raced around the wide sweeping circle, skidding to a halt at an angle across the middle of the Harrowford exit.

Leaping from his vehicle, he held up his hands, palms forwards and walked toward the stunned drivers, their vehicles crazily askew after avoiding the pursuit.

"Who do we have to assist from the Harrowford end Inspector?" Sir Angus asked.

"Two double crewed Whiskey vehicles Sir, Lima's Two and Four out of 'D' Division, there on 'snatch' at the Broughton Road junction."

"How far away?" Sir Angus asked.

The Inspector considered for a moment. "Three miles…perhaps a little more Sir."

Sir Angus frowned as he quickly calculated presumed speed and distance. "Lima Two to remain to provide a sterile area, Four to assist if you please."

The Inspector nodded to his operator. "Make it happen, quick as you like."

*****

Alan noticed the first faint signs of smoke and the pungent smell of burning rubber and his eyes were drawn to the rear nearside wheel of the Cortina. A vortex of grey smoke swirled around the outer edge of the tyre. "He's knocked himself out of true." Alan thought to himself, as both vehicles flashed through the imposing stone pillars of the City Gates.

As they left the City boundary and entered rural countryside, the road narrowed to a single carriageway. Alan pushed on, harrying his target with close proximity and a practised weaving motion.

The smoke now billowed from the rear of the Cortina and Alan's windscreen was slapped with small slivers of rubber. The Rover's V8 growled pleasingly, finally being given its 'head' after months of routine patrol speeds.

Alan looked ahead. The road was clear, all the way to the Broughton lights, two miles or more away.

To the right, a wide grass verge, a small, dry stone boundary wall and lush grassland, sweeping down toward the river, dotted here and there with grazing cattle a few of which raised their heads at the sound of the siren then resumed their grazing with indifference. To the left, the high stone wall surrounding the grounds of the Harrowford Hall estate and a deep soak away ditch, capturing the water draining from the raised woodland and diverting it away from the road.

Alan reached for the 'handsfree' stalk to update the operator, but paused as he looked ahead and saw the unmistakable square front of a Ford Granada approaching, its headlights flashing and the bank of blue lights rippling brightly across its roof as it set off from the junction up ahead.

There was a loud report as the Cortina's tyre finally failed. The rear end of the vehicle slumped and the outer tyre wall flapped crazily out from the wheelarch.

Alan could see his quarry now fighting with the steering wheel as the rear of his vehicle began its slow death waltz, first one way, then the other, slewing wildly across the carriageways.

Silence.

All sound suddenly muted except for a strange ringing in his ears.

Alan felt a chill down his back and he shuddered as Barney's face appeared, ethereal, wraithlike in his mind's eye.

The 'Aide' smiled, a boyish grin, childlike. His cheeks, not yet assailed by the razor's edge, still covered in fine down like, wisps of fair hair. "Take him Alan, take him for me. Now's your time."

The ghostly vision and the whispering voice faded and the clamour of the pursuit resumed.

The Cortina slewed toward the nearside grass verge and Alan seized the opportunity.

Slamming the gear lever forwards, he stepped down hard on the accelerator pedal. The V8 howled in protest, but three and a half litres surged the two ton vehicle past the rear of the failing Cortina.

Alongside now and Alan, from his elevated driving position glanced down into the interior of the Ford.

Lyburn's nostrils were flared, his skin shone from a thin film of sweat, the eyes were the same ones he had seen previously, but this time, they did not dart away furtively, this time he saw something new, something satisfying…Fear.

Alan wrenched at the steering wheel and the Range Rover slammed into the front wing of the Cortina. The result was inevitable.

The Cortina was shunted violently sideways. It slid across the road surface and the front nearside wheel dropped into the deep ditch at the side of the road. It was irretrievable. There was a sickening dull crump as the front wing ploughed into the soft grass at the far side of the ditch.

As the headlight exploded inwards, the wing buckled, the distorted metal edge digging a deep furrow into the soil beneath. The rear wheels of the Cortina lifted clear away from the road surface as momentum was overcome by friction. The vehicle pivoted on its new fulcrum point and a hail of debris was thrown into the air. Clods of grass torn away at their roots, mixed with a cloud of soil and a huge plume of steam from the ruptured radiator.

Alan slammed his foot down hard onto the brake pedal; the Range Rover shuddered to a halt as the rear end of the Cortina dropped back onto its wheels with a loud groan and keeled over at a crazy angle.

Alan was aware of the driver's door of the Cortina being thrown open and the seconds became as minutes.

All fluid motion oozed through what seemed to be a viscous quagmire of time. He felt his right hand against the door handle and the fingers of his left against the seat belt release. There was a rushing sound in his ears, the yelping of his sirens faded to a thick, resonant warble as time slowed further.

Out through the door, his feet firmly on the road surface, no weakness in his knees. Forwards to the front of his vehicle, keeping the Range Rover's huge steel engine block between him and his target. His thumb against the press stud, a flick and his hand curling around the grip, the suede lining of the holster giving up the revolver effortlessly. No fumbling, his hands surprisingly steady and through the rushing of blood in his ears, the voice of Sergeant Forbes, his firearms instructor. *"Ten yards gentlemen, thirty feet, so sayeth Mr Greenwood. Normal urban combat has historically been conducted at ten yards or less, you'll be shaking like a shitting dog and panting like a newlywed, so aim for the largest part of the body."*

Into his stance, legs apart, his forearms resting on the bonnet. Alan felt the heat from the trembling metal and felt his heart pounding fit to burst.

His quarry stumbled from the Cortina and fell to his knees as his legs failed him.

'Midnight' shot a panicked glance to his left, to the high stone wall behind him and the dense wooded area beyond as his feet scrambled to gain a foothold on the damp grass. He heard the approaching Granada's sirens growing ever louder. They were upon him. He knew that they'd soon be out of their cars with their big assed shotguns and he instinctively knew it was over.

He reached into the pocket of his jacket.

Alan saw a momentary glint of sunlight on chrome.

There was a single sharp report and the passenger window of the Range Rover exploded. A second crack and a dull, metallic thud as a round punctured the door skin. More wild shots, his target's arm flailing wildly and brief flashes of white light.

Alan felt the pressure of the trigger against his finger.

No verbal challenge given and no one there to say it wasn't. Both eyes open, his target crystal clear, the ribbed barrel of the .38 a blur.

A single breath taken and for the briefest of moments, Alan imagined that he once again smelled the fetid stench of the river Foyle.

Here it was then…the moment of truth.

Finally, here was atonement for failing Corporal McBurney and uncompromising vengeance for Barney. No frozen fear, no hesitation.

Twice he squeezed in rapid succession and the .38 barked in response.

The 158 grain semi wadcutter round tore into 'Midnight's' throat at almost a thousand feet per second. He was punched backwards, falling halfway into the open door cavity. He sucked frantically for breath but felt only a searing pain exploding in his chest, as the second round thudded home.

His revolver fell from unfeeling fingers, a coppery salt taste invaded his mouth and through a grey veil falling over his eyes, he saw a uniformed shape approaching, but hazy and opaque. He gave a single cough and felt a mist of warm blood falling back onto his face, the sound of the approaching sirens fading, then darkness.

## **Epilogue**

The bells of the City Parish church have ceased their sorrowful tolling, the last hymn has been sung, the eulogies given.

The polished oak coffin sits, clamped tight in place within the hearse that will carry him through the City streets, the same streets now lined with a thousand of his colleagues, heads bowed, in dress uniforms and white gloves. A sentinel every ten paces.

The casket, sitting amongst a sea of flowers, is draped with the Force flag, in the center of which has been placed a cap, its black peak polished to brilliance.

The cap is adorned with a pristine white cotton cover.

The heavy oak doors to the church are opened. The dignitaries and ranking Officers pass beneath the Gothic arch and out into the bright, crisp, sunlight and slowly descend the steps to the street where the Queen's piper patiently waits, his kilt fluttering in the slight breeze, the drones resting across his shoulder.

The entourage descends, slowly, in dignified fashion, passing between the Honour Guard all standing rigidly to attention. Traffic men in their dress uniforms, campaign medals worn, white tops and gloves. Each salutes as the Chief Constable and his lady Wife pass, she, supporting the arm of a weeping Mother.

The Chief halts momentarily as words are whispered, a request made. An arm is gently taken in support and the Honour Guard is approached.

The Chief points and words are spoken in hushed tones. A hand is outstretched, offered in friendship.

Alan bows his head respectfully and takes the hand. It feels hard and calloused even through the cotton of his white gloves. It is a farmer's hand.

The steel grey eyes that make contact are reddened with grief, yet glisten with pride. A word of thanks through quivering lips as the hand is shaken, slowly, firmly.

He turns away to join the Chief and his mourning Wife. He pauses, turns again and stares hard. He gives a single nod of respect before re-joining the entourage.

An engine starts and with a single barked command, the uniforms lining either side of the street stiffen and come to attention.

The piper's cheeks balloon and the drones awaken. He walks slowly before the creeping hearse and the skirling lament is played. 'Flowers of the Forest' and from one of the Honour Guard, hot salt tears, running down his cheeks in rivulets and dripping from his hard set chin.

No spray whipped up from the Moray Firth to disguise them, no wind swept Scottish rain to wash them away.

Printed in Great Britain
by Amazon.co.uk, Ltd.,
Marston Gate.